Innovation, Growth and Intellectual Property Rights in the Global Economy

World Scientific Studies in International Economics

(ISSN: 1793-3641)

World Scientific Studies in International Economics includes works dealing with the theory, empirical analysis, and evaluation of international economic policies and institutions, with topics covering international macroeconomics and finance, international trade theory and policy, as well as international legal and political economy. Monographs and edited volumes will comprise the core of the publications.

Vol. 85 *Innovation, Growth and Intellectual Property Rights in the Global Economy*
by Edwin L.-C. Lai (Hong Kong University of Science and Technology, Hong Kong)

Vol. 84 *Not Just Neighbors: The Remarkable Economic Relationships in North America*
by Raymond Robertson (Texas A&M University, USA)

Vol. 83 *Strategic Trade Policy*
by Jota Ishikawa (Gakushuin University, Japan)

Vol. 82 *Technology Transfer, Foreign Direct Investment, and the Protection of Intellectual Property in the Global Economy*
edited by Kamal Saggi (Vanderbilt University, USA)

Vol. 81 *Globalization, Firms, and Workers*
edited by Ann E. Harrison (University of California, Berkeley, USA) &
Keith E. Maskus (University of Colorado Boulder, USA)

Vol. 80 *Foundational Essays in Immigration Economics*
by George J. Borjas (Harvard University, USA)

Vol. 79 *Firms and Workers in a Globalised World: Larger Markets, Tougher Competition*
by Gianmarco I. P. Ottaviano (Bocconi University, Italy)

Vol. 78 *Broadening Trade Theory: Incorporating Market Realities into Traditional Models*
by James Markusen (University of Colorado, Boulder, USA)

Vol. 77 *Economic Effects of Antidumping*
edited by Thomas J. Prusa (Rutgers University, USA)

Vol. 76 *Policy Analysis and Modeling of the Global Economy: A Festschrift Celebrating Thomas Hertel*
edited by Peter Dixon (Victoria University, Australia),
Joseph Francois (University of Bern, Switzerland) &
Dominique van der Mensbrugghe (Purdue University, USA)

Vol. 75 *Competition, Innovation and Trade*

The complete list of the published volumes in the series can be found at
https://www.worldscientific.com/series/wssie

85 World Scientific Studies in International Economics

Innovation, Growth and Intellectual Property Rights in the Global Economy

Edwin L.-C. Lai
Hong Kong University of Science and Technology, Hong Kong

World Scientific
NEW JERSEY • LONDON • SINGAPORE • BEIJING • SHANGHAI • HONG KONG • TAIPEI • CHENNAI • TOKYO

Published by

World Scientific Publishing Co. Pte. Ltd.
5 Toh Tuck Link, Singapore 596224
USA office: 27 Warren Street, Suite 401-402, Hackensack, NJ 07601
UK office: 57 Shelton Street, Covent Garden, London WC2H 9HE

Library of Congress Control Number: 2026001703

British Library Cataloguing-in-Publication Data
A catalogue record for this book is available from the British Library.

World Scientific Studies in International Economics — Vol. 85
INNOVATION, GROWTH AND INTELLECTUAL PROPERTY RIGHTS IN THE GLOBAL ECONOMY

ISBN 978-981-98-2653-7 (hardcover)
ISBN 978-981-98-2654-4 (ebook for institutions)
ISBN 978-981-98-2655-1 (ebook for individuals)

For any available supplementary material, please visit
https://www.worldscientific.com/worldscibooks/10.1142/14683#t=suppl

Desk Editors: Soundararajan Raghuraman/Yipeng Hu

Typeset by Stallion Press
Email: enquiries@stallionpress.com

To the memory of my parents, Shuxin and Yi

About the Author

Edwin L.-C. Lai is Professor Emeritus of Economics at the Hong Kong University of Science and Technology (HKUST). He has been Senior Research Economist and Adviser at the Federal Reserve Bank of Dallas, a consultant with the World Bank, and a visiting fellow at Princeton University. He has served as an Associate Editor of *Review of International Economics* and has published numerous papers in leading economics journals. His work is widely cited. He was named a 2024 Top Scholar by ScholarGPS based on his lifetime record, which has placed him in the top 0.5% of all scholars worldwide in the research area of intellectual property. He is the sole author of the book *One Currency, Two Markets: China's Attempt to Internationalize the Renminbi*. The English edition was published in 2021 by Cambridge University Press, while the Chinese edition was published in April 2025 by Fudan University Press.

Contents

Introduction

This book is a collection of papers about the analysis of innovation, growth, intellectual property protection (IPP) and the relationship among them, with an emphasis on the relevance to the global economy. Most of the papers in this volume are theoretical in nature, although some use data to calibrate the models. Although some papers in this book were published quite some time ago, the topic of "innovation, growth and intellectual property rights (IPRs) protection in the global economy" continues to be an exciting area of economic research today. I strongly believe that the reader will find in this collection valuable gems of ideas on which to build new models to answer new questions.

Most people know quite well what innovation and growth are, but IPP may require more explanation. There are many types of IPRs, e.g. patents, copyrights, trademarks and trade secrets. In some papers in this book, I will focus mostly on patent protection. However, unless stated otherwise, IPRs in this book include all forms of intellectual property rights as long as they affect the incentive to innovate. Even patent protection has many dimensions, such as patent length, breadth, enforcement, scope, exhaustion, compulsory licensing requirements and subject matter, among others. In most of the analysis in this book, when we speak of the strength of IPP, one can interpret it as a policy package that includes patent length and breadth, protection of trademarks, copyrights and trade secrets, and the degree of enforcement, unless otherwise stated. Accordingly, a strengthening of IPRs means a change in the whole package of policies in favor of the innovators.

In some industries, IPP is essential for providing incentives for innovators to undertake innovation. These are called IPRs-sensitive industries. The definition of this set of industries is based on subjective judgement (with justification). Based on my reading of Maskus and Penubarti (1995), Lee and Mansfield (1996), and Smith (1999) and especially Maskus (2000), a reasonable list of patent-sensitive industries includes chemicals, electromedical machines, special industry machines, electric microcircuits, metal-working machines, measuring and control instruments, and data processing equipment. Besides, among other things, alcoholic beverages, perfume and cosmetics are considered trademark-sensitive, and printed matter and sound recordings are considered copyright-sensitive.

For IPRs-sensitive industries, IPP has a first-order impact on innovation. Sustained innovation in turn affects long-term growth. As foreign goods' IPRs are affected by the IPP of the home country, one can infer that the strength of IPP of a country affects imports of IPRs-sensitive goods. Therefore, IPRs is trade-related. For this reason, the international coordination of IPRs fell under the auspices of the World Trade Organization when it was established in 1995. The TRIPS agreement under the WTO provides rules governing IPP of member countries. As the North (the more developed countries) and South (the less developed countries) have very different innovative capacities and sizes of market for IPRs-sensitive goods, they have very different incentives to protect IPP. The TRIPS agreement is therefore an attempt to resolve the tension between the North and the South in this regard. Some of the papers in this book are related to the above issues.

Innovation is an important driver of growth. Therefore, endogenous rate of innovation leads to endogenous rate of growth. The endogenous growth literature consists of many papers that explain this nexus between innovation and growth. Some chapters in this book adopt this approach and so they are fundamentally innovation-driven endogenous growth models. Therefore, to the extent that IPP has a first-order impact on innovation, it is an important driver of growth as well.

Besides the macroeconomic, general-equilibrium analysis of IPP, innovation and growth, there can also be microeconomic, partial-equilibrium analysis of how IPP impacts the incentive to innovate, the rate of innovation or welfare. Some papers in this book adopt this partial-equilibrium approach.

IPRs is also closely related to law. One important legal issue concerning IPRs is the "exhaustion"of patent rights. One paper in this book address the issue of "domestic exhaustion" (i.e. whether patent rights in the country are exhausted upon first sale of the good in that country) and another addresses the issue of "international exhaustion" (i.e. whether parallel imports are legal without the authorization of the patent-owner).

Patent protection is an imperfect instrument in many ways. The following are just some examples. First, ideally, the optimal degree of patent protection should vary by industry, as the parameters that determine the optimal degree of patent protection are different across industries. But then that would be impossible to achieve in practice as it is hard to reach a consensus on how to calculate the optimal degree of patent protection in each industry. Thus, the political hurdle of providing different IPP across industries is too high. Second, the existence of "blocking patents" — patents that infringe on each other — not only makes it hard to demarcate patent rights in the real world but also makes the analysis of the effects of patents rather complicated. Third, patent trolls — patents that are not exploited to produce any goods or processes but just for profiteering when other firms infringe upon the patents — create deadweight losses in the patent system. Fourth, there can be problems if patents are excessively broad. The papers in this book abstract from these issues. In these papers, I assume that there is only one patent standard that applies to all industries, and I take the stance that complications arising from phenomena such as blocking patents and patent trolls have only second-order effects on the questions at hand. However, I am not apologetic about this. Almost all the papers in this collection are conceptual models, and I am mostly only interested in the first-order impacts of a strengthening or weakening of IPP on the variables of interest (e.g. rate of innovation) without questioning where the strengthening or weakening of IPP comes from. I leave the analysis of blocking patents, patent trolls and other microeconomic details of patenting behaviors and patenting phenomena to other people and to my own future research.

Although many papers in this volume were published many years ago, I believe they are still relevant today. There are two main reasons.

First, some of the issues addressed by these papers continue to be relevant today. For example, one result from the paper "Patent Length and Rate of Innovation" is that when the government designs IPP so as to maximize the rate of innovation, it offers too much IPP from the welfare point of view. This result is quite general and therefore as relevant today as when it was published back in 1996. Another example is the paper "Parallel Imports and Price Controls". It argues that legalization of parallel imports of pharmaceuticals from Canada, where there were price controls, would raise the control-price in Canada and increase the profits of drug companies in the US. This is a controversial theory, but the issue is as relevant today as when the paper was published in 2008. It can continue to stimulate further research. Today, the debate about the effects of legalization of parallel imports on the incentive to innovate in the innovating country, on welfare and on the pricing and availability of drugs in the country with price controls is still going on. Since the publication of our paper, many theoretical and empirical studies have been carried out. Most notably, Reisinger *et al.* (2019) pointed out that when the innovating country and price-control country have similar preferences, they are able to replicate our result that the innovating firms have higher incentive to innovate under parallel imports, as the price-control country will raise its control-price so as to ensure that the drug is available. However, when the two countries have very dissimilar preferences, they found that the innovating firm will have lower incentive to innovate. On the empirical front, Dubois and Sæthre (2020) found that parallel imports would lower the profits of the innovating firm. Nonetheless, one effect captured by our model is confirmed empirically by their work — that retailers in the price-control country have the incentive to foreclose consumers' access to some drugs under parallel imports. Presumably, this may exert pressure on the government to raise the controlled price in the long run. The above are just two examples. Other papers in this book contain principles that are rather general and therefore continue to be relevant today.

Second, although the economic reality of the world has changed, and we require new theories to guide the analysis of new issues, the best way to construct new theories is to build on the existing ones. The papers in this book provide such a basis to build new models. What are the new issues? The most prominent new political-economic reality of the world is the rapid rise of China as an economic power in the last four and a half decades, the trade war between China and the US, and the abandoning of the WTO-led rules-based world trading system by the US under Donald Trump. These developments are closely related to the topics of the papers in this book. First, in the last four and a half decades, China underwent extremely fast economic growth unprecedent in human history at the same time as it opened up to trade with the rest of the world at an enormous scale and underwent breathtaking technological progress at a pace unseen in history. This technological progress was accompanied by the establishment of a patent system which quickly evolved and improved over time to become one that is as sophisticated as those of the advanced industrialized countries. One can even say that the legal rights provided to patent-owners in China today are almost as strong as they are in the West. The fast rate of technological progress of China is also accompanied by the fast growth of the number of patents granted. The growth rate is so fast that China has now become the country that grants the largest number of patents per year, surpassing the US and Japan. Second, during the same period, China increased its share of investment in R&D in GDP substantially and engaged in many initiatives to subsidize innovation and promote the creation of patents. Third, since April 2, 2025, the global trading system has been badly damaged by the Trump administration of the US. At the same time, the Trump administration escalated the tariff war with China by imposing (or threatening to impose) exorbitant tariff on all Chinese exports to the US. At the core of the global trading system is the World Trade Organization, which is responsible for international coordination of tariffs, trade and intellectual property protection. The question is as follows: Is it still meaningful to talk about international coordination of trade and IPP policies when the largest player is not interested in it anymore?

These new circumstances inspire new questions:

How does the establishment of a well-designed patent system help achieve the optimal amount of innovation in a developing country such as China? Specifically, how does the introduction of patent protection affect the rate of innovation and welfare in a large developing country like China? How does subsidies on innovation and promotion of patent creation affect the rate and quality of innovation as well as welfare of a developing country such as China?

In the absence of international coordination of IPP (such as TRIPS), when the largest and most innovative country in the world erects high trade barriers against the rest of the world, how does it affect the rate of innovation in the largest country itself and that in the rest of the world? How is the answer different when there is TRIPS and it is fully enforced?

When the largest and most innovative country in the world disregards WTO rules and erects high trade barriers against the rest of the world so as to maximize its own welfare, but the rest of the world continues to honor WTO rules (including TRIPS agreement), how does it affect the global trading and IPP equilibrium?

This book consists of four parts. They are as follows: I. International Policy Coordination in IPP. II. North–South trade, FDI and IPP. III. Endogenous growth models and IPP. IV. Microeconomics of IPP and innovation. In each part, I will provide a preview by first describing the common theme of the papers there and the major research questions posed by the papers, and finally a summary of each paper in the part.

Part 1. International Policy Coordination in IPP

Innovation is an important driver of growth, and many innovations are sensitive to the degree of intellectual property rights protection (hereinafter IPP). In a world where countries trade with each other, domestic IPP policies have international implications, affecting the rate of innovation, growth and trade flows of domestic and foreign countries alike. The chapters in this part are related to these issues. The major questions that these papers attempt to answer are as follows: How is a country's incentive to protect IPRs different when it engages in international trade than when it does not? How is the incentive for a less developed country different from that of a more developed country? Should there be international coordination in IPP when countries trade patent-sensitive goods with each other? If so, what is the optimal degree of international IPP? How well does the theory explain the real world?

This part consists of four papers corresponding to Chapters 1, 2, 3 and 4, respectively. Chapter 1 (Lai, 2008) is a non-technical presentation of the results and intuition behind the main messages to be delivered in Chapters 2, 3 and 4. The chapter presents data to show that there was a wide IP protection gap between the North (the set of more developed countries) and the South (the set of less developed countries) and proposes a theory to explain why. It goes on to explain why countries have different incentives in protecting intellectual property under an open economy as opposed to a closed economy. The existence of cross-border externalities arising from domestic IP protection means that countries tend to provide too little IP protection than is globally desirable. This is the theoretical basis for the need for international coordination of IP protection. Finally, the article cautions against excessive IP protection.

Chapter 2 is the paper "International Protection of Intellectual Property"(Grossman and Lai, 2004). In that paper, we study the incentives that governments have to protect intellectual property in a trading world economy. We consider a world economy with ongoing innovation in two countries that differ in market size and in their capacities for innovation. National patent policies are determined in a non-cooperative game of patent protection between countries. We assume that there is national treatment, in the sense that the home country has to offer foreign firms the same treatment as domestic firms. National treatment implies that when the home country lengthens IPRs protection, it increases the profits of foreign innovators and the welfare of foreign consumers without creating any deadweight loss in the foreign country. Thus, under national treatment, there is a positive cross-border externality as a country increases its IPRs. Consequently, each country offers too little IPP in equilibrium. An international patent agreement would be globally welfare-improving if it increases the global level of IPP relative to the equilibrium level. We also find that intellectual property is better protected in the North than in the South if the former has a larger market and greater innovative capability. Concerning international patent agreements, we conclude that harmonization of patent policies is neither necessary nor sufficient for global efficiency. The paper was one of the first to consider a Nash game of the simultaneous choice of IPRs protection between two trading partners and use the model to analyze what international regime of IPRs protection would be globally efficient.

Chapter 3 is the paper "Theory of International Policy Coordination in Protection of Ideas"(Lai, 2008). In that chapter, I put forward a framework to analyze the underlying sources of national policy failures regarding intellectual property rights (IPRs) protection, the need for international coordination and how the coordination should be done. I also analyze whether global harmonization of IPRs standards is necessary or sufficient for achieving the maximization of global welfare. Then, I move on to analyze the Agreement on Trade-Related Aspects of Intellectual Property Rights (TRIPS), which was a monumental effort to establish rules governing IPRs policies across member countries of the World Trade Organization (WTO). I discuss what TRIPS was supposed to do and what it has actually achieved, with reference to my theoretical framework. I explain that it is desirable for IPRs to be included in world trade talks and be negotiated along with other trade issues. I offer analyses on the extensions of the basic model by introducing political economy and trade barriers, as well as allowing countries to discriminate against foreign firms. Finally, I comment on further potential extensions such as the introduction of foreign direct investment (FDI) or technology licensing, parallel imports, cumulative innovations, subject matter of patent protection and costs of implementation of IPP. The main thrust of the basic model is that, provided that there is free trade and non-discrimination of foreign firms, there exist positive cross-border externalities as a country strengthens its IPRs protection since it raises the profits of foreign firms and the welfare of foreign consumers without causing any deadweight loss on foreign soil. This implies that national governments tend to provide too little IPRs protection compared with the global optimum. The model also implies that a country with higher innovative capability and larger domestic market would provide stronger IPRs. Thus, it is not surprising that the South to protect IPRs less than the North in the absence of international coordination. These basic results largely continue to hold under various extensions.

This paper is a chapter of a volume edited by Maskus (2008). To facilitate the reader, it may be useful to quote Maskus's introduction to this paper:

"Edwin Lai's chapter analyzes comprehensively the normative issues involved in reaching international agreements on intellectual property rights. As is well known, economic theory justifies multilaterally negotiated agreements to cut straightforward trade barriers, such as tariffs, because individual countries would choose not to reduce them to levels that would jointly maximize global welfare. Acting rationally but alone, the government of one country would not take into account the costs its high tariffs impose on other nations. This equilibrium requires coordinated policy intervention, in the form of the WTO or regional trade agreements, to achieve substantially freer trade.

"Lai probes deeply into this policy coordination problem for patents, organizing his discussion around the theoretical framework he developed in a fundamental contribution with Gene Grossman (Grossman and Lai, 2004). Again, in setting individual patent policies (here the duration of patents), countries will take into account their own market sizes and innovation capacities, but will not consider the impacts on consumers and innovators abroad. An increase in one nation's patent length raises both domestic and foreign innovation incentives and affects the balance of consumer impacts in both locations between monopoly pricing and new goods. Governments fail to account for their policy spillovers across borders and, while larger and more technologically capable economies would have longer patent lengths in the uncoordinated equilibrium, all countries adopt policies that are weaker than globally optimal. In short, there is an argument for a global agreement to strengthen patents, which arguably the TRIPS Agreement has achieved.

"This issue is considerably more complex than suggested by this description and Lai offers far broader perspective. For example, that stronger patents in both developed, (the "North") and developing (the "South") countries may be required for a global optimum does not imply that they should be harmonized with identical standards. Perhaps more importantly, if both North and South raise their patent strength the net global welfare gains may not be distributed between them in a way that both regions gain. Rather, it is possible, even likely, that the South will be made worse off because the monopoly pricing its consumers face is not offset by much increase in domestic innovation if its firms have a significant disadvantage in that regard. Accordingly, it may be necessary for North to compensate South with some other form of welfare gain, perhaps through greater market access in the broader WTO accord. Lai offers an interesting analysis of whether TRIPS and the WTO have established such an outcome.

"The author analyzes a number of extensions of the basic issue, including whether an international IPRs agreement is likely to be optimal if individual countries significantly favor business interests in their policy weights, the implications of abandoning the national-treatment principle in a patent agreement. He also offers insights from the model about how to model specific patent-related issues, such as parallel imports and the choice of protected subject matters. The chapter raises a host of interesting analytical questions to which further theoretical and empirical research could be fruitfully applied."

Chapter 4 is the paper "Would Global Patent Protection be too weak without International Coordination?" (Lai and Yan, 2013). In some sense, it is a sequel to Grossman and Lai (2004). In fact, it is a substantial extension of Grossman and Lai by incorporating more features in the model so that it can be tested with the data. In the standard model of Grossman and Lai (2004), cross-border positive policy externalities result in countries choosing a combination of patent strengths that is weaker than optimal from a global perspective. This paper introduces three new features to the analysis: trade and FDI barriers, firm heterogeneity and political economy considerations in setting patent policies. Based on calibration, we find that there would be global under-protection of patent rights when there is no international policy coordination. The empirical fact that firm revenues follow a fat-tailed distribution implies that the barriers to exploit inventions internationally are quite low despite the fact that only a small fraction of firms sell overseas and an even smaller fraction of firms carry out FDI as a result of trade barriers. Despite the existence of trade barriers, the free-rider problem becomes very serious when there is a large number of country-players in the patent-setting game. Furthermore, requiring all countries to harmonize their patent standards with the equilibrium standard of the most innovative country (the US) does not lead to global over-protection of patent rights. One implication of this conclusion is that the most innovative country should subsidize other countries to induce them to increase their IPRs protection. This subsidy can take the form of, say, allowing other countries greater market access to the most innovative country.

Part 2. North–South Trade, FDI and IPP

This part focuses on North–South relationship. In this part, I focus on the interaction between the less developed region (South) and the more developed region (North) of the world, who trade with each other. This is a relevant angle for examining the TRIPS agreement of the WTO signed in 1995, as the main thrust of the TRIPS agreement is to require the South to substantially raise its IPP standard to narrow the gap between the North and the South in this regard. Suppose North is the sole or main source of innovation while the South consists solely or mainly of imitators. The major research questions posed by the papers in this part are as follows: How does TRIPS affect the long-term growth rate of the world? How does IPP in the South affect the rate of FDI from the North to the South and the rate of innovation by the North? How does the impact of Southern IPP on Northern rate of innovation depend on whether production is transferred via imitation by the South (without FDI) or FDI by the North? Does the South have any incentive to voluntarily increase its degree of IPP so as to harmonize with that of the North? If not, does there exist a possibility for a quid pro quo, in which the North opens its market to the South in exchange for stronger IPP to be adopted by the South? Do tariffs on patent-sensitive goods play a similar role as IPP? If so, how are the effects of tariffs in the imitator country different from those of tariffs in the innovator country?

This part consists of three papers corresponding to Chapters 5, 6 and 7, respectively. Chapter 5 is the paper "International Intellectual Property Rights Protection and Rate of Product Innovation"(Lai, 1998a). The world consists of the North and the South. The North innovates and the South only imitates. There is perfect IPP in the North but imperfect IPP in the South. Using a dynamic general equilibrium model of the international product cycle, we found that the effects of strengthening intellectual property rights protection (IPP) in South depend crucially on the channel of production transfer from North to South. Stronger IPP in South increases the rate of product innovation, production transfer and Southern relative wage if foreign direct investment (prior to imitation by the South) is the channel of production transfer but has opposite effects if production is transferred through imitation by the South without foreign direct investment by the North. The main point of the paper is that the effects of strengthening IPP in the South depends crucially on how production is transferred in the product cycle. Before this paper, the literature assumed that imitation without foreign direct investment was the dominant form of production transfer from North to South. This paper therefore filled a gap in thinking about the relationship among Southern IPP, international production transfer and Northern rate of innovation in the product cycle in the long run.

This paper also shows that IPP in South is trade-related, which provides a rationale for the WTO to include the TRIPS agreement under its auspices. One possible extension is to introduce tariffs in each country. In April 2025, Donald Trump announced that he was going to impose substantial tariffs on imports from many developing countries, e.g. 46% on Vietnam and 49% on Cambodia. A particularly relevant thought experiment in the context of our model is to extend the model to see how an increase in North's tariff on Southern imports affects the rate of production transfer from the North to the South and the relative wage of the South.

Chapter 6 is the paper "The North's intellectual property rights standard for the South?"(Lai and Qiu, 2003). In this paper, we build a North–South trade model to analyze international IPRs protection. There is free trade between the two regions of the world. Without any international agreement, the Nash equilibrium of the IPRs-setting game is that each country chooses its optimal degree of IPP given that chosen by the other country. By comparing the Nash equilibrium IPRs protection standard of the South (the developing countries) with that of the North (the developed countries), we find that the former is naturally weaker than the latter as it is reasonable to assume that the South has a lower innovative capability and a smaller market for innovation-intensive goods. Moreover, we show that both regions can gain from an agreement that requires the South to increase its IPRs standards to narrow the gap with those of the North (which benefits the innovation-intensive sectors of the North) and the North to lower its trade barriers against imports of traditional goods from the South (which benefits the traditional-goods sector of the South). This demonstrates the merits of multi-sectoral negotiations. Under the second Trump administration, many developing countries are threatened with substantially higher tariffs when exporting to the US unless they have something to offer to the US. An implication of our analysis in this context is that this Trump policy will harm the developing countries, which either face reduced access to the American market or have to agree to increased protection of IPRs over and above the level required by the TRIPS (e.g. paying more for innovation-intensive goods developed by the US). Either one of these outcomes would be detrimental to developing countries.

Chapter 7 is the paper "Protection of Trade for Innovation: The Roles of Northern and Southern Tariffs"(Qiu and Lai, 2004). This is a partial-equilibrium trade model with two countries in the world. The North stands for the innovator country and the South stands for the imitator country. We consider an industry where there is on-going innovation. Tariffs and IPP in the industry are the variables of interest. In each country, under imperfect competition, given the IPP of the innovator country and the imitator country, a small increase in tariff from zero increases producer profits and government revenue but reduces consumer surplus. But there is one additional benefit to the innovator country (and maybe to the world as well) when it imposes a sufficiently small import tariffs in the industry — it increases the rate of innovation and therefore increases welfare. It can even increase global welfare if the IPP in both the innovator and imitator countries are weak. So, the tariff in the innovator country is an imperfect substitute for IPP in either country. Tariff in the imitator country, however, will always be detrimental to global welfare.

We show that unlike a tariff in the imitator country, a tariff in the innovator country supplements IPRs protection and is not necessarily a beggar-thy-neighbor policy. The globally optimal tariff in the innovator country increases as IPRs protection in the innovator country or the imitator country decreases. Global welfare may rise as the innovator-country tariff increases but necessarily declines as the imitator-country tariff increases. This suggests that pushing for freer trade in the imitator-country is more urgent than in the innovator-country in innovation-intensive sectors where IPRs protections are weak in both regions. We should reiterate that in this paper we are not trying to argue for increasing trade protection. Rather, the message we would like to convey is that trade protection by the imitator country is more detrimental to world welfare than by the innovator country in innovation-intensive sectors where IPRs protection in both countries are weak. Therefore, it may be worthwhile for the innovator country to subsidize the tariff reduction of the imitator country.

Part 3. Endogenous Growth Models and IPP

This part focuses on the role of R&D investment in driving the long-term growth rate and the impacts of IPP policies, in a closed economy. By and large, there are two types of R&D-driven endogenous growth models: the expanding-variety type and the quality-improvement type. The first paper in this part is an expanding-variety-type model. In this type of endogenous growth model, it is typical that in equilibrium there is a constant R&D to output ratio and a constant endogenous steady-state growth rate. As in most dynamic models, the policy shock will typically lead to transitional dynamics that need to be taken into account in fully understanding its impact. The second paper in this part is a hybrid of expanding-variety-type and quality-ladder-type models, in the sense that a new product gradually becomes obsolete and eventually driven out of the market. The main questions that these papers ask are as follows: How does IPP impact the long term growth rate? How to overcome the challenge of analyzing the transitional dynamics? Does there exist an optimal degree of IPP when the transitional dynamics are taken into account? Under what condition does the decentralized market allocate too little (or too much) resources to R&D? What are the positive and negative externalities when a firm carries out R&D? How do the results of our analysis change when we allow products to be driven out of the market as they become obsolete gradually?

The two papers in this part correspond to Chapters 8 and 9, respectively. Chapter 8 is the paper "Intellectual Property Rights Protection and Endogenous Economic Growth" (Kwan and Lai, 2003). The main purpose of the paper is to examine the impact of IPRs protection on economic growth and welfare. To achieve this aim, we make use of an expanding-variety-type R&D-based endogenous growth model based on the "laboratory equipment" model of Rivera-Batiz and Romer (1991). One central feature of the model of Rivera-Batiz and Romer (1991) is that knowledge spillovers from past innovations lower the cost of future innovations. This leads to a constant rate of innovation and growth in steady state. Thus,

IPP, which governs knowledge spillovers, plays a pivotal role in long-term growth and welfare. We analyze the transitional dynamics of a shock in IPRs protection and account fully for the loss in current consumption and gain in consumption growth due to a tightening of IPRs protection. We find that there exists an optimal degree of IPRs protection in our model. We then calibrate our model by US data and found that under-protection of IPRs is much more likely than over-protection. Moreover, in the case of over-protection, the welfare losses are trivial; whereas in the case of under-protection, the welfare losses can be substantial. This paper was one of the first to implement the "laboratory equipment" model using data and the first to conclude, based on calibration, that the under-protection of IPP was one important reason for the under-investment of R&D in the US.

Chapter 9 is the paper "Schumpeterian Growth with Gradual Product Obsolescence" (Lai, 1998b). The motivation of the paper is to build a Schumpeterian model of creative destruction that captures innovation as both the birth of a new product and a destructive force in rendering the gradual obsolescence of the existing products. The model in this paper captures several important aspects of the real world: (i) gradual obsolescence of goods in the form of gradually declining net profit derived from each product until it is phased out, (ii) expanding variety of goods over time and (iii) both dynamic and static internal increasing returns to scale of production. To eliminate the scale effect, Jones's (1995) specification that gives rise to a "semi-endogenous" rate of innovation is adopted. In that specification, R&D confers both positive externalities via intertemporal knowledge spillovers and negative externalities via research duplication. To be consistent with a constant rate of innovation in steady state, the ratio of R&D to GDP has to be increasing over time in steady state. The most interesting finding of the paper is that, when the research duplication effect is small (large) relative to the intertemporal knowledge spillover effect in R&D, the decentralized market delivers insufficient (excessive) obsolescence and allocates too little (much) labor to R&D, while a small subsidy (tax) to innovation is welfare-improving. All these results hold because the positive knowledge spillover externalities overwhelm (is overwhelmed by) the negative research duplication externalities. The model can possibly be calibrated with data to find out empirically whether too little resources have been allocated to R&D and therefore whether R&D subsidies are warranted.

Part 4. Microeconomics of IPP and Innovation

While endogenous growth models are typically general-equilibrium macroeconomic models, microeconomic analysis can provide the micro-foundation that provide the justification for macroeconomic models. Sometimes, a partial-equilibrium microeconomic analysis provides important insights, which can later be incorporated into a general-equilibrium macroeconomic model. In fact, there is a rich literature in industrial organization that focusses on the microeconomic analysis of IPRs and innovation. The questions that we ask in the first two papers are as follows: How do profit-maximizing firms and utility-maximizing consumers interact to determine the effects of IPP on the rate of innovation and consumer welfare? Does there exist a degree of IPP that maximizes the rate of innovation? Does there exist a degree of IPP that maximizes welfare? If both answers are yes, is the IPP that maximizes the rate of innovation stronger or weaker than one that maximizes welfare? In a world with an innovating North and a non-innovating South, does international exhaustion of patent rights (i.e. legalizing parallel imports) in the North necessarily lowers the rate of innovation there? Does it necessarily benefit the South? There is also a literature in law and economics on IPP. The third paper in this part belongs to this category. The questions that this paper attempts to answer are as follows: In a patent regime in which patent rights are exhausted upon first sale of the patented good regardless or any contractual restrictions imposed by the patent-owner, how does the patent regime affect consumer surplus, producer surplus and social welfare? How is the social welfare compared with a regime in which the patent-owner is allowed to opt out of patent exhaustion upon first sale and impose contractual restriction on future re-sale? In the second regime above, how does the existence of transactions costs of contractual enforcement (e.g. via licensing) affect the result? The answers to these questions indicate that there are more dimensions to patent protection than the length and breadth the a patent. Therefore, macroeconomic modeling of patent protection needs to take into account such subtlety in order to build a realistic model of the world.

The three papers in this part correspond to Chapters 10, 11 and 12. Chapter 10 is the paper "Patent Length and the Rate of Innovation" (Horowitz and Lai, 1996). This paper models the effect of patent length on the rate of innovation and consumer welfare. We find that the patent length that maximizes the rate of innovation exceeds that which maximizes consumer welfare. We show a countervailing effect of patent length upon the "size" and "frequency" of innovation. Longer patents increase the size but decrease the frequency of innovation. The patent lengths that maximize the rate of innovation and welfare represent balance points between size and frequency. The intuition for the patent length that maximizes the rate of innovation to be larger than that which maximizes consumer welfare hinges on the fact that the patent length affect consumer welfare through a direct channel and an indirect channel. In the direct channel, an increase in patent length lowers the frequency of innovation, lowering consumer welfare. In the indirect channel, an increase in patent length affects the rate of innovation, which in turn impacts on consumer welfare positively if the rate increases (but negatively if the rate decreases). Calculus tells us that at the patent length where the rate of innovation is maximized, the indirect effect is zero. But at that patent length, the direct effect is negative. At the patent length where rate of innovation is maximized, consumer welfare has already fallen from its peak value. Therefore, the rate of innovation-maximizing patent length is longer than the consumer-welfare-maximizing one. In other words, a policy that targets maximizing the rate of innovation will choose too high a patent length for those who want to maximize consumer welfare.

Chapter 11 is the paper "Parallel Imports and Price Controls" (Grossman and Lai, 2008). Price controls create opportunities for international arbitrage. Many have argued that such arbitrage, if tolerated, will undermine intellectual property rights and dull the incentives for investment in research-intensive industries such as pharmaceuticals. We challenge this orthodox view and show, to the contrary, that the pace of innovation often is faster in a world with international exhaustion of intellectual property rights than in one with national exhaustion. This sounds like a counter-intuitive result. The key to our conclusion is to recognize that governments will make different choices of price controls when parallel imports are allowed by their trade partners than they will when they are not. There are two reasons. First, the legalization of parallel trade opens up the possibility that a manufacturer will refuse to serve the foreign market where the control price is too low, in order to mitigate or avoid reimportation. Second, the legalization of parallel trade forces the foreign government to raise its controlled price so as to provide enough profits (and therefore incentives) for the home-country firms to carry out R&D. It cannot free-ride on the IPRs granted by the home-country anymore. For both these reasons, the foreign government has to raise its controlled price sufficiently. Our analysis shows that the result is that international exhaustion of patent rights leads to higher profits for home-country manufacturers and higher consumer surplus in the home country. There are two hypotheses that are potentially testable empirically. First, legalization of parallel imports does not reduce the incentives to innovate. Second, legalization of parallel imports induces the non-innovating countries to raise their controlled price. It seems that the evidence for the first has been weak so far but there are some evidence in support of the second.

Chapter 12 is the paper "An Economic Model of Patent Exhaustion" (Ivus *et al.*, 2020). It is about the law and economics of IPRs. The doctrine of patent exhaustion implies that the authorized sale of patented goods "exhausts" the patent rights in the goods sold and precludes additional license fees from downstream buyers. Courts have considered absolute exhaustion (AE), in which the patent owner forfeits all rights upon an authorized sale, and presumptive exhaustion (PE), in which the patent owner may opt-out of exhaustion (and thereby reserve the patent rights so that it can prevent future re-sale of the patented good) via contract. In May 2017, the Supreme Court ruled that a patent owner's decision to sell a product exhausts all of its patent rights in that item, regardless of any contractual restrictions the patent owner imposes upon the sale of the patented good to a customer. In other words, the Supreme Court affirmed AE and disallowed PE. This paper analyzes the welfare implications of a switch from PE to AE. This paper offers the first economic model of domestic patent exhaustion that incorporates transaction costs in licensing downstream buyers and considers how the shift from absolute to presumptive exhaustion affects social welfare. We show that when transaction costs are high, the patent owner has no incentive to individually license downstream users, and absolute and presumptive exhaustion regimes are equivalent. But when transaction costs are at the intermediate level, the patent owner engages in mixed licensing, individually licensing high-valuation buyers and uniformly licensing low-valuation buyers. In this case, absolute exhaustion is socially optimal. Finally, presumptive exhaustion is socially optimal when social benefits from buyer-specific pricing outweigh social costs from transaction cost frictions in individualized licensing, which requires sufficiently low transaction costs.

References

Maskus, K. E. (2000). *Intellectual Property Rights in the Global Economy*, Washington, DC: Institute for International Economics.

Maskus, K. (2008). Introduction, in Maskus, K. E. (ed.), *Intellectual Property, Growth and Trade*, Frontiers of Economics and Globalization, Vol. 2, Elsevier, Amsterdam, The Netherlands.

Maskus, K. E. and Penubarti, M. (1995). How trade-related are intellectual property rights? *Journal of International Economics* 39, 227–248.

Lee, J.-Y. and Mansfield, E. (1996). Intellectual property protection and U.S. foreign direct investment, *The Review of Economics and Statistics* 78(2), 181–186.

Smith, P. J. (1999). Are weak patent rights a barrier to U.S. exports?, *Journal of International Economics* 48, 151–177.

Dubois, P. and Sæthre, M. (2020). On the effect of parallel trade on manufacturers' and retailers' profits in the pharmaceutical sector, *Econometrica* 88(6), 2503–2545.

The papers included in this volume are reprinted with revisions and permission from the original publishers. They are listed in the following.

Chapter 1. Edwin Lai. 2008. "Intellectual property protection in a globalizing era." *Economic Letter*, 3(3) (March 2008), Federal Reserve Bank of Dallas.

Chapter 2. Gene M. Grossman and Edwin L.-C. Lai. 2004. "International protection of intellectual property." *American Economic Review* (December 2004), pp. 1635–1653.

Chapter 3. Edwin L.-C. Lai. 2007. "Theory of international policy coordination in protection of ideas." In Keith E. Maskus (ed.) *Intellectual Property, Growth and Trade*. Frontiers of Economics and Globalization, Vol. 2, Published by Emerald Group Publishing Limited in 2007, and Elsevier Publisher in 2008.

Chapter 4. Edwin L.-C. Lai and Isabel K.M. Yan. 2013. "Would global patent protection be too weak without international coordination?" *Journal of International Economics* (January 2013), pp. 42–54.

Chapter 5. Edwin L.-C. Lai. 1998a. "International intellectual property rights protection and rate of product innovation." *Journal of Development Economics* (February 1998), pp. 133–153.

Chapter 6. Edwin L.-C. Lai and Larry D. Qiu. 2003. "The North's intellectual property rights standard for the South?" *Journal of International Economics*, 59 (2003), pp. 183–209.

Chapter 7. Larry D. Qiu and Edwin L.-C. Lai. 2004. "Protection of trade for innovation: The roles of Northern and Southern tariffs." *Japan and the World Economy*, 16 (2004), pp. 449–470.

Chapter 8. Yum K. Kwan and Edwin L.-C. Lai. 2003. "Intellectual property rights protection and endogenous economic growth." *Journal of Economic Dynamics and Control*, 27 (2003), pp. 853–873.

Chapter 9. Edwin L.-C. Lai. 1998b. "Schumpeterian growth with gradual product obsolescence." *Journal of Economic Growth* (March 1998), pp. 81–103.

Chapter 10. Andrew W. Horowitz and Edwin L.-C. Lai. 1996. "Patent length and the rate of innovation." *International Economic Review* (November 1996), pp. 785–801.

Chapter 11. Gene M. Grossman and Edwin L.-C. Lai. 2008. "Parallel imports and price controls." *RAND Journal of Economics*, 39(2) (Summer 2008).

Chapter 12. Olena Ivus, Edwin L.-C. Lai and Ted Sichelman. 2020. "An economic model of patent exhaustion." *Journal of Economics and Management Strategy*, 29(4) (Winter 2020), pp. 816—833. With an Online Appendix.

Part 1

International Policy Coordination in IPP

Chapter 1

Intellectual Property Protection in a Globalizing Era*

Innovation is key to global growth and rising living standards. Most technologies originate in the more-developed countries (nominally, the North), making the pace of diffusion to the rest of the world a critical factor in the well-being of less-developed nations (the South).

Technologies will diffuse quickly only if the South's consumers can afford them. Yet, as our world becomes more globalized, technology- and knowledge-intensive products are increasingly subject to patent rights and other intellectual property (IP) laws that maintain high prices.

Even staunch free-market advocates accept protecting intellectual property as necessary to stimulate innovation. Some analysts, however, worry that overly strong IP laws could restrict the South's access to technology, adversely affecting living standards.

These concerns contribute to the inherent tensions of protecting IP in a globalizing era. The North, being the technology-originating countries, wants the South to strengthen its IP rights, but the South resists, citing unfairness. International agreements that seek to strengthen the South's IP protection aren't likely to succeed without attendant commitments to ensure developing nations' access to affordable knowledge goods.

*By Edwin Lai. Originally published in *Economic Letter*, 3(3) (March 2008), Federal Reserve Bank of Dallas.

1 IP Protection Gaps

In 2007, Thailand decided some pharmaceuticals were unfairly expensive and threatened to impose compulsory licensing on drugs developed and sold by Western companies. In response, US and European producers dramatically lowered prices. This episode underscores the friction between North and South in an era of globalizing IP protection.

Two factors contribute to the North–South divide on IP protection. First, the North specializes in innovation- or knowledge-intensive industries, such as pharmaceuticals, computers, precision machine tools and business software. The South relies more on producing traditional goods, such as textiles and toys.

Second, markets for the North's innovation-intensive goods have become increasingly globalized through trade liberalization, declining transport costs and new communications technologies.

Why have these two forces made IP protection more important? The answer lies in the relationship between IP protection and innovation. Basically, each innovation is an idea. Ideas have value, but they can often be copied at little cost.

Think of pharmaceutical formulas. Typically, developing new drugs involves huge investments of time and money, involving lengthy laboratory trials as well as testing on animals or humans.[1] Once a drug becomes available, however, imitators can analyze its chemical composition and produce it. Chemicals, data-processing equipment and software are other examples of IP-sensitive industries in which ideas can be copied quickly without significant cost.

If we rely on the market for innovation, IP protection is essential for incentives to introduce new products and technologies, a process that usually involves investing capital and labor in hopes of future profits. IP laws basically give temporary monopoly power to inventors, so they can at least retrieve the cost of their R&D investment.

---

[1] A Tufts University report stated that the average cost to develop and bring a new drug to the market was US$ 802 million in 2001 (Tufts Center for the Study of Drug Development, 2007).

These temporary monopolies — US patents last 20 years from date of filing — are important to sectors that contribute a lot to the US economy. In 2003, consumption of IP-sensitive goods was about 17% of GDP, and these industries' total output constituted 40% of goods and services exports. IP-sensitive sectors employed about 18 million US workers (Siwek, 2005).

Not all innovations require patent or copyright protection. Some products, such as Coca-Cola, aren't easy to reverse-engineer, and maintaining trade secrets may be sufficient when imitation lags are long relative to patent length. Patents require disclosure of technical details, so some firms are reluctant to obtain them for inventions that take a long time to copy.

Other innovations, such as new management methods, may not require formal IP protection. The first-mover advantage can keep innovators ahead of potential competitors, and imitation lags may be long enough for innovators to recapture investment costs. Moreover, well-established brand names or reputations can sustain the ability to earn economic rents for a long time.

While trade secrets and first-mover advantages have their place, innovation-intensive industries rely more heavily on legal forms of IP protection. Since the North specializes in these industries, it places greater importance on IP laws and grants stronger protection than the South does.

Timely, comprehensive data on IP protection and innovation are scarce, but several measures confirm the gap between developed and developing nations:

- The Ginarte–Park index of patent rights for a representative sample of countries in 2000 shows the strongest laws can be found in the US and other developed nations (Figure 1).[2] Among the top 15 in patent protection, only South Korea and Spain had per capita

[2]The Ginarte–Park index criteria include (i) coverage of the patent laws in the country, (ii) membership in international agreements, (iii) the risks of having patent rights forfeited in the country, (iv) enforcement as stipulated by the law, and (v) duration of protection. See Ginarte and Park (1997) and Park and Wagh (2002).

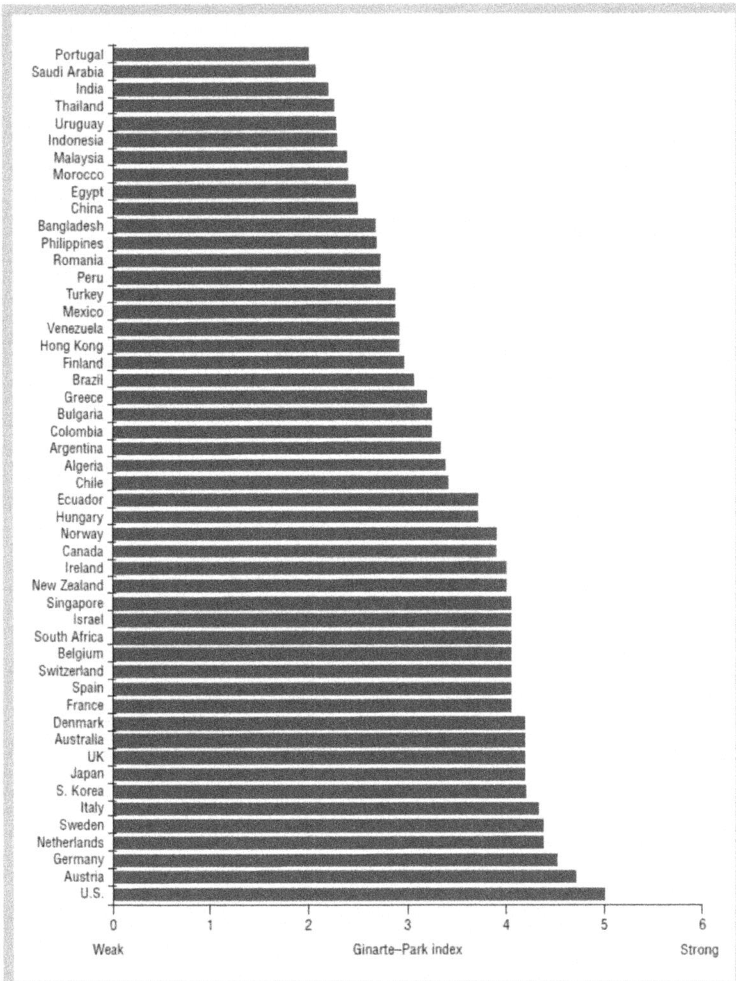

Figure 1. Patent rights vary among countries.
Source: Park and Wagh (2002).

incomes below US$ 22,100 a year in 2000. The group's average was US$ 24,100. The weakest protection was found among developing nations. Except for Portugal, the bottom 15 in strength of patent protection all had per capita incomes below US$ 10,500 a year. The group's average was US$ 6,674.

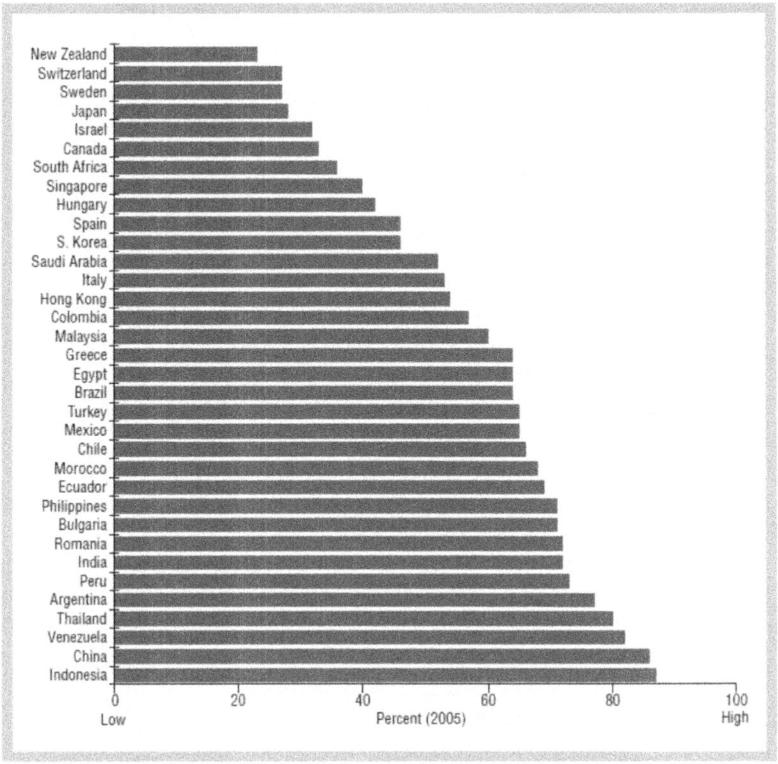

Figure 2. Nations differ on business software piracy rates.
Note: Data unavailable for Algeria, Australia, Austria, Bangladesh, Belgium, Denmark, Finland, France, Germany, Ireland, Netherlands, Norway, Portugal, UK, Uruguay and US.
Source: International Intellectual Property Alliance, iipa.com.

- The International Intellectual Property Alliance estimated piracy rates by looking at the difference between legally purchased and installed business software in 2005. Piracy rates are three times higher in some developing nations than they are in the most protective developed countries (Figure 2).
- Comparing these two measures shows that countries with strong patent rights tend to have high copyright compliance (defined as 1 minus the piracy rate). In addition to being closely correlated, the measures are weaker in less-developed countries (Figure 3).

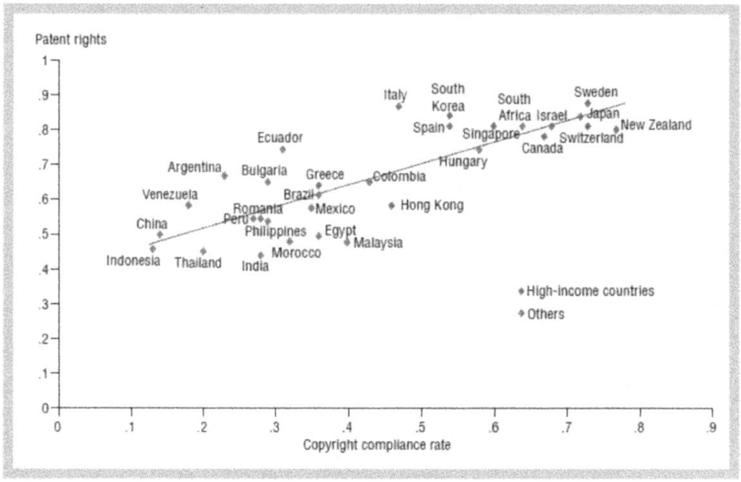

Figure 3. Intellectual property protection's North-South divide.
Notes: High-income countries are classified according to the World Bank's definition. Copyright data unavailable for Algeria, Australia, Austria, Bangladesh, Belgium, Denmark, Finland, France, Germany, Ireland, Netherlands, Norway, Portugal, UK, Uruguay and US.
Sources: Copyright compliance rate: International Intellectual Property Alliance, iipa.com. Patent rights: Park and Wagh (2002).

The variation of IP protection across countries emerges from fundamental economic differences. Firms in the North, which benefit from stronger IP laws, contend they lose profits in the South, where IP protection is weaker. Not surprisingly, the North advocates international harmonization of IP standards — that is, developing nations adopting developed countries' standards.

The South, however, is reluctant to harmonize, arguing that its stage of economic development doesn't justify highly protective IP standards. Moreover, developing nations contend that developed countries excessively protect IP to appease powerful IP lobbies at home.

2 Closed vs. Open Economies

Patent protection involves both benefits and costs. In examining the calculus that determines optimal patent length, we consider changes in societies' overall welfare that result from strengthening protections for innovators.

In an economy closed to international trade, increasing patent length allows more inventors to profit from investing in new ideas, speeding up innovation rates that benefit consumers with new, better or cheaper goods and services. Patent holders also benefit from higher profits. These positives constitute the *marginal benefit* of extending patent protection.

The downside is that consumers pay higher prices for longer periods — the *marginal cost* of extending patent protection.

When patent lengths are short, adding even a year of protection leads to relatively large increases in innovation rates. Inadequate patent protection had greatly discouraged innovation; therefore, even strengthening IP protection slightly can bring many low-cost inventions to market. The added benefits are large, eclipsing the burdens imposed by higher prices. So overall welfare rises.

Further increases in patent length will produce net benefits until incremental gains from faster innovation and profits (that is, the marginal benefit of extending patents) just balance incremental consumer burdens (that is, marginal cost of extending patents). This is the *optimal* patent length. Any further lengthening reduces overall welfare because the technology gains and added profits no longer outweigh the consumer burdens.

In closed economies, all the marginal costs and benefits of extending patent length accrue to domestic consumers and companies. When patent policies are purely domestic, North–South tensions don't arise.

Let's see how it changes when globalization introduces new actors — foreign consumers and foreign innovators.[3] In open

[3]We assume there are no trade barriers and that domestic and foreign firms are given the same IP protection in each country. But we assume that countries are not required to harmonize their IP with other countries. We further assume governments in a globalized world are committed to protecting foreign inventions as much as domestic ones. We call this the national treatment principle, which was respected by most countries even before the Trade-Related Aspects of Intellectual Property Rights (TRIPS) agreement of 1994.

economies that grant foreign and domestic firms the same patent rights, global innovators earn only a fraction of their profits in the home market. The rest come from foreign sales.

So lengthening patents in an open economy doesn't raise incentives to innovate as much as it does in a closed economy. What's more, increases in foreign firms' profits aren't counted in domestic welfare. Therefore, the marginal benefits of extending patent length are reduced in an open economy.

Economic logic leads to an important conclusion: In a globalized world without international coordination, each country's optimal patent length is shorter than it would be in a nonglobalized world. Open economies can rely partly on IP protection provided by foreign countries, and they can provide less protection than closed economies without hurting the incentives to innovate.

Globalization should benefit American consumers because US producers of IP-sensitive goods, such as pharmaceuticals, are able to sell to a larger market in which foreign countries at least partly foot the R&D bill. These companies have more incentive to develop new goods without seeking stronger domestic IP protection. At the same time, US consumers are potentially better off because American IP protection can be weaker and still provide the nation's innovators the same incentives. Easing domestic monopoly power would lead to lower prices without inhibiting the development of new technologies.

If countries trade freely, more innovative countries have greater incentive to offer greater patent protection — at least in the absence of international agreements. For these countries, the marginal benefit of extending patent length is higher because a larger share of innovation comes from domestic firms whose profits are counted in national welfare.

We do see this in practice. Measuring innovative capacity by patents issued to residents shows that eight of the top 10 most innovative countries are also among the top 10 in strength of patent rights protection. Eight of the bottom 15 countries in innovation are

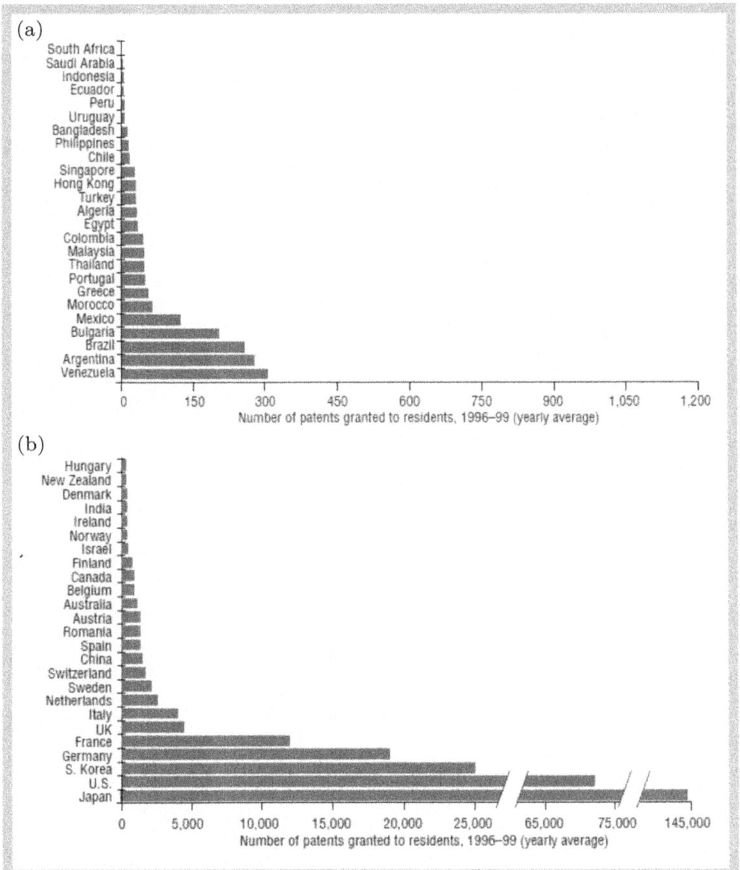

Figure 4. More innovative nations offer greater patent protection. (a) These countries tend to offer weaker patent rights. (b) These countries tend to offer stronger patent rights.

Source: World Intellectual Property Organization, http://www.wipo.int/portal/index.html.en.

among the bottom 15 in patent protection (compare Figure 4 with Figure 1).[4]

[4]We have to be careful with the Japanese statistic since Japan tends to grant a large number of narrow patents, unlike the US or EU. Nonetheless, Japan was among the top 10 most innovative countries.

If patent-sensitive goods are traded freely, countries with larger domestic markets for these products also have greater incentive to offer stronger patent protection because additional years of patent protection will spur more worldwide innovation.

This, too, we see in practice. Looking at consumption of patent-sensitive goods in 2000 shows that five of the top 10 countries in market size are among the top 10 in strength of patent rights. Six of the bottom 15 countries are among the bottom 15 in patent rights (compare Figure 5 with Figure 1).

The North offers more IP protection than the South because these developed nations have both higher innovative capability and larger domestic markets for patent-sensitive goods.[5] The North wants the South to harmonize its IP policies with the North, but the South doesn't have the same economic interest in protecting technology (Grossman and Lai, 2004).

Some developing countries fail to protect legitimate IP rights because of bad policy choices. But the fact that the South generally provides weaker protection than the North does at least partly reflects its rational choices.

3 International Coordination

Economic analysis suggests that the world might fail to adopt IP policies that achieve maximum economic gain from the global patent system. There are two reasons, but the underlying logic is the same: Protecting countries don't capture all the benefits of their actions.

First, national treatment commits countries to give the same protection to foreign and domestic firms, but domestic welfare doesn't include overseas producers. Second, as a country strengthens patent protection, it quickens the pace of innovation around the world, which makes foreign consumers better off without raising their burdens.

[5]Although the South may have higher population, the per capita demand for patent-sensitive goods is much lower because these goods are usually less affordable to low-income countries.

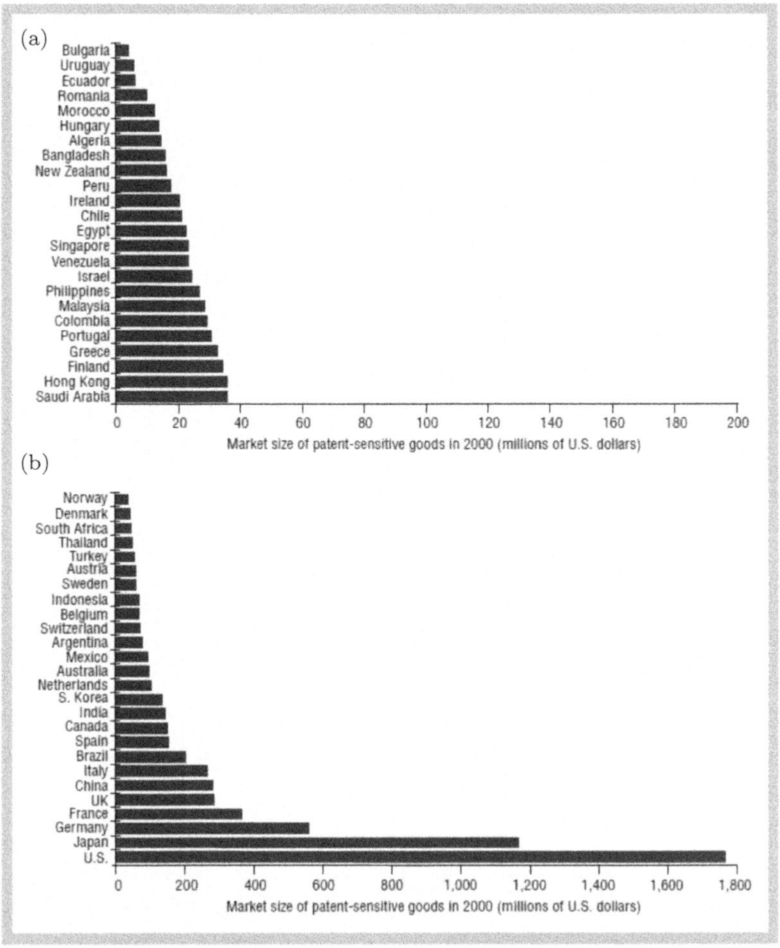

Figure 5. Large markets encourage stronger intellectual property laws. (a) These countries tend to have weaker IP laws. (b) Theses countries tend to have stronger IP laws.

Sources: Author's calculations.

We call the benefits conferred on foreign countries positive externalities. These two sources of positive externalities explain why international accords that require at least some countries to strengthen patent protection might increase global welfare.

The agreement on Trade-Related Aspects of Intellectual Property Rights (TRIPS), a pact requiring substantial stiffening of the

South's IP protection, was signed in 1994. It required all developed countries to adopt mini-mum IP standards by January 1, 1996. The corresponding deadlines were January 1, 2000, for all developing and transition economies, and January 1, 2006, for the least-developed countries.[6]

The TRIPS agreement effectively strengthens global IP protection by requiring some countries (mainly those in the South) to substantially raise IP protection while allowing others (mainly those in the North) to maintain or exceed their pre-TRIPS protection.[7]

The TRIPS agreement leads to significant wealth transfers between countries. The US, as the largest producer of innovation-intensive goods and services, receives the greatest benefit from foreign countries strengthening their patent protection to comply with the agreement (Figure 6).[8]

Because innovative firms sell to both regions and TRIPS increases global protection, the value of each patent increases. This creates incentives for more firms to innovate. As a result, globalization combined with international coordination can enhance the global rate of technological change.

The TRIPS agreement mainly requires raising IP protection in the South, which boosts the innovation rate without increasing the price burden on the North's consumers. This benefits the North at the expense of the South. To resolve this problem, the North agreed to open its markets for the South's exports of traditional goods. The possibility of reaching this quid pro quo proves that international IP agreements plus market opening can bridge the gap between North and South.

[6]The Doha Declaration of 2001 offered an extension to 2016 for pharmaceutical patent protection in the least-developed countries.

[7]Countries required by TRIPS to strengthen their patent protection would be reluctant to do it voluntarily. They have to be given incentives. Commentators argue that the North had given the South increased market access of low-tech goods in exchange for the South's acceptance of TRIPS (Reichman, 1995). Also see Lai and Qiu (2003).

[8]The estimates were based on patents existing at the time of study only. They would be higher today (McCalman, 2001).

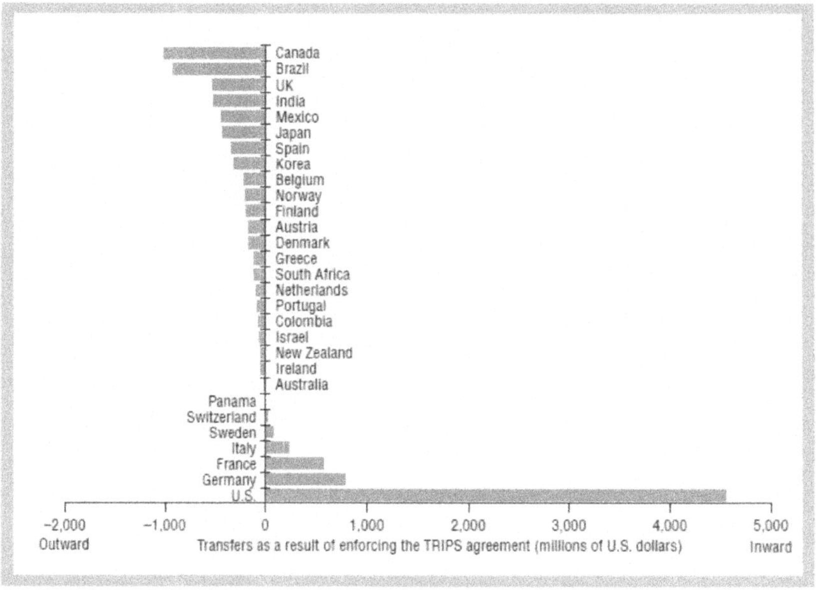

Figure 6. US benefits most from TRIPS agreement.
Source: McCalman (2001).

4 Excessive IP Protection

In the past quarter century, developed countries have greatly strengthened their IP protections. Supporters justify this by noting that the North has come to specialize in the production of innovation-intensive goods. At the same time, the TRIPS agreement commits developing countries to stronger IP protection.

Does the North strike the right balance between the costs and benefits of IP protection? Do the TRIPS requirements strike the right balance between costs and benefits for the South?

Those questions are hard to answer, but we can point to some potential dangers from IP protections that go too far:

- *Reducing access to affordable knowledge goods.* TRIPS requires less-developed countries to strengthen IP protection without attempting to ensure the South's access to knowledge goods. To reduce this problem, some commentators urge developing countries to use competition policy to counterbalance the anticompetitive aspects of IP protection. Others recommend that patent holders take more flexible approaches in the South.[9]

- *Privatizing basic scientific knowledge.* Imagine, for example, the burden on innovation if firms had to get permission to use calculus. Narrowing the availability of data and output from university research could shrink the "global knowledge commons" and slow scientific progress.
- *Privatizing traditional knowledge.* A lot of traditional knowledge has been around for many centuries. Carving up the rights to use it can curtail the ability of firms and individuals to innovate.
- *Excessive IP-related litigation.* The number of patent lawsuits has increased dramatically in recent decades. Before 1985, no more than 1,200 were initiated in any one year; by 2001, that number was around 2,500 (Jaffe and Lerner, 2004). In 2005, Microsoft reported spending about US$ 100 million a year to defend itself against lawsuits — 35–40 at any one time (McCullagh, 2005).
- *Broadening what can be patented.* In 1980, the US Supreme Court ruled that genetically engineered bacteria could be patented, establishing the precedent for life forms. Business methods, such as the one-click shopping method by Amazon.com, later became patentable.[10] So did computer programs. These trends contributed to the dramatic increase in the number of patents granted since the 1980s. Before 1985, the US awarded no more than 80,000 patents in any year. By 2000, that number was around 175,000 (Jaffe and Lerner, 2004).

The potential dangers of overprotection serve as warning that IP strengthening should be carried out with caution. Finding the right

[9] To help the South access essential medicine, some commentators suggest implementing price discrimination in pharmaceuticals in favor of the South, which presumably has higher income elasticity of demand for medicine. See, for example, Maskus and Reichman (2005).

[10] The one-click shopping method patent is often cited as an example of US authorities awarding a patent that is too obvious, violating one of the two major criteria in awarding patents — non-obviousness and novelty. Moreover, it's also too broad, critics say.

balance in IP protection is complex. Governments need to make sure scientific and economic progress isn't adversely affected.

In principle, a TRIPS-compliant IP system is good for many less-developed countries. A sound IP system would place these countries on a more sustainable development path. However, fully implementing TRIPS in the South can greatly increase costs of accessing technology. This can have tremendous implications on the South's growth and living standards. A more gradual and cautious approach in implementation would be advisable.

References

Ginarte, J. C. and Park, W. G. (1997). Determinants of patent rights: A cross-national study, *Research Policy* 26, 283–301.

Grossman, G. M. and Lai, E. L.-C. (2004). International protection of intellectual property, *American Economic Review* 94, 1635–1653.

Jaffe, A. and Lerner, J. (2004). *Innovation and Its Discontents*, Princeton, N.J.: Princeton University Press.

Lai, E. L.-C. and Qiu, L. D. (2003). The North's intellectual property rights standard for the South? *Journal of International Economics* 59(1), 183–209.

Maskus, K. E. and Reichman, J. H. (eds.) (2005). *International Public Goods and Transfer of Technology Under a Globalized Intellectual Property Regime*, New York: Cambridge University Press.

McCalman, P. (2001). Reaping what you sow: An empirical analysis of international patent harmonization, *Journal of International Economics* 55(1), 161–185.

McCullagh, D. (2005). Microsoft, Oracle call for patent reform, *CNET News.com*, 25 April 2005.

Park, W. G. and Wagh, S. (2002). Index of patent rights, in *Economic Freedom of the World: 2002 Annual Report*, The Fraser Institute, pp. 33–41.

Reichman, J. H. (1995). Universal minimum standards of intellectual property protection under the TRIPS component of the WTO agreement, *The International Lawyer* 29(2), 345–388.

Siwek, S. E. (2005). *Engines of Growth: Economic Contributions of the U.S. Intellectual Property Industries*, Economists Incorporated, Commissioned by NBC Universal.

Tufts Center for the Study of Drug Development (2007). *Outlook 2007 Report.*

Chapter 2

International Protection of Intellectual Property*

Abstract
We study the incentives that governments have to protect intellectual property in a trading world economy. We consider a world economy with ongoing innovation in two countries that differ in market size and in their capacities for innovation. After describing the determination of national patent policies in a non-cooperative regime of patent protection, we ask, Why is intellectual property better protected in the North than in the South? We also study international patent agreements by deriving the properties of an efficient global regime of patent protection and asking whether harmonization of patent policies is necessary or sufficient for global efficiency.

During the 1980's and early 1990's, the United States and several European countries expressed strong dissatisfaction with what they deemed to be inadequate protection of intellectual property in many developing countries. The developed countries made the upgrading of intellectual property rights (IPRs) one of their highest priorities for the Uruguay Round of trade talks. Their efforts bore fruit in the

*By Gene M. Grossman and Edwin L.-C. Lai. Originally published in *American Economic Review*, 94(5) (December 2004), pp. 1635–1653. The difference with the original published paper is that Proposition 5 has been revised.

Agreement on Trade-Related Aspects of Intellectual Property Rights (TRIPs), which was approved as part of the Final Act of the Uruguay Round.

TRIPs establishes minimum standards of protection for several categories of intellectual property. For example, in the area of new technology, it essentially harmonizes patent policies by requiring countries to grant patents to a broad class of innovations for a minimum of twenty years and to treat foreign and domestic applicants alike. The agreement also imposes new standards of enforcement, including the requirement of border controls, civil and criminal penalties in some circumstances, and expedited procedures for disciplining infringement. But IPRs remain a highly contentious issue in international relations, because many developing countries believe that TRIPs was forced upon them by their economically more powerful trading partners and that this move toward harmonization of patent and other IPR policies serves the interests of the North at the expense of their own.

In a country that is closed to international trade, the design of a system of IPRs poses a clear trade-off to a welfare-maximizing government. By strengthening the protection of intellectual property, a government provides greater incentives for innovation and thus the benefits that come from having more and better products. But, at the same time, it curtails potential competition for firms that have previously innovated and thus limits the benefits that can be realized from existing products. As Nordhaus (1969) argued, the optimal patent policy equates the marginal dynamic benefit with the marginal static efficiency loss.

But in an open economy, the trade-offs are not so clear cut. International trade spreads the benefits of innovation beyond national boundaries. This means that a country does not reap all of the global benefits that come from protecting intellectual property within its borders. Moreover, countries differ in their capacities for innovation due to differences in skill endowments and technical know-how. It is not obvious how a government ought to set its national IPR policy if some of the benefits of its national innovation accrue to foreigners, if its constituents benefit from innovations that are encouraged and take place beyond its boundaries, and if domestic and foreign firms differ in their ability to innovate.

Some previous research has addressed the question of whether a country with a limited capacity to innovate will benefit from extending IPRs to foreign inventors. Chin and Grossman (1990) and Deardorff (1992) investigated the welfare effects of extending patent protection from a country in which innovation takes place to another country that only consumes the innovative products. These papers treat the investment in R&D as a once-off decision, whereas Helpman (1993) models innovation as an ongoing process and associates the strength of the IPR regime with the flow probability that a given product protected by a patent in the North will be imitated in the South. He evaluates the welfare consequences of marginal changes in the rate of imitation. These papers do not, however, consider the simultaneous choice of IPR protection by trade partners, nor do they discuss what international regime of IPR protection would be globally efficient.[1]

In this paper, we study the incentives that governments have to protect intellectual property in a trading world economy. In our formal analysis, we associate the strength of IPR protection with an index variable that captures both the length of a country's patents and the stringency of its enforcement policies. We recognize that, in reality, governments choose packages of policies that include not only these instruments, but others such as patent breadth, limits on patentability, compulsory licensing requirements, copyright and trademark protections, and so on. We believe, however, that our analysis has broader relevance than would be implied by a literal interpretation of the model, because many of the factors that determine optimal patent duration and enforcement would also guide the choice of an optimal package of patent and copyright instruments in a setting in which governments choose from a wider range of policy tools.

[1] McCalman (2002) addresses some of these issues in a model of once-off innovation by a single firm in a developed economy. See also Lai and Qiu (2003), which we discuss at greater length below.

We consider a world economy with ongoing innovation in which there are two countries that differ in market size and in their capacities for conducting research and development. Innovators develop the designs for new products, each of which has a limited economic life. Patents, when fully enforced, provide inventors with exclusive rights to produce, sell and distribute their products within a country. We study a regime with national treatment, which means that the same protection is afforded to all inventors irrespective of their nation of origin.

We begin in Section 1 with the case of a closed economy. There we re-examine the trade-off between static costs and dynamic benefits that was first studied by Nordhaus. We derive a neat formula that characterizes the optimal patent policy in a closed economy and discuss the determinants of the optimal strength of patent protection. One interesting finding is that the optimal index of patent protection may be independent of or even decreasing in the size of the economy.

In Section 2, we describe the determination of national policies in a non-cooperative regime of patent protection. In this, we follow Lai and Qiu (2003), but with some differences that are better described after the model has been developed. After discussing the relationship between our paper and that one, we derive best response functions for the "North" and the "South," where the North is assumed to have a higher wage than the South, as well as possibly a larger market for innovative products and a greater capacity for innovation. We characterize the nationally optimal policies, compare the incentives for providing protection for intellectual property in an open economy to those that exist in a closed economy, and explain the strategic interactions between countries in the setting of their patent policies.

In Section 3, we ask, Why is IPR protection stronger in the North? If the capacity for R&D is greater in the North than in the South and the market for innovative products is at least as large there, then patent protection will be stronger in the North than in the South in a Nash equilibrium. We explain why relative market size and relative productivity in innovation matter for the relative incentives to protect intellectual property. Patents are a more potent instrument for stimulating innovation in the relatively larger market.

And a country that invents a smaller share of the world's innovative products will find more incentive to ease IPR protection so as to benefit local consumers at the expense of producers.

We study international patent agreements in Section 4. First we derive the properties of an efficient global regime of IPRs. An efficient patent regime is one that provides the optimal aggregate incentives for innovation to inventors throughout the world. These incentives can be achieved by various combinations of patent policies in the two countries, so there is no unique set of policies that is needed for global efficiency. However, different ways of achieving the optimal aggregate incentives have different implications for the distribution of welfare between the North and the South. Among combinations of policies that give the same overall incentives for global research, the North fares better, and the South worse, the stronger is patent protection in the South. An implication of our findings is that harmonization of patent policies is neither necessary nor sufficient for global efficiency. Moreover, starting from a non-cooperative equilibrium with stronger IPR protection in the North than in the South, an efficient agreement calling for harmonization of patent policies benefits the North quite possibly at the expense of the South.

In Section 5, we extend our analysis of both the non-cooperative and cooperative settings to a world with many trading countries. The many-country model is qualitatively similar to the two-country model, although the addition of more countries exacerbates the inefficiencies associated with non-cooperation. Our findings are summarized in Section 6.

1 A Simple Model of Innovation

In this section, we construct a simple model of ongoing innovation. We develop the model for a closed economy and use it to revisit the question of optimal patent policy that was first addressed by Nordhaus (1969). Our model yields a neat formula that characterizes the trade-off between the static costs and dynamic benefits of strengthening patent protection. The discussion of a closed economy lays the groundwork for the more subtle analysis of the international system that we undertake in the sections that follow.

The economy has two sectors, one that produces a homogeneous good and another that produces a continuum of differentiated products. The designs for the differentiated products result from private investments in R&D. Once a good has been invented, it has a finite economic life of length $\bar{\tau}$. That is, a new product potentially provides utility to consumers for a period of length $\bar{\tau}$ from the time of its creation, whereupon its value to consumers drops to zero.

There are M consumers with identical preferences. We shall refer to M as the "size of the market."[2] The representative consumer maximizes a utility function of the form

$$U(t) = \int_t^\infty u(z)e^{-\rho z}dz \tag{1}$$

where

$$u(z) = y(z) + \int_0^{n(z)} h[x(i,z)]di, \tag{2}$$

$y(z)$ is consumption of the homogeneous good at time z, $x(i,z)$ is consumption of the ith variety of differentiated product at time z, and $n(z)$ is the measure of differentiated products invented before z that still hold value to consumers at time z. We assume that $h'(x) > 0$, $h''(x) < 0$, $h'(0) = \infty$, and $-xh''(x)/h'(x) < 1$ for all x. The third assumption ensures a positive demand for every variety at any finite price. The fourth ensures that any firm producing a differentiated product charges a finite price.

A consumer maximizes utility by purchasing some of all varieties that are not yet obsolete. He chooses $x(i,z)$ so that $h'[x(i,z)] = p(i,z)$ for all i and z, where $p(i,z)$ is the price of variety i at

[2]In our model, demand for differentiated products does not vary with income. Thus, a rich country need not have a larger market for these goods than a poor country. Nonetheless, we prefer to think of the market for differentiated goods as being larger in the North than in the South. This could be rigorously justified within our model if we were to suppose that differentiated products provide utility only after a threshold level of consumption of the homogeneous goods has been reached. Then, a rich country may have more consumers who surpass the threshold.

time z. After the consumer makes all of his optimal purchases of differentiated products at time z, he devotes the remainder of his spending to the homogeneous good y. Spending is always positive in the equilibria we describe. This means that the interest rate is constant and equal to ρ, in view of the perfect intertemporal substitutability of good y in the preferences described by (1) and (2).

Manufacturing requires only labor. Any firm can produce good y with a units of labor per unit of output. All known varieties of the differentiated product also can be produced with a units of labor per unit of output.

The design of new varieties requires both labor and human capital. We take $\phi(z) \equiv F[H, L_R(z)] = \{b\,[L_R(z)/a]^{\beta} + (1-b)H^{\beta}\}^{1/\beta}$, where $\phi(z)$ is the flow of new inventions at time z, H is the (constant) stock of human capital, $L_R(z)$ is the amount of labor devoted to R&D, and a is a measure of labor productivity as before. This is, of course, a production function with a constant elasticity of substitution between labor and human capital. We assume that $\beta \leq 1/2$, or equivalently that the elasticity of substitution is less than or equal to two. This assumption is sufficient (but not necessary) to ensure that any patent policy that satisfies the first-order condition for an interior optimum also satisfies the second-order condition. Note that $\dot{n}(z) = \phi(z) - \phi(z - \bar{\tau})$, because the goods that were invented at time $z - \bar{\tau}$ become obsolete at time z.

The government grants the original designer of a differentiated product a patent of length $\tau \leq \bar{\tau}$. The government also chooses the vigor of its enforcement policy, which we index by $\omega \in [0, 1]$. For simplicity, we take ω to be the probability that a non-expired patent is enforced by the government at any moment in time.[3] If a live patent is enforced by the government, the holder enjoys exclusive rights to produce and sell the protected product in the local market.

We describe now the static and dynamic equilibrium for an economy that has a patent duration of τ and an enforcement rate of ω. In equilibrium, firms with enforced patents behave as

[3] Alternatively, we might interpret ω as being the fraction of the country's territory in which the patent is enforced.

monopolies. Each such firm faces an inverse demand curve from each of the M consumers with the form $p(x) = h'(x)$. The firm sets its price so that $(p-aw)/p = -xh''/h'$, where w is the wage rate and x is sales per consumer. This is the usual monopoly-pricing rule whereby the markup over unit cost as a fraction of the price is equal to the inverse demand elasticity. Optimal pricing yields the typical holder of an enforced patent profits of π per consumer and total profits of $M\pi$.

When a live patent is not enforced, competitors imitate the good costlessly. Then the product sells for the competitive price of $p = aw$ and generates no profits for the inventor. Similarly, once a patent expires, the price of the good falls to the competitive level and remains there until the good becomes obsolete. The homogeneous good always carries the competitive price of aw, which, because this good is the numeraire, implies that $w = 1/a$. In writing this condition, we implicitly assume that the economy's labor supply is sufficiently large that some labor remains for production of the homogeneous good after all derived demand for labor for producing differentiated products and conducting R&D has been satisfied.

Labor engages in manufacturing and R&D. The labor employed in manufacturing differentiated goods is just the amount needed to produce the quantities demanded at the equilibrium prices. The allocation of labor to R&D is such that its marginal value product in this activity is equal to the wage rate. Thus,

$$vF_L\left(H, L_R\right) = w, \tag{3}$$

where v is the value of a new patent. A patent is worth the discounted value of the expected profits it generates in the time before it expires, or

$$v = \frac{\omega M\pi}{\rho}\left(1 - e^{-\rho\tau}\right). \tag{4}$$

We see from (3) and (4) that an increase in either patent length or patent enforcement increases the value of a new patent, thereby drawing additional resources into R&D.

The final equilibrium condition equates savings with investment. Savings are the difference between national income $rH+wL+n_mM\pi$ and aggregate spending E, where r is the return to human capital, L is the aggregate labor supply, and n_m is the number of firms that hold live and enforced patents at a given time. All investment is devoted to R&D. This activity has an aggregate cost of $rH + wL_R$. Thus, we can write the equilibrium condition as $(rH + wL + n_mM\pi) - E = rH + wL_R$, or

$$E = w(L - L_R) + n_mM\pi. \tag{5}$$

Before proceeding to the government's maximization problem, it is useful to define an index of the strength of IPR protection afforded by the vector of policies (τ, ω). First, define $T \equiv (1 - e^{-\rho\tau})/\rho$ as the present discounted value of a flow of one dollar from time 0 to time τ. Then define $\Omega \equiv \omega T$. Clearly, (4) can be re-written as $v = M\pi\Omega$. Thus, Ω captures the overall incentives that government policy provides for the creation of new varieties. In what follows we use Ω as a measure of the strength of IPR protection.

Next, we derive an expression for aggregate welfare at date 0, the time at which a new (optimal) patent policy will be set by the government. By assumption, this patent protection applies only to goods introduced after time 0; those introduced beforehand are subject to whatever policy was in effect at the time of their invention.[4] Our derivation anticipates a stationary equilibrium in which the allocation of labor to R&D and thus the rate of innovation, ϕ, are constant over time. We substantiate this hypothesis in footnote 5 below. Note that in such a stationary equilibrium $n_m = \phi\Omega$.

At any moment, each consumer enjoys surplus of $C_m = h(x_m) - p_mx_m$ from his consumption of any good whose live patent is enforced and surplus of $C_c = h(x_c) - p_cx_c$ from any differentiated product

[4]It would never be optimal for the government to provide patent protection on goods that have already been invented. This would create deadweight loss without any offsetting social benefit. The government might wish to eliminate protection for goods that were invented under a different regime, but we assume that such expropriation of intellectual property would not be legal.

that is competitively priced, either because its patent has expired or because it is not enforced. Here, x_m and x_c are the amounts purchased by the consumer from a typical monopoly and competitive supplier, respectively, and p_m and p_c are the respective prices. We distinguish now between goods invented before time 0 and those invented afterward. The former yield some exogenous surplus that is unaffected by the new patent regime. Each good in the latter category yields each of the M consumers a discounted surplus of $C_m\Omega + C_c(\bar{T} - \Omega)$ over its useful life, where $\bar{T} \equiv (1 - e^{-\rho\bar{\tau}})/\rho$. Using (1), (2) and (5), and assuming that new goods are introduced at a constant flow ϕ after time 0, we calculate that aggregate welfare at time 0 is

$$W(0) = \Lambda_0 + \frac{w\,(L - L_R)}{\rho} + \frac{M\phi}{\rho}(C_m + \pi)\Omega + \frac{M\phi}{\rho}C_c(\bar{T} - \Omega), \quad (6)$$

where Λ_0 is the discounted present value of the consumer surplus and profits derived from goods invented before time 0.

We are now ready to derive the optimal patent policy for a closed economy. Note that aggregate welfare depends only on the index of patent protection Ω and not separately on the underlying policies τ and ω. This implies that patent duration and patent enforcement are perfect substitutes as instruments of IPR protection and it justifies our use of Ω as a measure of the strength of the IPR regime. Formally, we maximize $W(0)$ with respect to Ω, after recalling that $\phi = F(H, L_R)$ and that L_R is a function of Ω via (3) and (4).[5]

[5]Equivalently, we can maximize $\rho W(0)$ over the choice of Ω. Note that C_m, C_c and π do not depend on the strength of patent protection and thus do not depend on Ω. We can combine (3) and (4) to write $M\pi\Omega F_L\,(H, L_R) = w$, which allows us to solve for the functional relationship between the labor devoted to R&D and the policy variable Ω; denote it by $L_R(\Omega)$. Then, substituting this expression into (6) and rearranging terms, we can write the maxim and as

$$\rho W(0) = \rho\Lambda_0 + w\left[L - L_R(\Omega)\right] + MF\left[H, L_R(\Omega)\right]\left[(C_m + \pi - C_c)\,\Omega + C_c\bar{T}\right].$$

The first-order condition for a maximum requires

$$(C_c - C_m - \pi)MF\left[H, L_R(\Omega)\right] = \left\{MF_L\left[(C_m + \pi - C_c)\,\Omega + C_c\bar{T}\right] - w\right\}L_R'$$

It is more intuitive, however, to describe the social costs and benefits that derive from a marginal increase in patent protection from a given strength of protection Ω. The cost of strengthening patent protection is that the economy suffers the deadweight loss of $M\left(C_c - C_m - \pi\right)$ on each newly invented good for a greater fraction of the product's life. Considering that the constant flow of new products is ϕ per unit time, the total discounted marginal cost on all goods invented after time 0 is

$$\frac{\phi}{\rho} M\left(C_c - C_m - \pi\right).$$

The benefit to the economy of strengthening patent policy is that it encourages R&D, which in turn means a greater variety of differentiated products. Each differentiated product yields discounted consumer surplus of $MC_m\Omega$ during times when its patent is active and enforced and surplus of $MC_c(\bar{T} - \Omega)$ during times when it is competitively priced, where in each case the discounting is back to the time of invention. Now if we discount this flow of benefits back to time 0, and multiply by the number of new inventions induced by a marginal strengthening of the patent regime, we have the total marginal benefit, which is equal to

$$\frac{1}{\rho} \cdot \frac{d\phi}{dv} \cdot \frac{dv}{d\Omega} \cdot \left[MC_m\Omega + MC_c(\bar{T} - \Omega)\right].$$

Using (3) we calculate that

$$\frac{d\phi}{dv} = \gamma \frac{\phi}{v},$$

where γ is the ratio of the elasticity of research output with respect to labor to the elasticity of the marginal product of labor in R&D; i.e. $\gamma \equiv -\left(F_L\right)^2 / \left(FF_{LL}\right)$. The variable γ identifies the responsiveness of innovation to the protections afforded by the patent system. In general, it is a function of L_R and thus indirectly of the strength

---

from which (7) follows. In the appendix we show $\beta \leq 1/2$ is sufficient to ensure that the second-order condition is satisfied at any value of Ω that satisfies the first-order condition (7).

of patent protection Ω. With the CES research technology, $\gamma = [b/(1-b)(1-\beta)](L_R/aH)^{\beta}$. For the special case of a Cobb–Douglas technology (which is the limiting case of the CES as $\beta \to 0$), γ is a constant equal to the ratio of the cost share of labor to the cost share of human capital.

Next, we use (4) to compute that

$$\frac{dv}{d\Omega} = M\pi.$$

Substituting for $d\phi/dv$ and $dv/d\Omega$ in the expression for marginal benefit, and equating the result to the marginal cost, we derive an implicit formula for the optimal index of patent protection. We find that

$$C_c - C_m - \pi = \gamma \left[C_m + C_c \left(\frac{\bar{T} - \Omega}{\Omega} \right) \right] \tag{7}$$

at an (interior) optimal value of Ω.

From (7) we see that the optimal patent protection is stronger, the greater is the useful life of a product (larger $\bar{\tau}$), the more patient are consumers (smaller ρ), and the higher is the responsiveness of innovation to strengthened patent protection.[6] All of these findings accord well with intuition. One noteworthy feature of (7) is the relationship between market size and the optimal strength of patent protection. In a closed economy, the first-best level of R&D — that which maximizes discounted utility when all goods are competitively priced — typically is an increasing function of market size. This is because innovation is a public good, and the Samuelsonian rule for optimal provision of a public good calls for greater output when the benefits can be spread across more consumers. But the encouragement of innovation by patents achieves only a second best. According to (7), the size of the market M affects the optimal index of patent protection only through its effect on the supply elasticity of innovations. If γ is an increasing function of L_R, as it will be if

[6] The proof of these statements makes use of the second-order condition, which ensures that the right-hand side of (7) is a declining function of Ω.

$1/2 > \beta > 0$, then the optimal Ω is an increasing function of M. But if γ is a decreasing function of L_R, as it will be if $\beta < 0$, then the optimal Ω is a decreasing function of M. In the benchmark Cobb–Douglas case (with $\beta = 0$), γ is independent of L_R and therefore of market size. Then an increase in M enhances the marginal benefit of strengthening patent protection and the marginal cost of doing so in equal proportions. The optimal strength of patent protection in a closed economy with a Cobb–Douglas research technology is invariant to market size.

2 Noncooperative Patent Protection

In this section, we study the national incentives for protection of intellectual property in a world economy with imitation and trade. We derive the Nash equilibria of a game in which two countries set their patent policies simultaneously and noncooperatively. The countries are distinguished by their wage rates, their market sizes, and their stocks of human capital. The last of these proxies for their different capacities for R&D. We shall term the countries "North"and "South," in keeping with our desire to understand the tensions that surrounded the tightening of IPR protection in the developing countries in the last decade. Maskus (2000a, Chapter 3) has documented an increase in innovative activity in poor and middle-income countries such as Brazil, Korea, and China, so our model of relations between trading partners with positive but different abilities to conduct R&D may be apt for studying the incentives for IPR protection in a world of trade between such nations and the developed economies.[7] But our model may apply more broadly to relations between any groups of countries that have different wages and different capacities for research. Such differences exist, albeit to a lesser extent than between North and South, in the comparison of countries in Northern and Southern Europe, or the comparison of

[7]He also shows the extent to which patent applications in countries like Mexico, Brazil, Korea, Malaysia, Indonesia and Singapore are dominated by foreign firms, a feature of the data that figures in our analysis.

the United States and Canada. We do not mean the labels North and South to rule out the application of our analysis to these other sorts of relationships.

Before proceeding, we pause to discuss the relationship between the analysis that will be presented in this section and that contained in Lai and Qiu (2003), which covers some similar ground. Lai and Qiu also examine a non-cooperative game between two governments that set national patent policies. They do not, however, model how the resources used in innovation translate into new goods, but rather assume that at each moment in time the different goods that might be invented have different (exogenous) innovation costs. Specifically, the cost of making ϕ innovations is assumed to be an increasing, power function of ϕ. They also assume that demand for each differentiated product is iso-elastic and that the discount rate is zero. With our more general utility function and our explicit treatment of the R&D technology, we are able to explain when and why the countries' patent policies are strategic substitutes or strategic complements based on the technology for innovation — specifically, the substitutability between human capital and mobile resources in the R&D activity. Perhaps more importantly, we are able to provide an intuitive discussion of why and how a government's incentives for protecting intellectual property in an open economy differ from those it would face in a world without trade, whereas Lai and Qiu focus only on the algebra of a single, parameterized example of a trading economy.

2.1 The global IPR regime

The model is a natural extension of the one presented in Section 1. Consumers in the two countries share identical preferences. In each country, the representative consumer maximizes the intertemporal utility function in (1). The instantaneous utility of a consumer in country j now is given by

$$u_j(z) = y_j(z) + \int_0^{n_S(z)+n_N(z)} h[x_j(i,z)]di, \tag{8}$$

where $y_j(z)$ is consumption of the homogeneous good by a typical resident of country j at time z, $x_j(i,z)$ is consumption of the ith differentiated product by a resident of country j at time z, and $n_j(z)$ is the number of differentiated varieties previously invented in country j that remain economically viable at time z. There are M_N consumers in the North and M_S consumers in the South. While we do not place any restrictions on the relative sizes of the two markets at this juncture, we shall be most interested in the case where $M_N > M_S$.[8] It does not matter for our analysis whether consumers can borrow and lend internationally or not.

In country j, it takes a_j units of labor to produce one unit of the homogeneous good or to produce one unit of any variety of the differentiated product. New goods are invented in each region according to $\phi_j = F(H_j, L_{Rj}/a_j) = \left[b(L_{Rj}/a_j)^\beta + (1-b)H_j^\beta\right]^{1/\beta}$, where H_j is the human capital endowment of country j, L_{Rj} is the labor devoted to R&D there, and again we take $\beta \leq 1/2$. We assume that $a_N < a_S$, which means that labor is uniformly more productive in the North than in the South.[9] We also assume that the numeraire good is produced in positive quantities in both countries, so that $w_j = 1/a_j$ for $j = S, N$, and hence $w_N/w_S = a_S/a_N > 1$.

We now describe the IPR regime. In each country, there is *national treatment* in the granting of patent rights. Under national treatment, the government of country j affords the same protection $\Omega_j = \omega_j T_j$ to all inventors of differentiated products regardless of their national origins, where ω_j is the probability that a patent is enforced in country j (or the fraction of country j's market where a patent is enforced) at any moment in time, $T_j = (1 - e^{-\rho\tau_j})/\rho$, and τ_j is the length of the patents granted by country j. In other

[8]We remind the reader that market size is meant to capture not the population of a country, but rather the scale of its demand for innovative products.

[9]In Grossman and Lai (2002), we allowed the relative productivity of labor to vary in different uses; i.e. we allowed for Ricardian comparative advantage across the regions. This feature caused some subtle complications that we ignore here for the sake of simplicity and greater clarity.

words, we assume that foreign firms and domestic firms have equal standing in applying for patents in any country and that all patents are subject to the same enforcement provisions. National treatment is required by TRIPs and it characterized the laws that were in place in most countries even before this agreement.[10] In our model, a patent is an exclusive right to make, sell, use, or import a product for a fixed period of time (see Maskus, 2000a, p. 36). This means that, when good i is under patent protection in country j, no firm other than the patent holder or one designated by it may legally produce the good in country j for domestic sale or for export, nor may the good be legally imported into country j from an unauthorized producer outside the country. We also rule out parallel imports — unauthorized imports of good i that were produced by the patent holder or its designee, but that were sold to a third party outside country j.[11] When parallel imports are prevented, patent holders can practice price discrimination across national markets.

We solve the Nash game in which the governments set their patent policies once-and-for-all at time 0. These patents apply only to goods invented after time 0; goods invented beforehand continue to receive the protections afforded at their times of invention. So long

[10]National treatment is required by the Paris Convention for the Protection of Industrial Property, to which 127 countries subscribed by the end of 1994 and 164 countries subscribe today (see http://www.wipo.org/treaties/ip/paris/index.html). There were, however, allegations from firms in the United States and elsewhere that prior to the signing of TRIPS in 1994, nondiscriminatory laws did not always mean nondiscriminatory practice. See Scotchmer (2004) for an analysis of the incentives that countries have to apply national treatment in the absence of an enforcible agreement.

[11]The treatment of parallel imports under TRIPs remains a matter of legal controversy. Countries continue to differ in their rules for territorial exhaustion of IPRs. Some countries, like Australia and Japan, practice international exhaustion, whereby the restrictive rights granted by a patent end with the first sale of the good anywhere in the world. Other countries or regions, like the United States and the European Union, practice national or regional exhaustion, whereby patent rights end only with the first sale within the country or region. Under such rules, patent holders can prevent parallel trade. See Maskus (2000b) for further discussion.

as the governments cannot remove protections that were previously granted, the economy has no state variables that bear on its choice of optimal patent policies at a given moment in time. This means that the Nash equilibrium in once-and-for-all patents is also a subgame perfect equilibrium in the infinitely repeated game in which the governments can change their patent policies periodically, or even continuously. Of course, the repeated game may have other equilibria in which the governments base their current policies on the history of prior actions. We do not investigate such equilibria with tacit cooperation here, but rather postpone our discussion of cooperation until Section 4.

Let us describe, for given patent strengths Ω_N and Ω_S, the life cycle of a typical differentiated product. During an initial phase after the product is introduced, the inventor holds an active patent in both countries which is only partially enforced. The patent holder earns an expected flow of profits of $\omega_N M_N \pi$ from sales in the Northern market and an expected flow of profits of $\omega_S M_S \pi$ from sales in the Southern market, where π is earnings per consumer for a monopoly selling a typical brand. Notice that monopoly profits per consumer are the same for sales in both markets, because consumers share identical preferences. Also, they do not depend on where a good was invented or where it is produced, because the productivity gap between the countries exactly offsets the wage differential.[12] Each Northern consumer realizes a flow of expected surplus of $\omega_N C_m + (1 - \omega_N) C_c$ from his purchases of the good, where C_m is the surplus that a consumer derives from purchases of a good produced at a cost of $w_j a_j = 1$ and sold at the monopoly price p_m and C_c is the surplus he derives from a product sold for the competitive price of $p_c = 1$. Similarly, a Southern consumer realizes an expected flow of consumer surplus of $\omega_S C_m + (1 - \omega_S) C_c$ from his purchases of the good.

[12]In Grossman and Lai (2002), where we allowed for comparative technological advantages across different uses of labor, we were forced to consider separately situations in which direct foreign investment is and is not a possibility. However, our conclusions were qualitatively similar for the two cases.

After a while, the patent will expire in one country. For concreteness, let's say that this happens first in the South. Then the good will be legally imitated by competitive firms producing there, for sales in the local (Southern) market. The imitators will not, however, be able to sell the good legally in the North, because the live patent there, if enforced, affords protection from such infringing imports. When the patent expires in the South, the price of the good falls permanently to $w_S a_S = 1$, and the original inventor ceases to realize profits in that market. The flow of consumer surplus in the South rises to $M_S C_c$.

Eventually, the inventor's patent expires in the North. Then the Northern market can be served completely by competitive firms producing in either location. At this time, the price of the good in the North falls to $p_c = 1$ and households there begin to enjoy the higher flow of consumer surplus $M_N C_c$. The original inventor loses his remaining source of monopoly income. Finally, after a period of length $\bar{\tau}$ has elapsed from the moment of invention, the good becomes obsolete and all flows of consumer surplus cease.

2.2 The best response functions

We are now ready to derive the best response functions for the two governments. The best response expresses the strength of patent protection that maximizes a country's aggregate welfare as a function of the given patent policy of its trading partner. Consider the choice of Ω_S by the government of the South. This country bears two costs from strengthening its patent protection slightly. First, it expands the fraction of goods previously invented in the South on which the country suffers a static deadweight loss of $M_S(C_c - C_m - \pi)$. Second, it augments the fraction of goods previously invented in the North on which its consumers realize surplus of $M_S C_m$ instead of $M_S C_c$. Notice that the profits earned by Northern producers in the South are not an offset to this latter marginal cost, because they accrue to patent holders in the North. The marginal benefit that comes to the South from strengthening its patent protection reflects the increased incentive that Northern and Southern firms have to engage in R&D. If the welfare-maximizing Ω_S is positive and less than $\bar{T}$, then the marginal benefit *per consumer* of increasing Ω_S must match the marginal cost, which implies

$$\begin{aligned}&\phi_S(C_c - C_m - \pi) + \phi_N(C_c - C_m)\\ &\quad = \frac{\gamma_S\phi_S + \gamma_N\phi_N}{v} M_S\pi[C_m\Omega_S + C_c(\bar{T} - \Omega_S)],\end{aligned} \tag{9}$$

where $v = (M_S\Omega_S + M_N\Omega_N)\pi$ is the value of a new patent and γ_j is the responsiveness of innovation in region j to changes in the value of a patent (in elasticity form).

Similarly, in the North, the marginal benefit of strengthening patent protection must match the marginal cost at any interior point on the best response curve. The marginal cost in the North is different from that in the South, because the North's national income includes the profits earned by Northern patent holders but not those earned by Southern patent holders. The marginal benefit differs too, because the effectiveness of patent policy as a tool for promoting innovation varies according to the importance of a country's market in the aggregate profits of potential innovators and because the surplus from a typical product over its lifetime depends upon a country's patent regime. The condition for the best response of the North, analogous to (9) above, is

$$\begin{aligned}&\phi_S(C_c - C_m) + \phi_N(C_c - C_m - \pi)\\ &\quad = \frac{\gamma_S\phi_S + \gamma_N\phi_N}{v} M_N\pi\left[C_m\Omega_N + C_c(\bar{T} - \Omega_N)\right].\end{aligned} \tag{10}$$

Noting that $\gamma_S = \gamma_N = \gamma$,[13] the two best response functions can be written similarly as

$$C_c - C_m - \mu_i\pi = \gamma\frac{M_i\Omega_i}{M_S\Omega_S + M_N\Omega_N}\left[C_m + C_c\left(\frac{\bar{T} - \Omega_i}{\Omega_i}\right)\right] \quad \text{for } i = S, N, \tag{11}$$

[13]The fact that the two supply elasticities γ_S and γ_N are equal despite the differences in human capital endowments, in employment, and in labor

where $\mu_i = \phi_i/(\phi_S + \phi_N)$ is the share of world innovation that takes place in country i. This form of the best response function facilitates a comparison of the incentives that a government has for protecting intellectual property in a world with trade compared to those that exist when there is no trade, as expressed in (7). On the left-hand side of (11), the government of a open economy considers only a fraction of the profits that flow to patent holders to be an offset to the static cost of patent protection. On the right-hand side, the ability of an open economy to stimulate innovation with a given change in patent protection is a fraction of what it is in a closed economy, because inventors earn only part of their discounted profits within the country's borders. Both of these forces point to weaker patent protection in an open economy than would be optimal in the absence of trade. Against this, possibly, is the difference between the supply elasticities for innovation in the closed and open economies; the presence of a foreign country offering protection for innovators may increase the responsiveness of innovation to home patent policy if γ is an increasing function of L_R. However, with the CES research technology γ is in fact a *non-increasing* function of L_R whenever $\beta \leq 0$; i.e. when the elasticity of substitution between human capital

---

productivity is a property of the CES research technology. It follows from the observation that

$$\gamma_i = \frac{b}{(1-b)(1-\beta)} \left(\frac{L_{Ri}}{a_i H_i} \right)^{\beta}$$

and $vF_L(L_{Ri}/a_i, H_i) = w_i$, or

$$\frac{vb}{a_i} \left[b + (1-b) \left(\frac{L_{Ri}}{a_i H_i} \right)^{-\beta} \right]^{\frac{1-\beta}{\beta}} = \frac{1}{a_i}.$$

Combining the two, we find $\gamma_S = \gamma_N = \gamma$, where

$$\gamma = \frac{b}{1-\beta} \left[\left(\frac{1}{bv} \right)^{\frac{\beta}{1-\beta}} - b \right]^{-1}.$$

and labor is less than or equal to one. It follows that we have the following proposition.[14]

Proposition 1. *Let the research technology be* $\phi_i = [b(L_{Ri}/a_i)^\beta + (1-b)H_i^\beta]^{1/\beta}$ *in country* i*, for* $i = S, N$*. If* $\beta \leq 0$*, patent protection is weaker in each country in any Nash equilibrium than it would be if the country were closed to international trade.*

If the research technology in each country takes a Cobb–Douglas form (i.e. $\beta = 0$), the supply elasticity γ is a constant equal to $b/(1-b)$. Moreover, $\mu_i = H_i/(H_S + H_N)$ for any CES research technology.[15] Thus, both μ_i and γ are independent of the patent policies in the Cobb–Douglas case. It follows from (11) that the best response functions are linear and downward sloping in this case, and that the best response function for the South is steeper than that for the North, when the two are drawn in (Ω_S, Ω_N) space.

More generally, the best response functions need not be linear, but they must be downward sloping whenever $\beta \leq 0$; i.e. when the elasticity of substitution between human capital and labor in designing new products is less than or equal to one. Thus, the patent policies of the two countries are strategic substitutes in such circumstances. To understand the strategic interdependence between the governments in choosing their policies, consider the

[14]Suppose the government of an open economy were to choose the autarky strength of patent protection. The marginal cost of strengthening protection would be greater in the open compared to the closed economy, since $\mu_i < 1$. And, since $\gamma'(L_R) \leq 0$ and $M_i\Omega_i/(M_S\Omega_S + M_N\Omega_N) < 1$, the marginal benefit from strengthening the protection would be smaller in the open as compared to the closed economy. Thus, the marginal cost would exceed the marginal benefit in the open economy, which means that the government would have reason to reduce the index of patent protection from the autarky level.

[15]Note that

$$\phi_i = H_i \left[b \left(\frac{L_{Ri}}{a_i H_i} \right)^\beta + (1-b) \right]^{\frac{1}{\beta}}.$$

From the fact that $vF_L(L_{Ri}/a_i, H_i) = w_i$, we have that L_{Ri}/a_iH_i takes on a common value in the two countries; see footnote 13. It follows that ϕ_i is proportional to H_i, with the same factor of proportionality in both countries.

choice of patent protection by the South. Suppose the North were to strengthen its patent protection; i.e. to increase Ω_N. This would shrink the fraction of total discounted profits that an innovator earns in the South and so, ceteris paribus, reduce the responsiveness of global innovation to patent policy in the South. Moreover, the increase in Ω_N would draw labor into R&D in the North and South. If $\beta < 0$, the elasticity of innovation with respect to patent value would fall. The South would find that its market is relatively less important to potential innovators and that these innovators are less responsive to its patent policy. For both reasons, the marginal benefit to the South of strengthening its patent protection would fall and so the government would respond to the increase in Ω_N with a reduction in patent length or an easing of enforcement.

A situation of strategic complementarity (i.e. upward-sloping best response function) can arise only if the supply elasticity of R&D rises as the size of the research sector expands ($\beta > 0$) and then only if it rises sufficiently much to compensate for the decline in relative importance of a country's market that results when its trading partner strengthens its patent protection. It is straightforward to show that the two best response functions must slope in the same direction at any point of intersection. Thus, if the two patent policies are strategic complements in one country, they are strategic complements in both.

Returning to the case with $\beta \leq 0$, it is easy to show using (11) and $d\gamma/d\Omega_i \leq 0$ that the best response curve for the South must have a slope that is everywhere greater in absolute value than M_S/M_N, while the best response curve for the North must have a slope that is everywhere smaller in absolute value than M_S/M_N.[16] It follows

[16] We have not discussed the shape of the best response functions where they hit the axes or where the constraint that $\Omega_i \leq \bar{T}$ begins to bind. The best-response curve of the South becomes vertical if it hits the vertical axis at a point below $\Omega_N = \bar{T}$. It also becomes vertical if the South's best response is $\bar{T}$ for some positive value of Ω_N. Similarly, the best-response curve for the North becomes horizontal if either it hits the horizontal axis before $\Omega_S = \bar{T}$ or if the North's best response is $\bar{T}$ for some positive value of Ω_S. Thus, the best response curve for the

that the curve for the South must be steeper than that for the North at any point of intersection. This guarantees uniqueness of the Nash equilibrium and ensures stability of the policy setting game.

We summarize the most important findings in this section as follows.

Proposition 2. *Let the research technology be* $\phi_i = [b(L_{Ri}/a_i)^\beta + (1-b)H_i^\beta]^{1/\beta}$ *in country* i*, for* $i = S, N$*. If* $\beta \leq 0$*, then the two patent policies are strategic substitutes in both countries and there exists a unique and stable Nash equilibrium of the policy setting game.*

3 Why Is Patent Protection Stronger in the North?

Governments in the North typically provide stronger patent protection than their counterparts in the South.[17] In this section, we identify sufficient conditions under which patent protection in the North will be stronger than that in the South in the Nash equilibrium of a noncooperative policy game. Our goal here is to understand the reasons why the North may have a greater incentive to protect IPRs than the South. We shall also examine how the equilibrium patent policies respond to changes in the endowments of human capital and to changes in the size of the market in each region.

We organize our discussion of the national differences in equilibrium policy choices around the following proposition.[18]

Proposition 3. *Suppose* $M_N > M_S$ *and* $H_N > H_S$*. Then* $\Omega_N \geq \Omega_S$ *in any Nash equilibrium of the patent policy game. Moreover,* $\Omega_N > \Omega_S$ *unless* $\Omega_S = \bar{T}$*.*

South must be steeper than that for the North at any point of intersection, even if these additional segments of the best response functions are taken into account.

[17]See, for example, Ginarte and Park (1997) who have constructed an index of patent rights and have shown that this index is highly correlated with per capita GDP.

[18]Lai and Qiu (2003) provide conditions under which the Nash equilibrium patent duration is longer in the North than in the South. Recall, however, that their model is considerably less general than ours. Moreover, their conditions include that the North invents more goods at every moment than the South, whereas our Proposition 3 refers only to the primitives of the model.

The proposition is readily proved using the expressions for the best response functions in (11).[19] First, recall that with a CES research technology, $\mu_i = H_i/(H_S + H_N)$. Thus, $H_N > H_S$ implies $\mu_N > \mu_S$. The left-hand side of (11) is a decreasing function of μ_i. If we cancel the terms that are common to the two best response functions, the remaining expression on the right-hand side is an increasing function of M_i and a decreasing function of Ω_i. It follows that if $\mu_N > \mu_S$ and $M_N > M_S$, a pair of policies can be mutual responses only if $\Omega_N > \Omega_S$.

Our answer to the question in the section heading is that the North has a larger market for innovative goods and a greater capacity to conduct R&D. Why do these characteristics induce the Northern government to provide stronger patent protection in a noncooperative equilibrium than its counterpart in the South? The reasons are somewhat subtle.

Recall from the discussion in Section 1 that having a large market is not per se a reason for a government to grant stronger patent protection. The optimal patent strength in a closed economy can in fact be independent of or even decreasing with market size, because both the marginal benefit of stronger protection and the marginal costs of the associated distortions are proportional to M for given γ, and the supply elasticity may remain the same or even decline as more resources are employed in R&D. The role of market size in generating different incentives for the governments has to do, instead, with the relative effectiveness of the countries' policy instruments. If M_N is larger than M_S, innovative firms earn a majority of their profits in the North. Then, a given change in Ω_N will generate a larger response of global innovation than would the same change in Ω_S. Since patents generate deadweight loss in the country that affords the protection, the country that can more effectively stimulate innovation with a given strengthening of its patent protection will have an incentive to provide stronger protection, all else equal.

[19] There are some details involving corner solutions with $\Omega_S = 0$ or $\Omega_N = \bar{T}$ that we leave to the interested reader.

In our model, the endowment of human capital proxies for the capacity to conduct R&D. With $H_N > H_S$, a majority of the world's research is carried out in the North. As a consequence, a majority of the world's profits from innovative products accrue to residents of the North. In the North, the marginal cost of strengthening patent protection reflects the attendant loss in consumer surplus on all protected products less the profits that are captured by Northern producers. Similarly, the marginal cost of strengthening patents in the South reflects the loss of consumer surplus there less the profits captured by Southern producers. But since the Northern producers earn a majority of the profits, the offset to marginal cost is larger in the North than in the South. Accordingly, the government of the North has less of a temptation to ease patent protection than that of the South.

We turn next to the comparative static properties of the model. For this, we concentrate on the case in which the best response functions are downward sloping, which necessarily arises when (but not only when) $\beta \leq 0$.

Consider first the factor endowments. An equiproportionate change in H_S and H_N has no effect on μ_S or μ_N, and thus no effect on the best response functions or the Nash equilibrium. Policy outcomes change only when there is a change in the *relative* endowments of human capital in the two countries. Suppose H_S/H_N rises. This increases the share of innovation that occurs in the South (μ_S) and reduces the share in the North (μ_N). From (11) we see that the South's best response curve shifts to the right while the North's best response curve shifts downward. In Figure 1, we depict the original best response functions by SS and NN, respectively, and the shifted curves by $S'S'$ and $N'N'$. The equilibrium moves from E to E', with a reduction in the strength of patent protection in the North and an increase in patent protection in the South. This result is consistent with the Ginarte and Park (1997) finding that patent rights are positively correlated in a cross-national sample with secondary school enrollment rates and with the share of R&D in GDP.

We turn to the effects of market size. If M_S and M_N grow equiproportionately, the term $M_i\Omega_i/(M_S\Omega_S + M_N\Omega_N)$ on the right-hand side of (11) is not affected at the initial values of Ω_S and Ω_N. Then, if $\beta = 0$ (Cobb–Douglas research technology), γ also is constant, and there is no effect on patent policy in either country. However, if $\beta < 0$, the extra resources that are drawn into R&D reduce the supply elasticity of innovation with respect to the value of a patent. Then the index of patent protection falls in both countries. This is similar to our finding for a closed economy that, when $\beta < 0$, the optimal strength of IPR protection shrinks when the market for differentiated products expands.

Next consider an expansion in the size of the Southern market with no change in market size in the North. If $\beta = 0$, γ is constant, and an increase in M_S has qualitatively the same effects as an increase in μ_S; these effects are shown in Figure 1, where we see that the strength of patent protection in the South grows while that in the North shrinks. However, if $\beta < 0$, the increase in M_S reduces γ at the initial values of Ω_S and Ω_N. Relative to the situation depicted in Figure 1, there is a further downward shift in NN and an offsetting leftward shift in SS. Indeed, if the supply elasticity of innovation falls by enough, the SS curve might even shift to its left relative to its

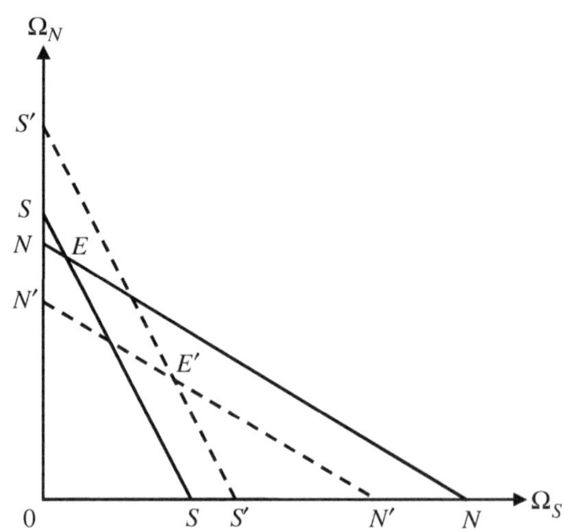

Figure 1. Comparative static effects of an increase in H_S/H_N.

initial location before the market expansion. In such circumstances Ω_S might fall as M_S grows.

4 International Patent Agreements

In this section, we study international patent agreements.[20] We begin by characterizing the combinations of patent policies that are jointly efficient for the two countries.[21] Then we compare the Nash equilibrium outcomes with the efficient policies, to identify changes in the patent regime that ought to be effected by an international treaty. Finally, we address the issue of policy harmonization. By that point, we will have seen that harmonization is neither necessary nor sufficient for global efficiency. We proceed to investigate the distributional properties of an agreement calling for harmonized patent policies and ask whether both countries would benefit from such an agreement in the absence of some form of direct compensation.

4.1 Efficient patent regimes

We shall begin by showing that the sum of the welfare levels of the two countries depends only on a measure Q of the *overall* protection afforded by the international patent system. This means that the same aggregate world welfare level can be achieved with different combinations of Ω_S and Ω_N that imply the same overall level of protection. One particular level of Q — call it Q^* — maximizes the sum of the countries' welfare levels. For a wide range of distributions

[20]See also McCalman (2002), who discusses globally efficient patent policies in his two-country extension of the Nordhaus (1969) model. Lai and Qiu (2003) consider whether the joint welfare of the two countries would be increased if the South were to extend its patents so as to be equal in length to those chosen by the North in a Nash equilibrium.

[21]Ours is a constrained efficiency, because we assume that innovation must be done privately and that patents are the only policies available to encourage R&D. We do not, for example, allow the governments to introduce R&D subsidies, which if feasible, might allow them to achieve a given rate of innovation with weaker patents and less deadweight loss.

of world welfare, efficiency is achieved by setting the individual patent policies so that the overall index of patent protection is Q^*.

In particular, let $Q = M_S\Omega_S + M_N\Omega_N$. This measure of global patent protection weighs the degree of patent protection in each country by the size of the country's market. A firm that earns a flow of expected profits of $\omega_S M_S \pi$ for a period of length τ_S in the South and a flow of expected profits of $\omega_N M_N \pi$ for a period of τ_N in the North earns a total discounted sum of expected profits equal to $Q\pi$. Thus, Q governs the allocation of resources to R&D in each country, regardless of the particular combination of patent policies in the separate countries.

Consider the choice of patent policies Ω_N and Ω_S that will take effect at time 0 and apply to goods invented thereafter. The expressions for the countries' gross welfare levels at time 0 are analogous to those for a closed economy, as recorded in equation (6). The aggregate welfare in country i, discounted to time 0, is given by

$$W_i(0) = \Lambda_{i0} + \frac{w_i(L_i - L_{Ri})}{\rho} + \frac{M_i(\phi_S + \phi_N)}{\rho}\left[\Omega_i C_m + (\bar{T} - \Omega_i)C_c\right] + \frac{\phi_i}{\rho}\pi\left(M_S\Omega_S + M_N\Omega_N\right), \quad \text{for } i = S, N, \tag{12}$$

where Λ_{i0} is the fixed amount of discounted surplus that consumers in country i derive from goods that were invented before time 0.

Summing the expressions in (12) for $i = S$ and $i = N$, we find that

$$\begin{aligned}\rho\left[W_S(0) + W_N(0)\right] &= \rho\left(\Lambda_{S0} + \Lambda_{N0}\right) + w_S(L_S - L_{RS}) \\ &\quad + w_N(L_N - L_{RN}) + (M_S + M_N)\bar{T}(\phi_S + \phi_N)C_c \\ &\quad - Q\left(\phi_S + \phi_N\right)\left(C_c - C_m - \pi\right). \end{aligned} \tag{13}$$

Since $v_S = v_N = \pi Q$, L_{RS} and L_{RN} are functions of Q.[22] The same is true of ϕ_S and ϕ_N. It follows that different combinations of Ω_S

[22]In country i, the allocation of labor to research is determined by

$$\pi Q F_L(L_{Ri}/a_i, H_i) = 1/a_i.$$

and Ω_N that yield the same value of Q also yield the same level of aggregate world welfare.[23]

If international transfer payments are feasible, then a globally efficient patent regime must have $M_S\Omega_S + M_N\Omega_N = Q^*$, where Q^* is the value of Q that maximizes the right-hand side of (13).[24] Notice that a range of efficient outcomes can be achieved without the need for any international transfers. By appropriate choice of Ω_N and Ω_S, the countries can be given any welfare levels on the efficiency frontier between that which they would achieve if $\Omega_S = 0$ and $\Omega_N = Q^*/M_N$ and that which they would achieve if $\Omega_S = Q^*/M_S$ and $\Omega_N = 0$.[25]

Although aggregate world welfare does not vary with the national policies ω_i and τ_i as long as $M_S\Omega_S + M_N\Omega_N = Q^*$, the countries fare differently under the alternative combinations of policies that can be used to achieve global efficiency unless compensating transfers take place. In particular, the welfare of the North increases and that of the South decreases as Ω_S is increased and Ω_N is decreased in such a way as to keep the weighted sum constant. It follows that, absent any international transfer payments, the countries have a strong conflict of interest over the terms of an international patent agreement.

---

[23]This result is anticipated by a similar one in McCalman (2002), who studied efficient patent agreements in a partial equilibrium model of cost-reducing innovation by a single, global monopolist.

[24]The first-order condition for maximizing $\rho[W_S(0) + W_N(0)]$ implies

$$C_c - C_m - \pi = \gamma\left\{C_m + C_c\left[\frac{(M_S + M_N)\bar{T} - Q^*}{Q^*}\right]\right\}.$$

The second-order condition is satisfied at $Q = Q^*$ when $\beta \leq 1/2$.

[25]This statement ignores the ceiling on patent lengths imposed by the finite economic life of differentiated products. A more precise statement is that a range of distributions of maximal world welfare can be achieved by varying Ω_S between $\Omega_S = \max\{0, (Q^* - M_N\bar{T})/M_S\}$ and $\min\{Q^*/M_S, \bar{T}\}$ while varying Ω_N between $\Omega_N = \min\{Q^*/M_N, \bar{T}\}$ and $\max\{0, \left(Q^* - M_S\bar{T}\right)/M_N\}$ in such a way that $M_S\Omega_S + M_N\Omega_N = Q^*$.

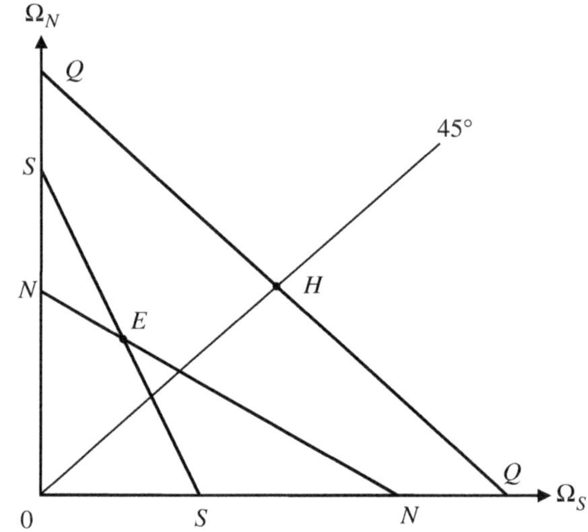

Figure 2. Comparison of Nash equilibrium and an efficient patent regime.

4.2 Pareto-improving patent agreements

How do the efficient combinations of patent policies compare to the policies that emerge in a noncooperative equilibrium? The answer to this question — which informs us about the likely features of a negotiated patent agreement — is illustrated in Figure 2. The figure depicts the best response functions and the efficient policy combinations on the same diagram.

In the figure, the efficient policy combinations are depicted by the line QQ.[26] We show this line being situated to the right of the SS curve and above the NN curve, which is a general feature of our model. The reasons are clear. Starting from a point on the South's best response function, a marginal strengthening of IPR protection in the South increases world welfare. Such a change in Southern policies has only a second-order effect on welfare in the South, but

[26]If international transfer payments are infeasible, the set of Pareto efficient policy combinations includes the segment of the vertical axis above its intersection with QQ and extending as far as the point $(0, \bar{T})$ and the segment of the horizontal axis to the right of its intersection with QQ and extending to $(\bar{T}, 0)$.

it conveys two positive externalities to the North. First, it provides extra monopoly profits to Northern innovators, which contributes to aggregate income there. Second, it enhances the incentives for R&D, inducing an increase in both ϕ_S and ϕ_N. The extra product diversity that results from this R&D creates additional surplus for Northern consumers.

By the same token, a marginal increase in the strength of Northern patent protection from a point along NN increases world welfare. Such a change in policy enhances profit income for Southern firms and encourages additional innovation in both countries. It follows, of course, that the QQ line must lie outside the Nash equilibrium. We record our finding in

Proposition 4. *Let* (Ω_S, Ω_N) *be an interior equilibrium in the non-cooperative policy game and let* (Ω_S^*, Ω_N^*) *be any efficient combination of patent policies. Then* $M_S\Omega_S^* + M_N\Omega_N^* > M_S\Omega_S + M_N\Omega_N$.

The proposition implies that, starting from any interior Nash equilibrium, an efficient patent treaty must strengthen patent protection in at least one country. It also implies that the treaty will strengthen global incentives for R&D and induce more rapid innovation in both countries.

4.3 Harmonization

Commentators sometimes claim that it is desirable to have universal standards for intellectual property protection and for many other national policies that affect international competition. The arguments for harmonization are not always clear, but they seem to be based on a desire for global efficiency. Yet it is hardly obvious why efficiency should require identical policies in countries at different stages of economic development. In this section, we examine the aggregate and distributional effects of international harmonization of patent policies. It should be noted that TRIPs essentially harmonizes patent policy by requiring all governments to grant patents of at least twenty years from date of filing and by requiring minimum standards of effective enforcement.

As should be apparent from the preceding discussion, harmonization of patent policies is neither necessary nor sufficient for global efficiency, regardless of whether international transfer payments are feasible or not. A regime of harmonized policies will only be efficient if the common index of patent protection in the two countries is such that $Q = Q^*$. And any combination of patent policies that provides the proper global incentives for R&D will be efficient, no matter whether the patent policies in the two countries are the same or not.

If patent protection is stronger in the North than in the South in an initial Nash equilibrium, then harmonization might be achieved either by a unilateral strengthening of patent laws in the South or by a combination of policy changes in the two countries. A unilateral increase in Ω_S is bound to harm the South (absent any side payments), because the equilibrium policy package is a best response by the South to the North's choice of patent laws and any unilateral deviation from a country's best response is, by definition, damaging to its interests.[27] As for harmonization that might be achieved through a combination of policy changes, we focus on a treaty that would achieve global efficiency. Such a treaty is represented by point H in Figure 2. Efficient harmonization surely requires a strengthening of patent protection in the South and in the world as a whole, since $\Omega_N > \Omega_S$ at E and QQ lies outside this point. If $\beta = 0$, it also requires a strengthening of patent protection in the North.[28] If $\beta < 0$, efficient harmonization may require a weakening of patent protection in the

[27]See also Lai and Qiu (2003), who consider the welfare effects of harmonizing IPR protection at the standard that would be chosen by the North in a non-cooperative equilibrium. In a model of once-off investment in R&D, they show that such a change in the South's policy from the Nash equilibrium level would benefit the North by more than it would harm the South.

[28]First, we note that when $\beta = 0$, point H lies above the intersection of the NN curve with the vertical axis. This can be seen by substituting $\Omega_N = \Omega_S$ in the first-order condition for maximizing $\rho\,[W_S(0) + W_N(0)]$ and comparing the resulting expression for $\Omega_N = Q^*/(M_N + M_S)$ with the expression for Ω_N that comes from (11) when $\Omega_S = 0$. Then, since the NN curve is downward sloping when $\beta = 0$, the fact that it starts below point H implies that the extent of patent protection in the North is greater at point H than it is at point E.

North.[29] If $M_N \geq M_S$ and $H_N \geq H_S$, the North definitely gains from efficient harmonization.[30] However, the South may be worse off at point H than in the Nash equilibrium at point E, unless some form of compensation is provided by the North. In general, the larger are M_N/M_S and H_N/H_S, the more likely it is that the South would lose from efficient harmonization.

Summarizing, we have[31]

Proposition 5. *Suppose $M_N \geq M_S$, $H_N \geq H_S$, and $\beta \leq 0$. Then efficient harmonization requires a strengthening of patent protection in the South and in the world as a whole. It requires a strengthening of patent protection in the North if $\beta = 0$, and may require a weakening of patent protection in the North if $\beta < 0$. The North necessarily gains from efficient harmonization, while the South may gain or lose.*

We conclude that harmonization has more to do with distribution than with efficiency, and that incorporation of such provisions in a treaty like TRIPs might well benefit the North at the expense of the South.[32]

---

[29] For further discussion of this case, see Boldrin and Levine (2009, Section 6).

[30] If $M_N \geq M_S$ and $H_N \geq H_S$, the common index of patent policy that maximizes the welfare of the North is greater than the common index of patent policy that maximizes aggregate world welfare. Therefore, the North gains from a unilateral increase in Ω_S that brings the Southern patent policy into conformity with the Nash equilibrium policy in the North, and further gains from an increase in the common policy until $Q = Q^*$.

[31] This proposition is different from the one in the original published version of the paper in American Economic Review. After the publication of the paper in AER, an error in the proposition was found. A corrigendum was published after that (see Grossman and Lai, 2006). This proposition takes into account the contents of the corrigendum. This correction does not affect the main thrust of the paper.

[32] McCalman (2001) estimates the income transfers implicit in TRIPs and finds that international patent harmonization benefits the United States at the expense of the developing countries as well as Canada, the United Kingdom and Japan. He does not, however, include in his calculations the benefits that countries derive from the global increase in innovative activities.

5 Patent Policy with Many Countries

In this section, we extend our analysis to a trading world with many countries. Our main finding is that adding countries exacerbates the free-rider problem that plagues the noncooperative policy equilibrium. Small countries are inclined to allow others to provide the incentives for innovation so as to avoid the deadweight losses in their home markets. In the limit, as the number of countries grows large and each one is small in relation to the world economy, the unique Nash equilibrium has universal patents of strength zero. Then, a patent treaty is critical for creating incentives for private innovation.

We assume that there are J countries, and that country i has market size M_i, human capital endowment H_i, and labor productivity $1/a_i$. The research technology in country i is $\phi_i = F\left(H_i, L_{Ri}/a_i\right) = \left[b[L_{Ri}/a_i]^{\beta} + (1-b)H_i^{\beta}\right]^{1/\beta}$, with $\beta \leq 1/2$. All consumers share the preferences given in (8).

Suppose that there is no cooperation between nations in setting their patent policies. In country i, either $\Omega_i = 0$ and the marginal cost of providing the first bit of patent protection exceeds the marginal benefit, $\Omega_i = \bar{T}$ and the marginal benefit of providing the last bit of patent protection exceeds the marginal cost, or $0 < \Omega_i < \bar{T}$ and the marginal benefit of strengthening patent protection equals the marginal cost. Equality between marginal benefit and marginal cost implies

$$C_c - C_m - \mu_i \pi = \frac{M_i}{Q}\gamma[\Omega_i C_m + C_c(\bar{T} - \Omega_i)], \tag{14}$$

where $Q = \sum_j M_j \Omega_j$ measures the strength of global patent protection in the Nash equilibrium.

Observe first that as $\mu_i \to 0$, the left-hand side of (14) approaches $C_c - C_m$; a small country captures virtually none of the monopoly profits from innovative products, so the marginal cost of a patent per consumer and product is the difference between the competitive and monopoly levels of consumer surplus. But as $M_i \to 0$, the right-hand side of (14) approaches zero, because a small country provides innovators with virtually none of their global profits and so worldwide innovation is hardly responsive to a change in such a country's patent policy. It follows that a small country will set its index of patent protection equal to zero in a Nash equilibrium.

If all countries choose positive patent strengths that are less than $\bar{T}$, equation (14) holds for every i. Then we can sum (14) across the J countries, which gives

$$J\left(C_c - C_m\right) - \pi = \gamma\left[C_m - C_c + \frac{C_c\left(\sum_j M_j\right)\bar{T}}{Q}\right]. \tag{15}$$

Then, for a given size of the world market, Q depends only on the *number* of countries J and not on the distribution of consumers and human capital across countries. Moreover, if $\beta \leq 0$, Q is a declining function of J; the greater is the number of countries, the weaker are the global incentives for innovation in a noncooperative equilibrium. As the number of countries grows large (holding constant the size of the world market), the aggregate incentives for innovation approach zero.[33] Evidently, the free-rider problem becomes increasingly severe as the number of independent decision makers in the world economy expands.

Finally, note that the requirements for global efficiency do not depend on the number of countries. Again, the sum of all national welfare levels is a function of the aggregate world incentive for innovation. This sum is maximized when

$$C_c - C_m - \pi = \gamma\left[C_m - C_c + \frac{C_c\left(\sum_j M_j\right)\bar{T}}{Q^*}\right]. \tag{16}$$

Thus, if international compensation is possible, an efficient global patent treaty will have $\sum_j M_j \Omega_j = Q^*$, where Q^* is solved from (16). Notice that Q^* must exceed Q, the aggregate patent protection in the Nash equilibrium. Even if international compensation is not

[33]Suppose Q were to approach a finite number as $J \to \infty$. Then γ would approach a finite number as well, and the right-hand side of (15) would be finite. But the left-hand side of (15) approaches infinity as $J \to \infty$.

feasible, an efficient agreement will have $\sum_j M_j \Omega_j = Q^*$ for a range of distributions of world welfare.

6 Conclusions

We have developed a simple model of endogenous innovation and have used it to study the incentives that governments face in choosing their patent policies. Our model features a familiar trade-off between the static benefits of competitive pricing and the dynamic benefits of increased innovation. For a closed economy, we derived a simple formula for the optimal strength of patent protection that relates the deadweight loss induced by a marginal strengthening of IPR protection to the surplus that results from the extra innovation.

In an open economy, differences in market size and differences in capacity for R&D generate national differences in optimal patent policies. We focused on policies that are applied with *national treatment*; that is, regimes that require equal protection for foreign and domestic applicants. A country's optimal patent policy is found by equating the sum of the extra deadweight loss that results from strengthening the IPR protection granted to domestic firms and the extra consumer surplus loss that results from expanding the fraction of imported goods that are subject to monopoly pricing with the benefits that flow from providing greater incentives for innovation to firms worldwide. A country's optimal IPR protection depends on the policies set by its trading partner, because the strength of foreign patent rights affects the responsiveness of global innovation to a change in a country's own patent policies.

We found that having a larger market for innovative products typically enhances a government's incentive to grant stronger patent rights. Also, a government's relative incentive to protect IPRs typically increases with its relative endowment of human capital. In a noncooperative equilibrium, patent protection will be stronger in the North than in the South if the North has a larger market for innovative products and a greater capacity for R&D.

Starting from a Nash equilibrium, countries can benefit from negotiating an international patent agreement. A treaty can ensure that national policies reflect the positive externalities that flow to foreign residents when a country tightens its patent laws. To achieve (constrained) efficiency, an international agreement must strengthen aggregate world patent protection relative to the Nash equilibrium. Harmonization of patent policies is neither necessary nor sufficient for the efficiency of the global IPR regime. If patent policies are harmonized at an efficient level, the move from a Nash equilibrium typically will benefit the North but possibly harm the South.

Our conclusions are essentially the same for a world with more than two countries. Countries with larger markets and more human capital will provide stronger IPRs in a noncooperative equilibrium than those with smaller markets and less human capital. Indeed, a country that is small in relation to the world economy has no incentive whatsoever to grant patents. The greater is the number of independent countries, the more severe is the free-rider problem inherent in the setting of national patent policies. Thus, the value of an international patent agreement grows with the number of independent sovereign decision makers.

Our analysis can be extended to more general environments. For example, in an earlier version of this paper (Grossman and Lai, 2002), we allowed for cross-national differences in relative labor productivity in the two industries. With comparative advantage in production, the productivity gap in the industry that produces differentiated products may not be offset by the gap in relative wages. Then the production costs for innovative products will be higher in one region or the other. This can create an asymmetry in the life cycle of a new good depending upon whether patents are longer in the North or in the South. We showed how such an asymmetry may generate multiple equilibria in the policy game.

Another possible extension would allow different preferences in different countries. With different demands, the marginal cost of strengthening IPR protection will vary around the globe. Then differences in the elasticities of demand for innovative products will be another factor that affects the governments' relative incentives for granting long patents or providing strict enforcement. Moreover, asymmetries in demand would be reflected in the characteristics of a globally efficient IPR regime. An efficient regime would equalize across countries the marginal deadweight loss associated with providing a given push to global innovation. Efficiency requires stronger patent protection in countries that have more inelastic demands for innovative products, all else the same.

Appendix

In this appendix we show that, for a closed economy, when Ω solves (7) and $\beta \leq 1/2$, the second-order condition for an optimal patent policy is satisfied. Similar calculations ensure that $\beta \leq 1/2$ is sufficient for the second-order condition to be satisfied for the best response given by (11) for an open economy.

Let us rewrite the first-order condition (7) as

$$\frac{\gamma}{\Omega}\left\{C_c\bar{T} - \Omega\left[(C_c - C_m) + (C_c - C_m - \pi)\frac{1}{\gamma}\right]\right\} = 0.$$

Since $\gamma/\Omega > 0$, the term in curly brackets must vanish at any local extremum. We will show that at any such point the term in curly brackets is a decreasing function of Ω; i.e. that

$$-\left[(C_c - C_m) + (C_c - C_m - \pi)\frac{1}{\gamma} - \Omega\frac{(C_c - C_m - \pi)}{\gamma^2}\frac{d\gamma(\Omega)}{d\Omega}\right] < 0. \tag{A.1}$$

This means that any point satisfying the first-order condition is a local welfare maximum. Since the welfare function is continuous and differentiable, it follows that there can be at most one local extremum point, and that the value of Ω that generates this point is the unique welfare-maximizing patent policy.

It is straightforward to calculate that

$$\gamma \equiv -\left[\frac{(F_L)^2}{FF_{LL}}\right] = \frac{b}{(1-b)(1-\beta)}\left(\frac{L_R}{aH}\right)^{\beta}$$

for the CES research technology. Meanwhile, $vF_L = w = 1/a$ and $v = M\pi\Omega$ imply that $F_L = 1/aM\pi\Omega$, or that

$$\frac{b}{a}\left[b + (1-b)\left(\frac{aH}{L_R}\right)^{\beta}\right]^{\frac{1-\beta}{\beta}} = \frac{1}{aM\pi\Omega}$$

in the CES case. Using these two equations, we can express γ as a function of Ω; we find that $\gamma = \left(\frac{b}{1-\beta}\right)\left[(bM\pi\Omega)^{\frac{-\beta}{1-\beta}} - b\right]^{-1}$.

We can now compute $d\gamma(\Omega)/d\Omega$, and substitute the resulting expression into the left-hand side of (A.1), which then becomes

$$\begin{aligned}\Psi = -\Bigg[&C_c - C_m - (1-\beta)(C_c - C_m - \pi)\\ &+ (C_c - C_m - \pi)\,(bM\pi\Omega)^{\frac{-\beta}{1-\beta}}\left(\frac{1-2\beta}{b}\right)\Bigg].\end{aligned}$$

But $\beta \le 1/2$ ensures that

$$\begin{aligned}\Psi &\le -\left[C_c - C_m - (1-\beta)(C_c - C_m - \pi) + (1-2\beta)\,(C_c - C_m - \pi)\right]\\ &= -\left[C_c - C_m - \beta(C_c - C_m - \pi)\right]\\ &< 0.\end{aligned}$$

So the second-order condition is satisfied when $\beta \le 1/2$ and the Ω that solves (7) — if it exists — is the unique welfare-maximizing patent policy.

Acknowledgment

The authors thank Doug Bernheim, Elhanan Helpman, Robert Lucas, Jr., Giovanni Maggi, Keith Maskus, Lars Svensson, and four anonymous referees for useful suggestions and comments. They are grateful to the U.S. National Science Foundation (grant nos. SES 9904480 and SES 0211748), the Hong Kong Research Grants Council (project nos. CityU 1145/99H and CityU 1235/00H), and the Department of Economics and Finance at City University of Hong Kong for financial support. Any opinions, findings, and conclusions or recommendations expressed in this paper are those of the authors and do not necessarily reflect the views of the National Science Foundation.

References

Boldrin, M. and Levine, D. K. (2009). Market size and intellectual property protection, *International Economic Review* 50(3), 855–881.

Chin, J. and Grossman, G. M. (1990). Intellectual property rights and North-South trade, in Jones, R. W. and Krueger, A. O. (eds.), *The Political Economy of International Trade*, Cambridge MA: Basil Blackwell Publishers, pp. 90–107.

Deardorff, A. V. (1992). Welfare effects of global patent protection. *Economica* 59(233), 35–51.

Ginarte, J. C. and Park, W. G. (1997). Determinants of patent rights: A cross-national study. *Research Policy* 26(3), 283–301.

Grossman, G. M. and Lai, E. L.-C. (2002). *International Protection of Intellectual Property.* National Bureau of Economic Research Working Paper No. 8794, Cambridge MA.

Grossman, G. M. and Lai, E. L.-C. (2006). International protection of intellectual property: Corrigendum. *American Economic Review* 96(1), 456.

Helpman, E. (1993). Innovation, imitation, and intellectual property rights. *Econometrica* 61(6), 1247–1280.

Lai, E. L.-C. and Qiu, L. D. (2003). The North's intellectual property rights standard for the South? *Journal of International Economics* 59(1), 183–209.

Maskus, K. E. (2000a). *Intellectual Property Rights in the Global Economy,* Washington, D.C.: The Institute for International Economics.

Maskus, K. E. (2000b). Parallel imports. *The World Economy* 23(9), 1269–1284.

McCalman, P. (2001). Reaping what you sow: An empirical analysis of international patent harmonization. *Journal of International Economics* 55(1), 161–185.

McCalman, P. (2002). National patents, innovation and international agreements. *Journal of International Trade and Economic Development* 11(1), 1–14.

Nordhaus, W. D. (1969). *Invention, Growth and Welfare: A Theoretical Treatment of Technological Change*, Cambridge MA: The MIT Press.

Scotchmer, S. (2004). The political economy of intellectual property treaties. *Journal of Law, Economics, and Organization* 20(2), 415–437.

Chapter 3

The Theory of International Policy Coordination in the Protection of Ideas*

Abstract

In this chapter, I put forward a framework to help us understand the underlying sources of national policy failures regarding intellectual property rights (IPR) protection, the need for international coordination, and how the coordination should be done. I also analyze whether global harmonization of IPR standards is necessary or sufficient for achieving globally welfare-maximizing policies. Then I move on to analyze the Agreement on Trade-Related Aspects of Intellectual Property Rights (TRIPS), which is a mighty effort to coordinate IPR policies across member countries of the World Trade Organization (WTO). I discuss what TRIPS was supposed to do and what it has actually achieved, with reference to my theoretical framework. I explain that it is desirable for IPR to be included in world trade talks and be negotiated along with other trade issues. I offer analyses on the extensions of the basic model by introducing political economy and trade barriers, as well as allowing countries to discriminate against foreign firms. Finally, I comment on further potential extensions such as introduction

*By Edwin L.-C. Lai. Originally published in Keith E. Maskus (ed.) *Intellectual Property, Growth and Trade* (Frontiers of Economics and Globalization, Volume 2), Emerald Group Publishing Limited, pp. 357–389. Copyright © 2007 Emerald Publishing Limited. It has been reprinted with revisions and permission from the original publisher. The difference with the original published paper is that Sections 3.2 and 5 have been updated and some items in the References section have been deleted or added accordingly.

of foreign direct investment (FDI) or licensing, parallel imports, cumulative innovations, subject matter of protection and costs of implementation. The main thrust of the basic model is that, provided that there is free trade and non-discrimination of foreign firms, there exist positive cross-border externalities as a country strengthens its IPR protection, since it raises the profits of foreign firms and the welfare of foreign consumers without causing any deadweight loss on foreign soil. This implies that national governments tend to provide too little IPR protection compared with the global optimum. The model also implies that a country with higher innovative capability and larger domestic market would provide stronger IPR. Thus, it is natural for the South to protect IPR less than the North in the absence of international coordination. These basic results largely continue to hold under various extensions.

1 Introduction

Why do we need international policy coordination? Typically, the answer is that in choosing their own policies individual governments do not take into account the effects those policies have on other nations. As a result, individual national policies are subject to a market failure arising from international externalities. The World Trade Organization (WTO) is a classic example of a body designed to facilitate international policy coordination — in this case, for trade-related issues. For example, Bagwell and Staiger (1999, 2002) and Staiger (1995) hold the view that terms of trade externalities are the core reason for having an organization such as the WTO. The optimal tariffs set by large countries seeking solely to maximize their own welfare are too high from the global welfare point of view, for no country considers the negative impact on export prices of its trading partners. Therefore, a multilateral institution that facilitates international coordination of trade policy to reduce tariffs can overcome this international policy failure and improve global welfare.

In this chapter, I address similar questions regarding the protection of intellectual property rights (IPR). Do we need international coordination of IPR? If so, where are the underlying sources of policy failure? How should the coordination be done? Is global harmonization of IPR standards the best means of achieving welfare-maximizing policies? If so, on what level should harmonization take place? The WTO contains an ambitious attempt to manage this problem. The Agreement on Trade-Related Aspects of Intellectual Property Rights (TRIPS) is an effort to coordinate IPR policies across member countries. What is TRIPS supposed to do and what has it actually achieved? Is it desirable for IPR to be included in world trade talks and be negotiated along with other trade issues?

In order to answer such questions, we need first to understand the nature of the problem at hand. What would the global policy equilibrium look like in the absence of international coordination of protection of ideas? What would the global optimum set of policies be? To answer these questions, I shall rely primarily on a simple model of policy formation with free trade and welfare-maximizing governments. I will see how tensions arise naturally in this context between technology-developing nations (the "North") and technology-importing countries (the "South"). Governments in he South naturally want to protect IPR less than the North does in Nash equilibrium. Next, I examine how the global optimum differs from the non-cooperative equilibrium. Then, I relax the assumptions of free trade and benevolent governments, analyzing the basic model in a world with trade barriers and firm-biased governments.

In the basic model I focus on international coordination in length and enforcement of patents in a world with free trade. However, IPR protection includes not only patents, but also copyrights and trademarks, among other things. Even if one focuses on only patent protection, there are other relevant issues, such as patent breadth, parallel trade, lobbying, trade barriers, and non-discrimination, which are not addressed in the basic model. How do these factors affect the optimal policy coordination? I will extend the basic model by incorporating some of these elements in the analysis. Towards the end of the chapter, I discuss other extensions to the basic model and speculate on how they might affects the major results.

The chapter is organized as follows. In Section 2, I briefly describe attempts at international coordination prior to, and including, the TRIPS Agreement. In Section 3, I review other papers that have analyzed policy coordination problems in the IPR context. I turn in Section 4 to my basic model, while in Section 5 I consider empirical evidence on its essential predictions. Further interpretation, extensions, and comments on potential extensions of the analysis are made in Sections 6–11, with concluding remarks in the final section.

2 The Development of Global Policy Coordination

Countries have long sought to coordinate their intellectual property policies, though the first major international efforts came in the late 19th century. The Paris Convention for the Protection of Industrial Property, which focuses primarily on patent protection, came into force in 1883. The Berne Convention for the Protection of Artistic and Literary Property, which focuses mainly on copyrights, was established in 1886. Both treaties were signed by a small number of countries with strong or emerging interests in IPR. These conventions have been renegotiated numerous times and their basic standards remain the essential framework of global IPR protection. A number of additional treaties have come into force over the intervening period, including the Madrid Agreement (covering registration and protection procedures in trademarks), the Rome Convention (covering protection for performers, broadcasters, and producers of audio recordings), and the Washington Treaty (aimed at protecting computer chip designs). Further, the World Intellectual Property Organization (WIPO), was elevated to the status of a United Nations specialized agency in 1974. Under its auspices a number of additional agreements have come into force, including the WIPO Copyright Treaty and the WIPO Performers and Phonograms Treaty, both negotiated in the late 1990s. WIPO is charged with facilitating negotiations on standards in intellectual property, overseeing the operation of its various conventions, serving as a clearinghouse for national laws in IPR, and accepting patent applications under the PCT and trademark applications under the Madrid Protocol.

While the international IPR system centered on WIPO and its various treaties is sophisticated and has been central in raising awareness about protection for technologies and information goods, it suffered from three serious shortcomings from the standpoint of global policy. First, virtually all international agreements on IPR within that system lacked any binding power to resolve disputes and commit countries to adopting and enforcing minimum standards. Second, the various conventions were based largely on a national treatment obligation, though even this mild form of non-discrimination was frequently subject to exceptions. This feature meant that the conventions failed to prevent countries from adopting weak standards of protection. Third, few of these conventions attracted significant numbers of countries, implying that they did not really extend the reach of IPR into much of the developing world.

Since the late 1980s, the United States, various EU countries and Japan began to exert ever higher pressure for other countries to adopt more stringent standards in protecting patents, trademarks, copyrights, and other elements in both the real world and the cyber-world. These efforts culminated in the signing of the Agreement on Trade-Related Aspects of Intellectual Property Rights (TRIPS), as part of the Uruguay Round of negotiations founding the WTO, in 1994. By January 1, 1996, all developed countries were required to adopt the universal minimum IPR standards set out in TRIPS. The corresponding deadline for all developing and transition economies was January 1, 2000, and that for the least-developed countries was January 1, 2006. The Doha Declaration of 2001 offered an additional extension to 2016 for pharmaceutical patent protection in the least-developed countries.

The TRIPS Agreement goes a long way toward resolving the three problems with the UN system mentioned above. Because it is part of the WTO, violations of IPR obligations accepted in TRIPS are now subject to binding dispute resolution procedures.[1] Second, it set out substantive minimum standards in all areas of intellectual property protection, which required virtually all nations, especially the developed countries, to strengthen their rules markedly. Third,

[1]This process is discussed in detail by Beshkar and Bond in their chapter in this volume.

because WTO membership is virtually universal, nearly all countries in the world are now bound by the IPR requirements in TRIPS. This applies equally to countries still acceding to the WTO, for they must adopt or exceed TRIPS standards. Thus, while TRIPS remains some distance from global harmonization of IPR, it has markedly strengthened and universalized international protection.

What does TRIPS cover? In general, there are three main aspects of coordination: national treatment, most-favored nation (MFN) treatment and a significant tendency toward harmonization of IPR standards. National treatment requires all members to treat nationals of other countries no less favorably than their own nationals. The MFN principle requires that advantages and privileges granted by a member to the nationals of any other country should be extended unconditionally to the nationals of all other WTO members. Harmonization refers to the establishment of universal minimum IPR standards. Note that these are minimum standards and countries are free to make their own regulations even more protective. In this sense TRIPS does not achieve full harmonization. The IPR standards to be coordinated cover patents, copyrights, trademarks, geographical indications, industrial designs, layout designs of integrated circuits, plant varieties, and trade secrets, among other things.[2]

It has been argued elsewhere (e.g. Maskus, 2000) that TRIPS is probably the most important international IPR agreement ever signed, because of the number of countries involved and the scope of changes implied, especially in the developing countries. Most importantly, TRIPS can be enforced by the WTO through the dispute settlement procedure. One country can impose trade retaliation on another country if the latter violates some TRIPS obligation and thereby nullifies or impairs the benefits of TRIPS that should be enjoyed by the former. Important as it is, formal economic analyses of TRIPS are scarce. Some legal scholars (e.g. Reichman, 1995) have argued that TRIPS is basically backward-looking in nature, enshrining what the developed world had been adopting before the

[2]See, for example, UNCTAD (1996, pp. 8–12) and Maskus (2000, pp. 18–19).

agreement was negotiated as the world minimum standard. Reichman goes on to argue that the reason the developing nations signed the TRIPS agreement was that the advanced industrial countries promised to open up their markets in agriculture and traditional goods in exchange for the former countries agreeing to abide by TRIPS.

3 Models of IPR Policy Coordination

3.1 Models of North-South IPR without coordination

There have been theoretical and empirical studies of the welfare effects of the global systems of IPR protection, mostly in the North-South setting. Both Chin and Grossman (1990) and Deardorff (1992) examine welfare effects of extending IPR protection from the North to the South. They find that many results depend on the size of the South's market. Their studies are based on two important assumptions. First, they assume that the South does not have innovative capability. Second, they examine only the case where the South has either full or no IPR protection. Diwan and Rodrik (1991) also consider various degrees of IPR protection in the North and the South. Interestingly, they find that to maximize global welfare, which is the equally weighted sum of the North's and the South's welfare, the rates of patent protection in the two regions must be identical. They emphasize the taste difference between the two regions and assume no innovative capability in the South. Helpman (1993) studies IPR protection, growth and welfare using a two-country general equilibrium model (with North and South), where the North specializes in innovation and the South specializes in imitation. He finds that tightening IPR protection in the South hurts the South and may or may not benefit the North.

How does IPR affect trade, foreign direct investment (FDI), licensing and technology transfer between the North and South? Drawing on the endogenous product-cycle model of Grossman and Helpman (1991, Chapter 11), Lai (1998) shows that an increase in the rate of imitation caused by a weakening of IPR protection leads to less FDI from the North to the South, as Northern firms prefer exporting so as to lower the risk of being imitated. This leads to a decrease in the rate of innovation and a decrease in the terms of trade of the South, as there is less technology transfer. Markusen (2001) shows that (intellectual) property rights enforcement may lead to a shift from exporting to a local subsidiary, and this mode shift improves the welfare of both the multinational corporation and the host country. Yang and Maskus (2001) examine the effects of IPR on licensing and innovation in the context of an international product-cycle model. Glass and Saggi (2002), on the other hand, study the effects of IPR protection on licensing versus direct investment, which in turn have an effect on economic growth.

An interesting empirical study by McCalman (2001) finds that TRIPS generates large income transfer between countries, with the total sum of net outward transfers from all countries equal to US$ 6.23 billion. The United States gets more than 70% of all inward transfers, followed distantly by Germany, France, and Italy. Surprisingly, developing countries account for only 40% of all the outward transfers. Even more surprisingly, the largest amounts of outward transfer come from Canada, Brazil, the United Kingdom, India, Mexico and Japan. This is certainly a mixed basket of Northern and Southern countries. This reveals the fact the many developed countries did not protect IPR as strongly as the United States before TRIPS came into being. However, McCalman does not estimate the total deadweight losses or the benefits that arise out of TRIPS, such as increased innovation, trade and technology transfer.

3.2 IPR-trade policy tradeoffs

How does IPR protection interact with trade policy? Since import barriers effectively subsidize domestic firms but tax foreign firms, they encourage innovation by domestic firms but discourage innovation by foreign firms. Qiu and Lai (2004) point out that in a world where the North specializes in innovation and the South in imitation, a Northern tariff is pro-innovation, and therefore is a substitute for IPR protection, while a Southern tariff discourages innovation, and therefore offsets IPR protection. They find that the globally optimal Northern tariff increases as IPR protection in the North or the South decreases. Consequently, global welfare may rise as the Northern tariff increases, but necessarily declines as the Southern tariff increases. Zigic (2000) finds a similar motive for the North to protect trade, and that a Northern tariff can be globally welfare improving, though he uses a more complicated four-stage game to demonstrate his result.

One has to bear in mind that the tradeoffs (or offsetting effects) between tariffs and IPR protection is true only for tariffs on IPR-sensitive goods. In a general-equilibrium model, tariffs on non-IPR-sensitive goods can penalize the domestic IPR-sensitive sector and discourage innovation. Conversely, tariffs on IPR-sensitive goods can have general-equilibrium effects on non-IPR-sensitive sectors. Welfare and growth analyses should take these effects into account.

3.3 IPR externalities and coordination problems

Central to the need for international coordination is the possible failure of self-serving national policies to deliver a globally efficient outcome. This is often linked to the existence of cross-border externalities. Noting the shortcomings of analyzing Southern IPR decisions as all-or-nothing in Chin and Grossman (1990) and Deardorff (1992), McCalman (2002) shows that when countries are allowed to set their own patent strengths, the non-cooperative equilibrium is globally suboptimal. He argues that global optimality requires that the country faced with a demand curve such that the ratio of deadweight losses to monopoly profits is lowest be the sole provider of IPR in the world. Therefore, when countries have to set their own national patents, their patent strengths are too low, due to the existence of two externalities. First is the free-rider effect, whereby all countries benefit from the IPR-strengthening policies of a single country, and second is the fact that the policy chosen by an individual country neglects to take into account the surplus that accrues elsewhere.

The relationship between IPR agreements and other trade agreements is captured in a theoretical analysis by Lai and Qiu

(2003). They point out that as a country protects IPR more, the rest of the world (ROW) gains because the ROW's innovating firms make more profit in the country that protects, and its consumers enjoy more new products at no extra costs. On the other hand, the loss in consumer surplus as a consequence of strengthening IPR is solely borne by the country that strengthens the protection. These externalities point to the suboptimality of the non-cooperative Nash equilibrium. The paper shows that, because of the externality created by the strengthening of Southern protection, it is globally welfare-improving for the South to strengthen IPR protection sufficiently to harmonize with the North's current level of protection, though it benefits the North at the expense of the South. This creates a case for a *quid pro quo* between the two regions: the North opens up its traditional goods market to the South in exchange for the South harmonizing IPR protection with the North. This paper will be discussed in more detail later in this chapter.

Casting the IPR coordination problem in a broader context, Scotchmer (2004a) studies the optimality of IPR treaty in a world where national governments have two technology-policy instruments: funding public R&D and negotiating an IPR treaty with foreign countries based on the principles of national treatment and, possibly, harmonization. She recognizes that total R&D in the world is too low in any non-cooperative equilibrium, as the benefits of R&D are partly enjoyed by foreigners. However, when comparing IPR protection and public spending on R&D, she concludes that an IPR treaty based on national treatment and harmonization would provide too much IPR protection and too little public R&D spending. This is because patent protection will encourage private firms to undertake R&D in order to earn profits abroad, while public sponsors are only interested in domestic consumer surplus. She therefore suggests that a better remedy to the problem of under-provision of total R&D is to seek international agreements on public spending for R&D, rather than negotiating treaties to strengthen IPR.

To guide empirical studies, a more detailed framework is needed to analyze the incentives to protect IPR in an open economy, why the strengths of IPR protection differ across countries, and whether and how international policy coordination is needed. Grossman and Lai (2004) is an attempt in this direction. The framework they use in the analysis of IPR is close to that of Lai and Qiu (2003). Grossman and Lai (2004), likewise, recognize the existence of positive cross-border externalities in IPR protection. The paper concludes that global welfare can be maximized by raising the strength of global IPR protection from the Nash-equilibrium level, where the strength of global IPR protection is defined as a variable proportional to the value of a global patent. There is a continuum of combinations of IPR strength in the two regions that can achieve a global optimum with Pareto improvements in welfare for both North and South. Whether or not strict harmonization is an element of this Pareto-optimal set depends on whether the North and the South are sufficiently similar in their innovativeness and the sizes of their domestic markets.

Although Grossman and Lai's (2004) paper generates valuable insights, the model may be regarded as too simple when used to answer the question "Would global patent protection be too weak without TRIPS?" Some commentators (such as Reichman, 1998, p. 588) think that patent protection was already too strong before TRIPS, while there is no hard evidence to show one way or the other. A straightforward application of Grossman and Lai (2004) would answer "yes" to the question. However, two important factors can create counteracting forces that reverse the answer to "no". They are government bias toward the interests of domestic firms and the existence of trade barriers. Lai and Yan (2013) is an attempt to model these questions. They conclude that under reasonable assumptions about the strengths of government-bias and trade barriers, global patent protection is still too weak in Nash equilibrium. In other words, global patent protection would still be too weak without international coordination and an agreement such as TRIPS can potentially improve global welfare.

Since the model in Grossman and Lai (2004) covers most of the issues in the literature, and can be easily extended to cover additional ones, I shall introduce a simple IPR coordination model based on that paper in the next section as a basis for analysis.

4 The IPR Coordination Model

I shall use the model set out in Grossman and Lai (2004) as my essential framework for analysis. First, I need to clarify that IPR protection includes not just patents, but also copyrights and trademarks, plus other devices that are similar to these canonical forms. I will, however, focus on patent protection in the formal analysis. The analysis of copyrights should follow the same principle, while trademarks should probably be analyzed differently. Second, bear in mind that not all innovations require patent or copyright protection. Some inventions, such as Coca-Cola, use trade secrets to protect their intellectual property, because the recipe is hard to reverse engineer from inspection of the product. Patent protection is offered in exchange for disclosure of technological detail. Therefore, trade secrets, rather than patent protection, are used when the imitation lag without disclosure is long relative to patent length. Other innovations, such as new management methods, may not seek any formal intellectual property protection, since the first-mover advantage is enough to keep the innovator ahead of other competitors. It takes time for rivals to imitate and the imitation lag may be long enough for the first inventor to make a sufficient profit to recapture investment costs. Moreover, the innovator might have already established a brand name or reputation that can sustain its ability to earn economic rents for a long period of time.

In the model to come, I assume that there will be no innovation without IPR protection since imitation is costless and can be done immediately. This is true to different extents in different industries. For example, imitation costs are quite low in many components of the pharmaceutical, chemical and biotechnology industries (Mansfield, 1986; Maskus, 2000). These industries are especially sensitive to patents. Similarly, digital products can be downloaded, copied and distributed at virtually zero cost, making content providers keen to be protected with copyrights. These two commercial complexes are often called IPR-sensitive industries.

4.1 Model preview

In the basic model, I consider a trading world with two countries that differ by the sizes of their domestic markets for IPR-sensitive goods and innovative capabilities. Assume also that consumers love more variety of differentiated goods, the blueprints of which are developed by investing in R&D. I consider ongoing product innovation done by firms in both countries. After a firm develops a new product, it seeks patent protection from each country separately. It follows that a firm's profits increase as the degree of patent protection in either country increases. Moreover, when a country's market is larger, a strengthening of IPR protection there generates more profits for firms in both countries. When more profits can be earned from owning patents, more firms will innovate, creating more variety for consumers.

I assume that the two countries' governments play a Nash game in setting their strengths of patent protection, taken here to be enforcement-adjusted patent length.[3] Given the duration of patent protection of the other country, each government chooses its duration of patent protection to maximize the present discounted value of the sum of domestic consumer welfare and the profits of domestic firms. This behavior generates the best-response function of each country. A government's best response strikes a balance between the marginal costs and marginal benefits of strengthening domestic patents, given the duration of protection of the other country.

The marginal costs of strengthening IPR protection arise from the fact that innovative firms charge monopoly prices instead of competitive prices for a larger fraction of the domestic market or product life. This market power increases prices domestic consumers

[3] "Enforcement-adjusted patent length" is defined as patent length multiplied by the probability that patent protection is enforced.

have to pay. It also increases domestic firms' profits but not by enough to offset the losses in consumer surplus, resulting in deadweight losses. Furthermore, each country is required to uphold the national treatment principle, under which domestic and foreign firms must be protected to the same extent. Thus, it loses more from IPR protection provided to foreign firms than from that accorded domestic firms, since the domestic government only cares about domestic firms' profits. Therefore, if a country innovates a smaller fraction of world goods than it consumes, its cost of strengthening patents is larger.

On the other hand, the marginal benefits of strengthening IPR protection arise from increasing the incentives of both domestic and foreign firms to innovate, thus providing more variety for domestic consumers. Because there is free trade, inventions from domestic and foreign firms are equally beneficial. For the same increase in length of patent rights, the country with the larger market provides more incentives for firms to innovate. Thus, the benefit a country reaps from strengthening its IPR protection is greater if the country's domestic market is larger.

When a country strengthens its patents, it increases the profits of foreign firms and also induces more inventions from all over the world, benefiting foreign consumers. Thus, a country's strengthening of IPR conveys positive spillovers to other countries. In other words, choosing policy on its own a country cannot capture all the benefits of its action. This is the key insight explaining why world IPR protection is too weak in the Nash equilibrium compared with the coordinated global optimum.

4.2 A North-South model of IPR choice

Here I present the formal model in some detail, referring the reader to Grossman and Lai (2004) for additional analysis. At any point in time, consumers are faced with a continuum of differentiated consumer products, which are the result of product innovations, and one outside good. There is ongoing innovation, the rate of which is endogenous. Each product has an exogenously given useful life of length $\bar{\tau}$. Define $\bar{T} = \frac{1-e^{-\rho\bar{\tau}}}{\rho}$, which is the present discounted value of one dollar from time 0 to $\bar{\tau}$. The two countries, North and South, each chooses its strength of patent protection, Ω_N and Ω_S, respectively, where $\Omega_j = \omega_j T_j$. The variable ω_j is the fraction of country j's market that protects patented goods and is interpreted as the degree of enforcement of patents. Variable $T_j = \frac{1-e^{-\rho\tau_j}}{\rho}$, where τ_j is patent length, is the present discounted value of one dollar from time 0 to τ_j.

Consumers in both countries have the same preferences. The utility function of a consumer in country j at time z is given by

$$u_j(z) = y_j(z) + \int_0^{n_S(z)+n_N(z)} h[x_j(i,z)]di$$

where $y_j(z)$ is consumption of the outside good, $n_k(z)$ is the measure of economically active differentiated goods that have been developed by country $k = N, S$, and $h[x_j(i,z)]$ is the utility derived from consumption of x_j units of differentiated good indexed by i at time z. For simplicity, we assume the demand curve faced by all consumers for all differentiated goods are the same. I make the usual assumptions sufficient to ensure that there is positive demand for all variety and that prices are finite. The number of consumers (market size) in North and South are M_N and M_S respectively. Note that the number of consumers is not necessarily the same as the population, for IPR-sensitive goods are typically normal goods with high income elasticity. Accordingly, they could have higher demand in richer countries than in poorer countries.

In steady state, free entry into the innovation business implies that at each date the returns to research capital $r_j H_j$ plus those of research labor $w_j L_{Rj}$ must equal the total value ($\phi_j v$) of the patents of all goods invented at that date: $r_j H_j + w_j L_{Rj} = \phi_j v$. Here H_j, the supply of research capital, is exogenous given, while r_j, the rate of return to research capital, L_{Rj}, the labor employed in research, ϕ_j, the flow of inventions from country j, and v, the value of a global patent, equal to $\pi\left(M_S\Omega_S + M_N\Omega_N\right)$, are endogenously determined.

The welfare of country i at time 0 consists of the welfare from consumption of goods that have been invented before time 0, Λ_{j0}, plus the present-discounted value of labor income, returns to capital, and consumer surplus derived from consumption of goods expected to be developed in each period in the future. This initial welfare measure for country j is then

$$W_j(0) = \Lambda_{j0} + \frac{w_j(L_j - L_{Rj})}{\rho} + \frac{M_j(\phi_S + \phi_N)}{\rho}\left[\Omega_j C_m + (\bar{T} - \Omega_j)C_c\right] + \frac{\phi_j}{\rho}\pi\left(M_S\Omega_S + M_N\Omega_N\right)$$

where L_j is supply of labor, π is the monopoly profit per consumer, C_c is consumer surplus under perfect competition, C_m is consumer surplus under monopoly, w_j is wage, and ρ is the time rate of preference, which is also equal to the interest rate as expenditure is constant over time. Of the variables in the above equation, only w_j, L_{Rj}, ϕ_S and ϕ_N are endogenously determined. The wage w_j is determined by trade and labor productivities. Stronger protection of IPR anywhere in the world would lead to increases in L_{Rj}, ϕ_S and ϕ_N, as stronger IPR protection under free trade induces more labor allocated to research in both countries and thus higher flows of innovation in both countries.

Labor is the only factor input in production of any good. Let a_j be the units of labor to produce one unit of any good in country j. Since the numeraire good is produced in both countries, and is freely traded, we have $w_N/w_S \equiv w = a_S/a_N$. Moreover, differentiated products have the same unit cost in each country. Assume for simplicity that the R&D function, $\phi_j = F\left(H_j, L_{Rj}/a_j\right)$, is Cobb–Douglas in research labor L_{Rj} and research capital H_j: $\phi_j = A\left(L_{Rj}/a_j\right)^b H_j^{1-b}$. Define γ_j to be the elasticity of the rate of innovation with respect to the value of a patent. When the R&D function is of the Cobb–Douglas type, $\gamma_j = \gamma = b/(1-b)$, which is a constant. Equilibrium in the labor market means that the value of marginal product of workers in R&D is equal to the wage, which determines the allocation of workers to R&D and manufacturing. Then an increase in patent value v leads to an increase in research labor L_{Rj}, which increases the rate of innovation ϕ_j. Under more general R&D functions, γ becomes endogenous and $\gamma'(v) \leq 0$ if there are weakly diminishing returns to innovation with respect to IPR protection. This is a more plausible scenario than a constant innovation elasticity.

Firms patent their goods separately in each country, but they all receive national treatment in each country. Countries choose their strengths of patent protection Ω_S and Ω_N. In the share of goods (ω_S, ω_N) where patents are protected, imitators cannot produce the goods locally, nor can an imitation good be imported and sold. When the patent expires, or when the patent is not protected because of lax enforcement, the good can be imitated, produced and sold freely.

Now I derive the best-response functions. To derive South's best response, note that the marginal cost (per consumer) to South consists of, first, increases in deadweight loss on goods invented in South, $C_c - (C_m + \pi)$, and, second, increases in the loss of consumer surplus on goods invented in North, $C_c - C_m$. The marginal benefit (per consumer) to South consists of, first, increases in the profits $M_S\pi$ of Southern innovators, which leads to an increase of ϕ_S, which in turn leads to greater consumer surplus for Southern consumers, and, second, increases in the profits $M_S\pi$ of Northern innovators, which leads to an increase in ϕ_N, and thus greater consumer surplus for Southern consumers. In other words, South's best response is given by

$$\begin{aligned}&\phi_S(C_c - C_m - \pi) + \phi_N(C_c - C_m)\\&\quad = \left(\frac{d\phi_S}{dv} + \frac{d\phi_N}{dv}\right) \cdot \frac{dv}{d\Omega_S}\left[C_m\Omega_S + C_c(\bar{T} - \Omega_S)\right]\end{aligned}$$

where the left-hand side is marginal cost and the right-hand side is marginal benefit. Define $\mu_j \equiv \phi_j/(\phi_S + \phi_N) = H_j/(H_S + H_N)$ for the Cobb–Douglas research function (indeed, for all CES research functions). Then this equation can be rewritten for country $j = N, S$

$$C_c - C_m - \mu_j\pi = \frac{\gamma M_j\left[C_c\bar{T} - (C_c - C_m)\,\Omega_j\right]}{M_S\Omega_S + M_N\Omega_N} \tag{1}$$

It is clear that the best-response function is downward sloping in (Ω_S, Ω_N) space. To understand the strategic interdependence between the governments, consider the choice of patent protection by the South. Suppose the North were to strengthen its patent protection, implementing a higher Ω_N. This would shrink the fraction of total discounted profits that any innovator earns in the South and so, *ceteris paribus*, would reduce the responsiveness of global innovation to patent policy in the South. Moreover, the increase in Ω_N would draw labor into R&D in both the North and South. Since the elasticity of innovation stays constant, the South would find that its market is relatively less important to potential innovators and that these innovators are less responsive to its patent policy. For both reasons, the marginal benefit to the South of strengthening its patent protection would fall and so the government would respond to the increase in Ω_N with a reduction in patent length or an easing of enforcement. Thus, foreign and home IPR protection policies are strategic substitutes given our assumption that innovation elasticity γ is independent of patent value v.

4.3 Nash equilibrium

The Nash equilibrium is shown in Figure 1. It is clear that the equilibrium is "stable" and unique when there is an interior solution. From equation (1), one can infer that a country with both larger M_j and μ_j has a higher equilibrium Ω_j. Thus, a country with a larger domestic market for IPR-sensitive goods and higher innovative capability protects patents more in equilibrium. Given that in

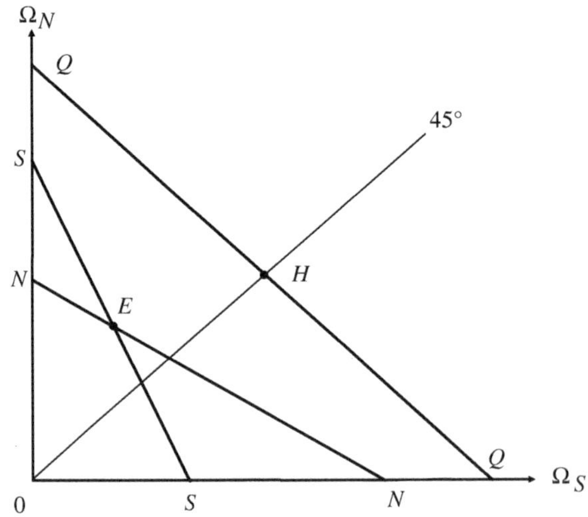

Figure 1. Comparison of Nash equilibrium and efficient patent regime.

practical terms the North has a larger market for IPR-sensitive goods, and higher innovative capability, it is natural to assume that $M_N > M_S$ and $\mu_N > \mu_S$. Then, it is not surprising that the North protects IPR more than the South does in equilibrium. This creates tension between the countries, as we shall discuss below.

Note that a country's equilibrium strength of protection is zero if its relative market size or relative innovativeness is small compared with the rest of the world. In other words, if either M_S/M_N or μ_S is too small, then the equilibrium Ω_S is equal to zero.[4] Similarly, there is an interior solution only when γ is sufficiently large. Otherwise, the South offers no protection in equilibrium. Since γ is the elasticity of rate of innovation with respect to the value of a patent, a large γ means that the differentiated goods are patent-sensitive. If the goods are not sufficiently patent-sensitive, the equilibrium strength of Southern protection Ω_S is zero.[5] This outcome would pertain if the set of protected subject matters include many non-patent-sensitive sectors, making γ too small.

4.4 Efficiency

To find the global optimum, we choose policies Ω_S and Ω_N that maximize $W_S(0) + W_N(0)$, where

$$\begin{aligned}\rho\left[W_S(0) + W_N(0)\right] = {} & \rho(\Lambda_{S0} + \Lambda_{N0}) + (L_S - L_{RS})w_S \\ & + (L_N - L_{RN})w_N + (M_S + M_N)\bar{T}(\phi_S + \phi_N)C_c \\ & - Q(\phi_S + \phi_N)(C_c - C_m - \pi).\end{aligned}$$

---

[4]We have not discussed the shape of the best-response functions where they hit the axes or where the constraint that $\Omega_j \leq \bar{T}$ begins to bind. The best-response curve of the South becomes vertical if it hits the vertical axis at a point below $\Omega_N = \bar{T}$. It also becomes vertical if the South's best response is $\bar{T}$ for some positive value of Ω_N. Similarly, the best-response curve for the North becomes horizontal if either it hits the horizontal axis before $\Omega_S = \bar{T}$ or if the North's best response is $\bar{T}$ for some positive value of Ω_S. Thus, the best-response curve for the South must be steeper than that for the North at any point of intersection.

[5]One can easily solve for $M_S\Omega_S$ from the best-response functions and observe that its value increases with γ. As γ becomes small, the value of $M_S\Omega_S$ becomes zero, given our assumption that $M_N > M_S$ and $\mu_N > \mu_S$.

in which $Q = M_S\Omega_S + M_N\Omega_N$ is the aggregate global strength of IPR protection. Observe that patent value $v = \pi(M_S\Omega_S + M_N\Omega_N) = \pi Q$, while the value of marginal product in innovation, $vF_L(H_j, L_{Rj}) = w_j = 1/a_j$ is constant. So, changes in Ω_S and Ω_N that leave Q unchanged do not affect labor allocation or innovation rates in either country or global welfare. The value of Q that maximizes global welfare defines the efficient combinations of Ω_S and Ω_N. Therefore, there is an efficiency frontier instead of an efficiency point. In fact, the first-order condition for maximization of $W_S(0) + W_N(0)$ is

$$C_c - C_m - \pi = \frac{\gamma(M_S + M_N)}{Q}\left[C_c\bar{T} - (C_c - C_m)\left(\frac{Q}{M_S + M_N}\right)\right], \tag{2}$$

which is linear in (Ω_S, Ω_N) space for the Cobb–Douglas research technology. If we compare equation (2) with equation (1), we see that the efficiency frontier lies outside both best-response functions, because of the externalities that we discussed before. Figure 1 shows this situation. The curve QQ is the efficiency frontier. For any given foreign strength of IPR protection, each country needs to protect more than its best-response level to achieve global efficiency.

If international transfer payments are feasible, then a globally efficient patent regime must have $M_S\Omega_S + M_N\Omega_N = Q^*$, where Q^* is the solution to equation (2). Notice that a range of efficient outcomes can be achieved without the need for any international transfers. By appropriate choice of Ω_N and Ω_S, the countries can be given any welfare levels on the efficiency frontier between that which they would achieve if $\Omega_S = 0$ and $\Omega_N = Q^*/M_N$ and that which they would achieve if $\Omega_S = Q^*/M_S$ and $\Omega_N = 0$.[6]

[6]This statement ignores the ceiling on patent lengths imposed by the finite economic life of differentiated products. A more precise statement is that a range of distributions of maximal world welfare can be achieved by varying Ω_S between $\Omega_S = \max\{0, (Q^* - M_N\bar{T})/M_S\}$ and $\min\{Q^*/M_S, \bar{T}\}$ while varying Ω_N between $\Omega_N = \min\{Q^*/M_N, \bar{T}\}$ and $\max\{0, (Q^* - M_S\bar{T})/M_N\}$ in such a way that $M_S\Omega_S + M_N\Omega_N = Q^*$.

Although aggregate world welfare does not vary with the national policies ω_j and τ_j as long as $M_S\Omega_S + M_N\Omega_N = Q^*$, the countries fare differently under the alternative combinations of policies that can be used to achieve global efficiency unless compensating transfers take place. In particular, the welfare of the North increases, and that of the South decreases, as Ω_S is raised and Ω_N is lowered in such a way as to keep the weighted sum constant. It follows that, absent any international transfer payments, the countries have a strong conflict of interest over the terms of an international patent agreement.

4.5 Pareto-improving patent agreements

The conclusion from Figure 1 is that efficiency requires strengthening patent protection in at least one country. Do all countries need to strengthen their protection under efficient harmonization? Suppose I maintain the plausible assumption that $M_N > M_S$ and $\mu_N > \mu_S$. More detailed analysis reveals that efficient harmonization must require the strengthening of IPR protection in the South, and in the world as a whole, as long as has there are weakly diminishing returns to patent protection in terms of inducing global innovation. Indeed, when the degree of diminishing returns is sufficiently high, efficient harmonization may not require strengthening of protection in the North (Boldrin and Levine, 2009; Grossman and Lai, 2006). However, it will require the North's strengthening of protection if γ is constant (i.e. the research function is Cobb–Douglas).

Do both countries necessarily gain from efficient harmonization? The answer is "no". Figure 2 shows the case when the North gains from efficient harmonization but the South loses. The more asymmetric the two regions are, i.e. the higher is M_N/M_S or H_N/H_S, the more likely is this outcome. If the countries are more symmetric it is more possible for both regions to gain from efficient harmonization.

4.6 Many countries

With many countries in the world the flavor of this analysis still holds. Specifically, a sufficiently small country (in a world with some large countries) will set its patent protection to zero in Nash

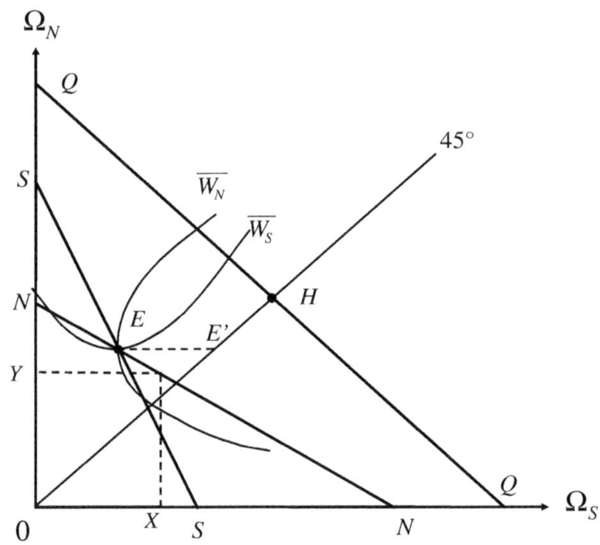

Figure 2. Who gains and who loses from harmonization of IPR protection?

equilibrium. Interestingly, the Nash-equilibrium global strength of patent protection is a declining function of the number of countries. The reason is that the greater the number of countries, the more serious is the free-rider problem. As a result global incentives for innovation are weaker in a noncooperative equilibrium. The efficiency frontier may be used to show that the greater the number of nations, the larger is the departure of global protection from the coordinated efficient level. It follows that a multi-country world would find it particularly hard to reach an agreement on efficient patent policies.

4.7 Main results

I summarize the main results of the model as follows. First, a country with a larger domestic market and higher innovative capability tends to protect IPR more in Nash equilibrium. Second, to achieve global efficiency, an international agreement must strengthen the aggregate world patent protection relative to the Nash equilibrium. Third, the problem of too-weak protection of IPR becomes more serious with an increase in the number of independent sovereign decision makers. Finally, harmonization is neither necessary nor sufficient for maximization of joint surplus of the world.

5 Empirical Studies on the Determinants of IPR Protection

With this analysis it becomes interesting to investigate how different patent rights are in the global economy. A number of empirical studies have been undertaken of this question, though most are *ad hoc* and reduced-form in nature, as I discuss next.

Ginarte and Park (1997) constructed an index of patent rights for 110 countries based on the laws and memberships in international agreements in each country for the years 1960 through 1990 at five-year intervals.[7] The authors then went on to analyze empirically the determinants of patent rights in 1965 through 1990 for 48 countries. When they put only GDP per capita on the right hand side, they found it to be a highly significant explanatory variable. However, when they additionally put in R&D/GDP and measures of schooling, political freedom, openness, and market freedom, they found GDP per capita to be insignificant, while R&D/GDP, openness and market freedom became significant. Interestingly, they did not include a domestic market-size variable as a determinant. Grossman and Lai's (2004) model suggests that this variable is an important determinant of patent rights.

Using an index constructed by Rapp and Rozek (1990), Maskus and Penubarti (1995) found that patent rights are positively related to GDP per capita and schooling. Later, using the index constructed by Ginarte and Park (1997), Maskus (2000, pp. 102–109) uncovered that GDP per capita (a proxy for the stage of economic development) affects patent rights in a non-monotonic manner — there is a U-shaped relationship between the two variables. In addition, scientists and engineers working in R&D as a percentage of labor force

[7]Park later added the data for 1995 and 2000. See, for example, Park and Wagh (2002).

(a proxy for innovative capability or human capital) has a significantly positive effect. Maskus argued, consistent with the theory above, that market size should matter for the strength of patents but did not find GDP to be significant.

The above empirical studies are not guided by any rigorous theory. Lai and Yan (2013) carry out an empirical study based on an extension of Grossman and Lai's (2004) theoretical model by introducing three new features to the analysis: trade and FDI barriers, firm heterogeneity and political economy considerations in setting patent policies. Based on calibration, they find that there would be global under-protection of patent rights when there is no international policy coordination. This result arises from the fact that, despite the existence of trade barriers, the free-rider problem becomes very serious when there is a large number of country-players in the patent-setting game. The empirical fact that firm revenues follow a fat-tailed distribution mitigates trade and FDI barriers a great deal, leading to low barriers to international exploitation of inventions. Thus, the cross-border externalities in strengthening national patent rights are high, despite the fact that only a small fraction of firms sell overseas (no more than say 15%) and an even smaller fraction of firms carry out FDI (no more than say 3%). Calibrating the model, they further find that requiring all countries to harmonize their patent strengths with the equilibrium strength of the most protective country (the US) does not lead to global over-protection of IPR. This is because the distribution of innovative capability among countries is not too skewed as to overcome the free-rider effect. If such an IPR harmonization scheme captures what the TRIPS has done, then there is no evidence that TRIPS leads to global over-protection of patent rights. In other words, TRIPS is globally welfare-improving. (This does not mean, however, that all countries would gain from such a harmonization. It only means that the sum of the gains for the gainers would exceed the sum of losses for the losers. Thus, distribution is still an issue in such a harmonization.)

What is the evidence for the existence of positive externalities in strengthening IPR protection? Externalities are difficult to pin down, since they do not leave any trace in the market, but the fact that the developed countries were willing to give market-access concessions to developing countries in the Uruguay Round in order for the latter to increase their IPR standards is consistent with the idea that such externalities exist.

6 What Has TRIPS Done?

It is possible to interpret TRIPS based on the above theoretical model. A number of views can be offered.

First, suppose we take the view of Reichman (1995) and others that TRIPS is backward-looking, in that it basically requires the South to adopt the pre-TRIPS standards of the North, without requiring much of an increase in standards in the latter. In other words, TRIPS requires harmonization of world IPR standards at the North's pre-TRIPS level. If we assume that the pre-TRIPS world is represented by the Nash equilibrium point E in Figure 2, then the effect of TRIPS is to move the world from point E to point E'. By comparing the latter point to the iso-welfare contours through the original point, it is clear that North gains and South loses, but global welfare improves.[8]

Second, suppose one takes the different view that TRIPS in fact required the South to harmonize with the North at the global efficiency frontier starting from the Nash equilibrium. Then the effect of TRIPS is to move the world from point E to H. In Figure 2, we have shown the case when the North gains and the South loses from such a global treaty. It is possible, however, that both the North and South gain from efficient harmonization. In that case, point H lies to the right of the $\overline{W_N}$ curve and above the $\overline{W_S}$ curve. By inspection, one can easily see that the more asymmetric are the two regions, the more likely it is that the South loses from efficient harmonization. Given the large differences in market sizes and innovative capabilities of the two regions, my considered conclusion is that the South likely loses from efficient harmonization. Even if this is true, it is still the

[8]South's consumers lose by paying higher prices, the North's producers gain higher profits, but all consumers gain from a larger variety of goods.

case that the North's gains outweigh the South's losses and global welfare increases as a result of this agreement.

Yet a third view of what TRIPS has done is that it requires the South to undertake partial harmonization and set IPR protection at a level such as X in Figure 2. Given that the South protects at level X, it is optimal for the North to protect at level Y, which remains stronger than the new South level. However, given that the North protects at Y, the South actually wants to protect at a lower level than X. But South is bound by TRIPS to maintain its protection at least at X. Therefore, TRIPS puts the world at $(\Omega_S, \Omega_N) = (X, Y)$. This view is consistent with the fact that TRIPS only sets minimum standards, which are binding for the South and not binding for the North. That is why in equilibrium some Northern countries choose to protect more than the minimum standard, while many Southern countries actually prefer to adopt lower standards than that required by TRIPS, though they cannot do so legally. Note that, compared with no agreement, it is still true that the North gains, the South loses, and global welfare increases.

It is important to emphasize that the best-response functions shown correspond to the post-TRIPS world. The analysis has been based on the assumption that these functions are the same both before and after TRIPS. However, it could be that the best-response functions of both regions in the post-TRIPS world have shifted from their earlier positions. One may suppose that at the time TRIPS was signed, governments actually anticipated the shifting of these curves in view of the continuous technological progress of the world and changes in the sizes of markets.

The second interpretation above is theoretically appealing, but unlikely to be true in practice. Unlike free trade, which is an easily located benchmark of economic optimality, the global efficiency frontier in IPR is not easily identifiable in practice. It is hard to argue that TRIPS is an economic optimizer. As the first and third interpretations demonstrate, it is possible to argue that TRIPS is globally welfare-improving without assuming that TRIPS actually achieves a global optimum.

If we adopt any of the above interpretations of TRIPS, its effect is to raise prices in South (and maybe also in North, to a lesser extent), raise profits of both Northern and Southern firms (with the majority being Northern ones), and increase the rate of innovation all over the world. Moreover, it increases trade in IPR-sensitive goods between countries. Suppose innovators respond to the increased incentives with a long time lag. Then, in the short-run the price hikes are the dominant effect. Southern consumers are the major losers while Northern firms are the major winners, as McCalman's (2001) results indicate. In the long run, it is predicted by the model that the increased rate of innovation will kick in and this effect will dominate the deadweight loss, an effect not captured by McCalman's study. The effect would hold as long as TRIPS put the world on or inside the efficiency frontier shown in Figure 2. That is, the dynamic gains will dominate as long as TRIPS does not result in over-protection of IPR in the world.

Scotchmer (2004b, pp. 334–336) offers an interesting alternative interpretation of what TRIPS has done. Because countries realize the inefficiency of individually choosing their own strengths of IPR protection, they decide to harmonize their standards. The question she asks is: "At what level do they harmonize?" Given the constraint $\Omega_S = \Omega_N = \overline{\Omega}$, she finds that a country prefers a higher harmonized $\overline{\Omega}$ the smaller and more innovative it is. Therefore, small and innovative countries such as Switzerland should be most enthusiastic about strengthening global IPR protection. The final outcome is a compromise among all countries.[9]

Is it possible to conceive of a Pareto-efficient agreement that is mutually beneficial to all countries? In fact, there is no reason why such an agreement cannot be reached, at least in principle. In Figure 2, we can always find a point on the efficiency frontier that lies above the South's iso-welfare line $\overline{W_S}$ and to the right

[9]In the context of my multi-country model, the country with higher μ_j/M_j prefers a higher $\overline{\Omega}$. This is the same conclusion as Scotchmer's.

of the North's iso-welfare line $\overline{W_N}$. At that point, the welfare of both South and North will be greater than in Nash equilibrium.[10] However, the real world consists of more than two countries, and in a multi-country world the Pareto-optimal set of strengths of IPR protection across countries contains combinations with very different degrees of protection among them. Such a Pareto-optimal agreement is complicated to write and hard to enforce.

7 Extension with Multi-Issue Negotiations

If a region's action confers positive externalities on another region, then the role of international policy coordination is to create a win-win situation so that both regions can be made better off by moving from the non-cooperative equilibrium to the cooperative outcome. Furthermore, if one accepts the presumption that TRIPS hurts the South and benefits the North, but the latter's gains outweighs the former's losses, then, in principle, one can imagine the North giving a lump-sum transfer to the South in exchange for its cooperation. In reality, however, rather than a transfer it is more feasible for the two regions to trade concessions with each other in multisectoral negotiations, such as in the WTO. It is widely believed that the South agreed to sign on to TRIPS only because the North offered additional market access for textiles, apparel and agricultural products (Reichman, 1995; Maskus, 2000). This shows the merits of multisectoral negotiations, in which all countries may benefit from the deal.

This possibility can be easily demonstrated with an extension of the basic model, as shown in Lai and Qiu (2003). In that paper, it is assumed that the North loses from a lowering of tariff t it imposes on imports from the South, but the South gains from the tariff reduction. This case can be motivated by assuming that each country has an endowment of some traditional good and that the autarky price of the good is lower in the South. Thus, that region has the comparative

---

[10]Note that the segment of the efficiency frontier enveloped between the iso-welfare line $\overline{W_S}$ and iso-welfare line $\overline{W_N}$ represent a "contract curve" of sorts.

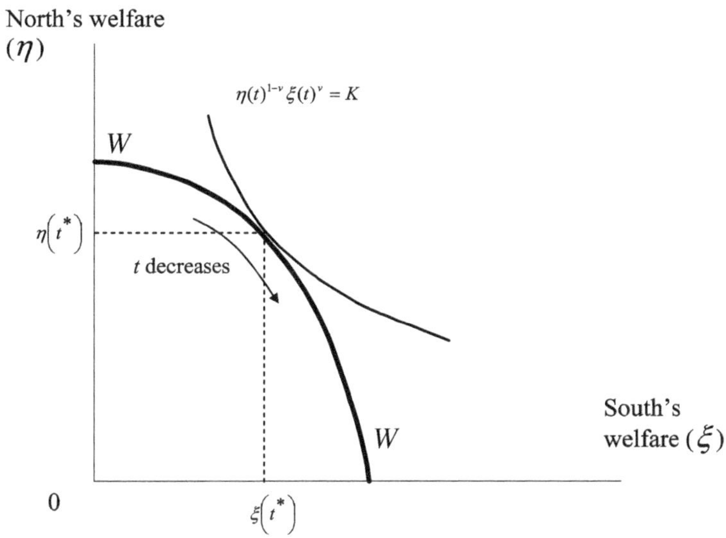

Figure 3. Nash Bargaining over t. The origin is the point with no agreement.

advantage in this sector. Since the North is large, its incentive is to drive down the price it pays for the good by setting a positive optimum tariff.

Suppose the two regions bargain simultaneously over whether the South adopts the North's pre-TRIPS patent policy and over the value of t. Then, adopting the Nash bargaining framework of analysis, the equilibrium is as shown in Figure 3. The function $\eta(t)$ is Northern welfare with TRIPS in place and with the Northern tariff set at t. The function $\xi(t)$ is the corresponding Southern welfare. The parameter v is South's bargaining power, K is a constant, and the curve WW is the welfare frontier. The outcome of Nash bargaining is a point on the welfare frontier such that $\eta(t)^{1-v}\,\xi(t)^{v}$ is maximized. This corresponds to the point $(\xi(t^*), \eta(t^*))$ in Figure 3. If the two countries fail to reach an agreement on t, then the South does not accept TRIPS. Since there is neither agreement in IPR nor in the tariff, this is the threat point of the bargaining game, corresponding to the origin of the graph. As shown in Figure 3, clearly both regions gain in equilibrium. The bargaining outcome is mutually beneficial since the total change in global welfare, taking into account both the

IPR agreement and the trade agreement, is positive. The stronger the bargaining power of the South, v, the deeper is the reduction in t, and the greater is the gain in global welfare.

Thus, there is a synergy between international policy coordination in technology protection and coordination in trade liberalization. This is reminiscent of the point made in Krugman and Obstfeld (2006, p. 237) that multisectoral trade negotiations help trade liberalization by playing the lobby supporting free trade, the exporting firms, against the lobby opposing free trade, the import-competing firms. In this case, multi-issue negotiations help trade liberalization by playing the North's protectionist import-competing firms against the exporters of intellectual property. It is precisely the possibility of engaging in such negotiations that makes the WTO an effective body in facilitating global trade liberalization.

8 Relationship with the Literature on Coordination of Trade Policy

Bagwell and Staiger (1999, 2002) hold the view that terms of trade externalities are the core reason for the WTO because Nash equilibrium tariffs are suboptimal from the global welfare point of view. According to Bagwell and Staiger (2002, p. 3), "...the purpose of a trade agreement [such as the GATT or WTO] is to offer a means for governments to escape from a terms-of-trade-driven Prisoners' Dilemma". The reason is that "...a government (of a large country) is assumed to set its import tariff in order to maximize national welfare, while recognizing that some of the cost of the tariff falls upon foreign exporters whose products sell at a lower world price (i.e. at a diminished terms of trade). This 'terms of trade externality' naturally leads governments to set unilateral tariffs that are higher than would be efficient" (Bagwell and Staiger, 2002, p. 3.). In the case of IPR protection, we also have a Prisoners' Dilemma game, but the externality is positive. The TRIPS agreement, together with the agreement to lower trade barriers in the North's traditional goods sector, allows the governments to escape both forms of the Prisoners' Dilemma.

In fact, unlike Bagwell and Staiger, I do not need to assume that countries are large in the analysis of IPR protection, which makes the patent story more compelling. Bagwell and Staiger and others develop a dynamic version of this line of analysis. They conclude that, in a repeated game, the trade agreement is self-enforcing since the cooperative outcome can be supported as a subgame perfect equilibrium of the dynamic tariff-setting game as long as the discount factor is sufficiently large (see, for example, Staiger, 1995; Bagwell and Staiger, 1997; Furusawa and Lai, 1999). There is no reason why the basic IPR model cannot also be analyzed from the perspective of a repeated game. Similar conclusion would be drawn, namely that the cooperative outcome is self-enforcing when the discount factor is sufficiently large.

9 Extension with Firm-Bias and Trade Barriers

The conclusion that global IPR protection is too weak in the absence of international agreement can be met with skepticism. Many people point to the strong pharmaceutical lobbies in Washington to justify why they think global patent protection before TRIPS must have been already too strong rather than too weak. Moreover, the existence of trade barriers weakens the international spillovers that one nation confers on foreign countries when it strengthens domestic IPR protection. Therefore, I address here two key simplifications of the basic model: that governments put equal weights on consumer welfare and firm profits and that there are no trade barriers. In reality, governments are often biased in favor of domestic firms and trade barriers are non-trivial. Omitting these factors can bias the conclusion that global IPR protection is too weak in the non-cooperative equilibrium. Obviously, whether the conclusion of the basic model can be overturned depends on how large are the magnitudes of these two effects. The analytical task is to find out what values of firm-biasedness and trade barriers can sustain the original conclusion that there is under-protection of IPR in Nash equilibrium, and then judge whether these values are plausible. This analysis is done by Lai and Yan (2013), which I explain briefly next.

Let y be the probability that an invention by a domestic firm is sold in a foreign market (call it the "import penetration rate"). This is an inverse measure of foreign trade barriers. In fact, if I assume that there is an iceberg trade cost equal to a fraction t of the production cost, then this formulation is equivalent to having $y = (1+t)^{-\epsilon+1}$, where ϵ is the price elasticity of demand for each differentiated good. So assume that there is a constant-elasticity demand curve faced by each consumer. Let $1 + a$ be the weight a government puts on domestic profits when a weight of one is put on domestic consumer surplus in its objective function. The parameter a measures the firm-bias of governments. Note that this approach of assigning additional exogenous weight to firms as opposed to consumers is similar to what is done by Bagwell and Staiger (2002). They essentially put a weight of $1 + a$ on firms in the government's objective function, which they treat as a reduced form derived from the analysis of a political-economy equilibrium a la Grossman and Helpman (1994). Let v_i be the expected value of a patent of an invention by a firm in country i. Therefore, $v_i = \pi \left[\sum_{k\neq i} (yM_k\Omega_k) + M_i\Omega_i\right]$.

It is useful to consider a multi-country setting, as the number of independent decision-making governments plays a crucial role in whether there is under-protection of IP in Nash equilibrium. Let there be J countries in the set $\mathcal{N}$ of countries in the world. In a multi-country setting, the best-response function of country i is

$$\begin{aligned} &y\left(\sum_{j\neq i}\phi_j\right)(C_c - C_m) + \phi_i\,(C_c - C_m) - \phi_i\,(1+a)\,\pi \\ &= \left(\sum_{j\neq i}\gamma\frac{\phi_j}{v_j}\right)y^2\pi M_i f_i + \gamma\frac{\phi_i}{v_i}\pi M_i f_i \end{aligned} \tag{3}$$

where $f_i \equiv C_c\overline{T} - (C_c - C_m)\,\Omega_i$ is the present discounted value of per-person consumer surplus derived from a differentiated good over its product life. The left-hand side of the above equation is, in fact, the marginal cost per consumer in country i of strengthening IPR there. The first term is the loss in consumer surplus attributed to inventions from firms outside country i; the second term is the loss of consumer surplus attributed to inventions from country i; and the third term is the offsetting of the losses of consumer surplus by gains in profits of firms in country i. The right-hand side is the marginal benefit per consumer in country i. The first term is the increase in consumer welfare in country i due to increases in flows of innovations from firms outside country i; the second term is the increase in consumer welfare in country i due to the increase in flow of innovation from country i. If I define the left-hand side as $MC_i(a)$ and the right-hand side as MB_i, then $\frac{1}{M_i}\frac{\partial W_i(a)}{\partial \Omega_i} = MB_i - MC_i(a)$, where $W_i\,(a)$ is the Government i's objective function. (Hereinafter, I put an argument "a" after the name of a function if firm-bias affects the value of the function.)

It can be easily shown that the first-order condition for global welfare maximization with respect to the choice of Ω_i is given by

$$MC_i(a) + \pi a \phi_i - y\pi \left(\sum_{j \neq i} \phi_j \right)$$
$$= MB_i + \sum_{k \neq i} \left(\sum_{j \neq k} \gamma \frac{\phi_j}{v_j} \right) y^2 \pi M_k f_k + \sum_{k \neq i} \gamma \frac{\phi_k}{v_k} y \pi M_k f_k \quad (4)$$

The left-hand side of this equation is the marginal global cost borne by each consumer in country i of strengthening IPR protection in that country. The second term is the welfare that will not be taken into account when IPR protection in country i is chosen to maximize global welfare instead of to maximize government i's firm-biased objective (therefore it is an addition to marginal cost); the third term is the offsetting of the loss in welfare of country i due to increases in profits of firms outside of country i. The right-hand side is the marginal global benefit attributed to each consumer in country i of strengthening IPR there. The second term plus the third term is the increase in welfare of consumers outside of country i due to faster innovation outside of country i plus the increase due to faster innovation from country i. The cross-border externalities of IPR protection are captured by the third term on the left-hand side plus the second and third terms on the right-hand side. It is apparent that since an increase in trade barriers (a decrease in y) leads to less international spillovers, the likelihood of under-protection of IPR in equilibrium is lower. Likewise, an increase in firm-bias (an increase in a) reduces the gap between marginal global benefit and marginal national benefit, making under-protection of IPR less likely.

Let us define the left hand side of the first order condition above as MC_i^w and the right hand side of the equation as MB_i^w. It follows that $\frac{1}{M_i}\frac{\partial W^w}{\partial \Omega_i} = MB_i^w - MC_i^w$, where W^w is world welfare (without bias towards firm profits).

I define under-protection as a situation when, starting from Nash equilibrium, global welfare increases as a result of some positive changes in all $\{\Omega_i\}_{i \in \mathcal{N}}$ (where the magnitudes of increase are not necessarily equal). The point of the analysis is to come up with a sufficient condition under which, starting from Nash equilibrium $\{\Omega_i^E\}_{i \in \mathcal{N}}$, some coordinated increases in IPR protection of all countries is globally welfare-improving. Note that an increase in the strength of protection in all countries raises the values of all patents. This increases the global deadweight losses, but gives a boost to the rate of innovation. To simplify the analysis, I focus on changes in $\{\Omega_i\}_{i \in \mathcal{N}}$ such that $M_i d\Omega_i = d\overline{\Omega}$ for all i. I want to find a sufficient condition under which such changes lead to an increase in global welfare. In other words, I seek a condition under which the marginal global benefit outweighs the marginal global cost.

Bear in mind that equation (3) is equivalent to $\frac{1}{M_i}\frac{\partial W_i(a)}{\partial \Omega_i} = 0$, and equation (4) is equivalent to $\frac{1}{M_i}\frac{\partial W^w}{\partial \Omega_i} = 0$. Summing the left-hand side and the right-hand side of equations (3) over all i as well as both sides of (4) over all i, and comparing the two ensuing equations, it can be shown that

$$(J-1)\,y > a$$

is a sufficient condition under which, starting from Nash equilibrium, small increases in Ω_i such that $d\Omega_i = \frac{d\overline{\Omega}}{M_i}$ is globally welfare-improving, i.e. $\frac{dW^w}{d\overline{\Omega}} > 0$. A detailed proof of this result can be found in Lai and Yan (2013).

This last statement says that starting from each Ω_i being at the Nash equilibrium level, small increases in $\{\Omega_i\}_{i\in\mathcal{N}}$ such that $\frac{d\Omega_i}{d\Omega_j} = \frac{M_j}{M_i}$ for all $i \neq j$ leads to an increase in global welfare. Therefore, $(J-1)\,y > a$ is exactly the condition we are looking for. To check that this is a reasonable condition, note that in the special case of the basic model, when there are two countries ($J = 2$), $y = 1$ and $a = 0$, the condition is satisfied. Moreover, it accords with the intuition that the free-rider problem gets more serious when there are more countries playing the patent-setting game, for a larger J leads to more under-protection. It also is consistent with the notions that trade barriers weaken the cross-border externality of IPR protection, because a smaller y leads to less under-protection, and that stronger government bias towards patent-holding firms tends to strengthen patents, for a larger a leads to less under-protection.

What is a reasonable value for a? In the political-economy literature (Grossman and Helpman, 1994; Maggi and Goldberg, 1999), researchers have tried to estimate the weight the US government puts on campaign contributions when it puts a weight of unity on welfare. They rarely come up with a number more than 0.5. Since this is a preference parameter, it should be the same in the context of patent protection. Suppose there is a patent lobby, and suppose there is no consumer lobby, nor is there lobbying from other sectors of the economy. Then I can show that the value the government puts on contributions is exactly the same as a in our model (Lai and Yan, 2013).

What is a reasonable value for J? This is the number of independent government decision-makers in the patent-setting game. Thus, it is the number of countries in the world that consume and trade patent-sensitive goods, and that adopt neither zero nor full patent protection. To be conservative, let $J = 5$.

When $a = 0.5$ and $J = 5$, a sufficient condition for the Nash equilibrium to be under-protecting patents is $y > 0.1$. As stated earlier, y can be interpreted as a parameter derived from iceberg trade costs, such that $y = (1+t)^{-\epsilon+1}$. If the price elasticity of demand for a differentiated good ϵ is equal to 4, then $y > 0.1$ is equivalent to an iceberg trade cost t of less than or equal to 78% of the cost of production. This condition is likely to be satisfied for most products. So, based on this rough calculation, I conclude that global patent protection in the absence of international coordination is probably too weak.

10 Extension with Relaxation of National Treatment

One may argue that in a non-cooperative equilibrium, there is no incentive for a country to offer national treatment. One response to this criticism is that, before the TRIPS Agreement was signed and implemented, many countries were already members of WIPO and the Berne and Paris Conventions. These treaties required their members to adopt national treatment. A critique of this response is that these treaties were so loosely enforced that countries did not really abide by that commitment. Do the main conclusions of the basic model continue to hold if I relax the assumption of national treatment? It turns out that the answer is, for the most part, "yes". Specifically, a larger country has incentives to offer more IPR protection, the positive cross-border externalities of strengthening domestic IPR protection continue to exist, and harmonization is neither necessary nor sufficient for global efficiency. I briefly explain the analysis below.

I first compute the Nash equilibrium. Let Ω_{ij} be the strength of protection offered by country i on goods invented by country j, where $i, j = \{N, S\}$. The value of a patent of a good invented in country j is therefore given by $v_j = \pi\left(M_j\Omega_{jj} + M_i\Omega_{ij}\right)$, where $i \neq j$. Focusing on the protection of goods invented by country j, the best-response function of that country gives the optimal choice of Ω_{jj} given that country i chooses Ω_{ij}. That function is

$$C_c - C_m - \pi = \frac{\gamma}{M_j\Omega_{jj} + M_i\Omega_{ij}} M_j[\Omega_{jj}C_m + (\bar{T} - \Omega_{jj})C_c]; \qquad (5)$$

while the best-response function of country i, selecting its best choice of Ω_{ij} given that country j chooses Ω_{jj}, is

$$C_c - C_m = \frac{\gamma}{M_j\Omega_{jj} + M_i\Omega_{ij}} M_i[\Omega_{ij}C_m + (\bar{T} - \Omega_{ij})C_c]. \qquad (6)$$

Note that the innovative capability of a country does not affect its equilibrium strength of IPR protection when countries can optimally choose to offer differential treatments to domestic and foreign firms. If one adds equations (5) and (6), it is not hard to show that v_j is the same for all countries in equilibrium. That is, the equilibrium value of a patent is independent of where the good is invented. Since $M_j\Omega_{jj} + M_i\Omega_{ij} = M_i\Omega_{ii} + M_j\Omega_{ji}$ where $i \neq j$, we can infer from (5) that a country with a larger domestic market tends to protect the IPR of domestically-invented goods more than one with a smaller domestic market. Moreover, (6) implies that a country with a larger domestic market tends to protect the IPR of foreign-invented goods more than one with a smaller domestic market.

The globally efficient combinations of Ω_{jj} and Ω_{ij}, on the other hand, are determined by

$$\begin{aligned} C_c - C_m - \pi &= \frac{\gamma}{M_j\Omega_{jj} + M_i\Omega_{ij}} \times \{M_j[\Omega_{jj}C_m + (\bar{T} - \Omega_{jj})C_c] \\ &\quad + M_i[\Omega_{ij}C_m + (\bar{T} - \Omega_{ij})C_c]\} \\ &= \frac{\gamma}{Q_j} \times [\bar{T}C_c(M_i + M_j) - (C_c - C_m)Q_j] \end{aligned} \tag{7}$$

where $Q_j \equiv M_j\Omega_{jj} + M_i\Omega_{ij}$. Again, rather than being unique, there exists a continuum of efficient combinations, given by setting $M_j\Omega_{jj}+ M_i\Omega_{ij}$ equal to the solution of Q_j in (7). In Figure 4, we plot the best-response functions and efficiency frontier in $(\Omega_{jj}, \Omega_{ij})$ space, where $j = N$ and $i = S$. The curve $NN - NN$ is North's best-response function while $SN - SN$ is that of South. The curve $Q_N - Q_N$ is the efficiency frontier. Considering the first line of equation (7), it is obvious that the continuum of globally efficient combinations of Ω_{jj} and Ω_{ij} lies outside each of the best-response functions, which is remarkably similar to what is shown in Figure 1. The interpretation is that, given Ω_{ij}, country j's best response Ω_{jj} falls short of the global optimum and vice-versa. This situation is caused by cross-border positive externalities as a country strengthens IPR protection of a good invented either by the domestic firms or foreign firms. Therefore, there is under-protection of IPR in Nash equilibrium for each differentiated good.

Harmonization (in the sense that $\Omega_{ii} = \Omega_{jj}$) is certainly not sufficient for global efficiency. Neither is it necessary, since Q_j can be

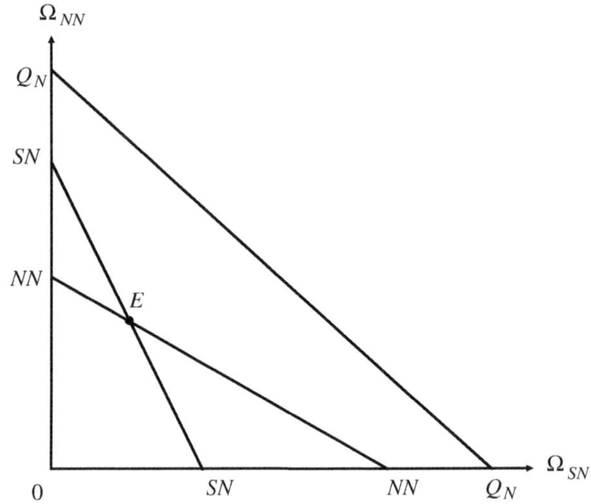

Figure 4. Best response functions and efficiency frontier corresponding to Northern goods.

at the efficiency level with Ω_{ij} small and Ω_{jj} large, or with Ω_{ij} large but Ω_{jj} small. Similarly, Ω_{ii} can be either large or small to attain global efficiency. Therefore, there is no need for $\Omega_{ii} = \Omega_{jj}$ to reach global efficiency. Along similar lines, it is easy to see that national treatment is neither necessary nor sufficient for global efficiency.

Left as an exercise for the reader is to prove that a country always protects domestically invented goods more than it does foreign-invented ones (i.e. $\Omega_{ii} > \Omega_{ij}$ for $i \neq j$). In fact, this result reflects an interesting history about copyrights in the United States. In the 18th century, American authors were not popular in the English-speaking world, including in the United States itself. In order to allow cheap reproduction of books by English authors, US policy basically did not offer copyright protection to their works. Even when the first copyright statute was enacted in 1790, no protection was offered to foreigners. It was not until American authors became internationally popular that the US government signed an agreement with Britain in 1890 to offer reciprocal granting of copyrights to each other with national treatment in both countries. As Scotchmer (2004a) argues convincingly, countries do not have incentives to offer national treatment when there is no reciprocity. Again, we can view the agreement between two countries of simultaneously offering national treatment and reciprocity to each other as one that facilitates escape from a Prisoners' Dilemma. In Nash equilibrium, countries tend to discriminate against foreign IPR holders and offer lower protection to them. This, however, is suboptimal and a Pareto improvement can be achieved by forcing each country to offer national treatment to the other.

11 Other Possible Extensions of the Basic Model

FDI or licensing. Imagine modifying the basic model above to allow for the effects of IPR on FDI or licensing. Suppose that in serving a foreign country's market, each innovator firm has two choices: exporting or producing the good there in a wholly-owned subsidiary. For simplicity, I assume that the firm can make the same profits from licensing the technology to an arm's-length partner. Thus, the effects of IPR on FDI and licensing are the same. The advantage of using FDI to serve a foreign market is that trade costs (including trade barriers and transportation cost) are saved. The disadvantage is that local firms can more easily invent around the patent, as proximity to information about manufacturing the good helps local firms develop commercially viable substitutes. In contrast, suppose that local firms cannot invent around a patent when the good is imported. For simplicity, assume that once a substitute is developed, the local market for the good turns from monopolistic to perfectly competitive. Suppose further that as a country strengthens IPR, the hazard rate at which local firms can successfully invent around the multinational firm's patent decreases. In equilibrium, foreign firms are indifferent between exporting to the local market and serving it through FDI. Moreover, the lower the hazard rate, the higher the equilibrium fraction of foreign goods serving the local market through FDI rather than exporting. Therefore, as a country strengthens IPR, not only does it induce more innovation from firms all over the world, it also increases FDI inflows.[11] It should be straightforward to figure out the best-response functions as well as the global efficiency frontier in this setting.

Strengthening IPR should give additional benefits to the domestic country because the increases in FDI inflows generates a saving in trade costs, which trickles down to lower prices paid by domestic consumers. Further, introduction of FDI into the basic model does not change the conclusion that there is under-protection of IPR in Nash equilibrium. The positive cross-border externalities of strengthening IPR continue to exist: As a country strengthens patents, foreign imports enjoy monopoly profits in more occasions. In addition, the expected duration of monopoly of an international firm is longer as the hazard rate of having the patent circumvented is lower. Lastly, as before, foreign consumers benefit from having more varieties to consume.

Parallel imports. Parallel imports (PI) are goods imported into a country without the authorization of the holder of intellectual property rights after the goods were legitimately sold outside the country.[12] Prohibition of PI by a country takes the form of denying "international exhaustion" of IPR. That is to say, the IP rights do not exhaust after first sale in the international market and any cross-border resale must be authorized by the rights holder. Clearly, denying international exhaustion allows the IPR holders to segment the foreign market from the domestic market, thus benefitting innovators. In short, a tighter PI policy can serve as a substitute for strengthening IPR protection. Interestingly, the TRIPS agreement does not harmonize PI policy at all. Article 6 states that "For the purposes of dispute settlement, nothing in the Agreement shall be used to address the issue of the exhaustion of IPRs, provided there is compliance with national treatment and most-favored nation treatment" (UNCTAD, 1996). One can view this omission as a

[11] This way of modeling the effects of IPR on FDI is borrowed from Lai (1998).
[12] The chapter by Ganslandt and Maskus in this volume deals comprehensively with parallel trade.

loophole of the TRIPS Agreement. A country that prefers to have weak IPR protection can abide by the minimum patent and copyright standards stipulated by TRIPS while undermining that protection by permitting parallel imports.

Since tight PI policy is a substitute for strong IPR protection, one would expect there to be over-provision of international exhaustion in the world as some countries tend to free-ride on other countries. The globally optimal degree of regulation of PI should therefore presumably be tighter than the Nash-equilibrium degree of regulation.

Cumulative innovation and breadth of patent. In the basic model, a crucial assumption was that innovation is not cumulative. In reality, however, development of new products often requires the inputs of the ideas embodied in patented goods. In that case, strengthening patent protection of goods with ideas used as inputs into other innovations increases the costs of future product development and could slow down the long-run rate of innovation. Here I consider one particular example to illustrate the economics of cumulative innovation, namely quality improvement on a "quality ladder". In the basic model, where inventions of completely new products are not substitutable with each other, the only relevant aspects of IPR protection are length and enforcement. In the quality-ladder model, innovations improve the quality of existing products. Here, two more aspects of IPR protection are important, namely the "minimum patentable inventive step" (MPIS)and the "leading breadth" (LB; Scotchmer, 2004b, pp. 84–88). The former is related to the concept of non-obviousness, and the latter to the concept of novelty. A higher MPIS means that an invention has to be more non-obvious (or more different from the state of the art) to be patentable. A higher LB means that an invention has to be more novel (again, more different from the prior art) for there to be non-infringement of the patent.

In the quality-ladder model, both aspects are measured by the size of the inventive step from the position of the latest art on the ladder. Further, they may be construed as two independent concepts. If the MPIS is higher than the LB, then all patents are non-infringing. If the LB is higher than the MPIS, then some patents may be infringing.[13] Consider, however, the simple case that MPIS is restricted to be always equal to LB, so that a patent never infringes on another patent. Then, an increase in LB in one country can confer a negative externality on foreign countries as it makes future quality-improvement innovations more costly to foreign firms. As the long-run rate of innovation is reduced, foreign consumers are worse off. Another possible source of negative externality of an increase in LB is that it can increase the duration of monopoly power enjoyed by each patent, which makes goods more expensive to foreign consumers, a deadweight loss. This can happen when the length of patent is longer than the time it takes for the next patentable product to appear in the market. As a result, the patent length is rather irrelevant in determining the duration of monopoly power. If these negative externalities dominate, then in Nash equilibrium the leading breadths in each country would tend to be too large compared with the global optimum, and international coordination should narrow them.

Subject matters. The analysis of the individual country's choice of subject matter to be protected is similar to that of patent length and of national treatment. An enlargement of the set of patentable subject matters induces more innovation (for patent-sensitive sectors), but it also gives monopoly powers to additional patent-holders for a certain duration of time. There are also positive cross-border externalities as foreign firms are given patent-protected monopoly power, and foreign consumers enjoy a larger variety of differentiated goods. Thus, the equilibrium set of protected subject matters would tend to be too small compared with the global optimum. Moreover, since countries differ in the their ability to

[13]There are many examples where, after a patent had been granted, it was successfully sued for infringement of another patent. Typically, the infringing patent-holder was ordered to pay a royalty to the patent-holder of the infringed patent, through bargaining, to compensate for the licensing of the technology from the latter to the former. In this case, the patentees are said to be holding 'blocking patents' (Scotchmer, 2004b, p. 86).

innovate in different areas of technology, each would tend to restrict the set of patentable subject matters to include only those in which it possesses high innovativeness. By doing so, the country effectively discriminates in favor of domestic firms. This is similar to the analysis of the extent of national treatment granted to foreign firms presented above. While it narrowed this possibility considerably from the prior condition, TRIPS still allows for some national autonomy in the choice of certain subject matters. This not only allows some countries to soften the negative welfare impact from the common patent length mandated by TRIPS, but also enables them to use the choice of protected subject matters to diminish the impact of the national-treatment requirement.

Costs of implementation. The costs of implementing stronger IPR per domestic consumer can depend on many things. If there are economies of scale in implementation, then the marginal cost is lower for a larger country. This reinforces the result of the basic model that larger countries tend to have incentives to protect IPR more. If the marginal costs of implementation are lower for countries that have a longer history of rule of law, such as the former colonies of Britain or France, they would have incentives to protect more. However, the costs of implementation have no effect on the positive externalities conferred on foreigners as a country strengthens its IPR protection. Therefore, the introduction of implementation costs does not alter the basic result that countries under-protect IPR in Nash equilibrium.

12 Conclusion

A good economic reason for international coordination of IPR protection is the existence of positive cross-border externalities, leading to under-protection in the global economy. This is true regardless of whether national treatment is required. However, the conclusion that uncoordinated levels of IPR are too low has to be tempered by the presence of trade barriers and lobbying by innovating firms, though a rough calibration exercise demonstrated that these factors are probably not enough to overturn it. The central conclusion of too-limited protection should be further tempered by the fact that many innovations are cumulative in nature.

The existence of cross-border positive externalities in IPR protection finds its parallel in the existence of cross-border negative externalities in tariff protection. While the former calls for cooperative strengthening of IPR, the latter calls for cooperative reduction in tariffs. One key difference between international coordination in trade policy and patent policy is that it is easy to identify and observe the efficiency benchmark of zero tariffs in the former area but difficult to identify in practice the efficiency benchmark in IPR policy coordination.

Ideally, international coordination should bring the world to the global efficiency point or frontier. Supposing one can identify the efficiency set in practice, efficient harmonization may very well benefit the North but hurt the South. A Pareto improvement can be reached in principle if the North makes a transfer to the South. In fact, the current practice in international coordination, implemented through TRIPS, can best be interpreted as requiring the South to harmonize with the pre-TRIPS standards of the North. This is probably not globally optimal, but perhaps is globally welfare-improving in the sense that the North's gains outweigh the South's losses. This possibility justifies multi-issue negotiations, whereby the South increases its IPR protection in exchange for the North opening its markets for agriculture and labor-intensive goods. This is a fair characterization of what was achieved in the Uruguay Round.

Coordination is more than harmonization (or establishing universal minimum IPR standards). It also includes non-discrimination through national treatment and the most-favored nation principle. Moreover, coordination includes enforcement, but since that is hard to monitor, full harmonization is harder to attain in practice than national treatment and MFN.

References

Bagwell, K. and Staiger, R. W. (1997). Multilateral tariff cooperation during the formation of customs unions, *Journal of International Economics* 42(1–2), 91–123.

Bagwell, K. and Staiger, R. W. (1999). An economic theory of GATT, *American Economic Review* 89, 215–248.

Bagwell, K. and Staiger, R. W. (2002). *The Economics of the World Trading System*, Cambridge MA: MIT Press.

Boldrin, M. and Levine, D. K. (2009). Market size and intellectual property protection, *International Economic Review* 50(3), 855–881.

Chin, J. and Grossman, G. M. (1990). Intellectual property rights and North-South trade, in Jones, R. W. and Krueger, A. O. (eds.), *The Political Economy of International Trade*, Cambridge MA: Basil Blackwell Publishers, pp. 90–107.

Deardorff, A. V. (1992). Welfare effects of global patent protection, *Economica* 59(233), 35–51.

Diwan, I. and Rodrik, D. (1991). Patents, appropriate technology, and North-South trade, *Journal of International Economics* 30, 27–47.

Ginarte, J. C. and Park, W. G. (1997). Determinants of patent rights: A cross-national study, *Research Policy* 26(3), 283–301.

Furusawa, T. and Lai, E. L.-C. (1999). Adjustment costs and gradual trade liberalization, *Journal of International Economics* 49(2), 333–361.

Glass, A. J., and Saggi, K. (2002). Licensing versus direct investment: Implications for economic growth, *Journal of International Economics*, 56(1), 131–153.

Grossman, G. M. and Helpman, E. (1991). *Innovation and Growth in the Global Economy*, MIT Press, Cambridge, Massachusetts, USA.

Grossman, G. M. and Helpman, E. (1994). Protection for sale, *American Economic Review* 84, 833–850.

Grossman, G. M. and Lai, E. L.-C. (2004). International protection of intellectual property, *American Economic Review* 94(5), 1635–1653.

Grossman, G. M. and Lai, E. L.-C. (2006). International protection of intellectual property: Corrigendum, *American Economic Review* 96(1), 456.

Helpman, E. (1993). Innovation, imitation, and intellectual property rights, *Econometrica* 61(6), 1247–1280.

Krugman, P. R. and Obstfeld, M. (2006). *International Economics: Theory and Policy*, 7th edn., Boston: Pearson Education, Inc.

Lai, E. L.-C. (1998). International intellectual property rights protection and rate of product innovation, *Journal of Development Economics* 55, 133–153.

Lai, E. L.-C. and Qiu, L. D. (2003). The North's intellectual property rights standard for the South? *Journal of International Economics* 59(1), 183–209.

Lai, E. L.-C. and Yan, I. K. (2013). Would global patent protection be too weak without international coordination? *Journal of International Economics* 89(1), 42–54.

Maggi, G. and Goldberg, P. (1999). Protection for sale: An empirical investigation, *American Economic Review* 89, 1135–1155.

Mansfield, E. (1986). Patents and innovation: An empirical study, *Management Science* 32(2), 272–280.

Markusen, J. R. (2001). Contracts, intellectual property rights, and multinational investment in developing countries, *Journal of International Economics* 53(1), 189–204.

Maskus, K. E. (2000). *Intellectual Property Rights in the Global Economy*, Washington, DC: Institute for International Economics.

Maskus, K. E. and Penubarti, M. (1995). How trade-related are intellectual property rights? *Journal of International Economics* 39, 227–248.

McCalman, P. (2001). Reaping what you sow: An empirical analysis of international patent harmonization, *Journal of International Economics* 55(1), 161–185.

McCalman, P. (2002). National patents, innovation and international agreements, *Journal of International Trade and Economic Development* 11(1), 1–14.

Park, W. G. and Wagh, S. (2002). Chapter 2: Index of patent rights, in *Economic Freedom of the World: 2002 Annual Report*, Vancouver: The Fraser Institute.

Qiu, L. D. and Lai, E. L.-C. (2004). Protection of trade for innovation: The roles of northern and southern tariffs, *Japan and the World Economy* 16(4), 449–470.

Rapp, R. T. and Rozek, R. P. (1990). Benefits and costs of intellectual property protection in developing countries, *Journal of World Trade* 24, 75–102.

Reichman, J. H. (1995). Universal minimum standards of intellectual property protection under the TRIPS component of the WTO agreement, *The International Lawyer* 29(2), 345–388.

Reichman, J. H. (1998). Securing compliance with the TRIPS agreement after U.S. v India, *Journal of International Economic Law* 29, 585–601.

Scotchmer, S. (2004a). The political economy of intellectual property treaties, *Journal of Law, Economics, and Organization* 20(2), 415–437.

Scotchmer, S. (2004b). *Innovation and Incentives*, Cambridge, MA: MIT Press.

Staiger, R. W. (1995). A theory of gradual trade liberalization, in Levinsohn, J., Deardorff, A. V., and Stern, R. M. (eds.), *New Directions in Trade Theory*, Ann Arbor MI: University of Michigan Press.

United Nations Conference on Trade and Development (UNCTAD) (1996). *The TRIPS Agreement and Developing Countries*, Geneva: UNCTAD.

Yang, G. and Maskus, K. (2001). Intellectual property rights, licensing, and innovation in an endogenous product cycle model, *Journal of International Economics* 53(1), 169–187.

Zigic, K. (2000). Strategic trade policy, intellectual property rights protection, and North-South trade, *Journal of Development Economics* 61, 27–60.

Further Reading

Hokeman, B. M. and Kostecki, M. M. (1995). *The Political Economy of the World Trading System*, Oxford: Oxford University Press.

Kwan, Y. K. and Lai, E. L.-C. (2003). Intellectual property rights and endogenous economic growth, *Journal of Economic Dynamics and Control* 27(5), 853–873.

Yang, Y. (1998). Why do Southern countries have little incentive to protect Northern IPRs? *Canadian Journal of Economics* 31(4), 800–816.

Chapter 4

Would Global Patent Protection Be Too Weak without International Coordination?*

Abstract

In the standard model with free trade and social-welfare-maximizing governments à la Grossman and Lai (2004), cross-border positive policy externalities result in countries choosing a combination of patent strengths that is weaker than optimal from a global perspective. This paper introduces three new features to the analysis: trade and FDI barriers, firm heterogeneity and political economy considerations in setting patent policies. Based on calibration, we find that there would be global under-protection of patent rights when there is no international policy coordination. The empirical fact that firm revenues follow a fat-tailed distribution implies that the barriers to exploit inventions internationally are quite low, despite the fact that only a small fraction of firms sell overseas and an even smaller fraction of firms carry out FDI as a result of trade barriers. Furthermore, requiring all countries to harmonize their patent standards with the equilibrium standard of the most innovative country (the US) does not lead to global over-protection of patent rights.

*By Edwin L.-C. Lai and Isabel K. M. Yan. Originally published in *Journal of International Economics* (January 2013), pp. 42–54. Copyright © 2013 by Elsevier B.V. It has been reprinted with revisions and permission from the original publisher.

1 Introduction

The global intellectual property rights (IPR) protection system was given a boost by the implementation of the TRIPS agreement (Agreement on Trade-Related Aspects of Intellectual Property Rights), which started a gradual process of IPR harmonization in 1995. This agreement effectively requires the strengthening of patent protection of many countries, and pushes the world IPR protection policies towards harmonization (albeit a partial one). TRIPS is unprecedented in its ability to coordinate international IPR protection, not least because of the large number of countries involved (it is under the auspices of the WTO) and its ability to enforce rulings due to the credible threat of punishment through trade sanctions. Given the tremendous repercussions of such a coordinated increase in the strengths of IPR protection, it is fair to ask whether TRIPS is really a solution to a global coordination problem. It is clear that TRIPS creates distributive effects among countries.[1] However, the more important question is whether global IPR protection was too weak before TRIPS. If it was, then TRIPS can potentially be globally welfare-improving and therefore it can potentially make all countries better off. For example, if less developed countries (LDCs) lose from the strengthening of their IPR and developed countries (DCs) gain from it, but the DCs' gains outweigh the LDCs' losses, then it can be mutually beneficial for the LDCs to accept (partial) harmonization of IPR standards with the DCs in exchange for the DCs' opening their markets to goods from the LDCs. However, if global patent protection was already too strong before TRIPS, then no such synergy exists between negotiations on trade-related IPR and other issues of global trade.

The objective of this paper is twofold. First, we address the question of whether global patent protection would be too weak if individual governments were left to decide their own level of protection in the absence of international coordination. Second, we

[1] McCalman (2001) has shown that the US was by far the largest beneficiary, followed by Germany and France as distant second and third beneficiaries. On the other hand, the greatest loser was Canada, followed by Brazil and UK.

want to know whether the patent policy harmonization mandated by the TRIPS offers too much global patent protection. Both questions are important for us to evaluate the welfare consequences of TRIPS. To answer these questions, we derive sufficient conditions for global under-protection or over-protection of IPR and calibrate the model to check whether the conditions are satisfied.

The theoretical framework of this paper builds on Grossman and Lai (2004) (henceforth G–L) who develop a non-cooperative game model with free trade and social-welfare-maximizing governments.[2] It explains how a global system of patent protection affects incentives to innovate and how it creates distortions (deadweight losses). In particular, their model provides a basic theory that explains (a) how the national levels of patent protection is determined in a non-cooperative equilibrium, and (b) what the optimal global system of patent protection would look like.

In the basic G–L model, in the absence of international coordination, countries play a Nash game in setting the strengths of patent protection. The best response function of a country's government is obtained by setting the strength of patent protection that equates the marginal costs (deadweight loss due to longer duration of monopoly pricing) and marginal benefits (increased incentives of innovation) of extending protection, given the strengths of protection of other countries. Each country confers positive externalities on foreign countries as it extends patent protection, because it increases profits of foreign firms in the home market, and increases consumer surplus of foreign consumers due to induced innovations. As a result, there is global under-protection of patent rights in Nash equilibrium relative to the global optimum. In fact, the degree of under-protection in

[2]We start with the working assumption that the world was in a non-cooperative equilibrium before TRIPS. There is no doubt that some countries attempted to coordinate their IPR policies somewhat even before TRIPS, but empirical studies have shown that even as late as 1990, market sizes and innovative capabilities significantly affected variation in the strengths of patent protection across countries, as would be expected of a world where each country sets its own optimal IPR standard.

Nash equilibrium increases with the number of independent decision-makers in the patent-setting game.

However, two factors prevent us from directly applying G–L's basic model to answer whether global patent protection would be too weak without international coordination. First, as discussed in the political economy literature, governments may put extra weight on profits as opposed to consumer surplus in their objective functions due to firm lobbying. We call this profit-biased preferences of governments. When governments put more weight on profits, the marginal cost of patent protection decreases since deadweight loss is smaller. Therefore, the strength of patent protection in Nash equilibrium is stronger. Second is the existence of trade barriers and firm heterogeneity. As the recent empirical trade literature documents, only a small fraction of (more productive) firms sell to foreign markets. Moreover, the firms that do sell overseas have to bear trade costs, which include market entry costs, transportation costs and import tariffs. When only a fraction of domestic firms would enter a foreign market, and when there are trade costs, the positive international externalities of patent protection is diminished. Both profit-bias and trade barriers tend to diminish the degree of global under-protection in Nash equilibrium relative to the global optimum. If these forces are strong enough, there may even be over-protection of patent rights in Nash equilibrium. Therefore, whether or not there is global under-protection of patent rights in the non-cooperative equilibrium is an empirical question. To answer this question, we extend the G–L model by introducing three new elements: trade barriers, firm heterogeneity in productivity and political economy considerations. We also allow for FDI/licensing to be alternative means of serving a foreign market besides exporting.[3]

The contributions of this paper are twofold, one theoretical and one empirical. On the theory front, we develop a model to analyze the interaction among innovation, firm heterogeneity, trade and FDI and patent protection in a unified framework. An innovator invests

[3]Some preliminary ideas of these extensions first appeared in Lai (2008).

in R&D and develops a new product. The labor productivity of the resulting production firm follows a Pareto distribution. Because of the existence of fixed costs of exporting and of FDI, only the most productive firms export to or carry out FDI in foreign countries. Because it offers greater profit potential, a country with a larger market or stronger patent protection attracts more foreign firms to sell there. Successes in exploitation of inventions internationally increase the profits of firms and induce more innovation. Thus, there is a positive connection between patent protection and market size in one country and innovation in another. However, this connection may be weakened by exporting or FDI barriers. Given the strengths of patent protection of other governments, each government chooses its patent strength to maximize its objective function, which is biased in favor of firm profits because of firm lobbying. Thus, the strength of patent protection and the probability that foreign inventions are exploited in each country are endogenously determined in the model.

On the empirical front, this paper uses data and parametric values estimated in the literature to calibrate the theoretical model so as to answer two empirical questions. First, we find that global patent protection is too weak without international coordination. There are two reasons: (a) Despite the existence of trade barriers, the free-rider problem becomes serious when there is a large number of independent country-players in the patent-setting game. (b) The empirical fact that firm revenues follow a fat-tailed distribution implies that the barriers to exploit inventions internationally are quite low, despite the fact that only a small fraction of firms sell overseas and an even smaller fraction of firms carry out FDI as a result of trade barriers. This implies that the positive cross-border externalities of patent protection remain quite high. The fat-tailed distribution of firm sizes and the fact that only the most productive firms carry out FDI overseas implies that FDI is a very important channel of international exploitation of inventions. Therefore, it must be taken into account in any modeling of international exploitation of technology. Second, we find that requiring all countries to harmonize their strengths of patent protection with the equilibrium strength of the most protective country does not lead to global over-protection of IPR. This is because the distribution of innovative capability among countries is not too skewed as to overcome the free-rider effect. We therefore conclude that there is no evidence that TRIPS leads to global over-protection of patent rights. (This does not mean, however, that all countries would gain from such a harmonization. It only means that the sum of the gains for the gainers would exceed the sum of losses for the losers. Thus, distribution is still an issue in such a harmonization.)

The present paper is similar in spirit to that of Eaton and Kortum (1999), though the model they use is different. Like them, we try to link together innovation, patenting and international exploitation of inventions. Unlike them, however, we focus on product innovation instead of productivity-enhancing inventions, and so productivity growth is not the focus of our analysis. Another difference is that, in our model, the benefits of inventions are spread mainly through exporting and FDI, whereas in their model the main mechanism of international exploitation of inventions is diffusion of knowledge. We focus on analyzing the market of patent-sensitive goods whereas they focus on the entire macroeconomy.

The structure of the rest of the paper is as follows. Section 2 augments the G–L model by introducing trade and FDI barriers, firm heterogeneity and firm lobbying. It derives the key equations for the non-cooperative equilibrium and those for the globally efficient patent regime for both the two-country and multi-country cases. In Section 3, we calibrate the multi-country model and investigate (i) whether there is global under-protection of IPR in the absence of international coordination and (ii) whether the harmonization mandated by TRIPS over-protects IPR globally. Section 4 concludes.

2 A Theory of Innovation and International Patenting

The theory described in this section is modified from Grossmanand Lai (2004) by introducing trade and FDI barriers, firm heterogeneity and profit-bias of governments.

In this section, we study the national incentives for protection of intellectual property in a world economy with innovation, international patenting, trade and imitation. We derive the Nash equilibrium of a game in which countries set their patent policies simultaneously and noncooperatively. Then we derive the globally optimal patent regime. This is followed by a comparison between the Nash equilibrium and the global optimum, and a discussion of the policy implications. For ease of exposition, we first start with a two-country case, and then generalize it to a multi-country one.

2.1 The setup

2.1.1 *Two-Country case*

The two countries are distinguished by their wage rates, their market sizes, and their stocks of human capital, which proxies for their different capacities for R&D. For the sake of convenience, we shall term the countries "North" and "South".

Consumers in the two countries share identical preferences. In each country, the representative consumer maximizes the intertemporal utility function. The instantaneous utility of a consumer in country j is given by

$$u_j(z) = y_j(z) + \int_0^{n_S(z)+n_N(z)} h[x_j(i,z)]di, \tag{1}$$

where $y_j(z)$ is consumption of the homogeneous good by a typical resident of country j at time z, $x_j(i,z)$ is consumption of the ith differentiated product by a resident of country j at time z, and $n_j(z)$ is the number of differentiated varieties previously invented in country j that remain economically viable at time z. We make the standard assumption that $h'[.] > 0$ and $h''[.] < 0$.[4] There are M_j

[4]We further assume that $h'(0) = \infty$, and $-xh''(x)/h'(x) < 1$ for all x. The first assumption ensures a positive demand for every variety at any finite price. The second ensures that any firm producing a differentiated product charges a finite price.

consumers in country j.[5] It does not matter for our analysis whether consumers can borrow and lend internationally.

In country j, it takes a_j units of labor to produce one unit of the homogeneous (numeraire) good. To capture firm heterogeneity, we assume that it takes $a_j c$ units of labor to produce one unit of a variety of differentiated good, where c is stochastic. It follows that c is the unit cost of a differentiated product when the cost of the homogeneous good is normalized to one. Each differentiated variety is produced by one firm (before its patent expires), and therefore the firm's productivity is equal to $1/c$. We further assume that $1/c$ follows the distribution $\Pr(\frac{1}{c} < x) = 1 - \left(\frac{b}{x}\right)^{\lambda}$ where $x \in [b, \infty]$, i.e. a Pareto distribution with a lower bound b and shape parameter λ. This implies that $\Pr(c < z) = (bz)^{\lambda}$ where $z \in [0, 1/b]$. The flow of new goods invented in each region is given by $\phi_j = \mathcal{F}(H_j, L_{Rj}/a_j) = B\,(L_{Rj}/a_j)^{\beta}\, H_j^{1-\beta}$, where B is a constant, H_j is a fixed input whose quantity determines the innovative capability of country j, and L_{Rj} is the labor devoted to R&D there. We assume that the numeraire good is tradeable with negligible trade costs, and that it is produced in positive quantities in both countries, so that wage in country j in equilibrium is given by $w_j = 1/a_j$, and hence $w_N/w_S = a_S/a_N$. Define $\overline{T} = (1 - e^{-\rho\overline{\tau}})/\rho$, where $\overline{\tau}$ is the product life of a differentiated good, and ρ is the time rate of discount.

2.1.2 *Multi-country case*

We now describe the IPR regime, trade barriers and profit-bias. Let us generalize the above description to a multi-country setting, and let there be J countries in the set $\mathcal{N}$ of country-players. In each country, there is *national treatment* in the granting of patent rights. Assume for simplicity that all unexpired patents are fully enforced. Under national treatment, the government of country j affords the same protection Ω_j to all inventors of differentiated products regardless

[5] We remind the reader that market size is meant to capture not the population of a country, but rather the scale of its demand for innovative products.

of their national origins, where $\Omega_j = (1 - e^{-\rho\tau_j})/\rho$, and τ_j is the length of the patents granted by country j. In our model, a patent is an exclusive right to make, sell, use, or import a product for a fixed period of time (see Maskus, 2000, p. 36). This means that, when good i is under patent protection in country j, no firm other than the patent holder or one designated by it may legally produce the good in country j for domestic sale or for export, nor may the good be legally imported into country j from an unauthorized producer outside the country. We also rule out parallel imports — unauthorized imports of good i that were produced by the patent holder or its designee, but that were sold to a third party outside country j. When parallel imports are prevented, patent holders can practice price discrimination across national markets.

The recent empirical trade literature documents that only a small fraction of firms export. To capture this phenomenon, we assume that firms are heterogeneous in labor productivities (more will be said about this later). Furthermore, each producer of differentiated goods is faced with trade barriers when selling abroad. They include: a fixed cost in exporting, which is denoted by F_{EX}, a fixed cost in setting up production facilities in a foreign country (which we call "carrying out FDI"), which is denoted by F_{FDI}, and a variable trade cost of the iceberg type (which consists of transport costs and import tariffs), which is equal to a fraction t of the production cost if a good is exported from one country to another. As a result, only a fraction of domestic firms will export to or set up production facilities in another foreign country. In this paper, we do not distinguish between FDI and licensing as they can be regarded as more or less equivalent. We assume that when an innovator licenses his technology to a foreign firm, he extracts all the rents from the latter. Assuming that the licensee has to bear the same fixed and variable costs of production, FDI and licensing are equivalent.[6] Hereinafter, therefore, "FDI" shall

[6]By and large, casual observation suggests that licensing is a relatively minor channel of exploiting an invention overseas, compared with exporting and FDI. Nonetheless, we believe that in analyzing certain markets where licensing is

mean "FDI or licensing". We assume that the demand of a typical consumer is given by $x = Ap^{-\epsilon}$ (where A is a constant, p denotes the price, and $\epsilon > 1$ denotes the price elasticity of demand), and define $y \equiv (1+t)^{-\epsilon+1}$, which is less than one. Therefore, y is an inverse measure of the variable trade cost.[7] As a first cut, we assume that each of the three parameters F_{FDI}, F_{EX} and t are the same across countries. It is assumed that not only is $F_{\text{FDI}} > F_{\text{EX}}$ but also $y \cdot F_{\text{FDI}} > F_{\text{EX}}$, which guarantees that firms who choose to carry out FDI in a foreign country always have the option of exporting but choose not to do so. Thus, we have a structure as depicted in Helpman *et al.* (2004). For any given foreign market, a firm with high unit cost of production will not sell to that market; a firm with a sufficiently lower unit cost will export to there, and a firm with a still lower unit cost will carry out FDI there. For any given firm, a sufficiently large foreign market or sufficiently strong patent protection there will induce the firm to export to that market; further increases in the market size or strength of patent protection there will eventually induce the firm to carry out FDI in that market. See Figure 1 for a graphical analysis. Define $\widetilde{\pi}(c)$ as the flow of monopoly profit per consumer as a function of a firm's unit cost c. The bold curve in Figure 1 is the upper envelope of the three profit lines corresponding to no exporting to k, exporting to country k besides selling domestically, and doing FDI in country k besides selling domestically, as described below the figure. When the value of $\widetilde{\pi}M_k\Omega_k$ lies in the range marked "Domestic Sales Only", the upper envelope corresponds to the profit from pure domestic sales. When $\widetilde{\pi}M_k\Omega_k$ lies in the range marked "Domestic Sales plus Exporting to k", the upper envelope corresponds to the profit from both export

pervasive one should include licensing as a separate mode of entry. This will be left to future research.

[7]The profit flow and consumer surplus per consumer are given by equations (A1) and (A2) in Appendix A. It can be easily shown from equations (A1) and (A2) that, for any given unit cost of production, the profit flow per consumer obtained by a firm in a foreign market is multiplied by a factor of y when an iceberg trade cost of t is incurred. So is the consumer surplus flow per consumer enjoyed by foreign consumers.

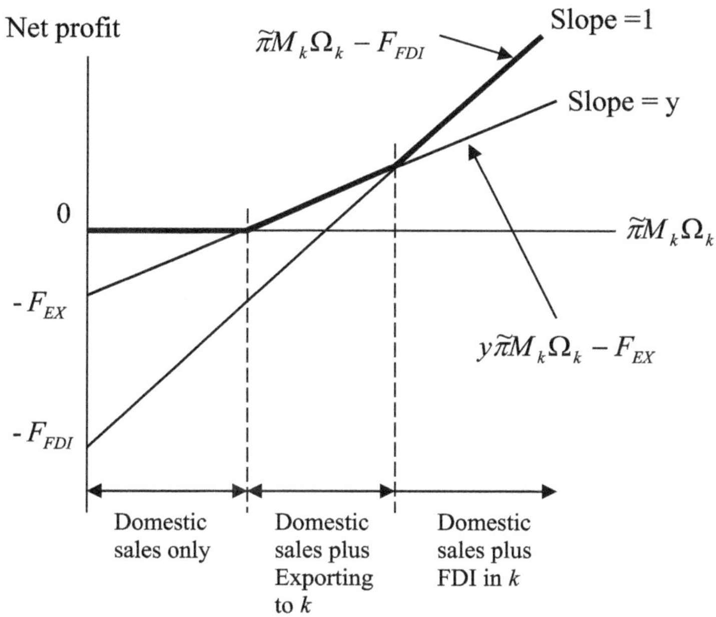

Figure 1. A foreign firm's decision concerning exporting to and carrying out FDI in country k.

Notes:

1. The horizontal line with vertical intercept 0 represents the net profit (normalized to zero) when a foreign firm does not sell to country k.
2. The line $y\tilde{\pi} M_k \Omega_k - F_{\mathrm{EX}}$ represents the net profit when a foreign firm exports to country k besides selling domestically.
3. The line $\tilde{\pi} M_k \Omega_k - F_{\mathrm{FDI}}$ represents the profit when a foreign firm carries out FDI in country k besides selling domestically.

and domestic sales. When $\tilde{\pi} M_k \Omega_k$ lies in the range marked "Domestic Sales plus FDI in k", the upper envelope corresponds to the profit from carrying out FDI and domestic sales.

Recent political economy models indicate that politicians' desire for campaign contributions tends to bias the objective function of a government in favor of the contributors. In our model, owners of research capital are owners of firms, who donate campaign contributions to politicians. Following the literature, we let $1 + a$ be the weight each government puts on domestic profits when a weight of one is put on domestic consumer surplus in its objective function.

Therefore, the parameter a measures the profit-bias of governments. It can also be interpreted as the weight a politician puts on campaign contribution when a weight of one is put on social welfare, given that his objective function is the weighted sum of the two terms. See, for example, Bagwell and Staiger (2004) and Grossman and Helpman (1994).

Define π as the (unconditional) mean profit flow per consumer for a monopoly selling a typical brand; define C_m as the (unconditional) mean surplus flow that a consumer enjoys from the consumption of a good produced at a unit cost of $w_j a_j c = c$ and sold at the monopoly price $p_m > c$; and define C_c as the (unconditional) mean surplus flow he enjoys from a product sold at the competitive price of $p_c = c$. It can be shown (in Appendix A) that

$$C_c = \left(\frac{1}{\epsilon - 1}\right)\left(\frac{\lambda}{1 - \epsilon + \lambda}\right) Ab^{\epsilon-1} \tag{2}$$

and

$$\pi = C_m = \Lambda C_c \quad \text{where } \Lambda \equiv \left(\frac{\epsilon - 1}{\epsilon}\right)^{\epsilon}. \tag{3}$$

Based on the assumption of $\Pr(c < z) = (bz)^{\lambda}$ above, it can be easily shown (in Appendix B) that the distribution of revenue per consumer $\widetilde{R}$ is Pareto with shape parameter $\frac{\lambda}{\epsilon-1}$:

$$\Pr(\widetilde{R} < \mathfrak{s}) = 1 - \left(A\Lambda b^{\epsilon-1}\right)^{\frac{\lambda}{\epsilon-1}} \cdot \mathfrak{s}^{-\frac{\lambda}{\epsilon-1}}, \quad \text{where } \mathfrak{s} \in \left(A\Lambda b^{\epsilon-1}, \infty\right).$$

Axtell (2001) finds that the size (number of employees) as well as revenue distribution of American firms followed a Pareto distribution $P(s, \alpha) : \Pr(x < s) = 1 - (s_0/s)^{\alpha}$ where $x \in (s_0, \infty)$. He finds that for size distribution, $\alpha = 1.059$, while for revenue distribution, $\alpha = 0.994$. In other words, the estimated α for both distributions are very close to one. Luttmer (2007) finds that all possible size distributions of firms have a tail similar to Pareto distribution, with analogous tail index (equivalent to Axtell's α and our $\frac{\lambda}{\epsilon-1}$) that must be slightly above one in order to fit the data. Based on the above empirical facts, we shall assume $\frac{\lambda}{\epsilon-1}$ to be larger than but close to one in our calibration below.[8]

Now, define θ_{EX}^{k} as the probability that a foreign firm can profitably export to or carry out FDI in country k; and define θ_{FDI}^{k} as the probability that a foreign firm can profitably carry out FDI in country k. According to our assumptions above, if a firm can profitably export to (carry out FDI in) a smaller foreign market it can also profitably export to (carry out FDI in) a larger foreign market. Therefore, the probability that a firm in a country can profitably export to (carry out FDI in) some foreign market(s) is equal to the probability that it can profitably export to (carry out FDI in) the largest foreign market. We further define the *(inverse) international barrier to exploiting an invention in country* k as

$$\theta^{k} = y\left(\theta_{\text{EX}}^{k}\right)^{\frac{1-\epsilon+\lambda}{\lambda}} + (1-y)\left(\theta_{\text{FDI}}^{k}\right)^{\frac{1-\epsilon+\lambda}{\lambda}} \quad \text{for } k = 1, 2, \ldots, J. \quad (4)$$

The economic meaning of θ^k can be understood as follows. We have assumed that a foreign producer gets a patent in country k whenever it sells there. It can be shown that in country k each consumer obtains an expected consumer surplus equal to $\theta^k C_m$ from each product developed in a foreign country, due to the existence of trade barriers in k.[9] Note that $\theta^k C_m < C_m$, as trade barriers in k not only increase the cost of serving country k market by foreign firms but also prevent some foreign firms from serving the market. Likewise, a

---

[8]Note that we preclude the cases with $\alpha < 1$, as this would correspond to infinite mean. We are most interested in the cases when the value of α is greater than one but very close to one.

[9]The expression for θ^k in (4) is obtained via the following equation:

$$\theta^{k} \int_{c=0}^{\frac{1}{b}} \widetilde{C}_m(c)\, dF(c) = \int_{c=c_{\text{FDI}}^{k}}^{c_{\text{EX}}^{k}} y\widetilde{C}_m(c)\, dF(c) + \int_{c=0}^{c_{\text{FDI}}^{k}} \widetilde{C}_m(c)\, dF(c)$$

where c_{EX}^{k} is the threshold unit-cost for exporting to country k; c_{FDI}^{k} is the threshold unit-cost for carrying out FDI in country k. $F(c) = (bc)^{\lambda}$ where $c \in [0, \frac{1}{b})$ is the c.d.f. of unit-cost c, $\widetilde{C}_m(c)$ is the realized flow of surplus per consumer. Thus, $\theta_{\text{EX}}^{k} = \left(b \cdot c_{\text{EX}}^{k}\right)^{\lambda}$ and $\theta_{\text{FDI}}^{k} = \left(b \cdot c_{\text{FDI}}^{k}\right)^{\lambda}$. Refer to Appendices A, B and C.

foreign firm can only earn an expected profit per consumer equal to $\theta^k \pi$ from country k market due to the existence of trade barriers.[10] Note that, for given θ^k_{EX} and θ^k_{FDI}, lower trade barriers (higher y) lead to higher θ^k, while a fatter tail distribution of firm productivity ($\frac{\lambda}{\epsilon-1}$ closer to one) leads to higher θ^k, as the firms that do export have a higher average productivity. Clearly, $\theta^k = 1$ (the model collapses to the case of free trade) when $\frac{\lambda}{\epsilon-1} = 1$, regardless of the values of t, F_{EX} and F_{FDI}.

It follows that the expected value of a patent of an invention by a firm in country i is given by

$$v_i = \pi \left[\sum_{k \neq i} \left(\theta^k M_k \Omega_k \right) + M_i \Omega_i \right] - \sum_{k \neq i} \left[\left(\theta^k_{\mathrm{EX}} - \theta^k_{\mathrm{FDI}} \right) F_{\mathrm{EX}} + \theta^k_{\mathrm{FDI}} F_{\mathrm{FDI}} \right] \quad \text{for } i = 1, 2, \ldots, J \tag{5}$$

In general $v_i \neq v_j$ for $i \neq j$. As F_{FDI} and F_{EX} are the same in all countries, it can be easily shown from (C1) and (C2) in Appendix C that, in equilibrium,

$$M_{\mathrm{US}} \Omega_{\mathrm{US}} \left(\theta^{\mathrm{US}}_{\mathrm{EX}} \right)^{\frac{1-\epsilon}{\lambda}} = M_k \Omega_k \left(\theta^k_{\mathrm{EX}} \right)^{\frac{1-\epsilon}{\lambda}} \quad \text{for all } k \neq \mathrm{US}. \tag{6}$$

and

$$M_{\mathrm{US}} \Omega_{\mathrm{US}} \left(\theta^{\mathrm{US}}_{\mathrm{FDI}} \right)^{\frac{1-\epsilon}{\lambda}} = M_k \Omega_k \left(\theta^k_{\mathrm{FDI}} \right)^{\frac{1-\epsilon}{\lambda}} \quad \text{for all } k \neq \mathrm{US}. \tag{7}$$

As $1 - \epsilon < 0$, equations (6) and (7) indicate that a country with stronger patent protection or a larger market tends to attract a higher fraction of foreign firms to sell to the country as well as a higher fraction of foreign firms to set up production facilities there.

Substituting the expressions for θ^k_{FDI} and θ^k_{EX} derived in Appendix C (i.e. equations (C1) and (C2)) into (5) and invoking

[10] This can be easily shown by replacing $\widetilde{C}_m(c)$ by $\widetilde{\pi}(c)$ in the equation in the last footnote.

(3) and (4), we can simplify (5) to

$$v_i = \pi \left[\sum_{k \neq i} \left(\frac{\epsilon - 1}{\lambda} \right) \theta^k M_k \Omega_k + M_i \Omega_i \right] \tag{8}$$

This is an interesting equation as v_i can be expressed in a very simple form though it has taken into account a myriad of factors including fixed costs of exporting and FDI, variable cost of exporting, heterogeneous firms and screening of firms by the market. The simplicity of the equation is attributed to the Pareto distribution of firm productivity.

2.2 The theory: two-country case

Let us describe, for given patent strengths Ω_N and Ω_S, the life cycle of a typical differentiated product developed in South. After the invention of a product, an innovator makes a productivity draw to find out her unit cost of production. Then, she will apply for and obtain a patent in each country. After that, she decides whether or not to sell overseas.[11] There is a probability θ_{EX}^N that she would be able to profitably sell to the Northern market. During an initial phase after the product is invented, the inventor holds an active patent in both countries. Even if a good is not sold in a foreign market, the innovator still has incentives to obtain a patent there, as it is costless to do so. Consequently, consumers cannot purchase a product before its patent expires in the country if the innovator does not sell it there.[12] The patent holder earns an expected flow of profits of $\theta^N M_N \pi$ from sales in the Northern market and an expected

[11]The assumption that a firm patents in all countries may be unrealistic. However, such a formulation simplifies the analysis without sacrificing the intuition. Moreover, the conclusions of the basic model are robust to an alternative formulation, as discussed below.

[12]We rule out compulsory licensing and working requirement here as they are not of first order importance in the context of our analysis. Important as these issues are, we believe they should be addressed in future research. By and large, researchers such as McFetridge (1998) observe that the number of compulsory licenses granted were generally small in most countries, and mainly concentrated in special types of products such as food and medicines.

flow of profits of $M_S\pi$ from sales in the Southern market. Each Northern consumer realizes a flow of expected surplus of $\theta^N C_m$ from his purchases of the good. A Southern consumer realizes an expected flow of consumer surplus of C_m from his purchases of the good.

After a while, the patent will expire in one country. For concreteness, let's say that this happens first in the South. We assume that local firms do not have to incur the fixed cost of market entry.[13] Therefore, the good will be legally imitated by competitive firms producing there for sales in the local (Southern) market. The imitators will not, however, be able to sell the good legally in the North, because the live patent there affords protection from such infringing imports. When the patent expires in the South, the price of the good falls permanently to $w_S a_S c = c$, and the original inventor ceases to realize profits in that market. The flow of consumer surplus in the South rises to $M_S C_c$.[14]

Eventually, the inventor's patent expires in the North. Then the Northern market can be served completely by competitive firms producing in the North. If the North has been served by the innovator, then, at this time, the price of the good in the North falls to $p_c = c$ and households there begin to enjoy the higher flow of consumer surplus $M_N C_c$. The original inventor loses his remaining source of monopoly income. If the North has not been served by the innovator, then at this time, the market begins to be served by competitive firms in the North. Finally, after a period of length $\bar{\tau}$ has elapsed from the moment of invention, the good becomes obsolete and all flows of consumer surplus cease.

Alternatively, one could assume that an innovator only patents in the countries in which she can profitably sell. This can be justified

---

[13] Melitz (2003), for example, makes a similar assumption.

[14] Since there is no cost of patenting, a firm always patents its good in all countries once it is developed. Once patented, the technology is disclosed. But the good cannot be legally imitated in that market until the patent expires. So, when a patent has expired consumer surplus is C_c whether a good was developed overseas or locally, as countries can always imitate foreign-developed goods when the patent has expired, and these imitated goods are produced locally, and so there is no trade barrier when imitated goods are sold.

by the assumption that there is a small cost of patenting in any country. This assumption will align with the fact that most inventions are patented only at home and only a fraction of inventions are patented internationally. To make the model consistent with the fact that trade and FDI are the major channels of international exploitation of inventions, we need to further assume that a domestic firm can technically imitate a foreign-developed product only if the good has previously been sold there. The alternative formulation based on these two assumptions will make the exposition more complicated and the intuition more obscure. Nonetheless, we carried out robustness check based on this alternative formulation and found that the numerical results are about the same, and the conclusions of the paper intact.[15] The results are reported in Appendix F.

2.2.1 *Nash equilibrium*

Here we solve the Nash game in which the governments set their patent policies once-and-for-all at time 0. These patents apply only to goods invented after time 0; goods invented beforehand continue to receive the protections afforded at their times of invention. Consider the choice of patent policies Ω_N and Ω_S that will take effect at time 0 and apply to goods invented thereafter. The expressions for the government objective function in country i, discounted to time 0, is given by

$$W_i(0) = \Lambda_{i0} + \frac{w_i L_i}{\rho} + (1+a)\frac{r_i H_i}{\rho} + \frac{M_i \phi_i}{\rho}\left[\Omega_i C_m + (\bar{T} - \Omega_i) C_c\right] + \frac{M_i \phi_{-i}}{\rho}\left[\theta^i \Omega_i C_m + (\bar{T} - \Omega_i) C_c\right]$$

[15]The intuition is that fat-tailed firm productivity distribution in a country implies that even though a small fraction of firms patent and sell to foreign markets, they are firms with exceptionally high productivities, and therefore foreign consumer surplus attributed to this country's inventions is very close to that when all firms patent and sell to all foreign markets. As $\lambda/(\epsilon - 1) \to 1^+$, the two formulations yield the same results.

$$= \Lambda_{i0} + \frac{w_i\left[L_i - (1+a)\,L_{Ri}\right]}{\rho} + \frac{M_i\phi_i}{\rho}\left[\Omega_i C_m + (\bar{T} - \Omega_i)C_c\right]$$

$$+ \frac{M_i\phi_{-i}}{\rho}\left[\theta^i\Omega_i C_m + (\bar{T} - \Omega_i)C_c\right] + \frac{\phi_i}{\rho}\pi\,(1+a)$$

$$\times\left[M_i\Omega_i + \theta^{-i}M_{-i}\Omega_{-i}\left(\frac{\epsilon-1}{\lambda}\right)\right], \quad \text{for } i = S, N, \tag{9}$$

where Λ_{i0} is the fixed amount of discounted surplus that consumers in country i derive from goods that were invented before time 0; X_{-i} or X^{-i} refers to the value of variable X pertaining to country j where $j \neq i$; r_i is the return to the factor H_i. The second equality arises from the fact that there is zero present-discounted profit for each firm, so that $r_i H_i + w_i L_{Ri} = \phi_i v_i$, where $v_i = \pi\left[M_i\Omega_i + \theta^{-i}M_{-i}\Omega_{-i}\left(\frac{\epsilon-1}{\lambda}\right)\right]$ is the value of a new patent developed in country i as shown in equation (8).

We are now ready to derive the best response functions for the two governments. The best response expresses the strength of patent protection that maximizes a national government's objective as a function of the given patent policy of its trading partner. We assume that country i's government treats θ^i_{EX}, θ^i_{FDI} and therefore θ^i as parametric as it chooses Ω_i. Consider the choice of Ω_S by the government of the South. This country bears two costs from strengthening its patent protection slightly. First, it expands the fraction of goods previously invented in the South on which the country suffers a static deadweight loss of $M_S[C_c - C_m - (1+a)\pi]$. Second, it augments the fraction of goods previously invented in the North on which its consumers realize expected surplus of $\theta^S M_S C_m$ instead of $M_S C_c$. Notice that the profits earned by Northern producers in the South are not an offset to the South's marginal cost, because they accrue to patent holders in the North. The marginal benefit accrued to the South from strengthening its patent protection reflects the increased incentive that Northern and Southern firms have to engage in R&D. If the objective-maximizing Ω_S is positive and less than $\bar{T}$, then the marginal benefit *per consumer* of increasing Ω_S must match the marginal cost, which implies

$$\begin{aligned}
&\phi_N(C_c - \theta^S C_m) + \phi_S\left[C_c - C_m - (1+a)\,\pi\right] \\
&= \frac{d\phi_S}{dv_S} \cdot \frac{dv_S}{d\Omega_S}\left[C_c\bar{T} - (C_c - C_m)\,\Omega_S\right] \\
&\quad + \frac{d\phi_N}{dv_N} \cdot \frac{dv_N}{d\Omega_S}\left[C_c\bar{T} - \left(C_c - \theta^S C_m\right)\Omega_S\right] \\
&= \gamma\frac{\phi_S}{v_S} M_S\pi\left[C_c\bar{T} - (C_c - C_m)\,\Omega_S\right] \\
&\quad + \gamma\frac{\phi_N}{v_N}\theta^S M_S\pi\left[C_c\bar{T} - \left(C_c - \theta^S C_m\right)\Omega_S\right],
\end{aligned} \tag{10}$$

where $\gamma = \frac{\beta}{1-\beta}$ is the elasticity of the flow of new products developed in each region with respect to the value of a patent, i.e. $\frac{d\phi_j}{dv_j} = \gamma\frac{\phi_j}{v_j}$; (8) implies that $v_S = \pi\left[M_S\Omega_S + \theta^N M_N\Omega_N\left(\frac{\epsilon-1}{\lambda}\right)\right]$ and $v_N = \pi\left[M_N\Omega_N + \theta^S M_S\Omega_S\left(\frac{\epsilon-1}{\lambda}\right)\right]$. On the other hand, (5) implies that $\frac{dv_S}{d\Omega_S} = M_S\pi$ and $\frac{dv_N}{d\Omega_S} = \theta^S M_S\pi$, as we assume that each government treats θ^i_{EX}, θ^i_{FDI}, θ^i $(i = N, S)$, F_{EX} and F_{FDI} as parametric.

It is straightforward to write down the condition for the best response of the North, analogous to (10) above, so we do not put it here in the interest of space.

If we define $\mu_i = \phi_i/(\phi_S + \phi_N)$, it can be easily shown that $\mu_i = H_i/(H_S + H_N)$ when $\frac{\lambda}{\epsilon-1} = 1$, which means that it is unaffected by patent policies in that case. Given that $\frac{\lambda}{\epsilon-1}$ is close to one, which is true empirically, we can show from (10) and its Northern counterpart that the best response functions are downward sloping, and that the best response function for the South is everywhere steeper than that for the North, when the two are drawn in $(\Omega_S,\ \Omega_N)$ space. This guarantees uniqueness of the Nash equilibrium and ensures stability of the policy setting game.

2.2.2 *Global optimum*

In this section, we study the welfare impacts of international patent policy coordination. We begin by characterizing the combination of patent policies that are jointly efficient for the two countries, which is called the global optimum. We then compare the Nash equilibrium outcome with the efficient policies, to identify changes in the patent regime that ought to be effected by an international agreement.

Let $Q_S = M_S\Omega_S + \theta^N\left(\frac{\epsilon-1}{\lambda}\right)M_N\Omega_N$. A Southern firm that earns a discounted sum of expected profits of $M_S\Omega_S\pi$ for a period of length τ_S in the South and discounted sum of expected profits of $\theta^N\left(\frac{\epsilon-1}{\lambda}\right)M_N\Omega_N\pi$ for a period of τ_N in the North earns a total discounted sum of expected profits equal to $Q_S\pi$. On the other hand, a Northern innovator earns total discounted sum of expected profits equal to $Q_N\pi$ where $Q_N = \theta^S\left(\frac{\epsilon-1}{\lambda}\right)M_S\Omega_S + M_N\Omega_N$.

Consider the choice of patent policies Ω_N and Ω_S that will take effect at time 0 and apply to goods invented thereafter. Equation (9) becomes an expression for welfare when $a = 0$. Summing the expressions in (9) for $i = S$ and $i = N$ with a set to zero, we find that

$$\begin{aligned}
\rho W^w &= \rho\left[W_S(0)|_{a=0} + W_N(0)|_{a=0}\right] \\
&= \rho\left(\Lambda_{S0} + \Lambda_{N0}\right) + w_S(L_S - L_{RS}) + w_N(L_N - L_{RN}) \\
&\quad + M_S\phi_S\left[\bar{T}C_c - \Omega_S\left(C_c - C_m - \pi\right)\right] \\
&\quad + M_S\phi_N\left\{\bar{T}C_c - \Omega_S\left[C_c - \theta^S C_m - \theta^S\left(\frac{\epsilon-1}{\lambda}\right)\pi\right]\right\} \\
&\quad + M_N\phi_N\left[\bar{T}C_c - \Omega_N\left(C_c - C_m - \pi\right)\right] \\
&\quad + M_N\phi_S\left\{\bar{T}C_c - \Omega_N\left[C_c - \theta^N C_m - \theta^N\left(\frac{\epsilon-1}{\lambda}\right)\pi\right]\right\}
\end{aligned} \tag{11}$$

where W^w denotes world welfare (without any bias in favor of firm profits).

There is clearly a tradeoff as patent strength is increased in either country. For example, as Ω_S increases there is a direct effect of an increase in the deadweight losses $M_S\Omega_S\left(C_c - C_m - \pi\right)$ per Southern invention and $M_S\Omega_S\left[C_c - \theta^S C_m - \theta^S\left(\frac{\epsilon-1}{\lambda}\right)\pi\right]$ per Northern invention, which lower global welfare. But there are indirect effects that tend to increase global welfare: an increase in Ω_S leads to an increase in Q_N (Q_S), which induces faster innovation in the North (South), thus increasing ϕ_N (ϕ_S) and L_{RN} (L_{RS}). These effects are globally welfare-improving as L_{RN} and L_{RS} are optimally chosen by firms. In fact, it can be shown that when $\frac{\lambda}{\epsilon-1}$ is sufficiently small, there exists a unique globally optimum combination of Ω_N and Ω_S.

How do the efficient combination of patent policies compare to the policies that emerge in a noncooperative equilibrium? The answer to this question — which informs us about the likely features of a negotiated patent agreement — is illustrated in Figure 2.

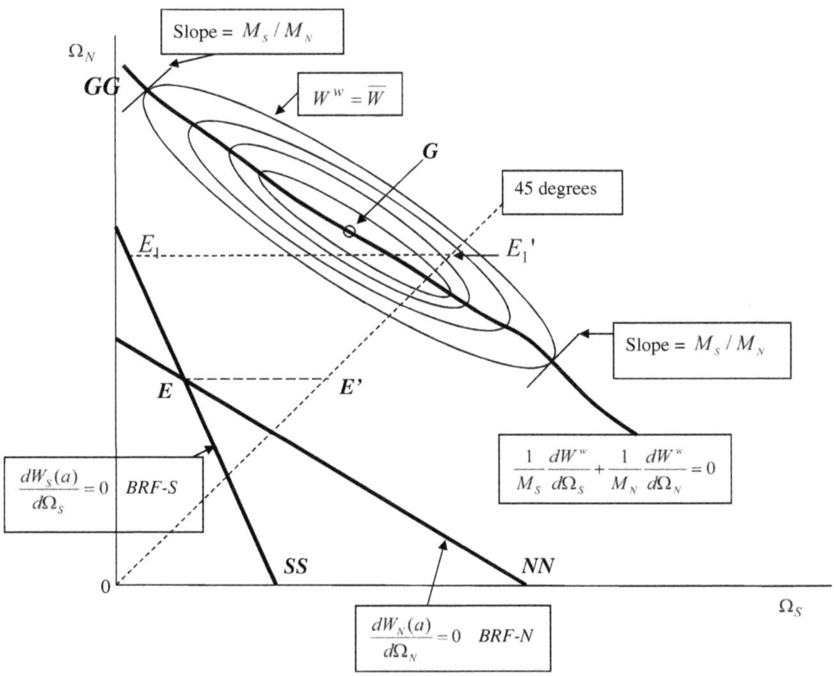

Figure 2. Relationship between the Nash equilibrium E and global optimum G. The curve $W^W = \overline{W}$ is an example of an iso-global-welfare line. *BRF-S* and *BRF-N* are the best response functions of South and North respectively. Starting from any point on an iso-global-welfare line to the left of GG (defined by $\frac{1}{M_S}\frac{dW^w}{d\Omega_S} + \frac{1}{M_N}\frac{dW^w}{d\Omega_N} = 0$), any small increase in Ω^N and Ω^S would increase the global welfare W^W. Hence, simultaneous increases of Ω^N and Ω^S from point E lead to an increase in global welfare. The globally optimal policy combination is depicted by point G. A movement from E to G is globally welfare-improving.

The figure depicts the best response functions and the efficient policy combination in the same diagram.

In this figure, the globally optimal policy combination is depicted by point G. The iso-global-welfare lines such as $W^w = \overline{W}$ around G are also shown. The diagram shows that simultaneous increases of Ω_N and Ω_S from point E lead to an increase in global welfare. That is, a movement from E to G is globally welfare-improving. This is true when a is small, i.e. when governments' profit-bias is weak. The reasons are clear. Starting from a point on the South's best response function curve SS, a marginal strengthening of IPR protection in the South increases the world's welfare when profit-bias is weak. This is because such a change in Southern policies has only a second-order effect on the welfare of the South, but it conveys two positive externalities to the North. First, it provides extra monopoly profits to Northern innovators, which contributes to the aggregate income there. Second, it enhances the incentives for R&D, inducing an increase in both ϕ_S and ϕ_N. The extra product diversity that results from this additional R&D creates additional surplus for Northern consumers.

By the same token, a marginal increase in the strength of Northern patent protection from a point along NN increases world welfare. However, both SS and NN shift out as a increases, but the position of G is independent of a. Therefore, if a is not "small", then it is possible that an efficient patent treaty may require all countries to reduce their strengths of patent protection. Whether or not a is small in practice is an empirical question, which we answer in Section 3.

We define global under-protection of patent rights to be a situation when global welfare rises as Ω_N and Ω_S are both raised from their Nash equilibrium levels. If there is global under-protection of patent rights, then starting from any interior Nash equilibrium, an efficient patent treaty must strengthen patent protection in both countries. It also implies that the treaty will strengthen global incentives for R&D and induce faster innovation in both countries.

2.3 The theory: multi-country case

Before bringing the model to the data, it is useful to extend the model to a multi-country setting, as the number of independent decision-making governments plays a crucial role in whether there is global under-protection of IPR in Nash equilibrium. Recall that there are J countries in the set $\mathcal{N}$ of country-players. Define $f_i \equiv C_c\overline{T} - (C_c - C_m)\,\Omega_i$ as the present discounted value of consumer surplus for a consumer in country i derived from the consumption of a home-developed differentiated good over its product life; and $f_i' \equiv C_c\overline{T} - \left(C_c - \theta^i C_m\right)\Omega_i$ as the corresponding expected consumer surplus derived from the consumption of a product developed by a foreign country.

2.3.1 *Nash equilibrium*

In a multi-country setting, the best-response function of country i is given by

$$\underbrace{\left(\sum_{j\neq i}\phi_j\right)\left(C_c - \theta^i C_m\right) + \phi_i\left[(C_c - C_m) - (1+a)\,\pi\right]}_{\text{marginal cost}}$$
$$= \left(\sum_{j\neq i}\frac{d\phi_j}{dv_j}\frac{dv_j}{d\Omega_i}f_i'\right) + \frac{d\phi_i}{dv_i}\frac{dv_i}{d\Omega_i}f_i$$
$$= \underbrace{\left(\sum_{j\neq i}\gamma\frac{\phi_j}{v_j}\right)\theta^i\pi M_i f_i' + \gamma\frac{\phi_i}{v_i}\pi M_i f_i}_{\text{marginal benefit}} \quad \text{for } i = 1, 2, \ldots, J \tag{12}$$

Equation (12) is analogous to (10). The *left-hand side* (LHS) of equation (12) is, in fact, the marginal cost per consumer in country i of strengthening IPR there. The first term is the loss in consumer surplus attributed to protection of inventions from firms outside country i; the second term is the loss of consumer surplus attributed to protection of inventions from country i, offset by the gains in profits of firms in country i (augmented by the profit-bias a). The *right-hand side* (RHS) or the last line of (12) is the marginal benefit per consumer in country i. The first term is the increase in expected consumer welfare in country i due to increases in flows of innovations from firms outside country i; the second term is the increase in consumer welfare in country i due to the increase in the flow of innovation from country i. If we define the left-hand side of (12) as $MC_i(a)$ and the right-hand side of (12) as MB_i, then $\frac{1}{M_i}\frac{dW_i(a)}{d\Omega_i} = MB_i - MC_i(a) =$ marginal net national benefit to i, where $W_i\,(a)$ is Government i's objective function. Hereinafter, we put an argument 'a' after the name of a function if profit-bias affects the value of the function.

Invoking equations (2), (3) and (8), equation (12) can be re-written as

$$\left(\sum_{j\neq i}\phi_j\right)\left(1-\Lambda\theta^i\right)+\left[1-(2+a)\,\Lambda\right]\phi_i$$
$$=\gamma\left\langle\sum_{j\neq i}\left\{\frac{\phi_j\theta^i M_i\left[1-\left(1-\Lambda\theta^i\right)\omega_i\right]}{\sum_{k\neq j}\left(\frac{\epsilon-1}{\lambda}\right)\left(\theta^k M_k\omega_k\right)+M_j\omega_j}\right\}\right.$$
$$\left.+\frac{\phi_i M_i\left[1-(1-\Lambda)\omega_i\right]}{\sum_{k\neq i}\left(\frac{\epsilon-1}{\lambda}\right)\left(\theta^k M_k\omega_k\right)+M_i\omega_i}\right\rangle\quad\text{for } i=1,2,\ldots,J \tag{13}$$

where $\omega_k \equiv \Omega_k/\overline{T}$ and $\Lambda \equiv C_m/C_c = \pi/C_c$. The endogenous variables are ω_i and θ^i for $i = 1,2,\ldots,J$. In order to solve for the values of ω_i for $i = 1,2,\ldots,J$, we also need equations (4), (6), and (7), as well as the calibrated value of θ^R_{EX} and θ^R_{FDI}, where the superscript R denotes the country with the largest market outside the US. It turns out that R is Japan. We shall adopt $\theta^R_{\mathrm{EX}} = 0.15$ and $\theta^R_{\mathrm{FDI}} = 0.03$ based on the estimates of the fractions of French and American firms that export and of those that carry out FDI in foreign countries, as provided in Eaton *et al.* (2004) (French) and

Bernard *et al.* (2003) (American). More discussion will be provided about this in the next section.

2.3.2 *Global optimum*

Next, we turn to the comparison between the Nash equilibrium and the global optimum. It can be easily shown that the first-order condition for global welfare maximization with respect to the choice of Ω_i is given by

$$M_i\left[MC_i(a)+\pi a\phi_i-\theta^i\left(\frac{\epsilon-1}{\lambda}\right)\pi\left(\sum_{j\neq i}\phi_j\right)\right]$$

$$=M_i\times MB_i+\sum_{k\neq i}\left(\sum_{j\neq k}\frac{d\phi_j}{dv_j}\frac{dv_j}{d\Omega_i}M_kf_k'\right)+\sum_{k\neq i}\frac{d\phi_k}{dv_k}\frac{dv_k}{d\Omega_i}M_kf_k$$

$$=M_i\times MB_i+\sum_{k\neq i}\left[M_k\left(\gamma\frac{\phi_i}{v_i}M_i\pi f_k'\right)\right.$$

$$\left.+M_k\left(\sum_{j\neq k,i}\gamma\frac{\phi_j}{v_j}\right)\theta^iM_i\pi f_k'\right]+\sum_{k\neq i}M_k\left(\gamma\frac{\phi_k}{v_k}\theta^iM_i\pi f_k\right) \quad (14)$$

The LHS of (14) (call it LHS_{14}) is the marginal global cost of strengthening IPR protection in country i. The second term inside the squared brackets ($\pi a\phi_i$) is the welfare that will not be taken into account when IPR protection in country i is chosen to maximize the global welfare instead of government i's profit-biased objective function (therefore it is an addition to marginal cost); the third term inside the squared brackets $\left(\theta^i\left(\frac{\epsilon-1}{\lambda}\right)\pi\left(\sum_{j\neq i}\phi_j\right)\right)$ reduces the global marginal cost as it takes into account the increases in profits of firms outside country i. The RHS (or the last two lines) of (14) (call it RHS_{14}) represents the marginal global benefit of strengthening IPR in country i. The second term and the third term are both increases in welfare of consumers outside country i. The second term is due to faster foreign rate of innovation, while the third term is due to faster domestic rate of innovation ("foreign" and "domestic" here are relative to each country other than country i). The cross-border externalities of IPR protection are captured by the third term inside the squared brackets on the LHS plus the second and third terms on the RHS. Let us define LHS_{14}/M_i as MC_i^w (marginal cost to the world) and RHS_{14}/M_i as MB_i^w (marginal benefit to the world). It follows that $\frac{1}{M_i}\frac{dW^w}{d\Omega_i} = MB_i^w - MC_i^w =$ marginal net global benefit from i.

Suppose we start with a world of Grossman and Lai (2004) where $a = 0$ and $y = 1$ (i.e. free trade). G–L have shown that there is global under-protection of IPR in Nash equilibrium, as the marginal net global benefit from i is larger than the marginal net national benefit to i. It is apparent that since an increase in the variable trade cost (i.e. a decrease in y, which in turn lowers θ^i for all i) leads to less international spillover, it narrows the net-benefits gap, thus lowering the likelihood of under-protection of IPR in equilibrium. Likewise, an increase in profit-bias (an increase in a) reduces the net-benefits gap, making under-protection of IPR less likely. Therefore, we expect that the lower is a and the higher is each θ^i, the more likely there is global under-protection of patent rights. This is exactly what equation (15) indicates below.

3 Calibration of the Model

3.1 Is there global under-protection of IPR?

We define under-protection as a situation when, starting from Nash equilibrium, global welfare increases when there are positive changes in some or all of the elements in the set $\{\Omega_i | \, i \in \mathcal{N}\}$. The point of the analysis is to come up with a sufficient condition under which, starting from Nash equilibrium $\{\Omega_i^E \big| \, i \in \mathcal{N}\}$, the simultaneous increases in IPR protection of some countries is globally welfare-improving. Note that increases in the strengths of protection in some countries raise the values of all patents. This increases global deadweight losses but encourages innovation. If there is global under-protection of patent rights, then the rate of innovation in the world is too low from a global welfare point of view.

In Appendix D, it is proved that a sufficient condition for global under-protection of IPR in Nash equilibrium is

$$a - \sum_{i \neq \max} \theta^i < 0 \tag{15}$$

where $\theta^{\max}$ is the largest θ^i among all countries. This is intuitive, as it means that the positive force that arises from profit-bias (measured by a) is weaker than the negative force that arises from cross-border externalities (measured by $\sum_{i \neq \max} \theta^i$), thus making the Nash equilibrium more likely to yield under-protection.

In what follow, we shall explain a calibration exercise that tries to find out whether the above sufficient condition (15) is satisfied. We shall solve equations (4), (6), (7) and (13) for $i = 1, 2, \ldots, J$ with parametric values calibrated using estimates in the literature.

As explained earlier, the parameter a can also be interpreted as the weight politicians put on campaign contributions. In the political-economy literature (Grossman and Helpman, 1994; Goldberg and Maggi, 1999; Gawande and Bandyopadhyay, 2000; Mitra *et al.*, 2002; Eicher and Osang, 2002; McCalman, 2004; Mitra *et al.*, 2006), researchers have estimated the weight the US government puts on campaign contributions given a weight of unity on social welfare. The estimates range from 0.000315 to 1.3333. For robustness check in the calibration exercise, we tried the values of $a = 0.000315$ (low profit-bias), 1 (strong profit-bias) and 1.3333 (very strong profit-bias).[16]

The parameter J denotes the number of independent government decision-makers in the patent-setting game. Thus, it is the number of countries in the world that consume and trade patent-sensitive goods, and that adopt neither zero nor full patent protection. In Table 1, we list the patent counts and market sizes of the twenty largest

[16]Since a a preference parameter, it should be the same in the context of patent protection. Suppose there is a patent lobby, and suppose there is no consumer lobby or lobbying from other sectors of the economy, it is easy to show that the value the government puts on campaign contributions is exactly the same as a in our model. A proof is available from the author upon request.

Table 1. Data on the market size of patent-sensitive goods and patent counts.

	Innovative capacity (ϕ)	Market size (M)
US	187.83	9.25
Japan	214.25	9.07
Germany	98.32	8.75
France	56.76	8.57
UK	52.08	8.45
China	0.06	8.45
Italy	24.24	8.43
Brazil	0.43	8.31
Spain	5.07	8.19
Canada	89.80	8.17
India	0.07	8.15
South Korea	55.34	8.13
Netherlands	65.15	8.02
Australia	31.91	7.99
Mexico	0.57	7.97
Argentina	1.06	7.88
Switzerland	167.53	7.85
Belgium	57.50	7.83
Sweden	122.82	7.77
Austria	50.25	7.76

Notes:

1. M is the logarithm of the average annual consumption (or absorption) of patent-sensitive goods in the country over the years 1996–1999.
2. ϕ is the average number of patents granted to residents of the country per year by the US Patent Office over the years 1996–1999 divided by the population of the country. The patent count of the US is adjusted for the home-bias effect discussed in Appendix E.

markets for patent-sensitive goods among the forty most innovative countries.[17] As (15) suggests, the more countries that are included in the game, the more likely the condition is satisfied. Therefore, it suffices to prove under-protection if we find that (15) holds for the

[17]Innovative capability is measured by the average number of patents granted to domestic residents of the country by the US patent office per year over the years 1996–1999 divided by population. Russia is not included due to the lack of reliable data. See Appendix E.

twenty countries with the largest markets for patent-sensitive goods. These countries are thus included in our empirical analysis. Hence, $J = 20$.

We proxy the market size (M_i) by the natural logarithm of the dollar value of the consumption of patent-sensitive goods in each country and proxy the innovative capability (ϕ_i) by the number of patents granted to residents of each country by the US patent office divided by the population of the country (we adjust for home bias of American patentees).[18] Data on M_i for 1996–1999 are obtained from Lai *et al.* (2007), and data on ϕ_i for 1996–1999 are from the website of World Intellectual Property Organization (WIPO).

θ^i_{EX} and θ^i_{FDI} are respectively the probabilities that foreign firms can sell to and carry out FDI in country i. Eaton *et al.* (2004) report that in 1986 only 17.4% of French manufacturing firms exported, and of those who exported, only 19.7% exported to ten or more countries. Moreover, in 1987, only 14.6 % of US manufacturing firms exported. Bernard *et al.* (2003) report that 79% of US manufacturing plants did not export at all in 1992. A summary of the existing studies in the literature indicates that 15–20% of manufacturing firms sell to foreign markets, of which about 1/5 produce in the foreign market in which they sell. (See, for example, Bernard *et al.*, 2009). Patent-sensitive goods are likely to be more tradeable than the average manufactured good. Therefore, to be conservative, we assume that 15% of American firms in the patent-sensitive industries sell to foreign markets, while 3% produce in the foreign countries in which they sell their goods. In other words, we set $\theta^{\text{Japan}}_{\text{EX}} = 0.15$ and $\theta^{\text{Japan}}_{\text{FDI}} = 0.03$ as Japan is the largest foreign market for US firms. The θ^i_{EX} and θ^i_{FDI} for other countries are determined endogenously by equations (6) and (7) respectively.

[18]We also tried using the patent counts without dividing by population to proxy for innovative capability, and the sufficient condition for under-protection (15) is still satisfied. But the rank order of ω^E_i matches more closely the actual rank order of the Ginarte–Park patent rights indexes (see Park, 2008) when we use patent counts divided by population.

We estimate γ, the elasticity of innovation rate with respect to patent value, based on the work of Boldrin and Levine (2009), who suggest a point estimate of around 4.[19] As we find that our results are robust to alternative values of γ, we just report the case of $\gamma = 4$ in this chapter.

Lai *et al.* (2007) estimate the parametric values of the elasticity of demand for patent-sensitive goods (ϵ) across thirty countries. These values average to 5.63. Given this, we assume $\epsilon = 5$. This coincides with the value implied by putting together the findings of literature that the shape parameter of the Pareto distribution of firm revenues ($\frac{\lambda}{\epsilon-1}$ in our model) is close to 1 and the finding of Simonovska (2011) that λ is approximately 4. For robustness, we also try a low elasticity scenario with $\epsilon = 1.5$ and a high elasticity scenario with $\epsilon = 9.28$. The upper value of 9.28 is obtained based on $\frac{\lambda}{\epsilon-1} \approx 1$ and the finding of Eaton and Kortum (2002) that λ is approximately 8.28.

Based on the empirical finding that $\lambda/(\epsilon - 1)$ is very close to one but above one, we report the cases of $\lambda/(\epsilon - 1) = 1$ and 1.049, as these two values lie roughly at the two ends of the spectrum of estimates obtained in the literature. Adopting this range also ensures that there are interior solutions to all endogenous variables of interest.

For the variable trade cost, we try a wide range of values from $t = 0$ (no iceberg trade cost) to 0.5 (very high iceberg trade cost). For the case $\lambda/(\epsilon - 1) = 1$, the results are invariant to the value of t.

Based on the above parametric values and data, we solve for the Nash equilibrium values of $\left\{\omega_i^E, \theta^i, \theta_{\text{EX}}^i, \theta_{\text{FDI}}^i \middle| \ i \in \mathcal{N}\right\}$ from equations (4), (6), (7) and (13) for $i = 1, 2, \ldots, J$. A summary of the calibration results are presented in Table 2. A wide range of values of profit-bias have been tried ($a = 0.000315, a = 1$ and $a = 1.3333$) but it has relatively minor effects on θ^i. So we only report the results for the most conservative case of $a = 1.3333$ in the interest of space. More tables of results are available from the authors upon request.

[19]Details of the derivation can be obtained from the authors upon request.

Table 2. Nash equilibrium and harmonized global optimum ($a = 1.333$).

	Trade cost $(t) = 0$											
	$\varepsilon = 1.5$				$\varepsilon = 5$				$\varepsilon = 9.28$			
	$\frac{\lambda}{\varepsilon-1} = 1$		$\frac{\lambda}{\varepsilon-1} = 1.049$		$\frac{\lambda}{\varepsilon-1} = 1$		$\frac{\lambda}{\varepsilon-1} = 1.049$		$\frac{\lambda}{\varepsilon-1} = 1$		$\frac{\lambda}{\varepsilon-1} = 1.049$	
	ω_i^E	θ^i	ω_i^E	θ^i	ω_i^E	θ^i	ω_i^E	θ^i	ω_i^E	θ^i	ω_i^E	θ^i
US	**0.373**	1	**0.423**	0.917	**0.529**	1	**0.588**	0.915	**0.561**	1	**0.621**	0.915
Japan	**0.367**	1	**0.418**	0.915	**0.520**	1	**0.597**	0.915	**0.550**	1	**0.633**	0.915
Germany	**0.285**	1	**0.318**	0.901	**0.368**	1	**0.418**	0.898	**0.384**	1	**0.439**	0.897
France	**0.246**	1	**0.267**	0.893	**0.298**	1	**0.331**	0.887	**0.307**	1	**0.344**	0.886
UK	**0.231**	1	**0.247**	0.889	**0.276**	1	**0.303**	0.882	**0.285**	1	**0.315**	0.881
China	**0.207**	1	**0.208**	0.881	**0.217**	1	**0.210**	0.867	**0.218**	1	**0.211**	0.864
Italy	**0.215**	1	**0.222**	0.884	**0.241**	1	**0.251**	0.874	**0.245**	1	**0.258**	0.873
Brazil	**0.189**	1	**0.181**	0.875	**0.196**	1	**0.168**	0.856	**0.196**	1	**0.035**	0.790
Spain	**0.176**	1	**0.161**	0.869	**0.182**	1	**0.040**	0.798	**0.182**	1	**0.044**	0.799
Canada	**0.214**	1	**0.228**	0.884	**0.279**	1	**0.308**	0.881	**0.291**	1	**0.325**	0.881
India	**0.170**	1	**0.148**	0.865	**0.171**	1	**0.052**	0.808	**0.170**	1	**0.056**	0.808
S. Korea	**0.192**	1	**0.193**	0.877	**0.232**	1	**0.239**	0.870	**0.239**	1	**0.250**	0.870
Netherlands	**0.182**	1	**0.180**	0.873	**0.226**	1	**0.231**	0.868	**0.234**	1	**0.244**	0.868
Australia	**0.163**	1	**0.142**	0.863	**0.182**	1	**0.037**	0.794	**0.185**	1	**0.038**	0.793
Mexico	**0.145**	1	**0.088**	0.842	**0.141**	1	**0.078**	0.823	**0.139**	1	**0.081**	0.822
Argentina	**0.133**	1	**0.064**	0.829	**0.127**	1	**0.082**	0.825	**0.125**	1	**0.084**	0.823
Switzerland	**0.208**	1	**0.231**	0.883	**0.323**	1	**0.367**	0.887	**0.346**	1	**0.395**	0.888
Belgium	**0.153**	1	**0.130**	0.858	**0.187**	1	**0.158**	0.851	**0.193**	1	**0.167**	0.851
Sweden	**0.177**	1	**0.181**	0.872	**0.257**	1	**0.280**	0.875	**0.273**	1	**0.302**	0.876
Austria	**0.140**	1	**0.094**	0.844	**0.166**	1	**0.049**	0.804	**0.170**	1	**0.048**	0.801
Harmonized global optimum	$\omega^* = 1$		$\omega^* = 1$		$\omega^* = 1$		$\omega^* = 1$		$\omega^* = 1$		$\omega^* = 1$	

(Continued)

Table 2. *(Continued)*

	Trade cost $(t) = 0.5$											
	$\varepsilon = 1.5$				$\varepsilon = 5$				$\varepsilon = 9.28$			
	$\frac{\lambda}{\varepsilon-1} = 1$		$\frac{\lambda}{\varepsilon-1} = 1.049$		$\frac{\lambda}{\varepsilon-1} = 1$		$\frac{\lambda}{\varepsilon-1} = 1.049$		$\frac{\lambda}{\varepsilon-1} = 1$		$\frac{\lambda}{\varepsilon-1} = 1.049$	
	ω_i^E	θ^i	ω_i^E	θ^i	ω_i^E	θ^i	ω_i^E	θ^i	ω_i^E	θ^i	ω_i^E	θ^i
US	**0.373**	1	**0.424**	0.904	**0.520**	1	**0.579**	0.862	**0.550**	1	**0.607**	0.851
Japan	**0.367**	1	**0.419**	0.903	**0.529**	1	**0.589**	0.862	**0.561**	1	**0.620**	0.851
Germany	**0.285**	1	**0.318**	0.889	**0.368**	1	**0.409**	0.845	**0.384**	1	**0.425**	0.834
France	**0.246**	1	**0.266**	0.881	**0.298**	1	**0.321**	0.834	**0.307**	1	**0.331**	0.823
UK	**0.231**	1	**0.246**	0.877	**0.276**	1	**0.293**	0.830	**0.285**	1	**0.302**	0.819
China	**0.207**	1	**0.206**	0.869	**0.217**	1	**0.197**	0.814	**0.218**	1	**0.194**	0.801
Italy	**0.215**	1	**0.221**	0.872	**0.241**	1	**0.240**	0.822	**0.245**	1	**0.243**	0.810
Brazil	**0.189**	1	**0.180**	0.863	**0.196**	1	**0.154**	0.804	**0.196**	1	**0.034**	0.735
Spain	**0.176**	1	**0.159**	0.857	**0.182**	1	**0.040**	0.752	**0.182**	1	**0.043**	0.743
Canada	**0.214**	1	**0.228**	0.872	**0.279**	1	**0.302**	0.830	**0.291**	1	**0.316**	0.819
India	**0.170**	1	**0.147**	0.853	**0.171**	1	**0.052**	0.761	**0.170**	1	**0.056**	0.752
S. Korea	**0.192**	1	**0.193**	0.865	**0.232**	1	**0.232**	0.819	**0.239**	1	**0.240**	0.808
Netherlands	**0.182**	1	**0.180**	0.861	**0.226**	1	**0.226**	0.817	**0.234**	1	**0.235**	0.807
Australia	**0.163**	1	**0.141**	0.851	**0.182**	1	**0.035**	0.746	**0.185**	1	**0.036**	0.735
Mexico	**0.145**	1	**0.084**	0.829	**0.141**	1	**0.075**	0.774	**0.139**	1	**0.076**	0.763
Argentina	**0.133**	1	**0.064**	0.818	**0.127**	1	**0.078**	0.775	**0.125**	1	**0.079**	0.764
Switzerland	**0.208**	1	**0.232**	0.871	**0.323**	1	**0.365**	0.836	**0.346**	1	**0.390**	0.826
Belgium	**0.153**	1	**0.130**	0.847	**0.187**	1	**0.155**	0.802	**0.193**	1	**0.161**	0.791
Sweden	**0.177**	1	**0.182**	0.860	**0.257**	1	**0.278**	0.825	**0.273**	1	**0.297**	0.815
Austria	**0.140**	1	**0.094**	0.833	**0.166**	1	**0.045**	0.754	**0.170**	1	**0.043**	0.742
Harmonized global optimum	$\omega^* = 1$		$\omega^* = 1$		$\omega^* = 1$		$\omega^* = 1$		$\omega^* = 1$		$\omega^* = 1$	

(Continued)

Notes for Table 2:

1. $\omega_i^{\bar{E}}$ denotes the patent protection of country i in Nash equilibrium. θ^i is defined as $y(\theta^i_{EX})^{\frac{1-\varepsilon+\lambda}{\lambda}} + (1-y)(\theta^i_{FDI})^{\frac{1-\varepsilon+\lambda}{\lambda}}$, where θ^i_{EX} and θ^i_{FDI} represent the probabilities of a foreign firm selling to and canying out FDI in country i respectively. ω^* denotes the globally optimal level of hammonized patent protection.
2. ε refers to the price elasticity of demand of a typical consumer. The value of $\varepsilon = 5$ is obtained from Lai, Wong and Yan (2007) and by putting together the findings of Axtell (2001) and Luttmer (2007) that the shape parameter of the Pareto distribution $\left(\frac{\lambda}{\varepsilon-1}\right)$ is close to but larger than 1 and the finding of Simonovska (2011) that λ is approximately 4. The alternative value of $\varepsilon = 9.28$ is obtained based on $\frac{\lambda}{\varepsilon-1} \approx 1$ and the finding of Eaton and Kortum (2002) that λ is approximately 8.28.
3. $\frac{\lambda}{\varepsilon-1}$ refers to the shape parameter of the distribution of firm revenues. Based on the data on US's firm size distributions in 1988–1997, Axtell (2001) obtain that $\frac{\lambda}{\varepsilon-1}$ is close to and larger than 1. A recent study by Luttmer (2007) finds that the shape parameter is also close to but larger than 1. We perform robustness check on $\frac{\lambda}{\varepsilon-1}$ by setting its upper end to 1.049.
4. "1+a" is the weight a government puts on domestic profits when a weight of one is put on domestic consumer surplus in its objective function. The parameter "a" measures the profit-bias of governments. It ranges from 0.000315 to 1.3333 in the literature (Goldberg and Maggi, 1999; Gawande *et al.*, 2000; Mitra *et al.*, 2002; Eicher and Osang, 2002; McCalman, 2004 and Mitra *et al.*, 2005). Since $a = 1.3333$ gives the most conservative case that makes it hardest for us to reach the under-protection conclusion, we only present this case here. Lower values of "a" yield an even larger degree of under-protection in Nash equilibrium.
5. Bold terms are the values for the variable ω_i^E.

As expected, a higher value of a is associated with a higher level of equilibrium strengths of IPR protection in each country $\{\omega_i^E\}$ as governments put more weight on the profits of patent-holders. Furthermore, from Table 2, we find that a higher t leads to lower probabilities of exploiting an invention in each country $(\{\theta^i\})$.

The calibration exercise yields two important results.

1. We find that the values of θ^i are above 0.7 for all countries under all scenarios. It follows that the sufficient condition for under-protection of IPR in the Nash equilibrium specified in equation (15) is satisfied under all parametric values considered. As a result, *we conclude that there is global under-protection of patent rights when there is no international coordination.* The main reason is the existence of a free-rider problem in the protection of patent rights, which becomes very serious when there is a large number of government-players in the patent-setting game. The value of θ^i_{EX} varies across countries, but never exceeds 0.2 under various sensitivity tests, while the values of θ^i_{FDI} for different countries are all below 0.04.[20]
2. If we ignored FDI/licensing, we would have severely overestimated the barriers to exploit an invention internationally. For example, in the case of the US firms selling to Japan, if the iceberg trade cost is $t = 0.5$, $a = 1.333$, $\frac{\lambda}{\epsilon-1} = 1.049$, $\epsilon = 9.28$, and if we accept the estimate that 15% of US firms sell to Japan and assume that they do not do FDI/licensing, then the estimated

[20]The relatively high value of θ^i we obtain is consistent with the finding of Eaton and Kortum (1999), who find that the extent of international diffusion of technology is about two-third of the way between total absence of diffusion and perfect diffusion. In our model, total absence of diffusion before a patent expires in country i corresponds to $\theta^i = 0$, while perfect diffusion before a patent expires corresponds to $\theta^i = 1$. Two-third of the way from the state of zero diffusion corresponds to $\theta^i = 0.67$ in our model.

θ^{Japan} is 0.032 [i.e. $(1+0.5)^{-9.28+1} \cdot (0.15)^{1-\frac{1}{1.049}}$].[21] If we take into account the fact that 1/5 of those firms that sell to Japan (i.e. 3% of all US firms) in fact carry out FDI/licensing, then the estimated θ^{Japan} is 0.851 [i.e. $(1+0.5)^{-9.28+1} \cdot (0.15)^{1-\frac{1}{1.049}} + \left[1-(1+0.5)^{-9.28+1}\right](0.03)^{1-\frac{1}{1.049}}$]. That is a huge difference. The errors in the estimation of θ^i of other countries would be equally large. In fact, *had we omitted FDI/licensing, we would have concluded that the sufficient condition for under-protection would not be satisfied*, as the magnitudes of the calibrated cross-border externalities would be really small. As the error becomes more serious as $\frac{\lambda}{\epsilon-1}$ gets closer to one, *the empirical fact that firm revenues follow a fat-tailed distribution implies that it is really important to include FDI as an alternative channel of exploiting an invention internationally (besides exporting)* in any empirical work.

3.2 Harmonization with the most protective country

Our analysis in the previous section indicates that there would be under-protection of IPR without international coordination. A natural question to ask is whether the current form of international coordination mandated by TRIPS is over-protective from a global welfare perspective. Adopting the views of Reichman (1995) and Lai and Qiu (2003), we assume that TRIPS requires all countries in the world to harmonize their IPR standards with the pre-TRIPS standards of the most protective country. We try to answer the above question based on this characterization of TRIPS.[22]

---

[21]This is the case when F_{FDI} is so large that $\theta^k_{\text{FDI}} \to 0 \; \forall k$.

[22]If one examines the Ginarte–Park patent rights index for the periods 1960–1990, 1995, 2000 and 2005 (refer to Park, 2008), one sees that the most protective country before TRIPS (i.e. 1960–1990) was the US, whose index was 4.14. By 2005, all developed or newly industrialized economies would have already adopted the patent standard required by TRIPS. The patent rights indexes for countries that adopt the minimum requirement mandated by TRIPS turned out to be about 4.1 (e.g. Israel 4.13, Australia 4.17, New Zealand 4.01, Norway 4.17). So harmonization with the pre-TRIPS standard of the US is more or less what the TRIPS mandated.

Suppose we sum up all the J first order conditions (14) and impose the restriction $\Omega_j = \Omega^* \ \forall j \in \mathcal{N}$ on this equation. The solution of Ω^* will then yield the harmonized patent strength that is globally efficient. Suppose country k is the most protective country in equilibrium, i.e. $\Omega_k^E = \max\{\Omega_j^E \big| j \in \mathcal{N}\}$. Then, $\Omega_k^E < \Omega^*$ is the necessary and sufficient condition that there is no over-protection of patent rights even if all countries harmonize their IPR standards with the most protective country in the world. We have already solved for Ω_k^E, which is Ω_{US}^E, in the earlier section. Adopting the same set of parametric values and the same set of countries as in the previous section, we compute the value of Ω^*. The values of Ω^* under different parameter values are provided in the last rows of Table 2. As the values of Ω^* are all close to 1, which exceeds the equilibrium protection strengths of all countries including the US in all cases, we conclude that $\Omega_{\text{US}}^E < \Omega^*$. This means that there is no global over-protection of IPR resulting from TRIPS.

The intuition of the above result is that the distribution of innovative capability among countries is not too skewed so that requiring all countries to harmonize their patent standards with that of the most protective (and most innovative) country in Nash equilibrium (i.e. the US) does not lead to over-protection of patent rights from the global welfare point of view. The situation in a two-country case is shown in Figure 2. It shows that global harmonization with the North's pre-TRIPS standard is a movement from point E to point E'. As E' is still inside the frontier GG, global welfare increases from E to E'. The North gains more than the South loses in this global IPR harmonization scheme, and global welfare increases. Taken together, the two results in this section indicate that TRIPS is globally welfare-improving.[23]

[23]If the distribution of innovative capability is too skewed, then the equilibrium may be at E_1 shown in Figure 2. In that case, a movement from E_1 to E_1' leads to over-protection.

4 Conclusion

On the theoretical front, we extend the Grossman and Lai (2004) model to analyze the interaction among innovation, firm heterogeneity, exporting, FDI and patent protection in a unified framework. On the empirical front, we find that there is global under-protection of patent rights in the non-cooperative equilibrium given the estimates of the profit-bias parameter in the political economy literature and the estimates of the barriers to international exploitation of inventions. Our conclusion to this question is robust to alternative parametric values obtained in the literature. This result arises from the fact that, despite the existence of trade barriers, the free-rider problem becomes very serious when there is a large number of country-players in the patent-setting game. The empirical fact that firm revenues follow a fat-tailed distribution mitigates trade and FDI barriers a great deal, leading to low barriers to international exploitation of inventions. Thus, the cross-border externalities in strengthening national patent rights are high, despite the fact that only a small fraction of firms sell overseas (no more than say 15%) and an even smaller fraction of firms carry out FDI (no more than say 3%). Calibrating the model, we find that requiring all countries to harmonize their patent strengths with the equilibrium strength of the most protective country does not lead to global over-protection of IPR. This is because the distribution of innovative capability among countries is not too skewed as to overcome the free-rider effect. If such an IPR harmonization scheme captures what the TRIPS has done, then there is no evidence that TRIPS leads to global over-protection of patent rights. In other words, TRIPS is globally welfare-improving. (This does not mean, however, that all countries would gain from such a harmonization. It only means that the sum of the gains for the gainers would exceed the sum of losses for the losers. Thus, distribution is still an issue in such a harmonization.)

Last but not least, in our calibration exercise, we find that omitting FDI/licensing as an alternative channel of exploiting an invention internationally (besides exporting) can severely over-estimate the barriers to international exploitation of inventions. Therefore, it is important to include both exporting and FDI in any model that attempts to explain international exploitation of technology.

The theoretical framework can possibly be exploited further to analyze empirically the relationship between innovation, trade barriers, market size, patent protection, and trade flows of patent-sensitive goods among countries. This is left to future research.

Appendix

A. Mean Values of Profit and Consumer Surplus

Define the unconditional means of the monopoly profit, the competitive consumer surplus and consumer surplus under monopoly, per consumer, as

$$\pi = \int_{c=0}^{\frac{1}{b}} \widetilde{\pi}(c)dF(c); \quad C_c = \int_{c=0}^{\frac{1}{b}} \widetilde{C}_c(c)dF(c);$$

$$\text{and} \quad C_m = \int_{c=0}^{\frac{1}{b}} \widetilde{C}_m(c)dF(c)$$

where c is the unit cost of production. $\widetilde{\pi}(c)$, $\widetilde{C}_c(c)$ and $\widetilde{C}_m(c)$ are monopoly profit, the competitive consumer surplus and consumer surplus under monopoly, respectively, expressed as functions of c. From Section 2.1.1, the c.d.f. of c is given by $F(c) = (bc)^{\lambda}$, where $c \in [0, \frac{1}{b}]$.

Recall that the demand of a typical consumer is $x = Ap^{-\epsilon}$ (where $\epsilon > 1$). It can be easily shown that

$$\widetilde{C}_c = \frac{Ac^{-\epsilon+1}}{\epsilon - 1}. \tag{A1}$$

Therefore,

$$C_c = \frac{A\lambda b^{\epsilon-1}}{(\epsilon-1)(1-\epsilon+\lambda)}.$$

Similarly,

$$\widetilde{\pi} = \widetilde{C}_m = \Lambda \widetilde{C}_c \quad \text{where } \Lambda \equiv \left(\frac{\epsilon - 1}{\epsilon}\right)^{\epsilon}$$

$$\text{and so} \quad \pi = C_m = \Lambda C_c. \tag{A2}$$

B. The Distributions of Firm Profits and Revenues

From Section 2.1.1, we have $\Pr(c < z) = (bz)^{\lambda}$, where $z \in [0, \frac{1}{b}]$. From Appendix A, we have $\widetilde{\pi} = A\left(\frac{1}{\epsilon-1}\right)\Lambda c^{-\epsilon+1}$. Therefore,

$$\Pr(\widetilde{\pi} < s) = 1 - \left(\frac{A\Lambda b^{\epsilon-1}}{\epsilon - 1}\right)^{\frac{\lambda}{\epsilon-1}} \cdot s^{-\frac{\lambda}{\epsilon-1}}, \quad \text{where } s \in \left(\frac{A\Lambda b^{\epsilon-1}}{\epsilon - 1}, \infty\right) \tag{B1}$$

and revenue per consumer $\widetilde{R} = (\epsilon - 1)\widetilde{\pi}$ follows a distribution

$$\Pr(\widetilde{R} < \mathfrak{s}) = 1 - (A\Lambda b^{\epsilon-1})^{\frac{\lambda}{\epsilon-1}} \cdot \mathfrak{s}^{-\frac{\lambda}{\epsilon-1}}, \quad \text{where } \mathfrak{s} \in (A\Lambda b^{\epsilon-1}, \infty).$$

C. Fixed Cost of Exporting and Probability of Exporting

Define c^k_{FDI} as the critical c for FDI to country k and c^k_{EX} as the critical c for exporting to country k. From Figure 1, we get

$$y\widetilde{\pi}(c^k_{\text{EX}})M_k\Omega_k = F_{\text{EX}}.$$

From Appendix A, we obtain

$$\widetilde{\pi}(c^k_{\text{EX}}) = \left(\frac{A\Lambda}{\epsilon - 1}\right)(c^k_{\text{EX}})^{-\epsilon+1}.$$

From Appendix B, we obtain

$$\theta^k_{\text{EX}} = \Pr(c < c^k_{\text{EX}}) = (b \cdot c^k_{\text{EX}})^{\lambda}.$$

From the above three equations we can obtain c^k_{EX} and θ^k_{EX} in terms of the exogenous variables and Ω_k:

$$\theta^k_{\text{EX}} = b^\lambda \left[\frac{y\Lambda A M_k \Omega_k}{F_{\text{EX}}(\epsilon - 1)}\right]^{\frac{\lambda}{\epsilon-1}} \quad \text{and} \quad c^k_{\text{EX}} = \left[\frac{y\Lambda A M_k \Omega_k}{F_{\text{EX}}(\epsilon - 1)}\right]^{\frac{1}{\epsilon-1}}. \quad \text{(C1)}$$

By the same token, we can obtain the following three equations

$$y\widetilde{\pi}(c^k_{\text{EX}})M_k\Omega_k - F_{\text{EX}} = \widetilde{\pi}(c^k_{\text{FDI}})M_k\Omega_k - F_{\text{FDI}},$$
$$\widetilde{\pi}(c^k_{\text{FDI}}) = \left(\frac{A\Lambda}{\epsilon - 1}\right)(c^k_{\text{FDI}})^{-\epsilon+1},$$
$$\theta^k_{\text{FDI}} = \Pr(c < c^k_{\text{FDI}}) = (b \cdot c^k_{\text{FDI}})^\lambda,$$

which allow us to obtain c^k_{FDI} and θ^k_{FDI} in terms of the exogenous variables and Ω_k:

$$\theta^k_{\text{FDI}} = b^\lambda \left[\frac{(1-y)\Lambda A M_k \Omega_k}{(F_{\text{FDI}} - F_{\text{EX}})(\epsilon - 1)}\right]^{\frac{\lambda}{\epsilon-1}} \quad \text{and}$$
$$c^k_{\text{FDI}} = \left[\frac{(1-y)\Lambda A M_k \Omega_k}{(F_{\text{FDI}} - F_{\text{EX}})(\epsilon - 1)}\right]^{\frac{1}{\epsilon-1}}. \quad \text{(C2)}$$

D. Proof of Condition (15)

Recall that the Nash equilibrium condition (12) is equivalent to $\frac{1}{M_i}\frac{dW_i(a)}{d\Omega_i} = 0$ while the global optimum condition (14) is equivalent to $\frac{1}{M_i}\frac{dW^w}{d\Omega_i} = 0$. *A sufficient condition for under-protection in Nash equilibrium is* $\sum_i \frac{1}{M_i}\frac{dW^w}{d\Omega_i} > 0$ *for all combinations of* $\{\Omega_i | i \in \mathcal{N}\}$ *that satisfy* $\sum_i \frac{1}{M_i}\frac{dW_i(a)}{d\Omega_i} = 0$. This is because $\sum_i \frac{1}{M_i}\frac{dW^w}{d\Omega_i} > 0 \Leftrightarrow \left(\sum_i \frac{1}{M_i}\frac{dW^w}{d\Omega_i}\right)\delta > 0$ where $\delta = M_i d\Omega_i \ \forall i$, which means that increasing each Ω_i slightly by an amount proportional to $1/M_i$ is globally welfare-improving. Furthermore, the set of equilibrium IPR $\{\Omega^E_i | i \in \mathcal{N}\}$ is obviously a subset of $\{\Omega_i | \sum_i \frac{1}{M_i}\frac{dW_i(a)}{d\Omega_i} = 0\}$. From equation (14), we know that the above sufficient condition is equivalent to

$$\sum_i \left[\pi a\phi_i - \theta^i\pi\left(\sum_{j\neq i}\phi_j\right)\right]$$
$$< \sum_i \left[\sum_{k\neq i}\left(\gamma\frac{\phi_i}{v_i}\pi M_k f_k' + \sum_{j\neq k,i}\gamma\frac{\phi_j}{v_j}\theta^i\pi M_k f_k'\right)\right.$$
$$\left. + \sum_{k\neq i}\gamma\frac{\phi_k}{v_k}\theta^i\pi M_k f_k\right] \tag{D1}$$

for all combinations of $\{\Omega_i\}_{i\in\mathcal{N}}$ that satisfy $\sum_i \frac{1}{M_i}\frac{dW_i(a)}{d\Omega_i} = 0$.

The RHS of (D1) is greater than zero, as there are positive cross-border externalities as a country strengthens its patent protection. Therefore, a sufficient condition for (D1) to hold is $\sum_i \left[a\phi_i - \theta^i\left(\sum_{j\neq i}\phi_j\right)\right] < 0$, a sufficient condition of which is $a - \sum_{i\neq \max}\theta^i < 0$. □

E. Data for Market Size (M) and Innovative Capability (ϕ)

The market size variable (M_i) is proxied by the natural logarithm of the average dollar value of consumption (or use) of patent-sensitive goods per year by country i over the years 1996–1999 (estimated by Lai *et al.*, 2007). Our choice of the set of patent-sensitive goods is mainly based on Maskus (2000), with some modifications. The set includes Chemicals, Electromedical machines, Special industry machines, Electric microcircuits, Metalworking machines, Measuring and control instruments, and Data processing equipment. The innovative capability variable (ϕ_i) is proxied by the average number of patents granted to the resident of country i by the US patent office per year over the years 1996–1999 (obtained from the WIPO website) divided by population. However, to adjust for home-bias of the US data, we calculate the US innovative capability as the mean of an upper bound and a lower bound. The upper bound is given by the yearly average of the actual number of patents granted to US residents by the US patent office, $P_{\text{US}}^{\text{US}}$, where P_i^j denotes the number of patents granted to residents of country i by country j. This is an upper bound because it probably over-states the innovative capability of the US because even relatively trivial inventions might be patented in the US by US residents as the cost of patenting and subsequent working of the patents by domestic residents is relatively low. This is the home bias effect. The lower bound estimate is obtained by the formula

$$\widetilde{P_{\text{US}}^{\text{US}}} = \frac{P_{\text{US}}^{\text{EPO}}}{P_{\text{Japan}}^{\text{EPO}}} \times P_{\text{Japan}}^{\text{US}}.$$

The idea is that the American capability to obtain patents relative to that of Japan in Europe is approximately equal to the American capability to obtain patents relative to that of Japan in the US. Comparison with Japan is chosen because its innovative capability is comparable to that of the US while other countries are much further behind. The reason for choosing patents awarded in Europe is because European countries have a longer tradition of patent protection and have patent systems similar to that of the US. Japan, on the other hand, has a more liberal patent system with narrower protection than in the US and Europe. Therefore, calibration with the Japanese patent counts is not done. The estimate $\widetilde{P_{\text{US}}^{\text{US}}}$ is considered a lower bound of US innovative capability as some useful American innovations are not patented overseas perhaps because they are relatively less significant (though may be still useful). This is just the opposite of the home bias effect.

The estimated innovative capability of the US is therefore calculated as

$$\widehat{\phi_{\text{US}}} = \frac{\widetilde{P_{\text{US}}^{\text{US}}} + P_{\text{US}}^{\text{US}}}{2}$$

After taking the above into account, we obtain Table 1, which shows the patent counts and market sizes of the twenty most innovative countries.

F. Alternative Formulation

If one adopts the alternative formulation explained just before Section 2.2.1, then equation (13) becomes

$$\left(\sum_{j\neq i}\phi_j\right)\left[\left(\theta^i_{EX}\right)^{\frac{\lambda-\epsilon+1}{\lambda}}-\theta^i\Lambda\right]+\left[1-(2+a)\,\Lambda\right]\phi_i$$

$$=\gamma\left\langle\sum_{j\neq i}\left\{\frac{\phi_j\theta^i M_i\left[\left(\theta^i_{EX}\right)^{\frac{\lambda-\epsilon+1}{\lambda}}-\left(\left(\theta^i_{EX}\right)^{\frac{\lambda-\epsilon+1}{\lambda}}-\theta^i\Lambda\right)\omega_i\right]}{\sum_{k\neq j}\left(\frac{\epsilon-1}{\lambda}\right)\left(\theta^k M_k\omega_k\right)+M_j\omega_j}\right\}\right.$$

$$\left.+\frac{\phi_i M_i\left[1-(1-\Lambda)\omega_i\right]}{\sum_{k\neq i}\left(\frac{\epsilon-1}{\lambda}\right)\left(\theta^k M_k\omega_k\right)+M_i\omega_i}\right\rangle$$

for $i=1,2,\ldots,J$

Moreover, the following set of equations is to be solved to obtain the globally optimal harmonized $\widetilde{\omega}$ for Section 3.2 (where $\Lambda\equiv\left(\frac{\epsilon-1}{\epsilon}\right)^{\epsilon}$, $J=$ number of countries).

$$\widetilde{\omega}\left\{\left(\sum\phi_j\right)\left[\sum\left(\widetilde{\theta}^i_{EX}\right)^{\frac{\lambda-\epsilon+1}{\lambda}}-2\Lambda\left(\sum\widetilde{\theta}^i\right)+(1-2\Lambda)\right]\right.$$

$$\left.-\sum\left[\phi_i\left(\widetilde{\theta}^i_{EX}\right)^{\frac{\lambda-\epsilon+1}{\lambda}}\right]+2\Lambda\sum\left(\phi_i\widetilde{\theta}^i\right)\right\}$$

$$=\gamma\sum_i\left\{\sum_{j\neq i}\left\langle\frac{\phi_j\widetilde{\theta}^i M_i\left[\left(\widetilde{\theta}^i_{EX}\right)^{\frac{\lambda-\epsilon+1}{\lambda}}-\left(\left(\widetilde{\theta}^i_{EX}\right)^{\frac{\lambda-\epsilon+1}{\lambda}}-\widetilde{\theta}^i\Lambda\right)\widetilde{\omega}\right]}{\sum_{k\neq j}\left[\left(\frac{\epsilon-1}{\lambda}\right)\widetilde{\theta}^k M_k\right]+M_j}\right\rangle\right.$$

$$\left.+\frac{\phi_i M_i\left(1-(1-\Lambda)\,\widetilde{\omega}\right)}{\sum_{k\neq i}\left[\left(\frac{\epsilon-1}{\lambda}\right)\widetilde{\theta}^k M_k\right]+M_i}\right\}$$

$$+\gamma\sum_{i}\left\{\sum_{k\neq i}\left\langle\frac{\phi_i M_k\left[\left(\widetilde{\theta}^k_{EX}\right)^{\frac{\lambda-\epsilon+1}{\lambda}}-\left(\left(\widetilde{\theta}^k_{EX}\right)^{\frac{\lambda-\epsilon+1}{\lambda}}-\widetilde{\theta}^k\Lambda\right)\widetilde{\omega}\right]}{\sum_{m\neq i}\left[\left(\frac{\epsilon-1}{\lambda}\right)\widetilde{\theta}^m M_m\right]+M_i}\right.\right.$$

$$\left.+\sum_{j\neq k,i}\frac{\phi_j\widetilde{\theta}^i M_k\left[\left(\widetilde{\theta}^k_{EX}\right)^{\frac{\lambda-\epsilon+1}{\lambda}}-\left(\left(\widetilde{\theta}^k_{EX}\right)^{\frac{\lambda-\epsilon+1}{\lambda}}-\widetilde{\theta}^k\Lambda\right)\widetilde{\omega}\right]}{\sum_{m\neq j}\left[\left(\frac{\epsilon-1}{\lambda}\right)\widetilde{\theta}^m M_m\right]+M_j}\right\rangle$$

$$\left.+\sum_{k\neq i}\left(\frac{\widetilde{\theta}^i\phi_k M_k\left[1-(1-\Lambda)\widetilde{\omega}\right]}{\sum_{m\neq k}\left[\left(\frac{\epsilon-1}{\lambda}\right)\widetilde{\theta}^m M_m\right]+M_k}\right)\right\}$$

$$\widetilde{\theta}^i = y\left(\widetilde{\theta}^i_{EX}\right)^{\frac{1-\epsilon+\lambda}{\lambda}} + (1-y)\left(\widetilde{\theta}^i_{FDI}\right)^{\frac{1-\epsilon+\lambda}{\lambda}} \quad \text{for } i = 1, 2, \ldots, J$$

$$M_{US}\cdot\left(\widetilde{\theta}^{US}_{EX}\right)^{-\left(\frac{\epsilon-1}{\lambda}\right)} = M_k\cdot\left(\widetilde{\theta}^k_{EX}\right)^{-\left(\frac{\epsilon-1}{\lambda}\right)}$$

for $k = 2, \ldots, 30$ (assume that k=1 for the US)

$$M_{US}\cdot\left(\widetilde{\theta}^{US}_{FDI}\right)^{-\left(\frac{\epsilon-1}{\lambda}\right)} = M_k\cdot\left(\widetilde{\theta}^k_{FDI}\right)^{-\left(\frac{\epsilon-1}{\lambda}\right)}$$

for $k = 2, \ldots, J$ (assume that k=1 for the US)

$$\widetilde{\theta}^{\text{Japan}}_{\text{EX}} = 0.15$$

$$\widetilde{\theta}^{\text{Japan}}_{\text{FDI}} = 0.03$$

The results are shown in Table A1. It can be seen that the results in Tables 2 and A1 are almost the same. Therefore, the conclusions of the basic model are robust to this alternative formulation.

Alternative Formulation Table A1. Nash equilibrium and harmonized global optimum ($a = 1.333$).

	Trade cost $(t) = 0$											
	$\varepsilon = 1.5$				$\varepsilon = 5$				$\varepsilon = 9.28$			
	$\frac{\lambda}{\varepsilon-1} = 1$		$\frac{\lambda}{\varepsilon-1} = 1.049$		$\frac{\lambda}{\varepsilon-1} = 1$		$\frac{\lambda}{\varepsilon-1} = 1.049$		$\frac{\lambda}{\varepsilon-1} = 1$		$\frac{\lambda}{\varepsilon-1} = 1.049$	
	ω_i^E	θ^i	ω_i^E	θ^i	ω_i^E	θ^i	ω_i^E	θ^i	ω_i^E	θ^i	ω_i^E	θ^i
US	**0.367**	1	**0.420**	0.915	**0.529**	1	**0.603**	0.915	**0.561**	1	**0.640**	0.915
Japan	**0.373**	1	**0.425**	0.917	**0.520**	1	**0.591**	0.915	**0.550**	1	**0.626**	0.915
Germany	**0.285**	1	**0.320**	0.902	**0.368**	1	**0.418**	0.897	**0.384**	1	**0.439**	0.897
France	**0.246**	1	**0.269**	0.893	**0.298**	1	**0.328**	0.886	**0.307**	1	**0.342**	0.885
UK	**0.231**	1	**0.249**	0.889	**0.276**	1	**0.301**	0.882	**0.285**	1	**0.313**	0.881
China	**0.207**	1	**0.209**	0.881	**0.217**	1	**0.203**	0.865	**0.218**	1	**0.202**	0.862
Italy	**0.215**	1	**0.224**	0.884	**0.241**	1	**0.247**	0.873	**0.245**	1	**0.253**	0.871
Brazil	**0.189**	1	**0.184**	0.875	**0.196**	1	**0.168**	0.856	**0.196**	1	**0.165**	0.853
Spain	**0.176**	1	**0.165**	0.870	**0.182**	1	**0.145**	0.849	**0.182**	1	**0.141**	0.846
Canada	**0.214**	1	**0.234**	0.885	**0.279**	1	**0.315**	0.882	**0.291**	1	**0.332**	0.882
India	**0.170**	1	**0.153**	0.866	**0.171**	1	**0.114**	0.839	**0.170**	1	**0.036**	0.791
S. Korea	**0.192**	1	**0.200**	0.878	**0.232**	1	**0.245**	0.871	**0.239**	1	**0.256**	0.870
Netherlands	**0.182**	1	**0.189**	0.875	**0.226**	1	**0.241**	0.870	**0.234**	1	**0.254**	0.869
Australia	**0.163**	1	**0.152**	0.865	**0.182**	1	**0.162**	0.853	**0.185**	1	**0.166**	0.851
Mexico	**0.145**	1	**0.107**	0.850	**0.141**	1	**0.063**	0.814	**0.139**	1	**0.064**	0.812
Argentina	**0.133**	1	**0.073**	0.834	**0.127**	1	**0.064**	0.815	**0.125**	1	**0.065**	0.813
Switzerland	**0.208**	1	**0.242**	0.884	**0.323**	1	**0.383**	0.889	**0.346**	1	**0.414**	0.890
Belgium	**0.153**	1	**0.144**	0.862	**0.187**	1	**0.183**	0.857	**0.193**	1	**0.193**	0.857
Sweden	**0.177**	1	**0.194**	0.874	**0.257**	1	**0.298**	0.877	**0.273**	1	**0.321**	0.878
Austria	**0.140**	1	**0.119**	0.854	**0.166**	1	**0.144**	0.847	**0.170**	1	**0.152**	0.847
Harmonized global optimum	$\omega^* = 1$		$\omega^* = 1$		$\omega^* = 1$		$\omega^* = 1$		$\omega^* = 1$		$\omega^* = 1$	

(Continued)

Alternative Formulation Table A1. *(Continued)*

	Trade cost $(t) = 0$											
	$\varepsilon = 1.5$				$\varepsilon = 5$				$\varepsilon = 9.28$			
	$\frac{\lambda}{\varepsilon-1} = 1$		$\frac{\lambda}{\varepsilon-1} = 1.049$		$\frac{\lambda}{\varepsilon-1} = 1$		$\frac{\lambda}{\varepsilon-1} = 1.049$		$\frac{\lambda}{\varepsilon-1} = 1$		$\frac{\lambda}{\varepsilon-1} = 1.049$	
	ω_i^E	θ^i	ω_i^E	θ^i	ω_i^E	θ^i	ω_i^E	θ^i	ω_i^E	θ^i	ω_i^E	θ^i
US	**0.367**	1	**0.421**	0.903	**0.529**	1	**0.597**	0.862	**0.561**	1	**0.628**	0.851
Japan	**0.373**	1	**0.425**	0.904	**0.520**	1	**0.585**	0.862	**0.550**	1	**0.613**	0.851
Germany	**0.285**	1	**0.320**	0.889	**0.368**	1	**0.412**	0.845	**0.384**	1	**0.426**	0.834
France	**0.246**	1	**0.268**	0.881	**0.298**	1	**0.322**	0.834	**0.307**	1	**0.328**	0.822
UK	**0.231**	1	**0.249**	0.877	**0.276**	1	**0.295**	0.830	**0.285**	1	**0.300**	0.818
China	**0.207**	1	**0.207**	0.869	**0.217**	1	**0.193**	0.813	**0.218**	1	**0.185**	0.799
Italy	**0.215**	1	**0.223**	0.872	**0.241**	1	**0.239**	0.821	**0.245**	1	**0.238**	0.809
Brazil	**0.189**	1	**0.182**	0.863	**0.196**	1	**0.158**	0.804	**0.196**	1	**0.146**	0.789
Spain	**0.176**	1	**0.163**	0.858	**0.182**	1	**0.136**	0.798	**0.182**	1	**0.120**	0.781
Canada	**0.214**	1	**0.234**	0.873	**0.279**	1	**0.311**	0.831	**0.291**	1	**0.323**	0.820
India	**0.170**	1	**0.151**	0.854	**0.171**	1	**0.033**	0.744	**0.170**	1	**0.041**	0.741
S. Korea	**0.192**	1	**0.199**	0.866	**0.232**	1	**0.241**	0.820	**0.239**	1	**0.246**	0.809
Netherlands	**0.182**	1	**0.188**	0.863	**0.226**	1	**0.238**	0.819	**0.234**	1	**0.245**	0.808
Australia	**0.163**	1	**0.151**	0.853	**0.182**	1	**0.157**	0.802	**0.185**	1	**0.154**	0.790
Mexico	**0.145**	1	**0.105**	0.838	**0.141**	1	**0.060**	0.766	**0.139**	1	**0.062**	0.755
Argentina	**0.133**	1	**0.068**	0.820	**0.127**	1	**0.062**	0.766	**0.125**	1	**0.063**	0.755
Switzerland	**0.208**	1	**0.243**	0.873	**0.323**	1	**0.383**	0.838	**0.346**	1	**0.408**	0.828
Belgium	**0.153**	1	**0.144**	0.851	**0.187**	1	**0.181**	0.807	**0.193**	1	**0.185**	0.796
Sweden	**0.177**	1	**0.195**	0.863	**0.257**	1	**0.298**	0.827	**0.273**	1	**0.315**	0.817
Austria	**0.140**	1	**0.118**	0.842	**0.166**	1	**0.143**	0.797	**0.170**	1	**0.144**	0.786
Harmonized global optimum	$\omega^* = 1$		$\omega^* = 1$		$\omega^* = 1$		$\omega^* = 1$		$\omega^* = 1$		$\omega^* = 1$	

(Continued)

Notes for Table A1:

1. $\omega_i^{\bar{E}}$ denotes the patent protection of country i in Nash equilibrium. θ^i is defined as $y(\theta^i_{EX})^{\frac{1-\varepsilon+\lambda}{\lambda}} + (1-y)(\theta^i_{FDI})^{\frac{1-\varepsilon+\lambda}{\lambda}}$, where θ^i_{EX} and θ^i_{FDI} represent the probabilities of a foreign firm selling to and canying out FDI in country i respectively. ω^* denotes the globally optimal level of hammonized patent protection.
2. ε refers to the price elasticity of demand of a typical consumer. The value of $\varepsilon = 5$ is obtained from Lai, Wong and Yan (2007) and by putting together the findings of Axtell (2001) and Luttmer (2007) that the shape parameter of the Pareto distribution $\left(\frac{\lambda}{\varepsilon-1}\right)$ is close to but larger than 1 and the finding of Simonovska (2011) that λ is approximately 4. The alternative value of $\varepsilon - 9.28$ is obtained based on $\frac{\lambda}{\varepsilon-1} \approx 1$ and the finding of Eaton and Kortum (2002) that λ is approximately 8.28.
3. $\frac{\lambda}{\varepsilon-1}$ refers to the shape parameter of the distribution of firm revenues. Based on the data on US's firm size distributions in 1988–1997, Axtell (2001) obtain that $\frac{\lambda}{\varepsilon-1}$ is close to and larger than 1. A recent study by Luttmer (2007) finds that the shape parameter is also close to but larger than 1. We perform robustness check on $\frac{\lambda}{\varepsilon-1}$ by setting its upper end to 1.049.
4. "1+a" is the weight a government puts on domestic profits when a weight of one is put on domestic consumer surplus in its objective function. The parameter "a" measures the profit-bias of governments. It ranges from 0.000315 to 1.3333 in the literature (Goldberg and Maggi, 1999; Gawande *et al.*, 2000; Mitra *et al.*, 2002; Eicher and Osang, 2002; McCalman, 2004 and Mitra *et al.*, 2005). Since $a = 1.3333$ gives the most conservative case that makes it hardest for us to reach the under-protection conclusion, we only present this case here. Lower values of "a" yield an even larger degree of under-protection in Nash equilibrium.
5. Bold terms are the values for the variable ω_i^E.

Acknowledgment

The authors would like to thank participants in seminars in Michigan State University, Kobe University, Erasmus University, and in European Trade Study Group Annual Conference in Warsaw, AEA Annual Meeting and Otago Workshop in International Economics, CES-ifo Area Conference on Global Economy in Munich 2011 for helpful comments. The work in this paper has been supported by the Research Grants Council of Hong Kong, China (General Research Funds Project No. 642210) and City University of Hong Kong. Lai would also like to thank the International Economics Section of Princeton University for their support while he was writing this chapter there.

References

Axtell, R. L. (2001). Zipf distribution of US firm sizes, *Science* 293, 1818–1820.

Bagwell, K. and Staiger, R. W. (2004). Multilateral trade negotiations, bilateral opportunism and the rules of GATT/WTO, *Journal of International Economics* 63(1), 1–29.

Bernard, A. B., Eaton, J., Jensen, J. B., and Kortum, S. (2003). Plants and productivity in international trade, *American Economic Review* 93(4), 1268–1290.

Bernard, A. B., Jensen, J. B., and Schott, P. K. (2009). Importers, exporters, and multinationals: A portrait of firms in the US that trade goods, in Dunne, T., Jensen, J. B., and Roberts, M. J. (eds.), *Producer Dynamics: New Evidence from Micro Data*, University of Chicago Press, Chicago, Illinois, USA.

Boldrin, M. and David, L. (2009). Market size and intellectual property protection, *International Economic Review* 50, 855–881.

Eaton, J. and Kortum, S. (1999). International technology diffusion: Theory and measurement, *International Economic Review* 40(3), 537–570.

Eaton, J. and Kortum, S. (2002). Technology, geography, and trade, *Econometrica* 70(5), 1741–1779.

Eaton, J., Kortum, S., and Kramarz, F. (2004). Dissecting trade: Firms, industries, and export destinations, *American Economic Review* (Papers and Proceedings) 94(2), 150–154.

Eicher, T. and Osang, T. (2002). Protection for sale: An empirical investigation: Comment, *American Economic Review* 92(5), 1702–1710.

Gawande, K. and Bandyopadhyay, U. (2000). Is protection for sale? A test of the Grossman-Helpman theory of endogenous protection, *Review of Economics and Statistics* 82, 139–152.

Goldberg, P. K. and Maggi, G. (1999). Protection for sale: An empirical investigation, *American Economic Review* 89, 1135–1155.

Grossman, G. M. and Helpman, E. (1994). Protection for sale, *American Economic Review* 84, 833–850.

Grossman, G. M. and Lai, E. L.-C. (2004). International protection of intellectual property, *American Economic Review* 94(5), 1635–1653.

Helpman, E., Melitz, M., and Yeaple, S. (2004). Export versus FDI with heterogeneous firms, *American Economic Review* 94(1), 300–316.

Lai, E. L.-C (2008). Theory of international policy coordination in protection of ideas, in Maskus, K. E. (ed.), *Intellectual Property, Growth and Trade*, Frontiers of Economics and Globalization, Vol. 2, Elsevier, Amsterdam, The Netherlands.

Lai, E. L.-C. and Qiu, L. D. (2003). The North's intellectual property rights standard for the South? *Journal of International Economics* 59(1), 183–209.

Lai, E. L.-C., Wong, S., and Yan, I. (2007). *International Protection of Intellectual Property: An Empirical Investigation*, Manuscript, November 2007.

Luttmer, E. G. J. (2007). Selection, growth, and the size distributions of firms, *Quarterly Journal of Economics* 122(3), 1103–1144.

Maskus, K. E. (2000). *Intellectual Property Rights in the Global Economy,* Washington D.C.: The Institute for International Economics.

McCalman, P. (2001). Reaping what you sow: An empirical analysis of international patent harmonization, *Journal of International Economics* 55(1), 161–185.

McCalman, P. (2004). Protection for sale and trade liberalization, *Review of International Economics* 12(1), 81–94.

McFetridge, D. G. (1998). Intellectual property, technology diffusion, and growth in the Canadian economy, in Anderson, R. D. and Gallini, N. T. (eds.), *Competition Policy and Intellectual Property Rights in the Knowledge Based Economy*, The Industry Canada Research Series, University of Calgary Press, Calgary, Canada.

Melitz, M. J. (2003). The impact of trade on intra-industry reallocations and aggregate industry productivity, *Econometrica* 71(6), 1695–1725.

Mitra, D., Thomakos, D. D., and Ulubasoglu, M. (2002). 'Protection for sale' in a developing country: Democracy versus dictatorship? *Review of Economics and Statistics* 84, 497–508.

Mitra, D., Thomakos, D. D., and Ulubasoglu, M. (2006). Can we obtain realistic parameter estimates for the 'protection for sale' model? *Canadian Journal of Economics* 39(1), 187–210.

Park, W. G. (2008). International patent protection: 1960–2005, *Research Policy* 37, 761–766.

Reichman, J. H. (1995). Universal minimum standards of intellectual property protection under the TRIPS component of the WTO agreement, *The International Lawyer* 29(2), 345–388.

Simonovska, I. (2011). *The Elasticity of Trade: Estimates and Evidence*, UC Davis Department of Economics, Working Paper #11-2.

Part 2

North-South Trade, FDI and IPRs Protection

Chapter 5

International Intellectual Property Rights Protection and the Rate of Product Innovation*

Abstract
Using a dynamic general equilibrium model of the international product cycle, we found that the effects of strengthening intellectual property rights protection (IPP) in South depend crucially on the channel of production transfer from North to South. Stronger IPP in South increases the rate of product innovation, production transfer and Southern relative wage if foreign direct investment is the channel of production transfer, but has opposite effects if production is transferred through imitation. Stronger IPP can be more broadly interpreted as any incentive given by South to encourage Northern FDI.

1 Introduction

According to the terms of the Uruguay Round of the General Agreement on Tariffs and Trade, less developed countries (LDCs, hereinafter called the 'South') are required to strengthen intellectual property rights protection (IPP) in their countries. To economists who are concerned with long-term economic growth, the immediate questions are: What are the long-term repercussions of this on

---

*By Edwin L.-C. Lai. Originally published in *Journal of Development Economics* (February 1998), pp. 133–153.

global rate of technological progress, technology diffusion and world distribution of income between the 'North' (the more advanced countries) and 'South'? As pointed out by Helpman (1993), if the rate of innovation is exogenous, it is quite clear that LDCs stand to lose from stronger IPP, since both the terms of trade and efficiency effects go against the welfare of the LDCs. He also finds that the steady state rate of innovation will be decreased as IPP is strengthened, provided that imitation is the only channel by which production is transferred to South. However, when he allows for the possibility of foreign direct investment (FDI) from North to South as a channel of production transfer, Helpman only deals with exogenous rate of innovation.

We think it is important to investigate the long-term effects of Southern IPP on the global rate of innovation and technology diffusion. Recently, there has been various attempts to model the long-term effects of IPP on the rate of product innovation, economic growth and terms of trade in the international product cycles (Vernon, 1966). Segerstrom *et al.* (1990) find that a lengthening of patent duration for Northern firms lowers the rate of product innovation. Grossman and Helpman (1991b) and Helpman (1993) find that strengthening IPP (or subsidy to imitation) in South has a negative effect on the rate of innovation when imitation is the only channel of international production transfer. In these three models, where R&D output is linear in research effort, and imitation is the only channel by which production is transferred to South, there is a positive feedback from the rate of imitation to the rate of innovation. As a result, a strengthening of IPP lowers the rate of innovation and the rate of production transfer.[1] All these results seem to go against

[1]In a paper where a 'quality ladder' model is employed for the analysis, Grossman and Helpman (1991a or Chapter 12 of 1991c) find similar result in the 'inefficient follower' case, viz. a reduction in the cost of Southern imitation increases the rate of innovation in North. In the 'efficient follower' case, where there is no positive feedback from the rate of imitation to the rate of innovation, subsidy to Southern imitation (which can be viewed as a weakened IPP) reduces the Northern rate

the intuition furnished by Schumpeter (1950) and his followers (such as Romer, 1991) that stronger protection of the fruit of R&D should encourage innovation.

The principal objective of this paper is to compare and contrast between the cases when (i) FDI and (ii) imitation is the channel of international production transfer, with respect to the long-run effects of IPP on rate of product innovation, rate of international production transfer and world income distribution. For the present endeavor, we adopt the 'product cycle' (Vernon, 1966 or Krugman, 1979) paradigm that North is the only source of innovation, and the only way South can acquire technology is through 'technology transfer' from North. We modify the model of Grossman and Helpman (1991b) and Helpman (1993), which study the North-South product cycle where South can only acquire new technology by imitating products produced in North. Our modifications are (i) to allow Northern firms to undertake FDI in South (a process called 'multinationalization'); and (ii) assume that, in the 'multinationalization' regime, Southern firms can imitate only after Northern firms transfer production to South.[2]

We find that the effects of IPP in South depends crucially on whether imitation or multinationalization (prior to imitation) is the channel of international production transfer from North to South. If *imitation* is the channel of production transfer, stronger IPP lowers the rate of innovation, rate of production transfer and wage of South relative to North; if *multinationalization (prior to imitation)* is the channel of production transfer, IPP *has exactly the opposite effects.* In fact, the latter effects hold even when both channels co-exist, as long as the rate of multinationalization is sufficiently large.

The first scenario mentioned in the last paragraph is that described in Grossman and Helpman (1991b) and Helpman (1993).

---

of innovation (Grossman and Helpman, 1991c, p. 323), a result similar to ones in this paper.

[2]We shall maintain the assumption that R&D output is linear in research effort.

According to this scenario, production is transferred to South only through imitation of goods produced in North. There are two counteracting effects of enforcing stronger IPP in South. First, it lowers the rate of imitation and prolongs the expected duration of monopoly of each Northern innovator. This raises the returns to innovation. Second, since firms produce longer in North, it raises the demand for Northern labor and Northern wage, and hence raises the cost of innovation. Thus, it lowers the profits from innovation at each date. As shown by Grossman and Helpman, it turns out that the the second effect dominates the first one, and the rate of innovation declines. The contribution of the present paper lies mainly in the analysis of the second scenario described in the last paragraph. Under this scenario, production is transferred internationally through multinationalization (prior to imitation). Northern firms move production to South to take advantage of the lower wage, which they balance against the probability that they will lose their monopoly to imitators after multinationalization. A stronger IPP in South increases the rate of innovation in two stages. First, it increases the expected lives of monopolies. However, because the resulting increase in demand for labor falls entirely on South, the return to innovation rises without a rise in cost. Second, since the return to multinationalization increases, firms will move more quickly to South. This lowers the demand for Northern labor, Northern wage, and costs, thus increasing the return to innovation further.

Section 2 presents a benchmark product cycle model with FDI as the channel of production transfer to South. Section 3 presents the reduced form equilibrium conditions and investigates the effects of IPP. Section 4 presents the case where imitation is the channel of production transfer. Section 5 concludes and discusses some caveats and extensions.

2 The Product Cycle Model with Foreign Direct Investment

In this paper, we are only concerned with the steady state, i.e. the long run equilibrium. For the present purpose, we are not interested in welfare analysis in transition. We define steady state as a state at which the growth rate of the economy is constant over time, generally termed the "balanced growth path".

There are two countries (North and South) in the world, where free trade is allowed. A Northern firm develops a product by incurring an upfront innovation cost. It then earns the opportunity to make a stream of future profits. There is infinite patent life in North and the South, but patent law enforcement in North is perfect while enforcement in South is imperfect. Therefore, there is no imitation by Northern firms, and imitation only occurs in South. It is assumed that imitation is costless. It is assumed that the efficiency of Southern labor in innovation is so much lower than that of North that, in equilibrium, only Northern firms will innovate.

There is only one factor input, labor. It is used for research and development (R&D) and production in North and for production only in South. At any instant, a number of differentiated products (denoted by n) have been developed by North. Each innovation takes the form of the introduction of a new differentiated product in the economy by a firm. In equilibrium Northern firms will transfer production to South through FDI, a process we call 'multinationalization', since wage is lower in South. In this paper, we do not differentiate between multinationalization through wholly owned subsidiary, partly owned subsidiary or technology licensing. We assume that under perfect foresight all three forms of production transfer yield the same gain to Northern innovator. Hereinafter, we speak of multinationalization as the setting up of a multinational corporation (MNC) by a Northern firm. Since Southern wage is lower, the Northern firm will stop production in the North once it has multinationalized production.

In this section, we assume that multinationalization (prior to imitation) is the only form of production transfer to South. In other words, a product will not be imitated until its production has been multinationalized by the innovator. We assume that after production is transferred to South (by multinationalization or otherwise), the unit labor requirement for production in South is the same as that in North. The only motivation for production transfer is the lower production cost in South. In Section 4, we shall investigate the case where imitation is the channel of production transfer to South.

2.1 The demand for goods

Following Grossman and Helpman (1991b), we assume there is a world representative agent (or, alternatively, one representative agent in each country) who chooses instantaneous expenditure $E(\tau)$ to maximize intertemporal utility at time t:

$$W = \int_t^{\infty} e^{-\rho(\tau-t)} \frac{U(\tau)^{1-\sigma} - 1}{1-\sigma} d\tau \tag{1}$$

subject to the intertemporal budget constraint[3]

$$\int_t^{\infty} e^{-r(\tau-t)} E(\tau) d\tau = \int_t^{\infty} e^{-r(\tau-t)} I(\tau) d\tau + A(t) \quad \text{for all } t \tag{2}$$

where $0 \leq \sigma \leq 1$ and $\sigma =$ intertemporal elasticity of substitution; ρ is the time rate of preference; r is the nominal interest rate; $U(\tau)$ is instantaneous utility at time τ; $E(\tau)$ is instantaneous expenditure at τ; $I(\tau)$ is instantaneous income at τ; $A(t)$ is the current value of assets at t. At each date τ, the agent takes $A(\tau)$, $I(\tau)$, r and prices of goods as given.

It is also assumed that, at any time t, the instantaneous utility[4] is

$$U(t) = \left\{ \int_0^{n(t)} [x(z)]^{\alpha} dz \right\}^{\frac{1}{\alpha}} \tag{3}$$

where $0 < \alpha < 1$; $x(z) =$ quantity of good z consumed and $n = n(t)$ also stands for the index of the most recently developed good existing in the world at time t.

The dynamic optimization problem specified by (1) and (2) can be reduced to a two-stage budgeting problem, where the agent solves

[3]The 'flow equation' implied from the 'stock equation' shown here is $I(t) - E(t) + rA(t) = \dot{A}(t)$.

[4]Alternatively, $U(\tau)$ can be regarded as quantity of final goods produced from a set of intermediate goods, with production function (3).

a dynamic optimization problem of allocating $E(t)$ over time, then solves a static optimization problem of choosing the various $x(z)$ subject to a budget constraint of $E(t)$ at time t.

It is shown in Appendix A that the dynamic optimization problem has a solution which yields the equation:

$$r = \rho - (1-\sigma)\left(\frac{1-\alpha}{\alpha}\right)\frac{\dot{n}}{n} + \frac{\dot{E}}{E} \tag{4}$$

where $\frac{\dot{E}}{E}$ is the growth rate of total expenditure on goods. Equation (4) implies that the more people discount the future, the higher the interest rate needs to be to maintain the amount of savings to sustain the same growth rate of expenditure. Define $\frac{\dot{n}}{n} = g$ in steady state. We normalize by setting $\frac{\dot{E}}{E} = \frac{\dot{n}}{n}$.[5] Hence, equation (4) becomes $r = \rho + \phi g$, where $\phi = 1 - (1-\sigma)(\frac{1-\alpha}{\alpha}) \leq 1$. We assume that $\alpha \geq 1 - \sigma$ (which will include the case of logarithmic utility in the intertemporal utility function stated in equation (1)) so that $0 \leq \phi \leq 1$. This will ensure the stability of the general equilibrium.[6]

The static optimization problem of the two-stage budgeting problem is:

$$\max_{x(z)} U(t)$$

s.t.

$$\int_0^n x(z)p(z)dz = E(t). \tag{5}$$

We hereafter drop the time argument t for convenience, unless otherwise stated.

---

[5]It can be shown that this is equivalent to setting the market value of each firm to one at each date.

[6]If $\phi < 0$, then more entry into innovation activity lowers interest rate, which can increase the profit rate of innovations, leading to even more entry. This would cause instability of the steady state equilibrium.

The standard solution to the static maximization problem (5) leads to

$$x(z) = \frac{p(z)^{-\epsilon}}{\int_0^n p(u)^{1-\epsilon} du} E \tag{6}$$

where $\epsilon = \frac{1}{1-\alpha}$ is the elasticity of substitution between any two goods, and $\epsilon > 1$.

We assume constant returns to scale production technology, and that the unit labor requirement for production is the same in both countries and for all goods. Due to the symmetry of all goods in the preference function (3), $x(z)$ is the same for all goods produced in the same country.

2.2 The steady state

At time t, there are n goods existing in the world, among which n_s goods have been multinationalized and n_N goods continue to be produced in North. Therefore, $n = n_s + n_N$. Moreover, $n_s = n_i + n_m$ where n_i = number of products imitated by South; n_m = number of products produced by Northern MNCs. Because of symmetry of all goods in the demand function, x_N stands for the demand for any good produced by a Northern firm, while x_m stands for the demand for any good produced by a Northern subsidiary (MNC) in South. The variables x_N and x_m are determined by demand function (6) when the prices of the n goods are known. Because transportation cost is zero and there are no trade barriers, the producer of a good always sells to the world market. Let π_N be the instantaneous profit of a Northern firm, and π_m be that of a MNC whose product has not been imitated at that instant. Wage rates in North and South are denoted by w_N and w_s respectively.

On the 'balanced growth path', $\frac{\dot{n}_s}{n_s} = \frac{\dot{n}_i}{n_i} = \frac{\dot{n}_m}{n_m} = \frac{\dot{n}}{n} = \frac{\dot{E}}{E} = g$, and g, $\frac{n_s}{n}$, $\frac{n_i}{n}$ and $\frac{n_m}{n}$ are constant over time. It can be deduced from (6) to (8) and symmetry of all $x(z)$ in the utility function that at steady state, π_N and π_m are constant over time. L_s and L_N are the exogenous supply of labor in South and North respectively.

2.3 Innovation and international technology transfer

We assume constant returns to scale in the production of each good. There are no fixed costs of production per period, nor are there transportation costs.

Assume for simplicity that each product is developed and produced by a different firm.[7] Firms compete with each other by setting prices. Assuming time separability of the intertemporal profits function, an innovator firm or MNC producing good z chooses price $p(z)$, given the prices of other goods, to maximize instantaneous profit $\pi(z)$, subject to the demand function (6). Therefore, a Northern firm or its subsidiary in South solves $\max_{p(z)} \pi(z) = x(z)[p(z) - c(z)]$ subject to the demand function (6), where $c(z)$ is the per unit production cost of good z.

Thus, we obtain from the first order condition the mark-up pricing rule for a Northern innovator or an MNC (Dixit and Stiglitz, 1977)

$$p(z) = \frac{c(z)}{\alpha} \tag{7}$$

The market power of a Northern firm or its subsidiary can be maintained as long as its IPR are protected. The North offers full IPP, while the South only offers partial IPP. Once a product is imitated (by Southern firms), no firms producing that product have any market power, and its price will be driven down to marginal cost, and no firms can make any profits from selling that product.

Without loss of generality, we assume that the unit labor requirement for production is one, so that

$$c(z) = w \tag{8}$$

where w = wage rate in the country where production of good z takes place.

[7]It is not necessary to have all products developed by different firms, but it is necessary to have sufficiently large number of firms so that we can ignore the effects of any single producer's action on the denominator of demand function (6).

Differentiating (5) with respect to time, invoking demand equation (6), mark-up pricing equation (7) and production cost function (8), and imposing the steady state condition $\frac{\dot{E}}{E} = \frac{\dot{w}}{w}$, it can be shown that the steady state growth rate of utility $\frac{\dot{U}}{U} = (\frac{1-\alpha}{\alpha})g = (\frac{1-\alpha}{\alpha})\frac{\dot{E}}{E}$.

2.3.1 *Innovation, multinationalization and imitation*

We define the (Poisson arrival) rate of imitation by Southern firms from MNCs as $\frac{\dot{n}_i}{n_m}$, denoted by $i\delta$; and the (Poisson arrival) rate of multinationalization as $\frac{\dot{n}_s}{n_N}$, denoted by ω. The rate $i\delta$ is the 'hazard rate', i.e. the probability that a multinationalized product will be imitated at the next instant. Similarly, ω is the 'hazard rate' at which a North-produced product will be multinationalized in the next instant.[8] The rate of multinationalization ω is endogenous, based on optimization of Northern firms, as shown below. The rate of imitation δi is composed of two parts. i is assumed to be exogenously determined by technology (i.e. by how quickly the technology can be reverse engineered given the complexity of the technology); while δ is a policy parameter determined by Southern authority. A smaller δ reflects a stronger IPP. When $\delta = 0$, patent law enforcement is perfect. When $\delta = 1$, there is no enforcement of patent laws. We can interpret this as follows. Of all attempts to imitate, only a fraction δ successfully slip through the surveillance of the patent authority in the South. In this case, a smaller δ means weaker criteria in convicting violators of patents in South. An alternative interpretation is that Southern authority will enforce patent laws in a fraction δ of illegally imitated products. All firms that is not imitated have equal chance of being imitated at any date. Therefore, all MNCs face the same

[8] If we assume the duration τ between the time of multinationalization and time of imitation to have an exponential distribution with cumulative density $\Pr(\tau \leq t) = 1 - e^{-i\delta t}$, then $i\delta$ is the 'hazard rate' or Poisson arrival rate at which a good will be imitated in the next instant provided that it has not been imitated. Similarly, the cumulative density function of $\hat{\tau}$, the duration between the time of innovation and time of multinationalization, is given by $\Pr(\hat{\tau} \leq v) = 1 - e^{-\omega v}$ where ω is the Poisson arrival rate at which the product will be multinationalized in the next instant. See also Helpman (1993) for a discussion of 'hazard rate'.

$i\delta$. The fractions δi and ω are both constant over time in steady state.

Knowing $i\delta$, a Northern firm will decide whether or not to multinationalize at each date. There is symmetry among all Northern firms. At any date, the equilibrium value of ω is the one that leaves all Northern firms indifferent between multinationalizing and continuing production in North. If ω is below the equilibrium value, the PDV of profits from multinationalizing is higher than that from continuing production in the North for each firm. Thus, more Northern firms transfer their production to South, leading to an increase of ω. If ω is above the equilibrium value, there are gains from moving production back to the North. As some firms move back to the North to seek higher profits, ω decreases. Therefore, ω is a stable equilibrium.[9]

The cost of innovation

Following Grossman and Helpman (1991b), the cost of innovation (product development) by a Northern firm is assumed to be

$$C_d = a_d \frac{w_N}{n} \tag{9}$$

where a_d is the cost parameter of innovation, $\frac{1}{n}$ captures the spillover effect of knowledge generated from past innovation on efficiency of current innovation. In other words, the efficiency of product development in North increases with n, which is a proxy for the cumulative knowledge generated as by-products of all past innovations in North (Romer, 1990).

Imitation

We assume that there is zero cost of imitation. Once a product is imitated, it will be sold at marginal cost. That is, the price of a

[9]There are other reasons for Northern firms to produce in North, where production cost is higher. For example, Vernon (1966) suggested that production needs to stay in North in the standardization period, when the product design, inputs, and production process need to be standardized for large scale, more mechanized production. However, if all multinationalization decisions are due to technological factors, such as this one, then ω would be exogenous.

South-imitated product is $p_s = w_s$. This is because price competition between the MNC and the imitator(s) will drive price down to marginal cost. The imitator hires from the same pool of labor as the MNC. Since all firms face the same cost of labor, the MNC loses all profits once the product is imitated.

2.3.2 *Pricing strategy of Northern firms and MNCs*

When production location is in North, a Northern innovator-producer firm prices at the monopoly level according to (7) and (8), so that the price of a Northern good is

$$p_N = \frac{w_N}{\alpha}. \tag{10}$$

After production has been transferred through multinationalization to South, the MNC sets price at the monopoly level:

$$p_m = \frac{w_s}{\alpha} \tag{11}$$

The demand function (6), production cost function (8), and mark-up pricing rules (10), (11) show that the profit of the MNC, π_m, and that of a Northern firm, π_N, are related by

$$\frac{\pi_m}{\pi_N} = \left(\frac{w_s}{w_N}\right)^{1-\epsilon} \tag{12}$$

In equilibrium, it must be true that $\frac{w_s}{w_N} < 1$, otherwise there is no incentive to shift production location to South. Since $\epsilon > 1$, it must be true that $\pi_m > \pi_N$ in equilibrium. It is shown below that this must be true in equilibrium.

2.3.3 *Multinationalization equilibrium*

The expected present discounted value (PDV) of profits of a Northern MNC *with* Poisson arrival imitation rate $i\delta$ is

$$\Pi_m = \frac{\pi_m}{r + i\delta} \tag{13}$$

For more detailed derivation and interpretation of the equation, refer to Appendix B and Lee and Wilde (1980).

Let Π_N be the PDV of profits for a Northern firm if the innovator never multinationalizes. It is clear that $\Pi_N = \pi_N/r$. Since in steady state equilibrium the typical firm is indifferent between multinationalization and continuing production in North, it must be true that the PDV of a Northern firm's profits is Π_N regardless of whether it eventually multinationalizes. Therefore $\Pi_N = \Pi_m$ in steady state equilibrium. Hence,

$$\frac{\pi_N}{\pi_m} = \frac{r}{\delta i + r} \tag{14}$$

The above equation shows that because of the risk of being imitated, the instantaneous profit of Southern MNC must be larger than that from Northern production in equilibrium.

2.3.4 *Northern free entry condition*

Finally, free entry and profit maximization of Northern firms imply that the expected PDV of profits in the future must be equal to the cost of innovation in steady state equilibrium. Therefore,

$$\frac{\pi_N}{r} = \Pi_N = \frac{a_d}{n} w_N \tag{15}$$

3 Solution of the Model

3.1 Reduced form equations in steady state

In this section, we want to find the reduced form of (i) Northern free entry condition and (ii) multinationalization equilibrium in terms of two variables, g and ω. Then we shall be able to find the effects of changes in the parameters on g, ω and other endogenous variables. Because unit labor requirement for all goods is one, as shown in (8), and price is constant mark-up over cost as shown in (10) and (11), we have $\pi_m = x_m(p_m - w_s) = x_m w_s(\frac{1-\alpha}{\alpha})$ where $x_m = \frac{L_m}{n_m}$ and L_m is the quantity of labor hired by MNCs (for production) in South; Similarly, $\pi_N = x_N w_N(\frac{1-\alpha}{\alpha})$ where $x_N = \frac{L_N^p}{n_N}$ and L_N^p = quantity of labor devoted to production in North.

Hence, we have

$$\pi_m = \frac{L_m}{n_m} w_s \left(\frac{1-\alpha}{\alpha}\right) \tag{16}$$

$$\pi_N = \frac{L_N^p}{n_N} w_N \left(\frac{1-\alpha}{\alpha}\right) \tag{17}$$

From Appendix C, it can be shown that

$$L_m = \frac{L_s}{\frac{\delta i}{g}\alpha^{-\epsilon} + 1} \tag{18}$$

In North the quantity of labor devoted to R&D is equal to $a_d \frac{\dot{n}}{n} = a_d g$ at each date. Therefore,

$$L_N^p = L_N - a_d g \tag{19}$$

Moreover, it can be shown that in steady state[10]

$$\frac{n_s}{n_N} = \frac{\omega}{g} \quad \text{and} \quad \frac{n}{n_N} = \frac{\omega}{g} + 1 \quad \text{and} \quad \frac{n_m}{n_N} = \frac{\omega}{g + i\delta} \tag{20}$$

Divide (17) by (16), and, in the resulting equation, substitute for $\frac{w_s}{w_N}$, $\frac{\pi_m}{\pi_N}$, L_m, L_N^p and $\frac{n_m}{n_N}$ from (12), (14), (18), (19) and (20) respectively, we obtain the reduced form of the multinationalization equilibrium in terms of g and ω:

$$\left[\frac{\omega}{g}\left(\frac{g + i\delta\alpha^{-\epsilon}}{g + i\delta}\right)\left(\frac{L_N - a_d g}{L_s}\right)\right]^{\alpha} = \frac{r}{\delta i + r} \tag{21}$$

To obtain the reduced form of Northern free entry condition in terms of g and ω, we invoke (15), (17), (19) and (20) to obtain

$$\left(\frac{1-\alpha}{\alpha}\right)(L_N - a_d g)\left(\frac{\omega}{g} + 1\right) = a_d r \tag{22}$$

[10]By definition, $\frac{n_s}{n_N} = \frac{n_s}{n - n_s} = \frac{\dot{n}_s}{n - n_s}\left(\frac{n_s}{\dot{n}_s}\right) = \frac{\omega}{g}$ in steady state. Moreover, $\frac{n_m}{n_N} = \left(\frac{n_m}{n_s}\right)\left(\frac{n_s}{n_N}\right)$. By definition, $\dot{n}_i = n_m i\delta$, which implies that $n_i g = n_m i\delta \Rightarrow (n_s - n_m)g = n_m i\delta \Rightarrow \frac{n_m}{n_s} = \frac{g}{\delta i + g}$. Hence, $\frac{n_m}{n_N} = \frac{\omega}{\delta i + g}$.

Therefore, we have obtained two equations (21) and (22) in two unknowns g and ω. We are now ready to carry out the comparative steady state analysis concerning the two variables.

3.2 Comparative steady states analysis

If we express $\frac{\omega}{g}$ in terms of g from (22) and substitute the expression into (21), we obtain

$$\left[\left(\frac{g+i\delta\alpha^{-\epsilon}}{g+i\delta}\right)\left(\frac{a_d r\left(\frac{\alpha}{1-\alpha}\right)-L_N+a_d g}{L_s}\right)\right]^{\alpha}=\frac{r}{\delta i+r} \tag{23}$$

where $r=\rho+\phi g$. It must be true that $L_N > a_d\rho\frac{\alpha}{1-\alpha}$ if North can sustain positive growth as a closed economy.[11] It is demonstrated in Appendix D that an increase in g leads to an increase in $\frac{\text{LHS}}{\text{RHS}}$ of the above equation.[12] On the other hand, an increase in δ leads to an increase in $\frac{\text{LHS}}{\text{RHS}}$ of the equation. It follows, from the implicit function theorem, that a decrease in δ leads to an increase in g. That is, a strengthening of IPP in South increases the rate of innovation in North. Moreover, from (22), an increase in g corresponds to an increase in $\frac{\omega}{g}$, which implies that ω must also increase. That is, the rate of multinationalization also increases with stronger IPP in South.

The intuition is as follows. Northern firms move production to South to take advantage of the lower wage, which they balance against the probability that they will lose their monopoly to imitators after multinationalization. A stronger IPP in South increases the rate of innovation in two stages. First, it increases the expected lives of monopolies. However, because the resulting increase in demand for labor falls entirely on South, the return to innovation rises without a rise in cost. Second, since the return to multinationalization increases, firms will move more quickly to South on the average

[11]Without production transfer to South, the equilibrium condition in North is $\frac{1-\alpha}{\alpha}(L_N-a_d g)=a_d(\rho+\phi g)$, which implies that $L_N > a_d\rho\frac{\alpha}{1-\alpha}$.

[12]LHS = left hand side; RHS = right hand side.

(rate of multinationalization increases). This lowers the demand for Northern labor, Northern wage, and costs, thus increasing the return to innovation further.

Relative wage between North and South
From (12) and (14),

$$\frac{w_s}{w_N} = \left(\frac{\pi_N}{\pi_m}\right)^{\frac{1}{\epsilon-1}} = \left(\frac{\rho + \phi g}{i\delta + \rho + \phi g}\right)^{\frac{1}{\epsilon-1}} \tag{24}$$

A decrease in δ leads to an increase in g, both leading to an increase in the relative wage in South. An increase in IPP leads to more production shifted to South, increasing the demand for Southern labor. Therefore, an increase in IPP leads to an increase in relative wage (or terms of trade) of South.

Result 1. *Stronger IPP leads to higher rate of innovation, higher rate of production transfer from North to South and higher wage of South relative to the North if multinationalization is the channel of international production transfer.*

It might be argued that the imitated products can only be sold in South since the products violate the patent laws of the North. In that case, an MNC loses its profits only in the Southern market when its product is imitated, and its profits in North are preserved. It is shown in an appendix, available from the author upon request, that the qualitative aspects of the results are preserved even with this modification.

4 Imitation as the Channel of Production Transfer

This section is essentially Grossman and Helpman's (1991b) model adapted to the environment of this paper. We now modify the model specified in Sections 2 and 3. Assume that instead of FDI, imitation is the only channel of production transfer from North to South. Let the (Poisson arrival) rate of imitation from North-produced products be $j\delta$. Since there is no multinationalization, $\omega = 0$, and $n_m = 0$. Therefore, the total number of goods imitated is n_s. Hence, $j\delta = \frac{\dot{n}_s}{n_N}$. In steady state, $g = \frac{\dot{n}_s}{n_s}$. Also, $n = n_s + n_N$ continues to hold. By the same token as before, we can derive the Northern free entry condition as

$$\frac{\pi_N}{j\delta + r} = \Pi_N = \frac{a_d}{n} w_N$$

the reduced form of which is

$$\left(\frac{1-\alpha}{\alpha}\right)(L_N - a_d g)\left(\frac{j\delta}{g} + 1\right) = a_d(\rho + \phi g + j\delta) \tag{25}$$

since $\frac{n}{n_N} = \frac{n_s}{n_N} + 1 = \frac{j\delta}{g} + 1$.

This equation is the same as the NN curve is Grossman and Helpman (1991b). Since discount must dominate growth in order for the intertemporal budget to be finite, it must be the case that $r > g$. Therefore, $\frac{\partial}{\partial \delta}(\frac{r+j\delta}{g+j\delta}) < 0$. It follows from (25) that a decrease in δ will *decrease* g. Hence, a stronger IPP in South leads to *lower* rate of product innovation in North, as in Grossman and Helpman (1991b) and Helpman (1993).

The intuition for the above result is: If South can only acquire technology by imitation of goods produced in North, there are two counteracting effects of enforcing stronger IPP in South. First, it lowers the rate of imitation and prolongs the expected duration of monopoly of each Northern innovator. This raises the returns to innovation. Second, since firms produce longer in North, it raises the demand for Northern labor and Northern wage and hence raises the cost of innovation. Thus, it lowers the profit from innovation at each date. As shown by Grossman and Helpman, it turns out that the second effect dominates the first one (as r is necessarily greater than g), and the rate of innovation declines.

Relative wage between North and South

Let x_s be the demand for a good produced by a Southern imitator. According to (6) and $p_s = w_s$, the demand for goods produced in South relative to that of North is

$$\frac{x_s}{x_N} = \left(\frac{w_s}{w_N/\alpha}\right)^{-\epsilon}$$

Since $L_S = n_S x_S$, and $L_N - a_d g = n_N x_N$, and $\frac{n_S}{n_N} = \frac{j\delta}{g}$, it can be easily shown that

$$\frac{w_S}{w_N} = \left(\frac{L_S}{L_N}\frac{g}{j\delta}\right)^{-\frac{1}{\epsilon}}\frac{1}{\alpha}.$$

From (25), a decrease in δ leads to a decrease in g, which in turn leads to a decrease in $\frac{j\delta}{g}$. It follows that $\frac{w_S}{w_N}$ decreases. Therefore, $\frac{w_S}{w_N}$ decreases as IPP is strengthened, a result opposite to that obtained in Section 3. Here, since imitation is the only channel of production transfer to South, stronger IPP in South lowers the number of products produced by South and hence lowers the demand for Southern labor, leading to lower relative wage of South.

Result 2. *Stronger IPP leads to lower rate of innovation, lower rate of production transfer from North to South and lower wage of South relative to the North if imitation is the channel of international production transfer.*

The summary of Results 1 and 2 is shown in the following table:

In Appendix E, we show the more general case that both imitation and multinationalization (prior to imitation) are channels of production transfer at the same time. Assuming that IPP is enforced to the same degree before or after multinationalization, it is shown that a stronger IPP has the impact as shown in the middle column of Table 1 when the rate of multinationalization is sufficiently large ($\omega \geq \rho$) or the rate of imitation (prior to multinationalization) is small. Therefore, we have

Table 1. Effects of stronger IPP.

	Channel of production transfer	
	Multinationalization	Imitation
Rate of Innovation	**increase**	**decrease**
Rate of Prod. Transf.	**increase**	**decrease**
Relative wage of S.	**increase**	**decrease**

Result 3. *If both imitation and multinationalization are channels of production transfer, stronger Southern IPP leads to higher rate of innovation in the North, higher rate of production transfer to the South and higher Southern relative wage as long as the rate of multinationalization is sufficiently high or the rate of pre-FDI imitation is small.*

5 Conclusion

The effects of IPP in South depends crucially on whether imitation or multinationalization (prior to imitation) is the channel of international production transfer from North to South. If imitation is the channel of production transfer, stronger IPP lowers the rate of innovation, rate of technology transfer and wage of South relative to North; if multinationalization is the channel of production transfer, IPP has exactly the opposite effects. The latter results hold even when both channels co-exist, as long as the rate of multinationalization is sufficiently large or the rate of imitation (prior to multinationalization) is sufficiently small. Therefore, the literature which focuses on imitation as the sole channel of production transfer from North to South can lead to misleading implications. The consequence of changes that increase the rate of Southern imitation of Northern goods on global economic growth, international technology diffusion and world income distribution can be very different from what this literature predicts.

Although our analysis has focused on the effects of IPP in the South, we can actually interpret IPP more broadly as any incentive given by South to encourage Northern FDI. Interpreted this way, our theoretical results can be tested empirically in a variety of situations.

We have abstracted from other key factors that affect the rate of multinationalization from North to South. For example, the rate of standardization of technology will constrain the rate of FDI, since a production can only be readily transferred to another country after the inputs, designs, etc. have been standardized in the home country, as suggested by Vernon (1966). Also, (the fear of) trade barriers such as tariffs and quotas imposed by another country will accelerate the rate of multinationalization of a production, as in the case of Japanese motorcycle firms setting up in Taiwan, or US and Japanese firms setting up in the European Union before its establishment.

There are some other important caveats. First, we have used a general equilibrium model with one 'knowledge-intensive' production sector. We have assumed that labor supply is constant in this sector in both North and South. Because of the absence of a non-knowledge-intensive sector, we cannot account for the effects of IPP on resource allocation between the knowledge-intensive and non-knowledge-intensive sectors, which will have repercussions on the rate of innovation and production transfer. This should be the goal of our next research. Second, we have not looked at the effects of IPP on the welfare of South, which is certainly a concern of policy-makers. Third, and not the least, the use of a product cycle ignores the possibility of endogenous innovation taking place in South. Our intuition is that a stronger IPP in South should encourage domestic innovation while discourage domestic imitation in South. It will be interesting to find out the effects of IPP on both the rate of imitation and innovation in South in a more general model where Southern firms choose between imitation and innovation.

There are several possible extensions of the paper in future work. First, we can make imitation costly, and, consequently, profitable in equilibrium. Second, for realism, we should capture the likely outcome that multinationals bear higher labor cost than local firms, though lower cost than firms in North. Third, multinationalization is a risky business when compared with production in North, and so there should be a risk premium associated with FDI. Fourth, both Northern firms and multinationals may face the risk of imitation. The imitation costs should be different in the two cases. An increase in IPP, which increases imitation costs, would likely affect the rate of innovation, total rate of production transfer, etc. in more interesting ways.

Appendix

A. Derivation of Equation (4)

From (3) and symmetry of all goods,

$$U = (nx^{\alpha})^{\frac{1}{\alpha}} = n^{\frac{1}{\alpha}}x = n^{\frac{1}{\alpha}}\frac{E}{np} = n^{\frac{1-\alpha}{\alpha}}\frac{E}{p} \tag{A1}$$

The current value Hamiltonian to the dynamic optimization problem (1) and (2) is

$$H = \frac{U^{1-\sigma}-1}{1-\sigma} + m[I(t) - E(t) + rA(t)]$$

where m is the current value Lagrangian multiplier. The first order condition is therefore

$$H_E = U^{-\sigma}\frac{\partial U}{\partial E} - m = 0$$

From (A1), $\frac{\partial U}{\partial E} = \frac{n^{\frac{1-\alpha}{\alpha}}}{p}$. Therefore,

$$m = \frac{U^{-\sigma}n^{\frac{1-\alpha}{\alpha}}}{p}. \tag{A2}$$

Another first order condition is

$$\dot{m} = \rho m - H_A = \rho m - rm = (\rho - r)m \tag{A3}$$

(A2) implies that $\frac{\dot{m}}{m} = -\sigma\frac{\dot{U}}{U} + (\frac{1-\alpha}{\alpha})\frac{\dot{n}}{n} - \frac{\dot{p}}{p}$. Substituting this into (A3), we obtain

$$\rho - r = -\sigma\frac{\dot{U}}{U} + \left(\frac{1-\alpha}{\alpha}\right)\frac{\dot{n}}{n} - \frac{\dot{p}}{p} \tag{A4}$$

Now, (A1) implies that

$$\frac{\dot{U}}{U} = \left(\frac{1-\alpha}{\alpha}\right)\frac{\dot{n}}{n} + \frac{\dot{E}}{E} - \frac{\dot{p}}{p} = \left(\frac{1-\alpha}{\alpha}\right)\frac{\dot{n}}{n}. \tag{A5}$$

The last equality comes from the fact that $npx = E$ which implies $pX = E$, where X is total labor devoted to production (which is constant over time in steady state). Substituting (A5) into (A4), and imposing the normalization $\frac{\dot{n}}{n} = \frac{\dot{E}}{E} = \frac{\dot{p}}{p}$, we obtain

$$\rho - r = (1-\sigma)\left(\frac{1-\alpha}{\alpha}\right)\frac{\dot{n}}{n} - \frac{\dot{E}}{E}. \qquad \square$$

B. Discounted Expected Profits of an MNC

We assume that the duration τ between the date of multinationalization and date of imitation is a random variable with exponential distribution, having a Poisson arrival rate δi:

$$\Pr(\tau \leq t) = f(t) = 1 - e^{-i\delta t}$$

Therefore,

$$\Pr(\tau = t) = f'(t) = i\delta e^{-i\delta t}$$

The expected PDV of profits of an MNC at the time of multinationalization is

$$\Pi_m = \int_0^{\infty}\left(\int_0^t \pi_m e^{-rs} ds\right)\Pr(\tau = t)dt$$

It is straightforward to show that the RHS is equal to $\frac{\pi_m}{r+i\delta}$.

C. Expression for L_m in Section 3

By definition,

$$\frac{L_s}{L_m} = \frac{n_i x_i + n_m x_m}{n_m x_m} = \frac{n_i}{n_m}\left(\frac{x_i}{x_m}\right) + 1$$

On the other hand, from (6) and (7),

$$\frac{x_i}{x_m} = \left(\frac{w_s}{w_s/\alpha}\right)^{-\epsilon} = \alpha^{-\epsilon} > 1.$$

Moreover,

$$\frac{n_i}{n_m} = \frac{\dot{n}_i}{n_m}\frac{n_i}{\dot{n}_i} = \frac{\delta i}{g}.$$

Hence, substituting the last two equations into the first equation, we obtain

$$L_m = \frac{L_s}{\frac{\delta i}{g}\alpha^{-\epsilon} + 1}.$$

D. Comparative Steady States Analysis in the Multinationalization Regime

To compute the effect of an decrease in δ on g, we shall use the implicit function theorem.

Let $P = \rho + \phi g$, $Q = g + i\delta$, $R = g - A$ and $S = \rho + \phi g + i\delta$, where $A = \frac{L_N}{a_d} - \rho(\frac{\alpha}{1-\alpha}) > 0$. Now,

$$\frac{\partial}{\partial g}\left(\frac{\text{LHS}_{23}}{\text{RHS}_{23}}\right) > 0 \quad \text{as long as} \quad \frac{\partial}{\partial g}\left(\frac{R^\alpha S}{PQ^\alpha}\right) > 0$$

where LHS_i (RHS_i) denotes left hand side (right hand side) of equation i. And

$$\frac{\partial}{\partial g}\left(\frac{R^\alpha S}{PQ^\alpha}\right) = \frac{1}{P^2Q^{2\alpha}}[PQ^\alpha(\phi R^\alpha + S\alpha R^{\alpha-1}) - R^\alpha S(P\alpha Q^{\alpha-1} + \phi Q^\alpha)]$$

$$= \frac{1}{P^2Q^{2\alpha}}[PQ^{\alpha-1}R^\alpha(\phi Q - \alpha S) + Q^\alpha S R^{\alpha-1}(\alpha P - \phi R)] \qquad \text{(D1)}$$

Now, $\phi Q - \alpha S = -[\alpha\rho - (1-\alpha)\phi g - (\phi - \alpha)i\delta]$, while $\alpha P - \phi R = \alpha\rho + A\phi - (1-\alpha)\phi g$. Since $A > 0$, the latter is positive as long as $0 \le \phi \le 1$ and $g < \frac{L_N}{a_d}$. The last inequality must be true since $\frac{L_N}{a_d}$ is the innovation rate when all labor in North is used for innovation. If $\phi Q - \alpha S > 0$, RHS_{31} is obviously positive. Suppose, however, that $\phi Q - \alpha S < 0$. The fact that $Q > R$ and $S > P$ implies that $PQ^{\alpha-1}R^\alpha < Q^\alpha S R^{\alpha-1}$. The assumption $\alpha \ge 1 - \sigma$ stated in Section 2.1 implies that $\phi \ge \alpha$. If $\phi Q - \alpha S < 0$, it is clear that $|\phi Q - \alpha S| < |\alpha P - \phi R|$. It follows from (D1) that $\frac{\partial}{\partial g}(\frac{R^\alpha S}{PQ^\alpha}) > 0$.

It is straightforward to show that $\frac{\partial}{\partial\delta}(\frac{\text{LHS}_{23}}{\text{RHS}_{23}}) > 0$. Therefore, by the implicit function theorem, $\frac{dg}{d\delta} < 0$, and stronger IPP leads to higher rate of innovation.

E. Both Multinationalization and Imitation Are Channels of Production Transfer

We assume that Southern firms can imitate from Northern firms or the subsidiaries of Northern firms in South. It is assumed for simplicity that all products are equally protected under Southern patent laws. However, it seems reasonable to assume that it is technically harder to imitate from Northern firms than from their subsidiaries in South when both are equally protected under Southern jurisdiction. Therefore, the imitation rate of North-produced product, $j\delta$, is assumed to be less than the imitation rate of MNC-produced product in South, $i\delta$, or $j < i$.

Hence, it is straightforward to show that the counterparts of (14), (21) and (22) are, respectively,

$$\frac{\pi_N}{\pi_m} = \frac{\delta j + r}{\delta i + r}$$

$$\left[\frac{\omega}{g}\left(\frac{g + i\delta\alpha^{-\epsilon}}{g + i\delta}\right)\left(\frac{L_N - a_d g}{L_s}\right)\right]^{\alpha} = \frac{\delta j + r}{\delta i + r}$$

$$\left(\frac{1-\alpha}{\alpha}\right)(L_N - a_d g)\left(\frac{\omega + \delta j}{g} + 1\right) = a_d(r + \delta j) \tag{E1}$$

The last two equations reduce to

$$\left[\left(\frac{g + i\delta\alpha^{-\epsilon}}{g + i\delta}\right)\left(\frac{a_d(r + \delta j)\left(\frac{\alpha}{1-\alpha}\right) - (L_N - a_d g)\left(1 + \frac{\delta j}{g}\right)}{L_s}\right)\right]^{\alpha}$$
$$= \frac{\delta j + r}{\delta i + r} \tag{E2}$$

The LHS of (E2) is re-written as

$$\left[\left(\frac{g+i\delta\alpha^{-\epsilon}}{g+i\delta}\right)\right.$$
$$\left.\times\left(\frac{\left[a_d\left(\frac{\alpha}{1-\alpha}\right)-\left(\frac{L_N-a_dg}{g}\right)\right]\delta j+a_dr\left(\frac{\alpha}{1-\alpha}\right)-(L_N-a_dg)}{L_s}\right)\right]^{\alpha}$$

Define $D \equiv a_d(\frac{\alpha}{1-\alpha}) - (\frac{L_N-a_dg}{g})$. It follows that $\frac{\partial}{\partial\delta}(\frac{\text{LHS}_{33}}{\text{RHS}_{33}}) > 0$ if $D \geq 0$. On the other hand, from (E1), $(\frac{1-\alpha}{\alpha})(L_N - a_dg) = a_d(\frac{r+\delta j}{\omega+g+\delta j})g$. Therefore, $D \geq 0$ iff $(\frac{1-\alpha}{\alpha})(L_N - a_dg) \leq a_dg \Leftrightarrow a_d(\frac{r+\delta j}{\omega+g+\delta j})g \leq a_dg \Leftrightarrow \omega + g \geq r = \rho + \phi g \Leftrightarrow \omega + (1-\phi)g \geq \rho$. A sufficient condition of the last inequality is $\omega \geq \rho$. Therefore, a sufficient condition for $\frac{\partial}{\partial\delta}(\frac{\text{LHS}_{33}}{\text{RHS}_{33}}) > 0$ is $\omega \geq \rho$. The other sufficient condition for $\frac{\partial}{\partial\delta}(\frac{\text{LHS}_{33}}{\text{RHS}_{33}}) > 0$ is, of course, when j is sufficiently small so that the effect of $j\delta$ on $\frac{\text{LHS}_{33}}{\text{RHS}_{33}}$ is small.

If North can sustain positive growth without multinationalization, then $L_N > a_d(\rho+\delta j)(\frac{\alpha}{1-\alpha})$. Hence, by a similar derivation as the one stated in Appendix D, $\frac{\partial}{\partial g}(\frac{\text{LHS}_{33}}{\text{RHS}_{33}}) > 0$. By the implicit function theorem, therefore, a sufficient condition for $\frac{dg}{d\delta} < 0$ is $\omega \geq \rho$. That is, stronger Southern IPP leads to higher rate of innovation in North as long as $\omega \geq \rho$, or if j is small.

Acknowledgment

The financial support of the project from John M. Olin Foundation is gratefully acknowledged. The author is grateful to helpful discussions and comments from Joseph E. Stiglitz, Robert W. Staiger, Paul M. Romer, Danyang Xie, Andres Rodriguez-Clare, Sean Durkin on earlier versions and Andrea Maneschi, Horst Raff and two anonymous referees on the current version.

References

Dixit, A. and Stiglitz, J. E. (1977). Monopolistic competition and optimum product diversity, *American Economic Review* 67, 297–308.

Grossman, G. M. and Helpman, E. (1991a). Quality ladder and product cycles, *Quarterly Journal of Economy* 106, 557–586.
Grossman, G. M. and Helpman, E. (1991b). Endogenous product cycles, *Economic Journal* 101, 1214–1229.
Grossman, G. M. and Helpman, E. (1991c). *Innovation and Growth in the Global Economy*, MIT Press, Cambridge, Massachusetts, USA.
Helpman, E. (1993). Innovation, imitation and intellectual property rights, *Econometrica* 61(6), 1247–1280.
Krugman, P. R. (1979). A model of innovation, technology transfer, and the world distribution of income, *Journal of Political Economy* 87, 253–266.
Lee, T. and Wilde, L. L. (1980). Market structure and innovation: A reformulation, *Quarterly Journal of Economics* 94, 431–436.
Loury, G. (1979). Market structure and innovation, *Quarterly Journal of Economics* 93, 395–410.
Romer, P. M. (1990). Endogenous technological change, *Journal of Political Economy* 98, S71–S102.
Romer, P. M. (1991). Increasing returns and new developments in the theory of growth, in Barnett, W. A., *et al.* (eds.), *Equilibrium Theory and Applications: Proceedings of the Sixth International Symposium in Economic Theory and Econometrics*, Cambridge: Cambridge University Press, pp. 83–110.
Schumpeter, J. A. (1950). *Capitalism, Socialism and Democracy*, Harper and Row, New York, USA.
Segerstrom, P., Anant, T. C. A., and Dinopoulos, E. (1990). A Schumpeterian model of the product life cycle, *American Economic Review* 80(5), 1077–1091.
Vernon, R. (1966). International investment and international trade in the product cycle, *Quarterly Journal of Economics* 80, 190–207.

Chapter 6

The North's Intellectual Property Rights Standard for the South?*

Abstract
We build a multi-sectoral North-South trade model to analyze international intellectual property rights (IPR) protection. By comparing the Nash equilibrium IPR protection standard of the South (the developing countries) with that of the North (the developed countries), we find that the former is naturally weaker than the latter. Moreover, we show that both regions can gain from an agreement that requires the South to harmonize its IPR standards with those of the North, and the North to liberalize its traditional goods market. This demonstrates the merits of multi-sectoral negotiations in the GATT/WTO.

1 Introduction

One important breakthrough of the Uruguay Round of the General Agreement on Tariffs and Trade (GATT) is the signing of the Agreement on Trade-Related Aspects of Intellectual Property Rights (the TRIPS Agreement), which stipulates that all members adopt a

*By Edwin L.-C. Lai and Larry D. Qiu. Originally published in *Journal of International Economics*, 59 (2003), pp. 183–209. Copyright © 2003 by Elsevier Science B.V. It has been reprinted with revisions and permission from the original publisher.

set of universal minimum standards on intellectual property rights (IPR) protection.[1] According to many observers (e.g. Reichman, 1995), most of the terms of the agreement are based on the prevailing standards in developed countries (the North) at the time of the negotiation. The major consequence is that developing countries (the South) have to strengthen substantially the legal protection of IPR. Based on this observation, it is often argued that the agreement "forces" the South to harmonize its IPR standards with those of the North.

The TRIPS Agreement has raised several questions. For example, has the South been doing too little to protect IPR (from the South's and the global welfare points of view)? What are the welfare consequences, for the South, the North and the world, from strengthening IPR protection in the South? From the global welfare point of view, does the South protect too much if it adopts the North's IPR standard? How can we make the TRIPS Agreement compatible with the South's incentive? Answers to these questions would help us address other important issues as well. For example, if raising the South's IPR standard improves the world's welfare, then the TRIPS can potentially make all regions better off. This paper deals with the above questions and issues.

We build a model with two regions in the world, the North and the South, which trade two types of goods, differentiated products and traditional products. Innovation and imitation are carried out in the differentiated-products sectors of both regions. We assume that the North and the South adopted their respective Nash equilibrium IPR standards before the TRIPS was put in place, and the TRIPS Agreement requires both regions to adopt the pre-TRIPS IPR standard of the North as a minimum standard. The cost-benefit

[1]See UNCTAD (1997) and Maskus (1998, 2000) for more about the TRIPS Agreement and related issues.

analysis we adopt is not fundamentally different from Nordhaus's (1969) classical work in which he calculates the optimal patent length. Like his analysis, our optimal IPR protection strikes an optimal balance between the gains from increased R&D efforts and the deadweight losses resulting from the prolonged monopoly power of the innovators. Based on our analysis, we find that the South's equilibrium IPR standard is naturally not as strong as that of the North. Moreover, it is globally welfare-improving for the South to raise its IPR standard to harmonize with the North's pre-TRIPS level. The major effects of the TRIPS are: the South's consumers lose by paying higher prices, the North's producers gain higher profits, but all consumers gain from a larger variety of goods. On balance, the South's welfare decreases, the North's increases, but the total welfare of the two regions rises, because of the existence of a positive inter-regional externality. The externality arises because an increase in a region's IPR protection raises the profits of firms and enlarges the product variety in another region without raising the deadweight loss in the latter. However, an agreement that requires the South to raise its IPR standard without compensation benefits the North at the expense of the South, and would not be compatible with the South's incentive.

Therefore, we extend the above IPR model to incorporate multi-sectoral bargaining between the North and South to show that multi-sectoral negotiations (or multi-issue negotiations) in GATT/WTO can be mutually beneficial to both regions. For example, it would benefit both regions for the South to harmonize its IPR standard with the North's, in exchange for the North lowering its import tariffs against South's exports of traditional products. In this case, multi-issue negotiations can achieve incentive-compatible and mutually beneficial outcomes while single-issue negotiations cannot, since it is globally welfare-improving for each side to make concessions on a different issue.

There have been many theoretical and empirical studies on the effects of IPR protection on innovation, trade, foreign direct investment and economic growth.[2] As far as we are aware, however, the present paper is among the first to assume that both the North and the South have innovative capabilities and to consider optimal degrees of IPR protection for the North, the South and the world as a whole. It is also among the first to analyze the merits of raising the South's IPR protection in the broader context of multi-sectoral (or multi-issue) negotiations, such as in the GATT or WTO. There are some other studies in the literature that are related to our study in one way or another. Both Chin and Grossman (1990) and Deardorff (1992) examine welfare effects of extending IPR protection from the North to the South. They find, as we do, that many results depend on the size of the South's market.[3] However, there are two notable differences between these papers and our study. First, they assume that the South does not have innovative capability. Second, they examine only the case in which the South has either full or no IPR protection. Diwan and Rodrik (1991) also consider various degrees of IPR protection in the North and the South. Interestingly, they find that to maximize the global welfare, which is the equally weighted sum of the North's and the South's welfare, the rates of patent protection in the two regions must be identical. They emphasize the taste difference between the two regions and assume no innovative capability in the South. Helpman (1993) uses a dynamic general equilibrium North-South model to study IPR protection, growth and welfare. He assumes that the North specializes in innovation and the South specializes in imitation. He finds that tightening IPR protection in the South hurts the South and may or may not benefit the North. We believe that this result needs to be modified if we

[2]See, for example, Mansfield (1986), Maskus and Penubarti (1995), Gould and Gruben (1996), Richardson and Gaisford (1996), Horowitz and Lai (1996), Lai (1998), and Glass and Saggi (2002). For example, Lai (1998) finds that, since stronger IPR protection in the South can increase the rate of innovation, there is a tradeoff between the dynamic gains and static losses from strengthening IPR protection in the South.

[3]In particular, Deardorff (1992) shows that global welfare will be reduced if the North's IPR standard is extended to a very large part of the South. In a related study, Yang (1998) argues that because of the free-rider problem existing among the Southern countries, the South's IPR protection is too weak.

take into account the South's innovative capability. We examine this issue in our partial equilibrium model, which is able to include a more detailed microeconomic analysis of firm and government behaviors.[4] Unlike our work, none of the above-mentioned papers deals with the incentive-compatibility issue of the South's concessions in IPR. Our result that multi-issue negotiation makes both the South and North better off echoes the recent literature on linkage issue related to international trade negotiations (see Horstmann *et al.*, 2001).

More recently, McCalman (2001) makes estimates of the transfer of income from consumers to producers (mostly a transfer from South to North) resulted from the TRIPS. However, he does not estimate the welfare gains from larger product variety, which can be substantial. As we argue below, such a gain would actually outweigh the deadweight loss so that a rise in the South's IPR protection is globally welfare-improving.[5]

The organization of the chapter is as follows. Section 2 lays out the basic features of the model and derives the Nash equilibrium pre-TRIPS IPR standards in the two regions. Section 3 examines the effect of varying the South's IPR protection standard on global welfare. Section 4 introduces a bargaining game between the two regions in a multi-sectoral negotiation. Section 5 summarizes the findings.

2 A Multi-Sectoral Model with IPR Protection

There are two regions in the world, the North and the South. The North has higher innovative capability than the South. There are two distinct regimes, the pre-TRIPS regime and the post-TRIPS

[4]Taylor (1993) has an interesting study on how firms in the North respond to lax IPR protection in the South by creating market-made protection, i.e. technology masquing.

[5]He finds that the net transfers the US receives from the TRIPS to be up to 40% of the gains associated with trade liberalization in the WTO, while the developing countries pay net transfers of up to 64% of the gains they receive from trade liberalization. The large amount of transfers involved shows that the IPR issue can indeed be an important leverage for the South to elicit trade concessions from the North.

regime. We assume that in the pre-TRIPS regime, the North and the South adopt their respective Nash equilibrium IPR standards. While the TRIPS Agreement covers extensive issues, it is a widely shared view that establishing a global minimum IPR standard is the key.[6] To capture the view that the TRIPS adopted the prevailing IPR standard of the North at the time of signing the agreement, we assume that in the post-TRIPS regime the North's pre-TRIPS IPR standard is set as the minimum standard for both regions. We shall derive the Nash equilibrium IPR standards in the pre-TRIPS regime in this section; in the next section, we evaluate welfare consequence of the TRIPS Agreement.

2.1 Preliminaries

There are two traded sectors in each region: a differentiated goods sector and a traditional good sector. First let us focus on the differentiated products sector. Consider one or many industries with very high potential for product innovation. Assume that any newly developed product will become obsolete after T periods.[7] Although IPR protection refers to a broad range of legal activities, here we use patent protection as representative of IPR protection. Region k's government sets a patent length T_k for $k \in \{s, n\}$, where s denotes the South and n denotes the North. We assume "national treatment", i.e. governments provide the same protection to all firms, regardless of where they are invented. This had been practiced by many countries even before TRIPS. All imitated products are prohibited from being produced or sold in region k for T_k periods. The time horizon is infinite. At the beginning of period 0, both governments announce and immediately enforce patent length of T_s and T_n respectively for all goods invented in or after period 0. In each period, potential innovators decide whether or not to make individual R&D investments. If they do, differentiated products will

[6]See Hoekman and Kostecki (1995) for example.

[7]T can be regarded as the length of the product cycle. After T periods, the product has no economic value.

be developed. We assume that innovators (i.e. firms) and consumers face exactly the same environment in every period. (We can imagine there is a pool of resources that can perform product development and production every period.) Thus, potential innovators will take the same R&D action in every period. In particular, the same *numbers* of differentiated products will be developed in every period. Let M_k be the number of differentiated products developed in region k in each period. We assume that the sets of products developed in the North and South are non-intersecting, and so a product developed in one region is different from any product developed in the other region. Products invented in different periods are necessarily different to qualify for IPR protection. The same firm could develop many products in many periods. Nonetheless, for ease of exposition, we treat different products (whether in the same period or not) as being invented by different firms.

Before period T, the numbers of differentiated products (invented under the new IPR regime) whose patents have expired as well as not expired change from one period to the next. After period T, these numbers become steady. Therefore, a steady state is attained after period T. To simplify the analysis, we assume that there is no discount of the future. Since there is no discounting, we can focus our attention on the steady-state flow welfare for the purpose of welfare analysis. This can be justified by "overtaking criterion" in dynamic optimization theory.[8] In every steady-state period, there are TM_s South-invented products that are economically viable and TM_n North-invented products that are economically viable, of which $T_s(M_s + M_n)$ products' patents are still in force in the South and

[8]See, for example, Burmeister (1980), pp. 249–250. Basically, with no discounting, a path $\{\hat{c}, \hat{k}, \dot{\hat{k}}\}$ overtakes the path $\{c, k, \dot{k}\}$ if $\lim_{T\to\infty} \int_0^T [u(\hat{c}) - u(c)]dt \geq 0$, where c is the control variable, k is the state variable, and $u(c)$ is the instantaneous welfare corresponding to the path $\{c, k, \dot{k}\}$. A feasible path $\{\hat{c}, \hat{k}, \dot{\hat{k}}\}$ is optimal if it overtakes all other feasible paths. It can be easily seen that if the steady state value of $u(\hat{c})$ is higher than that of any other feasible values $u(c)$, then $\{\hat{c}, \hat{k}, \dot{\hat{k}}\}$ overtakes all other paths, and is therefore optimal.

$T_n(M_s + M_n)$ products' patents are still in force in the North. Although the number of products is discrete, we treat it as continuous in our mathematical derivation for easier handling.

Following some previous work, we assume a quasi-linear utility function for the representative consumer. With free trade in differentiated products and the traditional product, the steady state flow utility of the representative consumer in region k (where $k \in \{s, n\}$) in period t is:

$$u_k(t) = T_k \left[\sum_{j \in \{n,s\}} \int_0^{M_j} x_{jk}(i)^\alpha \mathrm{d}i \right] + (T - T_k) \left[\sum_{j \in \{n,s\}} \int_0^{M_j} \widetilde{x_{jk}}(i)^\alpha \mathrm{d}i \right] + \left(a z_k - \frac{1}{2} e_k z_k^2 \right) + y_k,$$

where $0 < \alpha < 1$ and $\frac{2a}{e_k} \geq z_k \geq 0$.[9] Parameters a and e_k are positive constants; $x_{jk}(i)$ ($\widetilde{x_{jk}}(i)$, respectively) is the consumption of differentiated product i developed in region j and consumed in region k, whose patent has not expired (has expired, respectively); z_k is the consumption of a traditional product z (e.g. textile products) in region k. Finally, y_k is a competitively produced non-traded composite good, produced and consumed only in region k. The price of y_s is normalized to one.[10] Note that if $e_s \neq e_n$, then consumers in different regions will demand the differentiated and the traditional products in different ratios, even if prices are equal across regions. In particular, if $e_s < e_n$, a consumer in the South demands a higher ratio of traditional product to differentiated products than a consumer in the North does. In each period, each consumer in region k maximizes her utility subject to a

[9]For $\frac{2a}{e_k} < z_k$, the utility derived from good z is zero. We shall maintain the assumption that a is sufficiently large to avoid corner solutions.

[10]We assume that there is free trade in order to focus on IPR policy. Qiu and Lai (2001), on the other hand, compare South's and North's tariffs but treat IPR policy as given.

budget constraint, $I_k \geq T_k \left[\sum_{j\in\{n,s\}} \int_0^{M_j} p_{jk}(i)x_{jk}(i)\mathrm{d}i\right] + (T - T_k)$ $\left[\sum_{j\in\{n,s\}} \int_0^{M_j} \widetilde{p_{jk}}(i)\widetilde{x_{jk}}(i)\mathrm{d}i\right] + p_k(z)z_k + y_k$, where $p_{jk}(i)$ ($\widetilde{p_{jk}}(i)$, respectively) is the price of product i developed in region j and sold in region k whose patent has not expired (has expired, respectively); $p_k(z)$ is the price of product z sold in region k, and expenditure I_k is exogenously given. To simplify the notation, define $\epsilon \equiv 1/(1-\alpha)$ and $A \equiv (1-\alpha)\alpha^{(1+\alpha)\epsilon}$.

The instantaneous demand for products x (the differentiated products) whose patents have not expired, that for those whose patents have already expired, and that for product z (the traditional product) by the representative consumers are, respectively,

$$x_{jk}(i) = \left[\frac{p_{jk}(i)}{\alpha}\right]^{-\epsilon}, \quad \widetilde{x_{jk}}(i) = \left[\frac{\widetilde{p_{jk}}(i)}{\alpha}\right]^{-\epsilon} \quad \text{and} \quad z_k = \frac{a - p_k(z)}{e_k}.$$

When $a < p_k(z)$, $z_k = 0$. We shall maintain the assumption that a is sufficiently large to ensure interior solutions. Let N_k be a shift parameter on aggregate demand, which can be interpreted as the number of consumers in region k. (We shall assume that $N_n > N_s$. Note that this should not be literally interpreted as the North's population being higher, but rather that the size of the market for differentiated products is larger in the North, as will become clear next.) Thus, the corresponding aggregate demands are, respectively:

$$X_{jk}(i) = N_k\left[\frac{p_{jk}(i)}{\alpha}\right]^{-\epsilon}, \widetilde{X_{jk}}(i) = N_k\left[\frac{\widetilde{p_{jk}}(i)}{\alpha}\right]^{-\epsilon} \quad \text{and}$$

$$Z_k = N_k\left[\frac{a - p_k(z)}{e_k}\right].$$

Define $e_n \equiv e$ and $\eta_k \equiv eN_k/e_k$. Then, we can rewrite

$$Z_k = \eta_k\left[\frac{a - p_k(z)}{e}\right].$$

Therefore, N_s/N_n is the size of the market for differentiated products in the South relative to that of the North, and η_s/η_n is the size of South's market for the traditional product relative to that of the

North. Note that $\eta_n = N_n$ and $\eta_s = eN_s/e_s$. Assuming that $e_s < e_n$, so that the South's propensity to consume the traditional product relative to the differentiated products is higher, we have $\eta_s/\eta_n > N_s/N_n$. It is indeed plausible that $\eta_s/\eta_n > 1$ and $N_s/N_n < 1$. We shall discuss more about this in Section 4.

For simplicity, assume that the unit cost of production for all x products is constant and equal to one unit of good y in that region regardless of the location of production.[11] Hence, the per-period operating profit (i.e. profit not including innovation costs) of firm i based in region j selling in region k is $\pi_{jk}(i) = [p_{jk}(i) - 1]X_{jk}(i)$. Under IPR protection, firm i has a monopoly on product i. As a result, for products whose patents have not expired,

$$p_{jk}(i) = \frac{1}{\alpha}, \quad X_{jk}(i) = N_k\alpha^{2\epsilon}, \quad \text{and} \quad \pi_{jk}(i) = N_k A.$$

We assume imitation costs are zero. Therefore, for products whose patents have expired, prices are driven down to the unit cost of production because of imitation. Thus

$$\widetilde{p_{jk}}(i) = 1, \quad \widetilde{X_{jk}}(i) = N_k\alpha^{\epsilon}, \quad \text{and} \quad \widetilde{\pi_{jk}}(i) = 0.$$

To avoid unnecessary complexity, we omit the details of the production of traditional good z by using an endowment model. Moreover, we assume that the South is relatively more abundantly endowed with good z than the North in the sense that in every period, t, region k is endowed with $\eta_k\bar{z}_k$ units of the traditional good and that $\bar{z}_n < \bar{z}_s$. Therefore, in autarky, the price of good z would be lower in the South than in the North, and when there is free trade the South would export this good to the North. Let $\eta_s z_{ss}$ and $\eta_s z_{sn}$ be the quantities of the South-produced traditional good sold in South's market and exported to North's market, respectively, with $z_{ss}+ z_{sn} = \bar{z}_s$. Let τ be the tariff imposed on each unit of good z imported to the North. Assume that the demand intercept

[11] In general, labor costs are lower in the South than in the North while innovation costs are higher in the South than in the North. But, our emphasis here is on the North-South difference in innovation costs.

a is sufficiently large and that $\bar{z}_s - \bar{z}_n > \tau/e$. Then, we have the following equilibrium conditions for the traditional good sector in both markets:

$$p_n(z) = a - e(\bar{z}_n + \delta z_{sn}), \quad p_s(z) = a - ez_{ss} \quad \text{and}$$
$$p_n(z) = p_s(z) + \tau, \quad \text{where} \quad \delta \equiv \eta_s/\eta_n.$$

Solving the above equilibrium conditions gives

$$z_{sn} = \frac{e(\bar{z}_s - \bar{z}_n) - \tau}{e(1+\delta)} \quad \text{and} \quad p_n(z) = \frac{a(1+\delta) - e(\bar{z}_n + \delta\bar{z}_s) + \delta\tau}{e(1+\delta)}. \tag{1}$$

The total revenue per period from sector z is therefore $R_{zn} = \eta_n[p_n(z)\bar{z}_n + \tau z_{sn}]$ for the North and $R_{zs} = \eta_s p_s(z)\bar{z}_s$ for the South. Consumer surplus per period derived from this sector in the North and South are respectively $\frac{\eta_n}{2e}[a - p_n(z)]^2$ and $\frac{\eta_s}{2e}[a - p_s(z)]^2$. Note that the per-period quantities in the traditional-good sector are also the steady-state quantities.

The total steady state flow welfare in region k is

$$W_k = U_k + U_{zk},$$

where U_k is region k's steady state flow welfare derived from all sectors excluding sector z, where as U_{zk} is the steady state flow welfare in region k derived exclusively from sector z. We shall focus on the analysis of IPR protection in the rest of this section and in Section 3. Since IPR protection affects sector x only, and will not affect U_{zk}, we shall ignore sector z until Section 4.

2.2 Analysis of the Pre-TRIPS Regime

Based on the analysis in the preceding section, region k's (where $k \in \{s, n\}$) representative consumer's steady state flow utility at time t is

$$u_k(t) = T_k(M_s + M_n)(1-\alpha)\alpha^{2\alpha\epsilon} + (T - T_k)(M_s + M_n)(1-\alpha)\alpha^{\alpha\epsilon}$$
$$+ [a - p_k(z)]^2/(2e_k) + I_k.$$

The first term on the right hand side refers to goods whose patents have not expired, and the second term refers to goods whose patents have expired.

We now turn to the firms' profits. Assume that in each period the innovation costs of different products are different. Some goods are easier to develop and some goods are harder to develop. We index goods in ascending order based on the innovation costs, i.e. a good with a lower index i has a lower innovation cost than a good with a higher i. It is assumed that the innovation cost of product i based in region k is $a_k \cdot i^{1/b_k}$ where $a_k > 0$ and $0 < b_k < 1$ are parameters.[12]

All firms sell their products in both the South's and North's markets. Thus, the life-time profit of firm i based in region k (over the entire life of product i) is

$$\begin{aligned}\Pi_k(i) &= \int_0^{T_s} \pi_{ks}(i)\mathrm{d}t + \int_0^{T_n} \pi_{kn}(i)\mathrm{d}t - a_k \cdot i^{1/b_k} \\ &= (N_sT_s + N_nT_n)A - a_k \cdot i^{1/b_k}.\end{aligned}$$

In each period, the marginal firm in the North, M_n, and that in the South, M_s, are defined as firms that earn zero profit, i.e. $\Pi_n(M_n) = 0$ and $\Pi_s(M_s) = 0$, respectively. This leads to

$$M_n = \left(\frac{\mu}{a_n}\right)^{b_n} \text{ and } M_s = \left(\frac{\mu}{a_s}\right)^{b_s}, \text{ where } \mu \equiv (N_sT_s + N_nT_n)A.$$

Thus, M_s products are developed in the South and M_n products are developed in the North in each period. We define the steady state flow profits of a region in a period as the total life-time profits of all firms that innovate in that period. It turns out that these flow profits are equal to $\int_0^{M_k} \Pi_k(i)\mathrm{d}i$.

Before we proceed further, we now make two assumptions about the asymmetry between the two regions. First, we assume that $N_n > N_s$. Although we can consider the South's population to be

[12]We could instead use a more general cost function $f(i)$, where $f(0) \geq 0$, $f'(.) > 0$, $f''(.) > 0$. But our results would not be altered qualitatively. Nor would our results be affected qualitatively if the future were discounted.

higher than the North's, it is widely documented that the North's demands for innovative products, such as computers, pharmaceuticals and biotechnological products, are higher than those of the South. Second, we assume that the North has higher innovative capability such that in equilibrium $M_s < M_n$. There are many combinations of a_s, a_n, b_s and b_n that can lead to this very plausible equilibrium outcome. For example, $b_s = b_n$ & $a_s > a_n$, or $b_s < b_n$ & $a_s = a_n$, are sufficient conditions for $M_s < M_n$. It would be seen later that these two assumptions would lead to the result that the North protects IPR stronger than the South does.

The steady state flow welfare of region k is given by

$$W_k(T_s, T_n, M_s, M_n) = N_k u_k(t) + \int_0^{M_k} \Pi_k(i)\mathrm{d}i + R_{zk}$$

$$= N_k T_k[(M_s + M_n)(1-\alpha)\alpha^{2\alpha\epsilon}] + N_k(T - T_k)$$

$$[(M_s + M_n)(1-\alpha)\alpha^{\alpha\epsilon}] + N_k I_k + M_k(N_s T_s + N_n T_n)A$$

$$-\frac{b_k}{1+b_k} M_k^{(1+b_k)/b_k} + U_{zk}.$$

Each region chooses its IPR protection policy T_k strategically to maximize its welfare. To characterize the Nash equilibrium, we first obtain the policy reaction functions of the North and of the South. Since the reaction functions of the North and the South are symmetric up to the values of the parameters, let us focus on the South for the time being. Assuming an interior solution, the optimal response T_s for any given T_n is obtained from the following equation:

$$\frac{\mathrm{d}W_s}{\mathrm{d}T_s} = \frac{\partial W_s}{\partial T_s} + \frac{\partial W_s}{\partial M_s}\frac{\partial M_s}{\partial T_s} + \frac{\partial W_s}{\partial M_n}\frac{\partial M_n}{\partial T_s} = 0. \quad (2)$$

Note that

$$\frac{\partial W_s}{\partial T_s} = -N_s\{M_s[1-(1+\alpha)\alpha^{\alpha\epsilon}] + M_n(1-\alpha^{\alpha\epsilon})\}(1-\alpha)\alpha^{\alpha\epsilon} < 0.$$

That is, the marginal effect of lengthening IPR protection, given that the number of products remains unchanged, is negative. It is the sum of consumer losses and producer gains, which add up to a deadweight loss. We denote this social marginal cost of IPR protection in the South as $MC_s \equiv |\partial W_s/\partial T_s|$, which increases with T_s.

On the other hand, lengthening IPR protection in the South encourages more innovations in both the North and the South, which enlarges product variety and so raises consumer welfare. Thus,

$$\frac{\partial W_s}{\partial M_s}\frac{\partial M_s}{\partial T_s} = N_s[T - T_s(1-\alpha^{\alpha\epsilon})](1-\alpha)\alpha^{\alpha\epsilon}\frac{\partial M_s}{\partial T_s} > 0,$$
$$\frac{\partial W_s}{\partial M_n}\frac{\partial M_n}{\partial T_s} = N_s[T - T_s(1-\alpha^{\alpha\epsilon})](1-\alpha)\alpha^{\alpha\epsilon}\frac{\partial M_n}{\partial T_s} > 0,$$

the sum of which captures the social marginal benefit (MB_s) from extending T_s. Since

$$\frac{\partial M_s}{\partial T_s} = \frac{N_s A}{\mu} b_s M_s \quad \text{and} \quad \frac{\partial M_n}{\partial T_s} = \frac{N_s A}{\mu} b_n M_n,$$

the marginal benefit MB_s decreases in T_s.

The South's reaction function is therefore obtained from equating MC_s to MB_s, which is reduced to[13]

$$M_s[1-(1+\alpha)\alpha^{\alpha\epsilon}]+M_n(1-\alpha^{\alpha\epsilon}) = \frac{N_s A}{\mu}[T-T_s(1-\alpha^{\alpha\epsilon})](b_s M_s + b_n M_n). \tag{3}$$

Invoking symmetry, we obtain the reaction function of the North

$$M_n[1-(1+\alpha)\alpha^{\alpha\epsilon}]+M_s(1-\alpha^{\alpha\epsilon}) = \frac{N_n A}{\mu}[T-T_n(1-\alpha^{\alpha\epsilon})](b_n M_n + b_s M_s). \tag{4}$$

Equations (3) and (4) jointly determine the Nash equilibrium, denoted by T_s^* and T_n^*. Refer to Figure 1.

[13]The second-order condition for the South is automatically satisfied as it can now be easily checked that $\mathrm{d}^2 W_s/\mathrm{d}T_s^2 < 0$.

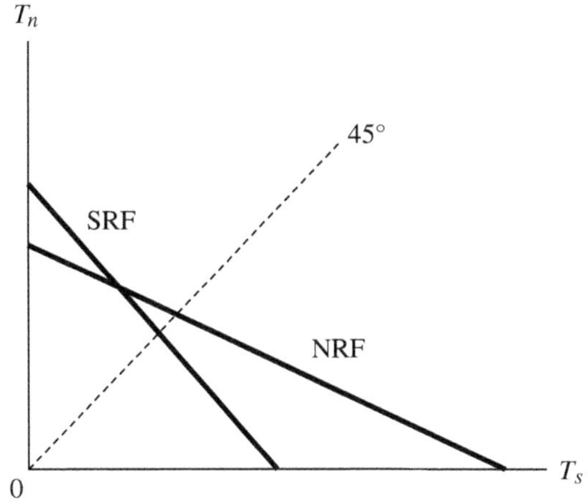

Figure 1. Pre-TRIPS Nash equilibrium IPR standards. NRF indicates the North's reaction function, while SRF indicates the South's reaction function.

Note that both the South's reaction function and the North's reaction function are downward sloping in the $(T_s,\ T_n)$ space. For example, the right hand side of equation (3) (hereinafter RHS(3)) decreases with both T_s and T_n, while the left hand side of equation (3) (hereinafter LHS(3)) increases with both T_s and T_n. Therefore, $(\mathrm{d}/\mathrm{d}T_n)[\mathrm{LHS}(3) - \mathrm{RHS}(3)] > 0$ and $(\mathrm{d}/\mathrm{d}T_n)[\mathrm{LHS}(3) - \mathrm{RHS}(3)] > 0$. By the Implicit Function Theorem, T_s decreases as T_n increases, as we move along the South's reaction curve in the (T_s, T_n) space. The same is true for the North's reaction function. Thus, stronger protection in the North makes it optimal for the South to protect less. The main reason for the substitution effect of the North's protection for the South's protection (as far as the South is concerned) is that as T_n increases, product variety is enlarged due to the greater incentive for firms to innovate, and so the $\mathrm{MC}_s(T_s)$ curve, which plots MC_s on a diagram with T_s on the horizontal axis, shifts up. This calls for a reduction of IPR protection in the South. On the other hand, the $\mathrm{MB}_s(T_s)$ curve, which plots MB_s on the same diagram, shifts down when consumers obtain increased product variety, due to the decreasing effect of variety on the marginal benefit. This also calls for a reduction of IPR protection in the South.

It can also be shown that the South's reaction curve is steeper than the North's reaction curve in the (T_s, T_n) space. Hence, the Nash equilibrium is stable (see Appendix A).

To compare the values of T_s^* and T_n^*, we first observe that because $M_n > M_s$, LHS(3) > LHS(4) for all T_s and T_n. Suppose we set $T_s = T_n = \xi$ in both (3) and (4). Then, RHS(3) < RHS(4) since $N_s < N_n$. Moreover, the RHS of both equations decreases with ξ, and the LHS of both equations increases with ξ. Hence, the value of ξ obtained from (3) is less than that obtained from (4). This, together with the fact that the South's reaction function is steeper than the North's reaction function, implies that the two curves must intersect at a point above the 45° line, which means that $T_s^* < T_n^*$ (see Figure 1).

The above analysis also indicates two reasons for $T_s^* < T_n^*$. First, the North has more innovations than the South ($M_s < M_n$), because the North has sufficiently higher innovative capability. Second, the North's market size is larger than the South's ($N_s < N_n$).

Next, we check the constraints on the parameters to ensure an interior solution of T_s^*. Note that a necessary and sufficient condition for $T_s^* > 0$ is that the value of T_n (given that $T_s = 0$) on the South's reaction function is greater than the value of T_n (given that $T_s = 0$) on the North's reaction function. A necessary condition for this inequality to hold is $N_n A[T - T_n(1 - \alpha^{\alpha\epsilon})] < N_s AT$, which, together with the condition $T \geq T_n$, implies $N_s/N_n > \alpha^{\alpha\epsilon}$. Therefore, the market in the South has to be sufficiently large compared with the market in the North in order for the South to have any incentive to protect IPR.

Finally, we examine the implications of market size for equilibrium IPR standards. We find that *the equilibrium IPR protection in the South (North) is stronger when the market in the South (North) becomes larger, or the market in the North (South) becomes smaller.* Mathematically,

$$\frac{\partial T_s^*}{\partial N_s} > 0, \frac{\partial T_s^*}{\partial N_n} < 0, \quad \frac{\partial T_n^*}{\partial N_n} > 0, \quad \text{and} \quad \frac{\partial T_n^*}{\partial N_s} < 0. \tag{5}$$

The proof is given in an appendix available from the authors upon request.

It is interesting to understand why the two market sizes have opposite impacts on the optimal IPR protection. The effects of N_n on the South's reaction function is that a larger market in the North results in greater product variety, which increases the marginal cost, MC_s, of the IPR protection in the South and lowers the marginal benefit, MB_s, of the IPR protection in the South, for any given T_n. Therefore, an increase in N_n shifts the South's reaction function inward. The effects of N_s on the South's reaction function is more complicated. On the one hand, a larger market in the South also leads to greater product variety, which should lessen the IPR protection in the South. On the other hand, there are more consumers in the South who benefit from increasing the IPR protection in the South, and, as a result, the marginal benefits, MB_s, of the IPR protection in the South increase. We find that this latter effect dominates the former one and thus an increase in N_s shifts the South's reaction function outward. By the same argument, an increase in N_n shifts the North's reaction function out, while an increase in N_s shifts the North's reaction function in. Consequently, we obtain the results given in (5).

We now conclude this section. Just like Chin and Grossman (1990), we also find that it is optimal for the South to protect IPR when its market is sufficiently large. Moreover, we find that as the market in the South grows, it is individually optimal for the South to strengthen its IPR protection. However, the South's incentive to protect IPR can never be as strong as the North's incentive so long as the North has a larger market for differentiated products and has more innovations than the South does.

3 The Post-TRIPS Regime and Global Welfare

In the post-TRIPS regime, both regions are required to adopt the North's pre-TRIPS IPR protection, T_n^*, as the minimum standard. We shall evaluate the welfare consequence of such a measure. But let us first identify the equilibrium in the post-TRIPS regime, i.e.

the equilibrium subject to the constraints $T_s \geq T_n^*$ and $T_n \geq T_n^*$. In other words, given that T_n^* is the minimum standard, what standards would the two regions adopt?

When governments adopt new IPR standards, the numbers of products invented in the regions in each period are different from those in the pre-TRIPS regime. Again, we can calculate the equilibrium policies based on the new steady-state welfare levels.[14] Thus, we can adopt a similar analysis as developed in Section 2.2. It can be easily shown that the unique post-TRIPS equilibrium is $T_s = T_n^*$ and $T_n = T_n^*$. That is, both regions simply adopt the North's pre-TRIPS IPR protection. The intuition is as follows. From the last section, we see that the North wants to lower T_n as the South increases T_s; conversely, the South wants to lower T_s as the North increases T_n. Therefore, as T_s is forced to increase from T_s^* to T_n^*, the North would want to reduce T_n below T_n^*. Given the constraint $T_n \geq T_n^*$, however, the optimal response for the North is $T_n = T_n^*$. Given that $T_n = T_n^*$, the South's unconstrained best response is $T_s = T_s^*$. However, under the constraint $T_s \geq T_n^*$, the best response of the South is $T_s = T_n^*$.

To evaluate world welfare, let us first define world (or global) welfare simply as the sum of the North's and the South's welfare, i.e. $W = W_s + W_n$. To evaluate whether the minimum IPR standard stipulated by TRIPS is welfare-improving for the world, we first find an expression for the effect of T_s on global welfare. Then, we discuss the properties of the globally optimal IPR standard of the South given that $T_n = T_n^*$. Finally, we evaluate the global welfare effect of increasing T_s from T_s^* to T_n^* given that $T_n = T_n^*$.

Based on the analysis in the last section, the North's steady state flow welfare at $T_n = T_n^*$ is given by

$$\begin{aligned} W_n(T_s, T_n^*, M_s, M_n) = {} & N_n(M_n + M_s)(1-\alpha)\alpha^{\alpha\epsilon}[T - T_n^*(1-\alpha^{\alpha\epsilon})] \\ & + N_n I_n + M_n(N_s T_s + N_n T_n^*)A \\ & - \frac{b_n}{1+b_n} M_n^{(1+b_n)/b_n} + U_{zn}. \end{aligned}$$

[14]The new steady state starts T periods after the TRIPS is invoked.

Recalling that $M_n = (\mu/a_n)^{b_n}$ where $\mu = (N_sT_s + N_nT_n)A$, we can easily see

$$\frac{\mathrm{d}W_n}{\mathrm{d}T_s} = \frac{\partial W_n}{\partial T_s} + \frac{\partial W_n}{\partial M_n} \cdot \frac{\partial M_n}{\partial T_s} + \frac{\partial W_n}{\partial M_s} \cdot \frac{\partial M_s}{\partial T_s} > 0. \tag{6}$$

A similar inequality can be shown for the South. Therefore, *a region always benefits from stronger IPR protection in the other region, i.e.* $\mathrm{d}W_n/\mathrm{d}T_s > 0$ *and* $\mathrm{d}W_s/\mathrm{d}T_n > 0$.[15] The benefit comes from enlarging product variety in both regions ($\partial M_k/\partial T_s > 0$ and $\partial M_k/\partial T_n > 0$, for $k = \{s, n,\}$) and increasing innovators' profits ($\partial \Pi_k(i)/\partial T_s > 0$ and $\partial \Pi_k(i)/\partial T_n > 0$, for $k = \{s, n,\}$). Specifically, with a stronger IPR protection in the foreign region, but with its own IPR protection unchanged, a region's consumers enjoy larger product variety with no price hikes (call it *variety spillover*), and its firms also receive more profits (call it *profit spillover*). There is, therefore, a positive inter-regional externality from strengthening IPR protection. Since a region's individually optimal IPR protection does not take into account this positive inter-regional externality, IPR is under-protected from the world's point of view if regions all adopt their individually optimal IPR standards as in the pre-TRIPS regime.

We now turn to consider the impact of increasing the South's IPR protection on global welfare given that $T_n = T_n^*$. Since $W(T_s) = W_n(T_s) + W_s(T_s)$, by (2) and (6), we have,

$$\frac{\mathrm{d}W}{\mathrm{d}T_s}|_{T_s=T_s^*} = \frac{\mathrm{d}W_s}{\mathrm{d}T_s}|_{T_s=T_s^*} + \frac{\mathrm{d}W_n}{\mathrm{d}T_s}|_{T_s=T_s^*} > 0. \tag{7}$$

That is, provided that there is no corner solution for T_s^*, slightly increasing the South's IPR protection from its individually optimal level T_s^* increases global welfare. This is due to the positive externality of IPR protection indicated above. This result supports the argument for increasing the South's IPR protection. The question is how much the South's IPR protection should be increased in order to achieve global welfare optimum.

---

[15]If, however, consumers from the two regions have different tastes for the products, it is possible that the North (South) cannot always benefit from stronger IPR protection in the South (North), as shown by Diwan and Rodrik (1991).

Differentiating $W(T_s)$ with respect to T_s gives

$$\begin{aligned}\frac{1}{(1-\alpha)\alpha^{\alpha\epsilon}N_s}\left(\frac{\mathrm{d}W}{\mathrm{d}T_s}\right) = &-(M_s+M_n)[1-(1+\alpha)\alpha^{\alpha\epsilon}] \\ &+\frac{A}{\mu}(b_nM_n+b_sM_s)\{N_s[T-T_s(1-\alpha^{\alpha\epsilon})] \\ &+N_n[T-T_n^*(1-\alpha^{\alpha\epsilon})]\}.\end{aligned} \tag{8}$$

We can easily check that $W(T_s)$ is concave in T_s, i.e. $\mathrm{d}^2W/\mathrm{d}T_s^2 < 0$ for all T_s. (Simply note that $\mathrm{d}W/\mathrm{d}T_s$ decreases with T_s.)

We next check if $\mathrm{d}W/\mathrm{d}T_s \geq 0$ at $T_s = T_n^*$. Substituting T_n^* for T_s in (8), then comparing the result with equation (4), we can show that it is indeed true that $\mathrm{d}W/\mathrm{d}T_s \geq 0$ at $T_s = T_n^*$. A formal proof is given in Appendix B. Defining the South's level of IPR protection that maximizes global welfare as $T_s^w \equiv \operatorname{argmax} W(T_n = T_n^*)$, we conclude that $T_s^w > T_n^*$. Therefore, *given that the North continues to adopt its pre-TRIPS Nash equilibrium IPR standard, global welfare is maximized when the South adopts an IPR standard which is stronger than that of the North.* Refer to Figure 2a and 2b.

Finally, we find that *the South's IPR protection that maximizes global welfare is an increasing function of the size of the South's market. Mathematically, we have* $\partial T_s^w/\partial N_s > 0$. The proof is given in an appendix available from the authors upon request. Intuitively, as N_s increases, there is a higher demand for North-innovated goods in the South (profit spillover is stronger) as well as a greater additional variety of differentiated products developed by the South from strengthening IPR (variety spillover is also stronger), and therefore the magnitude of the positive inter-regional externality of the South's IPR protection is greater. This calls for an increase in the South's IPR protection to internalize the externality.

The above result is somewhat consistent with the conclusion of Deardorff (1992), who finds that when the fraction of the world that is weak in IPR protection is larger, it is globally optimal to extend the strong IPR protection to more of these countries. What was not

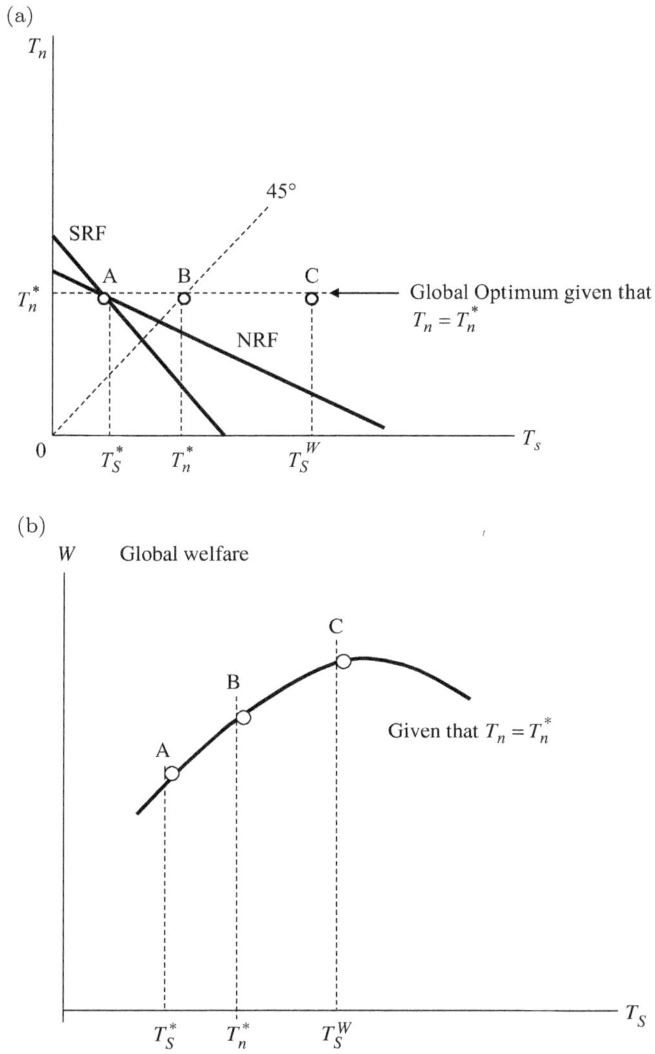

Figure 2. (a) The TRIPS versus global optimum. TRIPS moves the world from A to B, but the optimum is at C, given that $T_n = T_n^*$. Here, T_S^* indicates the South's pre-TRIPS patent length; T_n^* indicates the North's pre-TRIPS patent length; T_S^W indicates the South's patent length that would maximize global welfare given that the North keeps its pre-TRIPS patent length. (b) World welfare as South's patent length changes. Points A, B and C correspond to those in Figure 2a.

addressed by Deardorff (1992), but has been addressed by us, is that the globally optimal level of IPR protection by the South would be higher than the pre-TRIPS standard of the North even when the South has lower innovative capability than that of the North.

To conclude this section, we note that, given that the North is committed to the minimum standard, T_n^*, it would not be practical for the North to require the South to adopt any higher standard than that. This means that we can treat T_n^* as the upper bound of the minimum standard that the North can ask the South to adopt. Given this constraint, the TRIPS Agreement can be regarded as maximizing global welfare by requiring the South to adopt the North's pre-TRIPS standard, T_n^*, rather than anything lower, as the minimum IPR standard. It is in this sense that the TRIPS agreement is optimal.

4 Multi-Sectoral Negotiations

In this section, we analyze the merits of the TRIPS Agreement in the context of a multi-sectoral negotiation. We consider the case in which the North wants the South to increase its IPR protection while, in return, the South wants the North to lower its trade barriers to imports of traditional goods from the South. We have seen from previous analysis that while raising the IPR standard in the South from its Nash equilibrium level T_s^* to the North's Nash equilibrium level T_n^* is globally welfare-improving, the South itself loses from such an increase. To make the TRIPS Agreement incentive-compatible for the South, the North, which is the beneficiary region, has to compensate the South. While a lump sum income transfer from the North to the South would solve the incentive-compatibility problem theoretically, it is not practical. In the Uruguay Round, the South demanded increased access to the North's markets in which it has comparative advantage, such as textile products. This sector is represented by z in this model. In the model, increasing market access amounts to lowering tariff τ on the import of z. We will show that allowing better access to the North's market in exchange for the South's strengthening of IPR standard is not only a realistic channel to solve the incentive-compatibility problem of the TRIPS, but also superior to the (impractical) lump sum income transfer mechanism.

The steady state flow welfare associated with sector z in the North and the South are, respectively,

$$U_{zn}(\tau) = \eta_n \left[p_n(z)\bar{z}_n + \frac{1}{2e}(a - p_n(z))^2 + \tau z_{sn} \right],$$

$$U_{zs}(\tau) = \eta_s \left[p_s(z)\bar{z}_s + \frac{1}{2e}(a - p_s(z))^2 \right].$$

Again, with no discounting of the future, the steady state flow welfare can be the basis of welfare analysis.

Without cooperation/negotiation with the South, the North chooses a non-cooperative optimal tariff to maximize $U_{zn}(\tau)$. Given the market equilibrium outcome obtained in Section 2, we know that this optimal tariff is

$$\tau^* = \frac{e(1 + \delta - \delta^2)(\bar{z}_s - \bar{z}_n)}{2(1 + \delta) - \delta^2}.$$

The corresponding welfare for the North and the South when τ^* is imposed are denoted $U^*_{zn}(\tau)$ and $U^*_{zs}(\tau)$, respectively. It is easily seen that lowering τ will reduce the North's welfare in sector z but will increase the South's welfare in this sector:

$$\frac{\partial U_{zn}(\tau)}{\partial \tau} = \frac{\eta_n}{e(1 + \delta)}[e(1 + \delta - \delta_s^2)z_{sn} - \tau] > 0 \quad \text{for } \tau < \tau^*.$$

$$\frac{\partial U_{zs}(\tau)}{\partial \tau} = -\frac{\eta_s}{(1 + \delta)}(\bar{z}_s - z_{ss}) < 0 \quad \text{for all } \tau.$$

Recalling that U_k is region k's welfare derived from all sectors excluding sector z, we denote U^*_k as the equilibrium U_k under the pre-TRIPS regime (i.e. when both regions choose their Nash equilibrium IPR levels, T_n^* and T_s^*, respectively), and define U_k^c as the equilibrium U_k under the post-TRIPS regime (i.e. when both regions choose the minimum standard equal to T_n^*).

To model the multi-sectoral negotiation, we assume that the two regions bargain simultaneously over whether the South adopts the North's pre-TRIPS IPR standard as well as over the level of τ. The Nash bargaining model is adopted. Any agreement and bargaining outcome is assumed to last forever. Therefore, with no discounting, welfare consideration in the bargaining can be based on steady state flow welfare. Without having τ lowered, the South will not raise its IPR standard. So, the threat point of the bargain is such that the South maintains its pre-TRIPS IPR standard, while the North maintains tariff τ^*. To solve the bargaining problem, the tariff τ is chosen to maximize the product of two expressions that are functions of the net welfare improvements in the two regions, viz.

$$(U_n^c + U_{zn} - U_n^* - U_{zn}^*)^{(1-\upsilon)}(U_s^c + U_{zs} - U_s^* - U_{zs}^*)^{\upsilon},$$

where $\upsilon \in [0, 1]$ represents the South's bargaining power. For ease of exposition, let $\mathcal{N}(\tau) \equiv U_n^c + U_{zn} - U_n^* - U_{zn}^*$ and $\mathcal{S}(\tau) \equiv U_s^c + U_{zs} - U_s^* - U_{zs}^*$. It is clear that to satisfy the incentive-compatibility condition in the South, τ needs to be low enough for the South to gain sufficiently from the traditional sector to compensate for its loss in the differentiated-products sector. Since there is a natural lower bound, $\tau = 0$, for this policy, we need to assume that a, e and $\bar{z}_s - \bar{z}_n$ are sufficiently large. This will ensure that the traditional-good markets are sufficiently large, the optimal tariff τ^* is sufficiently large, and consequently, there are sufficient gains to the South from tariff-cutting by the North. This will in turn ensure that both $\mathcal{N}(\tau)$ and $\mathcal{S}(\tau)$ are positive.

To make sure that there indeed exists an interior solution to the bargaining game, we have to check that the welfare frontier is concave. The slope of the bargaining frontier is equal to $\mathrm{d}\mathcal{N}(\tau)/\mathrm{d}\mathcal{S}(\tau) = (\partial U_{zn}/\partial \tau)/(\partial U_{zs}/\partial \tau)$. First, the slope is equal to zero when $\tau = \tau^*$. Second, it can be easily shown that the slope is negative and increases in magnitude as τ decreases, i.e. as $\mathcal{S}(\tau)$ increases. This ensures that

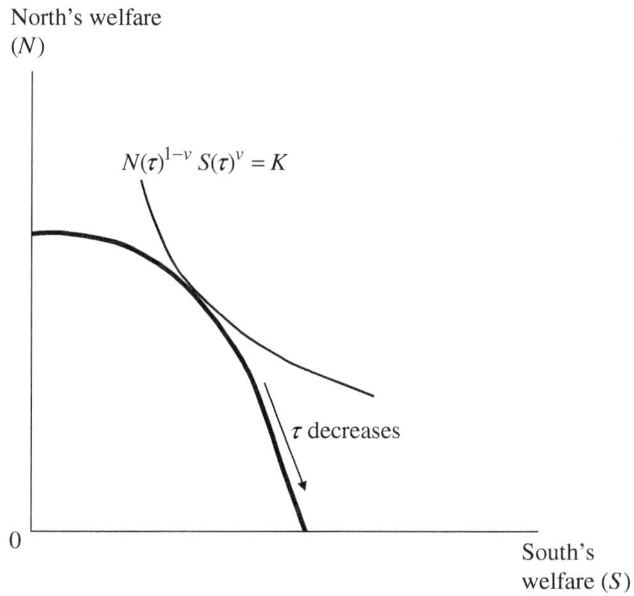

Figure 3. Nash bargaining over τ. The two regions bargain simultaneously over whether the South adopts the North's pre-TRIPS IPR and over the value of τ. The origin is the point with no agreement.

the frontier is strictly concave. So, if the first-order condition of the Nash bargaining yields $\tau^c \in [0, \tau^*]$, it is an optimal interior solution. Refer to Figure 3.

When $\tau = 0$, the slope of the welfare frontier is equal to $(1 + \delta - \delta^2)/\delta$, which is less than one as long as $\delta > 1$. To simplify things by ensuring that tariff reduction by the North is always globally welfare-improving, we assume that $\delta > 1$, i.e. the South's market for traditional good is larger than the North's. Therefore, any decrease in τ leads to an increase in $\mathcal{S}(\tau)$ with a magnitude greater than that of the concomitant decrease in $\mathcal{N}(\tau)$, so that global welfare is improved.[16]

[16]In our model, it is possible that $N_n > N_s$ while $\eta_s > \eta_n$, as long as e_s is sufficiently smaller than e_n. This simply reflects the fact that the South's consumers have, relatively speaking, a lower propensity to consume new products and a higher propensity to consume traditional products than their counterparts

The bargaining problem is equivalent to choosing τ to maximize $(1 - \upsilon)\ln(\mathcal{N}(\tau))+\upsilon\ln(\mathcal{S}(\tau))$, which yields the following first-order condition,

$$\frac{(1-\upsilon)}{\mathcal{N}(\tau)}\frac{\partial U_{zn}}{\partial \tau} + \frac{\upsilon}{\mathcal{S}(\tau)}\frac{\partial U_{zs}}{\partial \tau} = 0. \tag{9}$$

We are interested in how the bargaining outcome τ^c is affected by other factors and how global welfare is in turn affected by the bargaining outcome. First, it is straightforward to show that $\partial\tau^c/\partial\upsilon < 0$, that is, trade liberalization in the traditional-good sector in the North would be deeper when the South has more bargaining power. This is the usual outcome of Nash bargaining since a lower τ^c favors the South. Second, it can be easily shown that $\partial W/\partial\tau < 0$. That is, global welfare increases when the South has more bargaining power. This is because higher bargaining power for the South leads to deeper trade liberalization in the North, which improves global welfare.

We have seen that both an increase in T_s and a decrease in τ yield net gains to the world, which can then be split between the two regions through Nash bargaining. So, we can say that *since bargaining leads to* $\mathcal{N}(\tau^c) > 0$ *and* $\mathcal{S}(\tau^c) > 0$, *both regions benefit from the multi-sectoral negotiation, of which the TRIPS Agreement is an outcome.* Although we interpret the TRIPS Agreement as one that requires all regions to adopt a minimum IPR protection standard as defined by the North's pre-TRIPS protection level, the above result can be generalized as follows: *Both regions benefit from a bargain that involves the South raising its IPR protection standard to a pre-specified level* $T_s \in [T_s^*, T_n^*]$ *(while the North does not lower its pre-TRIPS IPR protection standard) on the one hand, and the North liberalizing trade in its traditional good sector on the other hand.* The proof of this general result can be obtained by simply repeating

in the North. Casual observation confirms the presumption that the North's market for new products is larger than the South's market, while the reverse is true for the market for traditional goods.

the above analysis. This result means that even if the regions find it impossible (e.g. for political reasons) to enforce a drastic set of concessions (with T_s set to T_n^*), they can agree on a less drastic set of concessions (with $T_s \in [T_s^*, T_n^*]$) and still end up with mutual gains in a multi-sectoral negotiation.

Finally, we examine each region's marginal gain from *increases* in T_s, for all $T_s \in [T_s^*, T_n^*]$. We have found in Section 3 that as long as $T_s \in [T_s^*, T_n^*]$, any increase in T_s would lead to an increase in U_n^c but a decrease in U_s^c (now we need to reinterpret U_k^c as the value of U_k when the South and the North adopt T_s and T_n^*, respectively), and the gain in the former outweighs the loss in the latter so that $U_n^c + U_s^c$ increases. We have also proved above that as long as $\tau \in [0, \tau^*]$, any decrease in τ would lead to an increase in U_{zs} but to a decrease in U_{zn}, and the gain in the former outweighs the loss in the latter so that $U_{zs} + U_{zn}$ increases. We have assumed that the traditional goods markets are sufficiently large and the differences between the regions in endowments of traditional good are sufficiently great that tariff-cutting in the North is sufficient to compensate the South for its increase in IPR protection. Consequently, we prove in Appendix C that *whenever the South is willing to increase T_s, the North is willing to reduce τ. On balance, as T_s increases, the marginal gain to the North is always positive (i.e. $\mathcal{N}(\tau)$ would increase), but the marginal gain to the South is positive (i.e. $\mathcal{S}(\tau)$ increases) only if v is sufficiently large or $\mathcal{S}(\tau)$ is sufficiently small.* This indicates that although raising the South's IPR protection T_s all the way to T_n^* is globally optimal and is in the best interest of the North, such a big move may not be in the South's best interest unless the South's bargaining power in the negotiation is sufficiently strong to elicit a large tariff reduction from the North. Otherwise, the South would prefer an agreement that requires $T_s = T_s^c < T_n^*$, since all the extra surplus from raising the IPR protection beyond T_s^c would accrue to the North. In other words, while both regions gain from the multi-sectoral negotiation, the South may be able to gain more if it has more freedom to choose the degree of IPR protection.

5 Summary and Conclusion

We find that it is globally welfare-improving for the South to increase its IPR protection above its (pre-TRIPS) Nash equilibrium level. Although this would hurt the South and benefit the North, the latter's gains are larger than the former's losses. Consequently, it can benefit both regions for the South to adopt the North's pre-TRIPS IPR standard, in exchange for the North lowering its import tariffs. We conclude, therefore, that the inclusion of IPR negotiations in GATT/WTO agendas is constructive.

We find that in the multi-sectoral negotiation it is globally optimal for the South to increase its IPR protection standard all the way to the North's level. However, it is not necessarily optimal for the South to do so. It is optimal for the South only if its bargaining power in the negotiation is sufficiently large to elicit a large enough tariff reduction by the North. Otherwise, the extra surplus generated from strengthened IPR protection will mostly benefit the North. In that case, if the South has the choice, it would prefer an agreement that binds it to a higher standard than before, but below that of the North. In other words, giving the South an "all-or-nothing" choice in either adopting the North's IPR standard or maintaining the old standard might diminish the South's gain from such a negotiation. It seems evident that the South was indeed presented with an "all-or-nothing" choice regarding IPR protection in the Uruguay Round of the GATT negotiations. If this is the case, we can say that the TRIPS Agreement requires the South to give up too much. It is therefore no wonder that many developing countries are not enforcing as high an IPR standard as the developed countries want while the developed countries seem to be retracting from their market access commitments. In spite of these seeming retractions, however, our result has demonstrated that both regions would still gain as long as they can eventually *willingly* enforce *some* bilateral concessions in both sectors. This again demonstrates the merits of multi-sectoral negotiations.

In future research, we hope to modify the existing model to a truly dynamic, and possibly general equilibrium one, and to consider interactions among trade policies, FDI policies and IPR policies in a unified model.

Appendix

A. Proof of the Stability of the Nash Equilibrium

To see this, totally differentiate (3) and (4) with respect to T_s and T_n. Note that by writing M_s and M_n as functions of μ, (3) can be expressed as a function of μ and T_s only, and thus,

$$\begin{aligned} \mathrm{d}[\mathrm{LHS}(3) - \mathrm{RHS}(3)] = {} & \frac{\partial}{\partial \mu}[\mathrm{LHS}(3) - \mathrm{RHS}(3)](N_s \mathrm{d}T_s + N_n \mathrm{d}T_n) \\ & - \frac{\partial}{\partial T_s}\mathrm{RHS}(3)\mathrm{d}T_s = 0. \end{aligned}$$

Since $(\partial/\partial\mu)[\mathrm{LHS}(3) - \mathrm{RHS}(3)] > 0$, and $(\partial/\partial T_s)\mathrm{RHS}(3) < 0$, the following inequality holds for the South's reaction function:

$$\left|\frac{dT_n}{dT_s}\right| > \frac{N_s}{N_n}.$$

Similarly, for the North, we have

$$\begin{aligned} \mathrm{d}[\mathrm{LHS}(4) - \mathrm{RHS}(4)] = {} & \frac{\partial}{\partial \mu}[\mathrm{LHS}(4) - \mathrm{RHS}(4)](N_s \mathrm{d}T_s + N_n \mathrm{d}T_n) \\ & - \frac{\partial}{\partial T_n}\mathrm{RHS}(4)\mathrm{d}T_n = 0, \end{aligned}$$

from which we conclude that the following inequality holds for the North's reaction function:

$$\left|\frac{dT_n}{dT_s}\right| < \frac{N_s}{N_n}.$$

Therefore, the South's reaction curve is steeper than the North's in the (T_s, T_n) space.

B. Proof of $\frac{dW}{dT_s}|_{T_s=T_n^*} > 0$

Suppose $\widehat{T}_n$ solves

$$M_n[1-(1+\alpha)\alpha^{\alpha\epsilon}]+M_s(1-\alpha^{\alpha\epsilon}) = \frac{N_nA}{\mu}[T-T_n(1-\alpha^{\alpha\epsilon})](b_nM_n+b_sM_s). \tag{B1}$$

where $M_n = \left(\frac{\mu}{a_n}\right)^{b_n}$ and $M_s = \left(\frac{\mu}{a_s}\right)^{b_s}$, where $\mu \equiv N_nT_nA$.

Comparing with equation (4), it is clear that $\widehat{T}_n > T_n^*$, since the North's reaction function is downward sloping, so that T_n increases as T_s decreases to 0. Now suppose $\widehat{T}_n'$ solves

$$\begin{aligned} &M_n[1-(1+\alpha)\alpha^{\alpha\epsilon}] + M_s(1-(1+\alpha)\alpha^{\alpha\epsilon}) \\ &\quad = \frac{N_nA}{\mu}[T - T_n(1-\alpha^{\alpha\epsilon})](b_nM_n + b_sM_s). \end{aligned} \tag{B2}$$

where $M_n = \left(\frac{\mu}{a_n}\right)^{b_n}$ and $M_s = \left(\frac{\mu}{a_s}\right)^{b_s}$, where $\mu \equiv N_nT_nA$.

We know that $\widehat{T}_n' > \widehat{T}_n$. This is because LHS($A2$) < LHS($A1$), while RHS($A2$) = RHS($A1$). Now, suppose $\widetilde{T}_n$ solves

$$\begin{aligned} &M_n[1-(1+\alpha)\alpha^{\alpha\epsilon}] + M_s(1-(1+\alpha)\alpha^{\alpha\epsilon}) \\ &\quad = \frac{(N_s+N_n)A}{\mu}[T - T_n(1-\alpha^{\alpha\epsilon})](b_nM_n + b_sM_s). \end{aligned} \tag{B3}$$

where $M_n = \left(\frac{\mu}{a_n}\right)^{b_n}$ and $M_s = \left(\frac{\mu}{a_s}\right)^{b_s}$, where $\mu \equiv (N_s + N_n)T_nA$.

We can prove that $\widetilde{T}_n > \widehat{T}_n'$. The proof is given below. Define $P \equiv A[T - T_s(1-\alpha^{\alpha\epsilon})]b_s$; $Q \equiv [1-(1+\alpha)\alpha^{\alpha\epsilon}]$; $R \equiv A[T - T_s(1-\alpha^{\alpha\epsilon})]b_n$ and $S \equiv (1-\alpha^{\alpha\epsilon})$. Equation (A2) can be written as

$$M_s\left(\frac{P}{AT_n} - Q\right) + M_n\left(\frac{R}{AT_n} - Q\right) = 0, \tag{B4}$$

where $M_n = \left(\frac{\mu}{a_n}\right)^{b_n}$ and $M_s = \left(\frac{\mu}{a_s}\right)^{b_s}$, where $\mu \equiv N_nT_nA$.

Now, we have

$$\begin{aligned}\frac{\partial \text{LHS}(A4)}{\partial N_n} &= \frac{\partial M_s}{\partial N_n}\left(\frac{P}{AT_n} - Q\right) + \frac{\partial M_n}{\partial N_n}\left(\frac{R}{AT_n} - Q\right)\\ &= \frac{M_s}{\mu} b_s T_n A \left(\frac{P}{AT_n} - Q\right) + \frac{M_n}{\mu} b_n T_n A \left(\frac{R}{AT_n} - Q\right)\\ &= \frac{M_s}{\mu} b_s T_n A \left(\frac{P}{AT_n} - Q\right) - \frac{M_s}{\mu} b_n T_n A \left(\frac{P}{AT_n} - Q\right)\\ &= \frac{M_s}{\mu} T_n A (b_s - b_n) \left(\frac{P}{AT_n} - Q\right)\end{aligned}$$

The third line of the above equation comes from using equation (A4). We are now ready to prove that the last line is greater than zero. If $b_n > b_s$, then equation (A4) indicates that $\frac{R}{AT_n} - Q > 0 > \frac{P}{AT_n} - Q$ since the two expressions must be of opposite signs; on the other hand, if $b_n < b_s$, then equation (A4) indicates that $\frac{R}{AT_n} - Q < 0 < \frac{P}{AT_n} - Q$. Both cases imply that the last line is greater than zero. Therefore, $\frac{\partial \text{LHS}(A4)}{\partial N_n} > 0$.

Now, it is quite clear that $\frac{\partial \text{LHS}(A4)}{\partial T_n} < 0$. Therefore, by the Implicit Function Theorem, we conclude that $\frac{\mathrm{d}T_n}{\mathrm{d}N_n} > 0$ for equation (A4) to hold. Now, (A3) is obtained from (A2) by changing N_n to $N_s + N_n$. Therefore, we can conclude that $\widetilde{T}_n > \widehat{T}'_n > \widehat{T}_n > T^*_n$. Since $(\partial/\partial T_n)[\text{RHS}(A3) - \text{LHS}(A3)] < 0$, and $\text{RHS}(A3) - \text{LHS}(A3) = 0$ at $T_n = \widetilde{T}_n$, it follows that $\text{RHS}(A3) - \text{LHS}(A3) > 0$ at $T_n = T^*_n$. Since $\text{RHS}(8)(\text{at } T_s = T^*_n) = \text{RHS}(A3) - \text{LHS}(A3)$ (at $T_n = T^*_n$), we conclude that $\frac{dW}{dT_s}|_{T_s = T^*_n} > 0$.

C. $\mathrm{d}\mathcal{N}/\mathrm{d}T_s$ and $\mathrm{d}\mathcal{S}/\mathrm{d}T_s$

Note that

$$\mathrm{d}\mathcal{S} = \mathrm{d}U^c_s + \mathrm{d}U_{zs} \quad \text{and} \quad \mathrm{d}\mathcal{N} = \mathrm{d}U^c_n + \mathrm{d}U_{zn}.$$

From the analysis in Section 3, we have

$$\frac{\mathrm{d}U^c_s}{\mathrm{d}T_s} < 0, \ \frac{\mathrm{d}U^c_n}{\mathrm{d}T_s} > 0, \ \left|\frac{\mathrm{d}U^c_s}{\mathrm{d}T_s}\right| < \left|\frac{\mathrm{d}U^c_n}{\mathrm{d}T_s}\right|.$$

From the analysis in Section 4, we have

$$\frac{dU_{zs}}{d\tau} < 0, \quad \frac{dU_{zn}}{d\tau} > 0, \quad \left|\frac{dU_{zs}}{d\tau}\right| > \left|\frac{dU_{zn}}{d\tau}\right|.$$

From equation (9), we have

$$\mathcal{S}(\tau)(1-\upsilon)\frac{\mathrm{d}U_{zn}}{\mathrm{d}U_{zs}} + \mathcal{N}(\tau)\upsilon = 0.$$

Since we want to find the effect of changes in U_n^c (due to changes in T_s) on $\mathcal{S}$ and $\mathcal{N}$, we totally differentiate the above equation with respect to τ and any other variables that are affected by T_s and τ.

$$(1-\upsilon)\frac{\mathrm{d}U_{zn}}{\mathrm{d}U_{zs}}d\mathcal{S} + \mathcal{S}(\tau)(1-\upsilon)\frac{\mathrm{d}}{\mathrm{d}\tau}\left(\frac{\mathrm{d}U_{zn}}{\mathrm{d}U_{zs}}\right)\mathrm{d}\tau + \upsilon\mathrm{d}\mathcal{N} = 0,$$

which implies

$$(1-\upsilon)\frac{dU_{zn}}{dU_{zs}}(dU_s^c + dU_{zs}) + \mathcal{S}(\tau)(1-\upsilon)\frac{d}{d\tau}\left(\frac{dU_{zn}}{dU_{zs}}\right)d\tau$$
$$+\upsilon(dU_n^c + dU_{zn}) = 0.$$

Note that changes in U_n^c and U_s^c are due to T_s while changes in U_{zn} and U_{zs} are due to τ. An increase in T_s leads to an increase in U_n^c and a decrease in U_s^c, thus prompting the North to decrease τ in the tariff negotiation, which in turn leads to an increase in U_{zs} and a decrease in U_{zn}, as will be shown below. Differentiating the equation with respect to T_s, we have

$$(1-\upsilon)\frac{\mathrm{d}U_{zn}}{\mathrm{d}U_{zs}}\left(\frac{\mathrm{d}U_s^c}{\mathrm{d}T_s} + \frac{\mathrm{d}U_{zs}}{\mathrm{d}\tau}\frac{\mathrm{d}\tau}{\mathrm{d}T_s}\right) + \mathcal{S}(\tau)(1-\upsilon)\frac{\mathrm{d}}{\mathrm{d}\tau}\left(\frac{\mathrm{d}U_{zn}}{\mathrm{d}U_{zs}}\right)\frac{\mathrm{d}\tau}{\mathrm{d}T_s}$$
$$+\upsilon\left(\frac{\mathrm{d}U_n^c}{\mathrm{d}T_s} + \frac{\mathrm{d}U_{zn}}{\mathrm{d}\tau}\frac{\mathrm{d}\tau}{\mathrm{d}T_s}\right) = 0.$$

Let $Y \equiv \left|\frac{dU_{zn}}{dU_{zs}}\right| > 1$. Recall that $\frac{dU_{zn}}{dU_{zs}} < 0$. From the above equation, we can solve for

$$\frac{\mathrm{d}\tau}{\mathrm{d}T_s} = \frac{(1-\upsilon)\frac{dU_s^c}{dT_s}Y - \upsilon\frac{dU_n^c}{dT_s}}{(1-\upsilon)\left[-Y\frac{dU_{zs}}{d\tau} - \mathcal{S}\frac{dY}{d\tau}\right] + \upsilon\frac{dU_{zn}}{d\tau}} < 0.$$

Therefore,

$$\frac{\mathrm{d}\mathcal{S}}{\mathrm{d}T_s}=\frac{\mathrm{d}U_s^c}{\mathrm{d}T_s}+\frac{\mathrm{d}U_{zs}}{\mathrm{d}\tau}\cdot\frac{\mathrm{d}\tau}{\mathrm{d}T_s}=\frac{-(1-\upsilon)\mathcal{S}\frac{dU_s^c}{dT_s}\frac{dY}{d\tau}+\upsilon\frac{dU_s^c}{dT_s}\frac{dU_{zn}}{d\tau}-\upsilon\frac{dU_n^c}{dT_s}\frac{dU_{zs}}{d\tau}}{(1-\upsilon)\left[-Y\frac{dU_{zs}}{d\tau}-\mathcal{S}\frac{dY}{d\tau}\right]+\upsilon\frac{dU_{zn}}{d\tau}}.$$

On the RHS of the above equation, the denominator is always positive. However, the numerator is greater than zero only if υ is sufficiently large or when $\mathcal{S}$ is sufficiently small, based on the inequalities obtained at the beginning of the proof and $\frac{\mathrm{d}Y}{\mathrm{d}\tau}<0$. Hence, the expression is positive if υ is sufficiently large or $\mathcal{S}$ is small. When $T_s=T_s^*$, $\tau=\tau^*$, and $\mathcal{S}=0$. Therefore, $\frac{\mathrm{d}\mathcal{S}}{\mathrm{d}T_s}>0$ at $T_s=T_s^*$. Given that, as T_s increases, $\left|\frac{dU_s^c}{dT_s}\right|$ and $\left|\frac{dY}{d\tau}\right|$ both increase, while $\left|\frac{dU_n^c}{dT_s}\right|-\left|\frac{dU_s^c}{dT_s}\right|$ decreases, and $\left|\frac{dU_{zs}}{d\tau}\right|-\left|\frac{dU_{zn}}{d\tau}\right|$ decreases, we conclude that $\frac{d\mathcal{S}}{dT_s}$ gets smaller as T_s increases. Therefore, $\mathcal{S}$ is maximized as T_s increases to a certain level. This level may not be much higher than T_s^* if υ is small. Thus, if υ is small, it is optimal for the South to increase its IPR protection only slightly. From the South's point of view, it is optimal to increase IPR protection all the way to T_n^* only when υ is sufficiently large so that $\frac{d\mathcal{S}}{dT_s}>0$ for any $T_s\in[T_s^*,T_n^*]$.

On the other hand,

$$\begin{aligned}\frac{\mathrm{d}\mathcal{N}}{\mathrm{d}T_s}&=\frac{\mathrm{d}U_n^c}{\mathrm{d}T_s}+\frac{dU_{zn}}{\mathrm{d}\tau}\cdot\frac{\mathrm{d}\tau}{\mathrm{d}T_s}\\&=\frac{(1-\upsilon)\left[-Y\frac{dU_n^c}{dT_s}\frac{dU_{zs}}{d\tau}+Y\frac{dU_n^c}{dT_s}\frac{dU_{zn}}{d\tau}-\mathcal{S}\frac{dY}{d\tau}\frac{dU_n^c}{dT_s}\right]}{(1-\upsilon)\left[-Y\frac{dU_{zs}}{d\tau}-\mathcal{S}\frac{dY}{d\tau}\right]+\upsilon\frac{dU_{zn}}{d\tau}}>0,\end{aligned}$$

because both the denominator and numerator are positive, based on the inequalities obtained at the beginning of the proof and $\frac{dY}{d\tau}<0$.

Acknowledgment

The authors are grateful for the helpful comments from participants in their presentations at City University of Hong Kong, Penn State University, Oregon State University, Rutgers University, Far Eastern Meeting of Econometric Society in Kobe, and the Midwest International Economics Conferences held at Purdue U. and U. of

Wisconsin-Madison. The work in this paper has been supported by the Research Grants Council of Hong Kong, China (Project no. CityU 1145/99H).

References

Burmeister, E. (1980). *Capital Theory and Dynamics*, Cambridge University Press, Cambridge, Massachusetts, USA.

Chin, J. and Grossman, G. M. (1990). Intellectual property rights and North-South trade, in Jones, R. and Krueger, A. O. (eds.), *The Political Economy of International Trade*, Oxford: Basil Blackwell, pp. 90–107.

Deardorff, A. V. (1992). Welfare effects of global patent protection, *Economica* 59, 35–51.

Diwan, I. and Rodrik, D. (1991). Patents, appropriate technology, and North-South trade, *Journal of International Economics* 30, 27–47.

Glass, A. J. and Saggi, K. (2002). Intellectual property rights and foreign direct investment, *Journal of International Economics*, 56(2), 387–410.

Gould, D. M. and Gruben, W. C. (1996). The role of intellectual property rights in economic growth, *Journal of Development Economics* 48, 323–350.

Helpman, E. (1993). Innovation, imitation, and intellectual property rights, *Econometrica* 61(6), 1247–1280.

Hoekman, B. M. and Kostecki, M. M. (1995). *The Political Economy of the World Trading System,* Oxford: Oxford University Press.

Horowitz, A. W. and Lai, E. L.-C. (1996). Patent length and rate of innovation, *International Economic Review* 37(4), 785–801.

Horstmann, I., Markusen, J., and Robles, J. (2001). *Multi-Issue Bargaining and Linked Agendas: Ricardo Revisited or No Pain No Gain*, NBER Working Paper #8347.

Lai, E. L.-C. (1998). International intellectual property rights protection and rate of product innovation, *Journal of Development Economics* 55, 133–153.

Mansfield, E. (1986). Patents and innovation: An empirical study, *Management Science* 32(2), 272–280.

Maskus, K. E. (1998). The international regulation of intellectual property, *Weltwirtschaftliches Archiv* 134(2), 186–208.

Maskus, K. E. (2000). *Intellectual Property Rights in the Global Economy,* Washington, DC: Institute for International Economics.

Maskus, K. E. and Penubarti, M. (1995). How trade-related are intellectual property rights? *Journal of International Economics* 39, 227–248.

McCalman, P. (2001). Reaping what you sow: An empirical analysis of international patent harmonization, *Journal of International Economics* 55(1), 161–186.

Nordhaus, W. (1969). *Invention, Growth, and Welfare*, Cambridge, Mass.: MIT Press.

Qiu, L. D. and Lai, E. L.-C. (2001). Trade and Intellectual Property Rights Protection: The Roles of Northern and Southern Tariffs, mimeo, Hong Kong University of Science and Technology.

Reichman, J. H. (1995). Universal minimum standards of intellectual property protection under the TRIPS component of the WTO agreement, *The International Lawyer* 29(2), 345–388.

Richardson, R. S. and Gaisford, J. D. (1996). North-South disputes over the protection of intellectual property, *Canadian Journal of Economics* 29, S376–S381.

Taylor, M. S. (1993). TRIPS, trade, and technology transfer, *Canadian Journal of Economics* 26(3), 625–637.

United Nations Conference on Trade and Development (UNCTAD) (1997). *The TRIPS Agreement and Developing Countries*, Geneva: UNCTAD.

Yang, Y. (1998). Why do Southern countries have little incentive to protect Northern IPRs? *Canadian Journal of Economics* 31(4), 800–816.

Chapter 7

Protection of Trade for Innovation: The Roles of Northern and Southern Tariffs*

Abstract
Using a North-South trade model with innovation and imitation, we investigate the interaction of intellectual property rights (IPR) protection and trade protection. We show that unlike a Southern tariff, a Northern tariff supplements IPR protection and is not necessarily a beggar-thy-neighbor policy. The globally optimal Northern tariff increases as IPR protection in the North or the South decreases. Global welfare may rise as Northern tariff increases, but necessarily declines as Southern tariff increases. This suggests that pushing for freer trade in the South is more urgent than in the North in innovation-intensive sectors where IPR protections are weak in both regions.

1 Introduction

Although innovation is conducive to economic growth, it is widely believed that markets do not provide appropriate incentives for innovation.[1] Nonetheless, there are many attempts to solve the

*By Larry D. Qiu and Edwin L.-C. Lai. Originally published in *Japan and the World Economy*, 16 (2004), pp. 449–470.

[1]Throughout this chapter, the words innovation and invention are used interchangeably, and so are the words innovate and invent.

problem of under-provision of new products and new production processes. In practice, governments have adopted various mechanisms to encourage innovation, including patents, R&D subsidization and patent buy-out.[2] Among those mechanisms, patents are used most widely and, along with copyrights and trademarks, are the major components of Intellectual Property Rights (IPR) protection. However, perhaps partly due to the myopic concerns of some interest groups over monopoly pricing, it is believed by many that even in developed countries (referred to here as the North) IPR protection is not strong enough from the social point of view, not to mention in less developed countries (referred to here as the South).[3] Thus, there are cries for stronger IPR protection from industries, and cooperative efforts have been made to strengthen IPR protection in many nations.[4] While most countries are strengthening IPR protection laws, there are many obstacles in enforcement. Some other mechanisms are potential supplements for weak IPR protection although they were not originally designed for such a purpose. This paper argues that trade policy measures are one of those mechanisms.

The reason why trade policy measures can potentially be used to supplement IPR protection measures is that IPR standards are usually slow to change while trade barriers can be erected relatively

[2]However, each of these mechanisms has its own shortcomings. Patents create monopolies and lead to social deadweight losses. Government subsidy of R&D is much better than the patent policy (Spence, 1984), but it cannot escape from the asymmetric information problem and always invites rent-seeking, which leads to inefficient subsidization. Patent buy-out could be potentially superior to the other two mechanisms, but it too may have drawbacks that have not yet come to light due to its short history and the lack of theoretical analysis. Kremer (1997) is one of the recent studies on patent buy-out.

[3]Kremer (1997) has a nice summary of the empirical literature on patents. Given the current patent system, social returns to innovation far exceed the private returns, suggesting that innovation is not encouraged sufficiently.

[4]In many recent international agreements, including the Uruguay Round, the European Union and the North American Free Trade Agreement, signatories are required to strengthen their national IPR protection over the next decade. See Maskus (1998) for some discussions on this.

quickly. Legislations to change IPR standards usually take a long time to enact because they need more debates, while trade barriers can often be imposed by the administration without going through the legislature, and they are very often non-noticeable to the public (e.g. administrative barriers).

Trade barriers, proxied by tariffs, can affect pricing decisions and profits of firms, which in turn affect incentives to innovate. Hence, tariffs can either supplement or offset IPR protection. It is therefore important to make a close, careful re-examination of tariffs when IPRs are not fully protected. The present study is motivated by this need. To carry out this reexamination, we establish a North-South trade model with innovation and imitation, in which both regions provide some degrees of IPR protection, captured by patent lengths, and trade protection, captured by tariffs. It is evident that the South has much lower inventive ability than the North's. For simplicity, therefore, we make the assumption that innovations originate only from the North.

The focus of the present paper is on the welfare effects of tariffs in the presence of innovation and imitation. Basically, we have obtained three results in this regard. First, there is a new rationale for a Northern tariff, besides terms-of-trade and rent-shifting considerations, which are well-documented in the trade literature.[5] When innovations concentrate in the North, a Northern tariff provides incentives for innovation and thus benefits consumers. Moreover, because of this effect, the optimal Northern tariff rate is always higher in the present model than in models without innovation. The tariff that is designed to capture this third effect is to promote innovation, not protect profits. A corollary of this effect is that a Northern tariff supplements IPR protection. In fact, weaker IPR protection in the North or the South not only calls for higher tariff protection in the North for the sake of Northern consumer

[5]There are some other economic justifications for tariffs, such as the infant industry argument and increasing returns to scale. Of course, one can also find arguments for tariffs in political economy.

welfare; it also calls for higher Northern tariff for the sake of world welfare.

Second, while a Northern tariff is pro-innovation, a Southern tariff, in contrast, is anti-innovation. This differentiates the two tariffs in an important way: a Southern tariff is a beggar-thy-neighbor policy, but a Northern one may not be. Third, global welfare declines as the South raises its tariff rate, but under some circumstances global welfare rises as the North increases its tariff rate. Hence, Southern tariffs are more detrimental to world welfare than Northern ones in innovation-intensive sectors where innovations concentrate in the North and IPR protection is weak in both regions. An example that comes to mind is internet-related products.[6]

Zigic (2000) finds a similar motive for the North to protect trade, and that a Northern tariff can be globally welfare improving. While he only focuses on the Northern market, our emphasis is the result that weaker IPR protection in the world calls for higher Northern tariffs for the sake of global welfare. Moreover, we emphasize the differing roles of Northern and Southern tariffs in a world where innovation concentrates in the North.

Our results have obvious policy implications. Note that in the real world the South maintains much higher trade barriers in general, and tariffs in particular, than the North. Our results, however, suggest that the opposite would lead to higher global welfare in certain sectors. The message that this study conveys is that it is more harmful to keep a high tariff in the South than in the North, and hence trade liberalization is more urgent and should be carried out at a faster pace in the South than in the North in certain well-defined sectors. From a policy point of view, it would benefit the North to subsidize trade liberalization of the South since Southern tariff reduction improves global welfare, and so the South's loss would be more than offset by the North's gain.

---

[6]In contrast, if tariffs are designed for the purpose of terms-of-trade improvement or profit-shifting, the Northern tariff and the Southern tariff are not qualitatively different.

There exists a rich literature on technology and trade, which mainly focuses on the interplay between innovation and international trade.[7] More recently, there have also been studies on the effects of IPR protection and trade policy. Taylor (1993), Maskus and Penubarti (1995), and Smith (1999) investigate whether strengthening IPR protection induces more trade flows. Horowitz and Lai (1996) and Lai (1998) analyze the effects of IPR protection on the rates of innovation. Grossman and Helpman (1991, Chapters 6 and 10) examine the response of innovation rates to trade and industrial policy. However, it is notable that studies on the welfare effects of the interaction of trade policy and IPR protection policy in the context of North-South trade are scarce. Chin and Grossman (1990), Diwan and Rodrik (1991), Deardorff (1992), Helpman (1993), and Lai and Qiu (2003) all examine how strengthening IPR protection in the South affects welfare in the North, the South, or both regions. As Grossman and Helpman (1995, p. 1327) point out, we still do not have a complete normative analysis of trade policy, especially for a large, open, innovating economy. We attempt to fill a gap in this literature by building a model to analyze the interaction between trade and IPR policies.[8]

The rest of the chapter is organized as follows. In Section 2, we construct a North-South trade model with innovation and imitation, and examine the policy effects on equilibrium amounts of innovation and imitation. Section 3 analyzes the Northern tariff. Section 4 compares the role of a Northern tariff with a Southern one. Finally, Section 5 concludes with a discussion of some caveats of the model.

2 The Model

Consider a world comprised of two regions, the North and the South, which differ only in their abilities to invent differentiated products.[9]

---

[7]Grossman and Helpman (1995) has a comprehensive survey of this literature.
[8]Zigic (2000) is also along this line.
[9]In the literature, it is common that one study focuses only on one type of innovation that either generates new products, improves the quality of existing products, or lowers production costs.

For analytical simplicity, we confine our study to an extreme case, which is not unrealistic, where innovation only takes place in the North.[10] In any period, there is a set of potential differentiated products to be invented, indexed by i within the range $[0, +\infty)$. Any differentiated product will become obsolete T periods after its invention. Beyond that, it loses its economic value. The IPR policy of a region is proxied by its patent length. A patent length of T_n, $T_n \leq T$, means that the Northern government prevents a patented product from being imitated or sold in the North within T_n periods after its invention.

Although the Northern government's IPR policy cannot be extended to the South, a differentiated product will not be imitated in the South within T_s periods after its invention, due to a natural imitation lag or the IPR protection by the Southern government. T_s periods after a product is invented, it can be (and will be) imitated and sold in the South.

The two regions trade with each other. The Northern government imposes a uniform specific tariff τ_n on all products imported from the South, and the Southern government imposes a uniform specific tariff τ_s on all products imported from the North.

In the beginning of period 1, the vector of policy instruments $\tau \equiv (T_n, T_s, \tau_n, \tau_s)$ are set by the governments. In each subsequent period, potential innovators then make their investment decisions. We assume that firms and consumers are faced with the same market

[10]The qualitative aspects of our results so derived remain robust even if we allow both regions to innovate and imitate as long as most of the innovation takes place in the North and most of the imitation occurs in the South. We have included a discussion on this in the concluding section. In fact, this is a common assumption in the literature, for example, Krugman (1979), Grossman and Helpman (1991, Chapter 11), and Helpman (1993). Grossman and Helpman (1995, p. 1327) also provide several reasons for this, "First, firms in the South have shown only limited ability to develop innovative products of their own. Second, several of the governments of less developed nations have been somewhat lax in their enforcement of foreign intellectual property rights. Finally, the low wage rates of the South make it an especially attractive place for copying some kinds of products, because successful imitators can expect to earn substantial profits in their competition against innovators who bear higher labor costs".

parameters in all periods, and so the same *number* of products will be invented in every period. Let M be the number of differentiated products invented in the North in each period. The same firm could invent more than one product in every period. Nonetheless, for ease of exposition, we treat different products (whether in the same period or not) as being invented by different firms. All differentiated products are necessarily different in order to be patented. We will show in Section 2.2 that by making an appropriate ordering the first M products will be invented in every period in equilibrium.

Before period T, the total number of products whose patents have not expired change from one period to the next. After period T, however, the number becomes steady. Therefore, a steady state is attained after period T. To simplify the analysis, we assume that there is no discount of the future. Since there is no discounting, we can focus our attention on the steady-state flow welfare for the purpose of welfare analysis. This can be justified by "overtaking criterion" in dynamic optimization theory.[11] In every steady-state period, there are $T_n M$ products whose patents have not expired in the North, $(T - T_n)M$ economically viable products whose patents have expired in the North, $T_s M$ products still maintaining monopoly power in the South, and $(T - T_s)M$ imitated products sold in the South. Although the number of products is discrete, we treat it as continuous in our mathematical derivation for easier handling.

Define t as the age of a product from the time of invention. Consumers in the two regions have identical utility function. In every steady-state period, consumers in each region j (with $j = n$ for the North and s for the South) derive utility from consuming the differentiated products and a composite traditional product[12]:

$$u_j = \sum_{t=1}^{T} \int_0^M x_j(i,t)^{\alpha} \mathrm{d}i + X_j, \quad 0 < \alpha < 1, \quad j = n, s,$$

[11]See, for example, Burmeister (1980), pp. 249–250.

[12]Specific utility functions are used in many other studies including Krugman (1979), Grossman and Helpman (1991, Chapter 11), and Helpman (1993).

where $x_j(i,t)$ is the consumption of product i with age t in region j, and X_j is the quantity of traditional good consumed by region j. In what follows, when it is unnecessary to keep the argument t in $x_j(i,t)$, we will drop it. To simplify the notation, we define $\epsilon = 1/(1-\alpha)$ and $A = (1-\alpha)\alpha^{(1+\alpha)\epsilon}$.

While the price of the traditional good is normalized to one in both regions, the price of differentiated product i with age t in region j is denoted by $p_j(i,t)$. Since there is no lending and borrowing, in each steady-state period, consumers in region j maximize the period's utility under the budget constraint: $E_j \geq \sum_{t=1}^{T}\int_0^M p_j(i,t)x_j(i,t)\mathrm{d}i + X_j$, where E_j is the (exogenous) total income spent on consumption by region j. Hence, the instantaneous demand for differentiated products of all ages is

$$p_j(i) = \alpha x_j(i)^{\alpha-1}, \quad j = n, s,$$

which has constant elasticity equal to ϵ. Note that the specific form of the utility function considered above implies that we confine our analysis to independent products. Allowing substitution among the differentiated products will greatly complicate the analysis without altering the results qualitatively.

2.1 The market

Let us consider the Northern market first. Suppose product i has been invented by a Northern firm, called it Northern firm i. The firm will be guaranteed a monopoly position in the Northern market for T_n periods and in the Southern market for T_s periods. To sharpen our focus on innovation, we assume that the innovation costs of different products vary (see next subsection), but their production costs are the same. Specifically, and for simplicity, assume identical and constant marginal cost of production, which is equal to c, for all firms in the North. Then, under IPR protection from the North, i.e. for Northern firm i with $t \leq T_n$, its steady-state flow operating profit (i.e. profit not taking into account the innovation costs) in the Northern market is $\pi_{nn} = (p_n - c)x_n$, where subscript nn stands for a Northern firm in the Northern market. In equilibrium (superscript

m standing for monopoly),

$$p_n^m = \alpha^{-1}c, \quad x_n^m = \alpha^{2\epsilon}c^{-\epsilon}, \quad \text{and} \quad \pi_{nn}^m = Ac^{-\alpha\epsilon}$$
$$\text{for a product with} \quad t \leq T_n. \tag{1}$$

After T_n periods, patent for product i expires in the North. Imitators start to enter the Northern market. Imitation is costly.[13] To simplify our analysis, but with little loss in generality, we assume equal imitation cost for all potential imitators and for all products. To focus on innovation and imitation costs, let us assume that the constant marginal cost of production in the South is also c.[14] Since the imitators face the same cost and demand for each product, there would be an equal number of entrants in all products.[15] Assume there are H Northern imitators and K Southern imitators for each product in equilibrium. Thus, the Northern innovator in the Northern market will face competition from the K Southern imitators and H Northern imitators after T_n periods. We assume that firms in the same market compete in quantity *à la* Cournot.[16] Consider the product markets for i. Each Southern imitator k has the following per-period export profit: $\pi_{sn} = [(p_n - c - \tau_n)]x_{sn}$, where x_{sn} is Southern imitator k's export volume (subscript sn stands for a Southern firm in the Northern market). The total export is Kx_{sn}. The Northern innovator and H Northern imitators each sells

[13]Empirical evidence indicates that imitation could be very costly, normally higher than 20% of the costs of innovation (Mansfield *et al.*, 1981). Glass and Saggi (2002) analyze the theoretical implications of costly imitation for innovation and foreign direct investment.

[14]The qualitative results do not change if we assume different production costs in the two regions, which is the case in our working paper Qiu and Lai (1999).

[15]This will be the case if imitation cost is not low and competition reduces market profit drastically. Moreover, in this model, if we explicitly allow imitators to choose products for imitation, they will choose to imitate different products. Limited resources also disallow a single imitator to imitate many products. All these tend to support the above assumption. Also imitation requires certain technology not owned by everyone.

[16]Changing from Cournot to Stackelberg model in the product market will not alter any of our results, since the effects of an increase in Northern tariff would be qualitatively the same. The analysis is available upon request.

x_{nn} to this market and has a per-period operating profit equal to $\pi_{nn} = (p_n - c)x_{nn}$. Hence, the total supply of product i in the Northern market is $x_n = (H+1)x_{nn} + Kx_{sn}$.

Denote $B(H,K) \equiv \epsilon\alpha^{\epsilon}(H+K+\alpha)^{\epsilon}$. The resulting equilibrium in the Northern market for product i is, for $T \geq t > T_n$,

$$\begin{cases} p_n = [(H+K+1)c + K\tau_n]/(H+K+\alpha), \\ x_n = \{\alpha(H+K+\alpha)/[(H+K+1)c+K\tau_n]\}^{\epsilon}, \\ x_{nn} = B(H,K)[(1-\alpha)c + K\tau_n]/[(H+K+1)c+K\tau_n]^{\epsilon+1}, \\ x_{sn} = B(H,K)[(1-\alpha)c - (H+\alpha)\tau_n]/[(H+K+1)c+K\tau_n]^{\epsilon+1}, \\ \pi_{nn} = B(H,K)[(1-\alpha)c + K\tau_n]^2/\{[(H+K+1)c+K\tau_n]^{1+\epsilon} \\ \qquad (H+K+\alpha)\}, \\ \pi_{sn} = B(H,K)[(1-\alpha)c - (H+\alpha)\tau_n]^2/ \\ \qquad \{[(H+K+1)c+K\tau_n]^{1+\epsilon}(H+K+\alpha)\}. \end{cases} \tag{2}$$

Clearly, from (2) we see that the Northern tariff reduces π_{sn} (i.e. $\partial\pi_{sn}/\partial\tau_n < 0$). Using condition $x_{sn} > 0$ or equivalently $(1-\alpha)c - (H+\alpha)\tau_n > 0$, we can show that

$$\frac{\partial\pi_{nn}}{\partial\tau_n} = \frac{KB(H,K)[(1-\alpha)c + K\tau_n]}{[(H+K+1)c+K\tau_n]^{2+\epsilon}} \times \left\{\frac{\epsilon[2(1-\alpha)c - (H+\alpha)\tau_n] + \alpha c}{H+K+\alpha}\right\} > 0. \tag{3}$$

A Northern tariff shifts profits from the Southern imitators to the Northern innovators and imitators. For products with $t \in (T_n, T]$, there are $H+1$ identical Northern firms (each with a marginal cost equal to c) and K identical Southern firms (each with a marginal cost equal to $c+\tau_n$) competing in the Northern market. As τ_n increases, the marginal cost for Southern firms increases. It is intuitive that the profits of all Northern firms increase while those of all Southern firms decrease.

We now examine the Southern markets. For products with $t \leq T_s$, Northern firm i, as a monopolist, exports its product to the South. Similar to (1), we have the following equilibrium (subscript ns stands for a Northern firm in the Southern market).

$$p_s^m = \alpha^{-1}(c+\tau_s), \quad x_s^m = \alpha^{2\epsilon}(c+\tau_s)^{-\epsilon}, \quad \text{and} \quad \pi_{ns}^m = A(c+\tau_s)^{-\alpha\epsilon}$$
$$\text{for products with} \quad t \le T_s. \tag{4}$$

A Northern innovator i with $t \in (T_s, T]$ (and with marginal cost $c+\tau_s$) competes against H Northern imitators (each with marginal cost $c+\tau_s$) and K Southern imitating firms (each with marginal cost c) in the Southern market. (Note that Northern firms with $t \in (T_s, T]$ can carry out imitation and sell in the South.)

For a product with $t \in (T_s, T]$, let x_{ns} and π_{ns} denote the steady-state flow output and operating profit, respectively, of the Northern innovator *and* all Northern imitators in the Southern market; while x_{ss} and π_{ss} denote the steady-state flow output and operating profit, respectively, of all Southern imitators in the Southern market. Hence, for a product with $t \in (T_s, T]$,

$$\begin{cases} p_s = [(H+K+1)c + (H+1)\tau_s]/(H+K+\alpha), \\ x_s = \{\alpha(H+K+\alpha)/[(H+K+1)c + (H+1)\tau_s]\}^{\epsilon}, \\ x_{ns} = B(H,K)[(1-\alpha)c - (K-1+\alpha)\tau_s]/[(H+K+1)c \\ \qquad + (H+1)\tau_s]^{\epsilon+1}, \\ x_{ss} = B(H,K)[(1-\alpha)c + (H+1)\tau_s]/ \\ \qquad \times [(H+K+1)c + (H+1)\tau_s]^{\epsilon+1}, \\ \pi_{ns} = B(H,K)[(1-\alpha)c - (K-1+\alpha)\tau_s]^2/\{[(H+K+1)c \\ \qquad + (H+1)\tau_s]^{1+\epsilon}(H+K+\alpha)\}, \\ \pi_{ss} = B(H,K)[(1-\alpha)c + (H+1)\tau_s]^2/\{[(H+K+1)c \\ \qquad + (H+1)\tau_s]^{1+\epsilon}(H+K+\alpha)\}. \end{cases} \tag{5}$$

Clearly, from (5) we see that the Southern tariff reduces π_{ns} (i.e. $\partial\pi_{ns}/\partial\tau_s < 0$). Using condition $x_{ns} > 0$ or equivalently $(1-\alpha)c - (K+\alpha-1)\tau_s > 0$, we can show that

$$\frac{\partial \pi_{ss}}{\partial \tau_s} = (H+1)\frac{B(H,K)[(1-\alpha)c + (H+1)\tau_s]}{[(H+K+1)c + (H+1)\tau_s]^{2+\epsilon}} \times \left\{\frac{\epsilon[2(1-\alpha)Kc - \alpha\tau_s] + \alpha c}{H+K+\alpha}\right\} > 0.$$

The Southern tariff shifts profits from the Northern innovator and imitators to the Southern imitators. For a product with $t \in (T_s, T]$, there are $H+1$ identical Northern firms (each with a marginal cost equal to $c+\tau_s$) and K identical Southern firms (each with a marginal cost equal to c) competing in the Southern market. As τ_s increases, the marginal cost for Northern firms increases. It is intuitive that the steady-state flow profits of all Southern firms increase while those of all Northern firms decrease.

In summary, we have derived the steady-state product market equilibria in the North for two distinct kinds of products (i.e. those with $t \leq T_n$ and $T \geq t > T_n$, respectively), and also in the South (those with $t \leq T_s$ and $T \geq t > T_s$, respectively). In particular, we have calculated each type of firm's steady-state flow operating profit derived from each market.

2.2 Innovation and imitation

We now turn to innovation and imitation in order to determine the number of products invented in each period. To this end, we examine a firm's profit over T periods. Thus, we will move away from the focus on the steady-state in this subsection. Northern firm i invests in R&D to invent product i if and only if the stream of operating profits over the entire T periods is sufficiently large to cover the innovation costs, and the imitators use the same criterion to decide whether or not to imitate. For convenience, we order the products in such a way that a product with a higher index i has a higher innovation cost. This could be due to the fact that the Northern firm with a higher i is less capable of innovation. Alternatively, this reflects economy-wide diminishing marginal returns to innovation activities or increasing marginal cost of innovation. Without loss of generality, we adopt the simplest possible innovation cost structure for product i: innovation cost $= bi$ where $b > 0$. We assume that the imitation cost for each imitator in each product is the same, being equal to $e > 0$.

We now consider innovation. Recall that under IPR protection, Northern firm i, if it invests in innovation, earns monopoly profit as given by (1) from its home market in the first T_n periods, and monopoly profit as given by (4) from export to the South in the first T_s periods. Its operating profit in the Northern market in each period after IPR protection expires is π_{nn} as given by (2) and in the Southern market is π_{ns} as given by (5). By definition, Northern firm i's net life-time profit (taking into account innovation costs) is

$$\Pi_n(i) = \pi_n - bi, \tag{6}$$

where the life-time operating profit is equal to

$$\pi_n = AT_n c^{-\alpha\epsilon} + AT_s(c+\tau_s)^{-\alpha\epsilon} + (T - T_n)\pi_{nn} + (T - T_s)\pi_{ns}. \tag{7}$$

Since only firms that earn positive profits would produce, the number of products invented in each period, M, must satisfy

$$\Pi_n(M) = 0. \tag{8}$$

Then all products with index $i \leq M$ will be developed.

2.3 Policy effects on innovation

Given policy parameters, the preceding subsection has characterized the possible equilibrium outcomes about innovation. In this subsection, we explore how various policy measures affect the innovation set. Although time is discrete, we treat time as continuous in analyzing the impacts of changing T_s and T_n.

Since (8) determines the equilibrium number of innovation, differentiating with respect to policy variable (parameter) $y = \{\tau_n,\ \tau_s,\ T_n,\ T_s\}$ yields the impact of the policy on innovation according to

$$\frac{\partial M}{\partial y} = \frac{1}{b}\frac{\partial \pi_n}{\partial y}. \tag{9}$$

The innovation set will expand if a policy raises Northern innovator's operating profit π_n. Eventually, we obtain

Proposition 1. *Innovation is encouraged by raising IPR protection in either region or raising tariffs in the North. Innovation is*

discouraged by raising tariffs in the South. Mathematically,

$$\frac{\partial M}{\partial T_s} > 0, \quad \frac{\partial M}{\partial T_n} > 0, \quad \frac{\partial M}{\partial \tau_n} > 0, \quad \frac{\partial M}{\partial \tau_s} < 0.$$

Proof. See Appendix. □

3 Northern Trade Protection: Protect Profits vs. Promote Innovation

At this point we switch our focus and turn to welfare analysis. In this section, we characterize the optimal Northern tariff and its relation to the degree of IPR protection. In particular, we argue that Northern tariffs not only shift profits but also encourage innovation. In the next section, we will compare and contrast the Northern tariff and the Southern tariff. In both sections, our primary purpose is to derive results that would not be obtained in conventional trade models, i.e. models without product innovation and imitation.

Based on (1) and utility maximization, the steady-state flow Northern utility derived from all the products with $t \leq T_n$ is

$$u_n(t) = T_n \int_0^M x_n^\alpha \mathrm{d}i = T_n M(1-\alpha)\left(\frac{\alpha^2}{c}\right)^{\alpha\epsilon} \tag{10}$$

Similarly, based on (2), the steady-state flow Northern utility derived from all the products with $t \in (T_n, T]$ is

$$\widetilde{u_n}(t) = (T - T_n)M(1-\alpha)\left[\frac{\alpha(H+K+\alpha)}{(H+K+1)c + K\tau_n}\right]^{\alpha\epsilon} \tag{11}$$

We use V_n to denote the total imports by the North in steady state, and it is given by

$$V_n = \sum_{t=T_n}^{T} \int_0^M x_{sn}(t)\mathrm{d}i = M(T-T_n)v_n,$$

$$\text{where} \quad v_n = KB(H,K)\frac{(1-\alpha)c - (\alpha+H)\tau_n}{[(H+K+1)c + K\tau_n]^\epsilon}.$$

We now calculate the steady-state flow welfare of the North, denoted by $W_n(\tau)$. It is defined as the sum of steady-state flow consumer utility, producer profits and tariff revenue from all invented products. The steady-state flow profits are the sum of Northern firms' profits derived in a steady-state period, which turn out to be equal to the sum of the life-time profits of all products that are invented in that period plus the sum of the life-time profits of all Northern imitators in both markets in that period. It is clear that this is equal to $\int_0^M \Pi_n(i)\mathrm{d}i + MH\left[\sum_{t=T_n}^{T}\pi_{nn}(t) + \sum_{t=T_s}^{T}\pi_{ns}(t) - e\right]$. Hence,

$$\begin{aligned} W_n(\tau) &= \sum_{t=1}^{T_n} u_n(t) + \sum_{t=T_n}^{T} \widetilde{u_n}(t) + \int_0^M \Pi_n(i)\mathrm{d}i + E_n + \tau_n V_n \\ &\quad + MH\left[\sum_{t=T_n}^{T}\pi_{nn}(t) + \sum_{t=T_s}^{T}\pi_{ns}(t) - e\right] = Mw_n(\tau) + E_n \end{aligned} \tag{12}$$

where

$$\begin{aligned} w_n(\tau) &= T_n(1-\alpha)\left(\frac{\alpha^2}{c}\right)^{\alpha\epsilon} + (T - T_n)(1-\alpha) \\ &\quad \times \left[\frac{\alpha(H+K+\alpha)}{(H+K+1)c + K\tau_n}\right]^{\alpha\epsilon} + \frac{b}{2}\pi_n + \tau_n(T - T_n)v_n \\ &\quad + H\left[(T - T_n)\pi_{nn} + (T - T_s)\pi_{ns} - e\right]. \end{aligned}$$

The Northern government's objective is to maximize Northern steady-state flow welfare by choosing a non-negative τ_n. Thus, assuming that the optimal tariff rate is an interior solution, it must satisfy the following first-order condition:

$$\frac{\partial W_n}{\partial \tau_n} = M\frac{\partial w_n}{\partial \tau_n} + w_n\frac{\partial M}{\partial \tau_n} = 0. \tag{13}$$

We examine each welfare term of (13) in turn. First,

$$\frac{\partial w_n}{\partial \tau_n} = (T - T_n)\left[-\alpha K \frac{[\alpha(H+K+\alpha)]^{\alpha\epsilon}}{[(H+K+1)c + K\tau_n]^{\epsilon}} + \left(H + \frac{1}{2}\right)\frac{\partial \pi_{nn}}{\partial \tau_n} + v_n + \tau_n \frac{\partial v_n}{\partial \tau_n}\right]. \tag{14}$$

Equation (14) is the welfare effect of the tariff that we usually see in models with imperfect competition but without innovation and imitation. The Northern tariff reduces consumer surplus, increases firms' profits, and generates government revenue. If import subsidy is not allowed, the optimal tariff could be zero or positive, depending upon whether the terms of trade are improved and how much profit is shifted from the foreign exporters to the local firms.[17] For the sake of exposition, let $\overline{\tau}_n$ be the optimal tariff rate when changes in innovation are ignored. Then, $\overline{\tau}_n = 0$ if $\partial w_n/\partial \tau_n \leq 0$ at $\tau_n = 0$ and $\overline{\tau}_n > 0$ otherwise.

We now turn to the second term of (13). Since $\partial M/\partial \tau_n > 0$ (by Proposition 1), Northern consumers benefit from larger product variety and more products will be exported by the North. These together raise Northern welfare.

We now combine all the effects discussed above for the first-order condition (13). Let τ_n^* be the optimal tariff rate that satisfies (13). Then, $\tau_n^* = 0$ if $\partial W_n/\partial \tau_n \leq 0$ at $\tau_n = 0$ and $\tau_n^* > 0$ otherwise. From the above analysis, we know $\partial W_n/\partial \tau_n > \partial w_n/\partial \tau_n$, and hence, $\tau_n^* \geq \overline{\tau}_n$. More specifically, whenever $\overline{\tau}_n > 0$, we must have $\tau_n^* > 0$ and $\tau_n^* > \overline{\tau}_n$; and in some cases, $\overline{\tau}_n = 0$, but $\tau_n^* > 0$. We summarize the above results in Proposition 2.

Proposition 2. *There is a new rationale for a Northern tariff. There is one more reason why a Northern tariff can raise Northern welfare above the level attainable by free trade in the present model, as compared with other trade models without innovation and imitation. Whenever it is optimal to impose a tariff, the optimal tariff rate in*

[17]Helpman and Krugman (1989, Chapter 6) have a nice analysis of this issue.

the presence of innovation and imitation is strictly higher than that in the absence of innovation and imitation.

What exactly is the new rationale for Northern tariff? Suppose T_s and τ_s are beyond the control of the Northern government. Note also the empirical fact that IPR policies are slow to change (e.g. a 17-year patent length has been in place and unchanged for many decades in the US). If the given IPR protection T_n is too low for the existing tariff τ_n, then an increase in τ_n can increase consumer welfare by encouraging innovation and thereby making a larger variety of goods available for consumption.

We demonstrate the above point below. To isolate the new motive for tariff protection, we exclude producer profits and tariff revenue in the Northern welfare function. That is, we focus only on the effect on consumer welfare. This enables us to focus on the case where a tariff is not for profit shifting or terms-of-trade improvement. We investigate how the optimal tariff rate τ_n^c, which maximizes Northern consumer welfare $\tilde{W}_n$, depends on the degree of IPR protection. Assume the second-order condition holds, i.e. $\partial^2\tilde{W}_n/\partial\tau_n^2 < 0$. By totally differentiating the first-order condition (13) (with W_n replaced by $\tilde{W}_n$, see Appendix C), we obtain

$$\frac{\partial\tau_n^c}{\partial T_n} = -\frac{\partial}{\partial T_n}\left(\frac{\partial\tilde{W}_n}{\partial\tau_n}\right) \Big/ \left(\frac{\partial^2\tilde{W}_n}{\partial\tau_n^2}\right),$$

$$\text{which implies } \operatorname{sgn}\left(\frac{\partial\tau_n^c}{\partial T_n}\right) = \operatorname{sgn}\left[\frac{\partial}{\partial T_n}\left(\frac{\partial\tilde{W}_n}{\partial\tau_n}\right)\right].$$

This sign is negative, and a similar relationship holds for τ_n and T_s (see Appendix C). Therefore, we have the following proposition:

Proposition 3. *The Northern tariff that maximizes Northern consumer welfare is higher if IPR protection in the North or IPR protection in the South is weaker. Mathematically,* $\partial\tau_n^c/\partial T_n < 0$ *and* $\partial\tau_n^c/\partial T_s < 0$.

Proof. See Appendix. □

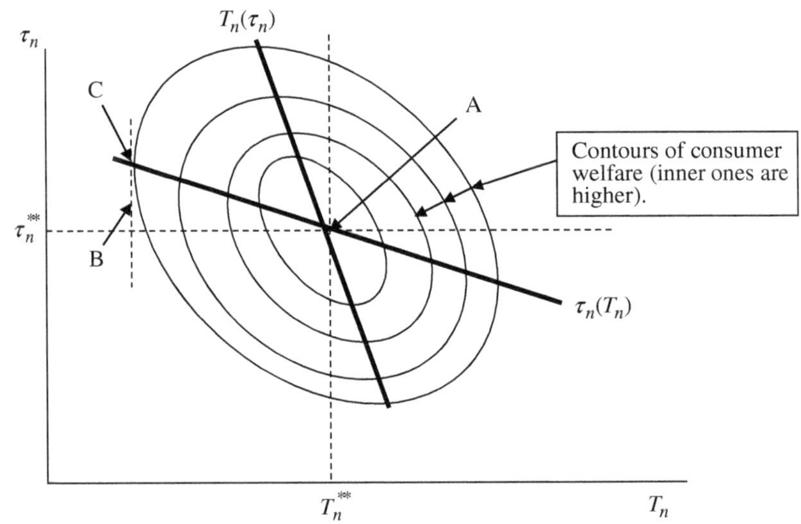

Figure 1. Optimal combination of T_n and τ_n for consumer welfare. $T_n(\tau_n)$ is the locus of all points with horizontal slopes. $\tau_n(T_n)$ is the locus of all points with vertical slopes. (T_n^{**}, τ_n^{**}) is the first best combination.

That an increase in import tariff can increase domestic consumer welfare is an interesting point, since most previous arguments for an optimal tariff are based on its effect on increased profits of firms and/or increased tariff revenue. Few previous theories have suggested that a higher tariff can increase consumer welfare.

In fact, an increased tariff to compensate for inadequate IPR protection is only a second best solution as far as the consumer welfare is concerned. The first best solution would be for both a tariff and IPR protection to be jointly optimally chosen to maximize consumer welfare. See Figure 1.

In the figure, it can be seen that the first best solution is at point A, denoted by (T_n^*, τ_n^*). The curve labeled $\tau_n(T_n)$ represents the optimal value of τ_n as a function of any given T_n. If T_n is lower (higher) than the first best, the optimal τ_n should be higher (lower) than the first best. The curve labeled $T_n(\tau_n)$ represents the optimal value of T_n as a function of any given τ_n. Again, if τ_n is lower (higher) than the first best, the optimal T_n should be higher (lower) than the first best.

The intersection of the two curves yields the first best solution for maximization of consumer welfare. Note that the first best optimal tariff is not $\tau_n = 0$ and the first best optimal IPR protection is not $T_n = T$. There are interior solutions to both. Suppose there is very little flexibility in the adjustment of T_n. Then curve $\tau_n(T_n)$ is the relevant one for our analysis. If T_n is too low for the existing τ_n, such as in point B, then consumer welfare can be improved with an increased τ_n by shifting to point C.

To understand intuitively how an increased Northern tariff can be used to (partly) supplement weak IPR protection, let us first compare the similar welfare effects resulting from an increase in Northern IPR protection and from a higher Northern tariff. Note that by excluding profits and tariff revenue the welfare is simply the consumer surplus, which decreases if the prices are higher but increases when there is larger product variety (i.e. a greater M). Since we cannot find any (costless) policy that will lower the prices and at the same time stimulate innovation, policy measures that maximize consumer welfare should be combined to strike a balance with prices being not too high and innovations being not too few. First, based on (12), we easily observe the two conflicting effects of increasing T_n. On the one hand, consumer surplus is reduced because all goods are charged at their monopoly prices for a longer period of time. On the other hand, M is larger and hence consumer surplus increases due to larger product variety. Second, those two conflicting welfare effects are also present when τ_n increases: An increase in the tariff results in higher prices paid by consumers for all products during the import periods and thus lowers consumer surplus; however, greater profits for the Northern innovators are assured by a higher tariff and therefore there are more innovations (i.e. M is larger), giving rise to greater consumer surplus. Clearly, the Northern tariff plays a similar role as Northern IPR protection and so the former can be used to supplement the latter when the Northern government has more flexibility to adjust its tariff rate than the patent length. For example, if IPR protection is too weak (T_n too small), meaning that M is not big enough from the consumers' point of view, we should raise the tariff to stimulate innovation. If, however, the IPR protection is already very strong (T_n very big), welfare can be increased by depressing the prices through lowering the tariff rate.

We now turn to the (partial) substitutability of τ_n for T_s. Unlike T_n, T_s has a single effect on Northern welfare through its influence on product variety: an increase of T_s raises M. Thus, as Southern IPR protection becomes weaker, the North can raise its tariff rate to at least partially compensate the Northern innovators, so that their innovations will not decrease too drastically. On the other hand, when Southern IPR protection becomes stronger, the North worries less about innovation incentives but more about high consumer prices, and thus the tariff rate should be lowered to dampen the prices.

To summarize this section, we have demonstrated (in Proposition 2) that there is a pro-innovation element in the optimal Northern tariff. This is a new justification (motive or rationale) for a Northern tariff. This effect of the tariff is to promote innovation, not protect profits. Moreover, in Proposition 3, we have shown that the optimal level of this tariff is higher (lower) if IPR protection, in the North or South, becomes weaker (stronger). Hence, we have identified the pro-innovation role of Northern tariffs, and its (partial) substitutability for IPR protection. In the next section, we shall compare the roles of Northern and Southern tariffs.

4 Trade Protection: By the North vs. by the South

The pro-innovation feature of the Northern tariff seems to imply that maybe the Northern tariff is desirable not only for the North but also for the world. What about the Southern tariff? If we allow tariff protection, which region should be allowed to use it, the North or the South? To answer these questions, we contrast the different welfare effects of the Northern tariff and the Southern tariff.[18]

[18]Recall that we have ascertained their different impact on innovation as summarized in Proposition 1.

First, let us look at the Southern tariff's impact on Northern welfare. Differentiating gives:

$$\frac{\partial W_n}{\partial \tau_s} = M\frac{\partial w_n}{\partial \tau_s} + w_n\frac{\partial M}{\partial \tau_s}. \tag{15}$$

First, note that using (12) we have

$$\frac{\partial w_n}{\partial \tau_s} = \frac{\partial \pi_n}{\partial \tau_s} = (T - T_s)\frac{\partial \pi_{ns}}{\partial \tau_s} < 0.$$

Thus, the first term of (15) is negative. This is the familiar profit-shifting result in the strategic trade literature and it has captured the total effect in the conventional trade model of imperfect competition without innovation and imitation. Thus, a foreign tariff is detrimental to home welfare because it reduces the home producers' profits.

Second, we turn to the second term of (15), which is negative according to Proposition 1. This shows that in the present model with innovation and imitation, the Southern tariff is more harmful to the North than in the conventional model. To see this, recall from Proposition 1 that an increase in τ_s shrinks the innovation set because the Southern tariff reduces Northern firms' profits. As a result, in the North, consumers have a smaller product variety and the government collects less tariff revenue. Northern welfare unambiguously decreases. Based on this analysis we immediately establish the following proposition:

Proposition 4. *A Southern tariff is a beggar-thy-neighbor policy. Its adverse effect on Northern welfare is more serious in the present model with innovation and imitation than in the conventional model without innovation and imitation.*

We now consider the impact of a Northern tariff on Southern welfare. We first derive the Southern steady-state flow welfare. Similar to (10) and (11), we obtain the steady-state flow utility derived from all products with $t \leq T_s$

$$u_s(t) = T_s M(1-\alpha)\left(\frac{\alpha^2}{c+\tau_s}\right)^{\alpha\epsilon},$$

and the steady-state flow utility derived from all products with $T \geq t > T_s$

$$\widetilde{u_s}(t) = (T - T_s)M(1-\alpha)\left[\frac{\alpha(K+\alpha)}{(K+1)c+\tau_s}\right]^{\alpha\epsilon}.$$

The total import by the South is

$$V_s = Mv_s, \quad \text{where } v_s = T_s A(c+\tau_s)^{-\alpha\epsilon}$$
$$+ (T - T_s)B(H,K)\left\{\frac{(1-\alpha)c - (K+\alpha-1)\tau_s}{[(H+K+1)c + (H+1)\tau_s]^{\epsilon+1}}\right\}.$$

The steady-state flow profits of all Southern imitators are equal to

$$\Pi_s = MK\left[\sum_{t=T_s}^{T}\pi_{ss}(t) + \sum_{t=T_n}^{T}\pi_{sn}(t) - e\right] = MK(\pi_s - e),$$
$$\text{where } \pi_s = (T - T_s)\pi_{ss} + (T - T_n)\pi_{sn}. \tag{16}$$

The Southern steady-state flow welfare, denoted by $W_s(\tau)$, is defined as the sum of the flow consumer surplus, producer profit and tariff revenue. Hence,

$$W_s(\tau) = \sum_{t=1}^{T_s} u_s(t) + \sum_{T_s}^{T}\widetilde{u_s}(t) + \Pi_s + \tau_s V_s = Mw_s(\tau) + E_s \tag{17}$$

where

$$w_s(\tau) = T_s(1-\alpha)\left(\frac{\alpha^2}{c+\tau_s}\right)^{\alpha\epsilon} + (T - T_s)(1-\alpha)$$
$$\times\left[\frac{\alpha(H+K+\alpha)}{(H+K+1)c + (H+1)\tau_s}\right]^{\alpha\epsilon}$$
$$+ K[(T - T_s)\pi_{ss} + (T - T_n)\pi_{sn} - e] + \tau_s v_s.$$

Differentiating with respect to τ_n, we obtain

$$\frac{\partial W_s}{\partial \tau_n} = M\frac{\partial w_s}{\partial \tau_n} + w_s\frac{\partial M}{\partial \tau_n}. \tag{18}$$

The first term on the right-hand side of (18), which is equal to $MK(T - T_n)\partial\pi_{sn}/\partial\tau_n$, is negative, being the result of profit shifting. Because of this, Southern welfare is reduced. However, the second term is positive, which tends to increase Southern welfare. The Northern tariff expands the innovation set, which in turn also gives rise to a larger imitation set. As a result, in the South, consumers enjoy larger product variety, there are more imitators earning positive profits, and the government collects more tariff revenue. All these lead to greater welfare for the South.

It is manifest from the above analysis that because the Northern tariff is pro-innovation, its adverse effect on Southern welfare, if any, is smaller in the present model with innovation and imitation than in the conventional model without innovation and imitation. Depending on the relative degrees of the positive and negative effects, the Northern tariff may even increase Southern welfare, in which case it is no longer a beggar-thy-neighbor policy.

In fact, it is not only a possibility that the South can benefit from a Northern tariff. We can actually show that it is really true for some values of τ_n. As W_s is a multivariable function including τ_n, whether $\partial W_s/\partial\tau_n > 0$ or not depends on various combinations of many parameters and so finding the necessary and sufficient conditions is intractable. Nevertheless, our purpose is to show that under some meaningful conditions a Northern tariff is beneficial to the South. Proposition 5 provides some results on this.

Proposition 5. *Given all other parameter values, there exists a unique* $b_0 > 0$ *such that* $\partial W_s/\partial\tau_n > 0$ *if and only if* $b < b_0$.

Proof. See Appendix. □

It is clear why we need the condition for b. When b is sufficiently small, increasing innovators' market profits will lead to a large increase in innovation M. This benefit to Southern consumers more than offsets the loss of Southern profits due to an increase in the Northern tariff. That is, when b is sufficiently small, the second positive term in (18) is greater than the first negative term in absolute value, leading to an increase in welfare in the South as τ_n increases.

We have found that tariffs imposed by the North and the South have very different consequences on the other region. How, then, are they different in affecting global welfare? A related question is: If we allow just one region to impose a tariff, should it be the North or the South? The above analysis seems to indicate the desirability (or lower undesirability) of the Northern tariff over the Southern tariff. In the rest of this section, we seek an explicit answer to this question.

Steady-state flow global welfare is the sum of Northern welfare and Southern welfare, and so it is defined as

$$W(\tau) = W_n(\tau) + W_s(\tau) \ = Mw(\tau) + E_n + E_s,$$
$$\text{where } w(\tau) = w_n(\tau) + w_s(\tau).$$

Differentiating with respect to the Southern tariff rate, we obtain

$$\frac{\partial W(\tau)}{\partial \tau_s} = M\frac{\partial w}{\partial \tau_s} + w\frac{\partial M}{\partial \tau_s} < 0.$$

The first term on the right-hand side is negative. This is the result from conventional trade models without innovation and imitation, that any region's tariff lowers global welfare even if it may raise the policy-adopting region's welfare. The second term is also negative because the Southern tariff reduces Northern firms' innovation incentives and so is detrimental to both regions. Hence, the Southern tariff unambiguously reduces global welfare, and it reduces global welfare more in the presence of innovation and imitation than in the absence of innovation and imitation.

Differentiating global welfare with respect to the Northern tariff rate, we obtain

$$\frac{\partial W(\tau)}{\partial \tau_n} = M\frac{\partial w}{\partial \tau_n} + w\frac{\partial M}{\partial \tau_n}. \tag{19}$$

The first term on the right-hand side is negative. However, the second term is positive, because Northern protection increases product variety and thus both regions benefit. Therefore, innovation reduces the detrimental effect of the Northern tariff on global welfare. It is even possible that global welfare is improved by raising Northern tariff if the positive innovation effect is sufficiently strong. We show this below.

Suppose τ_n^w (with no restriction on its sign) maximizes global welfare, then $\partial W(\tau)/\partial\tau_n = 0$ at $\tau_n = \tau_n^w$, assuming $\partial^2 W(\tau)/(\partial\tau_n)^2 < 0$. Differentiating this first-order condition with respect to T_s, we obtain

$$\frac{\partial\tau_n^w}{\partial T_s} = -\frac{\partial}{\partial T_s}\left(\frac{\partial W}{\partial\tau_n}\right) \Big/ \frac{\partial^2 W(\tau)}{(\partial\tau_n)^2} \quad \text{and so sgn}\left(\frac{\partial\tau_n^w}{\partial T_s}\right)$$
$$= \text{sgn}\left(\frac{\partial}{\partial T_s}\left(\frac{\partial W}{\partial\tau_n}\right)\right).$$

Then using (19), we have

$$\frac{\partial}{\partial T_s}\left(\frac{\partial W}{\partial\tau_n}\right) = M\frac{\partial}{\partial T_s}\left(\frac{\partial w}{\partial\tau_n}\right) + \frac{\partial w}{\partial\tau_n}\frac{\partial M}{\partial T_s} + w\frac{\partial}{\partial T_s}\left(\frac{\partial M}{\partial\tau_n}\right) + \frac{\partial M}{\partial\tau_n}\frac{\partial w}{\partial T_s} < 0$$

since the first term on the RHS is zero (using (6)–(8)) and the third term is also zero (using (6)–(8)), while the second and the last terms are both negative ($\partial w/\partial\tau_n < 0$, $\partial M/\partial T_s > 0$, $\partial M/\partial\tau_n > 0$, $\partial w/\partial T_s < 0$).[19]

As a result, $\partial\tau_n^w/\partial T_s < 0$. *That is, for weaker IPR protection in the South, the Northern tariff which is required to maximize global welfare should be higher, for otherwise the amount of innovation would be too small. The same result holds for the IPR protection in the North:* $\partial\tau_n^w/\partial T_n < 0$. (Proof is the same as the Southern IPR).

It remains to show that τ_n^w is positive under certain conditions. While general conditions are difficult to obtain, by focusing on the

[19]The last inequality, $\partial w/\partial T_s = AT_s(c+\tau_s)^{-\alpha\varepsilon}/2-(H+1/2)\pi_{ns}+(1-\alpha)[\alpha^2/(c+\tau_s)]^{\alpha\varepsilon}-(1-\alpha)[\alpha(H+K+\alpha)/[(H+K+1)c+(H+1)\tau_s]^{\alpha\varepsilon}-K\pi_{ss}+A\tau_s(c+\tau_s)^{-\alpha\varepsilon}-B(H,K)\tau_s\ \{[(1-\alpha)c-(K+\alpha-1)\tau_s]/[H+K+1)c+(H+1)\tau_s]^{(\varepsilon+1)} < 0$, can be confirmed by intuition: given that innovation is not changed (i.e. M is fixed here), increasing patent length increases patent holders' profits, reduces imitators profits, reduces consumer surplus, and *reduces* social welfare.

following parameter values as an example: $\alpha = 0.5$, $T = 30$, $T_n = 20$, $b = 2$, $e = 1$, $c = 1$, $H = K = 1$ and $\tau_s = 0$, we obtain,

$$\frac{\partial W}{\partial \tau_n} = \frac{25}{16(3+\tau_n)^4}[(9-2\tau_n)(1+2\tau_n)w$$
$$+ (39 - 384\tau_n - 224\tau_n)M] > 0 \text{ at } \tau_n = 0 \quad \text{and for all} \quad T_s.$$

This shows $\tau_n^w > 0$. When τ_n is sufficiently large, it is sure that increased Northern tariff will reduce global welfare. But the above results have shown that for a range of $\tau_n \in [0, \tau_n^w)$, global welfare continue to increase as the North raises its tariff. This range is larger if the IPR protection is weaker (T_s is smaller or T_n is smaller). Hence, we have

Proposition 6. *A higher Northern tariff supplements weak IPR protection in the world, in the sense that a weaker IPR protection in the North or the South raises the globally optimal Northern tariff.*

A corollary of the above proposition is that, starting from a point of optimal Northern tariff for given levels of T_s and T_n, an increase in Northern tariff will be globally welfare-improving in the face of a decrease in IPR protection in one of the regions. This result is in sharp contrast to the role of an increase in Southern tariff, which always reduces global welfare. Therefore, we conclude that Southern tariffs are more detrimental to world welfare than Northern ones in innovation-intensive sectors where innovations concentrate in the North, and IPR protections are weak in both regions. One example that comes to mind is internet-related products.

The (partial) substitutability of the two instruments, Northern IPR protection and Northern tariff, for the sake of world welfare is apparent, since the effects of the two policies are very similar. A stronger IPR protection in the North increases the profits of the Northern innovators at the expense of Northern consumer welfare, and results in an increase in deadweight loss in the North. This is the marginal cost of Northern IPR protection. The marginal benefit of Northern IPR protection is the increase in the number of innovations, which benefits both Northern and Southern consumers. The optimal Northern IPR protection would strike a balance between the two effects. An increase in Northern tariff protection increases the profits of Northern innovators and Northern imitators, and increases the deadweight loss in the North. This is the marginal cost of Northern trade protection. The marginal benefit of Northern trade protection is again an increase in number of innovations. An optimal Northern tariff would strike a balance between the two effects. Therefore, the two policies have similar effects on world welfare. A Northern tariff should be a less effective tool for encouraging innovation, in the sense that for the same increase in deadweight loss, the increase in innovator profits is smaller, since some increase in profits go to Northern imitators as well. Thus, the optimal Northern tariff may not be positive, but it is more likely so when T_n and T_s are both small.

5 Concluding Remarks

In a North-South trade model with innovation and imitation, we have shown how trade policy and IPR policy in the two regions affect innovation and imitation. The central message from this study comes from its answers to the question: what are the differing roles of Northern and Southern tariffs in a world with innovation and imitation, where innovations concentrate in the North? We have argued that unlike conventional trade models without innovation and imitation, the Northern tariff protects not only profits but also innovation and thus supplements weak IPR protection as a second best policy. Because of the consideration of innovation and imitation, the effects of Northern tariff and Southern tariff are qualitatively different. The former may not be a beggar-thy-neighbor policy but the latter is. Global welfare declines as the South raises its tariff, but under some circumstances it rises as the North raises its tariff. Hence, Northern tariffs are less harmful to world welfare than Southern ones in innovation-intensive sectors where innovations concentrate in the North, and IPR protection in the world is weak. Moreover, it would benefit the North to subsidize trade liberalization of the South in these sectors, since the South's loss would be more than offset by the North's gain.

Under imperfect competition, if we take into account innovation and imitation, there is one more motive for tariff protection in the North — improving consumer welfare by encouraging more innovation. This is an interesting finding since few previous analyses have pointed out that tariff protection can improve consumer welfare through encouraging more innovations. The underlying point is that, from the consumer welfare point of view, taxing at least some of the imitators can serve as a partial substitute for strengthening a weak IPR protection regime. This general principle holds in a closed economy as well as a global economy with trade.

What about the robustness of the results? As any other economic model, this one is built upon a number of assumptions. Among these, those deserving attention are the specific utility function, the absence of price competition between products, and the location where innovation takes place. Let us focus our discussion on the implications of allowing innovation to take place in the South. We conjecture that the qualitative aspects of our results would continue to hold if (a) IPR protection is much stronger in the North than in the South, (b) the ability to innovate is much higher in the North than in the South. Condition *a* alone would have resulted in much more innovation in the North than in the South even if both regions have an equal ability to innovate. Their difference in innovative ability described in *b* further widens the gap. Therefore, we would have the situation in which the North does most of the innovation and the South does only a little bit. Then, the effects of a Northern tariff and a Southern tariff would be similar to what have been presented in this paper. Finally, assuming the South has lower imitation cost would not alter our results.

There are two more caveats worth mentioning. First, our model is set in a partial-equilibrium environment, with expanding-variety type of innovation. This analysis is appropriate for certain purposes, yet may not be appropriate for others. When innovation is of the quality-improvement kind, a tariff increases the profits of an existing vintage, whose patent has expired, more than it increases the profits of a new (yet to be invented) vintage, whose profits are unaffected by the tariff. As a result, Arrow's "replacement effect" becomes more severe with a tariff, which reduces the incentive to innovate by the innovator of the existing vintage. Therefore, a tariff can reduce innovation. Second, if tariffs are imposed on a sufficiently large segment of the economy so that general-equilibrium effect cannot be ignored, a Northern import tariff can possibly deter innovation. This is because more production will stay in the North, which competes for resources (workers) for R&D, raising wage and lowering the returns to innovation, thus reducing innovation. Despite these caveats, however, we believe the model can apply to certain important sectors of the economy.

We should reiterate that in this paper we are not trying to argue for increasing trade protection. Rather, the message we would like to convey is that trade protection by the South is more detrimental to world welfare than by the North in innovation-intensive sectors where IPR protection in both regions are weak, such as the internet-related products. Therefore, the North should perhaps subsidize trade liberalization in the South.

Acknowledgment

We would like to thank Leonard K. Cheng, Mary E. Lovely and Bill Polley for helpful comments. We also benefit from presentation at the Midwest International Economics Conference held at Purdue University (1999) and seminars at Hitoshubashi University, Osaka University and the University of Hong Kong. An earlier version of this paper was circulated with the title "Trade and Intellectual Property Rights Protection: By Whom and for What?" The work in this paper has been supported by the Research Grants Council of Hong Kong, China (Project No. CityU 1145/99H).

Appendix

A. Proof of Proposition 1

Based on (6) and (8) we have

$$M = \frac{\pi_n}{b}, \tag{A1}$$

where π_n is given in (7). From (A1), differentiating M with respect to T_n and T_s, respectively, yields

$$\frac{\partial M}{\partial T_n} = \frac{\pi_{nn}^m - \pi_{nn}}{b} > 0 \quad \text{and} \quad \frac{\partial M}{\partial T_s} = \frac{\pi_{ns}^m - \pi_{ns}}{b} > 0.$$

The inequalities hold because the Northern innovator's monopoly profit is greater than its profit from oligopolistic competition.

Again, differentiating (A1) with respect to τ_n and τ_s, respectively, yields

$$\frac{\partial M}{\partial \tau_n} = \frac{(T - T_n)}{b}\frac{\partial \pi_{nn}}{\partial \tau_n} > 0 \quad \text{and} \quad \frac{\partial M}{\partial \tau_s} = \frac{(T - T_s)}{b}\frac{\partial \pi_{ns}}{\partial \tau_s} < 0. \qquad \square$$

B. Proof of Proposition 3

Since the profit term and tariff revenue term do not show up in the welfare function we define consumer welfare as

$$\tilde{W_n} = M(1-\alpha)\tilde{w_n} + E_n$$
$$\text{where} \quad \tilde{w_n} = T_n\left(\frac{\alpha^2}{c}\right)^{\alpha\epsilon} + (T - T_n)\left[\frac{\alpha(H + K + \alpha)}{(H + K + 1)c + K\tau_n}\right]^{\alpha\epsilon}.$$

Then the first order condition for an optimal Northern tariff τ_n is equivalent to

$$M\frac{\partial \tilde{w_n}}{\partial \tau_n} + \tilde{w_n}\frac{\partial M}{\partial \tau_n} = 0. \qquad \text{(B1)}$$

Moreover,

$$\epsilon\frac{\partial}{\partial T_n}\left(\frac{\partial \tilde{W_n}}{\partial \tau_n}\right) = M\frac{\partial}{\partial T_n}\left(\frac{\partial \tilde{w_n}}{\partial \tau_n}\right) + \tilde{w_n}\frac{\partial}{\partial T_n}\left(\frac{\partial M}{\partial \tau_n}\right)$$
$$+ \left(\frac{\partial \tilde{w_n}}{\partial \tau_n}\right)\left(\frac{\partial M}{\partial T_n}\right) + \left(\frac{\partial \tilde{w_n}}{\partial T_n}\right)\left(\frac{\partial M}{\partial \tau_n}\right). \qquad \text{(B2)}$$

Note that

$$\frac{\partial \tilde{w}_n}{\partial \tau_n} = -\alpha\epsilon K(T - T_n)\frac{[\alpha(H+K+\alpha)]^{\alpha\epsilon}}{[(H+K+1)c + K\tau_n]^{\epsilon}}, \quad \frac{\partial}{\partial T_n}\left(\frac{\partial \tilde{w}_n}{\partial \tau_n}\right)$$
$$= -\left(\frac{1}{T - T_n}\right)\frac{\partial \tilde{w}_n}{\partial \tau_n}.$$

From (7) and (8) we can obtain

$$\frac{\partial M}{\partial \tau_n} = \left(\frac{T - T_n}{b}\right)\frac{\partial \pi_{nn}}{\partial \tau_n} > 0, \quad \frac{\partial}{\partial T_n}\left(\frac{\partial M}{\partial \tau_n}\right) = -\left(\frac{1}{T - T_n}\right)\frac{\partial M}{\partial \tau_n}.$$

Substituting these into (B2) and using the first order condition (B1), we can immediately see that the sum of the first two terms of (B2) is equal to zero.

Recall from Proposition 1 that $\partial M/\partial \tau_n > 0$ and $\partial M/\partial T_n > 0$. And also note that consumer surplus decreases as T_n or τ_n increases, that is $\partial \tilde{w}_n/\partial T_n < 0$ and $\partial \tilde{w}_n/\partial \tau_n < 0$. We know that the third and fourth terms of (B2) are negative. The rest of the proof becomes obvious.

The proof of $d\tau_n^c/dT_s < 0$ is the same as above and so is omitted. □

C. Proof of Proposition 5

Let

$$\Phi \equiv \frac{\partial w_s}{\partial M} = T_s(1-\alpha)\left(\frac{\alpha^2}{c+\tau_s}\right)^{\alpha\epsilon} + (T - T_s)(1-\alpha)$$
$$\times \left[\frac{\alpha(H+K+\alpha)}{(H+K+1)c + (H+1)\tau_s}\right]^{\alpha\epsilon}$$
$$+ K[(T - T_s)\pi_{ss} + (T - T_n)\pi_{sn} - e] + \tau_s v_s > 0.$$

Using (6) and differentiating (8) with respect to M, gives $\partial M/\partial \tau_n = (1/b)(T - T_n)(\partial \pi_{nn}/\partial \tau_n)$. Then differentiating (17) with respect to

τ_n yields

$$\frac{\partial W_s}{\partial \tau_n} = MK(T - T_n)\frac{\partial \pi_{sn}}{\partial \tau_n} + \frac{1}{b}(T - T_n)\Phi\frac{\partial \pi_{nn}}{\partial \tau_n}. \tag{C1}$$

From (2), we obtain

$$\frac{\partial \pi_{sn}}{\partial \tau_n} = -\frac{B(H,K)[(1-\alpha)c - (H+\alpha)\tau_n]}{[(H+K+1)c + K\tau_n]^{2+\epsilon}} \cdot \left\{ \frac{2\alpha[(H+K+1)c + K\tau_n] + (1+\epsilon)K[(1-\alpha)c - (H+\alpha)\tau_n]}{H+K+\alpha} \right\} < 0.$$

Using this and (3) in (C1), we obtain that

$$\frac{\partial W_s}{\partial \tau_n} > 0 \quad \text{iff} \;\; b < b_0 \quad \text{where}$$

$$b_0 \equiv \frac{[(1-\alpha)c + K\tau_n]\{\epsilon[2(1-\alpha)c - (H+\alpha)\tau_n] + \alpha c\}\Phi}{M[(1-\alpha)c - (H+\alpha)\tau_n]\{2\alpha[(H+K+1)c + K\tau_n] + (1+\epsilon)K[(1-\alpha)c - (H+\alpha)\tau_n]\}} > 0.$$

This completes the proof. □

References

Burmeister, E. (1980). *Capital Theory and Dynamics*, UK: Cambridge University Press.

Chin, J. and Grossman, G. M. (1990). International property rights and North-South trade, in Jones, R. W. and Krueger, A. O. (eds.), *The Political Economy of International Trade*, Cambridge, MA: Basil Blackwell, pp. 90–107.

Deardorff, A. V. (1992). Welfare effects of global patent protection, *Economica* 59, 35–51.

Diwan, I. and Rodrik, D. (1991). Patents, appropriate technology, and North-South trade, *Journal of International Economics* 30, 27–47.

Glass, A. J. and Saggi, K. (2002). Intellectual property rights and foreign direct investment, *Journal of International Economics* 56, 387–410.

Grossman, G. M. and Helpman, E. (1991). *Innovation and Growth in the Global Economy*, Cambridge, MA: MIT Press.

Grossman, G. M. and Helpman, E. (1995). Technology and trade, in Grossman, G. M. and Rogoff, K. (eds.), *Handbook of International Economics*, Vol. III, Amsterdam: Elsevier Science B.V.

Helpman, E. (1993). Innovation, imitation and intellectual property rights, *Econometrica* 61, 1247–1280.

Helpman, E. and Krugman, P. R. (1989). *Trade Policy and Market Structure*, Cambridge, MA: The MIT Press.

Horowitz, A. W. and Lai, E. L.-C. (1996). Patent length and rate of innovation, *International Economic Review* 37, 785–801.

Kremer, M. (1997). *Patent Buy-Out: A Mechanism for Encouraging Innovation*, NBER Working Paper No. 6304.

Krugman, P. R. (1979). A model of innovation, technology transfer, and the world distribution of income, *Journal of Political Economy* 87, 253–266.

Lai, E. L.-C. (1998). International intellectual property rights protection and rate of product innovation, *Journal of Development Economics* 55, 133–153.

Lai, E. L.-C. and Qiu, L. D. (2003). The North's intellectual property rights standard for the South? *Journal of International Economics* 59, 183–209.

Mansfield, E., Schwartz, M., and Wagner, S. (1981). Imitation costs and patents: An empirical study, *Economic Journal* 91, 907–918.

Maskus, K. E. (1998). The international regulation of intellectual property, *Weltwirtschaftliches Archiv* 134, 186–208.

Maskus, K. E. and Penubarti, M. (1995). How trade-related are intellectual property rights? *Journal of International Economics* 39, 227–248.

Qiu, L. D. and Lai, E. L.-C. (1999). *Trade and Intellectual Property Rights Protection: By Whom and for What?* Hong Kong University of Science and Technology, Working Paper No. 99.1.

Smith, P. J. (1999). Are weak patent rights a barrier to U.S. exports? *Journal of International Economics* 48, 151–177.

Spence, M. (1984). Cost reduction, competition and industry performance, *Econometrica* LII, 101–121.

Taylor, M. S. (1993). TRIPs, trade and technology transfer, *Canadian Journal of Economics* 26, 625–638.

Zigic, K. (2000). Strategic trade policy, intellectual property rights protection, and North-South trade, *Journal of Development Economics* 61, 27–60.

Part 3

Endogenous Growth Model and IPRs

Chapter 8

Intellectual Property Rights Protection and Endogenous Economic Growth*

Abstract

The main purpose of the chapter is to examine the impact of intellectual property rights (hereinafter IPR) protection on economic growth and welfare. To achieve this aim, we make use of an expanding-variety type R&D-based endogenous growth model. We work out the transitional dynamics of a shock in IPR protection and account fully for the loss in current consumption and gain in consumption growth due to a tightening IPR protection. We find that there exists an optimal degree of IPR protection in our model. We then calibrate our model by US data, and found that under-protection of IPR is much more likely than over-protection. Moreover, in the case of over-protection, the welfare losses are trivial; whereas in the case of under-protection, the welfare losses can be substantial.

1 Introduction

The main purpose of the paper is to examine the impact of intellectual property rights (hereinafter IPR) protection on economic growth and welfare. To achieve this aim, we make use of an expanding-variety

---

*By Yum K. Kwan and Edwin L.-C. Lai. Originally published in *Journal of Economic Dynamics and Control*, 27 (2003), pp. 853–873. Copyright © 2002 by Elsevier Science B.V. It has been reprinted with revisions and permission from the original publisher. The difference with the original published paper is that a corrigendum is added at the end.

type R&D-based endogenous growth model *a la* Romer (1990). The simplest way to model IPR protection is to assume that imitation is costless, and that stronger IPR protection lowers the rate of imitation. This is the approach we adopt here.[1]

The conventional wisdom in the literature about strengthening IPR protection is that it encourages investment in R&D, yet depresses current consumption. Since there is a tradeoff between current loss in consumption and future gain in growth rate, there is a possibility of the existence of an optimal degree of IPR protection. The existence and properties of such an optimum, however, have not been confirmed before in the endogenous growth literature, partly because it involves a full characterization of the transitional dynamics of the rate of innovation and fraction of goods imitated in the economy. If transitional dynamics are not considered, and one focuses only on the steady state, then the welfare analysis is misleading. In fact, steady state welfare is maximized when growth rate of consumption is maximized. This will be achieved by protecting IPR fully and forever. Obviously, such a corner solution is intuitively unappealing and also counter-factual, since the transitional welfare gains and losses are not taken into account. This paper shows that once transitional dynamics are taken into account, there exists a finite optimal degree of IPR protection.

One contribution of our paper is that we compute the optimal IPR by working out the transitional dynamics of a shock in IPR protection and accounting fully for the loss in current consumption and gain in consumption growth due to a tightening of IPR protection. Specifically, we find that when the government announces an immediate increase in IPR protection, there is an immediate drop in current consumption and an immediate increase in the rate of growth of consumption, as well as overshooting of the rate of innovation. The instantaneous fall in consumption is caused by an expansion of the R&D sector, which bids up interest rate and induces more saving.

[1] If we assumed that imitation is costly, then tightening IPR protection amounts to increasing the cost of imitation. In that case, we believe similar results would obtain.

On the other hand, higher investment in R&D leads to higher growth of consumption following the initial level drop. At the optimal level of IPR, the marginal cost due to current consumption loss is equal to the marginal gain due to consumption growth. We are able to compute this optimal level of IPR, the existence and significance of which has not been established in the literature.

Another contribution of our paper is that it estimates the welfare loss due to deviation of the current IPR protection in the US from the optimal level. We conclude that under-protection of IPR is potentially a very important reason for under-investment of R&D. This is complementary to other work in the literature (e.g. Jones and Williams, 1998, 2000). To assess quantitatively the welfare significance of optimal IPR protection, we calibrate our model by US data on long-term growth rate, mark-up factor in manufacturing industries, time rate of preference and intertemporal elasticity of substitution. The calibration results indicate that there is under-protection of IPR (relative to the optimal level) within plausible range of parameter values, and that under-protection of IPR is much more likely than over-protection. More complete computation indicates that in the case of over-protection, the welfare losses are trivial; whereas in the case of under-protection, the welfare losses can be substantial. One interpretation of this result is that the US should protect IPR much more than it currently does.

Our specification of R&D draws from the "laboratory equipment" model used in Rivera-Batiz and Romer (1991). The dynamic analysis is similar to that of Helpman (1993). Helpman studies the effect of IPR protection in the South on the welfare of the North and the South in a two-region global economy. Contrary to our main objective, he does not attempt to find whether there is an optimal degree of IPR, nor is he interested in whether there is under-protection of IPR in the global economy.[2]

[2]In fact, it is not clear whether there exists a globally optimal IPR in his model. Stronger IPR in the South actually reduces the rate of innovation in his model with Southern imitation and endogenous rate of innovation.

There are by and large two types of R&D-based endogenous growth models: expanding-variety type and quality-ladder type. O'Donoghue and Zweimuller (1998) construct a quality-ladder type R&D-based endogenous growth model in the tradition of Grossman and Helpman (1991a) and Aghion and Howitt (1992). They merge the patent-design literature and endogenous-growth literature incorporating both length and breadth of patent in the quality ladder. They point out the short-comings of the partial equilibrium patent-design analyses, which omit the general equilibrium effects. One of these effects is that when multiple industries use patent protection, the monopoly distortion effect can be greatly diminished. In our model, rather than the tradeoff between static and dynamic efficiency, the central issue is the tradeoff between loss in current consumption and gain in consumption growth when IPR protection is strengthened across industries. Futagami *et al.* (1996) study optimal patent length in a Grossman–Helpman type quality-ladder model. Although they identify an optimal patent length under certain conditions, there is no transitional dynamics as in our model. Nonetheless, their work is an interesting complement to our paper.

Our result suggests that there is under-investment in R&D due to under-protection of IPR. This under-investment result echoes that of Jones and Williams (1998), who find that the US under-invested in R&D by a factor of two to four. Jones and Williams (2000) is an attempt to account for the relative importance of the various externalities that are responsible for the deviation of the market equilibrium from the optimal level of R&D, such as knowledge spillovers, "stepping on toes" effect, and creative destruction. Our quantitative result points out that under-protection of IPR is another important reason for under-investment of R&D. Our contention that IPR protection is an important determinant of growth is echoed by the work of Jones (2001), who argues that property rights protection is responsible for the emergence of the "industrial revolution" in the 20th century.

Our closed-economy result should be readily extended to an international setting. For example, Lai (1998a) finds that the rate of innovation increases with stronger IPR in both the North and the South as long as DFI (direct foreign investment) is the major channel of international technology diffusion. Accordingly, an optimal degree of IPR should also exist in a global economy. However, in a two-country setting, there are additional issues to be addressed, e.g. How are the effects of Southern IPR protection different from those of Northern protection?; and, Should there be harmonization of IPR standards? Moreover, the channel through which international technology diffusion occurs can affect the results.[3]

Section 2 lays out the model, and derive the dynamics when there is an immediate increase of IPR protection. The optimal degree of IPR protection is derived. In Section 3, we calibrate the model to the US economy. Since closed form solution is not possible, we solve the dynamic general equilibrium numerically, and compute the optimal degrees of IPR protection that correspond to different assumed actual monopoly durations of the innovators. Section 4 concludes with some discussion on future extensions.

2 The Model

The model is a dynamic general equilibrium one, with expanding-variety type R&D as the engine of growth. There is only one final good, which can be used for consumption, for production of intermediate goods, and for R&D, which is needed to invent new varieties of intermediate goods. The production function for the final good is characterized by an expanding variety of producer intermediates of the form:

$$Y = L^{1-\alpha} \int_0^A x(i)^\alpha \mathrm{d}i, \qquad 0 < \alpha < 1 \tag{1}$$

where Y is the quantity of final good; L is labor input; $x(i)$ is the variety of producer intermediates with index i; and A, the number of varieties, increases over time as a result of innovations. The final good market is perfectly competitive.

[3]These channels can include DFI, imitation, or licensing of technology. Contrary to Lai (1998a), when DFI does not play a central role in international technology diffusion, stronger Southern IPR can lead to lower rate of innovation, such as in Helpman (1993), Grossman and Helpman (1991b) and Glass and Saggi (2002).

The intermediate good market is monopolistically competitive *a la* Dixit and Stiglitz (1977), Ethier (1982) and Romer (1990). Sellers are innovators of intermediate goods and buyers are final good producers. There is no uncertainty in innovation. Motivated by the prospect of monopoly profit, an innovator invests in β units of final good and obtains a blueprint of a new variety. It then earns the opportunity to produce the new intermediate good at unit marginal cost (i.e. the cost of one unit of final good) and sell the differentiated intermediate good at a profit-maximizing markup of $1/\alpha$.

To allow a role for IPR protection, following Helpman (1993), we assume an imitation process of the form

$$\dot{A}_c = \mu(A - A_c), \qquad \mu > 0 \tag{2}$$

The variable A_c is the number of goods that have been imitated; whereas $A - A_c$ is the number of goods that have not been imitated and thus available for imitation. The parameter μ captures the strength of IPR protection, with higher value meaning weaker protection. It is the hazard rate at which the market power of an intermediate good producer disappears at the next date, given that its market power has not been eroded so far. This rate is defined as the rate of imitation. The rate of imitation is dependent on many factors. One way to capture explicitly all these factors is to decompose μ into two terms: $\mu \equiv \iota\delta$, where ι is the natural rate of imitation (the rate of imitation when there is no IPR protection at all), and $0 < \delta < 1$ is an index of the strength of IPR protection provided by the government, with higher δ representing weaker protection. Full IPR protection implies that $\delta = 0$, and no IPR protection implies that $\delta = 1$. The parameter ι is dependent on the level of technology, use of masking or other measures by the innovator to prevent or delay imitation, the stock of human capital, entrepreneurship, entry barriers, anti-trust policies, etc. The parameter δ is dependent on patent length and breadth, laws on trademark, copyrights and trade secrets, and enforcement of IPR. Although μ is influenced by an array of factors, we assume that government IPR policy only affect δ, while ι is assumed to be constant. Therefore, we regard μ as a parameter that can be controlled by the government through its IPR policy. Hereinafter, we shall refer to a tightening of IPR protection as a decrease in μ (caused by a decrease in δ).[4]

Once a product is imitated, we assume that competition will drive the price down to marginal cost. Thus, we can classify the intermediate goods into two groups: goods with index $i \in (0, A_c)$ are the imitated ones that are competitively priced, and the rest, with index $i \in (A_c, A)$, that are still under monopoly. The demand functions for the two groups are

$$x(i) = \begin{cases} L\alpha^{1/(1-\alpha)} \equiv x_c, & i \in (0, A_c) \\ L\alpha^{2/(1-\alpha)} \equiv x_m, & i \in (A_c, A) \end{cases} \tag{3}$$

Clearly, $x_m < x_c$, which reflects the usual monopoly distortion in resource allocation. To simplify the analysis, we assume that imitation is costless.[5] It follows that the resource constraint for the

[4]The imitation (or technology diffusion) function we adopt, with constant hazard rate of imitation, has been used by others, such as Grossman and Helpman (1991b) and Eaton and Kortum (1999). Eicher (1999) contends that the level of human capital of the host country affects the international rate of diffusion of technology. As mentioned above, the existence of effects other than IPR protection in affecting the rate of imitation is not denied in our model, and can be easily incorporated into the model if necessary to address other questions.

[5]Assuming costly imitation would make the analysis more complicated without altering the basic conclusion of the paper, namely, there is under-protection of IPR and under-investment in R&D in the US economy. The reasons are as follows. First, Assuming non-trivial cost of imitation implies that there is an under-estimation of welfare gains from increasing IPR, as there are resources to be saved by reducing imitation effort. Thus, *our estimate of the welfare gains from strengthening IPR is a lower bound. However, this actually strengthens our central conclusion that there is under-protection of IPR.* Second, the assumption of non-trivial imitation cost makes the analysis less tractable: when imitation cost is non-trivial, the post-imitation market would become imperfectly competitive in equilibrium, making the analysis more complicated. Finally, imitation costs may well be quite low in reality. Mansfield *et al.* (1981) finds that the cost of imitation on the average is about 0.6 times the cost of innovation. However, with the advent of the knowledge-based economy, there are more and more products for which the costs of imitation are very small compared with the cost of innovation (e.g. duplication of software), and Mansfield's estimates of average imitation costs are probably outdated by now.

economy can be written as

$$Y = C + \beta\dot{A} + A_c x_c + (A - A_c)x_m \tag{4}$$

where C is aggregate consumption.

Taking into account μ and the instantaneous profit at each future date, a potential innovator decides whether or not to enter into the innovation business. Under the assumption of free entry into the innovation business, the present discounted value (PDV) of net profits of an innovator is equal to zero in equilibrium. That is, the rate of return to innovation, r_m, must be equal to the real interest rate adjusted for imitation risk:

$$r_m = r + \mu \tag{5}$$

From (3) it follows that the rate of return $r_m = (L/\beta)$ $\alpha^{2/(1-\alpha)}(1/\alpha - 1)$. The value of a firm equals to the cost of innovation if there are no barriers to entry in the innovation business. Therefore, the PDV of the net profits of a firm is zero. If there are entry barriers in the innovation business, the PDV of net profits of an innovator is positive. The higher the barriers, the larger the PDV of net profits.

The representative consumer, who also owns the firms, is assumed to choose a consumption path $c(t)$ to maximize the utility function

$$U = \int_0^\infty \left[\frac{c(t)^{1-\theta} - 1}{1-\theta}\right] e^{-\rho t}\mathrm{d}t, \quad \theta > 0 \tag{6}$$

subject to the usual life-cycle budget constraint with asset value equal to the value of the firms. Applying standard optimal control arguments and making use of (5), we can write the consumer optimality condition as

$$\gamma_c \equiv \frac{\dot{C}}{C} = \frac{1}{\theta}(r_m - \mu - \rho) \tag{7}$$

2.1 Transitional dynamics

Define $g \equiv A_c/A$ and $h \equiv C/(\beta A)$. The variable g is the fraction of goods that have been imitated and thus $g \in [0, 1]$. The variable h is a scaled and normalized version of consumption C.

Using (1)–(4) and (7), it can be shown that the dynamics of the market equilibrium can be summarized by two differential equations:

$$\begin{cases} \dot{g} = \mu(g^{-1} - 1) + \gamma_1 g + \gamma_2 h + \gamma_3 \\ \dot{h} = \gamma_c + \gamma_1 g + \gamma_2 h + \gamma_3 \end{cases} \tag{8}$$

where $\gamma_1 \equiv -r_m[\alpha^{-1/(1-\alpha)} - \alpha^{-1} - 1] < 0$; $\gamma_2 \equiv 1$; $\gamma_3 \equiv -r_m(1+\alpha)/\alpha < 0$.[6] Equations (8) is an ordinary differential equation system of which a stable solution is determined by an initial condition at $t = 0$ and a boundary condition at $t = \infty$. The boundary condition is given by the steady state

$$g^* = \frac{\mu}{\gamma_c + \mu}, \quad h^* = -\frac{\gamma_1}{\gamma_2} g^* - \frac{\gamma_c + \gamma_3}{\gamma_2} \tag{9}$$

Note that if $\mu = 0$, (8) is linear and admits a closed form solution. Figure 1 depicts the system's phase diagram which summarizes the transitional dynamics. The two curves corresponding to $\dot{g} = 0$ and $\dot{h} = 0$ always intersect, though not necessarily at positive h. A sufficient condition for the existence of a positive steady state is the $\dot{h} = 0$ curve having a positive intercept, i.e. $\gamma_c + \gamma_3 < 0$. The phase diagram reveals that the dynamic system is saddle-path stable. Along the stable arm, if the economy starts from point X at which g and h are below the steady state, both g and h will rise monotonically along the transitional path. Similarly, starting from point Y at which g and h are above the steady state, both g and h decline monotonically during the transition.

2.2 Comparative dynamics around the steady state

We can learn more about the transitional dynamics by linearizing the differential equation system around the steady state. The linearized

---

[6] Although γ_1, γ_2 and γ_3 are independent of μ, changes in μ have both a static effect (level effect) and a dynamic effect (growth effect). See Section 2.2 for more detail.

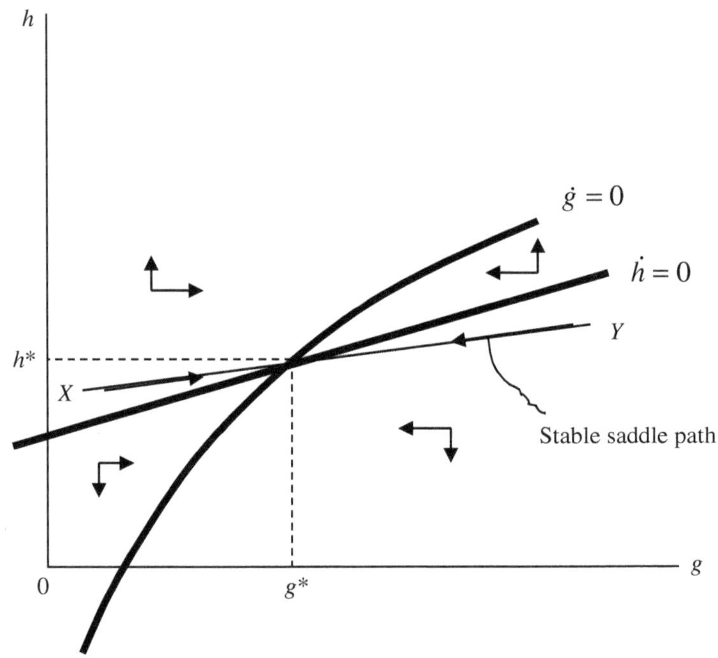

Figure 1. Transitional dynamics.

version can be written as

$$\begin{bmatrix} \dot{g} \\ \dot{h} \end{bmatrix} = M \cdot \begin{bmatrix} g - g^* \\ h - h^* \end{bmatrix} \tag{10}$$

where M is a 2×2 matrix with the (i, j) element a_{ij} being

$$a_{11} = -\mu \cdot (g^*)^{-2} + \gamma_1 < 0; \quad a_{12} = a_{22} = \gamma_2 > 0; \quad a_{21} = \gamma_1 < 0 \tag{11}$$

Let λ_1 and λ_2 be the two eigenvalues of M. Since $\lambda_1 \lambda_2 = |M| = -\mu\gamma_2(g^*)^{-2} < 0$, λ_1 and λ_2 must be real and opposite in sign. This means that the dynamic system is saddle-path stable, confirming the qualitative conclusion of the phase diagram. Solving the characteristic equation $|M - Ix| = 0$, the two eigenvalues are

$$\lambda_1 = \frac{1}{2}\left[(a_{11} + a_{22}) + B^{1/2}\right], \quad \lambda_2 = \frac{1}{2}\left[(a_{11} + a_{22}) - B^{1/2}\right] \tag{12}$$

where $B = (a_{11} + a_{22})^2 - 4|M| > 0$. Since the two eigenvalues are of opposite sign, it follows that $\lambda_1 > 0$ and $\lambda_2 < 0$. The general solution of the linearized system is

$$\begin{cases} g(t) - g^* = b_1 \nu_{11} e^{\lambda_1 t} + b_2 \nu_{12} e^{\lambda_2 t} \\ h(t) - h^* = b_1 \nu_{21} e^{\lambda_1 t} + b_2 \nu_{22} e^{\lambda_2 t} \end{cases} \tag{13}$$

where $[\nu_{1i} \quad \nu_{2i}]'$ is the eigenvector corresponding to λ_i, $i = 1, 2$, and b_1 and b_2 are constants to be determined by boundary conditions. Using the initial condition $g(0)$ and the asymptotic boundary condition $g(\infty) = g^*$, which characterizes the stable saddle-path, it follows that $b_1 = 0$ and $b_2 = g(0) - g^*$. Normalize $\nu_{12} = 1$ and write $\nu_{22} \equiv \nu$ and $\lambda_2 \equiv \lambda < 0$, we have

$$\begin{cases} g(t) = g^* + [g(0) - g^*]e^{\lambda t} \\ h(t) = h^* + [g(0) - g^*]v e^{\lambda t} \end{cases} \tag{14}$$

Let us determine the sign of ν. By definition,

$$\begin{bmatrix} a_{11} & a_{12} \\ a_{21} & a_{22} \end{bmatrix} \begin{bmatrix} 1 \\ \nu \end{bmatrix} = \lambda \begin{bmatrix} 1 \\ \nu \end{bmatrix} \tag{15}$$

Solving for ν, and using (11) and (12), it follows that

$$v = (\lambda - a_{11})/a_{12} = -a_{21}/(a_{22} - \lambda) > 0 \tag{16}$$

By combining the two equations in (14), we obtain the "policy function" $h(g)$ (as in dynamic programming) which is nothing but the equation for the stable saddle-path on the phase diagram:

$$h(g) = (h^* - \nu g^*) + \nu g \tag{17}$$

Thus, around the steady state, $h'(g) = \nu > 0$ so that the stable saddle-path is upward sloping, confirming what we have found from the phase diagram. Now, let us evaluate the impact of a change in μ on the paths of g and h. Using (7) and (9), it is straightforward to check that both g^* and h^* increase with μ:

$$\frac{\partial g^*}{\partial \mu} = \frac{\theta\gamma_c + \mu}{(\gamma_c + \mu)^2\theta} > 0, \quad \frac{\partial h^*}{\partial \mu} = -\frac{\gamma_1}{\gamma_2}\frac{\partial g^*}{\partial \mu} + \frac{1}{\theta\gamma_2} > 0 \tag{18}$$

For analytical tractability, following Helpman (1993), we consider the first order response of (g, h) to changes in μ by differentiating (14) with respect to μ, while ignoring the impact of μ on λ and ν:

$$\frac{\partial g(t)}{\partial \mu} = (1 - e^{\lambda t})\frac{\partial g^*}{\partial \mu} \geq 0 \tag{19}$$

$$\frac{\partial h(t)}{\partial \mu} = \frac{\partial h^*}{\partial \mu} - ve^{\lambda t}\frac{\partial g^*}{\partial \mu} = F(t) \cdot \frac{\partial g^*}{\partial \mu} + \frac{1}{\theta\gamma_2} > 0 \tag{20}$$

where $F(t) \equiv \{-\gamma_1\gamma_2(1-e^{\lambda t}) + \gamma_1\lambda\}/\{\gamma_2(\gamma_2 - \lambda)\} > 0$. In particular, at $t = 0$, $\partial g(0)/\partial\mu = 0$, implying that there is no jump in g as μ decreases (IPR protection tightens). However, $\partial h(0)/\partial\mu > 0$, which means that there is a downward jump in h as μ decreases. On the phase diagram, such a downward jump of the initial h shows up as a downward shift of the entire stable saddle-path as illustrated in Figure 2. Suppose we start from X on the saddle-path $h(g; \mu)$

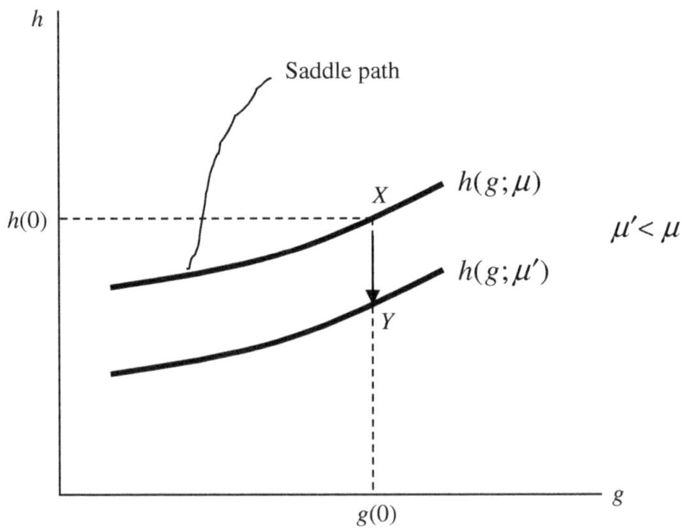

Figure 2. The shift of the saddle path as μ changes.

corresponding to a certain value of μ. Now suppose IPR protection is tightened so that $\mu \downarrow \mu'$. The value $h(0) \equiv h(g(0); \mu)$ is no longer on the equilibrium path; rather, the equilibrium initial h should take a discrete downward jump from X to Y, with the size of the jump given by $\partial h(0)/\partial\mu$. Since X is arbitrary, this implies that the entire saddle-path must shift downward as shown. Alternatively, the downward shift of the saddle-path can be discerned by differentiating the policy function (17) with respect to μ. Note that the entire saddle-path is changed as μ changes, as shown in Figure 2. The downward jump of C at $t = 0$ cannot be accounted for without solving for the entire new equilibrium saddle-path.

For $t > 0$, we see that $\partial g(t)/\partial\mu > 0$ and $\partial h(t)/\partial\mu > 0$. Thus, following a fall in μ (tightening IPR protection), both g and h fall at each point in time and converge to the new steady state. Figure 3 illustrates the comparative dynamics on the phase diagram, whereas Figures 4 and 5 show the time paths of g and h as IPR is tightened. In this model, the transitional dynamics of (g, h) is monotone, unlike Helpman (1993) in which the transitional adjustment may be non-monotone.

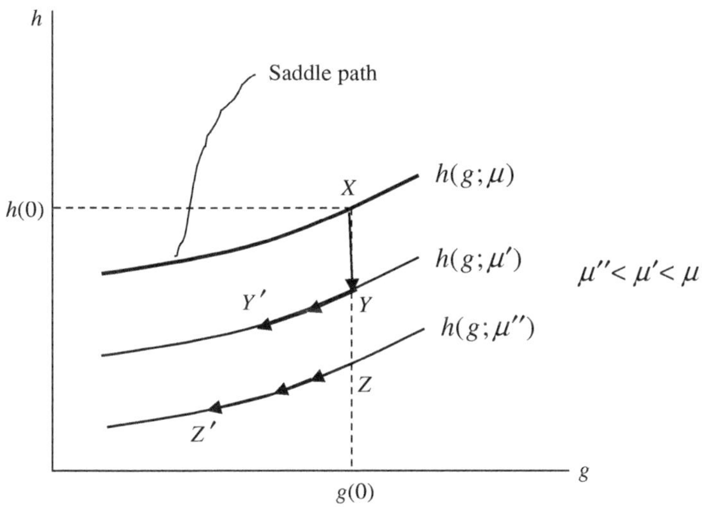

Figure 3. Transitional dynamics of g and h when there is a shock in μ.

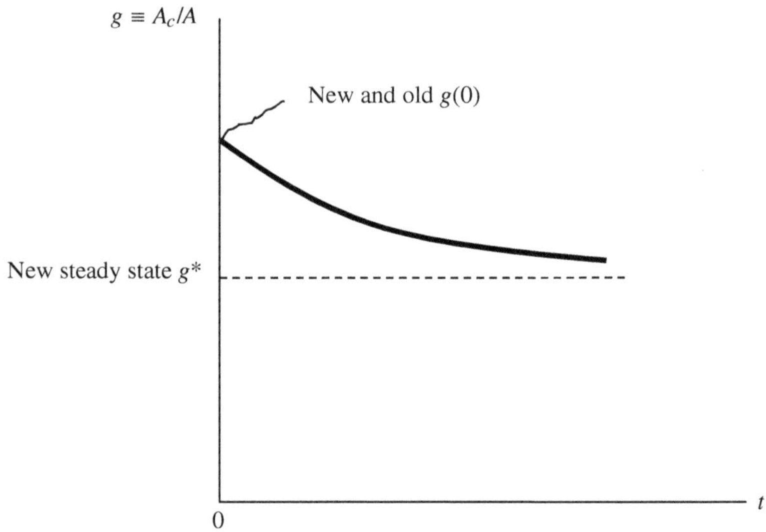

Figure 4. The time path of g with a tightening of IPR protection at $t = 0$.

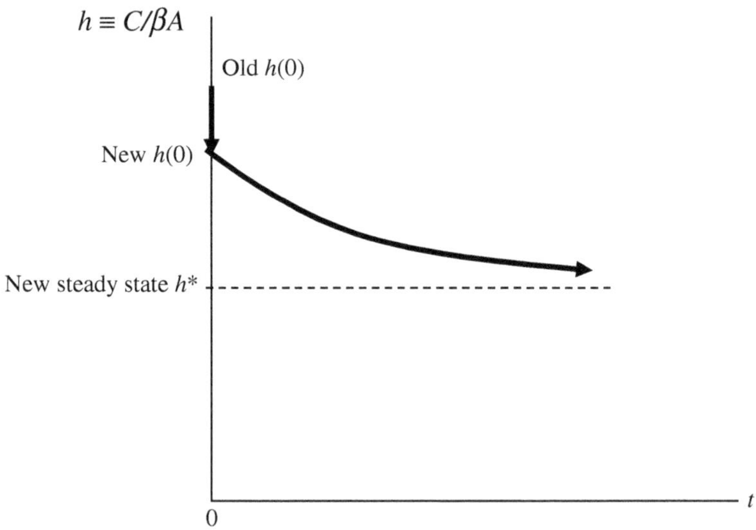

Figure 5. The time path of h with a tightening of IPR protection at $t = 0$.

We can say more about the impact of changes in μ on the innovation rate $\dot{A}/A$. Starting from (4) and making use of (1) and (3), we can write

$$\frac{\dot{A}}{A} = -\gamma_1 g - \gamma_2 h + \beta_3 \tag{21}$$

where $\beta_3 \equiv (L/\beta)\alpha^{2\alpha/(1-\alpha)}(1-\alpha^2) > 0$. Differentiating (21) with respect to μ and making use of (18)–(20), and (16), it can be shown that

$$\frac{\partial}{\partial \mu}\left(\frac{\dot{A}}{A}\right) = H(t) - \frac{1}{\theta} < 0,$$

where

$$H(t) \equiv -\frac{\partial g^*}{\partial \mu}\left[\frac{\gamma_1 \lambda}{\gamma_2 - \lambda}\right] e^{\lambda t} < 0 \tag{22}$$

Clearly, $H(t) \uparrow 0$ as $t \to +\infty$. This implies that there will be an initial over-shooting of the innovation rate $\dot{A}/A$ as μ is lowered (IPR protection is tightened). As t increases, $\partial(\dot{A}/A)/\partial\mu$ gradually approaches the long run value $-1/\theta = \partial\gamma_c/\partial\mu$. Figure 6 depicts

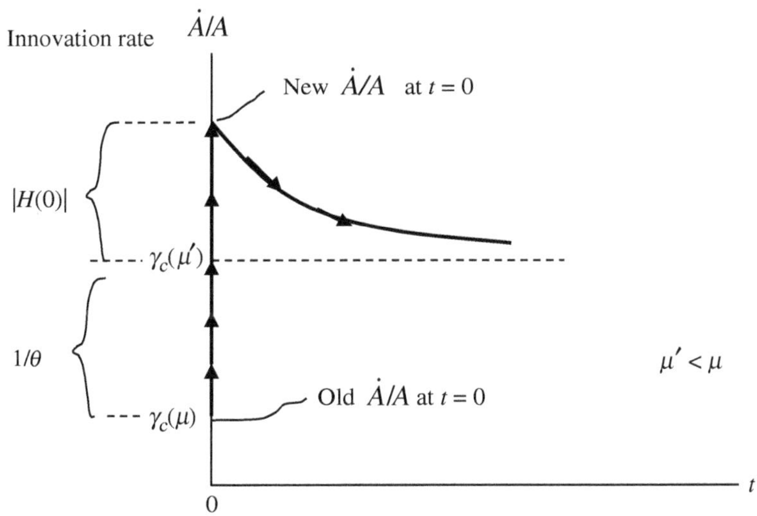

Figure 6. The impact of tightening IPR protection (lower μ) on the innovation rate.

the dynamic adjustment path of the innovation rate in response to tightened IPR protection. The economy starts out at a steady state at which the innovation rate is equal to $\gamma_c(\mu)$, given a certain level of IPR protection corresponding to μ. The new, tightened IPR protection level (with the corresponding $\mu' < \mu$) implies a higher steady state growth rate $\gamma_c(\mu') = \gamma_c(\mu) + 1/\theta$. The innovation rate initially overshoots by the amount $|H(0)|$ and then gradually converges to the new steady state growth rate.

2.3 Tightening IPR protection — Current loss vs. future gain

Tightening IPR protection will induce an immediate loss of current consumption arising from the expansion of the R&D sector, but a gain in future consumption as a result of more investment in R&D, which induces faster innovation and faster growth. More precisely, there will be a downward level shift of the entire consumption path, but the path will become steeper as a result of faster growth. We have already seen the consumption level shift in Figure 2, because $h \equiv C/(\beta A)$ is nothing but a scaled and normalized version of consumption C. To see more clearly the tradeoff between current and future consumption, let us find out the equilibrium consumption path. The consumer optimality condition (7) requires that equilibrium consumption grows at the rate $\gamma_c[\mu] = (r_m - \mu - \rho)/\theta$ which depends negatively on μ: $C(t) = C(0)\exp(\gamma_c[\mu]t)$. Rewrite $h(t)$ as $h[t;\mu]$ to emphasize its dependence on μ, by definition of h, we can write the equilibrium consumption path as $C(t) = \beta A(0)h[0;\mu]\exp(\gamma_c[\mu]t)$. Taking logarithm and differentiating with respect to μ, we have

$$\frac{\partial \ln C(t)}{\partial \mu} = \frac{1}{h(0)}\frac{\partial h[0;\mu]}{\partial \mu} + \frac{\partial \gamma_c[\mu]}{\partial \mu} \cdot t \tag{23}$$

The first term on the right hand side of (23) measures the extent of the consumption level shift at $t = 0$, where $\partial h[0;\mu]/\partial \mu > 0$ is given by (20) above. Such a level shift in the consumption path signifies the loss in current consumption from tightening IPR protection. Since

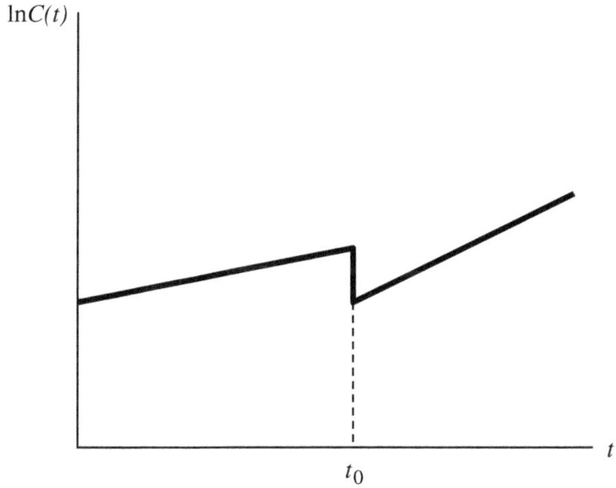

Figure 7. The time path of $C(t)$ when a tightening of IPR protection is announced at date t_0.

$\partial\gamma_c[\mu]/\partial\mu = -1/\theta$, the second term on the right hand side of (23) measures the steepening of the consumption path, which represents the gain in consumption growth from tightening IPR protection. Figure 7 displays the time path of $C(t)$ before and after a tightening of IPR protection is announced.

Unlike the innovation rate which exhibits overshooting behavior, the consumption growth rate has no transitional dynamics. Along the transitional path, the fraction of sectors that have competitive pricing is falling, reducing the quantity of goods demanded, and releasing resources for innovation. And yet these adjustments take place while insulating consumption growth from their effects. This somewhat peculiar feature of the model stems from specific functional forms employed (e.g. the Dixit–Stiglitz expanding variety form (1)) and the very simple imitation technology (2) which features a constant hazard rate μ. The no arbitrage condition (5) pins down the real interest rate r as the difference between the constant rate of return to innovation $r_m = (L/\beta)\alpha^{2/(1-\alpha)}(1/\alpha - 1)$ and the constant hazard rate μ. A constant real interest rate in turn implies, via the Ramsey optimal consumption rule (7), a constant rate of consumption growth without transitional dynamics. Transitional dynamics in consumption growth exists if we specify a more sophisticated imitation technology that features a time-varying hazard rate. Following a suggestion in Helpman (1993, footnotes 5), we have experimented with an imitation function of the form $\dot{A}_c = \mu A_c^{\phi}(A - A_c)^{1-\phi}, 0 < \phi < 1$, which features a time-varying hazard rate $\dot{A}_c/(A - A_c) = \mu[A_c/(A - A_c)]^{\phi}$. Other than generating transitional dynamics in consumption growth and significantly complicating the analytical derivations, using this more general imitation function does not change the results in this paper in any major way. The results with such a function are reported by the authors elsewhere. It may appear that, since the new steady state growth rate is attained immediately, it is straightforward to calculate the welfare and therefore the optimal IPR analytically. This is not the case because the loss in current consumption, namely the one-shot fall in $C(0)$, cannot be obtained unless the entire new saddle-path is calculated, which can be done exactly only by numerical method.

2.4 Optimal IPR protection

The tradeoff between the loss in current consumption and gain in consumption growth naturally leads to the possibility of an optimal IPR protection — optimal in the sense of maximizing the representative agent's utility. In our model this amounts to choosing $\mu = \mu^*$ such that utility (6) is maximized, subject to the law of motion of equilibrium consumption. As shown above, the equilibrium consumption path is $C(t) = \beta A(0)h[0;\mu]\exp(\gamma_c[\mu]t)$. Substituting $c(t) \equiv C(t)/L$ into the utility function (6), evaluating the relevant integrals and taking logarithm, the optimal μ can be characterized by

$$\mu^* = \arg\max_{\mu} \begin{cases} s(1-\theta)\ln h[0;\mu] - s\ln(\rho - \gamma_c[\mu](1-\theta)), & \theta \neq 1 \\ \ln h[0;\mu] + \gamma_c[\mu]/\rho & \theta = 1 \end{cases} \tag{24}$$

where

$$s = \begin{cases} 1 & \text{if } 1-\theta > 0 \\ -1 & \text{if } 1-\theta < 0 \end{cases} \tag{25}$$

Note that $\rho - \gamma_c(1-\theta) > 0$ as dictated by the transversality condition from the consumer optimal control problem. Referring to

Figure 3, different μ corresponds to different saddle-path with the corresponding $h(g_0;\mu) = h[0;\mu]$, as indicated by points X, Y, and Z. The trailing terms in (24), $-s\ln(\rho - \gamma_c[\mu](1-\theta))$ and $\gamma_c[\mu]/\rho$, reflect the utility of the consumption path from a starting point (say Z) to the corresponding steady state (say Z'). For an interior optimum, μ^* satisfies

$$\frac{\partial \ln h[0;\mu^*]}{\partial\mu} = -\left(\frac{1}{\rho - \gamma_c[\mu^*](1-\theta)}\right)\frac{\partial\gamma_c[\mu^*]}{\partial\mu} \qquad \text{for all } \theta > 0 \tag{26}$$

We have shown that the left hand side is greater than zero. Also, $\partial\gamma_c[\mu^*]/\partial\mu = -1/\theta < 0$, so the right hand side is greater than zero too. In fact, we can call the left hand side the marginal costs and the right hand side the marginal benefits of tightening IPR protection. The marginal costs come from a decrease in current consumption, and the marginal benefits come from an increase in consumption growth, which results in higher utility in the future.

3 Model Calibration

In this section, we calibrate the model to the US economy to get some idea about its practical relevance. In particular, we are interested in solving for μ^*, which parameterizes the optimal IPR protection level, and quantifying its welfare implications. As can be seen from (24), the objective function depends on $h[0;\mu]$ which is nothing but the policy function (i.e. the stable saddle-path) evaluated at $g(0)$. Rather than relying on the approximate solution in (17), we solve for the policy function numerically from the differential equation system (8) in our calibration exercise. Readers not interested in the numerical computation may skip the following sub-section without loss of continuity.

3.1 Numerical solution

By taking the ratio of the two differential equations in (8), we obtain a differential equation in (g, h) space which characterizes the two saddle-paths (one stable, one unstable) of the system:

$$h'(g) \equiv \frac{\mathrm{d}h}{\mathrm{d}g} = \frac{\dot{h}}{\dot{g}} = \frac{\gamma_1 g + \gamma_2 h + \gamma_c + \mu + \gamma_3}{\mu g^{-1} + \gamma_1 g + \gamma_2 h + \gamma_3} \equiv \frac{H(g)}{G(g)} \tag{27}$$

with initial value $h(g^*) = h^*$. The last identity gives the definitions of $H(g)$ and $G(g)$. The two saddle-paths are distinguished by their slopes at g^*, but (27) alone is not sufficient to pin down the stable path because $h'(g^*) = H(g^*)/G(g^*) = 0/0$. To calculate the slope of the stable path around the steady state, we use the L'Hopital's rule to evaluate $h'(g^*) = H'(g^*)/G'(g^*)$, and then write it in terms of the coefficients a_{ij} of the linearized system (10) as:

$$h'(g^*) = \frac{a_{21} + a_{22}h'(g^*)}{a_{11} + a_{12}h'(g^*)} \tag{28}$$

The two roots of the quadratic equation (28) are

$$h'(g^*) = \frac{-(a_{11} - a_{22}) \pm \sqrt{(a_{11} - a_{22})^2 + 4a_{12}a_{21}}}{2a_{12}} = \frac{\lambda_i - a_{11}}{a_{12}} > 0, \quad i = 1, 2 \tag{29}$$

where the second equality can be verified by substituting (12) for λ_1 and λ_2, the two eigenvalues of the linearized system. From the phase diagram we know that the stable path is flatter than the unstable path, so that the required slope must be the smaller root. Since $\lambda_1 > 0$ and $\lambda_2 < 0$, it follows that the slope of the stable path is $(\lambda_2 - a_{11})/a_{12}$ which is simply ν, the second component of the normalized eigenvector corresponding to the negative eigenvalue of the linearized system (see (16)).

Standard numerical algorithms are available for solving (27) which is an initial value problem in ordinary differential equation (e.g. Press *et al.*, 1992, Chapter 16). We use numerical routines in module nag_ivp_ode_rk in NAG Fortran 90 library (release 3, 1998) which implements a variable-step Runge–Kutta method. In searching over the optimal μ, each evaluation of the objective function in (24) with respect to μ requires the differential equation (27) be solved once to yield $h[0; \mu]$. That is, the differential equation solver has to be embedded within the optimization routine. We perform the computation on a Pentium PC with programs written in Gauss and Fortran 90. The computer programs are available upon request for replication.

3.2 Calibration result

We calibrate the model with US data. To tie down the two preference parameters, θ (intertemporal substitution) and ρ (discount factor), we make use of the consumer optimality condition (7) with the steady state growth rate, γ_c, and the real interest rate, r, equated to the observed values in the post-war era. Following King *et al.* (1988) we set $\gamma_c = 0.016$, the common trend annual growth rate of output, consumption and investment, and $r = 0.065$, the average real return to equity. Since both ρ and θ are positive, it follows that $0 < \theta < r/\gamma_c \approx 4$. θ is usually assumed to exceed one in the literature. We will consider $\theta \in [1, 4]$ as in Stokey (1995). For each θ in the interval, the consumer optimality condition then implies a unique ρ.

We need the initial state $g(0)$ to compute $h[0; \mu] = h(g(0); \mu)$ in (24). Assuming the US economy is currently at a steady state, corresponding to a particular value μ_0 (to be determined later), we set $g(0) = g^* \equiv \mu_0/(\gamma_c + \mu_0)$ using (9). The imitation rate μ_0 is calibrated to reflect the IPR protection level currently in place. We relate μ_0 to the duration T of a finite-life monopoly:

$$\frac{1}{\mu_0 + r} = \int_0^T e^{-rt} \mathrm{d}t \tag{30}$$

The left-hand-side is the expected present value of a profit stream of \$1 for a perpetual monopoly that faces a hazard rate of imitation μ_0. The right hand side is the certainty equivalence (CE) of the same profit stream for a finite-life monopoly that lasts only up to T. In other words, T is the certainty-equivalent duration of a monopoly position, given the risk of being imitated as indicated by μ_0. Given $r = 0.065$, we can assign a value for T (in years) and then back out the corresponding μ_0. The advantage of this approach is that we have better idea about the plausible range of T than μ_0. For example,

$T = 17$ years (the current (1995) patent length in US) corresponds to $\mu_0 = 0.032$.

The technology parameter α has two interpretations: labor share $1 - \alpha$ and markup ratio $1/\alpha$. For the purpose of this chapter, the markup interpretation seems to be more appropriate. The labor share interpretation, however, has the advantage of allowing us to fix α almost unambiguously by using the conventional labor share value of 0.6, which implies a markup ratio of 2.5. Hall (1986) estimates the markup ratios of some fifty industries at the two-digit SIC code level, covering all sectors of the US economy, and concludes that in most industries the markup ratio is above 1.5 and in a few it exceeds 3. We will consider markup ratio $1/\alpha \in [1.25, 2.5]$ and use Hall's estimate of 1.6 for the whole manufacturing industry as the benchmark value. The remaining unknown parameter is the ratio L/β. Given r and μ_0, the zero profit (no arbitrage) condition determines the rate of return $r_m = r + \mu_0$. The ratio L/β can then be solved from the expression $r_m = (L/\beta)\alpha^{2/(1-\alpha)}(1/\alpha - 1)$.

For illustrative purposes, Table 1 reports the optimal IPR protection levels and their welfare implications for three assumed levels of IPR protection currently in place (i.e. three values of μ_0 that correspond to 5, 10 and 17 years of CE monopoly duration, respectively). These figures are chosen for the following reasons. Eaton and Kortum (1999), based on Mansfield *et al.* (1981), estimate that the imitation rate for technology patented at home is about 0.23. This is equivalent to about four years of CE monopoly duration in our model. So, we pick a CE monopoly duration of 5 years as

Table 1. Average markup.

$r = 0.065, \gamma_c = 0.016, 1/\alpha = 1.6, \theta = 2.5$	(a)	(b)	(c)
Current IPR protection level μ_0	0.032	0.071	0.169
(CE monopoly duration in years corresp. to μ_0)	(17)	(10)	(5)
1. Deviation from optimal IPR protection: $\ln(\mu_0/\mu^*)$	1.78	1.97	2.02
2. Optimal growth rate (%)	2.67	4.04	7.47
3. Consumption level shift (%)	−20.36	−26.04	−29.85
4. Welfare gain (%)	17.16	33.65	55.57

one example. Another example for illustration is assuming that the current (1995) patent length of 17 years represents the CE monopoly duration of existing IPR protection level. Mansfield *et al.* would probably regard this as too long.[7] The third example chosen is 10 years, about midway between 5 and 17 years. The markup ratio and the intertemporal substitution parameter are set at the benchmark values of 1.6 and 2.5, respectively. Column (a) of Table 1 assumes that current IPR protection represents a CE monopoly duration of 17 years. Row 1 indicates that the corresponding $\mu_0 = 0.032$ is way above the optimal μ^*, which means that IPR is currently under-protected. Rows 2–4 report what would happen if optimal IPR protection were pursued. The steady state growth rate would accelerate to 2.67% (Row 2), comparing with the current growth rate of 1.6%; this is the gain in consumption growth from tightening IPR protection to the optimal level. There will be a loss in current consumption, however, leading to a downward level shift of the consumption path. The extent of such consumption level shift, as reported in Row 3 for the normalized consumption variable h at the steady state, is 20.36%. The welfare gain in consumption growth will of course outweigh the loss in current consumption, and the net gain in welfare is 17.16% as reported in Row 4. Columns (b) and (c) assume weaker levels of current IPR protection, corresponding to CE monopoly durations of 5 and 10 years, respectively. As can be seen, the extent of the under-protection is greater, the weaker is the current IPR protection level. The reason is that, given the real interest rate r fixed at the observed value, a higher risk of imitation μ_0 implies that the underlying rate of return to innovation r_m must also be higher. The higher rate of return to innovation generates a wealth effect and an intertemporal substitution effect. The wealth effect motivates the benevolent social planner to take more current consumption and

[7]They report that "... patent protection seems to have only a limited effect on entry in about half of the cases ..." and "... it seems to have a very important effect in a minority of them. For about 15% of the innovations, patent protection was estimated to have delayed the time when the first imitator entered the market by 4 years or more".

hence implies weaker optimal IPR protection. The intertemporal substitution effect, on the other hand, favors future consumption and hence implies stronger optimal IPR protection. Under our calibrated parameter values, the intertemporal substitution effect dominates the wealth effect.

Table 2 reports the results for a high markup ratio of 2.5, which corresponds to the value of α determined by appealing to the conventional labor share value $1 - \alpha = 0.6$. Comparing with Table 1, it can be seen that a higher markup ratio implies slightly stronger optimal IPR protection. To check robustness, we also report in Table 3 the case for a low markup ratio of 1.25. Comparing the three tables, it can be seen that the results, especially the welfare implications, are rather robust with respect to different markup ratios. The results in Tables 1–3 all suggest under-protection of IPR, and the welfare loss can be quite substantial. Will there ever be over-protection? If yes, is the welfare loss simply a mirror image of the

Table 2. High markup.

$r = 0.065, \gamma_c = 0.016, 1/\alpha = 2.5, \theta = 2.5$	(a)	(b)	(c)
Current IPR protection level μ_0	0.032	0.071	0.169
(CE monopoly duration in years corresp. to μ_0)	(17)	(10)	(5)
1. Deviation from optimal IPR protection: $\ln(\mu_0/\mu^*)$	1.87	2.06	2.12
2. Optimal growth rate (%)	2.69	4.08	7.56
3. Consumption level shift (%)	−18.22	−23.10	−26.38
4. Welfare gain (%)	18.63	35.43	57.19

Table 3. Low markup.

$r = 0.065, \gamma_c = 0.016, 1/\alpha = 1.25, \theta = 2.5$	(a)	(b)	(c)
Current IPR protection level μ_0	0.032	0.071	0.169
(CE monopoly duration in years corresp. to μ_0)	(17)	(10)	(5)
1. Deviation from optimal IPR protection: $\ln(\mu_0/\mu^*)$	1.73	1.92	1.97
2. Optimal growth rate (%)	2.66	4.02	7.43
3. Consumption level shift (%)	−21.30	−27.41	−31.54
4. Welfare gain (%)	16.32	32.62	54.63

under-protection case? How sensitive is our conclusion with respect to different parameter values?

We have performed extensive numerical computation to investigate the issues raised above. As mentioned before, the result is insensitive to variations in the markup ratio $1/\alpha$. We thus concentrate on θ, the intertemporal substitution parameter, and μ_0, the current imitation rate, which parameterizes the current degree of IPR protection. Figure 8 depicts the log deviation of μ_0 from the optimal level μ^* over wide ranges of θ and T, the CE monopoly duration (in years) that corresponds to μ_0. The over-protection region is highlighted by triangles. As can be seen, over-protection happens only when the current IPR protection is already very strong, to the extent that a monopoly position is expected to last over 50 years. For most industries this is certainly not a plausible degree of

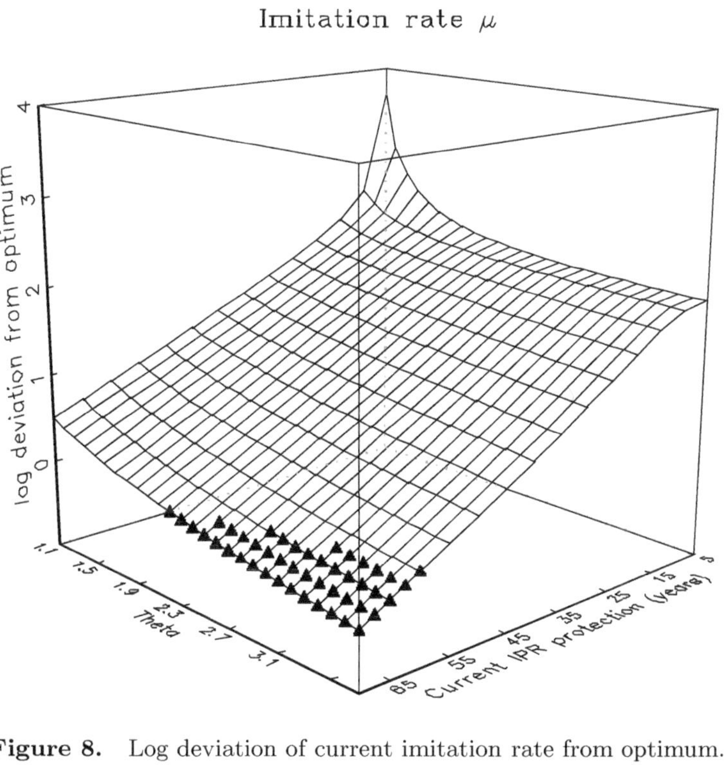

Figure 8. Log deviation of current imitation rate from optimum.

current IPR protection. But it is interesting to note that the current US copyright protection is indeed 50 years, and that Coca-Cola has been successfully safeguarding its secret formula for more than 100 years! Figure 9 depicts the welfare gain from pursuing optimal IPR protection, for the same ranges of θ and T values as in Figure 8. It can be seen that the welfare loss is trivial for the over-protection region. In fact, for T over 35 years, the welfare loss from sub-optimal IPR protection has already become trivial, as indicated by the flat region in Figure 9. The reason is that when T is already very high (i.e. μ_0 very small), given the real interest rate fixed at the observed value, the zero profit condition implies a low rate of return to innovation. There is thus not much growth effect to exploit by tightening IPR protection in the under-protection case. In the over-protection case, pursuing optimal IPR protection amounts to raising the level of the consumption path at the expense of the growth rate.

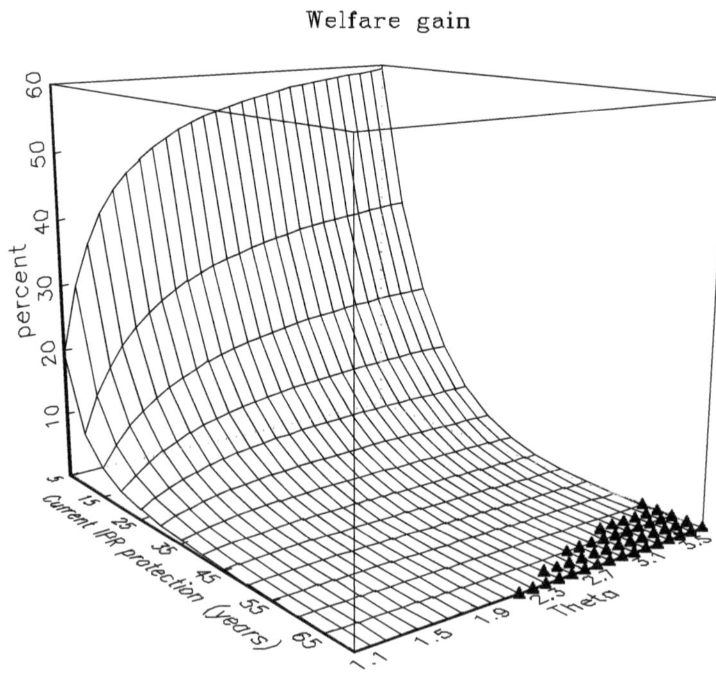

Figure 9. Welfare gain from pursuing optimal IPR protection.

As is well known from growth theory, the elasticity of welfare with respect to level effect is a lot smaller than that of growth effect. Therefore, the welfare gains from correcting over-protection of IPR is very small.

4 Concluding Remarks

It must be borne in mind that our model is, in a sense, a metaphor that tries to capture the fact that development of new intermediate goods increases labor productivity, and that strengthening IPR protection lengthens the average duration of monopoly position of the innovators of these intermediate goods. A few caveats need to be mentioned.

First, recall that we treat IPR protection as the part of "imitation rate" (rate at which monopoly profit is eroded) that can be influenced by government policy. This is a policy package that includes patent length and breadth, protection of trademarks, copyrights and trade secrets, and the degree of enforcement. Some may argue that even anti-trust policies can sometimes be treated as IPR polices. Accordingly, a strengthening of IPR in the US means a change in the whole package of policies in favor of the innovators. Consequently, any change in only one dimension of the package, e.g. an increase of patent length from 17 years to 25 years, might have limited effect on the overall protection of IPR.[8]

Second, just like other one-sector, highly aggregated, macroeconomic models, ours cannot capture things such as sectoral differences. However, we gain in tractability, which allows us to calibrate the model using easily available macroeconomic data.

Third, we have made use of a very simple model to illustrate the tradeoff between loss in current consumption and gain in

[8]Note that the CE monopoly duration in our model is different from the patent length. A change of the CE monopoly duration from, say, 17–25 years has a much higher effect on IPR protection in the economy than a change of the patent length from 17 to 25 years, since many sectors are not covered by patents, and the degree of enforcement is not perfect.

consumption growth due to increase in IPR protection. While we gain from simplicity of the model, we might not have sufficiently captured certain important aspects of the economy. For example, the expanding variety model is subject to the criticism that it fails to capture obsolescence of goods — goods stay in the market forever. The absence of obsolescence might lead to an over-estimation of the degree of IPR under-protection that we have found to prevail in the real world. However, it is straightforward to show that the qualitative aspects of the results would be preserved if an exogenous rate of obsolescence is incorporated in the present model. It is endogenous obsolescence that is of substantive interest and has not been captured in this paper. We would extend the current model to incorporate endogenous obsolescence along the line of Lai (1998b) and the result would be reported elsewhere.

Recently, there has been debate on how to reconcile the historical trend of increasing R&D-to-output ratio and a constant growth rate (see for example, Jones, 1995; Kortum, 1997). Our model features constant R&D to output ratio, which is at odds with the fact. However, we believe our results will not be altered qualitatively even if we adopted a modification such as in Jones (1995), which features increasing R&D to output ratio.[9]

Another extension we are carrying out is to assume a more general imitation technology to capture the fact that the rate of imitation is dependent also on the knowledge accumulated from past imitations. In this way, we allow for transitional dynamics of the hazard rate when there is a shock to IPR protection. Preliminary results show that this would give rise to multiple steady states and substantially richer transitional dynamics. It would be interesting to examine the qualitative and quantitative impact of changes in IPR protection in such a more general and presumably more realistic model.

[9]However, if we did that, long-term growth would not be driven by R&D, which would be inconsistent with our original premise that IPR protection should have long-term growth effect.

Acknowledgment

The authors would like to thank Eric Bond, Ping Wang, Isaac Erhlich, Kar-yiu Wong, two anonymous referees, and participants in the brown bag seminar in City University of Hong Kong and International Conference on "Innovation, Appropriate Strategies and Economic Policy" held in Paris, 1999 (especially Professor J. Hellier) for helpful discussions and constructive comments. The work in this paper has been supported by the Research Grants Council of Hong Kong, China (Project No. CityU 1145/99H).

References

Aghion, P. and Howitt, P. (1992). A model of growth through creative destruction, *Econometrica* 60, 323–351.

Cysne, R. P. and Turchick, D. (2012). Intellectual property rights protection and endogenous economic growth revisited, *Journal of Economic Dynamics & Control* 36, 851–861.

Dixit, A. and Stiglitz, J. (1977). Monopolistic competition and optimum product diversity, *American Economic Review* 67, 297–308.

Eaton, J. and Kortum, S. (1999). International technology diffusion: Theory and measurement, *International Economic Review* 40, 537–570.

Eicher, T. (1999). Training, adverse selection and appropriate technology: Development and growth in a small open economy, *Journal of Economic Dynamics and Control* 23, 727–746.

Ethier, W. (1982). National and international returns to scale in the modern theory of international trade, *American Economic Review* 72, 389–405.

Futagami, K., Mino, K., and Ohkusa, Y. (1996). Patent Length and Economic Growth, Mimeo, Ritsumeikan University, Kobe University and Osaka City University.

Glass, A. J. and Saggi, K. (2002). Intellectual property rights and foreign direct investment, *Journal of International Economics*, 56(2), 387–410.

Grossman, G. and Helpman, E. (1991a). Quality ladders in the theory of growth, *Review of Economic Studies* 58, 43–61.

Grossman, G. and Helpman, E. (1991b). *Innovation and Growth in the Global Economy* (MIT Press, Cambridge, Massachusetts), Chapter 11.

Hall, R. (1986). Market structure and macroeconomic fluctuations, *Brookings Papers on Economic Activity* 2, 285–322.

Helpman, E. (1993). Innovation, imitation and intellectual property rights, *Econometrica* 61, 1247–1280.

Jones, C. (1995). R&D-based models of economic growth, *Journal of Political Economy* 103, 759–784.

Jones, C. (2001). Was the Industrial Revolution Inevitable? Economic Growth Over the Very Long Run? Mimeo, Stanford University, March.

Jones, C. and Williams, J. (1998). Measuring the social return to R&D, *Quarterly Journal of Economics* 113, 1119–1135.

Jones, C. and Williams, J. (2000). Too much of a good thing? the economics of investment in R&D, *Journal of Economic Growth* 5, 65–85.

King, R., Plosser, C., and Rebelo, S. (1988). Production, growth and business cycles I: The basic neoclassical model, *Journal of Monetary Economics* 21, 195–232.

Kortum, S. (1997). Research, patenting, and technological change, *Econometrica* 65, 1389–1419.

Lai, E. (1998a). International intellectual property rights protection and rate of product innovation, *Journal of Development Economics* 55, 133–153.

Lai, E. (1998b). Schumpeterian growth with gradual product obsolescence, *Journal of Economic Growth* 3, 81–103.

Mansfield, E., Schwartz, M., and Wagner, S. (1981). Imitation costs and patents: An empirical study, *Economic Journal* 91, 907–918.

O'Donoghue, T. and Zweimuller, J. (1998). Patents in a Model of Endogenous Growth, Mimeo, Cornell University and University of Zurich.

Press, W., Teukolsky, S., Vetterling, W., and Flannery, B. (1992). *Numerical Recipes in C: The Art of Scientific Computing*, 2nd Edn. (Cambridge University Press, Cambridge).

Rivera-Batiz, L. and Romer, P. (1991). Economic integration and endogenous growth, *Quarterly Journal of Economics* 106, 531–555.

Romer, P. (1990). Endogenous technological change, *Journal of Political Economy* 98, S71–S102.

Stokey, N. (1995). R&D and economic growth, *Review of Economic Studies* 62, 469–489.

Chapter 9

Schumpeterian Growth with Gradual Product Obsolescence*

Abstract
The model in this paper captures several important aspects of the real world: (i) gradual obsolescence of goods in the form of gradually declining net profit derived from each product until it is phased out; (ii) expanding variety of goods over time; and (iii) both dynamic and static internal increasing returns to scale of production. To eliminate the scale effect, Jones's specification that gives rise to a "semi-endogenous" rate of innovation is adopted. The most interesting finding of the paper is that, when the research duplication effect is small (large) relative to the intertemporal knowledge spillover effect in R&D, the decentralized market delivers insufficient (excessive) obsolescence and allocates too little (much) labor to R&D, while a small subsidy (tax) to innovation is welfare-improving. All these results hold because the positive knowledge spillover externality overwhelms (is overwhelmed by) the negative research duplication externality.

1 Introduction

Endogenous growth models that try to capture the Schumpeterian process of creative destruction usually feature the complete

---

*By Edwin L.-C. Lai. Originally published in *Journal of Economic Growth*, 3 (March 1998), pp. 81–103.

destruction of rents of firms producing lower quality products once a higher quality product is developed (Aghion and Howitt, 1992; Grossman and Helpman, 1991, Chapter 4; Segerstrom, 1991).[1] In these models, lower quality and higher quality products are perfect substitutes; therefore, lower quality products become obsolete immediately once a higher quality product is introduced into the market. On the other extreme, there are R&D-based endogenous growth models where growth is driven by the expansion of product variety (Romer, 1990; Grossman and Helpman, 1991, Chapter 3). In these models, although the market share of older goods are lowered by the introduction of a new variety, all goods will exist in the market forever.[2] Casual observation, however, suggests that goods become obsolete gradually as an economy grows.

We believe a richer Schumpeterian growth model should capture quality improvement, expansion of variety and gradual obsolescence of goods. With such a model, we would be able to endogenize not only the rate of innovation and growth, but also the rate of obsolescence and length of product cycles. In this paper, we modify an R&D-based growth model to capture these features and to analyze their effects on the properties of such a class of R&D-based model regarding policies, rate of innovation, the length of product cycles, welfare, etc.

The model in this paper captures the existence of both static and dynamic internal increasing returns to scale, as is well-documented in empirical studies. These increasing returns result from the interaction of a sunk cost of innovation, a quasi-fixed cost of production (overhead cost due to the presence of working capital) at each date, and a constant marginal cost of production. The utility function of consumers is CES, with newer goods carrying higher weights than older goods, because newer goods are more sophisticated. As a

---

[1] For the original explanation of the idea of creative destruction, see Schumpeter (1976).

[2] The latter feature is basically an artifact of the Dixit–Stiglitz utility/production function, which, while being mathematically very tractable, has a "love-of-variety" property. See Dixit and Stiglitz (1977).

result, the instantaneous profit of a good declines over time, and is eventually phased out of the market when the firm's instantaneous gross profit is too small to cover the instantaneous quasi-fixed cost.

Endogenous growth models with gradual product obsolescence are not new. However, for the sake of tractability, the early models with this feature are mostly learning by doing models with perfect spillovers. The advantage of this type of model is it allows the authors to assume perfect competition in the product market (Stokey, 1988; Young, 1991). Young's (1993) model is the first true hybrid of (Schumpeterian) R&D-based and learning by doing models, with imperfect competition in the product market and gradual phasing out of goods. His focus is on the interaction of invention and learning by doing as well as on how market size influences the bottleneck of growth. Our focus, however, is on the impacts of different types of taxation/subsidy and of exogenous changes within the framework of a purely R&D-based growth model.

Keppler (1996) depicts a rich model that explains the empirical regularities concerning how entry, exit, market structure and innovation vary from the birth of an *industry* through its maturity. In our model, we emphasize how optimizing behavior of agents and firms determines steady-state innovation, entry and exit of *products* in a broadly defined industry. We focus on how the length of the market-determined product cycle deviates from the social optimum and on the policy remedies.

This chapter modifies an expanding-variety R&D-based growth model (Romer, 1990; Grossman and Helpman, 1991) to incorporate an asymmetrical CES specification for the index of consumption (with more recent products being more valuable) and an overhead cost of production at each date. These features allow for a limited lifespan of a product, which starts at the top-of-the-line when first introduced, and finishes its life as lowest quality. We have found a way to incorporate meaningful vintage products into a model of growth while keeping it tractable. We believe the steady state equilibrium captures the salient features of the product cycle — a product which starts as technologically innovative is gradually eclipsed by newer and more advanced products until it eventually disappears from the market altogether.

Jones (1995b) refutes the scale effect of the original frameworks of Romer (1990) and Grossman and Helpman (1991). Therefore, to eliminate the scale effect, we adopt Jones's (1995a) specification that leads to a "semi-endogenous" rate of innovation.

Our model captures several important aspects of the real world: (i) there is gradual obsolescence of goods in the form of declining net profit derived from each product until it is phased out; (ii) there is expanding variety of goods over time; (iii) there are both dynamic and static internal increasing returns to scale of production. There are several Interesting results. First, an increase in any exogenous variable that positively affects the steady state rate of innovation leads to a(n) decrease (increase) in the equilibrium (socially optimal) fraction of obsolete products. Second, when the research duplication effect in R&D is small (large) relative to the intertemporal knowledge spillover effect, the decentralized market delivers insufficient (excessive) obsolescence and allocates too little (much) labor to R&D, while a small subsidy (tax) to innovation is welfare-improving. These results hold because the positive knowledge spillover externality overwhelms (is overwhelmed by) the negative research duplication externality. When the research duplication effect in R&D is small (large) relative to the intertemporal knowledge spillover effect, the net external effect of obsolescence is positive (negative), and the product cycle is too short (long).

Section 2 lays down the main body of the model and solve for the endogenous variables. Section 3 compares the social optimum with the market equilibrium. Section 4 concludes the chapter.

2 The Model

In this chapter, we are only concerned with the "balanced growth" steady state in which the rate of innovation is constant over time. There is one primary factor, labor, which can be used to undertake innovation (product development) or production of goods.

Labor here, however, should be interpreted as skilled labor or "human capital" that can work both in the production or R & D sector. There is one industrial sector (or, alternatively, M identical sectors) in which innovation takes the form of quality improvement. Each good contains a number of features each of which contributes to the utility function of a consumer. An innovation is defined as the development of a product that incorporates some additional feature to the most sophisticated existing product. In principle, there is an infinite number of potential features and potential goods that can be developed. There is no uncertainty in the R&D process.[3] At any given time, only a finite number of goods has been developed.

2.1 The demand side

Following Grossman and Helpman (hereinafter G–H) (1991, Chapter 3) we assume that a representative agent chooses total expenditure and consumption of goods at each date to maximize the standard Ramsey intertemporal utility

$$W(t) = \int_t^\infty e^{-\rho(\tau-t)} \log U(\tau) d\tau \qquad (1)$$

subject to the intertemporal budget constraint[4]

$$\int_t^\infty e^{-r(\tau-t)} E(\tau) d\tau = \int_t^\infty e^{-r(\tau-t)} I(\tau) d\tau + A(t) \quad \text{for all } t \qquad (2)$$

where r = interest rate; $U(\tau)$ = instantaneous utility at time τ; $E(\tau)$ = instantaneous expenditure at τ; $I(\tau)$ = instantaneous income at τ; $A(t)$ = value of assets at t. At each date τ, the agent takes $A(\tau)$, $I(\tau)$, r and prices of goods as given. Instantaneous utility at

[3]The absence of uncertainty in the R&D process, while unrealistic, simplifies the analysis and allows us to focus on the issues this paper wants to address.
[4]The "flow" version of this "stock" equation is $I(t) - E(t) + rA(t) = \dot{A}(t)$.

time t is given by[5]

$$U(t) = \left\{ \int_{n_o(t)}^{n(t)} [u(z)]^\alpha dz \right\}^{\frac{1}{\alpha}} \tag{3}$$

where goods in the continuum from index $n_o(t)$ to index $n(t)$ are the goods that exist in the market at time t (goods 0 to n_o have become obsolete at that date) and

$$u(z) \equiv u(x(z)) \equiv z^{\frac{1}{\beta}} x(z) \tag{4}$$

($0 < \alpha < 1$ and $0 < \beta$) is the subutility attributed to a good of index z. Good z contains one unit of each of the characteristics in the interval $(0, z)$, and $x(z)$ is the quantity of good z consumed. A good with a higher index has more features, and is considered "more sophisticated". The variable $n = n(t)$ denotes the most sophisticated good existing in the economy at time t.

Utility function (3) indicates that there is both a "love of variety" and a "love of sophistication" of goods. There is love-of-variety since the consumer is better off as long as more varieties are made available, even if the additional varieties are less sophisticated than the existing ones. There is love-of-sophistication because utility is increased by an increase in sophistication of any variety (measured by $z^{\frac{1}{\beta}}$ for good z), keeping the number of varieties (measured by $n - n_0$) unchanged. Although new goods are more sophisticated than old ones, the love-of-variety can be justified by the specialized function performed by each good. A good that has fewer features is assumed to be more specialized in (and thus better at) performing certain tasks than a more sophisticated good.

The dynamic optimization problem specified by (1), (2), (3) and (4) can be broken down into an intra-temporal optimization problem at time t of choosing $x(z)$ to maximize $U(t)$ subject to the instantaneous budget constraint (for given $n(t)$), and the

[5]Alternatively, $U(t)$ can be regarded as quantity of final goods produced from a set of intermediate goods, with production function (3).

intertemporal optimization problem of choosing a time path of $E(t)$ to maximize W subject to the demand function of $x(z)$ (determined by intra-temporal optimization on the demand side) and the prices of goods $p(z)$ (determined by intra-temporal optimization on the supply side).

The intra-temporal consumer optimization problem is

$$\underset{x(z)}{\text{Max}} \; U(t)$$

s.t.

$$\int_{n_o(t)}^{n(t)} x(z)p(z)dz = E(t) \tag{5}$$

The intertemporal optimization problem will be solved after we have solved the instantaneous problems on the demand side and the supply side. We thereafter drop the time argument t for convenience, unless otherwise stated.

From the first order condition of the maximization problem (5), and some simple manipulation, we obtain the demand function $x(z)$ of good z,

$$x(z) = \frac{p(z)^{-\epsilon} z^{\gamma}}{\int_{n_o}^{n} p(s)^{1-\epsilon} s^{\gamma} ds} E \tag{6}$$

where $\epsilon = \frac{1}{1-\alpha} > 1$, and $\gamma = \frac{\alpha}{\beta(1-\alpha)}$. The parameter $\epsilon = \frac{1}{1-\alpha}$ is the elasticity of substitution between any two goods. So, ϵ increases with α. Other things being equal, the distribution of demand among goods of different degrees of sophistication is the result of consumers' compromise between the love-of-variety and the love of sophistication of goods. The greater α is, the less is the love of variety of goods. Similarly, the greater β is, the less is the love of sophistication.

2.2 The supply side

For tractability, all we need is to assume that there is a sufficient number of firms so that no single firm's action can significantly affect the denominator of (6). For ease of exposition, we adopt the stricter assumption that no two goods are produced by the same firm. Labor cost is the only variable cost of production. However, there are two non-variable costs: (i) before starting production, a firm needs to incur a sunk cost of product development; and (ii) as long as the firm stays in business, the firm needs to incur a quasi-fixed cost at each date. This quasi-fixed factor can be thought of as such capital as testing equipment, quality control equipment, general purpose equipment (such as measuring devices, control devices), etc. For the sake of convenience, we shall simply call this quasi-fixed factor "capital". We assume that there is no depreciation of the capital and that there is a perfect second hand market for it. Therefore, a firm is indifferent between renting the capital or owning it for as long as it needs it. For ease of exposition, we can proceed with our analysis assuming that the firm purchases the capital when it starts producing a good and sells the capital when it stops producing the good. The quasi-fixed cost at each date is then the rental cost of capital, the value of which will be derived later.

Following Jones's (1995a) approach, we assume that the technology of research is constant returns to scale with respect to the quantity of labor devoted to R&D at the firm level. However, productivity of labor in R&D is positively affected by knowledge in society and negatively affected by the total quantity of labor devoted to R&D in society (due to negative externality of R&D duplication). Hence, the number of new products developed by a firm is given by

$$\frac{1}{a}(l_n)n^{\phi}L_n^{\lambda-1},$$

where "a" is a measure of unit labor requirement in R&D, $0 < \phi < 1$, $0 < \lambda < 1$, l_n is labor devoted to product development at the firm level, and L_n is the aggregate quantity of labor devoted to R&D in society. The term $L_n^{\lambda-1}$ captures the negative externalities occurring because of duplication in the R&D process. In equilibrium, when aggregating over all firms in the economy, $L_n = \sum l_n$. The term n^{ϕ} captures the positive externalities of knowledge on the productivity of labor employed in innovation, since n is a proxy for knowledge, as in Romer (1990).

Therefore, in equilibrium, the total number of new products developed in the economy at date t is given by

$$\dot{n} = \frac{1}{a} n^{\phi} L_n^{\lambda}. \tag{7}$$

The rate of innovation is given by $\frac{\dot{n}}{n} = \frac{1}{a} n^{\phi-1} L_n^{\lambda}$. In steady state, $\frac{\dot{n}}{n}$ is constant, therefore, $\lambda N = (1-\phi)g$, where $N \equiv \frac{\dot{L}_n}{L_n}$, which is exogenous in steady state, and g is the steady state rate of innovation. This impies that

$$g = \frac{\lambda N}{1-\phi}. \tag{8}$$

The steady state rate of innovation is higher when the rate of growth of research population N is higher, the negative externality of R&D duplication with respect to research population $1-\lambda$ is weaker, and the positive knowledge spillovers effect of R&D ϕ is stronger. Although profit-maximizing firms innovate out of profit motive, the rate of innovation, and therefore growth, is determined by variables that we usually regard as exogenous.

The labor productivity in innovation is $\frac{\dot{n}}{L_n} = \frac{1}{a} n^{\phi} L_n^{\lambda-1}$. If we define labor productivity in innovation as $\frac{m}{a}$, then

$$m = n^{\phi} L_n^{\lambda-1}$$

The growth rate of m is equal to the growth rate of labor productivity in innovation. From the previous equation, the steady state growth rate of m is $\frac{\dot{m}}{m} = \phi g - (1-\lambda)N = \phi g - (1-\phi)g(\frac{1-\lambda}{\lambda}) = \psi g$, where $\psi \equiv 1 - (\frac{1-\phi}{\lambda}) < 1$. We see that $\psi > 0$ only when $\lambda > 1-\phi$, that is, labor productivity in innovation grows in steady state only when negative externalities of research duplication are sufficiently weak and/or the positive externalities of knowledge spillovers are sufficiently strong.

Similarly, we assume that $\dot{K} = \frac{1}{b}(L_K) n^{\phi} L_n^{\lambda-1}$ in the aggregate, where "b" is a measure of the unit labor requirement in production of capital; K is a measure of the quantity of capital in the economy, and L_K is the labor devoted to production of capital. Therefore, labor productivity in production of capital is $\frac{\dot{K}}{L_K} = \frac{1}{b}n^{\phi}L_n^{\lambda-1} = \frac{m}{b}$. That is, labor productivity in capital production is subject to the same negative and positive externalities as labor productivity in research. Note that assuming the same technology in production of blueprints and capitals is equivalent to saying that each innovation amounts to designing and building a "factory" which enables an innovator firm to produce a differentiated product using labor as the variable factor and the capital in the "factory" as a fixed factor. Moreover, a fraction $\frac{b}{a+b}$ of the "factory" is re-usable and re-sellable in the second hand market. This will be made clear below.

Following the above modification to Romer (1990) and Grossman and Helpman (1991, Chapter 3), we obtain the total non-variable costs to be paid by an innovator-cum-producer before it starts production:

$$C_d = (a+b)\frac{w}{m} \tag{9}$$

where "a" and "b" are constants. As implied from the above discussion, $\frac{a}{m}$ is the unit labor requirement for product development, and $\frac{b}{m}$ is the unit labor requirement for production of capital.[6] w is the wage rate. Contrary to Romer (1990), the non-variable costs include not just the cost of developing a "blueprint", but also the rental cost of a unit of capital at each date.

In addition to the non-variable costs, we assume that at each production date there is a constant labor requirement per unit of output (equal to one for all goods). Therefore, there are both static and dynamic internal increasing returns to scale of production.

The market structure is monopolistically Competitive, thus each firm has certain market power over the submarket of its good. Firms maximize the present discounted value of profits. Because of time separability of the intertemporal profit function, each firm chooses price, given the prices of other goods, to maximize instantaneous gross profit $\pi(z)$, subject to the demand function (6). Therefore, a

[6] In equilibrium, the market value of a piece of capital is equal to the cost of its production because of the competitive market.

producer solves

$$\underset{p(z)}{\text{Max}} \; x(z)\{p(z) - c(z)\} \tag{10}$$

s.t. the demand function (6), where $c(z)$ is the cost per unit of output, which is equal to w because the unit labor requirement is equal to one. We obtain from the first order condition the mark-up pricing rule

$$p(z) = \frac{c(z)}{\alpha} = \frac{w}{\alpha} \tag{11}$$

where $w =$ wage rate.

Using the results of the intra-temporal optimization problem, we obtain the first order condition for the intertemporal optimization as the Euler equation:

$$r = \rho + \frac{\dot{E}}{E}.$$

The above equation states that growth rate of E will be higher when consumers are less impatient (more willing to invest in the future), for any given r. We normalize by setting $w = m$. In other words, the wage paid to workers is always proportional to labor productivity in innovation (i.e. the number of new designs produced per worker). This implies that the price of a new design at any time is the same, meaning that a new design is the numeraire of the economy at any time. This normalization will imply that E/n is constant over time in steady state. We can then re-write the above equation as

$$r = \rho + g. \tag{12}$$

2.3 Obsolescence

An innovator invests in R&D to develop a blue-print, which enables him to produce a new, differentiated product. It then earns the opportunity to make a stream of future profits. In steady state, the instantaneous profit (gross of capital cost) of a good diminishes over time because of the gradual introduction of more sophisticated goods. Free entry ensures that no firms can earn any discounted net profits.

On the balanced growth path, the steady state is characterized by $\frac{\dot{n}}{n} = \frac{\dot{n}_o}{n_o}$ so that n_o and n are in constant ratio with each other at all times. The number of variety $n - n_o$ therefore increases at the rate of $\frac{\dot{n}}{n}$. We define $\xi \equiv \frac{n_o}{n}$, the steady state fraction of goods that has become obsolete.

Using the demand function, production cost functions and mark-up pricing rule, namely (6) and (11), we can shown that the instantaneous gross profit of a firm producing good z, when the most sophisticated good is n (remember that $z < n$), is

$$\pi(z,n) = \pi(n,n)\left(\frac{z}{n}\right)^{\gamma} \tag{13}$$

where

$$\pi(n,n) = \frac{E(\gamma+1)(1-\alpha)}{n(1-\xi^{\gamma+1})} \tag{14}$$

and instantaneous gross profit is defined as $\pi(z,n) \equiv x(z)$ $[p(z) - c(z)]$.

In steady state, the initial instantaneous gross profit of any good when it is first introduced, $\pi(n,n)$, is constant over time since $\frac{E}{n}$ and $\frac{n_o}{n}$ are constant over time. According to (13), for given z, $\pi(z,n)$ decreases exponentially over time at a rate of γg in steady state, since n is increasing at a rate of g. Let γ be called the "coefficient of obsolescence". Therefore, the present discounted value (PDV) of the future gross profits of the firm falls at an exponential rate of $\gamma g + g + \rho$. The capital of a firm is resellable (to a new firm) in a perfectly competitive second hand market. Assuming no depreciation of the capital, its current value at time t is equal to $\frac{w(t)}{m(t)}b$, which is constant over time. Therefore, the PDV of the resale value of the capital of a firm falls at an exponential rate of $\rho + g$, which is slower than the rate of decline of the PDV of gross profits. It is therefore clear that, *at some point*, the firm would find it optimal to sell its capital rather than continue operating the firm. Specifically, a firm will stop producing a product as soon as the marginal benefits of waiting (the time derivative of the resale value of the capital of the firm) are smaller than the marginal costs of waiting (the time derivative of the PDV of the future gross profits of the firm).

Let t_d be the time when good z is developed and t_o be the time when good z becomes obsolete; then $T = t_o - t_d$ is the age of good z at the time of obsolescence (i.e. T is the length of the "product cycle"). It can be shown that at steady state, when $\frac{\dot{n}}{n} = \frac{\dot{n}_o}{n_o} = g$,

$$\xi \equiv \frac{n_o}{n} = e^{-g(t_o - t_d)} = e^{-gT} \tag{15}$$

In Appendix B, it is shown that the marginal benefits of waiting is equal to the marginal costs of waiting when

$$\pi(n, n)e^{-(\gamma g + g + \rho)T} = (\rho + g)\frac{wb}{m}e^{-(\rho + g)T}$$

which implies

$$\pi(n, n)\xi^{\gamma} = (\rho + g)\frac{wb}{m}. \tag{16}$$

We shall refer to this as the obsolescence condition. The left hand side (LHS) is the instantaneous gross profit at the date of exit, while the right hand side (RHS) is the rental cost of capital at the date of exit. The firm exits when the instantaneous gross profit is just enough to cover the quasi-fixed cost at that date. This confirms the equivalence between the firm renting capital and its owning the capital for as long as the good is produced.

2.4 Zero profit condition of innovators

Free entry without barriers implies that no firm can make any net profit. In equilibrium, therefore, the PDV of gross profits plus the PDV of the resale value of the capital of the innovator is equal to sum of innovation cost and purchase price of capital. Hence,

$$\int_{t_d}^{t_o} e^{-r(\tau - t_d)}\pi(n(t_d), n(\tau))d\tau + \frac{w}{m}be^{-r(t_o - t_d)} = (a + b)\frac{w}{m}$$

As shown previously, in steady state, $\pi(n(t_o), n(\tau))$ diminishes at an exponential rate of γg with respect to τ. This, together with

(15), implies that the above equation is reduced to

$$\frac{\pi(n,n)}{(\rho+g+\gamma g)}(1-\xi^{\frac{\rho}{g}+1+\gamma})+b\frac{w}{m}\xi^{\frac{\rho}{g}+1}=(a+b)\frac{w}{m}$$

This is a zero profit condition for the innovator. The first term on the LHS is the PDV of the stream of instantaneous gross profits of a firm, with the factor $1-\xi^{\gamma+1+\frac{\rho}{g}}$ accounting for the fact that the stream of profits will terminate upon obsolescence. The term $\rho+g+\gamma g$ is the discount factor that includes both the interest rate $\rho+g$ and the rate of obsolescence γg (which is in fact the rate of capital loss due to obsolescence). The second term on the LHS is the PDV of the resale value of the capital of the firm.

Using (16) and the above zero profit condition, we obtain

$$\frac{\pi(n,n)}{\gamma g+g+\rho}\left(\frac{\rho+g+\gamma g\xi^{\gamma+\frac{\rho}{g}+1}}{\rho+g}\right)=(a+b)\frac{w}{m} \tag{17}$$

The term in parentheses on the LHS is greater than one, indicating that the PDV of total returns to the firm is greater than the PDV of gross profits from sales of goods, because of the positive resale value of the capital.

2.5 Market-determined value of ξ

Dividing (17) by (16) yields

$$\frac{\rho+g+\gamma g\xi^{\gamma+1+\frac{\rho}{g}}}{\rho+g+\gamma g}=(\frac{a+b}{b})\xi^{\gamma} \tag{18}$$

where g is expressed as a function of λ, N and ϕ in (8). In Appendix A, it is shown that the above equation can be represented by a downward sloping curve DE in the (N,ξ) or (g,ξ) space, given a, b, λ and ϕ, as shown in Figure 1. That is, a greater N corresponds to a smaller value of ξ — a higher growth rate of the research population, which leads to a higher steady state rate of innovation, corresponds to a smaller equilibrium fraction of obsolete products in steady state. This relationship is shown in Figure 1 as the curve DE (for "Decentralized Equilibrium"). Let us call the value of ξ under decentralized equilibrium ξ_{DE}. Hereinafter, all variables with

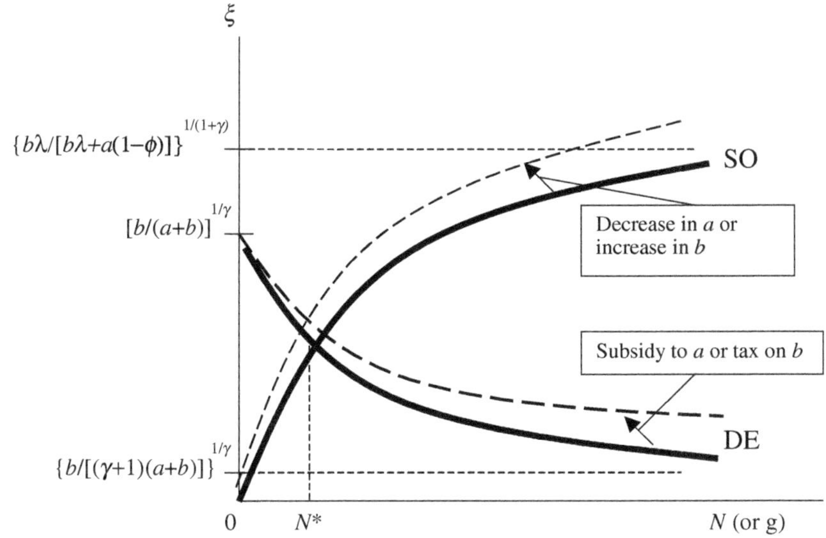

Figure 1. Relationship between the SO and DE Curves
Given a, b, λ, ϕ, γ, the curves will cross if $\lambda/(1-\phi) > (a+b)/[a(\gamma+1)]$.

subscript DE (SO) are associated with "decentralized equilibrium" ("social optimum").[7]

The intuition is as follows. As g increases, the rate of obsolescence γg also increases, which implies that the instantaneous gross profit falls more rapidly. In order for the firm to break even, the initial gross instantaneous profit of a new product must increase. As a result, the instantaneous gross profit has to fall to a lower fraction of initial level when the firm exits from the market.[8] This fraction is exactly equal to ξ^γ, as shown in (16). Therefore, a higher g corresponds to a lower ξ in a decentralized market.

From (15), it is not clear whether the length of the product cycle T_{DE} increases or decreases as g increases (which leads to a decrease in ξ_{DE}). However, it is demonstrated by Mathematica that

[7]As $g \to \infty$, the value of ξ_{DE}, call it $\xi_{\min}$, is defined by $\frac{1+\gamma\xi^{\gamma+1}}{1+\gamma} = (\frac{a+b}{b})\xi^\gamma$. It is hard to get a closed form solution to $\xi_{\min}$, but it can be shown that $\xi_{\min} \in ([(\frac{1}{1+\gamma})(\frac{b}{a+b})]^{\frac{1}{\gamma}}, [\frac{b}{(\gamma+1)a+b}]^{\frac{1}{\gamma}})$. The lower bound of $\xi_{\min}$ is shown in Figure 1.

[8]It is easier to understand this intuition if one pretends that r is independent of g. Although this is not true, the intuition is the same.

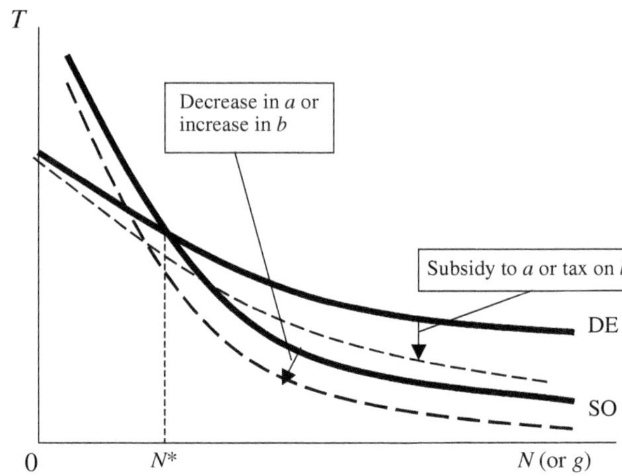

Figure 2. Comparison of lengths of product cycle between social optimum and decentralized equilibrium
Given a, b, λ, ϕ, γ, the curves will cross if $\lambda/(1-\phi) > (a+b)/[a(\gamma+1)]$. The DE curve is found to be downward sloping based on numerical simulation by Mathematica.

$T_{\rm DE}$ decreases as g increases for all the combinations of parametric values that have been tried. This result is consistent with casual observation that, in many sectors of the capitalistic economy, as the rate of innovation increases the length of product cycle shortens, while the fraction of obsolete products decreases.

A subsidy to innovation lowers the value of "a" faced by firms. For given λ, N and ϕ, this leads to an increase in $\xi_{\rm DE}$ (and decrease in $T_{\rm DE}$, according to (15)). Similarly, a tax on working capital increases the value of "b" faced by firms and leads to an increase in $\xi_{\rm DE}$ and decrease in $T_{\rm DE}$. See Figure 2, for the relationship between $T_{\rm DE}$ and g. Hence, we have

Result 1. *An increase in λ, N or ϕ leads to an increase in g, but a decrease in $\xi_{\rm DE}$ and $T_{\rm DE}$. A subsidy to innovation, or tax on working capital, leads to an increase in $\xi_{\rm DE}$ and a decrease in $T_{\rm DE}$.*

3 Social Optimum vs. Decentralized Equilibrium

We shall compare the socially optimal value of ξ with the decentralized market equilibrium value, then assess whether the competitive equilibrium carries too much inertia or momentum. We shall discuss the various externalities that lead to the divergence of the market equilibrium from the social optimum. The following analysis is similar to that of Grossman and Helpman (1991, Chapter 3, pp. 67–74).

To obtain the socially optimal path, we first of all solve a static problem of allocating resources to producing the various existing goods. Then we solve the dynamic problem of determining the growth of n over time. Let X be the aggregate output of manufactured goods. The static problem for the central planner is

$$\max_{x(z)} U = \left\{ \int_{n_o}^{n} [z^{\frac{1}{\beta}} x(z)]^{\alpha} dz \right\}^{\frac{1}{\alpha}} \quad \text{s.t.} \int_{n_o}^{n} x(z) dz \leq X$$

The Lagrangean of the above optimization problem is

$$\mathcal{L} = \left\{ \int_{n_o}^{n} [z^{\frac{1}{\beta}} x(z)]^{\alpha} dz \right\}^{\frac{1}{\alpha}} + \lambda \left[X - \int_{n_o}^{n} x(z) dz \right] \tag{19}$$

where λ is the shadow value of one unit of labor.

From the first order condition, it is straightforward to show that

$$\frac{x(z)}{X} = \frac{z^{\gamma}}{\int_{n_o}^{n} z^{\gamma} dz} \tag{20}$$

Substituting this into the expression for U above, we obtain

$$U = X \left(\frac{n^{\gamma+1} - n_o{}^{\gamma+1}}{\gamma + 1} \right)^{\frac{1-\alpha}{\alpha}} \tag{21}$$

From the above equation, log U expressed as a function of X, ξ and n is

$$\begin{aligned} \log U(X, \xi, n) = \left(\frac{1-\alpha}{\alpha} \right) [(\gamma + 1) \log n - \log (1 + \gamma) \\ + \log(1 - \xi^{\gamma+1})] + \log X \end{aligned} \tag{22}$$

Equation (9) says that the unit labor requirement for product development is $\frac{a}{m}$ and the unit labor requirement for the production of new capital is $\frac{b}{m}$. Since each firm needs one unit of capital for production, the quantity of new capital required is $\dot{n} - \dot{n}_0$, because old capital supplied from obsolete firms satisfies part of the demand in the market. Therefore, total labor in the economy devoted to R&D and the production of new capital at each date is equal to $(\frac{a}{m})\dot{n} + (\frac{b}{m})(\dot{n} - \dot{n}_0) = L_n + \frac{b}{a}L_n(1-\xi)$. It follows that

$$X = L - L_n - \frac{b}{a}L_n(1-\xi) \tag{23}$$

In the dynamic problem, the central planner maximizes $\int_0^{\infty} e^{-\rho\tau} \log U(X, \xi, n) d\tau$ subject to the labor constraint (23) and R&D technology (7). The current value Hamiltonian of this dynamic optimization problem is

$$\begin{aligned}\mathcal{H} = &\left(\frac{1-\alpha}{\alpha}\right)[(1+\gamma)\log n - \log(1+\gamma) + \log(1-\xi^{\gamma+1})] \\ &+ \log\left[L - L_n - \frac{b}{a}L_n(1-\xi)\right] + \theta\left(\frac{1}{a}n^{\phi}L_n^{\lambda}\right)\end{aligned} \tag{24}$$

where θ is the costate variable that represents the (current) shadow value of variety, L_n and ξ are the control variables, and n is the state variable.

3.1 Optimal ξ

In Appendix C, it is shown that the optimal ξ is characterized by [9]

$$\frac{\lambda g}{\rho + (1-\phi)g} = \left[\frac{a + b(1-\xi)}{b(1-\xi^{\gamma+1})}\right]\xi^{\gamma}, \tag{25}$$

where g as a function of λ, N, and ϕ is given in (8). The above equation can be represented by an upward sloping curve in the (N, ξ) or (g, ξ) space, given a, b, λ and ϕ. That is, an increase in the growth rate of research population, which leads to an increase in the steady state rate of innovation, corresponds to an increase in the

[9] Refer to G–H (1991, Chapter 3, p. 71) for a similar derivation procedure.

optimal fraction of obsolete products in society. This curve is shown in Figure 1 as SO (for "Social Optimum").[10]

Intuitively, an increase in ξ phases out older goods today but makes it possible to allocate more resources to develop sophisticated goods for the future. Therefore, it trades off less variety today for more variety tomorrow. As g gets larger, the positive marginal effect of ξ on tomorrow's variety increases (since knowledge stock grows faster, making labor more efficient in R&D in future) relative to its negative marginal effect on today's variety. Hence, the optimal ξ increases with g.

From (15), we know that an increase in g, which leads to an increase in ξ_{SO}, implies that T_{SO} decreases. That is, the optimal length of the product cycle falls as g increases, as shown in Figure 2. From (25) and (15), we conclude that ξ_{SO} increases and T_{SO} decreases as "a" decreases or "b" increases. Hence we have

Result 2. *An increase in λ, N or ϕ leads to an increase in g, an increase in ξ_{SO} and a decrease in T_{SO}. A decrease in "a" or an increase in "b" leads to an increase in ξ_{SO} and a decrease in T_{SO}.*

In Figure 1, we see that, for given a, b, λ and ϕ, since DE is downward sloping and SO is upward sloping in the (N, ξ) or (g, ξ) space, they intersect exactly once as long as the asymptotic level of SO is greater than that of DE. This is true when $\frac{\lambda}{1-\phi} > \frac{(a+b)}{a(\gamma+1)}$.[11] That is, if $\frac{\lambda}{1-\phi}$ is sufficiently large, then $\xi_{\text{DE}} > \xi_{\text{SO}}$ when g is small, and $\xi_{\text{DE}} < \xi_{\text{SO}}$ when g is large. This means the market-determined product cycle is too short (or there is "excessive momentum" in the obsolescence process) when g is small and the market-determined product cycle is too long (or there is "excessive inertia" in the obsolescence process) when g is large. Figure 2 basically describes the same phenomenon. Note that although both the DE and SO

[10]As $N \to \infty$, the value of ξ_{SO}, call it $\xi_{\max}$, is defined by $\frac{\lambda}{1-\phi} = [\frac{a+b(1-\xi)}{b(1-\xi^{\gamma+1}}]\xi^{\gamma}$. It is hard to obtain a closed form solution to $\xi_{\max}$, but we can show that $\xi_{\max} \in ([\frac{b\lambda}{b\lambda+(a+b)(1-\phi)}]^{\frac{1}{\gamma}}, [\frac{b\lambda}{b\lambda+a(1-\phi)}]^{\frac{1}{\gamma+1}})$. The upper bound of $\xi_{\max}$ is shown in Figure 1.

[11]This sufficient condition is derived from subtracting the upper bound of $\xi_{\min}$ for DE from the lower bound of $\xi_{\max}$ for SO obtained from footnotes 7 and 10 and restricting the expression to be greater than zero.

curves are downward sloping in Figure 2, the SO curve is above the DE curve for $N < N^*$ but below DE for $N > N^*$, for the reason depicted in Figure 1: for the same g, $\xi_{\text{DE}} > \xi_{\text{SO}}$ iff $T_{\text{SO}} > T_{\text{DE}}$, since $\xi = e^{-gT}$.

The finding that there is excess momentum (excess inertia) in the obsolescence process when the steady state rate of innovation is small (large) makes sense: In the extreme case that the rate of innovation is zero, it is certainly optimal to have no obsolescence of goods, because of the love-of-variety of consumers. However, there will be obsolescence in the market because the instantaneous gross profits of the least sophisticated goods are too small to cover the quasi-fixed cost of production.

The intuition for the divergence between ξ_{DE} and ξ_{SO} is as follows. There are three externalities as a firm exits from the market: (a) A negative externality on today's variety (*current variety effect*) — the number of today's older variety decreases; (b) a positive externality on profits of other firms today (*profit-creation effect*) — the profits of firms that remain in the market increase because there is less competition; and (c) a positive externality on future variety (*future variety effect*) — the firm's exit makes it possible to allocate more resources to develop more sophisticated variety in the future. Such allocation results in positive externality when $\frac{\lambda}{1-\phi}$ is sufficiently large.[12] When $g = 0$, externality (c) is zero, but (a) dominates (b), and so the market delivers too much obsolescence.[13] As g grows, (c) becomes more significant, since the labor efficiency in R&D increases in the future as the knowledge stock grows faster. Eventually, (c) overwhelms (a), the market begins to deliver too little obsolescence.

---

[12] A larger λ implies that the externality resulted from duplication of research is less serious. A larger ϕ implies that the externality resulted from intertemporal knowledge spillovers is stronger. Both effects tend to increase the net positive externality of resource allocation to R&D. To understand more about the externality of allocation of labor to R&D, see the discussion above Result 5.

[13] Note that when all goods carry equal weights in the Dixit–Stiglitz CES utility function (see Dixit and Stiglitz, 1977), (a) and (b) just cancel each other (See Grossman and Helpman, 1991, p. 70). In that case, an exit always results in a positive externality.

Hence, we have

Result 3. *Suppose* $\frac{\lambda}{1-\phi}$ *is sufficiently large that* $\frac{\lambda}{1-\phi} > \frac{(a+b)}{a(\gamma+1)}$. *For given a and b, when g is sufficiently small,* $\xi_{\rm DE} > \xi_{\rm SO}$ *and* $T_{\rm DE} < T_{\rm SO}$ *(i.e. the product cycle is too short in the decentralized equilibrium). When g is sufficiently large,* $\xi_{\rm DE} < \xi_{\rm SO}$ *and* $T_{\rm DE} > T_{\rm SO}$ *(i.e. the product cycle is too long in the decentralized equilibrium).*

On the other hand, if $\frac{\lambda}{1-\phi}$ is too small, the DE and SO curves will not cross, and $\xi_{\rm SO}$ is always less than $\xi_{\rm DE}$. This is true when $\frac{\lambda}{1-\phi} < \frac{a}{(1+\gamma)(a+b)-b}$.[14] In other words, when the degree of research duplication is too strong, the market always delivers too much obsolescence, because it has too much incentive to allocate resources from production of older goods to development of new sophisticated products. Hence, we have

Result 3A. *If* $\frac{\lambda}{1-\phi} < \frac{a}{(1+\gamma)(a+b)-b}$, *then* $\xi_{\rm SO} < \xi_{\rm DE}$ *for all g.*

Therefore, if $\frac{\lambda}{1-\phi} < 1$, it is possible that $\xi_{\rm SO} < \xi_{\rm DE}$ when γ gets sufficiently small.

3.2 Fraction of labor allocated to research $\frac{L_n}{L}$

With regard to the social optimum, we have, from (C4) in Appendix C,

$$\frac{a}{b}\left(\frac{L}{L_n}-1\right) = \left(\frac{\alpha}{1-\alpha}\right)\left[\frac{1-\xi^{\gamma+1}}{(\gamma+1)\xi^{\gamma}}\right] + (1-\xi). \tag{26}$$

where ξ varies directly with g as given in (25).

It is clear from the equation that an increase in optimal ξ is associated with an increase in optimal $\frac{L_n}{L}$. From Result 2, we know that an increase in λ, ϕ or N is accompanied by an increase in the optimal ξ. Therefore, we conclude that an increase in λ, ϕ or N leads to an increase in the socially optimal $\frac{L_n}{L}$.

[14]This sufficient condition is obtained from imposing the restriction that the upper bound of $\xi_{\rm max}$ for SO be smaller than the lower bound of $\xi_{\rm min}$ for DE obtained from footnotes 7 and 10.

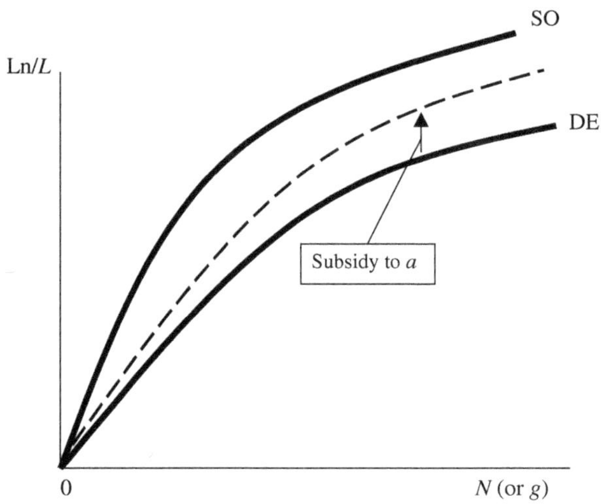

Figure 3. Comparison of labor allocation to R&D between social optimum and decentralized equilibrium
a, b, λ, ϕ, γ are given. The DE curve is found to be upward sloping based on numerical simulation using Mathematica. The SO curve is above the DE curve when $\lambda/(1-\phi)$ is sufficiently large.

With regard to the decentralized equilibrium, Appendix D shows:

$$\frac{a}{b}\left(\frac{L}{L_n}-1\right)=\left(\frac{\alpha}{1-\alpha}\right)\left[\frac{1-\xi^{\gamma+1}}{(\gamma+1)\xi^{\gamma}}\right]\left(\frac{\rho+g}{g}\right)+(1-\xi). \qquad (27)$$

Using Mathematica, we find that the RHS of the above equation decreases with g, noting that ξ is a function of g as given in (18). Together with (8), we can conclude that an increase in λ, ϕ or N leads to an increase in $(\frac{L_n}{L})_{\mathrm{DE}}$. A subsidy on innovation decreases the value of "a" faced by firms, but not the actual resource requirements for R&D. Therefore, the value of "a" on the RHS of (18) decreases, leading to a higher ξ_{DE}, for given g, which in turn leads to a higher $(\frac{L_n}{L})_{\mathrm{DE}}$, according to equation (27). This is shown in Figure 3.

Therefore, we have

Result 4 (Numerical). *An increase in λ, N or ϕ leads to an increase in g, and increases in $(\frac{L_n}{L})_{\mathrm{SO}}$ and $(\frac{L_n}{L})_{\mathrm{DE}}$. A subsidy on innovation leads to an increase in $(\frac{L_n}{L})_{\mathrm{DE}}$.*

Jones (1995a) suggests that $(\frac{L_n}{L})_{\rm SO}$ diverges from $(\frac{L_n}{L})_{\rm DE}$ for three reasons: (a) When $\phi > 0$, $(\frac{L_n}{L})_{\rm SO} - (\frac{L_n}{L})_{\rm DE}$ increases with ϕ, reflecting a positive externality due to the knowledge spillovers from previous research. (b) When $1 - \lambda > 0$, $(\frac{L_n}{L})_{\rm SO} - (\frac{L_n}{L})_{\rm DE}$ decreases with $1 - \lambda$, which reflects a negative externality due to duplication of research by different firms. (c) $(\frac{L_n}{L})_{\rm SO} - (\frac{L_n}{L})_{\rm DE}$ increases with α, reflecting monopoly price markup, which causes too little labor to be devoted to research. Jones (1995a) finds that $(\frac{L_n}{L})_{\rm SO} < (\frac{L_n}{L})_{\rm DE}$ when $1 - \lambda$ is sufficiently close to one (i.e. λ close to zero) and $(\frac{L_n}{L})_{\rm SO} > (\frac{L_n}{L})_{\rm DE}$ when $1 - \lambda$ is sufficiently close to zero (i.e. λ close to one).

Our findings are similar. From (26) and (27), we can deduce that a sufficient condition for $(\frac{L_n}{L})_{\rm SO} > (\frac{L_n}{L})_{\rm DE}$ when g is large is $\frac{\lambda}{1-\phi} > \frac{(a+b)}{a(\gamma+1)}$.[15] Recalling that $g = \frac{\lambda N}{1-\phi}$, we conclude that $(\frac{L_n}{L})_{\rm SO} > (\frac{L_n}{L})_{\rm DE}$ when $\frac{\lambda}{1-\phi}$ is sufficiently large. This is exactly the condition that guarantees that there is insufficient obsolescence in the decentralized equilibrium when g is large.[16] Using Mathematica, we also confirm that $(\frac{L_n}{L})_{\rm SO} < (\frac{L_n}{L})_{\rm DE}$ when $\frac{\lambda}{1-\phi}$ is sufficiently small. Therefore, we have

Result 5. *The decentralized market allocates too little labor to research when* $\frac{\lambda}{1-\phi} > \frac{(a+b)}{a(\gamma+1)}$ *and* g *is sufficiently large. It is also demonstrated numerically that the decentralized market allocates too much labor to research when* $\frac{\lambda}{1-\phi}$ *is sufficiently small.*

Results 4 and 5 are summarized by Figure 3.

Let us now consider how government policies can improve welfare. Note that there are now two market-determined variables the values of which can diverge from the social optima — the fraction of labor allocated to R&D and the fraction of obsolete goods. Therefore,

[15] $(\frac{L_n}{L})_{\rm SO} \to 0$ and $(\frac{L_n}{L})_{\rm DE} \to 0$ as $N \to 0$. On the other hand, a sufficient condition for $(\frac{L_n}{L})_{\rm SO} - (\frac{L_n}{L})_{\rm DE} > 0$ as $N \to \infty$ is for $\xi_{\rm SO} > \xi_{\rm DE}$ as $N \to \infty$, a sufficient condition of which is $\frac{\lambda}{1-\phi} > \frac{(a+b)}{a(\gamma+1)}$, which is derived in footnote 11.

[16] This confirms our point given earlier (just before Result 3) that the future variety effect of obsolescence is positive only when the allocation of labor to research results in positive externality.

any government remedy has to take care of the divergence in both variables. When $\frac{\lambda}{1-\phi} > \frac{(a+b)}{a(\gamma+1)}$ and g is sufficiently large that $\xi_{\mathrm{DE}} < \xi_{\mathrm{SO}}$, a small subsidy to innovation (which lowers the value of "a" faced by firms) will increase the market-determined ξ and push it towards the optimal value, according to Result 1. It also increases the market-determined $\frac{L_n}{L}$ towards the socially optimal value provided that $\frac{\lambda}{1-\phi}$ is sufficiently large, according to Results 4 and 5. Since there are no other distortions that cause the decentralized outcome to deviate from the social optimum, a small innovation subsidy will be welfare-improving when $\xi_{\mathrm{DE}} < \xi_{\mathrm{SO}}$.

When $\frac{\lambda}{1-\phi}$ is large but N is sufficiently small that $\xi_{\mathrm{DE}} > \xi_{\mathrm{SO}}$, a small tax on innovation (which increases "a" faced by firms) will decrease the market-determined ξ, pushing it towards the socially optimal value, but it will also decrease the market determined $\frac{L_n}{L}$, pushing it away from the optimal value when $\frac{\lambda}{1-\phi}$ is sufficiently large. Therefore, the welfare consequence of such a effect is not obvious. However, when $\frac{\lambda}{1-\phi}$ or N is sufficiently small, g is very small, and $\xi_{\mathrm{DE}} - \xi_{\mathrm{SO}}$ is very large, but the deviation between $(\frac{L_n}{L})_{\mathrm{SO}}$ and $(\frac{L_n}{L})_{\mathrm{DE}}$ approaches zero. Therefore, it is clear that a small tax on innovation is welfare-improving when $\frac{\lambda}{1-\phi}$ or N is sufficiently small. Hence we have

Result 6. *A small subsidy to innovation is welfare-improving when* $\frac{\lambda}{1-\phi} > \frac{(a+b)}{a(\gamma+1)}$ *and* g *is sufficiently large that* $\xi_{\mathrm{DE}} \leq \xi_{\mathrm{SO}}$. *A small tax on innovation is welfare-improving when* $\frac{\lambda}{1-\phi}$ *or* N *is sufficiently small.*

Hence, a subsidy to innovation is not always welfare-improving, as in Grossman and Helpman (1991). In fact, even when $(\frac{L_n}{L})_{\mathrm{SO}} > (\frac{L_n}{L})_{\mathrm{DE}}$, a subsidy to innovation is not always welfare-improving, because the subsidy could lead to further divergence between ξ_{DE} and ξ_{SO}, the welfare effect of which is negative. The latter welfare effect can dominate when g is small.

Note that a large $\frac{\lambda}{1-\phi}$ indicates that the research duplication effect is small relative to the intertemporal knowledge spillovers effect. The main message of this paper is that Results 3, 3A, 5 and 6 show the crucial importance of this parameter in determining the divergence between the optimal and equilibrium variables in the economy. Recalling that $g = \frac{\lambda N}{1-\phi}$, we have the following corollary from these Results:

Corollary 1. *When* $\frac{\lambda}{1-\phi}$ *is sufficiently large (small),* $\xi_{\mathrm{SO}} > (<) \xi_{\mathrm{DE}}$, $(\frac{L_n}{L})_{\mathrm{SO}} > (<) (\frac{L_n}{L})_{\mathrm{DE}}$ *and a small subsidy (tax) to innovation is welfare-improving.*

It is also worth mentioning the role of γ and N. A corollary from Results 3, 5 and 6 is

Corollary 2. *When* N *and* γ *are sufficiently large,* $\xi_{\mathrm{SO}} > \xi_{\mathrm{DE}}$, $(\frac{L_n}{L})_{\mathrm{SO}} > (\frac{L_n}{L})_{\mathrm{DE}}$ *and a small subsidy to innovation is welfare-improving. This is true regardless of the value of* $\frac{\lambda}{1-\phi}$.

Intuitively, when consumers value new goods more (i.e. γ increases), and knowledge accumulates more quickly (i.e. g increases as N increases), the positive external effects of allocating labor to R&D increase. When γ and N are sufficiently large, $(\frac{L_n}{L})_{\mathrm{SO}} > (\frac{L_n}{L})_{\mathrm{DE}}$. This type of externality has not received much attention in the literature.

4 Discussion and Caveats

Our model is a Schumpeterian growth model that captures a rich array of features in the real world: endogenous innovation, gradual obsolescence of goods, expanding variety of goods, and both dynamic and static internal increasing returns to scale in production. The most interesting finding is that, when the research duplication effect in R&D is small (large) relative to the intertemporal knowledge spillover effect, the decentralized market delivers insufficient (excessive) obsolescence and allocates too little (much) labor to R&D, and a small subsidy (tax) to innovation is welfare-improving. All these results hold because the positive externality due to knowledge spillover overwhelms (is overwhelmed by) the negative externality due to research duplication. We also find that when consumers' love-of-sophistication of new goods is stronger and the growth rate of research personnel is higher, the positive externality of R&D

increases. This externality due to consumers' aspiration of new products has not received enough attention in the literature.

There are a couple of caveats. Certain features of the model are not totally consistent with the real world. In the model, the newest product has the highest market share and the oldest one the smallest. In the real world, it is usually the products of medium age that have the largest market share because firms need to acquire enough production experience in order to attain the full potential of an innovation. We believe we can modify our model to capture this by allowing for a learning or reputation-building period for any new product, or some lagged response of consumers to better products which has just been introduced into the market.

Second, in this model, the number of active products in the market increases exponentially. Some may not find this very plausible. This feature is an artifact of the specific functional form of knowledge spillover *a la* Romer (1990) and Jones (1995a). There are other utility functions that can generate sustained exponential growth in steady state, yet with a fixed number of goods in the market. We believe the same qualitative results will be obtained.[17]

For future work, we can extend this model to a North-South product cycle trade model where the South imitates Northern products which may or may not have become obsolete in the North. Depending on the technological capability of the South relative to that of the North, different patterns of international division of labor between the North and South in production of goods can emerge. We can then evaluate whether countries still unambiguously gain from trade, what determine the world rate of innovation and the effects of certain tax policies on growth and welfare.

---

[17]For example, we could use the instantaneous utility function

$$U = \left\{ \int_{n_o}^{n} [\lambda^z x(z)]^\alpha dz \right\}^{\frac{1}{\alpha}}$$

In that case, there will be sustained exponential growth with a constant $n - n_o$ in steady state even when there is no knowledge spillover of the Romer type.

Appendix

A. The Slope of the DE Curve

It is straightforward to show that $\frac{\partial}{\partial\xi}\left(\frac{\rho+g+\gamma g\xi^{\gamma+1+\frac{\rho}{g}}}{\xi^{\gamma}}\right) = \frac{\gamma(\rho+g)(\xi^{\gamma+\frac{\rho}{g}+1}-1)}{\xi^{\gamma+1}} < 0$. Also, $\frac{\partial \mathrm{LHS}_{18}}{\partial g} < 0$, as shown below.

Let $\phi(\xi, g) = \frac{\rho+g+\gamma g\xi^{\gamma+1+\frac{\rho}{g}}}{\rho+g+\gamma g}$. Hence,

$$\frac{\partial\phi(\xi,g)}{\partial g} = \frac{1}{(\gamma g+g+\rho)^2}\left\{(\gamma g+g+\rho)\left[\gamma\xi^{\frac{\rho}{g}+1+\gamma}+\gamma\xi^{\frac{\rho}{g}+1+\gamma}\left(\frac{\rho}{g}\right)\right.\right.$$
$$\left.\left.\times\log\left(\frac{1}{\xi}\right)\right]-(\rho+g+\gamma g\xi^{\frac{\rho}{\gamma}+1+\gamma})(\gamma+1)\right\}$$

which tends to $\frac{-1}{\gamma g+g+\rho}$ as ξ tends to 1.

Moreover,

$$\frac{\partial}{\partial\xi}\frac{\partial\phi(\xi,g)}{\partial g} = \frac{\partial}{\partial g}\frac{\partial\phi(\xi,g)}{\partial\xi} = \frac{\partial}{\partial g}\gamma\xi^{\frac{\rho}{g}+\gamma}$$
$$= \gamma\xi^{\frac{\rho}{g}+\gamma}\left(\frac{\rho}{g^2}\right)\log\left(\frac{1}{\xi}\right) > 0 \quad \text{for } 0<\xi<1.$$

Hence, $\frac{\partial\phi(\xi,g)}{\partial g} < 0$ for the entire relevant range of ξ, viz. $\xi \in [0, 1]$, as shown in Figure A1.

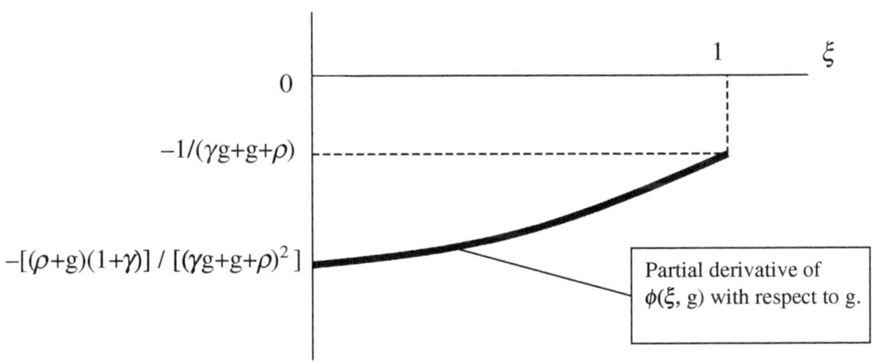

Figure A1. Diagram related to the proof in Appendix A.

Therefore, by the implicit function theorem, $\frac{d\xi}{dg} < 0$ for $0 < \xi < 1$ and $g \neq \infty$.

B. Optimal Timing of Obsolescence

Let B be the PDV of the benefit of reselling the capital of the firm at time t_0; and C be the PDV of the opportunity cost of reselling the capital at t_0. Because of perfect competition in the capital market, the resale value of the capital is always equal to the cost of producing it, which is wb/m, which in turn equals b, because of the normalization $w = m$. The value of C is the PDV of the worth of the firm. Therefore,

$$B = be^{-(\rho+g)(t_o-t_d)}$$

and

$$\begin{aligned} C &= \int_{t_o}^{\infty} \pi(n,n)e^{-(\rho+g+\gamma g)(\tau-t_d)}d\tau \\ &= \pi(n,n)\left[\frac{e^{-\gamma g(t_o-t_d)}e^{-(\rho+g)(t_o-t_d)}}{\gamma g+g+\rho}\right] \end{aligned}$$

where $\pi(n,n)$ is invariant over time, as shown in (14).

In steady state,

$$\frac{\partial B}{\partial t_o} = -[(\rho+g)be^{-(\rho+g)(t_o-t_d)}]$$

$$\frac{\partial C}{\partial t_o} = -\pi(n,n)e^{-(\rho+g+\gamma g)(t_o-t_d)}.$$

$$\frac{\partial^2 B}{\partial t_o^2} = (\rho+g)^2 be^{-(\rho+g)(t_o-t_d)}$$

$$\frac{\partial^2 C}{\partial t_o^2} = (\gamma g+g+\rho)\pi(n,n)e^{-(\rho+g+\gamma g)(t_o-t_d)}.$$

It is clear that at the time when $\frac{\partial B}{\partial t_o} = \frac{\partial C}{\partial t_o}$, $B > C$ and $\frac{\partial^2(B-C)}{\partial t_o^2} < 0$. Therefore, both the first and second order conditions of maximization are satisfied. This implies that the optimal timing of selling the capital of the firm is given by the equation immediately above (16).

C. Derivation of Social Optimum

Recall that

$$\mathcal{H} = \left(\frac{1-\alpha}{\alpha}\right)[(1+\gamma)\log n - \log(1+\gamma) + \log(1-\xi^{\gamma+1})]$$
$$+ \log\left[L - L_n - \frac{b}{a}L_n(1-\xi)\right] + \theta\left(\frac{1}{a}n^{\phi}L_n^{\lambda}\right)$$

From the above current value Hamiltonian, the first order condition with respect to n (i.e. $\dot{\theta} = \rho\theta - \frac{\partial\mathcal{H}}{\partial n}$) can be written as

$$\frac{\dot{\theta}}{\theta} = \rho - \left(\frac{1-\alpha}{\alpha}\right)\left(\frac{\gamma+1}{n\theta}\right) - \frac{\phi}{a}n^{\phi-1}L_n^{\lambda}. \tag{C1}$$

Following Grossman and Helpman (1991, Chapter 3), we define $M \equiv \theta n$, the shadow value of the total amount of variety. Substitute for $\frac{\dot{\theta}}{\theta}$ from $\frac{\dot{\theta}}{\theta} = \frac{\dot{M}}{M} - \frac{\dot{n}}{n}$ and $g = \frac{1}{a}n^{\phi-1}L_n^{\lambda}$, we obtain

$$\dot{M} = [\rho + (1-\phi)g]M - \left(\frac{1-\alpha}{\alpha}\right)(\gamma+1).$$

The only path of M that satisfies the above equation as well as the transversality condition is

$$M = \left(\frac{1-\alpha}{\alpha}\right)\left[\frac{\gamma+1}{\rho+(1-\phi)g}\right]. \tag{C2}$$

Substituting for $g = \frac{1}{a}n^{\phi-1}L_n^{\lambda}$ and for $M = n\theta$, the first order condition with respect to L_n (i.e. $\frac{\partial\mathcal{H}}{\partial L_n} = 0$) can be written as

$$\frac{\lambda Mg}{L_n} = \frac{1+\frac{b}{a}(1-\xi)}{L - L_n - \frac{b}{a}L_n(1-\xi)} \tag{C3}$$

where M is given by (C2). The RHS is the marginal effect of L_n on $\log X$. The LHS of the above equation is the marginal effect of L_n on the shadow value of new varieties $\theta\dot{n}$.

The first order condition with respect to ξ (i.e. $\frac{\partial \mathcal{H}}{\partial \xi} = 0$) is

$$\frac{\frac{b}{a}L_n}{L - L_n - \frac{b}{a}L_n(1-\xi)} = \left(\frac{1-\alpha}{\alpha}\right)\left[\frac{(\gamma+1)\xi^\gamma}{1-\xi^{\gamma+1}}\right] \tag{C4}$$

Eliminating $\frac{L_n}{L - L_n - \frac{b}{a}L_n(1-\xi)}$ between the previous two equations, we get (25).

D. Equilibrium Fraction of Labor Allocated to R&D

Labor is inelastically supplied at a quantity of L at each date. Therefore, from (11), total labor content of the sum of all the instantaneous variable costs of production at each date is:

$$X = \int_{n_o}^{n} \frac{c(z)}{w}x(z)dz = \frac{\alpha}{w}\int_{n_o}^{n} p(z)x(z)dz = \frac{\alpha}{w(1-\alpha)}\int_{n_o}^{n} \pi(z,n)dz.$$

Substituting (13) into the above equation, and simplifying, we obtain

$$X = \frac{\alpha}{(1+\gamma)(1-\alpha)}(1-\xi^{\gamma+1})\pi(n,n)\frac{n}{w}, \tag{D1}$$

which implies that

$$\pi(n,n) = \left(\frac{1-\alpha}{\alpha}\right)\frac{w}{n}\Phi, \tag{D2}$$

where $\Phi = \frac{(1+\gamma)X}{1-\xi^{\gamma+1}}$ and $\frac{\Phi}{n}$ is the labor content of the instantaneous variable cost of production for good n at the time of innovation. In other words, instantaneous gross profit of good n is simply a mark-up factor $\frac{1-\alpha}{\alpha}$ times the wage bill at that date.

To obtain the reduced form of the obsolescence condition (16), we simply substitute (D2) into (16) then invoke (23) and the normalization equation $w = m$:

$$L - L_n - \frac{b}{a} L_n (1-\xi) = b\frac{n}{m}\left(\frac{1-\xi^{\gamma+1}}{\xi^\gamma}\right)\left(\frac{\alpha}{1-\alpha}\right)\left(\frac{1}{1+\gamma}\right)(\rho+g)$$

Since $g = \frac{L_n^\lambda}{an^{1-\phi}}$ and $m = \frac{n^\phi}{L_n^{1-\lambda}}$, it can be shown that $\frac{n}{m} = \frac{L_n}{ag}$. Substituting this into the above equation, and re-arranging, we obtain

$$\frac{a}{b}\frac{L}{L_n} - \frac{a}{b} = \left(\frac{\alpha}{1-\alpha}\right)\left[\frac{1-\xi^{\gamma+1}}{(\gamma+1)\xi^\gamma}\right]\left(\frac{\rho+g}{g}\right) + (1-\xi)$$

which is the same as (27).

Acknowledgment

The financial support of the project from John M. Olin Foundation is gratefully acknowledged. I am grateful to helpful discussions and comments of earlier drafts from Joseph E. Stiglitz, Robert W. Staiger, Gene Grossman, Paul M. Romer, Danyang Xie, Leonard Cheng, Andrea Maneschi and participants of the 7th World Congress of the Econometric Society in Tokyo in 1995. I would like to thank John Roland and Roberto Penaloza Pesantes for helping proofreading the manuscript.

References

Aghion, P. and Howitt, P. (1992). A model of growth through creative destruction, *Econometrica* 60, 323–351.

Barro, R. and Sala-i-Martin, X. (1994). *Quality Improvements in Models of Growth*, NBER Working Paper No. 4610, January.

Dixit, A. and Stiglitz, J. E. (1977). Monopolistic competition and optimum product diversity, *American Economic Review* 67, 297–308.

Grossman, G. and Helpman, E. (1991). *Innovation and Growth in the Global Economy*, MIT Press, Cambridge, Massachusetts, USA, Chapter 3.

Jones, C. I. (1995a). R&D-based models of economic growth, *Journal of Political Economy*, 103(4), 759–784.

Jones, C. I. (1995b). Time series tests of endogenous growth models, *Quarterly Journal of Economics*, 110(2), 495–525.

Lai, E. L.-C. (1998). International intellectual property rights protection and rate of product innovation, *Journal of Development Economics*, 55(1), 133–153.

Romer, P. M. (1990). Endogenous technological change, *Journal of Political Economy*, 98(5), Part 2 (Oct, 1990), pp. S71–S102.

Schumpeter, J. A. (1976). *Capitalism, Socialism and Democracy*, Harper and Brothers, New York, USA.

Segerstrom, P. (1991). Innovation, imitation, and economic growth, *Journal of Political Economy* 99, 807–827.

Stokey, N. L. (1988). Learning by doing and the introduction of new goods, *Journal of Political Economy* 96(4), 701–717.

Young, A. (1991). Learning by doing and the dynamic effects of international trade, *Quarterly Journal of Economics* 106(2), 369–406.

Young, A. (1993). Invention and bounded learning by doing, *Journal of Political Economy* 101(3), 443–472.

Part 4

Microeconomics of IPP and Innovation

Chapter 10

Patent Length and the Rate of Innovation*

Abstract
This chapter models the effect of patent length on the rate-of-innovation and consumer welfare. We find that the patent length that maximizes the rate-of-innovation exceeds that which maximizes consumer welfare. We show a countervailing effect of patent length upon the "size" and "frequency" of innovation. Longer patents increase the size, but decrease the frequency of innovation. The patent lengths that maximize the rate-of-innovation and welfare represent balance points between size and frequency. The divergence of the welfare maximizing and rate-of-innovation maximizing patent lengths has important policy implications that we briefly explore.

1 Introduction

In a sweeping review of US technology and patent policy in 1988, the House Committee on Science and Technology repeatedly states the objective of increasing the "pace of technical change".[1] This emphasis

---

*By Andrew W. Horowitz and Edwin L.-C. Lai. Originally published in *International Economic Review* (November 1996), pp. 785–801. Copyright © 1996 by Wiley. The authors would like to thank David Wildasin, E. Young Song, Robert Driskill, James Foster, Jennifer Reinganum, Sam Kortum, Robert Margo and anonymous referees for helpful comments. Remaining errors are the authors'.

[1]See House Report Number 100-1093. The objective of increasing the pace of technical change is consistent with the stated objective of the first US patent law (1790), to wit: "to promote the progress of science".

on the *rate of innovation* departs from much of the theoretical patent literature, which focuses instead on the consumer surplus-deadweight loss tradeoff. Nordhaus (1969), in his seminal work on invention and welfare, sets the tone of this literature by developing a model in which patent length determines the "size" of innovation. The "optimal patent length" is that which induces an innovation of welfare-maximizing size. More recently, papers by Gilbert and Shapiro (1990), Klemperer (1990), and Gallini (1992), examine the interplay of the patent breadth and length instruments in determining optimal patent structure.

Another strand of the literature explores the effect of patent length in dynamic settings. Judd (1985) develops a general equilibrium model of continuous product innovation and finds that patents (or imitation lags) of infinite duration may achieve too much, too little, or the socially optimum level of innovation. He also demonstrates that finite-life patents may induce undamped oscillations in innovation. Jovanovic and Rob (1990) explore the link between discovery, imitation, and business cycles in a partial equilibrium model. They do not, however, discuss patent protection. Mookherjee and Ray (1991) develop a partial equilibrium model of successive innovation with focus on the timing of innovation as the rate of diffusion varies. Chou and Shy (1993) present a multiproduct, overlapping-generation model of product innovation in which the saving of the young can be allocated to innovation. However, only the polar cases of one-period and infinite patent length are considered, and the welfare-maximizing patent length is not identified.

While the analyses discussed above have provided important insights, they do not focus on the effect of patent length on the rate of innovation or *the relationship between the rate of innovation and consumer welfare.* This nexus, which was a central concern of Schumpeter (1939), is intertwined with the stated objective of patent law and is the primary focus of our analysis.

We model innovation as movement by a leading firm up a "product quality ladder". Higher positions on the ladder are associated with higher quality products. Imitating firms may follow the leader up the ladder, but are constrained in the dimension of time by patents.[2] We define the *size* of an innovation as the distance traveled on the product ladder and the *frequency* of innovation as the average number of innovations per-period. We define the *rate of innovation* as the average distance traveled up the product ladder per-period, which is the product of the size of innovation and the frequency of innovation. Many of the earlier models focused exclusively on the size of innovation, ignoring the effect of patents on innovation frequency.

Our model identifies a unique patent length that maximizes the rate of innovation. Patent length either too short, or too long, will weaken innovative incentives. We then derive the patent length that maximizes consumer welfare. We find that, in general, the patent length that maximizes the rate of innovation is longer than that which maximizes consumer welfare. This divergence creates a tension between the stated objective of patent law (to maximize the rate of innovation) and the more intuitive objective of maximizing consumer surplus.

The existence of finite patent lengths that maximize the rate of innovation and consumer welfare are attributable to the countervailing effects of patent length on the size and frequency of innovation. Longer patent length increases the size but decreases the frequency of innovation. For short patent length, the decrease in size of innovation dominates the increase in frequency, causing the rate of innovation to fall. For long patent length, the decrease in frequency dominates the increase in size, again resulting in a falling rate of innovation. At an intermediate patent length, these forces are balanced so as to maximize the rate of innovation.

---

[2]In practice, patent protection depends on the time to circumvent the patent, as well as statutory length. If competitors' are unable to circumvent a patent before its expiration, statutory length is the time measure of protection. If circumvention occurs before expiration, then the time to circumvent is the appropriate measure of protection. In either case the strength of protection may be measured in time units as the interval between innovation and the erosion of the leader's market power.

The trade-off between size and frequency also generates the existence of a finite welfare-maximizing patent length. However, the decline in the frequency of innovation as patent life is extended affects consumers both directly (due to discounting) and indirectly (through its effect on the rate of innovation). Consequently, from a welfare perspective, the balance point between the size and frequency of innovation occurs at a shorter patent length. That is, the patent life that maximizes consumer welfare is shorter than that which maximizes the rate of innovation.

The chapter is organized as follows: Section 2.1 motivates the model. Section 2.2 formally specifies the consumer and firm problems and derives the preliminary results. Section 2.3 derives the relationship between patent length and the rate of innovation. Section 2.4 demonstrates the existence of patent lengths that maximize the rate-of-innovation and consumer welfare. Section 2.5 examines the relationship between the patent lengths that maximize consumer welfare and the rate-of-innovation. Section 3 concludes.

2 The Model

2.1 Motivation

Our objective is construction of the simplest model capable of providing meaningful insight into the effect of patent length on the rate of innovation and welfare. We consider a product quality ladder with an innovating firm which obtains patents defined in the dimension of time as it climbs the ladder. Potential imitators stand ready to copy products whose patent protection has ceased. The presence of a single innovator approximates specialization of the innovative and imitative activities. Our quality ladder model is similar to that employed by Grossman and Helpman (1992); see also Aghion and Howitt (1992), and Segerstrom (1991). However, in contrast to the fixed rung property of the Grossman and Helpman ladder, we allow the innovator to traverse the ladder in arbitrary increments. That is, we employ a continuous ladder.

Products along the continuous ladder are perfect substitutes in the sense that there exists a quality-adjusted price at which consumers are indifferent between different positions on the ladder. Thus, though the leader adopts a limit-pricing strategy that prevents actual entry, the market is fully contestable. The threat of imitation disciplines the leader and induces behavior that approximates that under actual imitation.

2.2 Preliminaries

Consider a continuous product ladder with a single specialized innovative leader. The marginal cost of innovation, C, is assumed constant and is incurred in the dimension of distance traveled on the product ladder. Thus, the cost of traveling distance "d" up the product ladder is $C * d$. There exist potential imitators whose ability to produce along the product ladder is constrained in the dimension of time by a patent of length τ. That is, if the leader develops a product at time t, potential imitators cannot begin producing the product until time $t + \tau$. When the patent expires, we assume the cost of imitation is zero.[3] The unit cost of production (as distinct from innovation costs) along the product ladder are also constant at "η" per unit. We index time by $t = -1, 0, 1, 2, \ldots$, and designate $t = 0$ as the first period in which innovation can occur. The product existing at $t = -1$ represents a preexisting technology.

The demand side of the market consists of a representative consumer who maximizes utility in each period subject to a budget constraint. Let I_t be the set of all products that exist at time t, where $i \in I_t$ indexes a particular good. Let $v(i)$ be the *position* of good i along the quality ladder. Consumer valuation of the *quality* of good i is represented by the function: $q(i) = \lambda^{v(i)}, (\lambda > 1)$. Without loss of generality we assume that the quality of the preexisting product is 1. The *quantity* of good i consumed at time t is denoted as $x(i, t)$. The consumer's problem is to choose a quantity (x), of each good

[3]This can be thought of as an approximation of an industry in which imitation costs are very low. For example, in the pharmaceutical industry products are often simply chemical compounds. Reproduction by other firms once the patent has expired is typically straightforward.

i from the set of available goods at time $t(I_t)$, subject to a budget constraint. That is,

$$\max_{(x(i,t))_{i\in I_t}} U(t) = \sum_{i\in I_t} q(i)x(i,t)$$
$$\text{subject to } \sum_{i\in I_t} p(i,t)x(i,t) = E, \tag{1}$$

where $p(i,t)$ is the price of good i at t, and E is exogenously determined total consumer expenditure during each period.[4]

Firms engage in price competition each period. Since (1) implies that products of different qualities are perfect substitutes for each other and unit costs are constant along the product ladder, there exists a limit-pricing equilibrium in which only the highest-quality product will be produced. This equilibrium can be thought of as an approximation of one where entry actually occurs, in the sense that the leader is disciplined in price by the potential entrants.[5]

Let $n(t)$ be the *position* (along the quality ladder) of the highest-quality product existing at time t. That is, $n(t) = \max\{v(i) \mid i \in I_t\}$. Let $m(t)$ be the position (along the quality ladder) of the most advanced product that can be imitated at time t, given the patent law. Under limit pricing the leader, who produces only the highest-quality product, will set a price of

$$p_n = \eta\lambda^{n-m} - \varepsilon \quad (\varepsilon > 0, \varepsilon \to 0) \tag{2}$$

where the time arguments are suppressed and p_n will henceforth refer to the price of the most advanced product available at a given time (recall that $\boldsymbol{\eta}$ is the unit cost of production). The lowest price at which the (potential) imitator will produce the good at position m is $p_m = \boldsymbol{\eta}$, where (again suppressing the time argument) p_m is the price

[4]As with many patent models in the industrial organization literature, ours is a partial equilibrium analysis. Such an analysis allows us to solve for a steady-state rate of innovation for all patent lengths, and compare the patent length that maximizes the rate of innovation with that which maximizes welfare.

[5]This is essentially a contestable market argument.

of the most advanced product that can be imitated. By adopting the limit-pricing strategy (2), the leader will capture the whole market, since the marginal utility per dollar for the good at position n exceeds that for the good at position m:

$$\frac{MU_n}{p_n} = \frac{\lambda^n}{\eta\lambda^{n-m} - \varepsilon} > \frac{\lambda^m}{\eta} = \frac{MU_m}{p_m}. \tag{2a}$$

Moreover, there is no incentive for the leader to price below $n\lambda^{n-m} - \varepsilon$ since it faces unitary price elasticity of demand below the limit price. Hence, there is a corner solution and specialization in consumption of the most advanced product. The net revenue (i.e. profit before innovation costs are subtracted) of the leading firm at time t is therefore

$$\begin{aligned}\pi_t &= (p_n - \eta)x_n = \left(p_n - \frac{p_n}{\lambda^{n-m}}\right)x_n = \left(1 - \frac{1}{\lambda^{n-m}}\right)p_n x_n \\ &= \left(1 - \frac{1}{\lambda^{n-m}}\right)E \end{aligned}\tag{3}$$

with $t = 0$ designated as the first period during which innovation occurs. After an innovation, the patent law dictates the position of the imitative threat. The complete description of the imitative threat is

$$m(t) = 0 \quad \text{for } 0 \leq t < \tau \tag{4a}$$

$$m(t) = n(t - \tau) \quad \text{for } t \geq \tau \tag{4b}$$

Equation (4a) is simply an initial condition that says an imitator may not begin movement up the product ladder until the patent on the leader's first product expires at $t = \tau$.[6] Thereafter, the imitator's position on the product ladder at time $t \geq \tau$ is that which the leader occupied τ periods ago (i.e. $n(t - \tau)$).

[6]Note that the initial condition must specify the position of the imitative threat from time 0 to $\tau - 1$.

Using equations (1) through (4) we can now write period t consumer utility compactly as follows[7]:

$$U(t) = \begin{cases} \dfrac{E}{\eta} & \text{for } 0 \leq t < \tau \\ \dfrac{E}{\eta}\lambda^{n(t-\tau)} & \text{for } t \geq \tau \end{cases} \tag{5}$$

We now explore the effect of τ on firm behavior.

2.3 Patent length and the rate of innovation

Returning to the firm's problem, the leader maximizes the present discounted value of the stream of profits given in (3) by choosing a position on the product ladder each time period. That is, the leader maximizes

$$\max_{\langle n(t)\rangle_{\tau=0}^{\infty}} \sum_{t=0}^{\infty} \delta^t [\pi_t(n(t), m(t)) - C[n(t) - n(t-1)]] \tag{6}$$

subject to (4a) and (4b), where $0 < \delta < 1$ is the discount factor; C is the marginal cost of innovation, and we normalize by setting $n(-1) = 0$. Note that innovative cost is imposed in the dimension of distance traveled on the product ladder: $n(t) - n(t-1)$.

The first-order condition with respect to $n(t)$ is[8]:

$$\delta^t \frac{\partial \pi_t}{\partial n(t)} + \delta^{t+\tau} \frac{\partial \pi_{t+\tau}}{\partial n(t)} - C\delta^t + C\delta^{t+1} = 0 \quad \text{for } t \geq 0 \tag{7}$$

[7]To see this first note that since only one product is consumed we can substitute (2) into the budget constraint of equation (1) to obtain an expression for $x(n,t)$. Then substitute $x(n,t)$ and $q(n) = \lambda^n$ into the objective function of (1). Recall that the quality of the preexisting product is 1. Then for $t < \tau$, invoking (4a) yields the upper part of (5). For $t \geq \tau$, invoking (4b) yields the lower part of (5).

[8]This procedure assumes perfect foresight on the part of the firm. To see that (6) is in fact concave, note that each row of the Hessian contains only two nonzero elements; one on the diagonal (which is negative) and one τ spaces to the right of the diagonal element. Using Laplace expansion, it is immediate that Hessian is negative-definite (see, for example, Chiang, 1984, pp. 94–95). An implicit constraint, which is subsequently seen to be nonbinding, is that $n(t)$ cannot decrease over time.

Using (3), (4a), and (4b), equation (7) becomes

$$[\lambda^{m(t)-n(t)} - \delta^{\tau}\lambda^{n(t)-n(t+\tau)}]E\ln\lambda = C[1-\delta] \quad \text{for } t \geq 0 \tag{8a}$$

The left side of (8a) is the marginal revenue of innovating the product $n(t)$, which is decreasing in $n(t)$. The right side reflects the marginal cost of innovation, which is constant. Rearranging equation (8a) and invoking (4b) we obtain:

$$\lambda^{n(t-\tau)-n(t)} = \frac{C(1-\delta)}{E\ln\lambda} + \delta^{\tau}\lambda^{n(t)-n(t+\tau)} \quad \text{for } t \geq \tau \tag{8b}$$

Now by the same procedure, the first-order condition with respect to $n(t+\tau)$ can be written as:

$$\lambda^{n(t)-n(t+\tau)} = \frac{C(1-\delta)}{E\ln\lambda} + \delta^{\tau}\lambda^{n(t+\tau)-n(t+2\tau)} \quad \text{for } t \geq \tau \tag{8c}$$

Substituting (8c) into (8b) we obtain

$$\lambda^{n(t-\tau)-n(t)} = \frac{C(1-\delta)}{E\ln\lambda}[1+\delta^{\tau}] + \delta^{2\tau}\lambda^{n(t+\tau)-n(t+2\tau)} \quad \text{for } t \geq \tau \tag{8d}$$

Continuing recursive substitution of the first-order conditions with respect to $n(t+2\tau), \ldots, n(t+\phi\tau)$ yields

$$\lambda^{n(t-\tau)-n(t)} = \frac{C(1-\delta)}{E\ln\lambda}\left(1+\delta^{\tau}+\delta^{2\tau}+\cdots+\delta^{\phi\tau}\right) + \delta^{(\phi+1)\tau}\lambda^{n(t+\phi\tau)-n(t+(\phi+1)\tau)} \tag{8e}$$

for $t \geq \tau$, and integer ϕ.

Note that the last term on the right term of (8e) tends to zero when ϕ goes to infinity and (8e) becomes

$$\lambda^{n(t-\tau)-n(t)} = \frac{C(1-\delta)}{(1-\delta^{\tau})\,E\ln\lambda} \quad \text{for } t \geq \tau \tag{8f}$$

With the initial condition (4a), and the first-order condition (8a), equation (8f) indicates that the leading firm's optimal program consists of a series of discrete innovations of constant size at intervals of τ.[9] This behavior has a natural interpretation: the leading firm times the introduction of new products to coincide with the expiration of patents on earlier vintage products. The size of innovation undertaken each τ periods is:

$$n(t) - n(t-\tau) = \frac{1}{\ln\lambda}\ln\left[\frac{(1-\delta^{\tau})\,E\ln\lambda}{C(1-\delta)}\right]. \tag{8g}$$

Note that since δ is less than one, size is increasing in patent length. Letting $d(t)$ denote the size of innovation in period t, the complete innovation decision rule can be written as

$$d(t) = \begin{cases} \dfrac{1}{\ln\lambda}\ln\left[\dfrac{(1-\delta^{\tau})\,E\ln\lambda}{C(1-\delta)}\right] & \text{for } t = 0, \tau, 2\tau, 3\tau, \ldots \\ 0 & \text{otherwise} \end{cases} \tag{8h}$$

Having established that an innovation of constant size occurs once every τ periods, the frequency of innovation is $1/\boldsymbol{\tau}$. Since the rate-of-innovation is the product size and frequency, it is constant. Let z denote the rate of innovation. Then for given λ, δ, and C the rate of innovation is:

$$z = (n(t) - n(t-\tau))/\tau.$$

Substituting this expression into (8f) yields:

$$\lambda^{-z\tau} = \frac{C(1-\delta)}{(1-\delta^{\tau})E\ln\lambda} \tag{9}$$

The unique z which satisfies (9) given parameters τ, δ, λ, and C, is the profit-maximizing rate of innovation. Solving (9) for z we obtain

$$z = \ln\left[\frac{(1-\delta^{\tau})E\ln\lambda}{C(1-\delta)}\right]\frac{1}{\tau\ln\lambda} \tag{10}$$

[9]To see this note that (4a) and (8a) yield $\lambda^{-n(t)} = C[1-\delta]/\ln\lambda\,[1-\delta^{\top}]$ for $0 \le t \le \tau$. Thus the leader innovates at $t = 0$, and remains at $n(t) = [1/\ln\lambda]\ln[\ln\lambda\,[1-\delta^{\tau}]\,/C[1-\delta]]$ for $0 \le t < t$. Using (4b) and (8f), it is clear that the leader innovates again at $t = \boldsymbol{\tau}, 2\boldsymbol{\tau}, 3\boldsymbol{\tau}, \ldots$. More generally, (8f) can be employed to completely characterize the time path of $n(t)$ for any initial conditions over the entire interval $0 \le t \le \boldsymbol{\tau}$.

Equation (10) is the fundamental description of the rate of innovation in our model. Note that this rate of innovation is independent of initial conditions (equation (4a)). Inspection of (10) reveals the following necessary condition for a positive rate of innovation

$$(1-\delta^{\tau})E\ln\lambda > C(1-\delta) \tag{11}$$

If this inequality is reversed z will be negative, which we may interpret as a corner solution in which the rate of innovation is zero. Looking to the left side of (11), we see that consumers must have sufficient quality preferences (large enough λ), or the firm will have no incentive to innovate. The left side of (11) also reveals the existence of minimum patent length ($\tau^{\min}$), above which a perpetual sequence of discrete innovations will occur. Specifically, $\tau^{\min}$ is the smallest τ that satisfies inequality (11). It is immediate that in the absence of a patent law ($\tau = 0$), the rate of innovation will be zero. Inequality (11) also indicates the maximum marginal cost of innovation (in terms of the other parameters) at which the rate of innovation will be positive.

2.4 The rate of innovation and welfare-maximizing patent lengths

We have now obtained an expression relating the rate of innovation (equation (10)) to patent length, and identified restrictions on parameters that ensure ongoing innovation. The question now arises; does there exist a patent length that maximizes the rate of innovation? Inspection of equation (10) reveals the countervailing effects of patent length (τ) upon the rate of innovation (z) that are necessary for the existence of an extreme point. An increase in τ decreases the frequency of innovation, which has a negative influence on the rate of innovation. On the other hand, a larger τ increases the size of innovation, which exerts a positive influence on the rate of innovation. The existence of a patent length that maximizes the rate of innovation requires a balancing of these two effects. Proposition 1 of the Appendix demonstrates that just such a balance point exists and that z is approximated by the form indicated

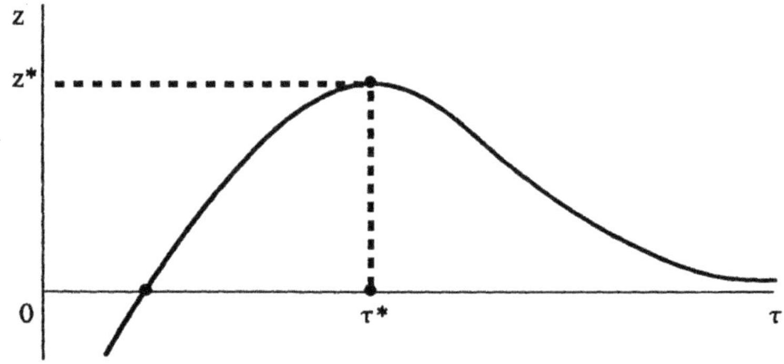

Figure 1. Rate of innovation plotted against patent length.

by Figure 1. For ease of exposition we treat the patent length, τ, as a real number.[10]

We have now established the existence of a patent length that maximizes the rate of innovation. Is there a patent length that maximizes consumer welfare? If so, how does it compare to the patent length that maximizes the rate of innovation? To answer these questions, first recall from equation (5) that instantaneous consumer utility for time $s \geq \tau$ has the form $U(s) = (E/\eta)\lambda^{n(s-\tau)}$ and $U(s) = E/\eta$ for $0 \leq s < \tau$. Further recall that since innovation occurs every τ periods

$$\lambda^{n(j\tau)} = \lambda^{n(j\tau+1)} = \cdots = \lambda^{n((j+1)\tau-1)} = \left[\frac{(1-\delta^{\tau})E\ln\lambda}{C(1-\delta)}\right]^{j+1}$$

for all $j = 0, 1, \ldots, \infty$. Then assuming for simplicity that the consumer's subjective discount factor is the same as the discount

[10]Since the time period is arbitrary, it can be made as short as desired. For example, time (and hence patent length) can be defined in units of months, hours, or even nanoseconds. As the units become shorter, our approximation becomes arbitrarily close to the integer mapping. Formally, we are examining an "extension" of z in which z is "embedded". See Saaty (1970, pp. 20–26) for a formal discussion of the use of extensions as approximations of integer mappings.

factor employed by the firm (δ), intertemporal utility is

$$w(\tau) = \sum_{s=0}^{\infty} U(s)\delta^s = \sum_{j=0}^{\infty} \sum_{s=j\tau}^{(j+1)\tau-1} \delta^s \left(\frac{E}{\eta}\right) \left[\frac{(1-\delta^\tau)\, E \ln\lambda}{C(1-\delta)}\right]^j. \quad (12)$$

With some manipulation it can be shown that

$$\sum_{s=j\tau}^{(j+1)\tau-1} \delta^s = \left[\frac{1-\delta^\tau}{1-\delta}\right] \delta^{j\tau} \quad \forall j = 0, 1, 2, \ldots . \quad (13)$$

Since δ^s is the only term in which the time index "s" appears on the right-hand side of (12), we may substitute (13) into (12) to obtain the following expression for consumer welfare as a function of patent length:

$$w(\tau) = \sum_{j=0}^{\infty} \left[\frac{1-\delta^\tau}{1-\delta}\right] \delta^{j\tau} \left(\frac{E}{\eta}\right) \left[\frac{(1-\delta^\tau) E \ln\lambda}{C(1-\delta)}\right]^j . \quad (14)$$

Note that the index "j" does not measure time. Rather "j" can be interpreted as denoting distinct vintages of product, each of which occupies the position of "most advanced" (and is consumed) for τ periods. With some manipulation (see Proposition 2 of the Appendix), equation (14) can be rewritten as:

$$w(\tau) = \left[\frac{1-\delta^\tau}{1-\delta}\right] \left(\frac{E}{\eta}\right) \frac{1}{1 - \left[\frac{(1-\delta^\tau)\delta^\tau E \ln\lambda}{C(1-\delta)}\right]} \quad (15)$$

Proposition 2 of the Appendix also demonstrates that the graph of (15) over a real domain has the form illustrated in Figure 2.[11]

The intuition for the existence of a welfare-maximizing patent length is closely related to that of the rate-of-innovation maximizing patent length. As patent length is extended, consumer welfare increases so long as the increased size of innovation dominates the decreased frequency (from a welfare perspective). At the balance

[11] See footnote 11 for a justification of this approximation.

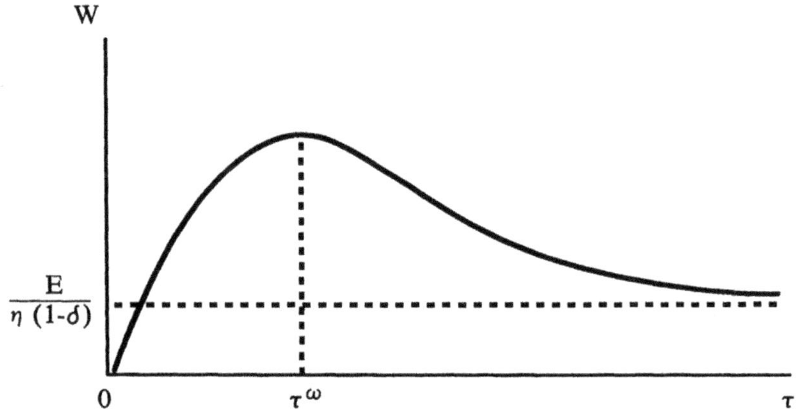

Figure 2. Consumer welfare plotted against patent length.

point of this trade-off, a welfare maximum is achieved. We formally analyze this trade-off in the following section.

2.5 Rate of innovation and welfare-maximizing patent lengths: Relationship and policy implications

The natural question at this point is the relationship between the patent length that maximizes the rate of innovation (τ^*) and that which maximizes consumer welfare (τ^ω). To help answer this question, define $B = [[C(1-\delta)]/[E \ln \lambda]]^{1/2}$. Inequality (11) indicates that 1 is an upper bound on B. If $B > 1$, we have a corner solution with a rate of innovation of 0. Intuitively, at this corner either costs are too high or discount factor, income, or the taste parameters are too low to warrant innovation by the firm. In Proposition 3 of the Appendix we show that there also exists a lower bound on B of 1/2. If $B < 1/2$ then w is infinite, and $\boldsymbol{\tau}^\omega$ is not defined. Proposition 3 of the Appendix establishes that for any parameter values for which τ^* and τ^ω are defined (i.e. $B^{\in}(1/2,\ 1)$), $\tau^* > \tau^\omega$, as shown in Figure 3.

Figure 3 indicates that the patent length that maximizes the rate of innovation will, in general, exceed the length that maximizes

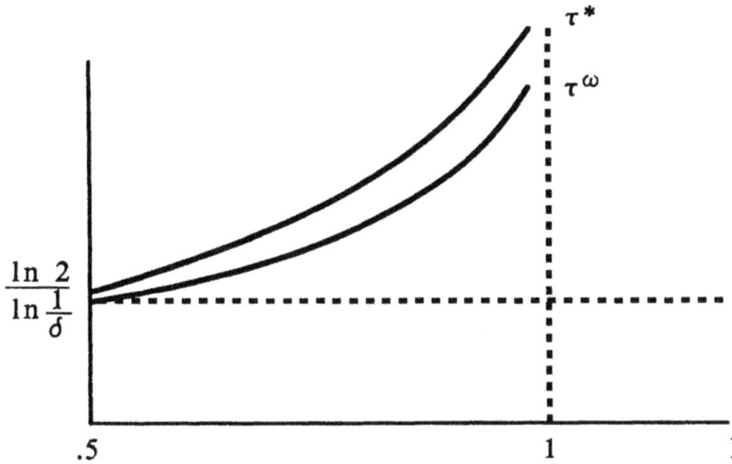

Figure 3. Consumer-welfare-maximizing patent length (τ^w) and innovation-rate-maximizing patent length (τ^*) plotted against "B", where "B" is defined in the first paragraph of section 2.5.

consumer welfare.[12] The motivation for this divergence can be illuminated by substituting (10) into (15) to obtain:

$$w(z(\tau),\tau) = \left[\frac{E}{\eta(1-\delta)}\right]\left[\frac{1-\delta^\tau}{1-(\lambda^z\delta)^\tau}\right] \tag{16}$$

The change in (16) with respect to τ can be expressed as

$$\frac{dw}{d\tau} = \left(\frac{\partial w}{\partial \lambda^z}\right)\left(\frac{\partial \lambda^z}{\partial z}\right)\left(\frac{dz}{d\tau}\right) + \left(\frac{\partial w}{\partial \tau}\right) \tag{17}$$

Equation (17) reveals that the change in w with respect to τ is the sum of two distinct components. The first component reflects the indirect influence of τ on w through z. This influence is embodied in the product of three derivatives. The first two elements of this product capture the effect of z on w, which is always positive since z (the rate of innovation) varies positively with consumer utility (see equation (5)). The sign of the third element ($dz/d\tau$) depends on

[12]The τ^* and τ^ω functions of Figure 3 are again real approximations of integer values.

the trade-off between size and frequency discussed in the previous section. The second component of (17), $\partial w/\partial\tau$, is the direct effect on welfare of less frequent innovation. This component is always negative due to consumer discounting. Hence, the trade-off between the size and frequency of innovation again determines the maximizing patent length. However, from the welfare perspective, the balance point between size and frequency (τ^{ω}) occurs before τ^*. To see this, simply note that at $\tau = \tau^*, dz/d\tau = 0$ and welfare are already falling in patent length (since $\partial w/\partial\tau < 0$). The divergence between τ^* and τ^{ω} is therefore attributable to consumer discounting. While size affects w only through z, frequency operates through two channels: through z and through consumer discounting.

From a policy perspective, divergence of the patent length that maximizes welfare and that which maximizes the rate of innovation creates a tension in the choice of patent length. If, consistent with the explicit Congressional objective, patent length is chosen to maximize the rate of technological advance, a price in consumer welfare must be paid.

3 Conclusion

The objective of this chapter is to identify the patent length that maximizes the rate of innovation and compare it with the patent length that maximizes consumer welfare. Our model suggests these patent lengths are distinct, and that the patent length that maximizes the rate of innovation exceeds that which maximizes welfare. Though our model is simple, the fundamental mechanism responsible for the existence of maximizing patent lengths, and their divergence, is intuitive, and should be operative in more complex formulations. Specifically, increases in patent length have countervailing effects on the size and frequency of innovation. A longer patent length increases the size, but decreases the frequency, of innovation. The patent length that maximizes the rate of innovation balances the size and frequency effects. Similarly, the patent length that maximizes consumer welfare balances the size and frequency effects from a welfare perspective. The rate of innovation and welfare balance points differ because of the more powerful effect of frequency on consumer welfare. A decrease in the frequency of innovation reduces welfare directly through discounting, and indirectly through its effect on the rate of innovation. Hence, reduced frequency dominates increased size at a lesser patent length from the welfare perspective.

The divergence in the patent lengths that maximize welfare and the rate of innovation raise a number of important policy questions. In addition to patents, the government employs a complex set of tax and regulatory incentives to influence firms' decisions to innovate. Could these instruments be used to offset the "distortion" created by choosing a patent life that maximizes the rate of innovation rather than consumer welfare? Though analysis of this question is beyond the scope of the current paper, our model provides a framework for broaching such coordination issues. The model can also be employed to explore variations in the maximizing patent length as tastes, production costs, or time preferences change. Such an exercise would be suggestive of how patent lengths might vary across industries in an ideal world. In-depth analysis of these issues will be the object of future research.

Appendix

Proposition 1. *The extension of z (equation (10)) to the real line (call it Z) has the following properties:*

(i) *Z has a unique positive stationary point that is a maximum.*
(ii) *$Z \to 0$ as $\tau \to \infty$.*
(iii) *$dZ/d\tau > 0$ when τ is sufficiently small.*

Proof. (i) Differentiating Z with respect to τ, yields:

$$\frac{dZ}{d\tau} = \frac{1}{\tau \ln \lambda}\left(\frac{-1}{\tau}\ln\left[\frac{(1-\delta^{\tau})\,E\ln\lambda}{C(1-\delta)}\right] + \frac{\delta^{\tau}\ln\frac{1}{\delta}}{1-\delta^{\tau}}\right) \tag{A1}$$

Setting (A1) equal to zero and manipulating yields

$$(\delta^{-\tau}-1)\ln\left[\frac{(1-\delta^{\tau})E\ln\lambda}{C(1-\delta)}\right] = \tau\ln\frac{1}{\delta} \tag{A2}$$

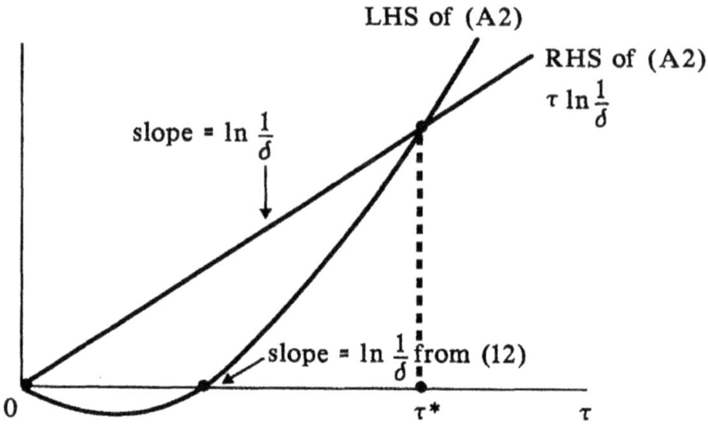

Figure A1. Determination of innovation-rate-maximizing patent length (τ^*) by plotting the LHS and RHS of Equation (A2) against patent length (τ).

Define the LHS of (A2) as the function $LA2(\tau)$, and RHS of (A2) as the function $RA2(\tau)$. To demonstrate the existence of a unique *positive* τ that satisfies (A2), ($\tau = 0$ is a trivial solution to (A2)), differentiate $LA2(\tau)$ to obtain:

$$\frac{dLA2}{d\tau} = \left(\delta^{-\tau} \ln\left[\frac{(1-\delta^{\tau})E\ln\lambda}{C(1-\delta)}\right] + 1\right) \ln\frac{1}{\delta} \tag{A3}$$

By (11), $(dLA2/d\tau) > 0$, for all $Z > 0$. Furthermore $d^2LA2/d\tau^2 > 0$ for all $\tau > 0$, establishing the convexity of $LA2(\boldsymbol{\tau}) \cdot RA2(\boldsymbol{\tau})$ is simply a ray from the origin with slope $\ln(1/\delta) > 0$. Figure A1 plots the $LA2(\tau)$ and $RA2(\tau)$.

Hence, there exists a unique, positive τ^* at which $dZ/d\tau = 0$. From (10) and (A2) we see that

$$Z^* = \frac{\delta^{\tau^*} \ln\frac{1}{\delta}}{(1-\delta^{\tau^*})\ln\lambda} \tag{A4}$$

Therefore, Z^* is positive and unique. We now demonstrate that the stationary point, τ^*, is a maximum of Z.

(ii) From (10), as $\tau \to \infty, Z \to 0$.

(iii) In (A1) it can be seen that as τ is sufficiently small, the term in the square brackets becomes one, and $dZ/d\tau > 0$.

Thus, since τ^* is unique, it must be a maximum and $Z(\tau)$ takes the form illustrated in Figure 1. ■

Proposition 2. *The extension of* w *(equation* (15)*) to the real line (call it* W*) has the following properties:*

(i) W *has a unique maximum.*
(ii) $W(0) = 0$ *and* $W(\tau) = E/\eta(1-\delta)$ *as* $\tau \to \infty$*.*

Proof. (i) From equation (14) we have

$$\begin{aligned} W(\tau) &= \left[\frac{1-\delta^\tau}{1-\delta}\right]\left(\frac{E}{\eta}\right)\sum_{j=0}^{\infty}\delta^{j\tau}\left[\frac{(1-\delta^\tau)E\ln\lambda}{C(1-\delta)}\right]^j \\ &= \left[\frac{1-\delta^\tau}{1-\delta}\right]\left(\frac{E}{\eta}\right)\sum_{j=0}^{\infty}\left[\frac{(1-\delta^\tau)\delta^\tau E\ln\lambda}{C(1-\delta)}\right]^j. \end{aligned} \quad \text{(A5)}$$

Inspection of (A5) reveals that a necessary condition for the existence of a finite W and, hence, a τ that maximizes welfare is

$$(1-\delta^\tau)\delta^\tau E\ln\lambda < C(1-\delta). \quad \text{(A6)}$$

Given that (A6) is satisfied, (A5) becomes

$$W(\tau) = \left[\frac{1-\delta^\tau}{1-\delta}\right]\left(\frac{E}{\eta}\right)\frac{1}{1-\left[\frac{(1-\delta^\tau)\delta^\tau E\ln\lambda}{C(1-\delta)}\right]}. \quad \text{(A7)}$$

which can be rewritten as

$$W(\tau) = \left[\frac{E}{\eta(1-\delta)}\right]\frac{1}{(1-\delta^\tau)^{-1}-\left[\frac{\delta^\tau E\ln\lambda}{C(1-\delta)}\right]}. \quad \text{(A8)}$$

Now define $\theta(\tau) = (1-\delta^\tau)^{-1} - A\delta^\tau$, where $A = \left[\frac{E\ln\lambda}{C(1-\delta)}\right]$. By inequality (A6), $A > 1$. Then we can rewrite (A7) as

$$W(\tau) = \left[\frac{E}{\eta(1-\delta)}\right]\frac{1}{\theta(\tau)}. \quad \text{(A9)}$$

The behavior of $W(\tau)$ thus depends on the properties of $\theta(\tau)$. Differentiating θ, we obtain

$$\frac{\partial\theta}{\partial\tau} = -(1-\delta^\tau)^{-2}\delta^\tau \ln\frac{1}{\delta} + A\delta^\tau \ln\frac{1}{\delta} \tag{A10}$$

which has an extreme point (call it τ^ω) where $-(1-\delta^\tau)^{-2} + A = 0$. Solving for τ^ω yields

$$\tau^\omega = \frac{1}{\ln\delta}\ln\left[1 - \left[\frac{C(1-\delta)}{E\ln\lambda}\right]^{1/2}\right]. \tag{A11}$$

Differentiating (A10) and simplifying, yields

$$\frac{\partial^2\theta}{\partial\tau^2} = \delta^\tau(\ln\delta)^2\left[(1-\delta^\tau)^{-2}\left[2(\delta^{-\tau}-1)^{-1}-1\right]+A\right]. \tag{A12}$$

Evaluating (A12) at $\boldsymbol{\tau}^\omega$ and simplifying, we find

$$\left.\frac{\partial^2\theta}{\partial\tau^2}\right|_{\tau=\tau^\omega} = 2\delta^{2\tau}(\ln\delta)^2(1-\delta^\tau)^{-3} > 0. \tag{A13}$$

Equation (A12) can also be used to demonstrate that a unique inflexion point (call it τ') of $\theta(\tau)$ exists[13]:

$$\tau' = -\frac{1}{\ln\delta}\ln\left[1 + \left[\frac{E\ln\lambda}{C(1-\delta)} - 1\right]^{-1/2}\right] \tag{A14}$$

With some manipulation it can be shown that $\tau' > \tau^\omega$. The final step in our characterization of the function $\theta(\tau)$ function is the evaluation of (A10) at the limits of τ. Using our definition of θ and (A10), we find that

$$\text{as} \quad \tau\to 0, \quad \theta\to\infty, \quad \partial\theta/\partial\tau \to -\infty$$

and

$$\text{as} \quad \tau\to\infty, \quad \theta\to 1, \quad \partial\theta/\partial\tau \to 0.$$

[13]A formal proof of the uniqueness of the inflexion point $\boldsymbol{\tau}'$ is available from the authors upon request.

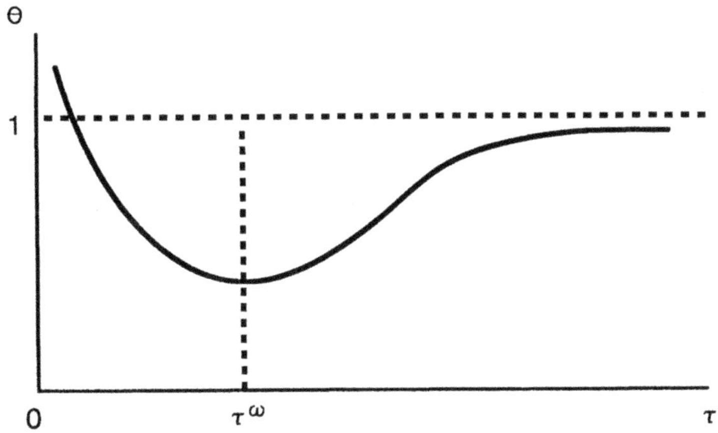

Figure A2. Plotting θ (which is inversely related to the consumer-welfare-maximizing patent length) against patent length. Please refer to Equation (A9).

Putting together these properties, the function $\theta(\tau)$ must have the form illustrated in Figure A2.

(ii) Now recalling (A9), $W(\boldsymbol{\tau}) \to 0$ as $\boldsymbol{\tau} \to 0$, and $W(\boldsymbol{\tau}) = E/[\eta(1-\delta)]$ as $\boldsymbol{\tau} \to \infty$. ■

Hence W(τ) has the approximate form illustrated in Figure 2 of the text.

Proposition 3. *$\tau^* > \tau^\omega$ for all values of B for which τ^* and τ^ω are defined (i.e. values of B consistent with inequalities* (11) *and* (A6)).

Proof. From (A11), τ^ω can be expressed as follows:

$$\tau^\omega = \frac{\ln\left[\frac{1}{1-B}\right]}{\ln\frac{1}{\delta}} \quad \text{where } B = \left[\frac{C(1-\delta)}{E\ln\lambda}\right]^{1/2} \tag{A15}$$

Figure A1 reveals that for any $\tau < \tau^*$, $RA2(\tau) > LA2(\tau)$. Similarly, for any $\tau > \tau^*$, $LA2(\tau) > RA2(\tau)$. Therefore, the direction of inequality between $RA2(\tau^\omega)$ and $LA2(\tau^\omega)$ establishes the relationship between τ^* and τ^ω. Inequality (11) establishes $B = 1$ as an upper bound on B for which τ^* is defined. Inequality (A6) establishes a lower bound of $B = 1/2$ for which W is finite and $\boldsymbol{\tau}^\omega$ is defined (since

$[(1-\delta^{\tau})\delta^{\tau}]^{1/2}$ has a maximum value of 1/2). Utilizing equation (A15) and noting that $\delta^{\tau^*} = 1 - B$, $LA2(\tau)$ can be expressed as $[-B/(1-B)]\ln B$ and $RA2(\tau)$ as $-\ln[1-B]$. The following inequality thus characterizes the relationship between τ^{ω} and τ^* for B $\in \left(\frac{1}{2}, 1\right)$.

$$B\ln B > (1-B)\ln(1-B) \Leftrightarrow \tau^{\omega} < \tau^* \qquad \text{(A16)}$$

Now define $\psi(B) = B\ln B - (1-B)\ln(1-B)$. Note that this function is continuous on the closed interval $B \in \left[\frac{1}{2}, 1\right]$. Using L'Hopital's rule $\psi(B) = 0$ at $B = 1$, and by inspection $\psi(B) = 0$ at $B = 1/2$. Differentiating $\psi(B)$ reveals an extreme point at $B = 0.839$. Now note that $\psi''(B) = (1-2B)/[B(1-B)]$, which is negative for all $B \in \left(\frac{1}{2}, 1\right)$. Thus $\psi(B)$ is concave and (A.16) is always satisfied on the interval $B \in \left(\frac{1}{2}, 1\right)\cdot$ By (A15), τ^{ω} is convex in B, yielding Figure 3 of the text. ■

References

Aghion, P. and Howitt, P. (1992). A model of growth through creative destruction, *Econometrica* 60, 323–351.

Chiang, A. C. (1984). *Fundamental Methods of Mathematical Economics*, 3rd edn., New York: McGraw-Hill.

Chou, C.-F. and Shy, O. (1993). The crowding-out effects of long duration of patents, *RAND Journal of Economics* 24, 304–312.

Gallini, N. T. (1992). Patent policy and costly imitation, *RAND Journal of Economics* 23, 52–63.

Gilbert, R. and Shapiro, C. (1990). Optimal patent length and breadth, *RAND Journal of Economics* 21, 106–112.

Grossman, G. and Helpman, E. (1992). *Innovation and Growth in the Global Economy*, Cambridge: MIT Press, Chapter 4.

Jovanovic, B. and Rob, R. (1990). Long waves and short waves: Growth through intensive and extensive search, *Econometrica* 58, 1391–1409.

Judd, K. (1985). On the performance of patents, *Econometrica* 53, 567–585.

Klemperer, P. (1990). How broad should the scope of patent protection be? *RAND Journal of Economics* 21, 113–130.

Mookherjee, D. and Ray, D. (1991). On the competitive pressure created by the diffusion of innovations, *Journal of Economic Theory* 54, 124–147.

Nordhaus, W. (1969). *Invention, Growth and Welfare*, Cambridge: MIT Press.
Saaty, T. (1970). *Optimization in Integers and Related Extremal Problems*, New York: McGraw-Hill.
Schumpeter, J. A. (1939). *Business Cycles*, New York: McGraw-Hill.
Segerstrom, P. S. (1991). Innovation, imitation and economic growth, *Journal of Political Economy* 99, 807–827.

Chapter 11

Parallel Imports and Price Controls*

Abstract
Price controls create opportunities for international arbitrage. Many have argued that such arbitrage, if tolerated, will undermine intellectual property rights and dull the incentives for investment in research-intensive industries such as pharmaceuticals. We challenge this orthodox view and show, to the contrary, that the pace of innovation often is faster in a world with international exhaustion of intellectual property rights than in one with national exhaustion. The key to our conclusion is to recognize that governments will make different choices of price controls when parallel imports are allowed by their trade partners than they will when they are not.

1 Introduction

Parallel trade occurs when a good protected by a patent, copyright, or trademark, having been legally purchased in one country, is exported to another without the authorization of the local owner of the intellectual property rights in the importing market (see Maskus, 2000b). Parallel trade represents a form of arbitrage whereby

*By Gene M. Grossman and Edwin L.-C. Lai. Originally published in *RAND Journal of Economics*, 39(2) (Summer 2008).

a legitimate product is shipped from the market intended by the intellectual property rights holder to another where it commands a higher price. Like other forms of arbitrage, parallel imports (also known as "grey-market imports" or "reimports") respond to international price differences that result from retailer price discrimination, vertical pricing restraints, or national differences in government price controls.

The propriety of parallel trade is a matter of intense policy debate in a number of countries and in the World Trade Organization (WTO). At present, WTO provisions allow member countries to establish their own rules for the "exhaustion" of intellectual property rights (IPR).[1] If a country opts for *national exhaustion* of IPR, a rights holder there may exclude parallel imports, because intellectual property rights continue until such a time as a protected product is first sold in that market. If a country instead chooses *international exhaustion* of IPR, parallel imports cannot be blocked, because the rights of the patent, copyright or trademark holder expire when a protected product is sold anywhere in the world. The United States practices national exhaustion for patents and copyrights, but permits parallel imports of trademarked goods unless the trademark owner can show that the imports are of different quality from goods sold locally or otherwise might cause confusion for consumers. The European Union provides for regional exhaustion of IPR whereby goods circulate freely within the trading bloc but parallel imports are banned from non-member countries. Japanese commercial law permits parallel imports except when such trade is explicitly excluded

---

[1]Article 6 of the Agreement on Trade-Related Aspects of Intellectual Property Rights (TRIPS) states that:

> For the purposes of dispute settlement under this Agreement, subject to the provisions of Articles 3 and 4, nothing in this Agreement shall be used to address the issue of the exhaustion of intellectual property rights.

by contract provisions or when the original sale is made subject to foreign price controls.[2]

Public debate about parallel imports has been especially heated in the area of prescription drugs. In the United States, where consumers, public health officials, and politicians have become increasingly concerned about the high and rising cost of medicine, bills that would introduce international exhaustion of patent rights for prescription drugs have been introduced in one or both houses of Congress in each of the last three sessions. In fact, in 2000, Congress passed a bill to permit reimportation of medicines. Although President Clinton signed the bill into law, his administration ultimately declined to implement it, citing concerns about consumer safety. New legislation was introduced to Congress in 2004 that would have forced deregulation of parallel imports of pharmaceuticals. In each case, the impetus for Congressional action came from public pressures to step up imports from Canada, where regulations and price controls have generated prices for prescription drugs significantly lower than those across the border.[3] Despite the continuing legal impediments to parallel imports, reimportation has been a growing source of pharmaceuticals supply in the United States due to increased personal trafficking and the proliferation of Internet purchases. By one estimate, parallel imports of prescription drugs from Canada amounted to US$1.1 billion in 2004, or about 0.5% of the US market (Cambridge Pharma Consultancy, 2004).

Parallel trade in pharmaceuticals features prominently in Europe as well, where it is the source of ongoing controversy. Differences in price regulations have resulted in significant variation in pharmaceutical prices across member countries of the European Union and the European Free Trade Association (Arfwedson, 2004; Kanavos

---

[2]Different national regimes of IPR exhaustion are described in more detail in Maskus (2000a, 2000b) and Arfwedson (2004).

[3]Maskus (2001) compares prices for similar doses of 18 drugs and finds lower prices in Canada than in the United States in 17 cases. The average price for these drugs in Canada was 63% of that in the United States.

and Costa-Font, 2005). Kanavos and Costa-Font, for example, report price differences for many products and country pairs of between 100% and 300%. Prices are highest in the countries with free or relatively free prices, which are Germany, the United Kingdom, Sweden, the Netherlands, and Denmark. These countries all have witnessed substantial growth in parallel importing, with reimports accounting for between 7% and 20% of their national expenditures on prescription drugs in 2002. The parallel exporters include Spain, France, Greece, Italy, and Portugal, all of which are countries with controlled prices or explicit price caps (Ganslandt and Maskus, 2004).

Opponents of parallel trade — of which there are many — are concerned that such trade undermines manufacturers' intellectual property rights.[4] The prevailing wisdom, expressed for example by Barfield and Groombridge (1998, 1999), Chard and Mellor (1989), Danzon (1997, 1998), and Danzon and Towse (2003), is that parallel trade impedes the ability of research-intensive firms such as those in the pharmaceuticals industry to reap an adequate return on their investments in new technologies. Their arguments seem to find support in more formal analyses, which offer only a few minor caveats. For example, Li and Maskus (2006) develop a model in which parallel trade creates competition in the home market between a manufacturer and its own distributor in a foreign market. They find that the distortions associated with parallel imports reduce the manufacturer's incentive to invest in cost reducing innovation at a prior stage. Szymanski and Valletti (2005) model an industry with vertical product differentiation and examine how parallel trade affects a firm's decision of whether to supply high quality products. They conclude that such trade diminishes the firm's incentive to invest in quality and may reduce welfare in both countries. In a related model, Valletti (2006) shows that parallel trade reduces investment when differential pricing is based purely on differences in

[4]Aside from any potential dynamic effects, parallel trade that undermines third-degree price discrimination can reduce world welfare by reallocating sales from markets with low demand elasticities to markets with high demand elasticities; see Malueg and Schwartz (1994).

price elasticities, but increases investment when differential pricing results from idiosyncratic costs of serving the two markets (that the manufacturer must bear, but an arbitrager can avoid). Finally, Rey (2003) examines parallel importing that may result from differential price regulation, as is most germane in the case of pharmaceuticals. He argues that such trade impedes a country's ability to accept high local prices in order to promote R&D when its trade partner prefers to set lower prices. As a result, world investment in technology is lower in his model when parallel trade is allowed than when it is banned.

In this chapter, we challenge the prevailing wisdom for the case (such as in pharmaceuticals) in which parallel trade is induced by different national price controls. We argue that the existing policy discussions and formal modeling overlook an important effect of national policy regarding the exhaustion of IPR. Whereas the papers in the literature that discuss parallel imports of pharmaceuticals in the presence of price regulation compare incentives for R&D in scenarios with and without parallel imports *for given levels of controlled prices*, we emphasize that a government will face different incentives in regulating prices in the presence or absence of arbitrage possibilities. This is so for two reasons. First, the admissibility of parallel trade introduces the possibility that a manufacturer will eschew low-price sales in the foreign market in order to mitigate or avoid re-importation. When arbitrage is impossible, the manufacturer is willing to export at any price above marginal production cost. But when the potential for arbitrage exists, the manufacturer may earn higher profits by selling only in the unregulated (or high-price) market than by serving both markets at the lower, foreign-controlled price. Accordingly, a switch from a regime of national exhaustion to one of international exhaustion can induce an increase in the controlled price as the foreign government seeks to ensure that its consumers are adequately served.

Second, the admissibility of parallel trade mitigates the opportunity for one government to free-ride on the protection of IPR granted by another. As we have shown in Grossman and Lai (2004), national policies to protect IPR often are strategic substitutes in a two-country (or many-country) policy-setting game; the greater is the protection afforded by one country, the less will be the optimal level of protection perceived by the other. In a world without parallel trade in which one government allows manufacturers to price freely in its market (or enforces a price ceiling at a relatively high level), the other government can hold the line on prices so as to benefit its local consumers and nonetheless enjoy the fruits of relatively high rates of innovation. But when arbitrage can occur, a low price cap in one country dulls incentives for investment worldwide. The government of a less-innovative country faces a different trade-off in setting its regulated prices in the presence or absence of arbitrage. As we will show, the deregulation of parallel imports in a highly-innovative economy always induces the government of its less-innovative trade partner to loosen its price controls.[5] In our analysis, the presumptive outcome is one in which deregulation of parallel imports generates both an increase in consumer surplus in the innovative country and an *increase* in the world pace of innovation. Thus, the more innovative country may face no trade-off at all between static and dynamic gains in its choice of regime for exhaustion of IPR. We find that typically the more innovative country gains from parallel trade, while the less innovative country loses.[6]

The starting point for our analysis is the two-country model of ongoing innovation and trade that we developed in Grossman and

[5]Indeed, Kanavos and Costa-Font (2005, p. 766) cite policy changes of this sort in some European countries in response to the growth of intra-European parallel trade in pharmaceutical goods. For example, they note that Portugal and Italy have in recent years moved their regulated prices for reimbursed medicines closer to average European prices, while France too has tended to allow freer pricing of highly innovative products.

[6]Pecorino (2002) makes a related though different point in a static model of sales and exports by a single firm. In his model, export prices are determined as a Nash bargain between the manufacturer and the foreign government. The possibility of reimportation strengthens the bargaining position of the manufacturer by lending credibility to the threat that he will not serve the foreign market. Accordingly, the monopolist's profits can be higher when parallel imports are allowed than when they are not.

Lai (2004) to study incentives that governments have to protect IPR in an open, world economy. In this model, firms devote resources to inventing horizontally differentiated goods with finite product lives. The greater is the global protection of IPR, as reflected in the duration of patents and the enforcement rate for live patents, the greater is the incentive for product development. The model yields a steady-state equilibrium in which the measure of differentiated products is constant. This measure responds to the policy regime. Here, we take the global regime for protection of patent rights as given, but introduce the possibility of price controls. That is, we assume that new pharmaceutical products receive similar patent protection in all countries (as indeed is dictated by the terms of the TRIPS agreement), but that existing international agreements do not prevent a country from regulating domestic prices of prescription drugs. We compare prices, profits and rates of innovation in a regime in which the high-price country allows parallel imports with those that arise when such trade is disallowed. We do so first under the assumption that the innovative "North" allows its firms to price freely and that no innovation takes place in "South".[7] Subsequently, we show that the main insights carry over to the case in which both countries regulate prices in a Nash equilibrium policy game, and also to the case in which innovation occurs in both countries provided that North conducts sufficiently more R&D than South.

We will argue that by allowing parallel imports, the North dulls the incentives in the South for free-riding on its protection of IPR. This argument does not require that the South be a single, large economy, as we initially assume. In fact, our results extend readily to a setting with several or many countries in the South. The size of a typical country in the South enters our analysis in several ways. If such a country is small (for example, because there are many such countries), there will be fewer consumers there to benefit from

[7]Whereas the geographic designations seem apt for Europe, the North American reader should not be confused by the fact that, in the context of our model, the United States is "North" and Canada is "South".

faster world innovation. But there will also be fewer consumers to be harmed by high local prices. These two effects of country size offset one another in our model, and so they do not affect a government's incentives in setting its price ceilings. The size of a country in the South can also affect the leverage that its governments has over world innovation and the risk it faces that its local market will not be served. The policies of a small country have little effect on R&D investment in a world without parallel trade, because each firm captures only a tiny share of its profits in such a market. Therefore, in a regime of national exhaustion of IPR in the North, the free-rider problem quickly grows more severe as the number of countries in the South expands. In contrast, when arbitrage is possible, a country that strictly controls prices impinges upon profit opportunities not only in its own small market, but also in other, larger markets to which the goods can be shipped. Accordingly, even a small country has considerable leverage over world innovation in such a setting. Note too that innovating firms may well be tempted to cut off supply from a very small market when goods can be transhipped from there to the North, but such firms have no reason to withhold supply from small markets in the absence of parallel trade. For these reasons, we find that the North's preference for international exhaustion of IPR extends to a world with multiple symmetric Southern countries and even to a world in which the typical such country is vanishingly small.

The remainder of the chapter is organized as follows. In the next section, we adapt the Grossman–Lai model of ongoing innovation to allow for price controls. We develop the model under the assumption that all innovation takes place in the North and that prices are regulated only in the South. In Section 3, we derive and discuss our main results, which compare prices, profits and rates of innovation under alternative regimes for exhaustion of IPR in which North does and does not allow parallel imports. Section 4 addresses circumstances in which North also may impose price controls and in which firms in South have the capacity to innovate and Section 5 extends the analysis to a world with several or many countries in the South. The final section summarizes our findings.

2 A Model of Ongoing Innovation

We consider an industry such as pharmaceuticals in which firms innovate by introducing new varieties of a differentiated product, all of which have finite economic lives. Our approach builds on Grossman and Lai (2004).

The world economy has two sectors, one that produces a homogeneous good and the other that produces a continuum of differentiated products. The designs for differentiated products are the outgrowth of investments in R&D. Each new product has a useful economic life of length $\bar{\tau}$, which means that it can provide utility to consumers for a period of that duration. When $\bar{\tau}$ years have elapsed from the time of invention, the product ceases to be of economic value.

There are two countries, North and South. Innovative products are consumed in both countries whereas (for now) all innovation takes place in North. In country j, $j = N$ (for North) or $j = S$ (for South) there are M_j consumers who demand the differentiated products of the innovating industry. The typical such consumer maximizes an intertemporal utility function of the form

$$U_j(t) = \int_t^{\infty} u_j(z)e^{-\rho(z-t)}\,dz \tag{1}$$

where

$$u_j(z) = y_j(z) + \int_0^{n(z)} h[x_j(i,z)]\,di, \tag{2}$$

$y_j(z)$ is consumption of the homogeneous good at time z, $x_j(i,z)$ is consumption of the differentiated product i at time z, and $n(z)$ is the number (measure) of differentiated products invented before time z that remains economically viable at z. As in Grossman and Lai (2004), we will refer to M_j as the "size of the market" in country j.

A consumer with the preferences represented by (2) maximizes utility by purchasing differentiated product i at time z up to the point where its marginal utility, $h'\,[x_j(i,z)]$ is equal to the local price of the good. After the consumer makes all of his optimal purchases of the economically viable differentiated products available at time z, he devotes residual spending (which we take to be strictly positive) to the homogeneous good. With spending on the homogeneous good assumed positive at every moment, (1) implies that the interest rate must be constant and equal to ρ. Then each household attains indirect utility equal to the present discounted value of lifetime spending plus the present discounted value of consumer surplus captured on purchases of differentiated products.

New varieties of the differentiated product result from a research activity that requires labor and a sector-specific factor that we call "research capital". We take $\phi_j(z) = \frac{1}{\beta}K_j^{1-\beta}L_{Rj}(z)^\beta$, where $\phi_j(z)$ is the flow of new products developed in country j at time z, K_j is the (fixed) stock of research capital in country j, and $L_{Rj}(z)$ is the (effective) labor devoted to research in country j at time z.[8] To capture a setting in which research capacity is highly concentrated in one country, we assume (for now) that $K_N > 0$ while $K_S = 0$. Note that the time derivative of $n(z)$ is $\dot{n}(z) = \phi_N(z) - \phi_N(z - \bar{\tau})$, because products invented at time $z - \bar{\tau}$ become obsolete at time z. In steady state, ϕ_N is constant and so $\dot{n}(z) = 0$.

Our earlier paper focused on the determination of patent lengths and enforcement rates in non-cooperative and cooperative international regimes of intellectual property protection. Here, we take the patent regime as given and assume that patent lengths have been harmonized by some international agreement such as TRIPS. Every inventor is awarded a patent of length $\tau < \bar{\tau}$ in both countries. We assume that patents are perfectly enforced.[9] By taking the terms of patent protection as given, we can focus most sharply on price controls and parallel trade as instruments of innovation policy.

[8]In Grossman and Lai (2004), we allow for a constant elasticity of substitution between labor and research capital that need not be equal to one. We find that most qualitative results do not depend on the size of this elasticity, as long as it does not exceed two.

[9]In Grossman and Lai (2004), where we allowed for imperfect enforcement, we showed how one could construct a single measure of strength of IPR protection that reflects both duration of patents and rates of enforcement. Here, we ignore the complications associated with imperfect enforcement for simplicity.

Once a variety has been invented, it can be produced in North with c units of labor per unit of output. We take North's wage as numeraire, so c also represents the marginal cost of production there. A firm that holds a live patent for an economically viable good has the sole right to produce that good and to make the first sale at home or abroad. Whether it can also prevent reimportation of goods that it initially sells in South depends on the prevailing regime for exhaustion of IPR. If North adopts national exhaustion, the patent holder can prevent parallel imports of units it sells to consumers (or distributors) in South. If North instead chooses international exhaustion, parallel imports cannot be barred. For simplicity, we ignore transportation and marketing costs. Therefore, price arbitrage is perfect in a regime that permits parallel trade.

Firms that hold live patents set prices for (initial) sales in each market. They do so after North has decided its regime for exhaustion of IPR and after the two governments have announced their pricing policies, if any. If the price that a firm charges for sales in a country exceeds the legal price ceiling there, no distributor or consumer will be able to purchase its product. If North adopts international exhaustion and a patent holder asks a higher price there than that for sales in South, it will lose the Northern market to parallel traders. Accordingly, a patent holder must charge a price for sales in each country no greater than the local price ceiling or its sales there will be zero, and it must charge identical prices in the two markets under international exhaustion or its sales in the higher-priced market will be zero.

We denote by $\pi(p)$ the profits that a patent holder makes per consumer when it charges the price p in some market and serves all local demand at that price. Note that consumers in both countries have identical demands, so these profits are the same (as a function of price) for sales in North and South. Similarly, $C(p)$ is the surplus that a consumer in either country enjoys when the differentiated product i is available at price p. Let $C_C = C(c)$ be the surplus per consumer when a differentiated product is available at the competitive price c, and let $C_M = C(p_M)$ be the surplus per consumer when the patent holder charges the unconstrained monopoly price p_M. As usual, the monopoly price is such that the markup over marginal cost as a fraction of price is equal to the inverse demand elasticity.[10]

Whenever a patent expires, the formerly-patented good can be produced by firms anywhere in the world at a unit cost of c. That is, we assume that any wage gap that exists between North and South reflects a difference in the productivity of labor in all of its uses. This, and the tradability of the numeraire good, allows us to measure Southern labor in efficiency units, with the wage per efficiency unit in South equal to that in North. Then the production cost for unpatented goods is the same in both places.[11]

We describe now the steady-state equilibrium for a given policy regime. In a steady state, the measure of differentiated products is constant. The products invented at time z replace the products that become obsolete at z, which are those that were invented at $z - \bar{\tau}$. The total number of viable products is $n = \phi_N \bar{\tau}$, with $n_M = \phi_N \tau$ of these under patent protection at any moment, and the remaining $n_C = \phi_N(\bar{\tau} - \tau)$ competitively priced. The patented goods carry a price p_N in North and p_S in South. These prices will reflect the policy regime in force, including the height of any price ceilings and whether North allows parallel imports. A Northern monopolist earns a flow of profits $M_N \pi(p_N) + M_S \pi(p_S)$ for a period of length τ, the present discounted value of which is

$$v = [M_N \pi(p_N) + M_S \pi(p_S)]\, T, \tag{3}$$

[10]We assume that the monopoly price is finite, which requires a demand elasticity greater than one at the relative point on the demand curve. For example, it would be sufficient that $-xh''(x)/h'(x) < 1$ for all x. We do not make the latter assumption as we did in Grossman and Lai (2004), because we wish to consider linear demands as a special case.

[11]More formally, let a_j and ca_j be the unit labor requirement in country j for producing the numeraire good and a differentiated good, respectively. Then, by the normalization $a_N = 1$, we have $w_N = 1$, $w_S = a_N/a_S$, and one efficiency unit of Southern labor is equal to a_S/a_N units of Southern labor. The price of an unpatented good, which is sold at cost under perfect competition, is equal to c in both countries. This assumption of equal production costs is not needed for our results, but it simplifies the exposition.

where $T \equiv (1 - e^{-\rho\tau})/\rho$ is the present value of a flow of one dollar from time zero to time τ. Firms in North deploy labor in R&D up to the point where the marginal value product in this activity is equal to the wage, or

$$v\left(K_N/L_{RN}\right)^{1-\beta} = 1. \tag{4}$$

Then, given this allocation of labor, the flow of new innovations is $\phi_N = \frac{1}{\beta}K_N^{1-\beta}L_{RN}^{\beta}$, from which the steady-state measure of differentiated products can be computed.

We assume that Northern firms are owned by households in North and, without further loss of generality, that investments in R&D are financed by aggregate savings there.[12] Spending in North, E_N, is the difference between national income Y_N and national savings, or between national income and national investment. National income comprises labor income, the return to research capital, and the flow of monopoly profits paid as dividends, so $Y_N = L_N + rK_N + n_M\left[M_N\pi(p_N) + M_S\pi(p_S)\right]$, where r is the return to research capital and L_N is the aggregate labor supply in North. Investment is devoted entirely to R&D, the cost of which is $L_{RN} + rK_N$. Therefore,

$$E_N = L_N - L_{RN} + n_M\left[M_N\pi(p_N) + M_S\pi(p_S)\right]. \tag{5}$$

In South, all income derives from wages and all is spent, so $E_S = L_S$, where L_S is South's labor supply measured in efficiency units.

We are ready now to describe the policy environment and the objective functions of the two governments. North's government faces an initial decision about its policy for exhaustion of IPR. Our analysis focuses on the relative merits of its alternative options.[13] We assume

[12]With quasi-linear preferences, our analysis would be unaffected if we were to introduce the possibility of international borrowing and lending. The constant interest rate equal to the discount rate makes consumers indifferent to the time profile of their spending.

[13]We could allow South's government to make a simultaneous choice of policy regarding parallel imports. However, inasmuch as prices of differentiated products are higher in North than South in all equilibria that we consider with national

that the choice of IPR exhaustion is a long-term commitment; i.e. the government decides once and for all whether it will tolerate or ban parallel imports. Subsequently, at each moment $z > 0$, the governments set their price regulations for goods invented at time z. A government can commit at time z to a price ceiling that will apply during the economic life of any good i invented at time z. Without this ability to pre-commit, both governments would be tempted to enact price ceilings at the competitive level c for every new good the moment after it is invented and, foreseeing this, firms would have no incentive to invest in R&D. The ability to pre-commit can be sustained, as usual, by an appropriate reputation mechanism.[14] We assume for the time being that North imposes no price controls or, equivalently, that its price ceiling for every good equals or exceeds the monopoly price p_M.

While in principle South's government could choose to set different price ceilings for goods invented at different times (or for different goods invented at the same time), it has no reason to do so. Therefore, we shall solve for a single price ceiling that is optimal for South for all goods and at all times, which however depends on what parallel trade regime is in effect. At time zero and thenceforth, the government of South chooses a price ceiling

exhaustion, there is no incentive for parallel trade to flow from North to South, and thus South's policy toward parallel imports is irrelevant.

[14]Our assumption that the government sets its pricing ceiling before firms make their R&D decisions suggests that the government has more incentive to commit than the firms, or is better able to do so. We believe the assumption is plausible in our context, because the government's policies affect many potential investors at each moment in time and even more investors over time. In contrast, an individual firm makes a single R&D decision at a given moment and may invest for only a limited period. Accordingly, the government has ample incentive to invest in a reputation for not expropriating IPR via price controls, whereas the individual firms have no reason to commit to high levels of investment and little to gain by committing not to invest. We emphasize, however, that our timing assumption is crucial to our argument. Without pre-commitment by the Southern government, international exhaustion of IPR would kill all incentives for innovation. Lack of pre-commitment ability in North would imply zero innovation also under national exhaustion of IPR.

to maximize the discounted value of the total consumer surplus that its households achieve on goods invented subsequently. Considering that the number of Southern consumers is M_S, that innovation will be constant over time at rate ϕ_N, and that each newly invented good spends the first τ years of its economic life as a patented good with (endogenous) price p_S and the remaining $\bar{\tau}-\tau$ years as an unpatented good with price c, the South government's objective is to maximize the present discounted value of the sum of spending and consumer surplus,

$$W_S = \frac{L_S}{\rho} + \frac{M_S\phi_N}{\rho}\left[TC(p_S) + (\bar{T} - T)\,C_C\right], \tag{6}$$

where $\bar{T} = (1 - e^{-\rho\bar{\tau}})/\rho$ is defined analogously to T.

In North, aggregate welfare is the present value of spending plus consumer surplus, and spending is augmented by profit income but diminished by the savings that finance R&D; see (5). Accordingly, the government of North will evaluate the alternative trade regimes with an eye toward maximizing

$$W_N = \frac{L_N - L_{RN}}{\rho} + \frac{\phi_N}{\rho}[TM_NC(p_N) + (\bar{T}-T)M_NC_C + T\Pi_N], \tag{7}$$

where $\Pi_N = M_N\pi(p_N) + M_S\pi(p_S)$ is the global profit flow earned by a typical Northern patent holder. The differences between (6) and (7) reflect that (i) the sizes of the two markets differ, (ii) profits accrue to firms in North but not to firms in South, and (iii) North devotes resources to R&D whereas South does not. In other words, as in Grossman and Lai (2004), the governments have different interests because the countries have different capacities for research and differently sized markets for innovative products.

In the next section, we discuss the optimal price control in South in a regime with national exhaustion of IPR (no parallel imports) and in a regime with international exhaustion. Then we compare the aggregate welfare in North under the alternative regimes, to shed light on its decision whether or not to allow parallel trade. We also discuss how parallel trade affects welfare in South.

3 Price Controls with and without Parallel Trade

Throughout this section, we assume that the government of North does not impose price controls and firms in South do not innovate. When North prohibits parallel imports, South can limit the prices of differentiated products in its market without any effect on the prices that these products carry in North. Such restraints will benefit Southern consumers and will not cause any loss of income for Southern households. However, they will reduce the incentives for innovation in North to an extent that depends on the size of the Southern market. We derive the optimality conditions for the South's price control in such circumstances and then turn to the more subtle calculus that arises when parallel imports are tolerated in the North. Then the government of South must recognize that Northern firms would prefer at some prices to sacrifice sales in the Southern market in order to curtail arbitrage. And, if patent holders set prices for initial sales in South that fall within the bounds of the price controls, the opportunities for arbitrage will affect prices in the North and thus the profits that the innovative firms can earn at home. After we derive the optimal price controls in the presence of arbitrage, we compare the welfare levels that result in each country under the alternative parallel trade regimes.

3.1 Optimal price ceiling with national exhaustion

Suppose that North prohibits reimportation of patented goods. With no price controls in North, each producer of a differentiated product charges the monopoly price p_M there for as long as its patent remains alive. In South, the monopolists can make positive profits at any price above c and will charge the highest price allowed under the price control, up to a maximum of p_M. Thus, South's government can choose the local price between c and p_M that maximizes W_S in (6), recognizing that the price determines both local consumer surplus $M_S C(p_S)$ and the flow of global profits per patent, $M_S \pi(p_S) + M_N \pi(p_M)$. The latter determines L_{RN}, which in turn determines the rate of innovation, via (4).

If the South sets a price control p_S above the marginal cost c, then the first-order condition implies

$$\frac{d\phi_N}{dv}\frac{dv^{\mathrm{ne}}}{dp_S}\left[TC(p_S) + \left(\bar{T} - T\right) C_C\right] + \phi_N TC'(p_S) = 0 \tag{8}$$

or, using (3), (4), $\phi_N = \frac{1}{\beta}\left(K_N^{1-\beta} L_{RN}^{\beta}\right)$ and the fact that $C'(p_S) = -x(p_S)$,

$$\frac{\beta}{1-\beta}\left[C(p_S) + \left(\frac{\bar{T} - T}{T}\right) C_C\right]\left[\frac{\pi'(p_S)}{x(p_S)}\right] = \pi(p_S) + m\pi(p_M), \tag{9}$$

where $v^{\mathrm{ne}} = [M_S\pi(p_S) + M_N\pi(p_M)]\,T$ is the value of a patent with national exhaustion of IPR in North, $x(\cdot)$ is the demand per consumer for the representative differentiated product as a function of its price, and $m \equiv M_N/M_S$ is the relative size of the Northern market. For m large, the right-hand side of (9) exceeds the left-hand side for all values of p_S above c. Then, South's government sets its price ceiling p_S^{ne} equal to c, where p_S^{ne} denotes the price ceiling in a regime with national exhaustion. Otherwise, p_S^{ne} is the value of p_S that solves (9).

The first-order condition (9) expresses the tradeoff between the benefit to South of the extra product diversity that results from greater innovation and the loss in surplus that Southern consumers suffer as a result of higher prices there. The term $\beta/(1-\beta)$ represents the elasticity of innovation ϕ_N with respect to the value of a patent v, and thus can be interpreted as the supply elasticity of R&D.[15] The government of South sets a more lenient price control (higher ceiling) when innovation is more responsive to profits, when product life is long relative to the duration of patents, and when the South's market is relatively large.[16]

[15]With $\phi_j = \frac{1}{\beta}K_j^{1-\beta}L_{Rj}^{\beta}$ and $v\left(\partial\phi_j/\partial L_{Rj}\right) = 1$,

$$\frac{\partial\phi_j}{\partial v}\frac{v}{\phi_j} = \frac{\beta}{1-\beta}\,.$$

[16]These claims rely on the second-order conditions being satisfied, which we assume to be the case.

3.2 Optimal price ceiling with international exhaustion

Now suppose that North permits parallel imports. If the price of a differentiated product in North were to exceed the (regulated) price of the same good in South, an arbitrage opportunity would present itself. We have assumed that shipping and distribution are costless, which means that no such arbitrage opportunities can persist in equilibrium. With international exhaustion, either a differentiated product must carry the same price in both markets or the price charged by patent holders for sales in the regulated market must be so high as to preclude sales there.

Under the threat of such arbitrage, a Northern patent holder faces a choice. It can set a price for sales in South that exceeds the price ceiling, thereby effectively cutting off supply from that region and eliminating any source of reimports. Or it can accept the competition from arbitrageurs and sell in both markets at a price less than or equal to the South's controlled price.[17] The former strategy allows

[17]Joseph Harrington points out that, in addition to setting a price for its sales to the South, a monopolist might wish to limit the quantity that it sells there. If a firm could direct sales only to those Southern consumers who value the product more than the monopoly price, then it would certainly wish to do so. However, the firm cannot legally charge a high price that would force these consumers to reveal themselves, and it will have no means to target sales to the high-valuation consumers without knowing who they are. Moreover, every resident of the South has positive demand at the controlled Southern price, because they can all resell the product at a profit in the North. When firms lacks the ability to identify consumers who will not engage in arbitrage, the profitability of limiting total sales to the South will depend upon the rationing mechanism that is used to allocate those sales.

One simple assumption supports our formulation, however. Suppose that the monopolists do not sell directly to consumers but instead sell to competitive retailers who have zero cost and no demand for the product for personal use. Perfect enforcement of the price ceiling implies that the the retailers will prefer to sell their entire allotment in the North as long as the price there exceeds the controlled price in the South. In such circumstances, a Northern firm maximizes profits either by setting a price in excess of the ceiling and selling nothing to the South, or else by setting the regulated price and satisfying all demand by Southern retailers.

the firm to earn maximal profits in the Northern market. The latter strategy affords (possibly) positive profits in South at the expense of diminished profits at home.

We define $\tilde{p}$ implicitly by

$$(M_N + M_S)\pi(\tilde{p}) = M_N\pi(p_M); \tag{10}$$

this is the price at which the two strategies yield equal profits. If the government of South sets a price ceiling below $\tilde{p}$, a Northern patent holder earns higher profits by selling at home at p_M and eschewing all sales in South than it does by selling in both markets at the maximum price allowed by South. It can achieve these profits, for example, by setting the price p_M for all sales. If the South's price ceiling instead exceeds $\tilde{p}$, the patent holder prefers to sell in both markets at the highest price allowed in South. It cannot be optimal for South's government to allow its market for differentiated products to be foreclosed. Accordingly, the government of South chooses its price ceiling p_S subject to the constraint that $p_S \geq \tilde{p}$.

Let us ignore the constraint for a moment. Then the first-order condition for the optimal choice of the South's price ceiling is given by

$$\frac{d\phi_N}{dv}\frac{dv^{\text{ie}}}{dp_S}\left[TC(p_S) + \left(\bar{T} - T\right)C_C\right] + \phi_N TC'(p_S) = 0,$$

which, with $v^{\text{ie}} = [(M_S + M_N)\pi(p_S)]\,T$, implies that

$$\frac{\beta}{1-\beta}\left[C(p^*) + \left(\frac{\bar{T} - T}{T}\right)C_C\right]\left[\frac{\pi'(p^*)}{x(p^*)}\right] = \pi(p^*), \tag{11}$$

where v^{ie} is the value of a patent with international exhaustion (and thus uniform pricing) and p^* is the price ceiling that South would enforce in a regime with parallel trade if it were subject to no constraints.

If $p^* > \tilde{p}$, the constraint that dictates a price ceiling high enough to ensure positive sales in South does not bind. Then the government optimally sets a maximum price of p^*. Otherwise, the governments sets the ceiling at $\tilde{p}$, the lowest level that generates positive supply.

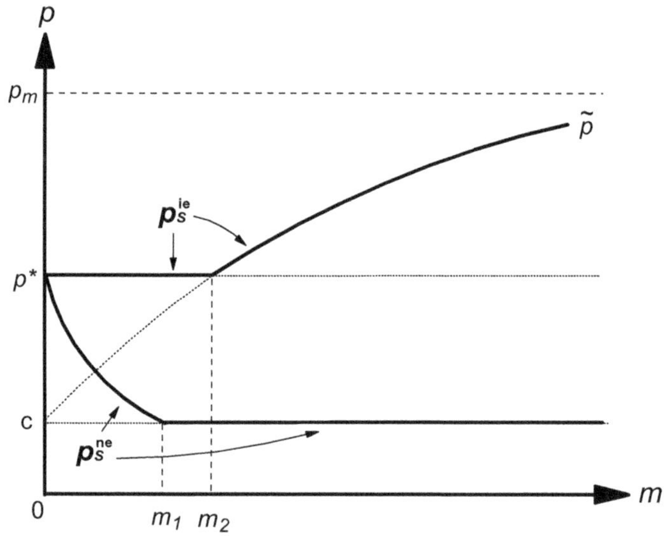

Figure 1. Price ceilings under alternative parallel trade regimes.

In other words, the optimal price ceiling for South in a regime in which North permits parallel imports is given by

$$p_S^{\text{ie}} = \max(\tilde{p}, p^*). \tag{12}$$

3.3 Comparing prices and profits in the alternative regimes

In Figure 1, we depict p_S^{ne}, p^* and $\tilde{p}$ as functions of m, the relative size of the Northern market. The price ceiling with national exhaustion p_S^{ne} is a decreasing function of m until it reaches c at some finite level of m, which we denote by m_1. South's government would never set a price ceiling below c, because patent holders would not serve the Southern market at prices below marginal production cost. Accordingly, $p_S^{\text{ne}} = c$ for all $m \geq m_1$. Notice that $p^* = p_S^{\text{ne}}$ when $m = 0$ inasmuch as the incentives facing the Southern government are the same in the two regimes when the Northern market is negligibly small. However, p^* is independent of m under international exhaustion; this is because arbitrage renders the effect of price controls on the incentives for innovation independent of the geographic distribution of world demand. Finally, (10) implies that $\tilde{p} = c$ at $m = 0$ and that $\tilde{p}$ is an increasing function of m for all $m > 0$. This is because patent holders will sell in South at any price equal to or exceeding marginal cost when the Northern market is negligibly small, but require an ever higher price to sell there (under the threat of arbitrage) as the Northern market grows relatively larger. Let m_2 be the level of m at which $p^* = \tilde{p}$.

The figure depicts p_S^{ne} and p_S^{ie} in bold. Evidently, we have

Proposition 1. *Suppose that South does not innovate and North imposes no price controls. Then $p_S^{\text{ie}} > p_S^{\text{ne}}$ for all $m > 0$.*

Intuitively, the prospect of arbitrage mitigates the ability of South to free ride on the intellectual property protection afforded by North. With more at stake in terms of the adverse effect of a price ceiling on the innovation rate, the South will accept higher domestic prices. And the gap between p_S^{ie} and p_S^{ne} is all the greater when, in the presence of parallel trade, the South is forced to set a price ceiling even higher than its preferred (unconstrained) choice to give patent holders reason to serve its market.

Now we are ready to compare the options facing North's government. We begin with $m < m_2$, so that $p^* > \tilde{p}$ and thus $p_S^{\text{ie}} = p^*$. Let us define the function

$$\Omega(p) \equiv \frac{\beta}{1-\beta}\left[C(p) + \left(\frac{\bar{T}-T}{T}\right)C_C\right]\left[\frac{\pi'(p)}{x(p)}\right].$$

Notice that the left-hand side of (9) is $\Omega(p_S^{\text{ne}})$ and the left-hand side of (11) is $\Omega(p^*)$. For some demand functions (more on this later), the following condition holds.

Condition 1. *Either $\Omega'' < 0$ or $|\Omega''/\Omega'| < |\pi''/\pi'|$ for all $p \in [c, p_M)$.*

In the appendix we prove the following lemma.

Lemma 1. *Suppose that South does not innovate, North imposes no price controls, $m < m_1$, and Condition 1 is satisfied. Then $(M_N + M_S)\pi(p^*) > M_N\pi(p_M) + M_S\pi(p_S^{\text{ne}})$.*

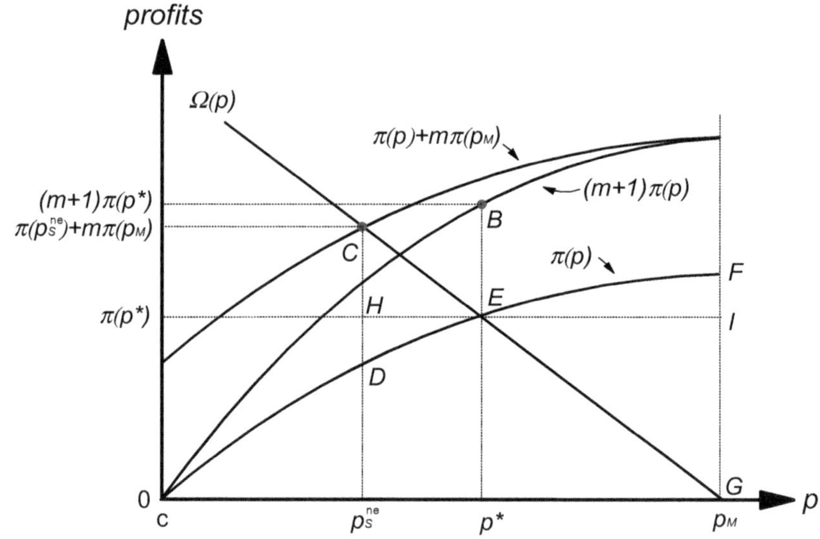

Figure 2. Global profits under alternative parallel trade regimes.

The consequent of Lemma 1 states that aggregate profits for a patent holder are greater when there is international exhaustion of IPR in North and South sets its price control at p^* than they are when there is national exhaustion and South sets its price control at $p_S^{\text{ne}} > c$. Figure 2, which depicts the case of a linear $\Omega(p)$ curve, may help us to understand why this is so. The concave $\pi(p)$ curve and the linear $\Omega(p)$ intersect at point E, which determines p^*. The figure also shows $(m+1)\pi(p)$ and $\pi(p) + m\pi(p_M)$. The intersection of $\Omega(p)$ and $\pi(p) + m\pi(p_M)$ at the point labelled C gives the price ceiling with national exhaustion, p_S^{ne}. Note that $(M_N + M_S)\pi(p^*) > M_N\pi(p_M) + M_S\pi(p_S^{\text{ne}})$ if and only if $(m+1)$ $\pi(p^*) > \pi(p_S^{\text{ne}}) + m\pi(p_M)$; i.e. if and only if the length of HD exceeds m times the length of FI. But $m = [\Omega(p_S^{\text{ne}}) - \pi(p_S^{\text{ne}})]/\pi(p_M)$ by (9), and so is represented in the figure by the ratio of the length of CD to the length of FG. Therefore, for the length of HD to exceed m times the length of FI, we need the ratio of HD to CD to exceed the ratio of FI to FG. But this is true, because the triangle CEH is similar to the triangle EIG, while the curve DEF is concave. If the $\Omega(p)$ curve passing through G and E instead were concave, the point C would lie to the southwest of the position shown, which would strengthen the argument. However, if the $\Omega(p)$ curve passing through G and E were convex, point C would lie to the northeast of the position shown. In this case, the length of HD would exceed m times the length of FI if and only if the absolute value of the curvature of $\Omega(p)$ were less than that of the curvature of $\pi(p)$, as provided in the second part of Condition 1.

Next we will show that, under Condition 1, $m_1 < m_2$, as depicted in Figure 1. Recall that m_1 is the smallest value of m for which $p_S^{\text{ne}} = c$ (South's government sets a price ceiling at the marginal production cost in the absence of parallel imports), while m_2 is the smallest value of m for which $\tilde{p} \geq p^*$ (the constraint on South's government to ensure positive supply in a regime with parallel imports binds). Suppose that $m_1 > m_2$. Then $(1 + m_2)\pi(p^*)$ exceeds $m_2\pi(p_M) + \pi[p_S^{\text{ne}}(m_2)]$ by Lemma 1, which in turn exceeds $m_2\pi(p_M)$ by the fact that $p_S^{\text{ne}}(m_2) > c$. But $m_2\pi(p_M) = (1+m_2)\pi[\tilde{p}(m_2)]$ by the definition of $\tilde{p}$. So $(1+m_2)\pi(p^*) > (1+m_2)\pi[\tilde{p}(m_2)]$, which implies that $p^* > \tilde{p}$ at m_2. But this contradicts the definition of m_2.

For m between m_1 and m_2, South's government sets a price ceiling of $p_S^{\text{ne}} = c$ in a regime with national exhaustion of IPR in North and a price ceiling of $p_S^{\text{ie}} = p^*$ in a regime with international exhaustion in North. With national exhaustion, aggregate profits per patent are $M_N\pi(p_M)$. With international exhaustion, profits are $(M_N + M_S)\pi(p^*)$, which exceeds $(M_N + M_S)\pi(\tilde{p})$ because $p^* > \tilde{p}$. But $(M_N + M_S)\pi(\tilde{p}) = M_N\pi(p_M)$ by the definition of $\tilde{p}$. It follows that global profits per patent are higher with international exhaustion than with national exhaustion for this range of values of m as well.

Finally, when $m \geq m_2$, $p_S^{\text{ne}} = c$ and $p_S^{\text{ie}} = \tilde{p}$. In either case, global profits are equal to $M_N\pi(p_M)$. We conclude that, under Condition 1, the value of a patent when North tolerates parallel imports is no less than the value of a patent when it bars such imports, and patents actually are more valuable with parallel trade whenever $m < m_2$. Innovation responds positively to the value of a patent. It follows that innovation is at least as great, and for small m is greater, in a regime with legal parallel trade.

We are now ready to address the North's choice of parallel trade regime and to evaluate the implications of this choice for welfare in South. Let W_N^j denote North's aggregate welfare (as defined in (7)) in regime j, for $j = \{ne, ie\}$. We have

Proposition 2. *Suppose that South does not innovate, North imposes no price controls, and Condition* 1 *is satisfied. Then* $W_N^{\text{ie}} > W_N^{\text{ne}}$.

Proof. We have already seen that the innovation rate ϕ_N is at least as great in a regime with international exhaustion in North as in a regime with national exhaustion. Also, $p_N^{\text{ne}} = p_M$ while $p_N^{\text{ie}} = \max[p^*, \tilde{p}] < p_M$, where p_N^j is the price of a patented differentiated product in North in regime j. So $C(p_N^{\text{ie}}) > C(p_N^{\text{ne}})$. Finally, note the term $\phi_N T\Pi_N - L_{RN}$ that appears in W_N. This is aggregate profits from all patents minus the cost of labor used in research. But $T\Pi_N = v$, the value of a patent, and the L_{RN} that is chosen in each regime maximizes $\phi_N v - L_{RN}$; see (4). It follows that $\phi_N^{\text{ie}} T\Pi_N^{\text{ie}} - L_{RN}^{\text{ie}} \geq \phi_N^{\text{ne}} T\Pi_N^{\text{ne}} - L_{RN}^{\text{ne}}$, because $\max_{L_{RN}} (\phi_N v - L_{RN})$ is increasing in v and the value of a patent is at least as great in a regime with international exhaustion as in a regime with national exhaustion. ■

Whereas North fares better by choosing international exhaustion (when Condition 1 is satisfied), this choice adversely impacts welfare in South. We record this observation in

Proposition 3. *Suppose that South does not innovate, North imposes no price controls, and Condition* 1 *is satisfied. Then* $W_S^{\text{ie}} < W_S^{\text{ne}}$.

Proof. With international exhaustion, the world price of a patented good is p_S^{ie}. In a regime with national exhaustion, it is feasible for South's government to set its price ceiling for patented goods at p_S^{ie}. This would generate the same consumer surplus in South as in a regime with international exhaustion and, because $p_S^{\text{ie}} < p_M$, more innovation and greater product diversity. Thus, by setting a price ceiling of p_S^{ie} in a regime with national exhaustion, South could achieve greater welfare than W_S^{ie}. Its optimal choice of p_S^{ne} must yield even greater welfare. ■

This leads us to ask how likely it is that Condition 1 will be satisfied. The expression for Condition 1 in terms of the primitive parameters of the model is rather complicated. But we can readily examine a pair of special cases that yield familiar demand functions.

Constant elasticity demand

Suppose that $h(x) = a^{1/\varepsilon}\left(\frac{\varepsilon}{\varepsilon-1}\right)x^{(\varepsilon-1)/\varepsilon}$ for $a > 0$, $\varepsilon > 1$. Then the demand function is $x(p) = ap^{-\varepsilon}$, which has a constant-elasticity form. The monopoly price in this case is a mark-up over marginal cost, or $p_M = c\varepsilon/(\varepsilon - 1)$. We calculate that

$$\Omega'(p) = -a\left(\frac{\beta}{1-\beta}\right)p^{-\varepsilon}\left[1 - \frac{\varepsilon(p-c)}{p}\right] - a\left(\frac{\beta}{1-\beta}\right)\frac{c\varepsilon}{p^2}\left[\frac{p^{1-\varepsilon}}{\varepsilon-1} + \frac{c^{1-\varepsilon}}{\varepsilon-1}\left(\frac{\bar{T}}{T} - 1\right)\right],$$

which is negative for all $p \in [c, p_M]$. Now we define $Z \equiv \Omega''(p)\pi'(p) - \Omega'(p)\pi''(p)$, and calculate

$$Z = -a^2c\varepsilon p^{-2(2+\varepsilon)}\left(\frac{\beta}{1-\beta}\right)\left\{p^2 + c^{1-\varepsilon}p^{\varepsilon}\left[c\varepsilon - (\varepsilon-2)p\right]\left(\frac{\bar{T}}{T} - 1\right)\right\},$$

which is negative for all $p \in [c, c\varepsilon/(\varepsilon - 1)]$. Since $\Omega'(p) < 0$ and $\pi'(p) > 0$ for all $p \in [c, p_M)$, $Z < 0$ implies $|\Omega''/\Omega'| < |\pi''/\pi'|$ and Condition 1 is satisfied. Notice that this is true for all values of $\varepsilon > 1$.

Linear demand

Suppose that $h(x) = A + ax/b - x^2/2b$ for $a > 0$, $b > 0$, and $a > bc$. This last parameter restriction ensures positive demand when a good is competitively priced. Then the demand function $x(p) = a - bp$ is linear and the monopoly price is $p_M = (a + bc)/2b$. We find that

$$\Omega'(p) = -\frac{1}{2}\left(\frac{\beta}{1-\beta}\right)\left[3a + bc - 4bp + \frac{(a-bc)^3\left(\frac{\bar{T}}{T}-1\right)}{(a-bp)^2}\right],$$

which again is negative for all $p \in [c, p_M]$. Now we calculate

$$\left|\frac{\Omega''(p)}{\Omega'(p)}\right| - \left|\frac{\pi''(p)}{\pi'(p)}\right| = \frac{2b - \left[\frac{(a-bc)^3\left(\frac{\bar{T}}{T}-1\right)b}{(a-bp)^3}\right]}{\left(\frac{3a}{2} + \frac{bc}{2} - 2bp\right) + \left[\frac{(a-bc)^3\left(\frac{\bar{T}}{T}-1\right)}{2(a-bp)^2}\right]} - \frac{2b}{a - 2bp + bc},$$

which is negative for all $p \in [c, (a + bc)/2b)$. Therefore, with linear demands too, Condition 1 is satisfied.

We conclude from these examples that Condition 1 is not unreasonable inasmuch as it always is satisfied for two families of commonly-used demand functions. When the condition is satisfied, the orthodox view that allowing parallel imports would retard innovation and harm a country that specializes in research is false. Once we recognize that this country's trade partners will regulate prices differently according to the prevailing policy on exhaustion of IPR, we find that the policy change induced by a switch to international exhaustion can easily be large enough to allow the innovating country to enjoy lower prices, greater profits, faster innovation, and higher welfare.

4 Extensions

In this section, we relax two of the simplifying assumptions that were used in the preceding analysis to highlight our main points. First, we allow for positive research capacity and thus active innovation activity in South. Second, we allow for the possibility that North may institute price controls of its own.

4.1 Innovation in south

In Section 3, we emphasized the asymmetries in research capacities by assuming that $K_S = 0$. Now we allow for $K_S > 0$, which, with the Cobb-Douglas technology for product development, ensures positive innovation in South. As before, we assume that any wage gap that exists between North and South matches a gap in labor productivity in all activities (including research). Then L_{RS} in the technology for product development in South measures the labor deployed in Southern research in efficiency units.

When South is endowed with research capital, the objective function for country j becomes

$$W_j = \frac{1}{\rho}\{L_j - L_{Rj} + (\phi_N + \phi_S)M_j[TC(p_j) + (\bar{T} - T)C_C] + \phi_j T\Pi_j\},$$

where $\Pi_j = M_N\pi(p_N) + M_S\pi(p_S)$ is the global profit earned by a typical producer in country j of a patented good when prices of such products in North and South are p_N and p_S, respectively. The expression for welfare reflects that households in country j derive consumer surplus from differentiated products produced anywhere in the world, but they derive profit income only from producers in their own country. Notice that $\Pi_S = \Pi_N$ under our assumption of wage equalization in efficiency units, and thus the value of a patent v is the same in both countries.

Firms in South hire (efficiency) labor to perform research up to the point where the marginal value product is equal to the wage, or $v(K_S/L_{RS})^{1-\beta} = 1$. Together with (4), the analogous condition for equilibrium investment in North, and the production function for innovation, $\phi_j = \frac{1}{\beta}L_{Rj}^{\beta}K_j^{1-\beta}$, this implies $\phi_N/\phi_S = K_N/K_S$. We let $\mu_j = K_j/(K_N + K_S)$ denote the fraction of the world stock of research capital located in country j. Then μ_j also is the fraction of world innovation that takes place in country j; i.e. $\mu_j = \phi_j/(\phi_N + \phi_S)$.

Still assuming that North does not regulate prices, South's government chooses p_S in a regime with national exhaustion of IPR to maximize W_S. The first-order condition that applies when $p_S^{\text{ne}} > c$ is

$$\frac{d}{dp_S}\{M_S(\phi_N + \phi_S)\left[TC(p_S) + (\bar{T} - T)\,C_C\right] + v\phi_S - L_{RS}\} = 0$$

or[18]

$$\left(\frac{\beta}{1-\beta}\right)\frac{C(p_S) + \left(\frac{\bar{T}-T}{T}\right)C_C}{\frac{x(p_S)}{\pi'(p_S)} - \mu_S} = \pi\,(p_S) + m\pi(p_M). \tag{13}$$

Note the similarity with (9), to which (13) reduces when $\mu_S = 0$.

We can similarly derive South's choice of price control that applies under international exhaustion of IPR when the constraint that $p_S^{\text{ie}} \geq \tilde{p}$ does not bind. The analog to equation (11) above is

$$\left(\frac{\beta}{1-\beta}\right)\frac{C(p^*) + \left(\frac{\bar{T}-T}{T}\right)C_C}{\frac{x(p^*)}{\pi'(p^*)} - (m+1)\mu_S} = \pi(p^*). \tag{14}$$

We define

$$\Lambda(p) \equiv \left(\frac{\beta}{1-\beta}\right)\frac{C(p) + \left(\frac{\bar{T}-T}{T}\right)C_C}{\frac{x(p)}{\pi'(p)} - \mu_S}.$$

Then (13) can be written as $\Lambda(p_S) = \pi(p_S) + m\pi(p_M)$, while the value of p^* that solves (14) must be bigger than the p that solves $\Lambda(p) = \pi(p)$; call the latter p^{**}.

We now introduce a modified version of Condition 1, namely

Condition 2. *Either* $\Lambda'' < 0$ *or* $|\Lambda''/\Lambda'| < |\pi''/\pi'|$ *for all* $p \in [c, p_M)$.

We can use exactly the same strategy and arguments as before to prove that if Condition 2 is satisfied and $p_S^{\text{ne}} > c$, then $(m+1)\pi(p^{**}) > m\pi(p_M) + \pi(p_S^{\text{ne}})$. But since $p^* > p^{**}$, this is sufficient to establish

[18]To derive (13), we use the fact that $dv^{\text{ne}}/dp_S = M_S T\pi'(p_S)$, $dC(p_S)/dp_S = -x(p_S)$ and $v(d\phi_S/dp_S) = dL_{RS}/dp_S$.

that $(m + 1)\pi(p^*) > m\pi(p_M) + \pi(p_S^{\text{ne}})$. In other words, with Condition 2 and $p_S^{\text{ne}} > c$, global profits per firm and the world innovation rate are greater with international exhaustion of IPR in North than with national exhaustion. It is also true as before that when $p_S^{\text{ne}} = c$, global profits per firm are at least as high with international exhaustion as with national exhaustion. And North enjoys higher consumer surplus with parallel trade. This establishes

Proposition 4. *Suppose that North imposes no price controls and Condition 2 is satisfied. Then* $W_N^{\text{ie}} > W_N^{\text{ne}}$.

Note, however, that Condition 2 may be more stringent than Condition 1. We compute for example that if the demand function $x(p)$ is linear, Condition 2 is satisfied for all parameters b, c and $a > bc$ when $\mu_S < 0.38$. If the demand function has constant elasticity ε then Condition 2 holds when $\mu_S < 1/2$ and both ε and $\bar{T}/T$ are sufficiently large. For example, if $\mu_S = 0.2$, Condition 2 is satisfied if $3.1\bar{T} + \varepsilon(1.9T - 2.3\bar{T}) < 1.9T$ or if $\varepsilon = 2$ and $\bar{T}/T > 1.3$.[19] Of course, Condition 2 must be satisfied for sufficiently small (but positive) μ_S. And while Condition 2 is sufficient for $W_N^{\text{ie}} > W_N^{\text{ne}}$, it is not a necessary condition for this outcome.

4.2 Price controls in north

Up until now, we have assumed that North does not impose any price controls of its own. This assumption can be rigorously justified if administering price controls imposes fixed costs, and if these costs fall in a range such that maintaining a regulatory program is worthwhile for South but not for North. Now we shall examine a policy environment in which the fixed costs of maintaining price controls, while not literally zero, are arbitrarily small.[20]

---

[19]The details of these calculations are available from the authors upon request.

[20]We make the assumption of small administrative costs to eliminate some unreasonable Nash equilibria of the regulation game that can otherwise arise when parallel imports are allowed. When regulatory schemes are costless, each country might impose the same low price ceiling and while both countries would

To simplify the exposition, we assume once again that all research capacity is concentrated in North. First consider the regulation game in a regime in which North does not allow parallel imports. In this case, the best response by South to a price ceiling p_N in North is given by the solution to

$$\left(\frac{\beta}{1-\beta}\right)\frac{C(p_S)+\left(\frac{\bar{T}-T}{T}\right)C_C}{\frac{x(p_S)}{\pi'(p_S)}}=\pi(p_S)+m\pi(p_N), \qquad (15)$$

if such a solution exists with $p_S > c$, and by $p_S^{\text{ne}} = c$ otherwise. In North, the maximization of W_N in (7) with respect to the choice of p_N implies

$$m\left(\frac{\beta}{1-\beta}\right)\frac{C(p_N)+\left(\frac{\bar{T}-T}{T}\right)C_C}{\frac{x(p_N)}{\pi'(p_N)}-1}=\pi(p_S)+m\pi(p_N). \qquad (16)$$

Notice that $p_N < p_M$ for all values of p_S.[21] This is because a price ceiling in North set just below the monopoly price causes only a second-order reduction in profits and so a negligible loss of product diversity, but generates a first-order gain in consumer surplus. Note too that $p_N^{\text{ne}} > p_S^{\text{ne}}$ as long as $m \geq 1$, which reflects the fact that monopoly profits accrue to households in North but not to households in South and that a country with a larger market provides more incentives to innovators for the same increment in the price ceiling.

Now consider the game that emerges when parallel imports are permitted by North. We define p_N^* as the uniform global price ceiling most preferred by the government of North[22] and p^* as the one most preferred by South, which once again is the value of p that solves (11). Note that $p_N^* > p^*$, because the two governments face

prefer to see higher prices of patented goods, neither has an incentive to raise its ceiling as long as the other's ceiling is unchanged.

[21]If $p_N = p_M$, then $\pi'(p_N) = 0$ and the left-hand side of (16) equals zero, while the right-hand side of (16) is strictly positive.

[22]That is,

$$p_N^* = \arg\max_p M_N\phi_N[TC(p)+(\bar{T}-T)C_c]+v\phi_N - L_{RN},$$

similar incentives except that monopoly profits accrue to households in North. If $(M_N + M_S)\pi(p^*) > M_N(p_M)$, then South will set a price ceiling of $p_S^{\text{ie}} = p^*$ and North will impose no price ceiling in the Nash equilibrium of the regulation game. In this case, South's government is unconstrained in its choice of price ceiling, and North's government has no reason to bear the (small) fixed cost of a regulatory program. If $(M_N + M_S)\pi(p^*) < M_N\pi(p_M)$ but $\tilde{p}$ (as defined in (10)) is less than p_N^*, then $p_S^{\text{ie}} = \tilde{p}$ and again North has no price ceiling in the Nash equilibrium. In this case, South is constrained and it chooses $\tilde{p}$, but North has no reason to introduce a price control because it would like to see South choose an even higher value of p_S^{ie} than this. Finally, if $(M_N + M_S)\pi(p^*) < M_N\pi(p_M)$ and $\tilde{p} > p_N^*$, then North sets a price ceiling such that the constrained government of South will choose $p_S^{\text{ie}} = p_N^*$ in order that its market be served.[23]

In the appendix, we prove the following proposition that compares global profits per firm, the values of a patent and rates of innovation in the alternative regimes.

Proposition 5. *Suppose that South does not innovate and Condition 1 is satisfied. Then* $(M_N + M_S)\pi(p_S^{\text{ie}}) > M_N\pi(p_N^{\text{ne}}) + M_S\pi(p_S^{\text{ne}}), v^{\text{ie}} > v^{\text{ne}}$, *and* $\phi_N^{\text{ie}} > \phi_N^{\text{ne}}$.

The proposition states that profits are higher, patents are more valuable, and innovation is faster when the North allows parallel imports than when it does not. The proof is tedious, because it requires separate consideration of five different cases depending on whether p_S^{ie} is equal to p^*, $\tilde{p}$, or p_N^*, whether p_S^{ne} equals or exceeds c, and whether p^* exceeds or falls short of p_N^{ne}. However, the reasoning is straightforward in several of these scenarios, which we describe now.

---

where $v = T(M_N + M_S)\pi(p)$, which implies that p_N^* is the solution to

$$\left(\frac{\beta}{1-\beta}\right)\frac{C(p_N^*) + \left(\frac{\bar{T}-T}{T}\right)C_C}{\frac{x(p_N^*)}{\pi'(p_N^*)} - \left(\frac{1}{m}+1\right)} = \pi(p_N^*).$$

[23]That is, North chooses p_N^{ie} so that $(M_N + M_S)\pi(p_N^*) = M_N\pi(p_N^{\text{ie}})$.

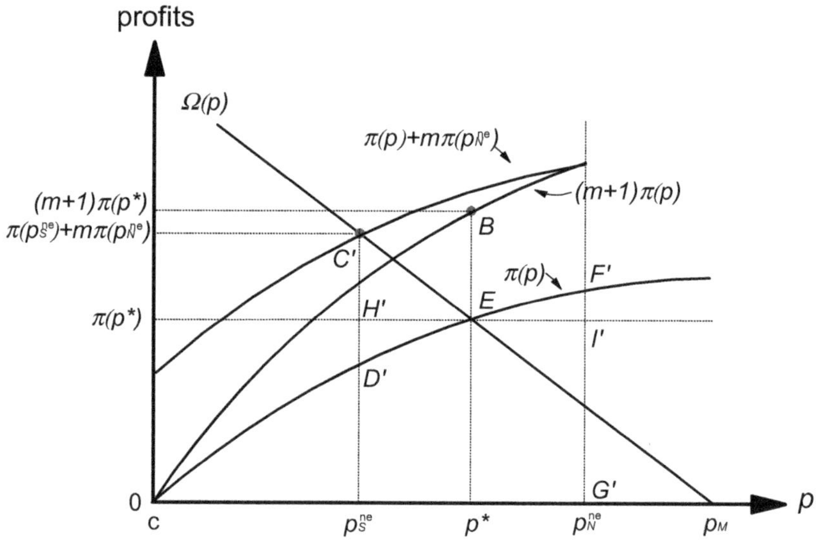

Figure 3. Profit comparison with northern price controls.

First, suppose that $p^* > p_N^{\mathrm{ne}}$; that is, an unconstrained South would choose a higher price ceiling under international exhaustion than North's Nash equilibrium price ceiling in the regulation game with national exhaustion. Since the prevailing world prices with international exhaustion are at least as high as p^*, and the prices in North and South with national exhaustion are both lower than p^*, global profits must be higher in the former regime than in the latter.

Next suppose that $p_S^{\mathrm{ie}} = p^* < p_N^{\mathrm{ne}}$ and $p_S^{\mathrm{ne}} > c$; i.e. the constraint on South's government to ensure positive supply of its market does not bind in either regime. Then it chooses p^* under international exhaustion and a price above marginal cost under national exhaustion. Now the argument is very similar to that used in proving the analogous result that applies when North eschews price regulation. Figure 3, like Figure 2, depicts a linear $\Omega(p)$ curve. When there is national exhaustion of IPR in North, the Nash equilibrium of the regulation game has $\Omega(p_S^{\mathrm{ne}}) = m\pi(p_N^{\mathrm{ne}}) + \pi(p_S^{\mathrm{ne}})$ which is represented by the point C' in the figure. South's choice of price ceiling with international exhaustion is found at E, where

$\Omega(p^*) = \pi(p^*)$. The comparison of global profits in the two equilibria now requires a comparison of the length of $H'D'$ with m times the length of $F'I'$. But the relative size of the two markets m is represented in Figure 3 by the ratio of the length of $C'D'$ to the length of $F'G'$. So, the concavity of $\pi(p)$ ensures that $(m+1)\pi(p^*) > m\pi(p_N^{\text{ne}}) + \pi(p_S^{\text{ne}})$. And, if $\Omega(p)$ is concave, or convex with curvature less in absolute value than that of $\pi(p)$, we reach the same conclusion.

A third case arises when $p_S^{\text{ie}} = \min[\tilde{p}, p_N^*]$ and $p_S^{\text{ne}} = c$; i.e. South would like to set a lower price ceiling in both regimes, but in each case it is constrained by the need to ensure positive supply of its market. In this scenario, the profits in North under international exhaustion are at least as large as $\pi(p_N^*)$ and those in South are positive. When parallel imports are forbidden by North, profits there are $\pi(p_N^{\text{ne}})$ while those in South are nil. But p_N^* exceeds p_N^{ne} for much the same reason that p^* exceeds p_S^{ne}; namely, North would choose a higher price were that price to apply to markets in both countries than the price it chooses when the price applies only at home. So patent holders earn higher profits in both countries under international exhaustion than under national exhaustion.

Although Proposition 5 gives conditions under which parallel imports promote innovation (by inducing changes in price regulation), these conditions do not guarantee a welfare gain for households in North. Contrary to the common wisdom that parallel imports would enhance consumer surplus but retard innovation, just the opposite can happen when North has price controls of its own in the absence of parallel trade, and the endogenous response of these controls is taken into account. If $p_S^{\text{ie}} = p^* < p_N^{\text{ne}}$, then consumer surplus in North is higher with international exhaustion than national exhaustion, and Northern welfare is unambiguously higher in the former regime than the latter. But if a ban on parallel trade leads North's government to set a reasonably tight price control in the Nash equilibrium of the regulation game, then a removal of the ban could lead to a rise in prices for Northern consumers.[24] If so,

[24]This could happen either because $p_S^{\text{ie}} = p^*$ and $p^* > p_N^{\text{ne}}$ or because $p_S^{\text{ie}} = \min[\tilde{p}, p_N^*] > p^*$ and $\min[\tilde{p}, p_N^*] > p_N^{\text{ne}}$.

the North still may benefit from parallel trade, but the realization of such a benefit would require that the gains from greater product variety exceed the losses from higher prices.

5 Several or Many Countries in the South

Until now, we have considered a two-country world with a single North in which firms invest in R&D and a single South with little or no such investment. We have argued that, by opening itself to parallel trade, the government of the North induces its counterpart in the South to set a higher price ceiling than otherwise. The South's choice of a high price ceiling reflects one of two considerations: either it wishes to ensure that its market is not cut off from innovative products or it seeks to preserve sufficient incentives for R&D. It may seem that the latter motivation rests on there being only one or a few countries in the South, because it requires that the government perceives a non-negligible influence of its own policy on the value of a patent. We address this issue by allowing for multiple Southern countries and show that, in fact, the conclusion does not require the presence of a large actor in the South.

Suppose that the South comprises n_S identical countries, each with a population of m_S consumers. Let $M_S = n_S m_S$ be the total population in the South and let $m = M_N/M_S$ be the relative size of the North, as before. We assume as in Section 3 that no innovation takes place in the South and that the North adopts no price controls, and we focus on symmetric Nash equilibria in which all the countries in the South set the same maximum price.[25]

As before, we are interested in the North's choice between national exhaustion and international exhaustion of IPR. With

[25] A symmetric Nash equilibrium always exists in the settings that we consider. In some cases — especially when the number of countries in the South is small — there may also exist asymmetric equilibria. However, the existence of such equilibria seems to require that the demand functions have special properties. Since our point can be seen most clearly when the Southern governments behave similarly, and since we have little to say about equilibrium selection when multiple equilibria exist, we choose to focus on the symmetric equilibrium.

several or many countries in the South, the relative attractiveness of these alternative regimes to North may hinge upon the permissibility of parallel imports in its various trade partners. One possible way for us to proceed would be to consider the simultaneous setting of policies toward parallel trade by the North and all Southern countries. However, analysis of the multi-stage game of choice of parallel trade regime followed by ongoing choices of price ceilings is complicated by the fact that pure-strategy equilibria do not exist in the price-control sub-games for all possible configurations of parallel trade policies.[26] Rather than delve into the complexities introduced by mixed strategies, we choose instead to treat the policies of the South with regard to parallel imports as exogenous. We will consider in turn the attractiveness to the North of allowing parallel trade under the alternative assumptions that all Southern countries prohibit parallel imports and that all Southern countries tolerate such imports.

5.1 National exhaustion of IPR in the south

Suppose the symmetric countries in the South all prohibit parallel imports. By doing so, each preserves autonomy in regulating its own internal prices without the risk that its decisions will be undermined by arbitrage. We consider in turn the alternative regimes available to the government of the North and then compare the two outcomes.

If the North also practices national exhaustion of IPR, each country in the South has the same first-order condition for its choice of a price ceiling (analogous to (8)), which for country i is given by

$$\frac{d\phi_N}{dv}\frac{dv^{\text{ne}}}{dp_i}\left[TC(p_i)+\left(\bar{T}-T\right)C_c\right]-\phi_N Tx(p_i)=0.$$

[26]In particular, we find that when $n_S - 1$ countries in the South practice national exhaustion of IPR, and the remaining country in the South plus the North practice international exhaustion of IPR, there exists no pure-strategy equilibrium in the second-stage game between the Southern countries. The described configuration of parallel trade policies arises naturally when considering a potential equilibrium in which all Southern countries choose national exhaustion and one contemplates a deviation to international exhaustion.

Note that

$$\frac{d\phi_N}{dv}\frac{v}{\phi_N} = \frac{\beta}{1-\beta}$$

is the elasticity of innovation supply with respect to the value of a patent and that

$$\left.\frac{dv^{\text{ne}}}{dp_i}\right|_{\mathbf{p}_{-i}} = Tm_S\pi'(p_i) = T\frac{M_S}{n_S}\pi'(p_i)$$

is the effect of a change in the price ceiling in country i on the value of a patent, where $\mathbf{p}_{-i}$ is the vector of prices in Southern countries other than i. With no parallel trade, each country affects world innovation in proportion to the size of its market. In a symmetric equilibrium, $p_i = p_S$ for all i, so $v^{\text{ne}} = T\left[M_S\pi(p_S) + M_N\pi\left(p_m\right)\right]$. Combining, as we have done before, gives

$$\frac{\beta}{1-\beta}\left[C(p_S) + \left(\frac{\bar{T}-T}{T}\right)C_C\right]\left[\frac{\pi'\left(p_S\right)}{x(p_S)}\right] = n_S[\pi(p_S) + m\pi(p_m)], \tag{17}$$

which is analogous to (9). The p_S^{ne} curve implicit in (17) again is downward sloping as a function of m and becomes horizontal at c. But notice that the right-hand side of (17) increases with n_S; this captures the declining influence of each Southern country on the world rate of innovation as the typical such country becomes smaller. An increase in n_S shifts the downward-sloping portion of the p_S^{ne} curve downward, and of course results in an intersection with c at a smaller value of m. This is shown in Figure 4, where the bold curves represent a case with $n_S > 1$ and the dotted curves apply for $n_S = 1$ and are reproduced from Figure 1 for reference.

Now suppose that the North instead practices international exhaustion of IPR. We first determine $\tilde{p}_i$, the critical price ceiling for country i at which the Northern monopolists are indifferent between supplying country i with innovative products and not, considering the arbitrage that results. We are looking for a symmetric equilibrium among the Southern countries; in such an equilibrium, $\tilde{p}_i = \tilde{p}$ for all i.

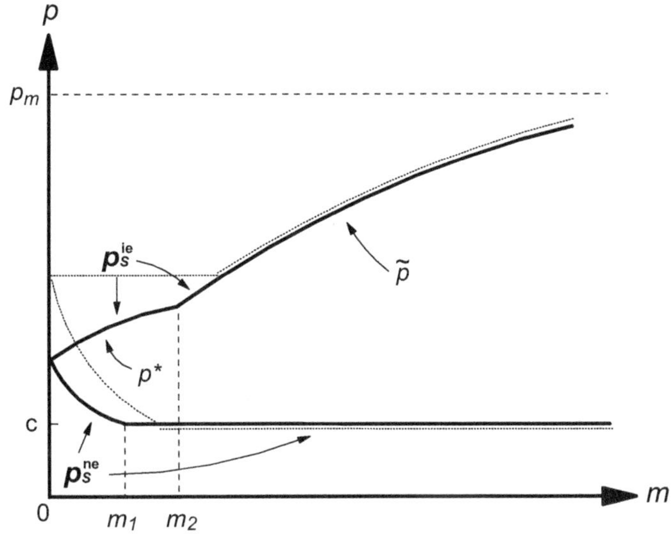

Figure 4. Price ceilings with several southern countries.

We will show that $\tilde{p}$ is the solution to

$$(M_S + M_N)\,\pi\,(\tilde{p}) = M_N\pi(p_m);$$

i.e. $\tilde{p}$ is independent of the number of countries in the South and has the same value as before.

To see this, notice first that if all Southern countries set a price ceiling above $\tilde{p}$, the Northern firms prefer to serve all of them to serve none (or some) of them, even considering the erosion of profits in the North that results from arbitrage. But if all Southern countries set a price below $\tilde{p}$, the Northern firms prefer to serve none than to serve some or all of them. They can extinguish supply to the South and the resulting arbitrage activity by charging the monopoly price p_M worldwide. Finally, and most relevantly, suppose that all countries in the South except country i set a price ceiling of $\tilde{p}$. Will country i be served if it sets a lower ceiling? If it does so, then i will have the lowest price and, by arbitrage, the price p_i will also prevail in the North. The other Southern countries have national exhaustion, so they will continue to pay $\tilde{p}$. By serving country i at price p_i and the remaining Southern countries at $\tilde{p}$, a Northern firm earns

$$(m_S + M_N)\,\pi(p_i) + (n_S - 1)\,\pi\left(\tilde{p}\right) < (M_S + M_N)\,\pi\left(\tilde{p}\right) = M_N \pi(p_m).$$

So the firm does better by serving none of the Southern countries than by serving some or all of them. In other words, if all Southern countries set a price ceiling of $\tilde{p}$, none has any incentive to lower its ceiling still further, because doing so would cause its market (and all others in the South) to be excluded from sales of innovative products.

Next we derive a new formula for p^*, the optimal price ceiling in a typical Southern country. We are looking for a symmetric equilibrium in which all Southern countries set p^*. But it must be a Nash equilibrium, which means that no Southern country has an incentive to deviate *when the other countries set* $p^* \geq \tilde{p}$. So, we assume that all Southern countries except i set $p^* \geq \tilde{p}$ as their price ceiling and examine a deviation by country i. When evaluated at p^*, such a deviation must not be profitable.

The tempting deviation for country i is to cut its price ceiling below p^*. If it does so, its price will be the lowest among all countries in the South and, by arbitrage, its price will also prevail in the North. But its price will not spill over to the other Southern countries, because, by assumption, these countries do not allow parallel imports. The trade-off facing country i is between the gain in consumer surplus that results from a lower price and the slowdown in innovation that occurs when firms earn lower profits in one Southern country *and in the North.* This trade-off is expressed in the marginal net benefit to country i from a small change in p_i, which is

$$\frac{d\phi_N}{dv}\frac{dv^{\text{ie}}}{dp_i}\left[TC\left(p_i\right) + \left(\bar{T} - T\right)C_c\right] - \phi_N T x(p_i).$$

The marginal profit change is $(M_N + m_s)\,\pi'(p_i)$ and so $dv^{\text{ie}}/dp_i = T\,(M_N + m_s)\,\pi'(p_i)$. Substituting, as before, and evaluating at $\mathbf{p}_{-i} = p_i = p^*$ (because the countries besides i choose p^* by assumption, and we are looking for a symmetric Nash equilibrium where country i also finds it optimal to set $p_i = p^*$) we find that the marginal net benefit vanishes when

$$\frac{\beta}{1-\beta}\left[C(p^*)+\left(\frac{\bar{T}-T}{T}\right)C_C\right]\left[\frac{\pi'(p^*)}{x(p^*)}\right]=\left[\frac{1+m}{\frac{1}{n_S}+m}\right]\pi(p^*). \quad (18)$$

Notice that this gives the same formula for p^* as (12) when $n_S = 1$ and that p^* is increasing in m when $n_S > 1$. An increase in the relative size of the North increases p^*, because each Southern country affects world innovation to an extent that depends on the share of the North plus one Southern market in a firm's global profits. As n_S rises, p^* falls. This again signifies the declining influence on innovation of the price ceiling in a typical Southern country as the number of countries grows. So the flat portion of p_S^{ie} falls, and of course, $\tilde{p} > p$ for a wider range of m's. Finally, note that when $m = 0$, the formula for p^* and for p_S^{ne} are the same. So the p_S^{ne} and p_S^{ie} curves continue to emanate from the same point; see Figure 4.

The figure shows that the Southern countries set higher price ceilings and accept lower consumer surplus when the North allows parallel imports than when it prohibits such trade, no matter how many countries are located in the South. There are two parts to the explanation for this finding. First, with international exhaustion of IPR in the North, each Southern country must set a price ceiling of at least $\tilde{p}$ (which is always greater than c) in order to ensure that Northern firms are willing to supply its market despite the arbitrage that occurs. In contrast, when national exhaustion of IPR prevails in the North, the only constraint on the price ceiling in a Southern country is that it must not fall below the marginal cost c at which goods are produced. Second, with national exhaustion of IPR in the North, the policies in a small Southern country have limited impact on innovation, because firms earn a small (perhaps tiny) share of their profits there. With international exhaustion of IPR, the incentives facing a Southern government bite when its price ceiling is the lowest among all Southern countries, in which case its policies determine the price not only in its own small market, *but also in the North.* Therefore, each country's potential influence over world innovation remains vital even as its own market becomes small.

We shall not repeat the remaining analysis of Section 3. Suffice it to say that a variant of Lemma 1 continues to hold under the same Condition 1.[27] That is, if Southern countries do not allow parallel imports, a patent holder earns greater aggregate profits when the North practices international exhaustion of IPR and the Southern countries set the price ceiling p^* defined in (18) than when the North practices national exhaustion of IPR and the Southern countries set their price ceilings at $p_S^{\text{ne}} > c$. Also, Proposition 2 applies with any number of countries in the South; with national exhaustion of IPR throughout the South, the North fares better by allowing parallel imports than by prohibiting them. Again, the key is the different behavior of the Southern governments under the alternative parallel trade regimes in the North. When the North practices international exhaustion of IPR, the countries in the South set higher price ceilings than under national exhaustion, which in turn leads to aggregate profits that are at least as high for Northern firms and innovation that is at least as fast. Since arbitrage delivers lower prices and greater consumer surplus in the North, $W_N^{\text{ie}} > W_N^{\text{ne}}$ no matter what is the size of a typical country in the South.

Note finally that the same conclusion applies in the limit, as the number of countries in the South grows large. With a continuum of small Southern countries, national exhaustion of IPR in the North leads the Southern countries to set a price ceiling of $p_S^{\text{ne}} = c$. International exhaustion of IPR in the North leads the Southern countries to set a price ceiling of $p_S^{\text{ie}} = \tilde{p}$.[28] By the definition of $\tilde{p}$, aggregate profits per firm equal $M_N \pi(p_M)$ in either case, which means that the value of patent and the rate of innovation are the same in either case. But the North enjoys greater

[27]The proof parallels that in Appendix A, except that now $k \equiv -n_S \pi'(p^*)/\Omega'(p^*)$, $\hat{\Omega}(p) \equiv k\left[\Omega(p)/n_S - \pi\left(p^*\right)\right]$, and $\hat{\pi}(p) \equiv \pi(p^*) - \pi(p)$. A detailed proof is available from the authors upon request.

[28]To make this statement, we need to show that $p^* < \tilde{p}$ for all $m > 0$ as n_S tends to infinity. First we note that $p^* = \tilde{p} = c$ when $m = 0$. By totally differentiating the implicit definitions for $\tilde{p}$ and p^* that apply as $n_S \to \infty$, we find that $d\tilde{p}/dm > dp^*/dm$ for all m. It follows that $\tilde{p} > p^*$ for $m > 0$.

consumer surplus at the lower price of $\tilde{p}$ that prevails with parallel imports than at the higher price of p_M that prevails without them.

5.2 International exhaustion of IPR in the south

The argument is simpler and more straightforward when the various countries in the South all permit parallel imports. Consider the choice of price ceilings by the Southern governments when the South practices international exhaustion of IPR and the North does not. Again we look for a symmetric equilibrium in which all Southern governments choose the price ceiling p_S^{ne}. Starting from a situation in which all but one of the Southern countries sets their ceilings at some p_S, the policy in the remaining country i will affect prices and allocations if and only if $p_i \leq p_S$; otherwise, parallel imports from the other Southern countries will make the choice of a high price ceiling by country i irrelevant. But if $p_i \leq p_S$, a marginal change in policy by country i will affect prices *in all countries in the South.* Therefore, the influence of country i on world innovation is exactly the same in these circumstances as would be the case if the South were one large country. It follows that the optimal choice of price ceiling for country i is the same as with one Southern country; the implicit formula for p_S^{ne} in a symmetric Nash equilibrium is given by equation (9).

Now suppose that the North permits parallel imports, so that international exhaustion of IPR prevails worldwide. It should be apparent that $\tilde{p}$ — the minimum price ceiling in a Southern country that allows for positive consumption — is the same as before. If all Southern countries but country i set a ceiling of $\tilde{p}$ as given in (10), and i sets its ceiling at $p_i < \tilde{p}$, a producer of innovative products earns higher profits by selling only in the North at the monopoly price p_M than by selling worldwide at the common (due to arbitrage) price p_i. Moreover, the price ceiling p^* that prevails in a symmetric equilibrium when m is not too large also is the same as when there is only one country in the South. If all Southern countries other than country i were to set the p^* given by (11) as their maximum price, a lower ceiling of $p_i < p^*$ would generate a world price of p_i in all markets via parallel trade, and thus would lead to lower welfare for country i than if it set a ceiling of p^*. And if all countries other than country i were to set a common price ceiling above the p^* given by (11), the best response for country i would be to set a ceiling of p^*.

In short, with tolerance of parallel imports throughout the South, the outcomes based on what the North chooses as its parallel trade regime are the same in any symmetric equilibrium as those that would arise were the South to be a single, unified country. Each Southern country's choice of price ceiling matters only when it is the lowest one, and when that is the case the policy determines prices and profit opportunities throughout the region. It follows from the analysis in Section 3 that the North fares better by allowing parallel imports than by forbidding such imports when the South uniformly practices international exhaustion of IPR, just as when it practices national exhaustion. Evidently, our results do not require that the number of countries in the South be small.

6 Conclusions

Many countries impose price controls on pharmaceutical products to hold down the cost of medicine to national health plans and local consumers. Such controls have generated sizable differences in the prices of similar drugs in different countries. The price gaps in turn create incentives for arbitrage in the form of "re-importation" or parallel trade.

Current trade rules leave the legality of such trade in the hands of the importing country. In many of these countries, the question as to whether intellectual property rights should be exhausted nationally or internationally has been highly controversial. Consumer advocates argue for parallel importation as means to temper monopoly pricing, while the pharmaceutical lobby points to the adverse effects of price controls on the returns to research. By allowing parallel imports, they claim, a country would import its trade partner's price controls and thereby undermine intellectual property and dampen incentives for innovation.

In this chapter, we have examined the welfare economics of parallel trade in a setting in which such trade is motivated by differential price controls. Our analytical framework is one in which the protection of IPR creates a static distortion due to monopoly pricing, but provides incentives for ongoing innovation. Our analysis takes off from the observation that governments face different incentives for regulating prices when parallel imports are allowed by their trade partners than when they are not. Therefore, an evaluation of the costs and benefits of allowing parallel imports should incorporate the indirect effects of the trade regime on the level of foreign price controls.

We considered a two-country world in which product development is highly (or entirely) concentrated in one country ("North") and compared outcomes when this country practices international versus national exhaustion of its patent rights. We found that the less innovative country ("South") always sets a more lenient price ceiling in the former regime than the latter. In other words, the prospect of arbitrage induces the low-price country to accept higher prices than otherwise. This is because arbitrage forces the country to export its price controls and so impedes its ability to free-ride on the research incentives provided by its trade partner This prediction of the model is consistent with the observation by Kanavos and Costa-Font (2005) that the growth of parallel trade in Europe has been accompanied by a relaxation of price controls in low-price countries such as Portugal, Italy and France, which now tolerate prices closer to European averages than they did before.

We first considered a setting in which South does no R&D and North imposes no price controls. We provided a sufficient condition under which global profit flows per patent, the value of a patent, and the pace of innovation are higher when North allows parallel imports than when it does not. Since reimportation also reduces prices in North, this country enjoys both higher surplus per product and greater product variety when it tolerates parallel trade. In contrast, the legalization of parallel imports by North spells a welfare loss for South, where the pain of higher prices outweighs the gain of faster innovation. We showed that our sufficient condition is satisfied by all linear and constant-elasticity demand functions.

Relaxing our assumptions of no Southern innovation and no Northern price regulation introduced some caveats but did not alter the gist of our conclusions. With positive but limited innovation in South, North still fares better by allowing parallel imports to cross its borders. When both countries impose price ceilings non-cooperatively in a world without parallel trade, a switch in trade regime again raises the return to R&D. However, in this case, faster innovation may come at the expense of higher drug prices in both countries.

Our results also extend to situations with several or many countries in the South. We examined symmetric equilibria in a model with multiple, identical Southern countries. We considered both the possibility that these countries tolerate parallel imports and the possibility that they do not. In either case, the North fares better by allowing parallel imports than by prohibiting them. Even a small Southern country has incentive to set a reasonable price ceiling when the North is open to parallel trade, because its policy influence extends via arbitrage to the large market of the North and because doing otherwise might lead Northern firms to set prices that preclude sales to its (small) market.

Lobbies for pharmaceutical firms have vigorously encouraged their trade authorities to negotiate the relaxation or elimination of foreign price controls. Our analysis suggests that legalizing the reimportation of prescription medicines, perhaps paradoxically, might further their cause.

Appendix

A. Proof of Lemma 1

Define $k \equiv -\pi'(p^*)/\Omega'(p^*)$, $\hat{\Omega}(p) \equiv k\,[\Omega(p) - \pi(p^*)]$, and $\hat{\pi}(p) \equiv \pi(p^*) - \pi(p)$. Note that $\hat{\Omega}(p^*) = \hat{\pi}(p^*) = 0$ and $\hat{\Omega}'(p^*) = \hat{\pi}'(p^*) = -\pi'(p^*)$. Thus, $\hat{\Omega}(p)$ and $\hat{\pi}(p)$ are tangent at $p = p^*$. Note too that $\hat{\pi}''(p) = -\pi''(p) > 0$, while $\hat{\Omega}''(p) = \Omega''(p) \gtrless 0$. If Condition 1 is satisfied, then $\hat{\Omega}(p) \leq \hat{\pi}(p)$ for all $p \in [c, p_m]$, with equality only at $p = p^*$.

Suppose Condition 1 is satisfied. Then

$$k\left[\Omega(p) - \pi(p^*)\right] \leq \pi(p^*) - \pi(p),$$

with equality only at $p = p^*$. Therefore

$$k\left[\Omega(p_S^{\mathrm{ne}}) - \pi(p^*)\right] < \pi(p^*) - \pi(p_S^{\mathrm{ne}}) \tag{A1}$$

and

$$k\left[\Omega(p_M) - \pi(p^*)\right] < \pi(p^*) - \pi(p_M). \tag{A2}$$

But $\Omega(p_M) = 0$, which, with (A1) and (A2), implies

$$\frac{\pi(p^*) - \pi(p_S^{\mathrm{ne}})}{\pi(p_M) - \pi(p^*)} > \frac{\Omega(p_S^{\mathrm{ne}}) - \pi(p^*)}{\pi(p^*)}.$$

This in turn implies

$$\frac{\Omega(p_S^{\mathrm{ne}}) - \pi(p_S^{\mathrm{ne}})}{\pi(p_M)} > \frac{\Omega(p_S^{\mathrm{ne}}) - \pi(p^*)}{\pi(p^*)}.$$

Recognizing that the left-hand side of this inequality is equal to m, we have

$$(m+1)\pi(p^*) > \Omega(p_S^{\mathrm{ne}}) = m\pi(p_M) + \pi(p_S^{\mathrm{ne}}).$$

B. Proof of Proposition 5

We distinguish five cases.

(i) $p^* > p_N^{\mathrm{ne}}$
Since $p_S^{\mathrm{ie}} \geq p^* > p_S^{\mathrm{ne}}$, $(m+1)\pi(p_S^{\mathrm{ie}}) \geq (m+1)\pi(p^*) > m\left(\pi p_N^{\mathrm{ne}}\right) + \pi(p_S^{\mathrm{ne}})$.

(ii) $p_N^{\mathrm{ne}} > p_S^{\mathrm{ie}} = p^* \geq \tilde{p}$ and $p_S^{\mathrm{ne}} > c$

Define k, $\hat{\Omega}(p)$ and $\hat{\pi}(p)$ as in the proof of Lemma 1. We have seen there that if Condition 1 is satisfied,

$$k\left[\Omega(p) - \pi(p^*)\right] \leq \pi(p^*) - \pi(p)$$

for all $p \in [c, p_M]$, with equality only at $p = p^*$. Therefore

$$k[\Omega(p_N^{\text{ne}}) - \pi(p^*)] < \pi(p^*) - \pi(p_N^{\text{ne}}). \tag{B1}$$

Since $\Omega(p_N^{\text{ne}}) > 0$, (A1) and (B1) imply

$$\frac{\pi(p^*) - \pi(p_S^{\text{ne}})}{\pi(p_N^{\text{ne}}) - \pi(p^*)} > \frac{\Omega(p_S^{\text{ne}}) - \pi(p^*)}{\pi(p^*) - \Omega(p_N^{\text{ne}})} > \frac{\Omega(p_S^{\text{ne}}) - \pi(p^*)}{\pi(p^*)}.$$

This in turn implies

$$\frac{\Omega(p_S^{\text{ne}}) - \pi(p_S)}{\pi(p_N^{\text{ne}})} > \frac{\Omega(p_S^{\text{ne}}) - \pi(p^*)}{\pi(p^*)}.$$

Recognizing that the left-hand side of this inequality is equal to m, we have

$$(m+1)\pi(p_S^{\text{ie}}) = (m+1)\pi(p^*) > \Omega(p_S^{\text{ne}}) = m\pi\,(p_N^{\text{ne}}) + \pi(p_S^{\text{ne}}).$$

(iii) $p_S^{\text{ie}} = \min[\tilde{p}, p_N^*]$ and $p_S^{\text{ne}} > c$
In part (ii) we established that Condition 1 ensures $(m+1)$ $\pi(p^*) > m\pi(p_N^{\text{ne}}) + \pi(p_S^{\text{ne}})$. Here, $\tilde{p} > p^*$ and $p_N^* > p^*$, so $p_s^{\text{ie}} > p^*$. Therefore, $(m+1)\pi(p_S^{\text{ie}}) > m\,\pi(p_N^{\text{ne}}) + \pi(p_S^{\text{ne}})$.

(iv) $p_S^{\text{ie}} = p^* < p_N^{\text{ne}}$ and $p_S^{\text{ne}} = c$
The fact that $p_S^{\text{ie}} \geq \tilde{p}$ implies $(m+1)\pi(p_s^{\text{ie}}) \geq m\pi(p_M) > m\pi(p_N^{\text{ne}}) = m\pi(p_N^{\text{ne}}) + \pi(p_S^{\text{ne}})$.

(v) $p_S^{\text{ie}} = \max[\tilde{p}, p_N^*]$ and $p_S^{\text{ne}} = c$

(a) Suppose that $\tilde{p} \geq p_S^{\text{ie}} = p_N^*$. Note that $p_N^* > p_N^{\text{ne}}$. Therefore $(m+1)\pi(p_S^{\text{ie}}) \geq m\pi(p_S^{\text{ie}}) \geq m\pi(p_N^*) > m\pi(p_N^{\text{ne}}) = m\pi(p_N^{\text{ne}}) + \pi(p_S^{\text{ne}})$.

(b) Suppose that $p_N^* \geq p_S^{\text{ie}} = \tilde{p}$. Then $(m+1)\pi(p_S^{\text{ie}}) = (m+1)$ $\pi(\tilde{p}) = m\pi(p_M) > m\pi(p_N^{\text{ne}}) = m\pi(p_N^{\text{ne}}) + \pi(p_S^{\text{ne}})$.

Acknowledgment

The authors are grateful to the U.S. National Science Foundation (Grant Nos. SES 0211748 and SES 0451712), the Hong Kong Research Grants Council (Project No. CityU 1476/05H), the Department of Economics and Finance at City University of Hong Kong, and the International Economics Section at Princeton University for financial support. We thank Pol Antràs, Joan Costa-Font, Joseph Harrington, Stefan Szymanski, Tommaso Valletti and two anonymous referees for comments on an earlier draft. Any opinions, findings, and conclusions or recommendations expressed in this paper are those of the authors and do not necessarily reflect the views of the National Science Foundation or any other organization.

References

Arfwedson, J. (2004). *Re-importation (Parallel Trade) in Pharmaceuticals*, Institute for Policy Innovation Policy Report 182, IPI Center for Technology Freedom.

Barfield, C. E. and Groombridge, M. A. (1998). The economic case for copyright and owner control over parallel imports, *The Journal of World Intellectual Property* 1, 903–939.

Barfield, C. E. and Groombridge, M. A. (1999). Parallel trade in the pharmaceutical industry: Implications for innovation, consumer welfare, and health policy, *Fordham Intellectual Property, Media & Entertainment Law Journal* 10, 185–265.

Cambridge Pharma Consultancy (2004). *Pricing and Reimbursement Review 2003*, Cambridge UK: IMS Health — Management Consulting.

Chard, J. S. and Mellor, C. J. (1989). Intellectual property rights and parallel imports, *The World Economy* 12, 69–83.

Danzon, P. M. (1997). *Pharmaceutical Price Regulation*, Washington, D.C.: The American Enterprise Institute Press.

Danzon, P. M. (1998). The economics of parallel trade, *PharmacoEconomics* 13, 293–304.

Danzon, P. M. And Towse, A. (2003). Differential pricing for pharmaceuticals: Reconciling access, R&D and patents, *International Journal of Health Care Finance and Economics* 3, 183–205.

Ganslandt, M. and Maskus, K. E. (2004). The price impact of parallel imports in pharmaceuticals: Evidence from the European Union, *Journal of Health Economics* 23, 1035–1057.

Grossman, G. M. and Lai, E. L.-C. (2004). International protection of intellectual property, *American Economic Review* 94, 1635–1653.

Kanavos, P. and Costa-Font, J. (2005). Pharmaceutical parallel trade in Europe: Stakeholder and competition effects, *Economic Policy* 44, 751–798.

Li, C. and Maskus, K. E. (2006). The impact of parallel imports on investment in cost-reducing research and development, *Journal of International Economics* 68(2), 443–455.

Malueg, D. A. and Schwartz, M. (1994). Parallel imports, demand dispersion, and international price discrimination, *Journal of International Economics* 37, 167–196.

Maskus, K. E. (2000a). *Intellectual Property Rights in the Global Economy,* Washington, D.C.: The Institute for International Economics.

Maskus, K. E. (2000b). Parallel imports, *The World Economy* 23, 1269–1284.

Maskus, K. E. (2001). *Parallel Imports in Pharmaceuticals: Implications for Competition and Prices in Developing Countries*, Final Report to the World Intellectual Property Organization, Geneva.

Pecorino, P. (2002). Should the US allow prescription drug reimports from Canada, *Journal of Health Economics* 21, 699–708.

Rey, P. (2003). *The Impact of Parallel Imports on Prescription Medicines*, Manuscript, University of Toulouse.

Szymanski, S. and Valletti, T. (2005). Parallel trade, price discrimination, investment, and price caps, *Economic Policy* 44, 705–749.

Valletti, T. M. (2006). Differential pricing, parallel trade, and the incentive to invest, *Journal of International Economics*, 70(1), 314–324.

Chapter 12

An Economic Model of Patent Exhaustion*

Abstract
The doctrine of patent exhaustion implies that the authorized sale of patented goods "exhausts" the patent rights in the goods sold and precludes additional license fees from downstream buyers. Courts have considered absolute exhaustion, in which the patent owner forfeits all rights upon an authorized sale, and presumptive exhaustion, in which the patent owner may opt-out of exhaustion via contract. This chapter offers the first economic model of domestic patent exhaustion that incorporates transaction costs in licensing downstream buyers and considers how the shift from absolute to presumptive exhaustion affects social welfare. We show that when transaction costs are high, the patent owner has no incentive to individually license downstream users, and absolute and presumptive exhaustion regimes are equivalent. But when transaction costs are at the intermediate level, the patent owner engages in mixed licensing, individually licensing high-valuation buyers and uniformly licensing low-valuation buyers. In this case, absolute exhaustion is socially optimal. Presumptive exhaustion is

---

*By Olena Ivus, Edwin L.-C. Lai and Ted Sichelman. Originally published in *Journal of Economics and Management Strategy*, 29(4) (Winter, 2020), pp. 816–833. Copyright © 2020 by Wiley Periodicals LLC. It has been reprinted with revisions and permission from the original publisher.

socially optimal when social benefits from buyer-specific pricing outweigh social costs from transaction cost frictions in individualized licensing, which requires sufficiently low transaction costs.

1 Introduction

Within the United States, the judge-made doctrine of "patent exhaustion" (sometimes termed the "first-sale" doctrine) implies that authorized sales of patented goods — e.g. by a manufacturer directly authorized by the patent owner — "exhausts" any rights of the upstream patent owner to seek payment from downstream buyers. However, in some instances, upstream patent owners attempt to contractually restrict downstream buyers — for example, prohibiting resale of the good — in order to preserve their right to collect additional license fees. Whether and under what circumstances such downstream contractual restrictions can overcome the doctrine of patent exhaustion has been the subject of many conflicting, and often vague, judicial decisions over the past century. The legal literature has qualitatively examined the arguments for and against absolute patent exhaustion, but the qualitative literature provides no clear framework to resolve the issue of whether absolute exhaustion increases or decreases overall welfare. In the economics literature, several scholars have examined the exhaustion doctrine in the international context but surprisingly, very few have advanced a formal model of domestic patent exhaustion.

This chapter offers the first economic model of domestic patent exhaustion that incorporates transaction costs in buyer-specific patent licensing, and also allows for two types of licensing of buyers by the patent owner — *individualized licensing* (buyer-specific) directly from the patent owner and *uniform licensing* via the manufacturer. In this context, we examine how a shift in domestic patent policy from absolute to presumptive exhaustion (which presumes exhaustion but allows the patent owner to opt-out via contract) affects social welfare.[1]

[1] Although we refer to patents here, our model is also applicable to exhaustion in the copyright context.

Our model is motivated by a transactional structure common in the high-technology industries addressed by the US Supreme Court in the patent exhaustion case of *Quanta Computer, Inc. v. LG Electronics, Inc.* (2008), which we discuss further below. In our stylized model of this transactional structure, there exists one patented component of a complex product. In order for a manufacturer to produce the good, it must enter into a license with the patent owner. We assume the patent provides market power to the patent owner, which in turn selects one of many competitive manufacturers to produce and sell the good. The patent owner thus licenses the component to only one manufacturer, making the manufacturer a monopolist in the market for the good.[2] Buyers differ in their willingness to pay for the good. Note that "buyers" are often themselves downstream manufacturers of their own complex product.[3] The price a buyer is charged depends on the regime of patent exhaustion.

Under absolute exhaustion (Regime AE), when the manufacturer sells the good to the buyer, the patent owner loses all rights to proceed against the buyer for patent infringement. Under presumptive exhaustion (Regime PE), the patent owner may opt out of exhaustion by imposing contractual restrictions on the buyer, in which case the buyer must enter into a license with the patent owner or risk patent infringement. We allow for two types of licensing of buyers in Regime PE — individualized and uniform — and assume that a license from the patent owner (of either type) provides the buyer with a right to use the good but not to resell it.[4] Precluding resale

[2]The patent owner will be able to extract all rents from the manufacturer when the patent owner has a monopoly position via the patent and there is a competitive manufacturing market.

[3]In the case of a downstream computer manufacturer (e.g. Dell) purchasing patented components from an upstream manufacturer of computer parts (e.g. Intel), our model would treat Dell as the "buyer" and Intel as the "manufacturer".

[4]These assumptions are consistent with the real-world practice of downstream patent licensing in a regime of presumptive exhaustion. Legally, there is no need to directly license buyers to impose downstream restrictions, and the cost of adding such restrictions in a license (of either type) is negligible.

in Regime PE implies arbitrage will not occur, and the patent owner and manufacturer can price discriminate between buyers in the first degree. Regime AE, by contrast, prevents contractual restrictions on buyers and as such, allows resale; consequently, pricing is uniform.[5] Importantly, we allow for a positive transaction cost in individualized licensing, which increases the unit cost of producing the final good for those who are licensed individually. This transaction cost is critical in determining the social welfare implications of patent exhaustion. It includes the time and effort involved in negotiating license fees and executing separate licensing agreements with individual buyers.[6]

The size of the transaction cost affects the patent owner's optimal licensing scheme in Regime PE. When the transaction cost is positive but not excessively high, the patent owner will engage in *mixed licensing*, individually licensing high-valuation buyers and uniformly licensing low-valuation buyers. Mixed licensing features a tradeoff between social benefits in the form of price discrimination and social costs generated by transaction cost frictions. Two insights, not recognized in the previous literature, arise. First, at intermediate levels of transaction costs, the patent owner does not fully internalize the social costs of licensing in its single-minded, private goal of rent maximization. Thus, when allowed to do so in Regime PE, the patent owner will succumb to the classic economic problem of rent dissipation, willing to burn up essentially all of a buyer's individual surplus in order to gain a penny of producer surplus. Secondly, at

---

[5]We discuss resale in more detail in Section 6. Also, we abstract away from the possibility that the patent owner enforces its licensing restrictions through a contract suit, which is not necessarily barred by absolute exhaustion, rather than a patent suit. As we explain in footnote 11, contractual suits are generally not as effective in these situations. To the extent contractual actions allow patent owners to "imperfectly" enforce downstream restrictions, our results would not change qualitatively, but the welfare effects of the exhaustion regimes would be less pronounced.

[6]We assume all parties know the buyer's type. We discuss information asymmetry in assessing the buyer's demand in Section 6.

sufficiently low levels of transaction costs, the patent owner's private incentive to maximize rents may lead to net social gains. Specifically, the ability of the patent owner to price discriminate implies that more buyers may gain access to the patented good than in Regime AE. In other words, while Regime PE burns up surplus in the transaction costs when the patent owner engages in individualized licensing, these costs may be worth the candle if enough additional producer surplus is generated and enough additional buyers gain access to the good. Our model shows that when transaction cost frictions are sufficiently low, presumptive exhaustion is optimal.

We briefly discuss extensions to our model in Section 6 and more formally discuss how to relax some of the assumptions in a supplementary online appendix.[7] In particular, we note that dynamic gains in promoting *ex ante* investment in product quality may outweigh any loss of static efficiency in Regime PE when the transaction cost is high. Regime PE is also more likely to dominate (in static terms) when licensing is via heterogeneous intermediaries (e.g. wholesalers, resellers), with each intermediary negotiating the license fees on behalf of a large number of buyers. But when there are information frictions, which act as an increase in transaction costs — such as information asymmetry in assessing the buyer's demand and search costs — Regime AE is more likely to dominate. Our results also hold qualitatively when we allow for a positive transaction cost in manufacturer licensing or substitutes for the patented component, consider goods comprising multiple patented components, or allow buyers to resell used patented products on a secondary market.

In the economics literature, Maskus and Chen (2004), Valletti (2006), Valletti and Szymanski (2006), Grossman and Lai (2008), and Saggi (2013, 2014) are valuable contributions that offer models of patent exhaustion. But these models are limited to parallel trade among countries and draw a distinction between the regimes of

[7] The supplementary online appendix can be found at the https://ssrn.com/abstract=3634038.

national and international exhaustion, under both of which the exhaustion is absolute. This is in contrast to recent legal decisions and case comments, which focused on the distinction between absolute and presumptive domestic exhaustion. Furthermore, the effects of international exhaustion cannot be easily adapted to the domestic context.[8]

Only one paper, Layne-Farrar *et al.* (2014), formally models domestic patent exhaustion. In that model, a patent owner can grant a license to an upstream manufacturer and, if absolute patent exhaustion does not apply, also to a downstream manufacturer. The model focuses on royalty allocation among the three parties but abstracts away from the issue of transaction costs in downstream licensing, which is a critical feature of our model.

Although the previous literature recognized that absolute exhaustion and presumptive exhaustion are equivalent when transaction costs are so prohibitive that there is no incentive for the patent owner to engage in downstream licensing, it did not describe the shift from prohibitive to intermediate to low levels of transaction costs (e.g. Layne-Farrar *et al.*, 2014). Rather, some scholars focused on how exhaustion solves the problem of rent dissipation burning up transaction costs (e.g. Mulligan, 2013), while others criticized exhaustion for preventing socially beneficial price discrimination (e.g. Kieff, 2018). No previous scholar has provided the means of determining, as our model does, when one of these competing interests dominates the other.

This paper's contribution to the literature is threefold. First is the modeling contribution. We offer the first economic model of domestic patent exhaustion that incorporates transaction costs in downstream licensing, an issue that has caused ongoing, unresolved debate in the legal literature. Our framework is rigorous yet simple and can be easily extended to study other aspects of patent exhaustion. Second, we identify the reasons why transaction costs place a wedge

[8]Brown and Norman (2003) discusses domestic exhaustion, but merely in the context of international trade.

between private and social welfare. The third major contribution is our detailed formal study of domestic exhaustion, particularly the distinction between absolute and presumptive exhaustion. This distinction has been the focus of recent legal decisions and qualitative scholarship, but — with the exception of Layne-Farrar *et al.* (2014) — has not been presented in the economic literature. We seek to bring the two strands of literature together to provide a formal model, with a variety of extensions.

The rest of the chapter proceeds as follows. Section 2 briefly provides a background on the doctrine of exhaustion. Section 3 sets up our model and outlines the patent exhaustion regimes. Section 4 solves for the equilibrium prices and license fees under each of the regimes, and Section 5 examines social welfare. Section 6 discusses extensions to our model, and Section 7 discusses the implications for policy. Section 8 concludes.

2 Background on the Doctrine of Exhaustion

So far in the US, the exhaustion doctrine's application and scope has been determined by case law. Despite many Supreme Court and lower court decisions, as of the mid-2000s, legal academics and practitioners were quite uncertain as to whether absolute or presumptive exhaustion should apply, with many seemingly conflicting opinions in the lower courts. To resolve this critical issue, the Supreme Court granted certiorari in *Quanta Computer, Inc. v. LG Electronics, Inc.* (2008). Here, the US Supreme Court examined the exhaustion doctrine in the context of computer microprocessors and memory. LG Electronics owned patents covering specific aspects of computer memory. LG licensed Intel, a manufacturer of computer chips, but in its license agreement to Intel, expressly reserved a license to any third party that sought to combine Intel products with its own or other third party products. For instance, if the license agreement were interpreted at face value, it would prevent Dell from combining its or other third party components with Intel's chips in order to manufacture a computer for sale to end-consumers, absent a separate, individualized license from LG, the patent owner, to Dell.

Given the prevalence of the form of transaction structure in the *Quanta v. LG*, we base our economic model on the facts in this case. As in our model, there is a single owner with market power (LG), which licenses manufacturers such as Intel.[9] The manufacturer, Intel, sells patented components to buyers, which are typically downstream manufacturers, such as Dell, Lenovo, and Asus, for use in a complex product, such as a computer. In Regime AE, assuming Intel's sale is authorized, Dell, Lenovo, and Asus can use Intel's chips — including reselling them to each other — without having to fear a patent suit from LG. In other words, absolute exhaustion trumps whatever ostensible restrictions were imposed on the use of the chips through the provision in LG's license to Intel precluding downstream third parties from combining Intel chips with third-party components. Knowing that buyers can resell the chips to one another — which for chips is relatively costless compared to the value of the chip — Intel will set a uniform price for the chip that reflects the maximum producer surplus it can earn from the buyers. LG will then extract some or all of that surplus through a licensing fee charged to Intel, based on the level of its market power enabled by its patents.

In contrast, in Regime PE, LG's licensing restrictions, if properly drafted, would preclude Dell, Lenovo, and Asus from using Intel's chips to manufacture computers unless each of these manufacturers entered into a separate license with LG. Because LG could impose restrictions in such a license on reselling the Intel chips to other manufacturers, LG could price discriminate among the buyers by charging different licensing rates based on each buyer's willingness to pay, as long as the transaction costs of such individualized licensing were less than the gain to LG. Indeed, given the ability to price discriminate in Regime PE, LG could reduce its license fee to Intel, which might cause Intel to reduce its chip prices in order to increase

[9]For simplicity, as noted earlier, we assume the patent owner has full monopoly power and there is a single manufacturer, but we examine the implications of relaxing these assumptions in Section 6.

overall sales by identifying new buyers (e.g. Acer) that were not able to afford the chips in Regime AE.

Yet, the Supreme Court never decided whether absolute or presumptive exhaustion applies in the *Quanta* case, because it essentially found that LG did not properly draft its licensing restrictions, mooting the issue. In other words, because LG's licensing restrictions were not properly drafted, Intel's sales were both authorized and without restriction as to its customers combining Intel chips with their own or third-party components. Although the court reaffirmed that exhaustion applies to domestic sales and held that patent exhaustion is triggered by, among other things, an authorized sale of a component that "substantially embodies" the patent in question — even if it does not completely practice the patent — the Supreme Court's decision did little to dispel the confusion about what constitutes "authorization" or whether a patent owner can impose contractual restrictions on downstream buyers to limit patent exhaustion.

The Supreme Court once again considered exhaustion in *Bowman v. Monsanto* (2013), with the unusual facts of whether the sale of a patented soybean seed to a farmer exhausts the right to essentially identical seeds generated by the soybean plant itself. Specifically, Bowman purchased the patented soybean seeds, subject to the contractual restriction that he not save and use any of the seeds produced by the soybean plant grown from the patented seeds. Rather than deciding whether absolute or presumptive exhaustion applies in this situation, the Court simply reiterated the longstanding rule that "the exhaustion doctrine does not extend to the right to "make" a new product". Because Bowman was essentially making a new product from the original seeds, exhaustion did not apply, and Monsanto's licensing restrictions were effective.

Finally, in *Lexmark Int'l, Inc. v. Impression Products, Inc.* (2017), the Supreme Court decided that absolute exhaustion applies to all authorized sales or products covered by US patents. Lexmark sold its printer cartridges under two pricing options: a "regular cartridge" at "list price" and a "return program cartridge" at a discount. The sale of the return program cartridge was accompanied by post-sale contractual restrictions that the cartridge was not to be reused or resold, whereas the regular cartridges could be freely reused or resold. In violation of these restrictions, Impression acquired used return program cartridges from Lexmark's customers within and outside the US and then altered and resold the cartridges in the US, undermining Lexmark's ability to implement differential pricing.[10]

Two key questions were presented in *Lexmark* regarding the scope of the patent exhaustion doctrine. First, whether the doctrine of absolute exhaustion applies to end Lexmark's patent rights upon its authorized sale of the cartridges to its customers, or whether presumptive exhaustion applies so that Lexmark's contractual restrictions on the cartridge's reuse and resale override the exhaustion doctrine and may be effectively enforced through a patent infringement lawsuit. Second, whether Lexmark exhausted its patent rights by selling its cartridges *outside* of the US, so that Impression can import the cartridges into the US and resell without being liable for patent infringement (so-called "international exhaustion").

The economic importance of these legal issues is underscored by the very large number of major companies that filed over forty amicus briefs at the Supreme Court. Intel, LG Electronics, Samsung, eBay, Amazon and other firms that rely on numerous patent-protected inputs to the products they produce or sell opposed presumptive exhaustion. They argued that allowing upstream patent owners to impose downstream contractual restrictions would require

[10]The transaction structure in *Lexmark* is relatively uncommon, because most patented products cannot typically be rebuilt at a low cost and essentially sold again as new. Rather, most patented products are either immediately consumed and "wasted" to zero value (e.g. pharmaceutical drugs) or the value is diminished very quickly and cannot be easily restored (e.g. computer chips). Although there is often a secondary, "used" market for the second class of patented goods by end-consumers, typically these resales do not have a large impact on the prices and royalties relating to the goods when sold anew. For these reasons, we ignore the *Lexmark*-style transaction and resale markets in this paper, though we extend our model to more general secondary, resale markets in the online appendix.

a downstream firm to "trace the patent rights of every component it purchases and then negotiate appropriate license arrangements with the component manufacturer (as well as any subcomponent manufacturer)". Such tracing and negotiation would in their view engender substantial transaction costs, diminishing the efficient distribution of patented goods. On the other side, the Pharmaceutical Research and Manufacturers of America (PhRMA), the Biotechnology Industry Organization (BIO), and the Intellectual Property Owners Association (IPO) opposed a broader scope of patent exhaustion. These organizations represent firms and individuals that depend substantially on patent rents and so not surprisingly, they argued that patent exhaustion should remain limited so as to allow firms to engage in domestic and geographical price discrimination.

In May 2017, the Supreme Court ruled in Impression's favor, holding that (1) a patentee's decision to sell a product exhausts all of its patent rights in that item, regardless of any restrictions the patentee purports to impose; and (2) an authorized sale outside the US, just as one within the US, exhausts all rights under the Patent Act. With this decision, the Supreme Court overturned the Federal Circuit's ruling that upstream patent owners may opt out of patent exhaustion via contractual restrictions, and that patent rights are not exhausted by an authorized sale abroad (even where no reservation of rights accompanies the sale). This decision also contravened the US government's position that a foreign sale authorized by the US patentee should exhaust US patent rights by default unless the patentee expressly reserved those rights.[11]

[11] The Supreme Court's decision left open the possibility of contractual actions to enforce downstream restrictions. If a licensee has exceeded the limitations in a license agreement directly executed between the patent owner and the licensee, the patent owner may be able to assert a contract claim. Nonetheless, patent owners tend to favor patent claims. First, patent claims offer a wider array and scope of remedies, particularly injunctive relief; while contract claims usually afford no consequential or punitive damages. Also, patent cases are tried in federal courts with a relatively uniform body of nationwide law, which is often preferred to state courts, which may vary widely in applicable law. Finally, to enforce downstream restrictions in contract, "privity" — that is, some direct

A common justification for exhaustion found in judicial decisions and legal scholarship (e.g. Skladony, 2007) is that once the patent owner is paid by a licensee for the use of a patented good, it has no right to further payment. As the US Supreme Court stated in *Bloomer v. Millinger* (1863), patent owners "are entitled to but one royalty for a patented machine". However, such contentions are more conclusory than evincible. There is no *a priori* reason to assume a single license to an intermediate manufacturer, reseller, or purchaser is sufficient to induce optimal investment. Perhaps, as the Federal Circuit stated in *Mallinckrodt, Inc. v. Medipart, Inc.* (1992), the patent owner charges less than the full value available under the proper scope of the patent to each licensee, so that in effect there is no double counting. Another justification for exhaustion — and one heavily relied upon by the US Supreme Court in *Lexmark' Int'l, Inc. v. Impression Products, Inc.* (2017) — is the general aversion to restraints on alienation; namely, that it is economically efficient to allow the sale and transfer of goods (e.g. Carrier, 2004). Katz (2016), for instance, explains that exhaustion can eliminate supernormal pricing for patented goods and thereby reduce deadweight loss. Perzanowski and Schultz (2011) argues that exhaustion can reduce situations of buyer "lock in" and diminish switching costs, by allowing users to more easily switch to competing technologies. Exhaustion can also reduce the rent dissipation that may occur when the transaction costs of licensing are high (Mulligan, 2016) and prevent

contractual relationship between the parties — is required. In *Lexmark*, for example, Lexmark (the patent owner) could not assert a contractual claim against Impression (the alleged infringer), because Impression purchased the cartridges from the Lexmark's customers rather than Lexmark itself. Although a patent owner can attempt to impose a "nested" set of downstream contracts so as to ensure privity with downstream parties, achieving as much is not a certainty and it raises transaction costs. This is especially so if the contractual "intermediaries" between the patent owner and downstream resellers are ordinary customers, which patent owners are typically averse to sue because of negative repercussions in the marketplace. So it is not surprising that patent owners vigorously oppose any exhaustion of the patent rights underlying such claims, or that the matter of exhaustion is of such great importance to downstream resellers and users.

anticompetitive practices (e.g. tying, resale price maintenance, and exclusive dealing), which can be imposed on downstream licensees via contract and may not survive antitrust scrutiny (Hovenkamp, 2016).[12] A counterargument is that absolute exhaustion can reduce overall efficiency by precluding the typically efficiency-enhancing effects of freedom of contract, particularly when the contractual restraints are vertical in nature (Kieff, 2008; Hovenkamp, 2011; Katz, 2016).[13] In this regard, presumptive exhaustion allows for price discrimination, which may reduce deadweight loss and increase incentives to innovate. Also, while absolute exhaustion could alleviate the restraints on alienation concerns, other instruments (such as the patent misuse doctrine and the antitrust laws) are more suitable for the purpose.[14]

Against that background, it is clear that US patent exhaustion policy is a serious and contentious issue, which is of fundamental importance in numerous industries (e.g. pharmaceutical drugs, semiconductors, software) and carries with it significant consequences for trade and welfare, both domestic and abroad. Yet the actual policy implications of patent exhaustion are far from clear.

3 Model Set-up

Consider a closed economy in a country populated with L buyers. Assume there exists a good y that has quality h.

---

[12]Indeed, many of the judicial opinions addressing patent exhaustion arise in the context of downstream tying restrictions. In *Henry v. A.B. Dick Co.* (1912), the US Supreme Court upheld downstream licensing restrictions that required purchasers to use the patentee-manufacturer's patented mimeograph machine with its unpatented supplies. Just five years later, in *Motion Picture Patents Co. v. Universal Film Mfg. Co.* (1917), the Court overruled its holding in *A.B. Dick Co.* by finding that a similar downstream restriction was invalid.

[13]Unlike horizontal restraints, vertical restraints do not constrain direct competitors (Meurer, 2003).

[14]We abstract away from these anticompetitive issues here and address exhaustion doctrine's most basic concern: the ability of the downstream buyer to use or resell the patented good in the absence of a separate license from the patent owner.

Buyers have vertical preferences and differ in their type ϕ, which determines their willingness to pay for goods of a certain quality.[15] A buyer of a type $\phi > p/h$ purchases one unit of good y of quality h at a price p and earns utility (i.e. individual consumer surplus) of $U(\phi) = h\phi - p$. A buyer of a type $\phi < p/h$ does not purchase good y and earns utility of zero. We assume that ϕ is uniformly distributed over the interval $[0, 1]$. Given uniform price p, the quantity demanded q is linear and is given by the number of buyers who purchase good y:

$$q = L\int_{p/h}^{1} d\phi = L\left(1 - \frac{p}{h}\right). \tag{1}$$

The production of good y requires one differentiated component, x, which is patented by a third-party patent owner. The patent provides market power to the patent owner, as there are no substitutes for x.[16] Besides the component x, labor and materials are the only other inputs into the production of y. The per-unit cost of labor and materials is constant and equal to γ. The fixed cost of production of y is zero.

We assume that a potential manufacturer of y will obtain a license from the patent owner to make and sell component x as part of good y. This is because a manufacturer can accurately estimate the probability of losing a patent infringement suit and given litigation costs, it is less costly to negotiate a license *ex ante* rather than risk being sued for patent infringement. The manufacturer will pay a license fee of λ_m per unit of x plus a lump sum fee of $\bar{\lambda}$ to the patent owner.

Ex ante, there is a large number of identical potential manufacturers of good y competing for the use of x. This competition among potential manufactures *ex ante* allows the patent owner to adjust $\bar{\lambda}$

---

[15]The model is a vertically differentiated model as in Shaked and Sutton (1982). It is also adopted in Valletti (2006), Valletti and Szymanski (2006), Saggi (2013), and Ivus and Lai (2018).

[16]We discuss how allowing for unpatented substitutes for x affects our results in Section 6 and present a more formal analysis in Section D in the online appendix.

so as to recover all profit from the licensed manufacturer(s) *ex post*, making the manufacturer(s) break even. The patent owner maximizes its rents from license fees by licensing x to only one manufacturer, thus making this manufacturer a monopolist in the market for y that it sells.[17]

We consider two legal regimes regarding patent exhaustion:

Regime AE — Absolute Exhaustion: When the manufacturer sells the good to the buyer, regardless of the patent owner's desires, the patent owner loses all rights to proceed against the buyer for patent infringement.

Regime PE — Presumptive Exhaustion: The patent owner loses all rights to proceed against the buyer for patent infringement unless the patent owner imposes downstream contractual restrictions on the buyer. If the patent owner imposes such restrictions, the buyer must enter into a license with the patent owner or risk patent infringement.

Regime AE prevents contractual restrictions on buyers and as such, allows resale. The patent owner licenses the manufacturer to give it the right to manufacture and sell the good. We assume that the patent owner's and the manufacturer's incentive to price discriminate is eroded by a perfect and costless arbitrage.[18] Consequently, the manufacturer will set a uniform price for the patented product.

In Regime PE, the patent owner may opt out of exhaustion (which is the default rule) by imposing downstream contractual restrictions. If the patent owner imposes a downstream contractual restriction that effectively restricts the use or sale of the patented component by a buyer, then in order to avoid a charge of patent infringement, the buyer needs to separately enter into a license with the patent owner. The patent owner can directly license the buyer or use an agent to do so (such as the manufacturer), but either way, the

[17]We assume the manufacturer has the capacity and distribution network to satisfy the total demand.

[18]In component-manufacturer markets, where concerns of patent licensing and exhaustion are most applicable, resale can occur at very low cost.

terms and price of the license can be customized to individual buyer. For simplicity, we assume that the individualized licensing (when profitable) is direct, i.e. between the patent owner and the buyer, without going through the manufacturer. Assuming the cost of opting out is zero, the patent owner has a choice between *uniform licensing* (which involves sublicensing all buyers via the manufacturer under a uniform manufacturer license), *individualized licensing* (which is buyer-specific, i.e. perfect price discrimination), or *mixed licensing* (which involves individualized licensing of some buyers and uniform licensing of others). Here, we assume that a license from the patent owner or the sublicense from the manufacturer provides the buyer with a right to use the good but not to resell it[19] and so, the patent owner and manufacturer can exercise first degree price discrimination among the buyers. However, there is a positive transaction cost in individualized licensing, t, which includes the time and effort involved in negotiating license fees and executing licensing agreements with individual buyers of different type. The transaction cost increases the unit cost of y to $\gamma + t$.[20] We assume that licensing via the manufacturer does not involve transaction cost. Thus, under uniform licensing, the patent owner avoids the transaction cost by licensing via the manufacturer. However, it also fails to extract all consumer surplus.

Another possibility is a regime of *Absolute No Exhaustion*, in which regardless of the patent owner's desires, buyers, upon purchase of the good from the manufacturer, receive no license to make, use, or sell the patented good, and must enter into a license with the patent owner or risk patent infringement. This regime is effectively equivalent to presumptive exhaustion if the transaction cost is zero. More importantly, no court has ever adopted it. As such, we ignore it.

[19]We assume that it is costless for the manufacturer to insert a sublicensing clause into its form agreement so as to provide downstream rights to buyers; and that both the manufacturer and buyers forgo negotiation over the sublicense clause.
[20]The patent owner's cost in negotiating and executing a single licensing deal with the manufacturer is negligible in comparison, and ignored for simplicity.

4 Equilibrium

The model has three stages. In Stage I, the government sets the exhaustion regime. In Stage II, depending on the exhaustion regime, the patent owner may implement a licensing scheme. In Regime PE, the patent owner chooses between uniform, individualized, and mixed licensing. Under uniform licensing, the patent owner will set the manufacturer license fee of λ_m per unit of x and a lump-sum fee of $\bar{\lambda}$, and will license all buyers via the manufacturer. Under individualized licensing, the patent owner will maximize the overall rent from licensing by setting the manufacturer license fees to zero ($\lambda_m = \bar{\lambda} = 0$), in order to have the most flexibility in setting the buyer-specific license fees λ_ϕ paid directly by buyers, and will then set λ_ϕ to extract all individual consumer surplus. Under mixed licensing, the patent owner will choose the marginal type ϕ^* and will individually license high-valuation buyers with type $\phi \in [\phi^*, 1]$ and uniformly license low-valuation buyers with type $\phi \in [p/h, \phi^*)$ via the manufacturer (since their individual licensing is too costly relative to their willingness to pay for the final good).[21] High-valuation buyers will pay the buyer-specific license fee λ_ϕ on top of the (uniform) manufacturer's price, and low-valuation buyers will be licensed via the manufacturer and will pay the manufacturer's price. In Regime AE, the patent owner chooses the manufacturer license fees but does not engage in individualized licensing. In Stage III, the manufacturer sets the price p on the good to be sold to buyers, taking into account the license fees. The model is solved using backward induction.

In the rest of this section, we consider Regime PE. When exhaustion is presumptive, the patent owner's choice of a licensing scheme depends on the size of the transaction cost in individualized licensing, t, and to show this, we examine the following three cases: zero transaction costs in Section 4.1; intermediate transaction costs in Section 4.2; and prohibitive transaction costs in Section 4.3.

[21]Such mixed-licensing is common in many industries, as it allows the patent owner to extract some value immediately downstream, and then further value from high-valuation users for which transaction costs are relatively unimportant.

The outcome in Regime AE is equivalent to that in Regime PE with prohibitive transaction costs, since the patent owner will not engage in individualized licensing in this case.

4.1 Regime PE with zero transaction costs

When $t = 0$, the patent owner will engage in individualized licensing. This follows since, as we show below, the patent owner's overall rent from individualized licensing, which is given by equation (6), exceeds that from uniform licensing, which is given by equation (5).

Uniform licensing

Consider first uniform licensing. In Stage III, the manufacturer sets a price p to maximize its profit Π (exclusive of $\bar{\lambda}$), which depends on λ_m and is given by:

$$\Pi = (p - \lambda_m - \gamma)q = (p - \lambda_m - \gamma)L\left(1 - \frac{p}{h}\right), \quad (2)$$

The profit maximizing price and from equation (1), the aggregate quantity demanded at this price are as follows:

$$p = \frac{1}{2}(h + \lambda_m + \gamma) \quad \text{and} \quad q = \frac{L}{2h}(h - \lambda_m - \gamma). \quad (3)$$

In Stage II, the patent owner chooses λ_m and sets $\bar{\lambda} = \Pi$ to extract all the rents from the manufacturer. The patent owner's overall rent is $R_m = \lambda_m q + \Pi$. Using equations (2)–(3), we obtain:

$$R_m = \frac{L}{4h}(h + \lambda_m - \gamma)(h - \lambda_m - \gamma). \quad (4)$$

Differentiating R_m with respect to λ_m and setting the derivative to zero, we find the optimal per-unit license fee: $\lambda_m = 0$.[22] The zero per-unit license fee allows the patent owner to avoid double marginalization and in doing so, maximize the manufacturer's profit, which is then extracted via a lump-sum license fee. A positive λ_m,

[22]The second order condition for maximization is satisfied as $\partial^2 R_m/\partial\lambda_m^2 = -1 < 0$.

by contrast, would reduce the aggregate quantity below the profit maximizing level.

The patent owner's overall rent from uniform licensing is thus as follows:

$$R_m = \frac{L}{4h}(h - \gamma)^2. \tag{5}$$

In Stage III, the manufacturer sets $p = (h + \gamma)/2$, which follows from equation (3) when $\lambda_m = 0$.

Individualized licensing

Consider now individualized licensing when $t = 0$. In Stage III, the manufacturer is left with zero residual consumer surplus to be extracted and so, will set the price p equal to the marginal cost γ. In Stage II, the patent owner will set λ_ϕ equal to the reservation price $p_\phi = h\phi$ net of the price charged by the manufacturer to buyers, $p = \gamma$. The marginal buyer type that maximizes the patent owner's rent from individualized licensing will be $\phi^* = \gamma/h$. Buyers with type $\phi \geq \gamma/h$, who are willing to pay at least γ, will be charged the price of $p_\phi = h\phi$ or equivalently, the price of γ paid to the manufacturer plus the licensing fee of $\lambda_\phi = h\phi - \gamma$ paid to the patent owner. The patent owner's overall rent from individualized licensing will be given by:

$$R_c = L\int_{\gamma/h}^{1}(h\phi - \gamma)d\phi = \frac{L}{2h}(h - \gamma)^2. \tag{6}$$

4.2 Regime PE with intermediate transaction costs

Suppose the transaction cost is positive. In this case, the patent owner can still capture the entire total surplus with individualized licensing but must internalize the transaction cost. Alternatively, if the patent owner engages in uniform licensing via the manufacturer, the patent owner will avoid the transaction cost but will fail to capture the entire total surplus via the manufacturer, since the manufacturer will set a single monopoly price. Both the patent owner and the manufacturer can price discriminate between buyers in the first degree at the transaction cost of t, but the two parties' incentive to do so is fully aligned (since the patent owner extracts all the rents from the manufacturer with a lump-sum fee). Hence, if individualized licensing of buyers is not optimal for the patent owner, it is not optimal for the manufacturer either, and so the manufacturer will choose to serve the buyers under a single monopoly price.

Mixed licensing

When t is positive but low enough to satisfy $t < (h - \gamma)/2$, the marginal buyer type that maximizes the patent owner's overall rent from licensing will be $\phi^* < 1$, and the patent owner will engage in mixed licensing, individually licensing high-valuation buyers with type $\phi \in [\phi^*, 1]$ and uniformly licensing low-valuation buyers with type $\phi \in [p/h, \phi^*)$. In Stage III, the manufacturer will be left with zero residual consumer surplus to be extracted from high-valuation buyers and so, its price for high-valuation buyers will equal to the unit cost of a good: $p^H = \gamma + t$. The price for low-valuation buyers, denoted by p^L, will be set to maximize the manufacturer's profit Π, which is given by:

$$\Pi = (p^L - \lambda_m - \gamma)q^L = (p^L - \lambda_m - \gamma)L\left(\phi^* - \frac{p^L}{h}\right), \qquad (7)$$

where q^L is the number of uniformly licensed low-valuation buyers, given by:

$$q^L = L\int_{p^L/h}^{\phi^*} d\phi = L\left(\phi^* - \frac{p^L}{h}\right). \qquad (8)$$

The profit maximizing price and the aggregate quantity demanded at this price are as follows:

$$p^L = \frac{1}{2}(h\phi^* + \lambda_m + \gamma) \quad \text{and} \quad q^L = \frac{L}{2h}(h\phi^* - \lambda_m - \gamma). \qquad (9)$$

In Stage II, the patent owner will set the buyer-specific license fee of $\lambda_\phi = h\phi - \gamma - t$ for high-valuation buyers and will earn the following overall rent from individualized licensing:

$$R_c = L\int_{\phi^*}^{1}(h\phi - \gamma - t)d\phi = \frac{L}{2}(1 - \phi^*)[h(1 + \phi^*) - 2(\gamma + t)]. \qquad (10)$$

The patent owner will also set the manufacturer license fee of λ_m per unit of x and a lump-sum fee of $\bar{\lambda} = \Pi$ and will earn the following rent from uniform licensing:

$$R_m = \lambda_m q + \Pi = \frac{L}{4h}\left[(h\phi^* - \gamma)^2 - \lambda_m^2\right] = \frac{L}{4h}(h\phi^* - \gamma)^2, \quad (11)$$

which follows since the optimal per-unit manufacturer license fee is $\lambda_m = 0$.

The patent owner's total rent from mixed licensing will be equal to $R_T \equiv R_m + R_c$. Differentiating R_T with respect to ϕ^* and setting the derivative to zero, we find the marginal buyer type[23]:

$$\phi^* = \frac{1}{h}(\gamma + 2t). \quad (12)$$

It is true that $\phi^* < 1$ when the transaction cost satisfies $t < (h-\gamma)/2$.

When $\phi^* = (\gamma + 2t)/h$, it follows from (9) that the price for low-valuation buyers is equal to $p^L = \gamma + t$, which is the same as the price for high-valuation buyers, $p^H = \gamma + t$. Hence in Stage III, the manufacturer will set a price of $p = \gamma + t$ for all buyers. High-valuation buyers with type $\phi \in [(\gamma+2t)/h, 1]$ will be licensed directly and pay the price of $p_\phi = h\phi$ or equivalently, the price of $p = \gamma + t$ paid to the manufacturer plus the license fee of $\lambda_\phi = h\phi - \gamma - t$ paid to the patent owner. Low-valuation buyers with type $\phi \in [(\gamma + t)/h, (\gamma+2t)/h)$ will be uniformly licensed via the manufacturer and will pay the price of $p = \gamma + t$ to the manufacturer.

Note that when $t > 0$, the patent owner will directly license fewer buyers when the exhaustion regime allows for mixed licensing, as opposed to when it requires individualized licensing of buyers by the patent owner. Under mixed licensing, the marginal buyer type is $\phi^* = (\gamma + 2t)/h$. Under individualized licensing, the marginal buyer type will be $\phi^* = (\gamma + t)/h$.[24]

[23] $dR_T/d\phi^* = -hL/2 < 0$. Therefore, the second order condition is satisfied as well.

[24] In Stage III, the manufacturer will set the price of $p = \gamma + t$ and in Stage II, the patent owner will set the buyer-specific license fee of $\lambda_\phi = h\phi - \gamma - t$. This is

Last, substituting $\phi^* = (\gamma + 2t)/h$ into equations (10) and (11), we obtain:

$$R_c = \frac{L}{2h}(h - \gamma - 2t)(h - \gamma) \quad \text{and} \quad R_m = \frac{t^2 L}{h}. \tag{13}$$

4.3 Regime PE with prohibitive transaction costs — Same outcome as in Regime AE

Suppose the transaction cost is high enough that $t \geq (h - \gamma)/2$. Then the marginal buyer type is $\phi^* = 1$ and all buyers will be licensed uniformly via the manufacturer, since the transaction cost is so high that individualized licensing is not profitable for the patent owner. In Stage II, the patent owner will set $\lambda_m = 0$ and extract all rents from the manufacturer with a lump-sump fee of $\bar{\lambda}$. In Stage III, the manufacturer will set the monopoly price of $p = (h + \gamma)/2$. The patent owner's overall rent will be equal to R_m, which is given by equation (5).

5 Welfare Analysis

We now compare the social welfare in Regime PE to that in Regime AE.

5.1 Regime AE

Figure 1 plots the linear demand function $q(p)$ given by equation (1) and shows the composition of the total surplus in Regime AE.

The manufacturer's price is equal to $p^{\mathrm{AE}} = (h + \gamma)/2$. At this price, a buyer with type $\phi > p^{\mathrm{AE}}/h$ purchases one unit of good y and earns utility $h\phi - p^{\mathrm{AE}}$. The number of buyers who purchase good y is q^{AE}. The consumer surplus is thus given by

perfect price discrimination and so, ϕ^* is the value of ϕ that solves $\lambda_{\phi^*} = 0$, i.e. yields zero rent from the marginal buyer to the patent owner.

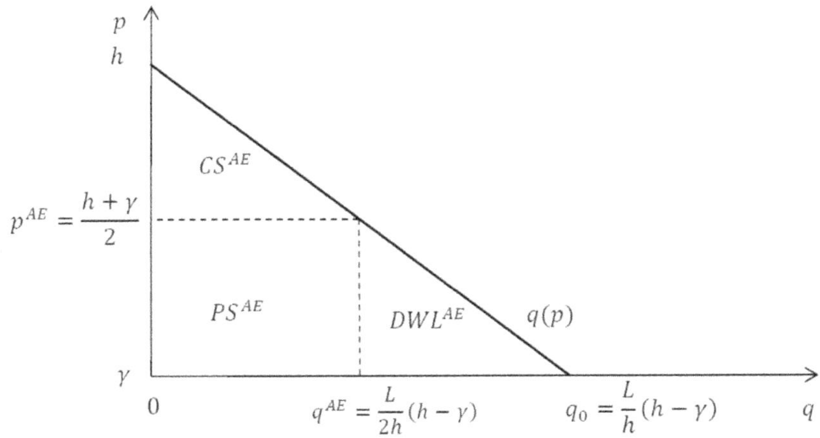

Figure 1. The composition of the total surplus in Regime AE.

$\mathrm{CS}^{\mathrm{AE}} = 0.5(h\Phi - p^{\mathrm{AE}})q^{\mathrm{AE}}$, or equivalently:

$$\mathrm{CS}^{\mathrm{AE}} = L\int_{p^{\mathrm{AE}}/h}^{1}(h\phi - p^{\mathrm{AE}})d\phi = \frac{L}{8h}(h-\gamma)^2. \tag{14}$$

The patent owner extracts all producer surplus from the manufacturer. The patent owner's rent is equal to $\mathrm{PS}^{\mathrm{AE}} = (p^{\mathrm{AE}} - \gamma)q^{\mathrm{AE}}$, which from equation (5) is equivalent to:

$$\mathrm{PS}^{\mathrm{AE}} = \frac{L}{4h}(h-\gamma)^2. \tag{15}$$

The uniform pricing creates a deadweight loss of $\mathrm{DWL}^{\mathrm{AE}} = S - \mathrm{CS}^{\mathrm{AE}} - \mathrm{PS}^{\mathrm{AE}}$, where S is the maximum potential surplus (i.e. the total surplus). The deadweight loss would be zero in the case of perfect price discrimination with no transaction cost. Then all consumer surplus would be extracted from buyers with type $\phi > \gamma/h$ with buyer-specific license fees of $\lambda_\phi = h\phi - \gamma$. The patent owner's rent (i.e. the producer surplus) would then be given by:

$$S = L\int_{\gamma/h}^{1}(h\phi - \gamma)d\phi = \frac{L}{2h}(h-\gamma)^2. \tag{16}$$

The deadweight loss in Regime AE is thus given by:

$$\mathrm{DWL}^{\mathrm{AE}} = L \int_{\gamma/h}^{p^{\mathrm{AE}}/h} (p^{\mathrm{AE}} - h\phi)d\phi = \frac{L}{8h}(h-\gamma)^2, \quad (17)$$

which is equivalent to $\mathrm{DWL}^{\mathrm{AE}} = 0.5(p^{\mathrm{AE}} - \gamma)(q_0 - q^{\mathrm{AE}})$, since q_0 buyers would have purchased good y at the price of γ but buyers who are willing to pay more than γ but less than p^{AE} are not served.

5.2 Regime PE

Figure 2 shows the composition of the total surplus in Regime PE. The market has two segments: (i) for low-valuation buyers with type $\phi \in (p/h, \phi^*)$, the demand is $q^L \equiv q(p;\phi^*)$, given by equation (8); and (ii) for high-valuation buyers with type $\phi \in [\phi^*, 1]$, the demand function can be expressed as the residual demand $q^H(p) = q(p) - q^L(p)$, where $q(p)$ is the total demand given by equation (1).

Low-valuation buyers will purchase q^{PE} units at the uniform price of $p^{\mathrm{PE}} = \gamma + t$ and will enjoy the consumer surplus of

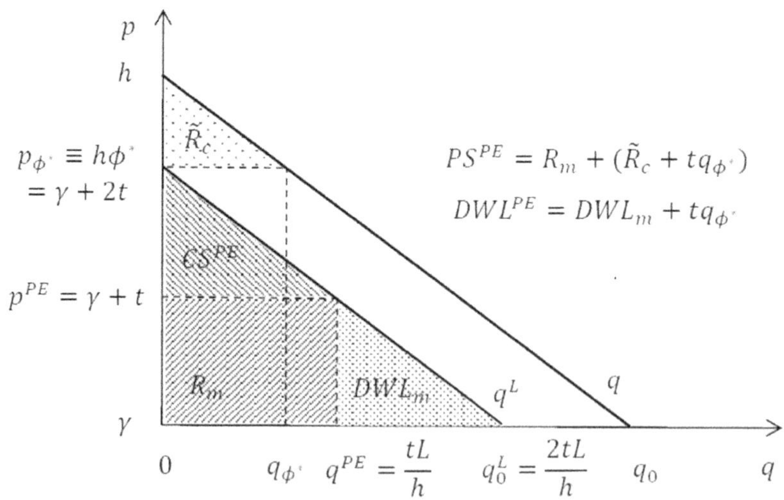

Figure 2. The composition of the total surplus in Regime PE.

$\text{CS}^{\text{PE}} = 0.5(p_{\phi^*} - p^{\text{PE}})q^{\text{PE}}$, which is equivalent to

$$\text{CS}^{\text{PE}} = L \int_{p^{\text{PE}}/h}^{\phi^*} (h\phi - p^{\text{PE}})d\phi = \frac{t^2 L}{2h}. \tag{18}$$

High-valuation buyers will purchase $q_{\phi^*} = L(1 - \phi^*) = L[1 - (\gamma + 2t)/h]$ units of y at the buyer-specific price of $p_\phi = h\phi$ and earn no consumer surplus.

The patent owner will extract all profit from the manufacturer and will earn $R_m = (p^{\text{PE}} - \gamma)q^{\text{PE}}$. The patent owner will also extract all consumer surplus from high-valuation buyers in the amount of $\tilde{R}_c = 0.5(h - h\phi^*)q_{\phi^*}$. The patent owner's overall rent from individualized licensing will be equal to R_c in equation (13), which is the sum of $\tilde{R}_c$ and the total amount of transaction costs paid by the buyers to the manufacturer, $\lambda_{\phi^*}q_{\phi^*} = (h\phi^* - \gamma - t)q_{\phi^*} = tq_{\phi^*}$. The producer surplus is equal to the patent owner's overall rent from mixed licensing, $R_T \equiv R_m + R_c$, which from equations (13) is given by:

$$\text{PS}^{\text{PE}} = \frac{t^2 L}{h} + \frac{L}{2h}(h - \gamma - 2t)(h - \gamma). \tag{19}$$

In Regime PE, deadweight loss arises from (i) uniform monopoly pricing by the manufacturer and (ii) positive transaction costs in individualized licensing. The maximum potential surplus S is given by equation (16) and so, the aggregate deadweight loss is as follows:

$$\text{DWL}^{\text{PE}} = S - \text{CS}^{\text{PE}} - \text{PS}^{\text{PE}} = \frac{tL}{2h}[2(h - \gamma) - 3t]. \tag{20}$$

In Figure 2, the aggregate deadweight loss is the area of the trapezoid with base $q_0 - q^{\text{PE}}$ and height $p^{\text{PE}} - \gamma$. It is equal to $\text{DWL}^{\text{PE}} = \text{DWL}_m + tq_{\phi^*}$, where $\text{DWL}_m = 0.5(p^{\text{PE}} - \gamma)(q_0^L - q^{\text{PE}})$ arises because buyers who are willing to pay less than p^{PE} will not be served and the total amount of transaction costs is tq_{ϕ^*}.

5.3 Comparison of the Regimes

When the transaction cost is prohibitive, i.e. $t \geq (h - \gamma)/2$, Regime PE is equivalent to Regime AE. Thus in what follows, we consider the case when $t < (h-\gamma)/2$. First, we compare the equilibrium prices and quantities across the two regimes. Proposition 1 follows.

Proposition 1. *It is true that* $q_{\phi^*}+q^{\mathrm{PE}} > q^{\mathrm{AE}}$. *Further,* $q^{\mathrm{PE}} < q^{\mathrm{AE}}$, $p^{\mathrm{PE}} < p^{\mathrm{AE}}$, *and these two cases are possible:*

(i) $q_{\phi^*} \geq q^{\mathrm{AE}}$ *and* $p^{\mathrm{AE}} \geq p_{\phi^*}$ *iff* $t \leq (h-\gamma)/4$;
(ii) $q^{\mathrm{AE}} > q_{\phi^*}$ *and* $p_{\phi^*} > p^{\mathrm{AE}}$ *iff* $t > (h-\gamma)/4$.

Fewer buyers pay uniform price in Regime PE, compared to Regime AE. But despite of this, more buyers are served in Regime PE overall, since some buyers are licensed individually by the patent owner. Not surprisingly, the number of buyers licensed individually is high when the transaction cost in individualized licensing is low enough that it satisfies $t \leq (h-\gamma)/4$. This is the case (i) at left in Figure 3. Further compared to p^{AE}, the manufacturer price in Regime PE is lower and in the case (i), the buyer-specific price is also lower.

We now compare the producer and consumer surplus across the two regimes. Proposition 2 follows.

Proposition 2. $\mathrm{PS}^{\mathrm{PE}} > \mathrm{PS}^{\mathrm{AE}}$ *and* $\mathrm{CS}^{\mathrm{PE}} < \mathrm{CS}^{\mathrm{AE}}$.

Proof. $\mathrm{PS}^{\mathrm{PE}} - \mathrm{PS}^{\mathrm{AE}} = L(h-\gamma-2t)^2/(4h) > 0$ and $\mathrm{CS}^{\mathrm{PE}} - \mathrm{CS}^{\mathrm{AE}} = L[4t^2 - (h-\gamma)^2]/(8h) < 0$.[25] ■

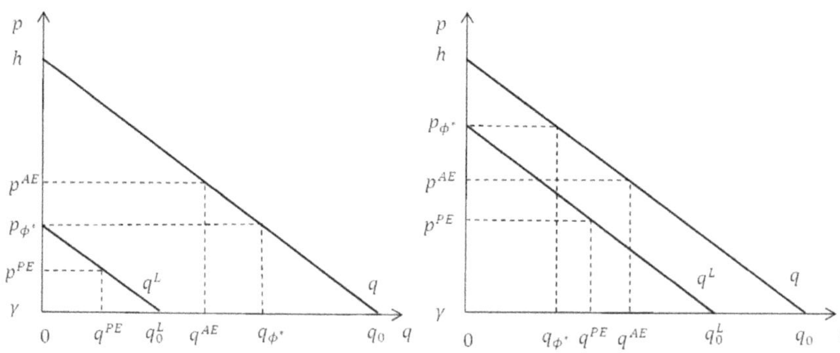

Figure 3. Price and quantity in Regime PE and Regime AE. Case (i) when $t \leq (h-\gamma)/4$, at left and case (ii) when $t > (h-\gamma)/4$, at right.

[25]The results follow from equations (14)–(15) and (18)–(19).

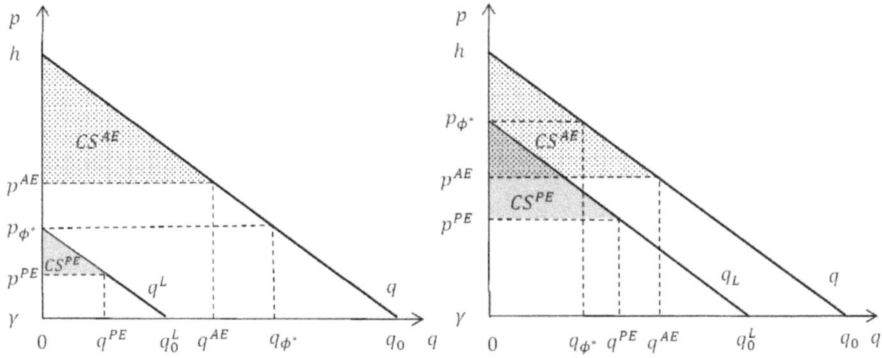

Figure 4. Consumer surplus in Regime PE and Regime AE. Case (i) when $t \leq (h - \gamma)/4$, at left and case (ii) when $t > (h - \gamma)/4$, at right.

Producer surplus is higher in Regime PE, which gives the patent owner more options. The patent owner's rent is highest under mixed licensing when $t > 0$, and when $t = 0$, it is highest under individualized licensing, which allows the patent owner to extract all consumer surplus from every paying buyer while incurring no transaction cost in this case. This confirms the standard proposition that price discrimination in the context of patent licensing is optimal in the absence of transaction costs. Regime AE, by contrast, does not permit licensing of individual buyers and so, restricts the patent owner's rent.

Figure 4 shows $\mathrm{CS}^{\mathrm{PE}}$ and $\mathrm{CS}^{\mathrm{AE}}$, with the low-$t$ case (i) at left and the high-t case (ii) at right.[26] Consumer surplus is lower in Regime PE, in which only low-valuation buyers (uniformly licensed) earn consumer surplus and the number of such buyers is relatively small ($q^{\mathrm{PE}} < q^{\mathrm{AE}}$). Importantly, though, the interests of buyers are conflicting: while low-valuation buyers prefer Regime PE, high-valuation buyers prefer Regime AE.

Last, we compare the deadweight loss across the two regimes. Proposition 3 establishes the result.

[26]These two cases are defined in Proposition 1.

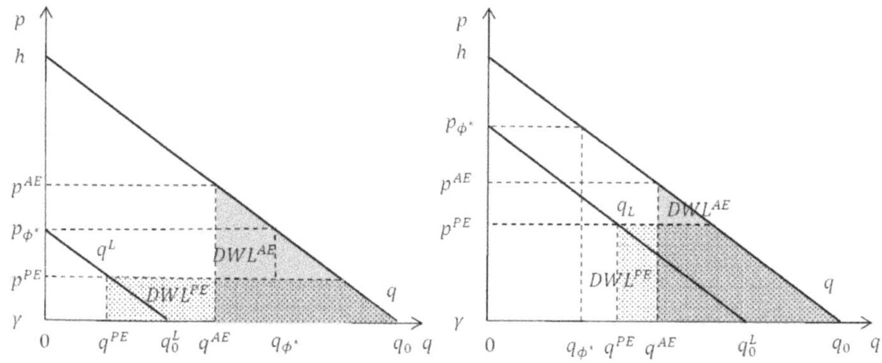

Figure 5. Deadweight loss in Regime PE and Regime AE. Case (i) when $t \leq (h-\gamma)/4$, at left and case (ii) when $t > (h-\gamma)/4$, at right.

Proposition 3. $\mathrm{DWL}^{\mathrm{PE}} < \mathrm{DWL}^{\mathrm{AE}}$ *iff* $0 \leq t < (h-\gamma)/6$ *and* $\mathrm{DWL}^{\mathrm{PE}} \geq \mathrm{DWL}^{\mathrm{AE}}$ *iff* $(h-\gamma)/6 \leq t \leq (h-\gamma)/2$.

Proof. The result follows since $\mathrm{DWL}^{\mathrm{PE}} - \mathrm{DWL}^{\mathrm{AE}} = L[8t(h-\gamma) - (h-\gamma)^2 - 12t^2]/(8h)$.[27] ∎

In Figure 5, $\mathrm{DWL}^{\mathrm{PE}}$ is the area of the trapezoid with base $q_0 - q^{\mathrm{PE}}$ and height $p^{\mathrm{PE}} - \gamma$, and $\mathrm{DWL}^{\mathrm{AE}}$ is the area of the triangle with base $q_0 - q^{\mathrm{AE}}$ and height $p^{\mathrm{AE}} - \gamma$. When t is small (at left), the deadweight loss is smaller in Regime PE. A large number of buyers are licensed individually in this case, which increases economic efficiency and with small t, does not add much to the deadweight loss in term of transaction cost frictions. As t rises, the number of individually-licensed buyers greatly falls, while the total amount of transaction costs rises. Consequently when t is large (at right), Regime PE produces a greater deadweight loss.

Figure 6 provides more intuition. On the right, $\mathrm{CS}^{\mathrm{PE}} + \mathrm{PS}^{\mathrm{PE}}$ is above $\mathrm{CS}^{\mathrm{AE}} + \mathrm{PS}^{\mathrm{AE}}$ when t is small, i.e. $t < (h-\gamma)/6$. Regime PE is socially optimal in this case, because the gain in producer surplus more than offsets the loss in consumer surplus. As t rises from zero on the left, the gain in producer surplus falls fast (since $\mathrm{PS}^{\mathrm{PE}}$ falls fast

[27] This follows from equations (17) and (20).

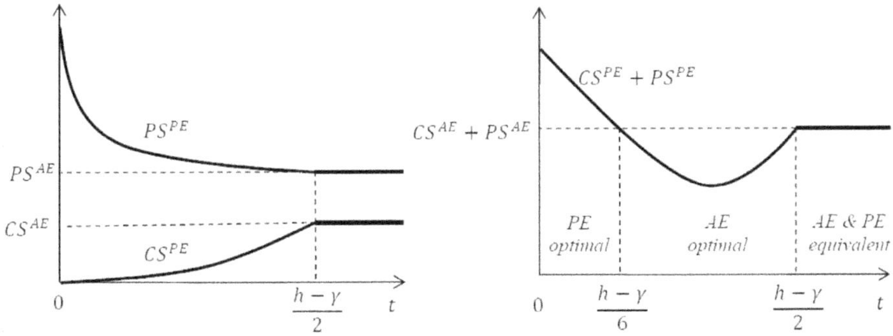

Figure 6. Consumer and producer surpluses in Regime PE and Regime AE in relation to the transaction cost.

and PS^{AE} does not change) while the loss in consumer surplus also falls but slowly (since CS^{PE} rises slowly and CS^{AE} does not change). Thus on the right, $\text{CS}^{\text{PE}} + \text{PS}^{\text{PE}}$ declines as t rises from zero and eventually falls below $\text{CS}^{\text{AE}} + \text{PS}^{\text{AE}}$. When $(h-\gamma)/6 < t < (h-\gamma)/2$, the total surplus in Regime PE is relatively small and so, Regime AE is socially optimal. When $t \geq (h-\gamma)/2$, the two regimes are equivalent.

As t falls from $(h-\gamma)/2$, the total surplus in Regime PE falls relative to that in Regime AE.[28] In other words, reducing the transaction cost from the prohibitive level increases the relative inefficiency of Regime PE; it is only after the transaction cost is sufficiently reduced that its further reduction starts contributing to the relative efficiency of Regime PE. When $t = (h-\gamma)/2$, the marginal buyer type is $\phi^* = 1$ and all buyers are licensed uniformly in Regime PE; in total $q^{\text{PE}} = L(h-\gamma)/(2h)$ buyers are served at the price $p^{\text{PE}} = (h+\gamma)/2$. Now suppose t is reduced by ε, where $\varepsilon < (h-\gamma)/6$. Then from equation (12), the marginal buyer type will fall to $\phi^* = 1 - 2\varepsilon/h$, and high-valuation buyers with type $\phi \in [\phi^*, 1]$ will be licensed individually. The total number of such buyers will be equal to $2\varepsilon L/h$. At the same time, the manufacturer's price will fall to $p^{\text{PE}} = (h+\gamma)/2 - \varepsilon$ and so, the number of uniformly-licensed

[28] $\text{CS}^{\text{PE}} + \text{PS}^{\text{PE}}$ falls as t falls in the range $(h-\gamma)/3 < t < (h-\gamma)/2$.

buyers will rise by $\varepsilon L/h$. That is, the number of individually-licensed buyers will increase twice as much as the number of uniformly-licensed buyers. A larger number of individually-licensed buyers will increase the deadweight loss from transaction cost frictions by $2\varepsilon^2 L/h$, but a larger number of uniformly-licensed buyers will reduce the deadweight loss from the manufacturer monopoly pricing by $\varepsilon^2 L/h$. The aggregate deadweight loss will thus rise.

6 Extensions

In this section, we discuss extensions to our model.

First, when assessing the welfare implications of patent exhaustion, it is important to understand how static effects interact with dynamic considerations. In a dynamic setting, producer surplus will generally drive the amount of *ex ante* innovation that the patent owner is willing to make. Indeed, if producer surplus is too low, the patent owner may not invent at all. In Section A in the online appendix, we examine how the patent owner's incentive to invest in product quality (a proxy for the overall *ex ante* innovation) compares across the two regimes. We show that dynamic efficiency rises in Regime PE, and these dynamic gains in promoting *ex ante* innovation may outweigh any loss of static efficiency when the transaction cost is high. We assumed that only the patent owner invests in product quality. When third parties also invest in product quality, Regime AE could also provide dynamic benefits, to the extent that absolute exhaustion lowers the costs of patented inputs for third parties. For cumulative innovation, two competing effects could arise: stronger patent protection in the form of presumptive exhaustion increases the initial innovator's profit but could render follow-on innovation more costly.[29] The optimal tradeoff between static and dynamic efficiencies will vary widely across industries and technologies.

Second, we abstracted away from intermediaries, such as wholesalers and resellers. This is justified when the manufacturer sells

[29]Denicolò (2000) assesses whether stronger patents promote welfare under cumulative innovation.

directly to buyers, exhaustion is presumptive, and the patent owner opts out, because in this case, a buyer may be required to enter into a separate licensing agreement with the patent owner. It is also justified when intermediaries are relatively homogeneous, purchasing and licensing on behalf of groups of buyers with similar distributions of the final product valuation. In Section B in the online appendix, we allow for intermediaries that purchase and license on behalf of the buyers, and assume that the intermediaries are heterogeneous in that they represent buyers of distinctly different willingness to pay for the final product. In addition, to make the model more realistic, we assume that the patent owner incurs a transaction cost when licensing to the manufacturer. Our results are qualitatively unchanged. In fact, it is more likely that Regime PE is socially optimal when each intermediary negotiates the license fees on behalf of a large number of buyers, thus saving in the transaction cost.

Third, we assumed that all parties are omniscient, particularly regarding the buyer's demand, but the patent owner may not be fully aware of the buyer's demand, particularly when the patented good is a mere component of a complex product. We consider information asymmetry in assessing the buyer's demand in Section C in the online appendix. We assume that the patent owner incurs an additional cost to determine the buyer's willingness to pay for the patented good. In this context, information asymmetry acts like an increase in the transaction cost of individualized licensing and so, reduces the efficiency of Regime PE. The conclusion is the same if a buyer has difficulty determining the product value (e.g. does not know if the product is subject to license fees) and the upstream patent owner chooses to incur a cost to reveal the product value to the buyer.

Another type of information asymmetry involves uninformed buyers unknowingly agreeing to downstream restrictions on the use of purchased goods. Here, the concern is that upstream licensors can impose socially harmful terms on such buyers to extract rents. Absolute exhaustion can help solve these market defects by making the restrictions effectively unenforceable in patent actions, but a broad-brush doctrine like exhaustion is not necessary in a situation where other instruments (such as the patent misuse doctrine or the unconscionability doctrine in contract law) can be used to render the terms unenforceable.

Fourth, we assumed that the patented component x has no substitutes. In Section D in the online appendix, we allow for unpatented imperfect substitutes for x. The existence of substitutes limits the power of the patent owner to act as a monopolist in setting license fees among competing manufacturers. If substitutes are perfect, then patents will provide no market power and the exhaustion doctrine — at least via its effect on a patent infringement suit — will be irrelevant. But if substitutes are imperfect, our qualitative results will still hold.

Fifth, we have assumed that buyers do not engage in arbitrage or resell used patented product on a secondary market. Indeed in the copyright context, some scholars (e.g. Heald, 2003) have justified the exhaustion doctrine on the grounds that it promotes a vigorous resale market, which benefits buyers.[30] In Section E in the online appendix, we assume that there is a second-hand market in which current buyers can buy used goods (with depreciated quality), which have been previously purchased by other buyers from the patent owner under uniform licensing (in Regime PE) or uniform pricing (in Regime AE), at a discounted price. The willingness of a buyer to pay for the new good is now constrained by the consumer surplus that the used good provides, but our qualitative results still hold.

Sixth, we consider goods with multiple components patented by different patent owners (e.g. computers, mobile phones, televisions, etc.). Scholars (e.g. Lemley and Shapiro, 2007) have been concerned with so-called anti-commons problems (e.g. hold-up and royalty stacking) in which a manufacturer is confronted with royalty payments and related transaction costs that may exceed the marginal value of the component. Assuming that these problems are notable for multi-component products — which is debatable (e.g. Barnett,

[30]Yet in the patent context, some goods cannot be resold after they are used, or the transaction costs of resale are too high to justify the practice. For instance, pharmaceutical drugs and downloaded mobile applications have no effective resale markets.

2015) — exhaustion can potentially ameliorate these concerns by reducing the number of inbound licenses needed to manufacture the product. We consider multi-component products in Section F in the online appendix. Our qualitative results still hold, although when the transaction costs in licensing and the number of patented components in a product are both high (especially when dealing with multiple patent owners requiring separate negotiations), Regime AE begins to be more attractive. This finding underscores our more general result that the relative efficiency of Regime PE is likely to vary widely by industry, technology, and product.

Last, we have assumed that the optimal outcome is the one that maximizes total surplus, foregoing any discussion of distributive benefits from an exhaustion regime. We find that Regime AE maximizes consumer surplus and so if the aim is to maximize consumer surplus — which is not standard in economic analysis, — then absolute exhaustion may be preferred. But we also find that low-valuation buyers prefer Regime PE. These buyers are often the least well-off and if one values their surplus more highly, then Regime PE may be optimal. Thus, despite some claims that distributive concerns support Regime AE, the reality is more nuanced.

7 Implications for Policy

Our findings explain some of the confusion surrounding the exhaustion doctrine and the differences between how exhaustion operates in the realm of copyright and patent law. In the copyright industries, where there are few intermediaries, large numbers of downstream buyers, and low prices for each work, one would expect high transaction cost inefficiencies dominating price discrimination benefits. In such industries, our model predicts the relatively vigorous enforcement of exhaustion. In the patent industries, however, there is much more variation. The mobile phone "app" industry, for example, appears closer to the copyright industries, while the semiconductor industry (with high-priced products and many intermediaries) is a better candidate for presumptive exhaustion. Like in many areas of patent law, an industry-specific set of rules is likely superior to an across-the-board rule (Burk and Lemley, 2003). Our model also shows — consistent with some qualitative scholarly treatments (e.g. Patterson, 2007) — that absolute exhaustion may make more sense with respect to end-consumers but less sense with respect to intermediaries (such as wholesalers and resellers), since the transaction cost involved in licensing these agents is relatively low.

In general, there is no *a priori* reason to favor absolute or presumptive exhaustion but rather, one regime or the other is more efficient depending on unique industry structures. Thus, assuming that judges can make relatively accurate determinations with respect to the underlying concerns — and also that contractual enforcement is generally not as efficient as patent enforcement of downstream restrictions — a contextual approach would be more fruitful than the one that precludes or allows opt-out in all cases. Based on our model, such an approach should examine three factors.

First is whether the costs in licensing downstream parties (including the negotiation, information, and search costs) are high relative to the value of the deal. A relatively high cost would support absolute exhaustion, because presumptive exhaustion would burn a large amount of social surplus in transaction cost and market frictions in this case. For instance, if a patent owner attempted to separately license each patient undergoing surgery with a particular patented surgical scalpel just prior to a surgical procedure, the transaction cost of such licensing would be high relative to the scalpel value. But if instead, the patent owner licensed large downstream manufacturers that assemble the patented component with other unpatented components en masse, the transaction cost of licensing might be relatively low. These differences in transaction costs help explain greater preference for absolute exhaustion in copyright as compared to patent law. In the copyright industries, there are few steps between the copyright owner and end-consumers, and enforcement is often against individual end-consumers; while in the patent industries, the number of steps between the patent owner and end-consumers is typically high, and enforcement is rarely against individual end-consumers.

Second, courts should determine if there is large information asymmetry between patent owners and buyers. Although this technically may be subsumed under the rubric of information and search costs, it could be difficult for courts to determine the magnitude of such costs. A useful proxy for the presence of substantial information asymmetry in this case is whether or not clear notice was provided to the downstream licensee. The absence of clear notice may support absolute exhaustion, all else being equal. With that said, because most defendants in patent infringement cases are sophisticated intermediaries, rather than individual end-consumers, the defendants typically are on actual or constructive notice of potential upstream patents that might be asserted against them. Furthermore, exhaustion applies only if the sale is authorized, which by definition requires a license between the patent owner and an upstream party in the supply chain. Sophisticated parties should be able to trace back through the supply chain to the original licensee and can demand indemnification from upstream sellers. Thus notice may be less important than appears at first blush.

Third, if transaction costs are large, courts should be more reluctant to allow opt-out when dealing with complex products comprising many separately patented components (such as computers or mobile phones), as compared to simple products comprising few patented components (such as agricultural seeds and pharmaceutical drugs). Product complexity can exacerbate the effects of high transaction costs. Also, the effects of exhaustion on complex product innovation are far from clear. Absolute exhaustion may reduce the surplus accruing to upstream patent owners, but it may also reduce the cost of using patented components in follow-on innovation and further commercialization by downstream parties, which is often required to achieve viability in complex-product industries (Sichelman, 2010).

Last, we note that there are other concerns, such as those premised on autonomy or distributive justice. For example, if courts wish to further the interests of consumers at the expense of overall welfare, then different considerations may apply.

8 Conclusion

This chapter examined how a shift in domestic patent policy from absolute to presumptive exhaustion (which presumes exhaustion but allows the patent owner to opt-out via contract) affects social welfare. It offered the first economic model of domestic patent exhaustion that allows for two types of licensing of buyers by the patent owner — individualized licensing and uniform licensing via the manufacturer — and incorporates transaction cost in buyer-specific patent licensing. The transaction cost, which includes the time and effort involved in negotiating license fees and executing licensing agreements with individual buyers, increases the unit cost of the final good.

The results show that when the transaction cost is low, presumptive exhaustion is socially optimal, because it allows welfare-enhancing price discrimination via individualized licensing. Conversely when the transaction cost is high, presumptive exhaustion leads to a greater loss of static efficiency, because the transaction cost frictions more than offset the benefit of price discrimination. Relaxing our model's key assumptions by-and-large does not affect our results.

Our findings confirm and expand upon qualitative results in the literature. First, we confirm the proposition in Mulligan (2013, 2016) that absolute exhaustion may reduce rent dissipation when the transaction cost of licensing is high, because it prevents the patentee from "burning up" large amounts of surplus via transaction costs in individualized licensing. We also show that absolute exhaustion can reduce product prices for buyers with high willingness to pay (Katz, 2016). Also, our results support the arguments in Kieff (2008) and Katz (2016) that absolute exhaustion can reduce social efficiency, since it prevents price discrimination via downstream licensing, and clarify that this occurs when the transaction cost in individualized licensing is low. On the other hand, our findings do not support the proposition in Layne-Farrar (2011) and Layne-Farrar *et al.*

(2014) that absolute exhaustion is likely to generate welfare losses in the face of transaction costs; in contrast, we show that absolute exhaustion *decreases* static inefficiency when the transaction cost in individualized licensing is high.

Whether absolute or presumptive exhaustion is more socially optimal is ultimately an empirical question that turns on the specific circumstances at hand. We suggest that courts adopt a contextual approach, allowing opt-out depending on the specific circumstances and considering three factors: (*i*) transaction costs, including negotiation, search, and information costs; (*ii*) information asymmetry; and (*iii*) product complexity.

Online Appendix for "*An Economic Model of Patent Exhaustion*"

Abstract

In this online appendix, we discuss extensions to our model of patent exhaustion. Section A examines how the patent owner's incentive to invest in product quality (a proxy for the overall *ex ante* innovation) in a regime of presumptive exhaustion compares to a regime of absolute exhaustion. In Section B, we allow for heterogeneous intermediaries that purchase and license on behalf of the buyers, and also assume that the patent owner incurs a transaction cost when licensing to the manufacturer. Section C considers information asymmetry in assessing the buyer's demand, and Section D allows for unpatented imperfect substitutes for the patented component. In Section E, we assume that there is a second-hand market in which current buyers can buy used goods (with depreciated quality), which have been previously purchased by other buyers from the patent owner at a discounted price. Section F considers multi-component products.

This Appendix discusses extensions to the model presented in "*An Economic Model of Patent Exhaustion*" by Lai Ivus and Sichelman.

A. Dynamic Effects and Quality-Feedback Mechanisms

Suppose the quality of good y depends on the quality of the component x, which is set by the patent owner prior to setting license fees. The optimal quality h will maximize the patent owner's producer surplus $\mathrm{PS}(h)$ net of the investment cost $H(h)$, where $d^2H/dh^2 > 0$ and $d^2H(h)/dh^2 > d^2\mathrm{PS}(h)/dh^2$. Differentiating $\mathrm{PS}^{\mathrm{AE}}$ and $\mathrm{PS}^{\mathrm{PE}}$, given by equations (15) and (19) in the paper, with respect to h, we find the marginal benefit of quality under each regime:

$$\frac{d\mathrm{PS}^{\mathrm{AE}}(h)}{dh} = \frac{L}{4h^2}\left(h^2 - \gamma^2\right) \quad \text{and}$$

$$\frac{d\mathrm{PS}^{\mathrm{PE}}(h)}{dh} = \frac{L}{2h^2}\left[h^2 - (\gamma + t)^2 - t^2\right].$$

At the optimal quality, the marginal benefit is equal to the marginal cost. To find an explicit solution, we assume the cost of investing in quality when $h > \sqrt{a/\xi}$ is given by $H(h) = (\xi h + a/h)/4$, where $a > \xi[(\gamma + t)^2 + t^2]$ and $\xi > 2L$.[31] Then the optimal quality is given by:

$$h^{\mathrm{AE}} = \left(\frac{a - L\gamma^2}{\xi - L}\right)^{1/2} \quad \text{and} \quad h^{\mathrm{PE}} = \left\{\frac{a - 2L[(\gamma + t)^2 + t^2]}{\xi - 2L}\right\}^{1/2}.$$

Since $h^{\mathrm{AE}} < h^{\mathrm{PE}}$,[32] the patent owner's *ex ante* investment into product quality is higher in Regime PE. If this positive impact on *ex ante* investment is strong, the gain in dynamic efficiency in Regime

[31] The parameter ξ is the fixed component of the marginal cost of quality and the parameter a measures the rate at which the marginal cost of quality rises as h rises. We restrict a and ξ to ensure that h^{AE} and h^{PE} exist. To complete the characterization of $H(h)$, we assume that $H(0) = 0$ and $H(h)$ is increasing in h when $h \in [0, \sqrt{a/\xi}]$.

[32] This result follows since $t < (h^{\mathrm{AE}} - \gamma)/2$, which is the necessary and sufficient condition for $h^{\mathrm{AE}} < h^{\mathrm{PE}}$.

PE will likely offset the loss of static efficiency in Regime PE with high transaction costs.

B. Licensing via Intermediaries and Manufacturer Transaction Costs

Assume a number of heterogeneous intermediaries which differ in the average valuation of their buyers: the first intermediary serves N buyers with the highest valuations, the second intermediary serves N buyers with the next highest valuations, etc. Suppose the patent owner incurs a fixed transaction cost t when licensing directly to each intermediary, and each intermediary can price discriminate among its buyers without incurring additional transaction costs. Then the transaction cost per buyer is equal to t/N. In Regime PE, in equilibrium, the patent owner will extract all the rents (consumer surplus) from the intermediary through a lump-sum license fee. Assuming further that the patent owner incurs a fixed transaction cost t_m when uniformly licensing buyers via the manufacturer, the lump-sum manufacturer licensing fee will be equal to $\bar{\lambda} = \Pi - t_m$, while the optimal manufacturer license fee per unit will still be $\lambda_m = 0$.

In Regime AE, allowing for $t_m > 0$ does not affect the manufacturer optimal price and quantity. Consumer surplus will also remain the same, but producer surplus (or the patent owner's rent extracted from the manufacturer) will fall and so, deadweight loss will rise:

$$\mathrm{CS}^{\mathrm{AE}} = \frac{L}{8h}(h-\gamma)^2; \quad \mathrm{PS}^{\mathrm{AE}} = \frac{L}{4h}(h-\gamma)^2 - t_m; \tag{B1}$$

$$\mathrm{DWL}^{\mathrm{AE}} = \frac{L}{8h}(h-\gamma)^2 + t_m. \tag{B2}$$

In Regime PE, the marginal buyer type will be $\phi^* = (\gamma + 2t/N)/h$.[33] High-valuation buyers with type $\phi \in [(\phi^*, 1]$ will be licensed individually, paying the buyer-specific price of $p_\phi = \lambda_\phi + \gamma + t/N$.

[33]We assume that $t/N < (h-\gamma)/2$ so that $\phi^* < 1$.

Low-valuation buyers with type $\phi \in [(\gamma+t/N)/h, \phi^*)$ will be licensed uniformly, paying the price of $p^{\mathrm{PE}} = \gamma + t/N$ and purchasing $q^{\mathrm{PE}} = tL/(Nh)$ units of the good. Allowing for $t_m > 0$ does not affect the patent owner's rent from individualized licensing (since the number of individually-licensed buyers remains the same), but the patent owner's rent from the uniform licensing falls to $R_m = t^2L/(N^2h) - t_m$ (since less profit will be extracted from the manufacturer). Consumer surplus, producer surplus, and the deadweight loss are thus as follows:

$$\mathrm{CS}^{\mathrm{PE}} = \frac{Lt^2}{2hN^2}; \qquad \mathrm{PS}^{\mathrm{PE}} = \frac{L}{2h}\left[\left(h - \gamma - \frac{2t}{N}\right)(h-\gamma) + \frac{2t^2}{N^2}\right] - t_m; \tag{B3}$$

$$\mathrm{DWL}^{\mathrm{PE}} = \frac{L}{2h}\left[\frac{2t}{N}(h-\gamma) - \frac{3t^2}{N^2}\right] + t_m. \tag{B4}$$

It follows from equations (B1)–(B4) that $\mathrm{PS}^{\mathrm{PE}} > \mathrm{PS}^{\mathrm{AE}}$, $\mathrm{CS}^{\mathrm{PE}} < \mathrm{CS}^{\mathrm{AE}}$, and $\mathrm{DWL}^{\mathrm{PE}} < \mathrm{DWL}^{\mathrm{AE}}$ iff $0 \leq t/N < (h-\gamma)/6$ and $\mathrm{DWL}^{\mathrm{PE}} \geq \mathrm{DWL}^{\mathrm{AE}}$ iff $(h-\gamma)/6 \leq t/N \leq (h-\gamma)/2$. Thus, Propositions 2 and 3 still hold qualitatively. Allowing for t_m reduces $\mathrm{PS}^{\mathrm{PE}}$ and $\mathrm{PS}^{\mathrm{AE}}$ by the same amount and does not affect $\mathrm{CS}^{\mathrm{PE}}$ and $\mathrm{CS}^{\mathrm{AE}}$. But allowing for intermediaries (which negotiate the license fees on behalf of a large number of buyers and in doing so, lower the transaction cost per buyer) increases the relative efficiency of presumptive exhaustion, making it more likely that $\mathrm{DWL}^{\mathrm{PE}} < \mathrm{DWL}^{\mathrm{AE}}$ for the same value of t.

C. Information Asymmetry in Assessing the Buyer's Demand

Suppose the patent owner incurs a "revelation" cost c_r to determine the buyer's type ϕ. Without paying c_r, the patent owner only knows that there are L buyers, with ϕ uniformly distributed over $[0, 1]$. Then the patent owner will engage in individualized licensing in Regime PE *iff* $\mathrm{PS}^{\mathrm{PE}} - \mathrm{PS}^{\mathrm{AE}} > Lc_r$, where Lc_r is the total revelation cost. Since $\mathrm{PS}^{\mathrm{PE}} - \mathrm{PS}^{\mathrm{AE}} = L(h-\gamma-2t)^2/(4h)$ (from Section 5.3), the patent owner will engage in individualized licensing in Regime PE if $t < t^*$, where $t^* = (h-\gamma)/2 - \sqrt{hc_r}$. In this case, the consumer surplus CS^{PE} will remain the same, as in equation (18) in the paper, while the producer surplus PS^{PE} will be given by equation (19) in the paper minus Lc_r. But if $t > t^*$, the patent owner will uniformly license all buyers.[34] The curve $CS^{PE} + PS^{PE}$ in Figure 6 will shift down by an amount Lc_r for $t < t^*$ and will overlap with $CS^{AE} + PS^{AE}$ for $t > t^*$. Propositions 2 and 3 will hold qualitatively provided c_r is small enough that $CS^{PE} + PS^{PE} > CS^{AE} + PS^{AE}$ at $t = 0$.[35] But when c_r is large, Regime AE will be socially optimal for any t.

Instead of incurring the revelation cost Lc_r *ex ante*, the patent owner may incur it *ex post*. Specifically, the patent owner may set a base upstream license fee λ_0 charged by the manufacturer, in addition to the downstream buyer-specific license fees λ_ϕ^D charged directly by the patent owner. The fee λ_0 will act as a costly screen, eliminating the need for the patent owner to determine the type of all buyers. When $t = 0$ for example, the manufacturer will set the price of $p = \gamma + \lambda_0$ in Stage III. High-valuation buyers with type $\phi > (\gamma + \lambda_0)/h$ will purchase the good at this price and will thus be easily identifiable. The total patent owner's revelation cost will thus fall to $c_r L(h - \gamma - \lambda_0)/h$. The patent owner will then set $\lambda_\phi^D = h\phi - \gamma - \lambda_0$ to extract all consumer surplus and earn the overall rent of $PS^{PE} = L(h - \gamma - \lambda_0)^2/(2h) + L(\lambda_0 - c_r)(h - \gamma - \lambda_0)/h$, i.e. the sum of the extracted consumer surplus and the total base rent net of c_r. The optimal base license fee will be $\lambda_0^* = c_r$, and the patent owner's overall rent at this base fee will equal to $PS^{PE} = L(h - \gamma - c_r)^2/(2h)$.

A similar information asymmetry arises when a buyer does not know its reservation price because, for example, it does not know if the product is covered by patents. In this case, prior to making a purchase, the buyer may do a costly search to identify any such patents and then negotiate a license fee with the patent owners. The buyer search cost will act like t in our model (assuming that it is roughly equivalent to the patent owner's revelation cost).

[34] If c_r is too large, the patent owner will adopt uniform licensing even if $t = 0$.
[35] The condition for this to be true is $c_r < (h - \gamma)^2/(8h)$.

In summary, the information asymmetry in assessing the buyer's demand makes it harder for the patent owner to set buyer-specific fees and so, increases the static efficiency of Regime AE. In this sense, asymmetric information acts like an increased transaction cost.

D. Substitutes for the Patented Component

If there exist unpatented imperfect substitutes for the patented component x, the willingness of a buyer to pay for the firm's good will be constrained by the consumer surplus that the rival goods provide. More formally, suppose that in addition to the firm in question (called Firm 1), there is a competitive fringe of rival firms that produce a homogeneous good. As before, there are L buyers of type ϕ uniformly distributed over $[0, 1]$. Let us call Firm 1's product "good 1" and the rivals' product "good 2", and use h_1 and p_1 (h_2 and p_2) to denote the quality and price of good 1 (good 2). Suppose $h_1 > h_2$. A buyer with type ϕ will purchase good 1 *iff* $h_1\phi - p_1 > h_2\phi - p_2$. In equilibrium, it must be that $p_1 > p_2$, and buyers with type $\phi \in [\frac{p_1-p_2}{h_1-h_2}, 1]$ will each buy one unit of good 1, while buyers with type $\phi \in [\frac{p_2}{h_2}, \frac{p_1-p_2}{h_1-h_2})$ will each buy one unit of good 2. It follows that

$$q_1 = L\left(1 - \frac{p_1 - p_2}{h_1 - h_2}\right) \quad \text{and} \quad q_2 = L\left(\frac{p_1 - p_2}{h_1 - h_2} - \frac{p_2}{h_2}\right).$$

Note that $q_1 < L(1 - p_1/h_1)$, which means that the existence of the substitute good shifts Firm 1's demand curve down, because the willingness to pay for good 1 falls.[36] But the demand curve for good 1 is still linear in p_1, and p_2 can be treated as parametric by Firm 1, since good 2 is priced at its marginal cost by a large number of perfectly competitive firms.[37] Since the results in Propositions 2 and 3 arise from a linear demand curve, Propositions 2 and 3 will continue

---

[36] The result that $q_1 < L(1 - p_1/h_1)$ follows since it must be true that $p_2/h_2 < p_1/h_1$ for $q_2 > 0$.

[37] If the fringe is monopolistically competitive (rather than perfectly competitive), p_2 can still be treated as parametric by Firm 1 as long as the number of firms in the fringe is large and the marginal cost of good 2 is the same for all firms in the fringe.

to hold qualitatively: Regime PE will be statically less efficient than Regime AE when t is large. The threshold t will be smaller than before and so, the range of t for which Regime PE is less efficient will be wider. This is intuitive since when the patent owner has low market power, it is not able to extract much consumer surplus with price discrimination for any given t.

E. Second-Hand Market

Suppose that in each period, in addition to new goods sold by the patent owner, there is a second-hand market in which current buyers can buy used goods (with depreciated quality), which have been previously purchased by other buyers from the patent owner under uniform licensing (in Regime PE) or uniform pricing (in Regime AE), at a discounted price. We justify that the used goods market is a competitive fringe by assuming that the used good has an alternative use and its price is equal to the price in the alternative-use market, which is assumed to be competitive. As before, in the current period, there are L buyers of type ϕ uniformly distributed over $[0,1]$. Let h, p, and q (h_u, p_u, and q_u) denote the quality, price and quantity of the new (used) good. Note that p_u is treated as parametric by firms and buyers in the current period, as the used-good market is perfectly competitive. A buyer with type ϕ will purchase the new good *iff* $h\phi - p > h_u\phi - p_u$. Let $h_d \equiv h - h_u > 0$ and $p_d \equiv p - p_u > 0$, and assume $h_d = \beta h$ where $\beta < 1$. A buyer obtains the utility of $U(\phi) = h\phi - p$ and $U_u(\phi) \equiv h_u\phi - p_u$ from consuming the new and used good respectively. Thus, $U_d(\phi) \equiv U(\phi) - U_u(\phi) = h_d\phi - p_d$ is the utility a buyer obtains from consuming the new good *beyond* the utility level that he would have obtained if he had consumed the used good. So, buyers with type $\phi \in [p_d/h_d, 1]$ will each buy one unit of the new good, while buyers with type $\phi \in [p_u/h_u, p_d/h_d)$ will each buy one unit of the used good. The demand curve for the new good becomes $q = L\int_{p_d/h_d}^{1} d\phi = L(1 - p_d/h_d)$.

Notice that all of the equations in Sections 3–5 in the chapter are completely determined by the demand curve $q = L(1 - p/h)$ and the marginal cost of production of good y, given by γ. As such, with suitable transformations of the variables, one can construct a one-to-one mapping between the equations in the model with a competitive fringe of used goods and the original model. For the demand curve, the transformation is from p and h to p_d and h_d. Further, in the model with a competitive fringe, let the marginal cost of production faced by the producer of the new good for the sake of profit maximization be γ_d. When profit is zero, $p = \gamma$ should correspond to $p_d = \gamma_d$, which implies that $\gamma_d = \gamma - p_u$. Thus, the equations in the model with a competitive fringe of used goods will correspond to the respective equations in Sections 3–5 in the chapter transformed by replacing U, h, p, and γ with U_d, h_d, p_d, and γ_d (but other variables such as ϕ and t will remain unchanged). In what follows, we offer proofs that this mapping is valid.

In Regime PE with intermediate transaction cost, in Stage III, the price for low-valuation buyers, p^L, will maximize the manufacturer's profit $\Pi_d = (p_d^L - \lambda_m - \gamma_d)L(\phi^* - p_d^L/h_d)$, which maps onto $\Pi = (p^L - \lambda_m - \gamma)L(\phi^* - p^L/h)$ in the original model. In Stage II, the patent owner will set the license fee of $\lambda_\phi = h_d\phi - \gamma - t + p_u$ for high-valuation buyers and will earn the rent of $R_c = L\int_{\phi^*}^1 [h_d\phi - \gamma - t + p_u]d\phi = 0.5L(1 - \phi^*)[h_d(1 + \phi^*) - 2(\gamma_d + t)]$ from individualized licensing, which maps onto $R_c = 0.5L(1-\phi^*)[h(1+\phi^*)-2(\gamma+t)]$. The marginal buyer type that maximizes the patent owner's total rent from mixed licensing will be $\phi^* = (\gamma + 2t - p_u)/h_d = (\gamma_d + 2t)/h_d$, which maps onto $\phi^* = (\gamma + 2t)/h$. It is true that $\phi^* < 1$ when $t < (h_d - \gamma + p_u)/2 = (h_d - \gamma_d)/2$, which maps onto $t < (h - \gamma)/2$. In Stage III, the manufacturer will set the monopoly price of $p_d = \gamma + t - p_u = p_d = \gamma_d + t$ for all buyers, which maps onto $p = \gamma + t$.

Low-valuation buyers will enjoy the following consumer surplus from the consumption of the new good (beyond the potential utility offered by the used good): $\text{CS}_d^{\text{PE}} = L\int_{p_d/h_d}^{\phi^*}(h_d\phi - p_d)d\phi = 0.5t^2L/h_d$, which maps onto $\text{CS}^{\text{PE}} = 0.5t^2L/h$ in the original model. The producer surplus (i.e. the patent owner's overall rent from mixed licensing) will be given by $\text{PS}_d^{\text{PE}} = [t^2L + 0.5L(h_d - \gamma_d - 2t)(h_d - \gamma_d)]/h_d$, which maps onto $\text{PS}^{\text{PE}} = [t^2L + 0.5L(h - \gamma - 2t)(h - \gamma)]/h$. The aggregate deadweight loss will be given by $\text{DWL}_d^{\text{PE}} = 0.5tL[2(h_d - \gamma_d) - 3t]/h_d$, which maps onto $\text{DWL}^{\text{PE}} = 0.5tL[2(h - \gamma) - 3t]/h$. Proposition 3 will now state that $\text{DWL}_d^{\text{PE}} < \text{DWL}_d^{\text{AE}}$ *iff* $0 \leq t < (h_d - \gamma_d)/6$ and $\text{DWL}_d^{\text{PE}} \geq \text{DWL}_d^{\text{AE}}$ *iff* $(h_d - \gamma_d)/6 \leq t \leq (h_d - \gamma_d)/2$. Thus, our conclusion concerning the optimality of Regime PE and Regime AE with regard to the magnitude of t will be qualitatively the same. Note that $h_d - \gamma_d < h - \gamma$ since $h_u - p_u$ (the potential utility offered by the used good to buyer type $\phi = 1$) must be positive. In other words, Figure 6 will still be valid, but the ranges of t for which Regime PE is optimal and Regime AE is optimal will be both smaller, while the range of t for which Regime PE and Regime AE are equivalent is larger. The first two ranges are smaller, the greater is the utility offered by the used goods to each buyer (i.e. when β or p_u is smaller).

F. Multi-Component Products

Suppose there are two patented components, x_1 and x_2, each of which is patented by a different patent owner, P_1 and P_2. The components x_1 and x_2 are intermediate goods manufactured by upstream manufacturers U_1 and U_2 and used in the production of the final good by a downstream manufacturer D. To produce the final good, D combines x_1 with x_2, materials, and factor inputs. Let ϕ_1 be the willingness of D to pay for x_1, which is derived from the profit motive of D. Then the "consumer surplus" derived from "consuming" x_1 should be interpreted as "profit" or "producer surplus" of D derived from using x_1. For example, D's willingness to pay for x_1 is equal to the price of the final good minus the unit input and material costs, and the per unit license fee paid to P_2 (which is the per unit producer surplus extracted by P_2). In general, this willingness to pay varies across different downstream manufacturers. Thus, the "total surplus" with respect to x_1 is the sum of the producer surplus of D and the producer surplus of P_1.

Our model is symmetric, with the result that in the presence of transaction cost t that is roughly fixed per component — and abstracting away from the increased producer surplus from additional downstream royalties — Regime PE will on balance reduce the total producer surplus of the two patent owners more than Regime AE.

If we further assume that the downstream license fees for multi-component products do not differ from a single-component product of equal value, then t in a multi-component product will cause more transaction cost friction and, hence, will burn up more surplus than in a single-component product. Therefore when t is large, there may be a stronger case in support of Regime AE for products with multiple components patented by different patent owners.

Multi-component products also shift incentives between pioneering and incremental innovation. In Regime AE, P_1 can only license U_1 but not D. But in Regime PE, D may need to obtain a license from P_1 (as well as P_2). Assuming for a moment that P_1 strikes the first license agreement with D, Regime PE increases the producer surplus of P_1 and reduces the producer surplus that can potentially be extracted by P_2. If the patents are asymmetric in their technological significance (e.g. if P_1 holds a foundational "upstream" patent that is essential to the final product, while P_2 holds a minor "downstream" patent covering an optional product configuration), then the distribution of surplus between P_1 and P_2 will have significant welfare implications, depending on the specific characteristics of the technology and other factors.

Acknowledgment

The authors thank Jonathan Barnett, Dan Burk, John Duffy, Jay Kesan, Mark Lemley, Robert Merges, Adam Mossoff, Zorina Khan, Michael Risch, Mark Schultz, and participants at the 2016 Patent Law Scholars Roundtable at the University of San Diego School of Law, the 2017 Searle Roundtable on Patents and Technology Standards at the Northwestern University, the 2017 Intellectual Property Scholars Conference at Cardozo School of Law, the 2017 HKUST Workshop on Law and Economics, and the Thomas Edison Innovation Fellowship Meeting in Austin, Texas, for helpful comments and discussions on earlier drafts. They especially thank Parth Sagdeo for his invaluable research assistance. This chapter is funded in part by a grant from the Center for Protection for Intellectual Property, Antonin Scalia Law School, George Mason University, but the contents are solely the responsibility of the authors.

References

Barnett, J. M. (2015). The anti-commons revisited, *Harvard Journal of Law & Technology* 29(1), 164–203.

Brown, D. K. and Norman, G. (2003). *Optimal Intellectual Property Rights Exhaustion and Humanitarian Assistance during a National Health Emergency*, Working Paper 0314, Department of Economics, Tufts University.

Burk, D. L. and Lemley, M. A. (2003). Policy levers in patent law, *Virginia Law Review* 89(7), 1575–1696.

Carrier, M. A. (2004). Cabining intellectual property through a property paradigm, *Duke Law Journal* 54(1), 1–145.

Denicolò, V. (2000). Two-stage patent races and patent policy, *The RAND Journal of Economics* 31(3), 488–501.

Grossman, G. M. and Lai, E. L.-C. (2008). Parallel imports and price controls, *The RAND Journal of Economics* 39(2), 378–402.

Heald, P. J. (2003). Mowing the playing field: Addressing information distortion and asymmetry in the TRIPS game, *Minnesota Law Review* 88, 249–314.

Hovenkamp, H. (2011). Post-sale restraints and competitive harm: The first sale doctrine in perspective, *NYU Annual Survey of American Law* 66, 487–547.

Hovenkamp, H. (2016). Patent exhaustion and federalism: A historical note, *Virginia Law Review Online* 102, 25–33.

Ivus, O. and Lai, E. L. C. (2018). *Patent Exhaustion Policy and International Production Sharing: Winners and Losers?* CESifo Working Paper.

Katz, A. (2016). The economic rationale of exhaustion: Distribution and post-sale restraints, in Calboli, I. and Lee, E. (eds.), *Research Handbook on IP Exhaustion and Parallel Imports*, Edward Elgar, Northampton, Massachusetts, USA, pp. 23–43.

Kieff, F. S. (2008). Quanta v. LG electronics: Frustrating patent deals by taking contracting options off the table, *Cato Supreme Court Review* 315–330.

Layne-Farrar, A. (2011). An economic defense of flexibility in IPR licensing: Contracting around first sale in multilevel production settings, *Santa Clara Law Review* 51, 101–137.

Layne-Farrar, A., Llobet, G., and Padilla, J. (2014). Patent licensing in vertically disaggregated industries: The royalty allocation neutrality principle, *Communications & Strategies* 1(95), 61–84.

Lemley, M. A. and Shapiro, C. (2007). Patent holdup and royalty stacking, *Texas Law Review* 85, 1991.

Maskus, K. E. and Chen, Y. (2004). Vertical price control and parallel imports: Theory and evidence, *Review of International Economics* 12(4), 551–570.

Meurer, M.J. (2003). Controlling opportunistic and anti-competitive intellectual property litigation, *Boston College Law Review* 44, 509–544.

Mulligan, C. (2013). A numerus clausus principle for intellectual property, *Tennessee Law Review* 80, 235–883.

Mulligan, C. (2016). Personal property servitudes on the internet of things, *Georgia Law Review* 50, 1121–1168.

Patterson, M. R. (2007). Contractual expansion of the scope of patent infringement through field-of-use licensing. *William and Mary Law Review* 49, 157–228.

Perzanowski, A. and Schultz, J. (2011). Digital exhaustion. *UCLA Law Review* 58, 889–946.

Saggi, K. (2013). Market power in the global economy: The exhaustion and protection of intellectual property, *The Economic Journal* 123(567), 131–161.

Saggi, K. (2014). Regional exhaustion of intellectual property, *International Journal of Economic Theory* 10(1), 125–137.

Shaked, A. and Sutton, J. (1982). Relaxing price competition through product differentiation, *The Review of Economic Studies* 49(1), 3–13.

Sichelman, T. M. (2010). Commercializing patents. *Stanford Law Review* 62(2), 341–413.

Skladony, W. P. (2007). Commentary on select patent exhaustion principles in light of the LG electronics cases, *IDEA* 47(3), 235–299.

Valletti, T. M. (2006). Differential pricing, parallel trade, and the incentive to invest, *Journal of International Economics* 70(1), 314–324.

Valletti, T. M. and Szymanski, S. (2006). Parallel trade, international exhaustion and intellectual property rights: A welfare analysis, *The Journal of Industrial Economics* 54(4), 499–526.

Author Index

Subject Index

E

F

G

H

I

K

Q

R

S

T

www.ingramcontent.com/pod-product-compliance
Ingram Content Group UK Ltd.
Pitfield, Milton Keynes, MK11 3LW, UK
UKHW061932100926
8556IPUK00007B/882